395.00

Legal Education

The International Library of Essays in Law and Legal Theory
Series Editor: Tom D. Campbell

Schools

Natural Law, Vols I & II *John Finnis*
Justice *Thomas Morawetz*
Law and Economics, Vols I & II *Jules Coleman and Jeffrey Lange*
Critical Legal Studies *James Boyle*
Marxian Legal Theory *Csaba Varga*
Legal Reasoning, Vols I & II *Aulis Aarnio and D. Neil MacCormick*
Legal Positivism *Mario Jori*
American Legal Theory *Robert Samuel Summers*
Postmodernism and Law *Dennis Patterson*
Law and History *David Sugarman*
Law and Language *Fred Schauer*
Sociological Theories of Law *Kahei Rokumoto*
Rights *Carlos Nino*
Law and Psychology *Martin Lyon Levine*
Feminist Legal Theory, Vols I & II *Frances Olsen*
Law and Society *Roger Cotterell*
Contemporary Criminological Theory *Francis T. Cullen and Velmer S. Burton Jr.*

Areas

Criminal Law *Thomas Morawetz*
Tort Law *Ernest J. Weinrib*
Contract Law, Vols I & II *Larry Alexander*
Anti-Discrimination Law *Christopher McCrudden*
Consumer Law *Iain Ramsay*
International Law *Martti Koskenniemi*
Property Law, Vols I & II *Elizabeth Mensch and Alan Freeman*
Constitutional Law *Mark V. Tushnet*
Procedure *D.J. Galligan*
Evidence and Proof *William Twining and Alex Stein*
Company Law *Sally Wheeler*
Privacy, Vols I & II *Raymond Wacks*
Lawyers' Ethics *David J. Luban*
Administrative Law *D.J. Galligan*
Child Law *Harry D. Krause*
Family Law, Vols I & II *Harry D. Krause*
Welfare Law *Peter Robson*
Medicine and the Law *Bernard M. Dickens*
Commercial Law *Ross Cranston*
Environmental Law *Michael C. Blumm*
Conflict of Laws *Richard Fentiman*
Law and Religion *Wojciech Sadurski*
Human Rights Law *Philip Alston*
European Community Law, Vols I & II *Francis Snyder*
Tax Law, Vols I & II *Patricia D. White*
Media Law *Eric Barendt*
Labour Law *David L. Gregory*
Alternative Dispute Resolution *Michael D.A. Freeman*

Legal Cultures

Comparative Legal Cultures *Csaba Varga*
Law and Anthropology *Peter Sack*
Hindu Law and Legal Theory *Ved Nanda*
Islamic Law and Legal Theory *Ian Edge*
Chinese Law and Legal Theory *Michael Palmer*
Socialist Law *W. Butler*
Common Law *Michael Arnheim*
Japanese Law and Legal Theory *Koichiro Fujikura*
Law and Development *Anthony Carty*
Jewish Law and Legal Theory *Martin P. Golding*
Legal Education *Martin Lyon Levine*
Civil Law *Ralf Rogowski*

Future Volumes
African Law and Legal Theory and Cumulative index.

Legal Education

Edited by
Martin Lyon Levine
UPS Foundation Professor of Law,
Gerontology, and Psychiatry
and the Behavioral Sciences
University of Southern California

Dartmouth
Aldershot · Hong Kong · Singapore · Sydney

© Martin Lyon Levine 1993. For copyright of individual articles please refer to the Acknowledgements. All rights reserved. No part of this publication may be reproduced, stored in a retrieval system, or transmitted in any form or by any means, electronic, mechanical, photocopying, recording, or otherwise without the prior permission of the publisher.

Published by
Dartmouth Publishing Company Limited
Gower House
Croft Road
Aldershot
Hants GU11 3HR
England

British Library Cataloguing in Publication Data
Legal Education. – (International Library
of Essays in Law & Legal Theory)
  I. Levine, Martin Lyon. II. Series
  340.07

ISBN 1 85521 247 1

Printed in Great Britain by Galliard (Printers) Ltd, Great Yarmouth

Contents

Acknowledgements   *ix*
Series Preface   *xi*
Introduction   *xiii*

PART I THE BEGINNINGS

1. Thomas Starkie (1833), 'Law Lecture', *Legal Examiner and Law Chronicle*, **2**, pp. 517–36.   5
2. Justice Oliver Wendell Holmes (1880), 'Book Notices: Langdell and Anson on Contract', *American Law Review*, **14**, pp. 233–5.   25
3. Christopher Columbus Langdell (1887), 'Harvard Celebration Speech', *Law Quarterly Review*, **3**, pp. 123–5.   29
4. Simeon E. Baldwin (1903), 'The Study of Elementary Law, The Proper Beginning of a Legal Education', *The Yale Law Journal*, **13**, pp. 1–15.   33

PART II WHAT IS A LAW SCHOOL FOR?

The University Ideal

5. Walter W. Cook (1927), 'Scientific Method and the Law', *American Bar Association Journal*, **13**, pp. 303–9.   53
6. Robert Maynard Hutchins (1934), 'The Autobiography of an Ex-Law Student', *The University of Chicago Law Review*, **1**, pp. 511–18.   61
7. James B. White (1982), 'The Study of Law as an Intellectual Activity', *Journal of Legal Education*, **32**, pp. 1–10.   69
8. John Henry Schlegel (1984), 'Searching for Archimedes – Legal Education, Legal Scholarship, and Liberal Ideology', *Journal of Legal Education*, **34**, pp. 103–10.   79
9. Paul D. Carrington (1986), 'The Dangers of the Graduate School Model', *Journal of Legal Education*, **35**, pp. 11–13.   87
10. Harry H. Wellington (1987), 'Challenges to Legal Education: The "Two Cultures" Phenomenon', *Journal of Legal Education*, **37**, pp. 327–30.   91

Public Policy

11. Chief Justice Harlan F. Stone (1924), 'The Future of Legal Education', *American Bar Association Journal*, **10**, pp. 233–5.   97
12. Leon H. Keyserling (1933), 'Social Objectives in Legal Education', *Columbia Law Review*, **33**, pp. 437–61.   101

13	David Riesman, Jr. (1941), 'Law and Social Science: A Report on Michael and Wechsler's Classbook on Criminal Law and Administration', *The Yale Law Journal*, **50**, pp. 636–53.	127
14	Myres S. McDougal (1947), 'The Law School of the Future: From Legal Realism to Policy Science in the World Community', *The Yale Law Journal*, **56**, pp. 1345–55.	145
15	Roscoe Pound (1951), 'Some Comments on Law Teachers and Law Teaching', *Journal of Legal Education*, **3**, pp. 519–32.	157
16	Charles L. Black, Jr. (1970), 'Some Notes on Law Schools in the Present Day', *The Yale Law Journal*, **79**, pp. 505–11.	171

Lawyering Skills

17	Judge Jerome Frank (1933), 'Why Not a Clinical Lawyer-School?', *University of Pennsylvania Law Review*, **81**, pp. 907–23.	181
18	K.N. Llewellyn (1935), 'On What is Wrong with So-Called Legal Education', *Columbia Law Review*, **35**, pp. 651–78.	199
19	Carrie Menkel-Meadow (1980), 'The Legacy of Clinical Education: Theories About Lawyering', *Cleveland State Law Review*, **29**, pp. 555–74.	227
20	Gary Bellow (1983), 'On Talking Tough to Each Other: Comments on Condlin', *Journal of Legal Education*, **33**, pp. 619–23.	247
21	Louis M. Brown (1985), 'If I Were Dean', *Journal of Legal Education*, **35**, pp. 117–22.	253

PART III LOOKING FOR ANSWERS BEYOND LAW

'Law And'

22	Lon L. Fuller (1948), 'What the Law Schools Can Contribute to the Making of Lawyers', *Journal of Legal Education*, **1**, pp. 189–204.	263
23	David Riesman (1968), 'In Memory of Harold W. Solomon: Comments on Southern California's Flyer in Legal Education', *Southern California Law Review*, **41**, pp. 506–13.	279
24	George L. Priest (1983), 'Social Science Theory and Legal Education: The Law School as University', *Journal of Legal Education*, **33**, pp. 437–41.	287

Humanism

25	Charles A. Reich (1965), 'Toward the Humanistic Study of Law', *The Yale Law Journal*, **74**, pp. 1402–8.	295

Justice, Moral Theory and Philosophy

26	Roscoe Pound (1952), 'Legal Education in a Unifying World', *New York University Law Review*, **27**, pp. 5–19.	305
27	William Robert Bishin (1965), 'Law, Language and Ethics', *Southern California Law Review*, **38**, pp. 499–502.	321

28   Christopher D. Stone (1968), 'Towards a Theory of Constitutional Law
      Casebooks', *Southern California Law Review*, **41**, pp. 1–18.   325

Economics and Law
29   Edmund W. Kitch (1983), 'The Intellectual Foundations of "Law and
      Economics"', *Journal of Legal Education*, **33**, pp. 184–96.   345
30   Guido Calabresi (1983), 'Thoughts on the Future of Economics in Legal
      Education', *Journal of Legal Education*, **33**, pp. 359–64.   359

PART IV   QUESTIONS AND CHALLENGES

Feminist Theory
31   Justice Ruth Bader Ginsburg (1982), 'Women's Work: The Place of
      Women in Law Schools', *Journal of Legal Education*, **32**, pp. 272–5.   369
32   Catharine W. Hantzis (1988), 'Kingsfield and Kennedy: Reappraising the
      Male Models of Law School Teaching', *Journal of Legal Education*, **38**,
      pp. 155–64.   373

Critical Legal Theory
33   Karl E. Klare (1982), 'The Law-School Curriculum in the 1980's: What's
      Left?', *Journal of Legal Education*, **32**, pp. 336–43.   385

Race and Critical Race Theory
34   Henry J. Richardson III (1974), 'Black Law Professors and the Integrity of
      American Legal Education', *The Black Law Journal*, **4**, pp. 495–505.   395
35   Angela D. Gilmore (1990), 'It is Better to Speak', *Berkeley Women's Law
      Journal*, **6**, pp. 74–80.   407

PART V   THE DEBATE IN THE COMMONWEALTH

Modernism
36   William Twining (1967), 'Pericles and the Plumber', *The Law Quarterly
      Review*, **83**, pp. 396–426.   419
37   Roderick A. Macdonald (1982), 'Curricular Development in the 1980s: A
      Perspective', *Journal of Legal Education* **32**, pp. 569–90.   451
38   Michael J. Trebilcock (1983), 'The Prospects of "Law and Economics": A
      Canadian Perspective', *Journal of Legal Education*, **33**, pp. 288–93.   473
39   Neil MacCormick (1985), 'The Democratic Intellect and the Law', *Legal
      Studies*, **5**, pp. 172–82.   479
40   Alan Hunt (1986), 'Jurisprudence, Philosophy and Legal Education –
      Against Foundationalism: A Response to Neil MacCormick', *Legal Studies*,
      6, pp. 292–302.   491

41	Honourable Mr. Justice Mark R. MacGuigan, P.C. (1989), 'The Public Dimension in Legal Education', *The Dalhousie Law Journal*, **12**, pp. 85–102.	503

Post-Modernism

42	Brenda Barrett (1986), 'What Should be Conserved?', *Law Teacher*, **20**, pp. 187–98.	523
43	Kate Green and Hilary Lim (1987), 'A Lib-Lib Pact: Silences in Legal Education', *Law Teacher*, **21**, pp. 256–62.	535
44	Christopher Stanley (1988), 'Training for the Hierarchy? Reflections on the British Experience of Legal Education', *Law Teacher*, **22**, pp. 78–86.	543

The Future

45	The Rt. Hon. Sir Ivor Richardson (1988), 'Educating Lawyers for the 21st Century', *Journal of Professional Legal Education*, **6**, pp. 111–16.	555

PART VI MAKING USE OF COMPETING VISIONS

46	Martin Lyon Levine (1980), 'Legal Education and Curriculum Innovation: Law and Aging as a New Field of Law', *Minnesota Law Review*, **65**, pp. 267–94.	563

Name Index 591

Acknowledgements

The editor and publishers wish to thank the following for permission to use copyright material.

The American Bar Association Journal for the essays: Walter W. Cook (1927), 'Scientific Method and the Law', *American Bar Association Journal*, **13**, pp. 303–9; Chief Justice Harlan F. Stone (1924), 'The Future of Legal Education', *American Bar Association Journal*, **10**, pp. 233–5.

Anglian Polytechnic University for the essays: Brenda Barrett (1986), 'What Should be Conserved?', *Law Teacher*, **20**, pp. 187–98; Kate Green and Hilary Lim (1987), 'A Lib-Lib Pact: Silences in Legal Education', *Law Teacher*, **21**, pp. 256–62; Christopher Stanley (1988), 'Training for the Hierarchy: Reflections on the British Experience of Legal Education', *Law Teacher*, **22**, pp. 78–86.

The Case Western Reserve University for the essays: James B. White (1982), 'The Study of Law as an Intellectual Activity', *Journal of Legal Education*, **32**, pp. 1–10. This essay appears in James Boyd White, *Heracles' Bow: Essays on the Rhetoric and Poetics of the Law*, published by the University of Wisconsin Press (1985). John Henry Schlegel (1984), 'Searching for Archimedes – Legal Education, Legal Scholarship, and Liberal Ideology', *Journal of Legal Education*, **34**, pp. 103–10; Paul D. Carrington (1986), 'The Dangers of the Graduate School Model', *Journal of Legal Education*, **35**, pp. 11–13; Harry H. Wellington (1987), 'Challenges to Legal Education: The "Two Cultures" Phenomenon', *Journal of Legal Education*, **37**, pp. 327–30; Roscoe Pound (1951), 'Some Comments on Law Teachers and Law Teaching', *Journal of Legal Education*, **3**, pp. 519–32; Gary Bellow (1983), 'On Talking Tough to Each Other: Comments on Condlin', *Journal of Legal Education*, **35**, pp. 619–23; Louis M. Brown (1985), 'If I Were Dean', *Journal of Legal Education*, **35**, pp. 117–22; Lon L. Fuller (1948), 'What the Law Schools Can Contribute to the Making of Lawyers', *Journal of Legal Education*, **1**, pp. 189–204; George L. Priest (1983), 'Social Science Theory and Legal Education: The Law School as University', *Journal of Legal Education*, **33**, pp. 437–41; Edmund W. Kitch (1983), 'The Intellectual Foundations of "Law and Economics"', *Journal of Legal Education*, **33**, pp. 184–96; Guido Calabresi (1983), 'Thoughts on the Future of Economics in Legal Education', *Journal of Legal Education*, **33**, pp. 359–64; Justice Ruth Bader Ginsburg (1982), 'Women's Work: The Place of Women in Law Schools', *Journal of Legal Education*, **32**, pp. 272–5; Catharine W. Hantzis (1988), 'Kingsfield and Kennedy: Reappraising the Male Models of Law School Teaching', *Journal of Legal Education*, **38**, pp. 155–64; Karl E. Klare (1982), 'The Law-School Curriculum in the 1980s: What's Left?', *Journal of Legal Education*, **32**, pp. 336–43; Roderick A. Macdonald (1982), 'Curricular Development in the 1980s: A Perspective', *Journal of Legal Education*, **32**, pp. 569–90; Michael J. Trebilcock (1983), 'The Prospects of "Law and Economics": A Canadian Perspective', *Journal of Legal Education*, **33**, pp. 288–93.

Cleveland State Law Review for the essay: Carrie Menkel-Meadow (1980), 'The Legacy of Clinical Education: Theories About Lawyering', *Cleveland State Law Review*, **29**, pp. 555-74.

Columbia Law Review Association for the essays: Leon H. Keyserling (1933), 'Social Objectives in Legal Education', *Columbia Law Review*, **33**, pp. 437-61; K.N. Llewellyn (1935), 'On What is Wrong with So-Called Legal Education', *Columbia Law Review*, **35**, pp. 651-78.

Alan Hunt (1986), 'Jurisprudence, Philosophy and Legal Education Against Foundationalism: A Response to Neil MacCormick', *Legal Studies*, **6**, pp. 292-302. Copyright © Alan J. Hunt.

Neil MacCormick (1985), 'The Democratic Intellect and the Law', *Legal Studies*, **5**, pp. 172-82. Copyright © Neil MacCormick.

New York University Law Review for the essay: Roscoe Pound (1952), 'Legal Education in a Unifying World', *New York University Law Review*, **27**, pp. 5-19.

Sweet & Maxwell Limited for the essays: Christopher Columbus Langdell (1887), 'Harvard Celebration Speech', *Law Quarterly Review*, **3**, pp. 123-5; William Twining (1967), 'Pericles and the Plumber', *Law Quarterly Review*, **83**, pp. 421-6.

University of Pennsylvania Law Review for the essay: Judge Jerome Frank (1933), 'Why Not a Clinical Lawyer-School?', *University of Pennsylvania Law Review*, **81**, pp. 907-23.

University of Southern California for the essays: David Riesman (1968), 'In Memory of Harold W. Solomon: Comments on Southern California's Flyer in Legal Education', *Southern California Law Review*, **41**, pp. 506-13; William R. Bishin (1965), 'Law, Language and Ethics', *Southern California Law Review*, **38**, pp. 499-502; Christopher D. Stone (1968), 'Towards A Theory of Constitutional Law Casebooks', *Southern California Law Review*, **41**, pp. 1-18. Reprinted with the permission of the Southern California Law Review.

The Yale Law Journal and Fred B. Rothman & Company for the essays: Simeon E. Baldwin (1903), 'The Study of Elementary Law, The Proper Beginning of a Legal Education', *The Yale Law Journal*, **13**, pp. 1-15; David Riesmans Jr. (1941), 'Law and Social Science: A Report on Michael and Wechsler's Classbook on Criminal Law and Administration', *The Yale Law Journal*, **50**, pp. 636-53; Myres S. McDougal (1947), 'The Law School of the Future: From Legal Realism to Policy Science in the World Community', *The Yale Law Journal*, **56**, pp. 1345-55; Charles L. Black Jr. (1970), 'Some Notes on Law Schools in the Present Day', *The Yale Law Journal*, **79**, pp. 505-11; Charles A. Reich (1965), 'Toward the Humanistic Study of Law', *The Yale Law Journal*, **74**, pp. 1402-8. Reprinted by permission of The Yale Law Journal and Fred B. Rothman & Company.

Every effort has been made to trace all the copyright holders, but if any have been inadvertently overlooked the publishers will be pleased to make the necessary arrangement at the first opportunity.

Series Preface

The International Library of Law and Legal Theory is designed to provide important research materials in an accessible form. Each volume contains essays of central theoretical importance in its subject area. The series as a whole makes available an extensive range of valuable material which will be of considerable interest to those involved in the research, teaching and study of law.

The series has been divided into three sections. The Schools section is intended to represent the main distinctive approaches and topics of special concern to groups of scholars. The Areas section takes in the main branches of law with an emphasis on essays which present analytical and theoretical insights of broad application. The section on Legal Cultures makes available the distinctive legal theories of different legal traditions and takes up topics of general comparative and developmental concern.

I have been delighted and impressed by the way in which the editors of the individual volumes have set about the difficult task of selecting, ordering and presenting essays from the immense quantity of academic legal writing published in journals throughout the world. Editors were asked to pick out those essays from law, philosophy and social science journals which they consider to be fundamental for the understanding of law, as seen from the perspective of a particular approach or sphere of legal interest. This is not an easy task and many difficult decisions have had to be made in order to ensure that a representative sample of the best journal essays available takes account of the scope of each topic or school.

I should like to express my thanks to all the volume editors for their willing participation and scholarly judgement. The interest and enthusiasm which the project has generated is well illustrated by the fact that an original projection of 12 volumes drawn up in 1989 has now become a list of some 60 volumes. I must also acknowledge the vision, persistence and constant cheerfulness of John Irwin of the Dartmouth Publishing Company and the marvellous work done in the Dartmouth office by Mrs Margaret O'Reilly and Sonia Hubbard.

TOM D. CAMPBELL
Series Editor
The Faculty of Law
The Australian National University

Introduction

Visions of the University Law School: International and Historical Perspectives

This anthology on legal education gathers together a sampling of representative, insightful or classic essays. In making the selections, a special effort has been made to include wide-ranging points of view, especially pieces from countries outside the US, important historical work, salient contributions which are not easily available, and contemporary critical perspectives.

The selections made, and the classifications deployed, are personal: as editor, I have included authors and work that attracted me, a conversation in print of voices across continents and generations. Material from outside the United States has been placed in a separate section, not just for ease of reference, but also to make a point for those who are unfamiliar with this literature. That international material of course reflects viewpoints which are also represented in separate sections in this book; such related essays should be read in tandem.

The guidelines for this series, the *International Library of Essays in Law and Legal Theory*, restrict the scope of source material to journals in the English language, excluding books, chapters in books and commission reports. Articles must be 'theoretical', a concept which, even if stretched, excludes empirical research, advocacy of various teaching methods or novel courses, and descriptions of legal education in various countries. The series rules also prohibit using excerpts of articles. Most long essays, and some seminal, widely-known, works – including some of my favourites – have had to be excluded to make room for a broader range of perspectives presented through briefer, less widely available, pieces. While striving for a balance among viewpoints, availability of suitable essays has sometimes skewed the results. At the end of this Introduction, I list some of the pieces that deserve to be read to supplement this collection.

This volume is intended to be useful to law professors and students interested in improving the law school curriculum, creating or reforming individual courses, planning research programmes, or rethinking the mission and social function of university legal education. It may also interest faculty outside legal education who wonder about that strange beast, the law school.

Does the Law School Belong in the University?

The theme of this volume is 'visions of the university law school'. Rather than unquestioningly accept the status quo, those involved in legal education should participate in the enduring debate over its proper role, challenging our own assumptions by listening to other voices, including those from other countries and other eras.

There has been continuing tension between the vision of the law school as a place for professional training of practising laywers, and the vision of it as a university school where law and the legal system are studied and original scholarship undertaken by faculty and students. Veblen, writing at a time when law schools generally taught just legal doctrine, thought that 'the law school belongs in the modern university no more than a school of fencing or dancing'.[1] Some still believe that the law school's only appropriate function is technical training for a vocation; while some boast of that, others conclude that a law school does not cohere with the liberal arts and research functions of the university proper.

Even the vocational mission of the law school, central as it is, does not mean that lawyers are best trained by learning just straight law. It is a commonplace maxim that law schools teach, not rules, but how to think like a lawyer: methods of analysis and expression, ways to read and think and argue. Preparation for successful practice is enhanced by learning broader perspectives. Thus excellent law study deciphers the actual workings and effects of the rule systems, explores the institutions and practices which create and enforce them, appraises their justifications and critiques, and develops and evaluates reforms.

These broader perspectives provide links with other university disciplines, placing the study of law among the other humanities and social sciences. Thus a school providing outstanding training for lawyering can simultaneously be a kind of mini-university, drawing on and contributing to sister disciplines.

A law school's vocational responsibilities do not make it stand out from the rest of the university; each Ph.D. programme preparing future university faculty is also a vocational school, teaching skills and a body of received knowledge. And law schools have become more scholarly: faculty engage, not only in descriptive research, but also in normative and sometimes empirical, cross-cultural or historical work; the better students edit a law journal while still in school and publish at least one piece of work of their own before graduation.

As in other professional schools, legal study and research enjoy some special benefits: the stimulus of confronting real-life problems, the rigour imposed by the constraints of working within actual social institutions, and the inspiration drawn from the ideals of the profession – ideals such as justice, fairness, peaceful resolution of disputes and a government of laws. The Romans spoke of 'juris prudentia' not of 'juris sapientia' because law is a practical wisdom.

Models of Legal Education

Law has been part of the university for as long as there have been universities. It is one of the founder disciplines comprising the central components of universities centuries before the appearance of such modern upstarts as sociology or comparative literature or biochemistry. The mediaeval universities graduated both Masters, the so-called *artists* who had studied in faculties of liberal arts and become Masters of Arts, and Doctors, who had studied in faculties of theology or law.

In the 18th and early 19th centuries, most legal education reflected two visions: a *practice* model, manifested in apprenticeship training that conveyed skills, ways of thinking and essential knowledge, and a *rule* model, using textbooks, lectures or a combination of the two to convey a body of doctrinal information. Chairs in the common law were created at a number of universities; Blackstone's Oxford lectures, published as a text, gave generations of lawyers an organized presentation of legal rules. The Scots taught law as a post-graduate study.

A famous tradition credits Langdell and Ames with revolutionizing law teaching by creating, in the late 19th century at Harvard, the case method. Even before Langdell, however, the case method had been developed by Clerke, who ran his own law school, and by Pomeroy at New York University and at Hastings.[2] The case method can be seen as part of a *principles* model. Law was divided into conceptual fields, each with its own set of principles, derivable by the inductive method from examination of an approved subset of cases. Questions of social policy and nonlegal data were generally thought to be excluded from this model.

Though spreading to dominate American legal education, Harvard's version of the case method was controversial from the first. Some other schools held to their traditional methods for years, while Holmes attacked it as overly abstract, even Hegelian. Its eventual predominance left room for a variety of movements in legal education: Roscoe Pound identified historical jurisprudence about 1890, economic interpretation at the turn of the century, logical analysis of rights about the time of World War I, then psychological realism, and by 1950 a 'rising cult' of natural law.[3]

A leading competitor to these models of legal education was the *policy* or functionalist model built on the legal realists' recognition that judges (and lawyers) are important shapers of the law. Its adherents thus made conscious attempts to cope with normative issues of what the law should be, often necessitating use of nonlegal as well as legal data. The Columbia Law School's extensive faculty debates and subsequent developments at Yale both emphasized the social functions of law rather than just the internal logic of its doctrine. Jerome Frank and Karl Llewellyn called for more teaching of craft skills: clinical legal education. Lasswell and McDougal's 'Law, Science and Policy' offered the most systematic proposal on how to teach future legal decision-makers to use their discretion to fashion wise public policy.

Current Visions

At the end of the 20th century, these models of legal education are supplemented by other visions. Law and economics represents a revival of interest in grand theories. Rationalist, utilitarian and scientific in its aspirations, it is intellectually related to the Lasswell-McDougal 'Law, Science and Policy' jurisprudence (though LSP was systematic rather than mathematical, and polytheistic as to the values to be maximized.) Competing with law and economics stand critical and humanistic perspectives, post-modernist demands to hear the voices of individuals and minorities identified by colour, ethnicity, gender and sexual orientation. Some new courses deal with women, minority racial groups, children and the elderly rather than with business or with intellectual abstractions; there are proclamations that the central work of law is with people.[4] Concern persists for morality and theories of rights and of justice, as well as attention to philosophical or literary approaches to issues of interpretation.

While the case method remains prototypical (at least among US first-year courses), there are many available teaching methodologies, including the lecture-text, legislative-statutory, historical, problem, conceptual, functional, transactional and (at least at Oxbridge) tutorial methods. Law courses may emphasize skills training, human relations skill, professional responsibility-values orientation, clinical exposure, integration of law and the social sciences, analysis of the judicial decision-making process, use of empirical methods or use of computers.

The continuing interest in clinical legal education manifests an interrelated set of concerns: exposing students to the real world and real clients; developing lawyer responsibility to clients; training in skills of trial advocacy, office counselling and negotiation; vivid teaching of substantive law; giving experience of ethical dilemmas *in vivo*, and fulfilling social responsibilities.

There is no consensus on what the law school should emphasize: debates abound among proponents of practical training, natural law, free-enterprise economics, radical and feminist criticism, varieties of communitarianism, and many other views. And legal doctrine, challenged though it is, is still taught everywhere – and not only in the law schools, but also through independent student study of 'black-letter' texts and through bar review courses. Summer clerkships for students, rotations for American associates, and pupillage for barristers, still provide apprenticeships. Thus the legal education which existed before the rise of university law schools still endures.

Scholarship

Does legal education harmonize with the research function of the university? Modern university research and the Ph.D. were developed in 19th-century German universities and The Johns Hopkins University. Law has had great scholars since Roman days, and it is an old idea that law is or should be a 'science'; however, legal research was long an enterprise of classification, rationalization and theory. Legal scholarship has only haltingly begun to study empirical assumptions underlying legal reasoning, the actual workings of legal regimes, and the causes and effects of changes in the law. One intellectual child of Veblen contends that fundamental research, 'about' law and grounded in normative issues of law reform, should be done to 'remove an embarrassment from the University'.[5]

Attempts to draw on the social science empirical tradition had abortive beginnings in a failed bid to start a legal research institute at The Johns Hopkins University, and in the work of several early scholars at Yale. The current interest in multidisciplinary study of the legal process is reflected in the existence of law teachers with dual training, in the appointment of nonlawyers to law faculties and lawyers to other departments, and cross-disciplinary team teaching. While economics is currently the most popular 'law-and-...' subject, psychology/psychiatry/psychoanalysis, philosophy, literary criticism and accounting are among other disciplines represented in American law schools. Worldwide, at least economics and philosophy have impact.

In past generations law schools produced relatively little scholarship and used large lecture-halls. With the increase in legal research, seminars and specialized electives, faculty-student ratios have changed and legal education has become as labour-intensive as other graduate education.

The External Context

Legal education is not a wholly autonomous enterprise. The external context – trends in society, the legal profession and higher education – creates both constraints and opportunities for the law school.

Each law school must take into account the changing needs of the community it serves, as well as the possibility of serving a wider community. Ambitious schools may seek out areas in which distinction can be achieved, having in mind social need, weakness of competition and existing strengths. Schools that formerly drew students from the locality, returned graduates to it, and engaged in research concerning local problems, may find themselves increasingly serving a wider region. The local community may also change, as agricultural regions become industrialized, new population groups emerge or a parochial home town becomes a base for international business transactions. The school may have to respond to the community's need for fewer lawyers, or better trained ones, or lawyers of wider perspectives.

An image of a certain state of society underlies much of traditional law school teaching: individual persons of means have disputes with other such individuals and turn for assistance to a lawyer likely to be in solo practice, who applies knowledge of the common law. Graduates of local law schools may still find themselves engaged in such a small town practice. The continuing modernization of society, however, renders that image less relevant for many law school graduates. Government increasingly regulates our affairs with multiplying complications. Lawyers and courts are consulted for solutions to more than individual disputes; it is not only in the United States that they may also have to deal with large-scale problems such as environmental impact, discrimination and conditions in prisons and mental hospitals. Those who need legal assistance may be involved, not so much in a single dispute, as in the complexities of an ongoing relationship, such as in labour-management negotiations or transactions with a regular business supplier. Much legal business in the future will involve relations between the individual and large organizations or bureaucracies (such as government agencies, large corporations, labour unions), or relationships among such behemoths. Preventive law – planning by lawyers to avoid disputes – will have increased importance.

More lawyers in the years ahead are likely to function within the context of large organizations: in private firms numbering hundreds of attorneys, with branch offices in many states or countries; in corporate law departments; in government agencies; in legal aid societies or public defender organizations; or through such third-party intermediaries as insurance carriers. Computers will be used increasingly as adjuncts to legal practice, both as aids to research (through systems like WESTLAW and LEXIS) and as necessary means of data management in massive lawsuits.

Private law and judge-made common law will increasingly be challenged to make room for public law involving government regulation, whose source is legislation and the administrative process. Traditionally there has been concern for due process and individual rights against the government; in the years ahead, with industry, unions, universities and other large organizations often functioning as 'private governments', lawyers and law schools will be concerned to protect fairness, equality and liberty in a bureaucratic civilization.

The growing interdependence of the world will also affect legal education. Many lawyers deal with business problems: as businesses increasingly engage in international transactions or organize their own corporations multinationally, their lawyers must take into account the laws of other nations. Just as law schools in any locality teach the legal system of the nation as a whole, so too law schools in each country will increasingly perceive the need for their students to be knowledgeable about regional regimes – like the EC or NAFTA – and the legal systems of the world.

These continuing trends will create curriculum issues for law schools in the years ahead.

Whom Do Law School Graduates Serve?

While previously legal services were readily accessible only to businesses and persons of means, in recent years there have been moves to increase access to the courts by poor and middle-income persons. In many nations, poor persons with civil disputes can often receive free legal assistance through government-funded legal services schemes; poor criminal defendants facing imprisonment have a right to free legal representation; and other persons of limited means can increasingly obtain legal assistance through prepaid legal insurance, low-cost legal clinics or similar means. As the delivery system for legal services is reformed, the demand for legal work will change concomitantly.

The distribution of work between lawyers and others is likely to change, a trend that is part of larger changes in the division of labour in society. Lawyers will frequently find that their work overlaps skills traditionally associated with other professionals, such as the accountant, manager or psychologist, and will find it useful to cultivate new skills, such as mediation or conflict resolution. Many work tasks that lawyers historically claimed for their own have in part shifted to other, perhaps cheaper, practitioners. Countries like England have begun rethinking their historic organization of the legal professions. From the position of the organized bar, changes in work allocation raise issues of the unauthorized practice of law and have in some countries led to 'treaties' with such groups as real estate brokers, accountants and title insurance companies. If graduates of local law schools find that many traditional tasks are performed by these nonlawyers, such schools must either upgrade or otherwise redefine the roles for which they train their students.

In some areas, there is an impending rise in the role of the legal paraprofessional or lawyer's assistant. Persons so trained may in the future no longer be regarded as 'paraprofessional', but as constituting a profession in their own right, forming their own firms to handle such matters as evictions, and hiring attorneys as needed to work for them. Paraprofessional training programmes can be compared with the law schools of the early 19th century, like Litchfield Law School, the first US law school. Students with or without college degrees receive legal training of a predominantly vocational nature, requiring a few months or a year, primarily in lecture or lecture-textbook form.

Alternative dispute resolution – called ADR or now sometimes simply called 'dispute resolution' – may dispense altogether with lawyers as we now know them. Neighbourhood justice centres, ombudspeople, patient advocates in hospitals, and organized programmes of mediation and conciliation may grow in prevalence. These processes and forums will seek to reconcile adversaries and settle quarrels without the skills, or the expense, of lawyers and judges as we know them. Law schools in the future may either withdraw from these processes or may train persons (whether or not called 'lawyers') to work with them.

There will also be differences in the extent to which various law schools embrace the wider definition of teaching and service envisaged in Chief Justice Vanderbilt's concept of the Law Centre.[7] In its contemporary version, such a centre might, for example, train court administrators, paraprofessionals, judges, practising lawyers, college and graduate students, as well as law students.

Financial Realities

What law schools can do is constrained by financial realities, which in large measure depend, directly or indirectly, on the ebb and flow of student demand. In the total pool of potential law school applicants, there are variations from period to period in the relative attractiveness of legal education compared to other professional and graduate schools and work opportunities. In a number of countries, the top law schools in particular have become extraordinarily selective, many local schools have reached the previous standards of the best schools, and a number of new schools have come into existence. The decline in sex discrimination has enabled many more women to seek professional roles.

Critics like Derek Bok complain that law schools attract too many of the most talented students, drawing them away from more productive fields. The force of such criticism depends on what law school graduates actually accomplish; it is less salient if they help coordinate business interaction, resolve disputes peacefully, and increase the justice and fairness which are important parts of the quality of life.

State and private law schools may both find it increasingly necessary to justify to representatives of a frugal public their high costs per student. Each discipline has its own set of reasons for deserving support, including traditional values, intellectual and cultural importance, and contribution to civilization. Legal educators will point out that law schools make an immediate contribution to the public good through legal research and the work of law school graduates. Since fewer resources are required than for some other fields, a relatively smaller university investment in a law school is needed to produce noticeable improvements in quality. Many graduates will be successful in practice, and their charity in later years may return to the university, many times over, the money invested in their schooling. And as legal education becomes less parochial, interdisciplinary research and teaching in law schools may benefit the college and other graduate and professional disciplines.

Technology

New technology is affecting the law schools. More and more schools teach the skills of computer-assisted legal research; students learn to use LEXIS and WESTLAW and word processors, as well as traditional printed indexes and office files. Law libraries increasingly use computerized bibliographic data bases, such as RLN and OCLC, and specialized data bases, as well as new data storage methods involving CD-ROM or other microforms (instead of hard copy) for material seldom consulted. There is likely to be a continuing, but slow, increase in the use of new technology in teaching: a few computer programs are already available to teach specific subjects. Immediate feedback on student clinical or classroom performance through video taping is now also feasible.

Leaders Must Make Choices

Leadership and creative planning are needed to make decisions intelligently; each school, by decision or drift, continually chooses its goals.

Choices on the future of a law school must be grounded in the aspirations and context of the individual academic community. They cannot be made as a matter of theory: each school has a unique situation at any given time. Each faculty has its own range of abilities, interests and ideals. Students, alumni, university administration, the local bench and bar, donors, government administrators and legislators, the larger society – each constituency has a sense of the identity of the school and is a bearer of its tradition and hopes. Each school has its own financial realities, reflecting previous decisions and influencing future ones, on quality, size and breadth of programme. And each has its own sense of vision.

The leadership of a school cannot be autocratic in shaping its goals. Though deans, presidents or vice chancellors may be looked to from all sides, they typically have much less power, and a more demanding task, than many business managers. Achievement of the school's goals requires the enthusiastic cooperation of many persons who should thus be involved in the ongoing process of planning. An educational leader must deal with a tenured faculty conscious of its own capacities and prerogatives, with a relatively fixed plant and product, and with the need to rely on philanthropic gifts or government subventions to meet a major portion of the budget.

Though deans and central administration may have limited power, they still must lead. Opportunities for leadership are available through the use of available points of leverage, such as setting the intellectual agenda, maintaining attention to long-term values, influencing decisions at hiring and 'up-or-out' stages, and allocation of discretionary funds and merit rises. Leadership can also be exercised through inspiration, encouragement and praise; the provision of opportunities for professional development; the structuring of participatory decision processes; and the identification of measurable objectives. The leader can facilitate change by promoting a sense of community, observing basic managerial efficiency and fiscal responsibility, and fighting for academic freedom and intellectual values.

Faculty, dean and central administration share the responsibilities of leadership. While it will take different forms in each school, leadership is required for law schools to deal successfully with the crucial issues they will face in the years ahead.

The Pursuit of Justice

An underlying mission that justifies public support of law schools is their contribution to the achievement of justice in the community, through the effects of their graduates' practice, faculty scholarship and public service activities.

Long before Roscoe Pound's criticisms at the turn of the century, there was widespread 'popular dissatisfaction with the administration of justice'. Many believe that too many lawyers are unethical, that civil disputes handled by lawyers through courts cost too much and take too long to be resolved, or that the law itself protects only the powerful or only certain parts of society. Lawyers' activities are thought to obstruct the finding of truth and the achievement of fairness through the exploitation of mere legal technicalities. There is periodic widespread criticism of specific criminal law practices or rules, such as plea-bargaining or exclusionary rules. Especially in the US, there is also widespread criticism of specific types of civil lawsuits, such as malpractice actions against doctors or personal injury cases, where a lawyer collects a contingent fee of one-third or more.

Law school courses and scholarship can identify abuses, injustice and anachronisms, and propose and evaluate reforms. They can develop students' abilities to communicate with the public, to listen and speak, promoting dialogue within the community on whether legal institutions adequately serve justice. They can study the values that underlie rules and practices, examining whether they are justified or rotten, and help to develop legal institutions that realize our finest values.

This Collection and Beyond

The prominent contemporary perspectives – such as critical legal studies, law and economics, feminist theory and critical race theory – have only short listings in this volume under their own headings, but they are also discussed under other headings, such as the Commonwealth section (Part V). Some essays that should be read in conjunction with this volume can readily be found elsewhere: Oliver Wendell Holmes (1897), 'The Path of the Law', *Harvard Law Review*, **10**, 457–78 (which was written as a piece on legal education) can be found in Robert Samuel Summers (1992), *American Legal Theory*, in the same series as this volume, and Duncan Kennedy (1982), 'Legal Education and the Reproduction of Hierarchy', *Journal of Legal Education*, **32**, 591–615 is in James Boyle (1992), *Critical Legal Studies* in the same series. Andrew S. Watson (1968), 'The Quest for Professional Competence: Psychological Aspects of Legal Education', *University of Cincinnati Law Review*, **37**, 91–166 and Duncan Kennedy (1970), 'Why the Law School Fails: A Polemic', *Yale Journal of Law and Social Action*, **1**, 71–90, as well as other examples of the subliterature on the psychology of legal education, have been reserved for the forthcoming volume on psychology and law in this series.

Because of its length, Harold D. Lasswell and Myres S. McDougal (1943), 'Legal Education and Public Policy: Professional Training in the Public Interest', *Yale Law Journal*, **52**, 203–95 could not be included here, nor do I have any articles from the symposium on it in *Virginia Law Review*, Volume 54 of 1968, though other essays do discuss the approach.

Among the many reports on legal education that deserve to be consulted are J. Redlich (1914), 'The Common Law and the Case Method in American University Law Schools'; the 1944 report of the Committee on Curriculum of the Association of American Law Schools, by Llewellyn and others (1945), 'The Place of Skills in Legal Education', *Columbia Law Review*, **45**, 345–91; and (1983), 'Law and Learning: Report to the Social Sciences and Humanities Research Council of Canada'.

Other articles unfortunately had to be omitted from this volume for reasons of space – even if they are classics. From the early period these include additional writing by Karl Llewellyn, specifically (1948), 'The Current Crisis in Legal Education', *Journal of Legal Education*, **1**, 211–20; also Brainerd Currie's account of the famous Columbia law faculty curriculum discussions: (1951), 'The Materials of Law Study', Parts I and II, *Journal of Legal Education*, **3**, 331–83, and (1955), Part III, *Journal of Legal Education*, **8**, 1–78.

Influential work of the 1960s and 1970s includes: Irvin C. Rutter (1968), 'Designing and Teaching the First-Degree Law Curriculum', *University of Cincinnati Law Review*, **37**, 9–166; Robert Redmount (1968), 'Humanistic Law Through Legal Education', *Connecticut Law Review*, **1**, 201–20 and (1972), 'A Conceptual View of the Legal Education Process',

Journal of Legal Education, **24**, 129–79; Robert Stevens's (1970) history, 'Two Cheers for 1870: The American Law School', *Perspectives in American History*, **5**, 405–35, expanded and revised in his (1983) book, *Law School: Legal Education in America from the 1850s to the 1980s*; Paul N. Savoy (1970), 'Toward a New Politics of Legal Education', *Yale Law Journal*, **79**, 444–504; Rand Rosenblatt (1970), 'Legal Theory and Legal Education', *Yale Law Journal*, **79**, 1153–78; Barry B. Boyer and Roger C. Cramton (1974), 'American Legal Education: An Agenda for Research and Reform', *Cornell Law Review*, **59**, 221–97; Jack Himmelstein (1978), 'Reassessing Law Schooling: An Inquiry into the Application of Humanistic Educational Psychology to the Teaching of Law', *New York University Law Review*, **53**, 514–60; Arthur Leff (1978), 'Law and', *Yale Law Journal*, **87**, 989–1011; Jerold S. Auerbach (1978), 'What Has the Teaching of Law to do with Justice?', *New York University Law Review*, **53**, 457–74; Stephen Guest (1979), 'Legal Education and Legal Theory', *Current Legal Problems*, **32**, 179–97.

Of work in the 1980s, limits set by a firm editor forced me to cut the following: Anthony T. Kronman (1981), 'Legal Scholarship and Moral Education', *Yale Law Journal*, **90**, 955–69; James R. Elkins (1983), 'On the Significance of Women in Legal Education', *ALSA Forum*, **7**, 290–316; John Henry Schlegel (1984), 'Langdell's Legacy, or the Case of the Empty Envelope', *Stanford Law Review*, **36**, 1517–33; John Goldring (1987), 'Babies and Bathwater: Tradition or Progress in Legal Scholarship and Legal Education', *University of Western Australia Law Review*, **17**, 216–56; William Twining (1988), 'Legal Skills and Legal Education', *Law Teacher*, **22**, 4–13; Carrie Menkel-Meadow (1988), 'Feminist Legal Theory, Critical Legal Studies, and Legal Education or the Fem–Crits Go To Law School', *Journal of Legal Education*, **38**, 61–86; and the many contributions by David Barnhizer, such as (1979), 'The Clinical Method of Legal Instruction: Its Theory and Implementation', *Journal of Legal Education*, **30**, 67–148 and (1989), 'The University Ideal and the American Law School', *Rutgers Law Review*, **42**, 109–76. A new symposium 'Legal Education' appeared just as this volume was going to press in *Michigan Law Review*, volume 91 of 1993.

Omitted here also are the debates on critical legal studies spawned by Paul Carrington's (1984) controversial counter-critique, 'Of Law and the River', *Journal of Legal Education*, **34**, 222–8, including those in *Journal of Legal Education*, Volume 35 of 1985. My respect for work of present and former colleagues is reflected in this volume's contents but, if room had only permitted, I would also have included Gary Bellow and Earl Johnson (1971), 'Reflections on the University of Southern California Clinical Semester', *Southern California Law Review*, **44**, 664–95; Michael J. Graetz and Charles H. Whitebread, II (1981), 'Monrad Paulsen and the Idea of a University Law School', *Virginia Law Review*, **67**, 445–6; and Susan Estrich (1992), 'Teaching Rape Law', *Yale Law Journal*, **102**, 509–20.

Worthy of attention also is the growing body of empirical work on legal education and law students, and descriptions of a variety of teaching methods and novel courses. A good deal of such work can be found in the pages of the *Journal of Legal Education*.

For early history, interesting is W. Wesley Pue (1989), 'Guild Training vs. Professional Education: The Committee on Legal Education and the Law Department of Queen's College, Birmingham in the 1850's', *American Journal of Legal History*, **33**, 241–87, in addition to material mentioned above. Those who think that Christopher Columbus Langdell was the initial discoverer must realize that Indians were there first.

Notes

1. Thorstein Veblen (1918), *The Higher Learning in America*, New York: B.W. Huebsch, reprinted 1965, 211.
2. See Clerke, Appendix to S. Warren (1st edition, London 1835; American edition, 1846), *A Popular and Practical Introduction to Law Studies*. On Pomeroy, see 1 P.C. Jessup (1938), *Elihu Root*, 61, 62; T.C. Barnes (1978), *Hastings College of the Law: The First Century*, 113, quoting Hastings College of the Law of the University of California (1928), *Golden Jubilee Book 1878–1928*, at 41. For a pre-Langdellian casebook, see E. Bennett and F. Heard (1856), *A Selection of Leading Cases in Criminal Law*.
3. Roscoe Pound (1951), 'Some Comments on Law, Teachers and Law Teaching', *Journal of Legal Education*, **3**, 519–532.
4. Virginia Anne Church (1975), 'The Real Business of Law Is People Not Cases: An Argument for Training Counselors', *Learning and the Law*, **2**, Spring, 54–60.
5. John Henry Schlegel (1984), 'Searching for Archimedes – Legal Education, Legal Scholarship, and Liberal Ideology', *Journal of Legal Education*, **34**, 103–10.
6. Chief Justice Arthur J. Vanderbilt (1952), 'The Mission of a Law Center', *New York University Law Review*, **27**, 20–31.

To Martha, with love

Part I
The Beginnings

LAW LECTURE.

(INNER TEMPLE, THOMAS STARKIE, ESQ.)

In my preceding lecture, I endeavoured to establish, as far as my ability and time would permit, the necessity, or, at least, the utility, of a more systematic attention to the law as a science. I was then obliged to defer the consideration of a question of importance, immediately connected with the former,—whether the law of England itself did not exhibit some peculiar defects, which might fairly be attributed to the want of scientific cultivation and of systematic arrangement. I purpose, in the course of the present lecture, to recur to this subject; but I wish, previously, to make a few further remarks in illustration and explanation of what I have already said.

I was anxious, on the occasion of my former lecture, to impress the danger of trusting too much to a knowledge of general rules, from whatever source and whatever authority they may be derived, which are not the results of the student's own observation and inquiries, or at least verified by such means. I repeat my former remark, that a work like the Commentaries, excellent as it is for many and most important purposes, is not to be read without this caution, that the student, when he learns principles from that source, has yet much to perform before he makes those principles his own, with a view to their useful and practical application. With respect to the application of the general principles of justice they are usually obvious; opinions do not usually differ concerning them; it is in the searching out the proper principles in confused and complicated cases of fact, to which the almost infinitely varied combinations and transactions of life constantly give rise, and in the skilful use of the discovered or acknowledged principle, for the defining the boundary line between right and wrong, that its practical excellency consists.

I shall, perhaps, best be able to explain and illustrate my meaning by particular instances, to show the practical inefficacy of mere general rules; and, for this purpose, I take, as the first subject which occurred to me in preparing my notes for this lecture, the subject of Slander and Libel.

In the Commentaries, vol. 3, p. 123, we find the extent of the legal remedy by action for slander, thus expressed. [*The learned Lecturer here read the passages referred to. p.* 123 *to* 126.]

I will now suppose, that these questions are proposed, or that they present themselves to the mind of a thinking student, who has thus made himself master of these principles, or rather rules.

1. Suppose that A. falsely says of B., that B., on such a day, assaulted and beat C. Will an action lie for such words without special damage?

2. Suppose that A. falsely says of B., that he is infected with the itch or cholera morbus. Will an action lie?

3. Suppose that A. is the heir-apparent of B., who has a large landed estate; and that C., with intent to cause B. to disinherit A. says that A. is a bastard. Will an action lie?

4. Suppose that A. publishes, in writing, concerning B. that he is a swindler. Will an action lie?

5. Suppose that A. publishes a caricature of B., or has him burnt in effigy, with intent to ridicule and disgrace him. Will an action lie, no special damage having been sustained?

Now, as to the first case, where an assault and battery are imputed, the student would find, that words are actionable which impeach a man of some *heinous crime*, as to say, that a man has murdered another, or is perjured. The student would naturally suppose, that the imputation of a mere assault was not actionable, the offence not being a heinous one, *ejusdem generis*, with murder or perjury, yet nothing can be more clear than that the imputation of any offence, in respect of which, if true, corporal punishment might be inflicted, would be actionable. And if the principle were to be extracted from the decisions, there being no written law on the subject, the boundary or limit would clearly appear. In ancient times, a man might be put on his trial, or, at least, might be consigned to prison for an offence of which he was charged, not by any open accuser, but by the common fame, as is expressly laid down by Glanville, who wrote, as is well known, in the reign of Henry II.; and as is stated in the Mirror to have been the *law* in the reign of Henry I. He says, ([1]) " time it was, that the law in favour of liberty gave a right of action against any one who, by a false report, endangered the liberty of another; " and as the principle extended to all reports which could thus endanger a man's liberty, and subject him to corporal punishment, so the law also has made, although, no doubt, with some fluctuations, every imputation to be actionable which could thus endanger a man's liberty. Here, then, although the reason on which the law was founded has, long since, in a great measure ceased, a recourse to the principle at once shows the extent to which the right of action for such words, without proof of special damage, extends, whilst the connection between the present law and the former practice, as to criminal proceedings, serve to illustrate each other, and to impress them on the memory.

Again, upon the question whether the imputation of being infected with a particular disease,—such as the scarlet fever, were actionable, without special damage, he would, probably, looking at the general rule as laid down in the Commentaries, conclude that it was, it being an infectious disease, whilst a reference to cases would show, that this was far too general a position, and that the rule was, in practice, confined to two particular instances of disorders, which, in former times, (as may be collected from history,) were the subject of terror and alarm.

Upon the question whether words of bastardy, spoken of an heir, were actionable, he would probably conclude, from the total omission of any mention of such a ground of action, that none would be maintainable; yet, in several instances, the contrary has been held, and although this is a remarkable instance illustrative of the common law reason for departing from the general rule, and giving an action to a party likely to suffer greatly from slanderous words, in case the *festinum remedium* were not allowed.

On the question whether, if one man publish of another, in writing, that he was a swindler, he would find it laid down generally, that *what has been said as to words spoken, will also hold, in every particular, with regard to libels in writing or printing, and the civil ac-*

---

(1) Glanville, p. 113.

tions consequent upon them; the conclusion, therefore, would be, that, as no action would lie for saying of a man that he was a swindler, neither would any action lie for publishing the same matter in writing; yet it has long been established, and before the time of the Commentaries, that the rule as to the actionable quality of written, was much more extensive than in the case of oral slander. It is true, indeed, that the distinction has, since then, been questioned, and that it has since been more certainly established than it had been before: still, however, taking the question to be then a doubtful one, it was well worthy of observation, for the sake of the principle involved, and, at all events, it justifies the remark, that Sir W. Blackstone was always desirous of exhibiting a regular and systematical rule, rather than notice defects and anomalies; and, according to the well-known rule observed by poets, he left untouched many points, which, when exhibited, might appear to be anomalous and ungraceful.

To my last remaining question, the student, finding it laid down, generally and positively, that, as to signs and pictures, it seems to be necessary always to show that some special damage has followed, he would answer accordingly, and adopt a rule as a peremptory and rigid rule, though contrary to the general principle already laid down as to written libels, tending to set a man in an odious or ridiculous light; for it is impossible to conjecture on what reasonable ground it could be held, that scurrilous representations of a man by pictures or signs, could differ at all, in this respect, from written libels, expressing the same offensive meaning.

Now, in every one of these cases, which are not extraordinary cases solely contrived with a view to puzzle or perplex, but such as might easily and naturally occur, the student would form an erroneous opinion. It is, then, perfectly clear, that much more must be done towards obtaining a practical knowledge of legal limits and boundaries, than to master such general rules as are so laid down, even by so great a proficient as Sir W. Blackstone; and that the student must either extract for himself, and from the cases, those principles which serve to define legal boundaries, or, which is not so profitable, adopt, after due consideration, the results of the labour of others who have undertaken the task.

It may be said, that minute accuracy on all points is not to be expected in a work so general as the Commentaries, which extends over far too wide a scope, embracing, indeed, the whole range of our political and civil constitution, to mark out legal limits and boundaries with precision; and that, consequently, the not enabling a student to answer a series of even ordinary and common questions, is by no means to be regarded as a defect. To this I fully accede; I readily admit the great excellence of the work; my object is simply to show, that it would not afford definite notions of the extent of the principles and rules of law; that these are to be learnt only by attentive and systematic reading.

Connected with the same subject, I think that the mode of treating the subject of libels, in reference to their criminal qualities, calls for remark. I do not conceive that offering such remarks requires any apology from me; for, independently of all other considerations, and were I merely commenting on the boundaries of this particular branch of the law, it would, most undoubtedly fall within my province to observe to my audience that I thought the law, on any particular subject, or any principle of the law, defectively, or ambiguously, or erroneously expressed; and that the student must not, even on so high an authority, adopt, as law, what is there asserted; but it is to a still further and more general extent essential, that I should enforce my general caution not to take too much upon trust, but to trace legal boundaries, if I may be allowed the expression, by his own legal perambulations.

I cannot but think it remarkable, that it should never have occurred to the learned commentator, that some limitation was necessary in laying down so broad a rule, which, it may be observed, carried the doctrine much further than it was ever carried in the disputed cases which gave rise to Mr. Fox's celebrated libel bill; for in none of these cases was it ever contended that the occasion of publishing might not constitute a defence; nor did any of them go to the length of asserting generally, that no facts were ever to be inquired into but the act of publication, and criminality of the matter. The charge to juries in the disputed cases, if I may so call them, were necessarily confined to the circumstances of the particular cases in which there was no evidence supplied, by the occasion of the publication, to show that it was not malicious. But numerous cases must suggest themselves, such as of confidential communications, of the publication of matters for the purpose of investigating a fact in which the party possesses an interest, which are not either actionable or indictable; *ex. gr. Delany v. Jones*, 4 Esp. C. 491, where a charge of bigamy was imputed.

I have also to observe that the learned commentator's allusions to the libel law are in some instances, and in reference to the very subject of libel, calculated to convey erroneous impressions, not only as to the practice, but even as to the principles of the Roman law.

VOL. II.   4 C

There is great reason for supposing that the offence of libel was not a capital offence by the Twelve Tables; the assertion that it was, rests entirely on a supposed extract from Cicero de Republicâ, to be found in St. Augustine's De Civitate Dei. There is strong circumstantial evidence to warrant the inference, that the law of the Twelve Tables was no more guilty of so sanguinary an enactment, than of the horrible enactment, also attributed to them, which was supposed to have directed that the body of an insolvent debtor should be cut into parts and distributed amongst his creditors; the law having, in truth, directed the cutting and dividing, not of the body, but what was much more acceptable to creditors, the property of the debtor. It would be difficult, in the absence of stronger and more express authority, to accede to the position that the decemviral code punished the offence of libel capitally.

The authority is weakened by the evidence that St. Augustine does not profess to communicate the exact words even of Cicero.

The shocking severity of such a law, in so early an age of the republic, affords intrinsic evidence, sufficient in the absence of the most direct authority, to question the existence of such a law. The Athenian laws, which were consulted by the framers of the law of the Twelve Tables, offered no precedent for such a law.

The law of the Twelve Tables punished the *hynecia*, a term which included libels, by a pecuniary fine. And the fact that Sylla, Augustus, and Tiberius punished those who were guilty of writing libels on illustrious persons with death, under the strained pretext of a violation of the *Lex læsæ Majestatis*, is strong to show that no general law then existed which awarded capital punishment; it is much more probable that they would have enforced or revived an obsolete law, than have incurred the odium of such a manifest abuse of a different law.

The observation also, as founded on the edict of Valentinian, is calculated to convey the impression that libel, generally, was the subject of capital punishment; whereas, in fact, the real object of capital punishment was an offender who had, if not accomplished, at least attempted to commit a species of assassination, through the medium of the law, by prefering a secret, anonymous, and false denunciation of a capital charge.

By the *fourth* constitution of the Theodosian code, " Famosa scriptio libellorum quæ *nomine accusatoris caret* minimè examinanda est, sed penitus abolenda, nam qui accusationis promotione confidat, liberâ potius intentione, quam captiosâ et occultâ conscriptione, alterius debet *vitam* in judicium devocare."

By the *eighth* "contumelia vero quæ caput alterius contra juris ordinem pulsat, depressa nostris legibus jaceat, intercidat *furor famosorum libellorum.*"

The *ninth*, which was the edict of Emperors Valentinian and Valens, afterwards imported into the Digest, clearly referred to the same offence of secret denunciation, adding as an encouragement to open accusation, " Sanè si quis devotionis suæ ac salutis publicæ custodiam gerat, nomen suum profiteatur, et quæ per famosum libellum persequenda putaverit *ore proprio edicat,*" &c.

I now proceed to notice some instances in our law in which inconvenience and uncertainty have arisen from want of more strict adherence to general and connected principles.

The want of system observable in our law, is, in the first place, in a considerable degree, attributable to the circumstance that our laws are derived from various sources, originating in remote times, applicable to very different circumstances, and most of all to the means adopted for getting rid of the inconvenience necessarily resulting from the adoption of exotic rules, calculated for other times, and very dissimilar circumstances.

It has been seen, from the masterly remarks made by Savigny, on the genius and spirit of the Roman law, that he attributes, and I believe truly attributes their excellence, as a system, to a gradual development of its scientific principles and constant adaptation to the increasing exigencies of society. From the time when, as poets feign, Numa received his simple laws at the fountain of the Goddess Ægeria, through all the varieties of political form exhibited in the history of that wonderful nation, there was no revolution which materially obstructed the gradual and progressive improvement of their laws. It is true that the Decemviral laws, or the laws of the Twelve Tables, were borrowed from Greece, or, at all events, that a deputation was sent to Athens, with a view to the framing of those celebrated laws. And here we may pause for a moment to contemplate this singular and important fact in the history of the Roman law. There is, perhaps, no instance to be found, in the annals of any country, of so earnest, so strong a desire, to establish good and perfect laws. Here we find a warlike athletic nation, if I may be allowed the expression, flourishing in all the pride and vigour of youth, employing the most rational and prudent means which could possibly be devised for providing a system of good and useful laws, not disdaining for that purpose, to consult even foreign sources, from which they knew that useful information might advantageously be derived. What has been the consequence? A code of laws has resulted, which, after the lapse of more than 2000 years from the time when its foundations were thus laid, remains the subject of veneration and respect even of those nations who, for good and wise reasons, unconnected with my present remarks, have refused to adopt that law as their own. To return, however, to the more immediate topic for consideration: the history of our own country in this respect, presents circumstances which afford an unfavourable and disadvantageous contrast with that of Rome. Rome, notwithstanding changes in political constitutions, through the several gradations of her regal, republican, and imperial constitutions, had yet the opportunity, through many centuries, of gradually improving on her ancient and simple laws, undisturbedly, in substance, by foreign invasion or intestine convulsion. I need not observe how different, in this respect, have been the state and condition of our own country, subject as its laws have been to successive and violent changes, under the Romans, Saxons, Danes, and Normans; and, divided as the country has been into a number of districts, each possessing its own peculiar laws and customs. This latter circumstance alone constitutes a remarkable difference between the laws of England and those of Rome; the latter, from a small beginning, enlarged her territories on every side; she, at the same time, extended her laws to her new subjects, and, to a greater or less degree, the privileges of Roman citizens; the result of which was, to a great extent, an uniformity of laws and customs; whilst, in this country, an immense variety of laws and local customs have immemorially prevailed, notwithstanding frequent attempts to assimilate them, and reduce them to consistency.

Of the confused multitude of our laws, even at so early a period as the reign of Henry II., Glanville's treatise affords convincing proof.

There can be no doubt that the greatest change, so far as regards the present state of our law, took place on the Norman conquest, for then, according to all accounts, and without entering upon the disputed question, whether the feudal law was then introduced for the first time, it is admitted, on all hands, that a very material change was effected by the notorious introduction of the feudal system, which, if it existed before, existed only under a very different and modified form.

The feudal law, however well adapted to the convenience of a vast extent of territory, parcelled out among the retainers of a warlike chief, in portions which rather resembled principalities than private estates, was little applicable to a country like England, where but few, though some such existed even after the Norman Conquest, and where the custom of gavelkind had, to a great extent, formerly prevailed, which was founded on a totally different principle. The doctines of open and notorious seisin and investiture by livery or by

Inner Temple.

entry, became almost ludicrous and absurd when applied as the law regulating the rights to small and inconsiderable portions of property. In after times, when the strictness of feudal restraints had partially relaxed, and when thus it came to pass, that the right to a grocer's shop or a coal-yard was to be governed by like rules as to livery of seisin, entry, ouster, and disseisin, as governed the rights of military tenants, whose possession was matter of continual notoriety and interest: the variety of the questions to which the system has frequently given rise, is not a little singular.

These, however, are considerations which it is not convenient to enter upon on the present occasion; my object is simply to point out the effect produced on our system of jurisprudence. The restraints and burdens which were imposed on the alienation and enjoyment of lands held under the feudal tenures, were found to be intolerably irksome and oppressive; the consequence was, that various subtle devices were practised and countenanced in the courts for evading them, until, by successive innovations, rules, as practised in this country, could scarcely be recognized by foreign jurists. Two great and important consequences, interesting in a theoretical and practical point of view, and materially connected with our present inquiry, were the result:—

In the first place, the English jurists having, to suit their own purposes, cut off and pruned away many of the rules of feudal law, seem for a long time to have purposely avoided all reference to the original and fundamental principles on which the system was founded, and which were still recognized in other countries. Their reasonings and analogies, therefore, founded, as they were, not on the real principles of enlightened law, but upon peremptory and arbitrary rules, which, whether attributable to feudal principles or not, they acquired without reference to those principles, their reasonings and deductions became necessarily subtle, intricate, and confused, from being no longer referable to true and simple principles.

The endeavours made to get rid of feodal restraints of conditional estates and estates tail, were not direct, but various and successful devices were practised to elude and evade them, by the technical aid of discontinuances, warranties, fines, and recoveries.

The consequences of once permitting any established laws or written ordinances to be virtually annihilated by any subtle and indirect means, can by no means be confined to the immediate consequences in respect of which the judicial may have encroached on the legislative functions. As a matter of principle, the results are infinitely more mischievous; a spirit of subtlety is thus tolerated and countenanced, and, it may be, wholly substituted, for sound straight-forward reason. All advancement of the law as a science is necessarily and completely obstructed, when the object to be obtained is not to apply plain and obvious principles of justice, or the rules founded on those principles, in a just and consistent manner, but to study law to evade existing rules by refined and subtle distinctions. The encouragement of attempts to evade the law by cunning and indirect practices, must necessarily and directly tend to bring its ordinances into contempt, and to weaken their virtue and their force, to degrade the law from the rank of a science, and to lay it open to all the mischievous practises which low cunning and chicanery can devise or suggest. Practices such as these are avowed without scruple by eminent men, and are even offered as an excuse for dispensing with any reference to original principles.—Butler, 22.

Mr. Hallam, in the second volume of his History of the Middle Ages, observes :—"The capacity of deciding legal controversies was now, (after the Norman conquest,) only to be found in men who had devoted themselves to that peculiar study; and a race of such men arose, whose eagerness, and even enthusiasm, in the profession of the law, were stimulated by the self-complacency of intellectual dexterity in threading its intricate and thorny mazes. The Romans are noted in their own country for a shrewd and litigious temper, which may have given a character to our courts of justice in former times. Something, too, of that excessive subtlety, and that preference of technical to rational principles, which runs through our system, may be imputed to the scholastic philosophy which was in vogue during the same period, and is marked by the same features.

"Those who are moderately conversant in our law will easily trace other circumstances, (other than a desire to get rid of innumerable and inconsistent precedents,) which have co-operated in producing that technical and subtle system which regulates the course of real property; for, as that formed almost the whole of our ancient jurisprudence, it is there we must seek its original character. But much of the same spirit pervades every part of the law; no tribunals of a civilized people ever borrowed so little, even of illustration, from the writings of philosophers or from the histories of other countries. Hence, law has been studied rather as an art than a science, with more solicitude to learn its rules and distinctions than to perceive their application to that for which all rules of law ought to have been made,—the maintenance of public and of private rights."

Though I cannot assent to Mr. Hallam's opinions in their full extent, because we have many branches of law which are founded on plain and just principles, it will be collected, that I assent to his observations in other respects.

Certain it is, that those branches of the law which attracted least attention in the times to which I allude, have not fared the worse for it in modern times. The laws relating to funded property, the different branches of commercial law, and even the laws relating to copyholds, which were little regarded in feudal times, have been placed upon far more liberal, consistent, and intelligible principles than those which are applicable to real estates of higher degree.

It was said of the late Baron Masseres, who was a skilful mathematician, that he prophesied that a particular college in the University of Cambridge would, at some period or other, excel all; for, he observed, they, at present, know nothing at all about the matter; they have nothing to unlearn, whilst every where else they must get rid of all they do know, before they can ever make a beginning in the science. Whether our ancestors acted on this principle or not, certain it is, that, in early times, they were more intent on evading existing laws, than in constructing new ones on plain and simple principles.

In the next place, want of system is observable in the statute law. The extemporaneous and desultory mode in which legislative alterations have been made, even in respect of the legal system itself, constitute at once a characteristic feature and prominent defect in our statute law. The mere local disunion and confusion of laws connected in spirit and subject-matter, is of itself a source of no inconsiderable inconvenience; not merely because the difficulty of access is increased, but that the laws themselves are thus rendered less intelligible; for no one can doubt, that the very order in which a series of legal rules, all dependent upon the same or on kindred principles is arranged, contributes greatly to illustrate and explain the true meaning of the legislator, and thus adds force and clearness to the law, and affords the most valuable aid for a true construction of that meaning, on occasions of doubt. I have laid little stress on the observation, that such a mode of legislation increases the difficulty of access. I must, however, remark, that, in some instances, a mode of reference from a later to a former statute, is inconvenient to a mischievous extent. I allude to the practice of repealing by a later statute a former statute, save and except so much as relates to a particular subject; this is, indeed, a very near approach to tying the living to the dead; the whole of the partially repealed statute remains an incumbrance to the statute book, (although great part of it is a mere dead letter,) and every subject of the realm is bound, at his peril, by careful and patient investigation, to rake out the living embers from the ashes of the half-consumed and smouldering statute.

On this subject I beg leave to refer to the observations made by Mr. Evans in his introduction to his translation of Pothier, pp. 62, 63.

Another observation, connected with my present topic, is the great extent to which a species of extempore and desultory legislation has been carried. Enactments, especially such as are of a criminal nature, have been usually passed, not upon a general consideration of the criminal code, as an entire and consistent whole, but on the spur of some particular exigency or occasion, which had attracted the attention, and excited public feeling, or popular indignation. A cook, for instance, commits a horrible and atrocious crime by poisoning a family; forthwith, a statute is enacted, directing that thenceforth those who murder by poison, shall be guilty of treason, and shall be boiled to death.—3 Inst. 48. Coventry Act.

It appears, (3 Inst. 48,) that this horrible punishment was inflicted on many persons, but, as Lord Coke observes, it was found to be too severe to last long. This, by the by, is not an unapt illustration of the mischief of enacting too severe punishments.—We find that, even in the case of so diabolical a crime as murder by poison, it is too severe to be retained.

The inconvenience resulting from this species of legislation is the multiplication of penal statutes, which are not founded on any general and consistent principles.

I shall not, on this occasion, notice particularly other and great defects in the system resulting from the same source; they are, for the most part, too obvious to require specific mention,—desultory laws, emanating from the different views which different individuals may entertain on various subjects of civil policy, and enacted in fact by so many legislative artisans, cannot possibly cohere as parts of one and the same uniform system. Congruity and uniformity, resulting from the separate unconnected efforts of so many individuals, each working on his own notions, would be almost miraculous;—it would be almost as reasonable to expect system from a concourse of atoms.

It appears from a report of a committee of the House of Commons, that there are about 150 acts relating to the stamp laws; many (I speak from the report of the committee,) are to be found in acts whose titles afford no clue to them, and which relate almost exclusively to subjects of a totally different nature, or comprise a variety of unconnected topics of legislation. This will be sufficiently apparent on referring to the titles and contents of the earlier acts. It would be superfluous to recite those acts, or to adduce further instances or details with a view to demonstrate the present very unsatisfactory arrangement of the statutable provisions relating to the revenue of stamps. Cov. cii. Four hundred and forty-five acts and parts of acts, were expressly repealed by the Registry Act, 6 G. 4, c. 105.

Further observation on this head may well be deemed to be unnecessary;—more than two centuries ago the bulk and the deformities of our statute law were the subject of great and serious complaint; even Lord Coke, the strenuous defender of the common law, vents many a splenetic remark upon a number of long and ill penned statutes. King James himself condescended to make their reformation the subject of a personal address in Parliament.

Want of system in our laws, is, in the next place, attributable to disregard of the statute law.

On this head I wish it to be observed, that I restrict this observation, most emphatically, to what has been the practice of the courts in former times; the inconvenience which has resulted from this source has long been felt and exceedingly lamented, and, at the present day, every one who is conversant with the practice of the courts, must have frequently witnessed an anxious wish, on the part of the learned judges of the superior courts, to carry into effect the intention of the framers of an act of Parliament, when it is clearly expressed, and to discover the real intention whenever the expression is ambiguous.

That a contrary tendency formerly prevailed, that it was the parent of doubt, uncertainty, and litigation, to say nothing of the contempt thus exhibited of all legislative authority, is now a matter of legal history, and may be exemplified in the weakening and even the overturning of many of the most important acts of the legislature. I may instance, in particular, the statute De donis Conditionalibus, (Westminster, 2, 2d,) the statute of uses,—the statute of limitations. In every one of these, and in many other instances, the plain letter and intention of the statutes was allowed to be defeated by manifest evasions, and it is scarcely necessary to observe at how great a sacrifice of legal certainty and principle. Those who have paid serious attention to the history of our law, so far as it is connected with the immediate subject of these observations, will not, I think, hesitate in attributing the results which I have alluded to, to something more than a wish to do justice at the expense of the statute law; they will discover, if I mistake not, a degree of impatience, if I may so express myself, of restraint by the statute law.

It appears to me that this unwillingness to be fettered by legislative restraint is not very difficult to be accounted for, and that it had its origin in the comparative intellectual superiority of the executive magistrates over the legislators of the day. Legislation, as a science, was little understood; a position in which, as far as the statutes, before his time, are concerned, I am borne out by the testimony of Lord Coke; the learning of the times was confined, in a great measure, to the clergy, who were, for a long period, judges as well as advocates, and subtle advocates too, and well versed in all the arts of pleading, which they had borrowed, if not from Norman practice, from the Roman law; what matter of surprise then can it be, that judges and advocates, who were well versed in the Roman law, who probably despised the law of England, who, in spite of the resistance of the barons, contrived to introduce and establish many of the principles and even legal forms of the Roman law, should be disposed to set little value on the simple ordinances of the statute law. But principles, modes of thinking, and habits once contracted, by any class of persons, will frequently remain long after the time when the peculiar circumstances which produced them have ceased to exist. Certain I am that, in former times, and times later than those of which I have just been speaking, a latitude of construction has been indulged in which would not be permitted at the present day.

The history of the law of Mortmain affords a striking illustration of my observations. It shows the difficulties the legislature of the times experienced, in carrying into effect an object of essential policy and convenience, against evasions which must have been ineffectual, if not to a certain extent countenanced by the courts. (¹)

Very nearly connected, in its origin, with the source to which I have just alluded, is the practice which, in former times, has prevailed to a great extent, of extending the rules of common law by construction. When it was found that, from change of circumstances, the common law rule or definition had become too narrow to satisfy the exigencies of justice, the more desirable course would probably have been, that the legislature should, by a distinct enactment, have altered the law as the demands of justice and public convenience required. Such has been the course pursued in modern times on the like occasions; and such is, no doubt, the course which would now be pursued. Unfortunately, however, as later experience has proved, the courts, instead of requiring or waiting for legislative aid, took it upon themselves to evade the difficulty, and, in effect, to re-model the ancient rules of law, by means of an artificial and constructive enlargement. Hence it is in the criminal law

---

(1) 2 Black. 268; Tyrrell, 11.

that we have constructive treasons, constructive breakings in burglary, constructive violence in robbery, constructive possession in larceny. The effect has been greatly to weaken the force of the common law rules; and when once known and ancient boundaries are exceeded by construction, it is impossible for any lawyer to say within what boundaries the overflow is to be limited.

The practice of enlargement by construction has not been confined to mere common law definitions; we have many enlargements even of criminal statutes, by decisions said to be founded on the equity of statutes. All these, in effect, amount to no more than so many judicial declarations, that the legislature had not been able to express their own meaning by their own words, and, therefore, that it was necessary that the judicial authorities should supply legislative defects. This principle was never perhaps carried to a greater extent than in *Poulter's case*, 11 Coke:—the prisoner had been convicted of arson, in burning a house at Newmarket, in consequence of which great part of the town of Newmarket was burnt. The question was, whether he was entitled to benefit of clergy, inasmuch as by the statute 4 & 5 Ph. and M. benefit of clergy was taken away expressly from accessaries before the fact only, and, after long debate, it was held, that by implication, benefit of clergy was taken away from the principal; an enormous position surely,—that the life of any man, under any circumstances, should be taken away, otherwise than by plain and express authority.

I may notice, by the way, the manner in which Lord Coke in this case speaks of the statute law. [*The learned Gentleman here read an extract from* 11 *Coke.*]

It is pretty plain, that his contempt for the statute was proportioned to his reverence and esteem for the common law. In civil cases, also, the same spirit has prevailed, and the courts of common law have been disposed to overleap the boundary prescribed by the statute law. It may suffice to adduce one or two instances, to show the uncertainty resulting from a departure from the boundary prescribed by a statute. The first is taken from the bankrupt laws.

Previously to the late alterations in the bankrupt laws, a fraudulent preference, except it were by deed, did not constitute an act of bankruptcy. But inasmuch as it seemed to the courts, that a trader by giving a preference on the eve of bankruptcy, in effect prevented that fair and equitable distribution of his property amongst his creditors, which it was the object of the bankrupt laws to effect; such a disposition, though, in fact, prior to the dividing line, the act of bankruptcy, which divested his property out of the vendee, and vested it in his assignees, was, in effect, an evasion of the bankrupt law, and a fraud on the bankrupt law, which ought not to be permitted; they therefore held, that such a transfer was fraudulent and void, as against creditors, and that the property thus transferred, though previous to the bankruptcy, vested in the assignees. This, after the legislature had laid down the rule, and had marked out the dividing point at which the trader's power to dispose of his property ceased, was a strong step beyond the legislative limit;—it was one which was productive of much litigation, inasmuch as all the circumstances of time, place, amount, intention, and purpose, by which a legal was to be distinguished from a fraudulent payment, were left undefined. The difficulties, however, on this head, are now in a great measure removed by the present bankrupt law, by which a fraudulent preference constitutes an act of bankruptcy.

Another instance, and that a modern one, occurred upon the statute of simony, *Fox* v. *Bishop of Chester*, 2 B. & C. 635, where it was held, that a contract entered into for the sale of a next presentation, the parties at the time knowing the incumbent to be at the point of death, and expecting a vacancy, was simoniacal. Abbott, C. J., in affirming the judgment of the Court below, observed:—"Our judgment is founded on the language of the statute 31 Eliz. c. 6, and the well-known principle of law, that the provisions of an act of parliament shall not be evaded by shift or contrivance."

Can it be said, that an agreement for the sale of a next presentation, at a moment when the incumbent is, and is also known to be, afflicted with a mortal disease, and also in extreme danger of his life is an evasion of the statute? If it be, it must be void according to general principles, and to the opinion expressed by Lord Hardwicke in the case of *Grey* v. *Hasketh*, and to the well known doctrine under the bankrupt laws, that a voluntary payment made by a man on the eve of bankruptcy to a favoured creditor is void.

Another circumstance which has occasioned inconsistency and obscurity into our legal system is the adoption, in former times, of principles and modes of reasoning of a subtle and recondite nature, somewhat tinctured by the conceits of the schoolmen. In this description may be included the rule as to the absolute verity of a record. It is undoubtedly consistent with reason and convenience that a record should be taken as indisputable evidence of the truth of the facts adjudicated, so far as the correctness of that judgment is concerned; but the rule was carried to the extent that different records should preserve an absolute consistency with each other, so that the law's abhorrence of inconsistency was upheld by the courts as tenaciously as Nature's abhorrence of a vacuum was by the schoolmen. The consequences were unreasonable and inconvenient. One was, that no accessory to a felony could be attainted before the conviction of the principal; they reasoned thus, if the accessory be found guilty, the record will necessarily aver and show the guilt of the principal. It may happen, that the principal may be tried and acquitted, and then there will be repugnant and inconsistent records. *A fortiori*, where the principal had been acquitted, the acquittal was made to operate conclusively in favour of the accessory. Consequently, the conviction of the principal was made to operate so conclusively against the accessory, that he was not permitted to negative the *corpus delicti* by evidence however strong.

It is obvious that all this proceeded on a mere fallacy—that a record possesses infallible certainty, for all purposes, of the fact which it contains; but, on plain and obvious principles of reason and justice it establishes no more than the truth of the facts found, so far as the legal consequences of the judgment are concerned. In this view of the case, an acquittal of the principal would be perfectly consistent with the conviction of the accessory; the record in the former case would show that, on the evidence adduced before the jury, on the trial of the party so charged, there was not sufficient evidence of the fact, whilst the record of the conviction of the accessory showed that, on his trial, there was sufficient evidence, and each might be perfectly correct according to the evidence adduced. The making the conviction of the principal to operate as conclusive evidence against the accessory, was, in after times, deemed to be too harsh a rule, and, consequently, it was held to afford *primâ facie* evidence only, leaving it open to the accessory to controvert the guilt of the principal, if he could, by evidence; and so the law remains to this day. Mitigated, however, as the rule is, it is in opposition to the great and general principle of evidence, that no man shall be bound, to any extent, by a verdict to which he is not privy, and where he had no opportunity of cross-examining or contradicting the witnesses on whose testimony the verdict was obtained. The rule is also attended with this inconsistency:—Upon the trial of the accessory, the confession of the principal would clearly be inadmissible evidence to prove the guilt of the principal, but yet the principal may have been convicted solely on his own confession; and thus, whilst the law excludes evidence of the confession of the principal altogether, it admits the record which may have been founded merely upon that confession, and places the alleged accessory in a worse situation than if the confession itself had been admitted; for, if the confession had been proved, an opportunity would have been afforded of rebutting the evidence, by showing that it had been drawn forth by improper means.

The rule relating to the stealing of annexations to the freehold, affords a specimen of scholastic reasoning, which has, in after times, very frequently called for the aid of the legislator. As the freehold could not possibly be stolen, the same rule was held to apply to portions of the realty, and annexations to the realty, when severed by the thief for the purpose of stealing, and even to deeds, and boxes or cases containing deeds, relating to the realty, for these, to use the quaint language of the times, were said to savour of the realty, *omne principale trahit ad se accessorium suum.* This was certainly a refined and subtle conclusion, that, because what was immovable could not be taken away, therefore, that which was severed should still be considered as retaining the quality of immobility.

Besides, it was admitted, that if, after severance, the severed portion was allowed to remain, to take it afterwards would be felony in the party who so severed it, by reason, (I presume,) of the property having, in the mean time, vested in the owner of the freeholds; but when does it so vest, if not instantly on severance? and, if it does not instantly on severance, then there is every requisite to constitute a complete felony.

It is not a little curious to observe the mischief resulting from this conceit, and the numerous statutes which have passed to obviate this difficulty in particular instances.

After having, because it was necessarily connected with my observations on the method of study, noticed some of the defects in our legal system, I feel relieved from a portion of a very considerable burden. I have discharged, in part, at least, a duty peculiarly incumbent on one who undertakes to assist others in forming sound and correct notions of the principles of our law, and one which would be strangely and perniciously neglected by any one who represented our system as more perfect than it really is. I have incidentally noticed some peculiar excellencies in the Roman law; these, however, are, in a considerable degree, referrible to circumstances connected with national history, over which neither legislators nor jurists had any control. The political revolutions which England has so often, in former times undergone, tended, no doubt, to extirpate the simple indigenous laws of our early ancestors, and certainly to introduce a succession and mixture of foreign ordinances, the attempt to connect which, necessarily occupied the attention of the legislature in some degree, of the courts to a still greater extent; and, therefore, greatly retarded and obstructed the cultivation of the law as a science, depending on the application of known and sure principles to the growing exigencies of society, in the manner sanctioned by experience.

It is by no means improbable, that the mischief and inconvenience experienced by our ancestors in the importation of foreign laws, created a degree of disgust and impatience on that score, which may well account for their reluctance in after times, and even long after the feudal system had been established under the Norman dynasty, to derive any aid from foreign sources. This is marked, not merely by their refusal to introduce such laws in after times, but even to refer, for the purposes of explanation, to those sources, by reference to which, and by which alone, those laws which had been transplanted, and become firmly fixed and rooted, could be satisfactorily and systematically explained, and completely understood.

This no doubt has been carried to a most remarkable, and even to an unreasonable extent. The quality of knowledge and its value are not diminished to ourselves, because they have been of benefit to an enemy, still less ought we to reject information, from whatever source derived, which tends to explain and elucidate laws which we have adopted as our own. If my theory be true, it is an instance, amongst many, to show how long, and to what an unwarrantable extent, prejudices may be carried, for ages, after the time when the original cause has ceased to exist. Be this as it may, I will conclude by observing that there is no more remarkable or admirable characteristic of our ancestors, than their strong, their devoted, and deep-rooted attachment to the excellent laws of their forefathers,—a feeling which no political convulsion was able to shake, and which outlived the greatest change which a nation could well suffer, under successful invasion by a powerful conqueror, bent, as far as he could be, on the subversion of our laws, the destruction of the forms of justice, even to the compelling the oppressed and injured suitor to urge his complaint for the obtaining of justice in a foreign tongue. Yielding, at length, to the pressure of persevering efforts made for the restitution of our ancient laws, the conquerors relaxed their grasp, and our ancestors were remitted to those rights for which they had so vigorously contended.

The allurements of the Roman law were little likely to prevail with our brave and hardy ancestors, who had with so much fortitude clung to their ancient customs; they wisely rejected a code which, however beautiful and admirable as a monument of antiquity, was ill-adapted to the manners and habits of the English, and those principles of rational freedom, which had then taken root, and from which afterwards sprung our admirable constitution. Century after

536   *Reviewal.*

century, may press into the dark abyss of eternity, but those principles ever remain; if they were dear to our ancestors, how much more dear and more estimable ought they to be to ourselves, who have learnt, not only from our own experience, but from the page of history, for so many centuries, how excellent, how excessively valuable they are, notwithstanding partial changes, such as every political as well as every natural body, in the course of human events, is destined to undergo: these constitute the soul which animates our political system and gives it sameness and identity, and which will serve as far as human wisdom, aided by the experience of past ages can foresee, to preserve it in undiminished vigour, the subject of admiration, and, what is more, the source of rational freedom and of social happiness to ages yet to come.

BOOK NOTICES.

A Selection of Cases on the Law of Contracts, with a Summary of the Topics covered by the Cases. By C. C. LANGDELL, Dane Professor of Law in Harvard University. Prepared for use as a Text-book in Harvard Law School. Second Edition. Boston: Little, Brown, & Co. 1879. Two vols. 8vo. pp. xviii, 1116.

Principles of the English Law of Contract. By Sir WILLIAM R. ANSON, Bart., M.A., B.C.L., of the Inner Temple, Barrister-at-Law, Vinerian Reader of English Law, Fellow of All Souls' College, Oxford. Oxford, at the Clarendon Press. 1879. One vol. 12mo. pp. xxxii, 358.

IT is a circumstance of note in the history of the English law of contract that two such books as these should fall to be chronicled at the same time. The little volume from the Clarendon Press, which would almost tempt a layman to read law by its attractive form, will delight lawyers by the merits of its style and matter. It is written by one who is at home with ideas, and who seizes with the readiness of a scholar every thing which is in the air. It is remarkably readable, its illustrations are new and most wisely chosen, and, without pretending to be a work of great originality, it gives proof of the writer's fresh and apprehensive intelligence on every page. It is also a model of proportion. Most works of the sort which rise above mediocrity show a bias in the direction of some particular doctrine, and develop that at the expense of others equally important. But here every thing receives its due and orderly attention, and every thing is seen in the clearest light.

Without holding one's self ready or bound to prove the proposition, one may suspect that the work owes some of its more penetrating qualities to Mr. Langdell's Appendix attached to the first edition of his Cases on Contracts. There was a deal of suggestive matter hidden away there in a few lines, sometimes, to be sure, almost as latent as the good law which Lord Coke tells us is expressed by Littleton's "&c.," but nevertheless to be found by the careful student. And now Mr. Langdell has published a second edition, and the brief index of the first has grown into a series of systematic discussions.

It is hard to know where to begin in dealing with this extraordinary production, — equally extraordinary in its merits and its limitations. No man competent to judge can read a page of it without at once recognizing the hand of a great master. Every line is compact of ingenious and original thought. Decisions are reconciled which those who gave them meant to be opposed, and drawn together by subtle lines which never were dreamed of before Mr. Langdell wrote. It may be said without exaggeration that there cannot be found in the legal literature of this country, such a *tour de force* of patient and profound intellect working out original theory through a mass of detail, and evolving consistency out of what seemed a chaos of conflicting atoms. But in this word "consistency" we touch what some of us at least must deem the weak point in Mr. Langdell's habit of mind. Mr. Langdell's ideal in the law, the end of all his striving, is the *elegantia juris*, or *logical* integrity of the system as a system. He is, perhaps, the greatest living legal theologian. But as a theologian he is less concerned with his postulates than to show that the conclusions from them hang together. A single phrase will illustrate what is meant. "It has been claimed that the purposes of substantial justice and the interests of contracting parties as understood by themselves will be best served by holding &c., . . . and cases have been put to show that the contrary view would produce not only unjust but absurd results. *The true answer to this argument is that it is irrelevant;* but" &c. (pp. 995, 996, pl. 15). The reader will perceive that the language is only incidental, but it reveals a mode of thought which becomes conspicuous to a careful student.

If Mr. Langdell could be suspected of ever having troubled himself about Hegel, we might call him a Hegelian in disguise, so entirely is he interested in the formal connection of things, or logic, as distinguished from the feelings which make the content of logic, and which have actually shaped the substance of the law. The life of the law has not been logic: it has been experience. The seed of every new growth within its sphere has been a felt necessity. The form of continuity has been kept up by reasonings purporting to reduce every thing to a logical sequence; but that form is nothing but the evening dress which the new-comer puts on to make itself presentable according to conventional requirements. The important phenomenon is the man underneath it, not the coat; the justice and reasonableness of a decision, not its consistency with previously held views. No one will ever have a truly philosophic mastery over the law who does not habitually consider the forces outside of it which have made it what it is. More than that, he must remember that as it embodies the story of a nation's development through many centuries, the law finds its philosophy not in self-consistency, which it must always fail in so long as it continues to grow, but in history and the nature of human needs. As a branch of anthropology, law is an object of science; the theory of legislation is a scientific study; but the effort to reduce the concrete details of an existing system to the merely logical consequence of simple postulates is always in danger of becoming unscientific, and of leading to a misapprehension of the nature of the problem and the data.

The preceding criticism is addressed to the ideal of the final methods of legal reasoning which this Summary seems to disclose. But it is to be remembered that the book is published for use at a law school, and that for that purpose dogmatic teaching is a necessity, if any thing is to be taught within the limited time of a student's course. A professor must start with a system as an arbitrary fact, and the most which can be hoped for is to make the student see how it hangs together, and thus to send him into practice with something more than a rag-bag of details. For this purpose it is believed that Mr. Langdell's teachings, published and unpublished, have been of unequalled value.

BOOK NOTICES.

Not only for this purpose, however, for even if Mr. Langdell's results should hereafter be overruled in particular cases, they will have done very nearly as much to advance the law as if they had been adopted. For they must be either adopted or refuted, they cannot be passed by. And a conclusion based upon the refutation of its opposite is very different from the same opinion based on ignorance of the arguments by which such an opposite could be maintained.

[3]

PROFESSOR LANGDELL.

Gentlemen of the Harvard Law School Association: I am very grateful for this unexpected greeting. You will be surprised to learn that this is the second time that your president has called upon me to speak for the Harvard Law School. The first time was nearly seventeen years ago, when I was about to assume the duties of Dane professor. And I do not know that I can do better than begin now where I left off then. On that occasion I called attention to the anomalous condition of legal education in English-speaking countries, the anomaly consisting in the fact that in those countries a knowledge of law had been acquired, as a rule, only or in connection with its practice and administration, while in all the rest of Christendom law has always been taught and studied in universities. And I ventured to express the opinion that the true interests of legal education in this country required that, in this respect, we should not follow longer in the footsteps of England, but should bring ourselves into harmony with the rest of the civilized world.

Since that time I have not concerned myself with legal education outside of Harvard Law School; but I have tried to do my part towards making the teaching and the study of law in that school worthy of a university; toward making the honourable institution of which we are celebrating the

250th anniversary a true university, and the law school not the least of its departments; in short, toward placing the law school, so far as differences of circumstances would permit, in the position occupied by the law faculties in the universities of continental Europe. And what I say of myself in this respect I may, with at least equal truth, say of all my associates.

To accomplish these objects, so far as they depended upon the law school, it was indispensable to establish at least two things—that law is a science, and that all the available materials of that science are contained in printed books. If law be not a science, a university will consult its own dignity in declining to teach it. If it be not a science, it is a species of handicraft, and may best be learned by serving an apprenticeship to one who practises it. If it be a science, it will scarcely be disputed that it is one of the greatest and most difficult of sciences, and that it needs all the light that the most enlightened seat of learning can throw upon it. Again, law can only be learned and taught in a university by means of printed books. If, therefore, there are other and better means of teaching and learning law than printed books, or if printed books can only be used to the best advantage in connection with other means; for instance, the work of a lawyer's office, or the proceedings of courts of justice, it must be confessed that such means cannot be provided by a university. But if printed books are the ultimate sources of all legal knowledge,—if every student who would obtain any mastery of law as a science must resort to these ultimate sources, and if the only assistance which it is possible for the learner to receive is such as can be afforded by teachers who have travelled the same road before him,—then a university, and a university alone, can afford every possible facility for teaching and learning law. I wish to emphasize the fact that a teacher of law should be a person who accompanies his pupils on a road which is new to them, but with which he is well acquainted from having often travelled it before. What qualifies a person, therefore, to teach law, is not experience in the work of a lawyer's office, not experience in dealing with men, not experience in the trial or argument of causes, not experience, in short, in using law, but experience in learning law; not the experience of the Roman advocate, or of the Roman prætor, still less of the Roman procurator, but the experience of the Roman jurisconsult.

My associates and myself, therefore, have constantly acted upon the view that law is a science, and that a well-equipped university is the true place for teaching and learning that science. Accordingly, the law library has been the object of our greatest and most constant solicitude. We have not done for it all that we should have been glad to do, but we have done much. Indeed, in the library of to-day one would find it difficult to recognise the library of seventeen years ago. We have also constantly inculcated the idea that the library is the proper workshop of professors and students alike; that it is to us all that the laboratories of the university are to the chemists and physicists, the museum of natural history to the zoologists, the botanical garden to the botanists.

From what I have already said, it easily follows that a good academic training, especially in the study of languages, is a necessary qualification for the successful study of law; that the study of law should be regular, systematic and earnest, not intermittent, desultory or perfunctory; and that the study should be prosecuted for a length of time bearing some reasonable proportion to the magnitude of the subject. Accordingly, to secure the first of these objects, we have established an examination for admission for such as are not graduates. To secure the third we have made three years of study necessary for a degree. To secure the second we have done several things. We have established a course of studies which we require to be pursued in the prescribed order. We have established annual examinations, to be held at the end of each year, in the work of that year. We require every candidate for a degree to pass his examinations in the studies of the first year at the end of his first year, as a condition of being admitted into the second year, and in the studies of the second year as a condition of being admitted into the third year; and we do not permit any one to pass his examinations in the studies of any year unless he has been regularly admitted into that year at the beginning of the year. In other words, we do not permit any one to pass examinations in any studies except those of the year to which he belongs. We have increased the amount of instruction in the last seventeen years, from ten hours a week to thirty hours a week. This enables us to give the whole of the three years' course every year, thus giving to each class its appropriate instruction.

The result of all these measures is that the school is strictly divided into three classes, each class doing the work which belongs to its year, and every man having the strongest possible inducement to do his work as it should be done and when it should be done.

Let it not be supposed that we are unmindful of the work of our predecessors. We should indeed be ungrateful if we were. We do not forget that they began with nothing, while we have enjoyed the fruits of all their labours. We do not wish to disguise the fact that we could not have done our work had we not had the work of our predecessors to build upon as a foundation.

Nor are we unmindful of the constant support and encouragement which we have received from the president of the university. He has never hesitated, wavered, or faltered when any responsibility was to be assumed or a work to be done.

Lastly, we are not unmindful of the support we have received from the students of the school, both while they were in the school and since they have left it. Without their support and co-operation the various measures to which I have referred (many of which could not have been expected to be popular measures) could never have been maintained.

It has been, in a great degree, the eagerness with which they have always encountered difficulties, the ability with which they have followed the subtlest lines of reasoning and detected the slightest flaws or sophistries in argument, and the persistence with which they have refused to be satisfied so long as any doubt remained to be cleared up, that has given to the instructors such success as they have achieved. Finally, it is almost wholly to their testimony, both while in the school and after leaving it, that the school is indebted for such public recognition as it has received.

YALE LAW JOURNAL

Vol. XIII   OCTOBER, 1903   No. 1

THE STUDY OF ELEMENTARY LAW, THE PROPER BEGINNING OF A LEGAL EDUCATION.*

The thought of our day moves mainly along two lines: the evolution in all things wrought by time, and the correlation of forces, whether of matter or of mind. To those interested in legal education, it has brought a new sense of the unity and permanence of what is essential in law, and of the passing and shifting character of all that is not essential in it. It has made law a larger thing. It has set in a larger place. It has correlated it to the whole family of social sciences, of which it is both child and king.

Legal science is the science dealing with the relations of man, as a member of organized political society, to that society and, through that society to mankind. But what is an organized political society? Out of what conditions does it arise? What differentiates it from human society at large?

These questions reach far. They belong to the domain of jurisprudence, and must be studied wherever and whenever that is taught.

But jurisprudence and law, as these terms are commonly used, are not convertible. Jurisprudence deals more with generals; law, more with particulars. Law schools have for their main office the imparting of such a knowledge of the legal principles and rules

---

*The greater part of this paper is taken from the annual President's address, delivered by the author before the Association of American Law Schools, August 26, 1903.

prevailing in some one particular political community as will justify the learner in professing his ability to expound and apply these in practice, against all comers, as occasion may arise.

What is it that has made the law of this particular society different from that of any other? In what does this difference consist? How shall principles and rules be so marshalled as best to show this? How shall their slow evolution be made clear? How much of accident, how much of order, has there been in their development? What light can be thrown on this by History, by the Philosophy of History, by Psychology, by Physical Geography?

But Law is both Science and Art—a philosophy and a trade. How does one best learn the trade-terms and trade-methods? How in a trade of word and argument does one best acquire that sleight of mind which takes the place of sleight of hand in the trades of handicraft?

Our trade-masters are the courts. How shall the apprentice be best taught to shape himself to such modes of approaching them as may serve most the advantage of clients—to such modes of learning the lessons they daily teach as will give him the real meaning of their judgments, the true *ratio decidendi* of their opinions?

Among English speaking peoples it is undisputed that Americans have thus far provided the best facilities for education for the bar. They were driven to it by the force of circumstances. Their system of government was one that rested, not on personal authority, not on historical tradition, not on political necessities, but on unwritten law, and it was a law higher than any which their legislatures could make or unmake. Who was to apply this higher law? Who was to say which, in any case of doubt, was the higher? On its proper understanding and execution, its just administration, its adaptation and re-adaptation, from time to time, to fast changing social conditions, hung the safety of the State. For all this it looked to its lawyers—made by inevitable circumstances both a creative and a conservative governing aristocracy. They were to lead in its Constitutional Conventions, in its legislatures. They were alone to officer its courts.

With these things in view, the American law student, as soon as the United States attained political independence, was subjected to a careful training. It was at first found in the office of some leader of the bar. Here was he first set to reading such works as Montesquieu, Grotius, Puffendorf, Vattel, Hale's History of the Common Law, the Institutes of Justinian, and perhaps a few books of the Pandects, and then given Blackstone's Commentaries. Wood's

THE STUDY OF ELEMENTARY LAW.

Institutes, and the later volumes of the English Law Reports.*
Whatever else might be omitted, in any case, Blackstone's Commentaries never were.

Soon came the first Law School, that at Litchfield, Connecticut, first opened in 1784, where instruction was given by elaborate lectures on the whole field of law, supported by references to leading cases in the reports. Later Law schools followed first the same method, and then added to it recitations from standard text-books. The great aim was to acquaint the student with the principles of law in such an order of arrangement, and with such reference to their historical development, as would best impress them permanently upon his mind. Cases were used mainly to support or illustrate antecedent propositions. They were regarded less as sources of law than as channels of law.

So far as office instruction went, it was in the same direction. For nearly a hundred years this was the history—the stationary history—of legal education in the United States. It ceased to be stationary in the seventh decade of the last century. A forward movement came which was marked by three great events:

---

*To illustrate the methods of this period, the course of reading may be compared taken by three young men, of whom two afterwards attained distinction, and one died in early youth:

Ezra Stiles, Jr. Harv. 1778, at Portsmouth. N. H. under Judge Parker, and New Haven. Conn., under Chas. Chauncey.

Burlamqui's *Principes de Droit Naturel;* Montesquieu, *de l'Esprit des Lois;* Lord Kames' History of Law; Blackstone; Wood's Maxims; Wood's Institutes; Co. Litt.; Bacon's Abr.; Hawkins' Pleas of the Crown; Gilbert's Evidence, Devises, and Tenures; Law of Bills of Exchange; Molley *de Jure Maritimo;* Hale's Abridgement; Lex Testamentorum; Sullivan's Lectures; Bohun's Institutes; Boot on Suits at Law; Offic. Cler. Pac.; Burn's Justice; Dalrymple's Institutions of the Laws of Scotland, etc.; Institutes of Justinian and part of the Pandects; Puffendorf; Poulton's Crim. Law; Salkeld's Rep.; 1 and 2 Burrow; part of Lord Raymond's, Holt's and Shower's Rep. See Literary Diary of Ezra Stiles, III, 420.

James Kent, Yale, 1781, Poughkeepsie, N. Y., under Judge Benson.
Grotius; Puffendorf; Smollett's, Hume's and Rapin's Histories of England; Hale. Hist. of the Comm. Law of England; Blackstone. See Memoirs of Chancellor Kent, 19.

John Quincy Adams, Harv. 1787, Newburyport, Mass., under Chief Justice Parsons.
Robertson's Hist. of Charles V, vol 1 (to get his account of feudalism); Vattel; Blackstone (read three times); Sullivan's Lectures; Wright's Tenures; Co. Litt. Wood's Institutes; Gilbert on Evidence; Foster's and Hawkins' Pleas of the Crown; Bacon's Pleas and Pleading; Institutes of Justinian; Buller's *Nisi* Prius; Barrington's Observations on the Statutes. See Proceedings of Mass. Hist. Soc., 2d Series, XVI, 315, *et seq.*

1. The creation of a committee on legal education, representing the whole American bar, and its report on that subject to the American Bar Association in 1879, urging a more scholarly and thorough training for the profession.[1]

2. The extension of the term of study required for a bachelor's degree, in two law schools,[2] to three years, and the offer, in another,[3] which still adhered to the two years' term, of two years more of advanced study for bachelors of law, leading to the degree of Doctor of Civil Law.[4]

3. The publication, in 1870, by Professor Langdell of Harvard, of the first case-book, which was prepared solely for use in law school instruction.

I have named these events in the reverse order of time, preferring what I deem their order in relative importance.

The first brought an influence to bear on courts and legislatures, which has proved irresisitible in advancing the requirements for admission to the bar.

The second helped greatly to make that advance possible, not only by leading to a general lengthening of the term of study, but by giving a higher legal education to those who were to become themselves law teachers, and forcing those who gave it to them, in order to be able to face their classes, to broaden their own reading and thought in new directions and in all directions.

The third proved to be the beginning of a new theory of legal instruction, according to which its main end from the beginning should be to encourage and assist the student in the study and analysis of judicial precedents, and he should be left to pick up and arrange the elementary principles of law, as he best can, for himself. This theory has been put in practice at several American law schools, and a system of instruction introduced, which is fundamentally different from that which formerly prevailed there, and from that which had ever prevailed at any seat of legal education in the history of the world.

"*Die Weltgeschichte ist das Weltgericht*" was the wise saying of a great poet. Was the world's judgment, formed and expressed

---

[1] By the American Bar Association, in 1878, Am. Bar. Ass'n Reports, II, 209-236.

[2] Those of Harvard and Boston Universities in 1876.

[3] That of Yale University in 1876.

[4] The history of the beginnings of the change of system, which has been since adopted in many other Schools, is given in the Journal of the Am. Social Science Association, XI, 123.

THE STUDY OF ELEMENTARY LAW.

during the long course of ages before 1870, wrong on this point, so vital to the question of what a sound legal education is?

But let us limit the inquiry more narrowly. There has never been a country in which this new mode of teaching law could have been possible, except Great Britain and its dependencies, and the United States and their dependencies. In no other is it so fully conceded that judges, if they do not make law, make it certain what law is. In no other is there such a mass of authoritative judicial opinion on every branch of public and private law.

In one respect, the United States offer a more favorable ground for putting Professor Langdell's theory into practice than Great Britain. Only in the United States do judicial opinions express the final word of the sovereign power. The courts of Great Britain must bow to the will of Parliament. The will of the Congress of the United States must bow to the courts of the United States. The will of the Legislature of each State must bow to the will of its highest court. Here, therefore, the opinions of the courts are, in Great Britain they are not, the ultimate source, in effect, of written authority.

On the other hand, the unity of the judicial system of Great Britain, with its one final court of appeals for all causes arising in the kingdom proper, and another final court of appeals for all causes arising in her dominions beyond the sea, avoids that conflict of authority which is the despair of American jurisprudence.

A prominent advocate of the case-book system said last year in a public address that whatever time students might devote to the study of elementary law was worse than wasted; that no knowledge was gained by it on which they could rely; and that the information acquired, if any, was necessarily superficial and misleading.* In his view, and in the view of quite a number of American law teachers, no book should be made the direct subject of class-room instruction in an American law school except a case-book.

The case-book is always a collection of cases on some particular topic. From its pages, aided by such explanations and additions as the teacher may be able to crowd into his hour, the student, under the new theory of legal education, must extract his knowledge of the elementary law relating to that branch; and after wrestling in succession with twenty such books on twenty topics, must be left to construct for himself an ordered and systematic body of the elementary law relating to all subjects, or perhaps be referred to one from an authoritative source, only at the close of his third year, as

*Reports of the American Bar Association, XXV, 749.

the last thing to look at before entering the bar, or as a proper precaution before meeting the State examiners.

Instruction as to the proper study and analysis of cases, as to their place in judicial history, as to their authority and the limits of it; instruction on particular topics in detail based largely or even wholly on case-books, but coming after a general knowledge of the nature of the topic and the outlines of its field have been otherwise acquired;—all this is useful and right. But can it be safe, can it be scientific, to skim over in a few lectures or leave for consideration in the closing months of a law school course that orderly statement and classification of legal conceptions and propositions which it is the purpose of elementary treatises to make, and without some familiarity with which no one, with the amplest library to consult, can know where to look for authority on any point? There are few lawyers who have had any considerable practice at the bar who will be in doubt as to the answer. They have found that what has helped them most has been the possession of clear general notions as to the whole field of law and the manner in which part of it is related to the rest. To give that, law schools must set before each incoming class the outlines of law in general, substantive and adjective, in orderly and scientific arrangement; and it should be done, if possible, by the best teacher in the faculty. Let the student start right, and he will come out right. Let him lean first on those who are wiser than he for accepted definitions and systematization of knowledge. Let him look for them to those who have made it their business to set them forth with precision, rather than to those who are only trying to decide a law suit, and to state their reasons as briefly as they can.

The main argument usually urged in favor of what for convenience may be called the case-system is that it is the inductive method; and that only inductive methods can be tolerated by modern science.

What is the meaning of the term "inductive method," as thus used to describe a method of learning law? It must be the method of proceeding from a study of particular decisions in particular law suits to ascertain by induction from these some general rule or rules of action, the application of which to a particular state of facts it was the purpose of each decision to make. It is, in the language of the logicians, a formal illation of a universal from singulars, produced by the mere action of the mind. It has little resemblance to a material illation of a universal from singulars, dependent upon an objective process of investigating particular facts. In studying legal problems, facts are mere conditions upon which the reason is

THE STUDY OF ELEMENTARY LAW.

to work, and have no intrinsic importance. Every judicial decision is, of course, a fact. But the fact that it was reached in a certain case is of no philosophic importance, except as it may illustrate the history of legal science; and that, to a beginner at least, is far more clearly shown by leading him to compare the institutional writers of successive centuries—Glanvil with Bracton, Blackstone with Kent.

Any commendation, therefore, of the inductive method as the only scientific manner of investigating natural phenomena and physical problems is irrelevant to the question of applying the inductive method in legal education. That method is all important in deriving certainties from uncertainties, the knowable from the unknown. But it is worthless, except as a mode of mental discipline, when applied to deriving known principles of law from recorded opinions of certain judges, of which these principles are, or are intended to be, the foundation, and in which they are generally named and stated with more or less of formal precision. When thus used, it becomes more properly a deductive method, proceeding from analysis to synthesis.

Bacon revolutionized the processes of philosophy with respect to the study of the physical world. He left them where Aristotle left them with respect to the study of reasoning from assumed premises to logical conclusions by pure laws of thought.[1] He left them as Aristotle left them, in their application to methods of legal education, and we have his own word for it. In his *de Dignitate et Augmentis Scientiarum*, the father of the inductive philosophy devoted a separate title[2] to the Sources of Law. Unless, he says, law is certain, it cannot be just. Hence, that law is best *quae minimum relinquit arbitrio judicis*.[3] His ideal to aim at was the formation of an official code of written law, stated with such clearness that he who runs might read it.[4] Meanwhile, for the better understanding of what the written law might leave doubtful, the judgments of the highest courts were to be looked to as the surest guide. They were to be arranged and digested in order of time, not in that of their subject-matter, since not only the decisions, but the times in which they were pronounced, were to be considered in estimating their due authority. This work was to be done at public cost, and not by any of the judges, lest they should stuff the book too full of their own opinions.[5]

---

[1] See Sir William Hamilton's Lectures on Logic, Lect. XVII.
[2] Lib. VIII. Cap. III.
[3] Works, Ed. of 1803, VII, 441.
[4] *Ibid.*, 453, Aphorism LXVIII.
[5] Works, VII, 457, Aphorisms LXXV, LXXVI.

Such works, however, were for the information of the lawyer or the citizen. So far as they set forth the rules of public law, they were also proper to be put in the hands of the student of law. Not so as to private law. This must be taught by institutional treatises, set out in clear and plain order, "not omitting some subjects and dwelling too long on others, but touching upon each briefly, so that to a student afterwards coming to read the whole body of the law nothing may appear wholly new, but as that of which some little notion had been previously imparted (*levi aliqua notione praeceptum*).[1]

No one who reads this chapter of Bacon's philosophy will question his attitude towards the teaching of elementary law. To quote his very words: "Youths and novices are to be prepared for receiving and imbibing more deeply and conveniently the knowledge and the difficulties of jurisprudence by institutes."[2]

He would also have in each country a book setting forth its legal rules, and after each of them, which is to be stated in brief and comprehensive words, adding illustrations and decisions of cases best fitted to explain it (*decisiones casuum maxime luculentae ad explicationem*).[3]

In the same vein, he has a word of caution for us who are law teachers. Lectures, he says, on law, and the exercises of those who are devoted to the study of law, should be so framed and ordered as all to tend rather to quieting than exciting questions and controversies as to what the law is. For now, and from a remote antiquity, too, it has been a kind of contest between all law teachers how to multiply doubts and questions as to law, as if for the sake of showing how bright they were.[4]

Bacon took pains himself to prepare an elementary law book for the benefit of students. His *Elements of the Common Law,* published in 1630,[5] came at once into use as a text-book, and held its place as such until the close of the next century.[6] In his preface to that work, he observes that he could think of no way in which he could essay to pay his debt to his profession so well as by collecting the

---

[1] *Ibid*, 458, Aphorism LXXXI.
[2] *Praeparendi sunt juvenes et novitii ad scientiam et ardua juris altius et commodius haurienda et imbibenda per institutiones.* Ibid.
[3] *Ibid*, 459, Aph. LXXXIV.
[4] *Ibid*, Aph. XCIII.
[5] Works, IV, 1-81.
[6] Theophilus Parsons dissuaded John Quincy Adams, when a student in his office, from reading it, saying that it taught rules rather than principles. Proc. Mass. Soc., 2d Series, XVI, 412.

THE STUDY OF ELEMENTARY LAW.

rules and grounds dispersed throughout the body of the laws of England, for—to quote his words—"Hereby no small light will be given in new cases and such wherein there is no direct authority, to sound into the true conceit of law by the depth of reason; in cases wherein the authorities do square[1] and vary, to confirm the law and to make it received one way; and in cases where the law is cleared by authority, yet nevertheless to see more profoundly into the reason of such judgment and settled cases, thereby to make more use of them for the decision of other cases more doubtful; so that the uncertainty of law, which is the most principal and just challenge that is made to the laws of our nation at this time, will by this new strength laid to the foundation, somewhat the more settle and be corrected."[2]

His book sets forth certain rules, it will be recollected, each being followed by a number of illustrations, often taken from reported cases. To these cases, however, he did not refer,[3] for, he says, "I judged it a matter undue and preposterous to prove rules and maxims, wherein I had the examples of Mr. Littleton and Mr. Fitzherbert, whose writings are the institutions of the laws of England; whereof the one forbeareth to vouch any authority altogether; the other never reciteth a book but when he thinketh the case so weak in credit of itself as it needeth surety."[4]

A great American lawyer and law teacher, speaking in the same vein, has said that cases do not make principles: they only illustrate them; and that the well trained student has a higher learning than they can furnish. "He does not," to quote his words, "need to wade through hundreds of volumes of books to see whether a particular point has been somewhere or other decided. He knows how it was decided, if it ever was, and how it *ought* to be decided if it never was."[5]

The term "case-lawyer" is justly one of reproach. What does it mean? He is a case-lawyer to whom the natural appeal to authority is to a volume of reports. He is a case-lawyer to whom a reported case is anything more than a statement of how a particular court decided a particular cause by applying particular rules to particular facts. If any such rule was a new one, the decision was wrong,

---

[1] i.e. in modern phrase, "square off," as one pugilist confronts another in fighting attitude.
[2] Works IV, 10.
[3] In the original edition.
[4] Op. cit., 13, 14.
[5] Edward J. Phelps, Orations and Essays, 83.

unless it be a rule consistent with and flowing from the reason of the law.

To what end is an opinion formally pronounced by a court of last resort? Certainly its primary office is not to constitute a source of supply from which law can be dug out by pains and difficulty. It is, on the contrary, at is best when it makes what the law as to a certain point is and how it applies to the case in hand most clear and easy of apprehension. Lord Bacon well observed that judgments *"anchorae legum sunt, ut leges republicae."*[1] They serve, that is, to hold the law firm in its place, just as the law serves to hold the State firm in its place. But the State was before the law, the law before the judgment. A case is worthless unless there is something which underlies it.

Fortunately for the student of law, these underlying propositions or principles are neither numerous nor obscure. In the words of the late Chancellor Hammond, in the able report to the American Bar Association in 1892 of its committee on Legal Education:

"No conception held in common by a large number of men such as the members of a State or great community can be very complex in its nature or difficult of comprehension. This may be taken for granted as one of the laws of thought. Consequently the fundamental notions out of which the rules of law are derived must be of this simple character, since it is in the general acceptance and uniformity of these notions that the common law exists as such."[2]

The case-system turns judges into oracles—or idols. It tends to put the student back into the ranks of those of former generations who thought of law only as a rule prescribed by a superior authority. If that be all of it, it may well be sought by going to the highest source of authority, and with us it is the courts that have the last word for the decision of every right or duty. But it was the right, the duty, or the absence of it, on which the decision hung: it is these that must be known before it can be comprehended.

In all instruction by the case-system, indeed, in actual practice, the teacher is compelled to supplement and support his work by reference to text-books, and statements of elementary propositions, and more or less of the proper classification of such propositions. The case-book may not begin, but conclude such a statement.[3]

---

[1] De Augmentis Scientiarum, Aphorism LXXIII.
[2] Reports of the American Bar Association, XV, 342.
[3] See, for an example of this, Professor Beale's Cases on the Conflict of Laws, at the end of the third volume of which comes a general exposition, covering forty-five pages, of the elementary conceptions and rules relating to that subject.

THE STUDY OF ELEMENTARY LAW.

The instructor is forced to begin with one, oral and therefore necessarily meagre, inadequate, and imperfectly apprehended.

Is he taking up a case-book on Torts? What are torts? Why are these cases classified together? The instructor or the casebook must first explain the division between Torts and Contracts, the nature of Quasi Contracts, of a legal obligation, of any obligation.

Is he carrying his class through a case-book on Criminal Law and Procedure? How do public wrongs differ from private ones? How does our law define this crime or that? What is burglary? Why send the inquirer to some ancient case for the answer, when the definition is better stated in every elementary treatise on the subject? It is a definition to be learned by heart. Let him learn it in its best form.

Is it said that he will remember it better or understand it better if he digs it out for himself from a series of cases? Is there not more danger that the conceptions acquired from the earlier ones may pre-occupy his mind, and obscure the closer and fuller ones given in the later? He is dealing, we must remember, with the grammar of law; with things that cannot be controverted; with things that every lawyer must know and have at his instant command.

The young man who has learned by heart a legal maxim or definition, of acknowledged authority and unexceptionable phrase, weighing every word, as weigh he must, in order to learn it, has put an arrow in his quiver that he will find his best weapon on a sudden call. I know I found it so when at the bar. I know that no argument now impresses me from the bar more than one proceeding from settled principles, with no reference to reported cases.

Who has ever opened the first book of the Institutes of Justinian, or of the Digest, without feeling his mind impressed by that stately sequence of definitions and foundation rules? They need no explanation, or at least to the Roman, they needed none. To him they proved themselves, and for the most part they are true for all men and all times.

In any country governed by an official code, it will hardly be questioned that that must be read by and, so far as it may need it, explained to every student of law. That code will have gathered into an orderly whole whatever is most important in such rules of conduct as may have been established by proper usage, judicial precedents, legislative action. Thereafter, all prior usage, precedent, legislation, will be studied by the beginner mainly for the help they give in understanding the just meaning and effect of the language of the code. The day may come when he will have the leisure and ability to look at them as part of national or universal history, but if it comes while he is yet preparing himself for admission to the bar, it will be in the closing stages of his preparation.

The same reasons, though with a less necessity, apply to the student of law in a country whose law is still unwritten. It is, as Sir Henry Maine has so well said, always and in every land written but unofficially by private hands, before it becomes a matter of public record. Courts are its echoes.*

The European system of legal education has always been founded on that of the Roman Empire. Roman law was taught as a system of deductive science. The *Corpus Juris* proceeds from assertions of principles to their application to various cases. The Institutes are a compendium of elementary law, prepared by law school professors, avowedly as a law school text-book. They are followed by the Digest, in which the same principles are more fully stated and illustrated. Then came the statute laws of recent times.

Can, indeed, in the nature of things, a science like law be intelligently taken up by one who has never been introduced to an acquaintance with its fundamental terms and conceptions?

It is said that Professor Agassiz was accustomed to begin his instructions in ichthyology by giving each student a fish and telling him to describe it. It was not a bad way. The teacher of physical science has this advantage over us. But can we learn algebra by having a quadratic equation flung at us, at the start, and being asked to explain it?

Some of our educational theorists undertook, a few years ago, to carry the "inductive system" into our primary schools. The multiplication table was no longer taught. Children were to be gently led to construct one for themselves, should they deem it useful, and only after fully apprehending the methods and processes on which it rested. They tell a story of a little girl—the product of this era—who was asked by an aunt how much seven times six made. "Oh, dear," was the reply, "I worked a week over that, last winter. I made up my mind it was either 40 or 42. I've forgotten which, and I don't care now, for we have got through multiplication."

---

*The respect which the courts feel for "elementary treatises of acknowledged authority," it may safely be said often exceeds that paid to any judicial opinions except their own. See Pennsylvania Co. v. Roy, 102 U. S., 451, 456: The Majestic, 166 U. S., 375, 386.

THE STUDY OF ELEMENTARY LAW.

There are those who would conduct our high schools on the same theory, and let the scholars study what they like and as they like, without the drudgery of laying a foundation first. A Massachusetts Latin school teacher has recently complained of the captious way in which college examiners mark the papers presented in English, and condition applicants for admission for mistakes in spelling or diction. Even if they were bad ones, he thought they should be overlooked, if the paper showed a sound appreciation of the subject from a literary point of view.

Germany, a few years ago, yielded somewhat to suggestions of this kind. In 1892, her system of secondary education was revised so as greatly to increase the use of the inductive method of instruction, and lessen the amount of grammatical and logical training previously required. The results were disastrous. Those who passed from the school to the university were found to be lacking, as compared with those of previous years, in clear thought and close reasoning. A general conference of the educational authorities was held at Berlin in 1900, to consider the situation, and in 1901 a new "School Order" was adopted, showing a decided reversion to the old usages, by adding seven hours a week more of gymnasium instruction in the Latin language.

If then we are to trust the experience of the world, to teach law by cases only, or by cases mainly, without first grounding the learner in the elements of the subject is, so far as scientific methods of instruction are concerned, to begin at the wrong end. It is to explain the foundation of a building by examining the roof, or rather by scrutinizing a few of the shingles.

Is the "case-system" to be adopted as a mode of mental discipline, or as strengthening the analytic faculty.

No serious study fails in some measure to discipline and reinforce the mind. But at the time of life which the law student has reached, and at the stage of education to which he must have attained, in order to be fit to enter on professional studies, mental discipline must be relegated to a secondary place.

The American high school or academy has pushed itself forward until the best of them now hold half the field formerly occupied by our older colleges, and the entire field now occupied by our weaker colleges. They have come to give to every American boy his best chance to acquire that texture of the mind which is the best gift of general education. It is, since the modern extension—the undue extension, I venture to think—of the elective system, in the fitting school, more than in the college, that habits of intellectual discipline are impressed. There are certain studies which must be pursued there, for the simple reason that entrance to college cannot otherwise be gained. Whether the boy likes them or dislikes them, he must become their master.

The best things we learn in early life are the hardest things and the least agreeable. Every man's life has its irksome duties, and he who has not learned in boyhood to do unwelcome tasks, and do them well, enters on his later years under a sad handicap. James Martineau said that the college study which had done him the greatest good was advanced mathematics, and that he took it because he hated it.

The students in the principal American law schools have had at least a high school education and that discipline, from enforced tasks performed during a course of years, for which it stands. If they have added a college course, further discipline has been also gained. High school and college are fields for discipline. It is, or ought to be, one of their main and peculiar ends. It is not and cannot be a main end for a law school to pursue. The law school requires, as a condition of entrance, what presupposes the possession of a fair degree of it. Its object is to teach law, and to invigorate the mind only as every science faithfully pursued strengthens the pursuer in the chase.

The report to the American Bar Association in 1892 of its committee on legal education, to which reference has been made, well expressed what then was, and I believe still is, the conviction of the legal profession, regarding the subject under consideration. The modern view (to summarize its conclusions) of the nature of human law leads directly to a natural and practical plan of elementary study. Its subject matter is those relations of men to the State or under the State to each other which are the necessary result of membership in a political community. These relations exist before the law and are regulated, not created, by it. They give rise to rights and duties. It makes no difference in practical effect whether the right or duty is so plain that all must own it, or one resting on some positive enactment. In either case, courts enforce it; in neither case do they create it. The elements of the law, therefore must be taught, and formally taught, to every student, with due regard to their history, but with first regard to their essential character.

There is a juristic encyclopedia, as the Germans phrase it, that must be mastered by whoever would be a true lawyer. It must receive his attention at the beginning of his course, and also at the

THE STUDY OF ELEMENTARY LAW.

close: at the beginning, as one must put every subject before a beginner, in outline; at the close, as he reviews his work, in its totality, scientifically considered, and yet in outline, too.

It is the natural and proper aim of the law-teacher to impress upon his classes the elements of law. If he has done that, and set them in their due relations, he has done well. It is not superficial work. It is the only foundation work. Principles, not cases, are the building stones of law, here and everywhere, now and always.

Simeon E. Baldwin.

Part II
What is a Law School For?

The University Ideal

[5]

SCIENTIFIC METHOD AND THE LAW

From Point of View of Present Day Ideas of Logic and of Scientific Method the "Traditional and Known Technique of the Common Law" is Grotesquely Inadequate for Legal Purposes—Can a Truly Scientific Method of Study be Applied to Law?—Fundamental Postulate of Such an Approach to Problem—Time Ripe for Establishment of School to Undertake Task*

By Walter W. Cook, L.L. M.
Professor of Law, Yale University; Visiting Professor of Jurisprudence, Johns Hopkins University

IN HIS address at the opening of The Johns Hopkins University Huxley expressed the view that a university ought to be a place in which knowledge is obtained without direct reference to its professional use. It is a striking fact that as yet no American university has ever undertaken work of this character in the legal field. Existing university schools of law are vocational institutions, engaged in preparing lawyers for the work of advising clients and carrying on litigation in the courts. In pointing this out, I do not mean to belittle in any way the importance of the work existing schools are doing, but merely to state a fact. To be sure, in a few of the schools arrangements have been made to lighten the teaching load of members of the faculty so that they may engage in legal research. In recent years also a few schools have added a year of graduate study to the curriculum, and in this year have permitted and encouraged, but not as a rule required, candidates for advanced law degrees to engage in what has been called legal research.

When about a generation ago the case method of studying law was introduced we were told that by its use the study of law had been made truly scientific. It was claimed that in the legal field it is the equivalent of the laboratory method in the physical sciences. That the lawyers produced under this method are better technicians than those turned out by the textbook and lecture methods, there can be no doubt. Whether, in a larger sense, they are scientifically trained members of a learned profession, is at least open to question. As one reads current legal discussions, whether in judicial opinions, textbooks, or periodicals, or listens to papers at bar association meetings, his doubt as to the scientific character of the legal thinking resulting from current legal education is increased.

At the present moment there are signs of unrest and dissatisfaction on the part of a few of the more thoughtful teachers of law. What, they are asking, would be involved in a truly scientific study of law? Can truly scientific methods of study be applied in our field of work? If so, to what extent can existing schools undertake work of the character described by Huxley, and to what extent must it be provided for in schools of a new type created especially for the purpose? In what follows I shall ask you to go with me on a voyage of exploration, in an attempt to answer these perhaps unanswerable questions. This inquiry is deemed to be of importance not merely for lawyers but for the community as a whole. To be sure, the evil effects of faulty laws are not so obvious as the consequences of defectively built bridges or bad sanitary arrangements. Nevertheless, complaints abound as to the inadequacy of our legal system to meet the demands of today. Forty-eight state legislatures and Congress grind out year in and year out a multitude of new laws; nearly a half hundred courts of last resort decide and write opinions about thousands of cases annually. The law grows more and more uncertain; delays in its administration multiply. Can we by taking thought perhaps discover at least some of the causes of our legal difficulties and do something to remedy them? The thesis which I shall attempt to support is that we can; but that this involves the application of truly scientific methods to the study of legal phenomena, something which has never yet been tried.

If we are to apply scientific methods to the study of law, so that we may proceed more intelligently, or at least less unintelligently, in our efforts to simplify and perhaps improve it, we must at the outset clarify our minds as to what these methods are. I approach the subject with diffidence and in all humility. Whatever I shall say is offered in the hope that it will call forth helpful criticism. At the outset perhaps the scientific members of the faculty will say that my boldness reminds them of the small boy who ventured to say to his mother: "Mother, what does God look like?" "Hush, dear, you must not ask such irreverent questions," was the reply. A little later the mother noticed the boy busy with pencil and paper. "What are you doing, dear?" "Drawing a picture of God." "But my son, no one knows what God looks like." "They will when I finish this picture." When I have finished drawing my picture, I hope that my friends who work in fields which are recognized as possessing a truly scientific technique will compare my attempt not with the effort of the small boy but with what we may imagine he may have attempted when in later years he had grown into an artist, and on being asked, "What are you drawing now?" perhaps replied, "I am drawing a picture which I hope will make folks think about God." Let me then ask you to think with me about scientific methods and their possible application or adaptation to the study of law, in the hope that perhaps we may be able to reach a tentative working hypothesis, upon the basis of which at least worth while experimental work can be carried on.

It is common to say that beginning with the early years of the seventeenth century scientific workers abandoned the rationalistic approach of the middle ages and entered upon the study of the empirical facts of

*Commemoration Day Address. Reprinted from The Johns Hopkins Alumni Magazine, Vol. xv, No. 3, March, 1927.

antecedents and consequences, appealing to experiment and what is called the inductive method. Like most broad generalizations, this proves upon examination to be misleading unless taken with many qualifications and limitations. It will be found that much of the rationalistic approach remained until the present century. Consider the situation in physics a generation ago. We were told by leading scientists of that day that atoms were indestructible units out of which an indestructible universe was built. It was believed that in a certain sense finality had been reached; that one consistent scheme of interpretation of the physical universe which would apply to all cognizable occasions had been attained. This idea influenced workers in other fields. Biologists, for example, struggled, perhaps some are still struggling, with the problem, given configurations of matter with locomotion in space as assigned by physico-chemical laws, to account for living organisms. The laws of the conservation of energy, of mass, of matter, were apparently established on a firm basis. The phrase, "As unchangeable as the law of gravitation," expressed the dominant attitude of mind. As Whitehead has said, it was the dullest period in science in the last three hundred years.

Had one scanned the horizon, as indeed Pearson, Mach, and Poincaré were already doing, he might have detected signs of a coming change. Indeed, as men look back now they perhaps wonder that those signs were not seen and understood by more. The reason, I venture to suggest, lies near at hand. Underlying all variant systems of thought in a given epoch there are always certain fundamental assumptions which are unconsciously presupposed. As Whitehead says, "Such assumptions appear so obvious that people do not know what they are assuming because no other way of putting things has ever occurred to them." It is believed that there underlay the scientific thought of the period to which we are referring an assumption of the validity of the logic of Aristotle, at least in its more essential features. Fundamentally, as I understand it, that logic assumes two things; (1) that in some way or other we can arrive at certain propositions which we know are factually true of the world in which we live; these propositions being either general or universal truths or particular truths—e.g., All men are mortal; Socrates is a man. These constitute the premises of our syllogisms. (2) That by combining these general and particular truths in accordance with the laws of the syllogism we can arrive at new truths about the world by deduction, without new observation.

Based upon this logical system there had come down to the modern world the system of Euclidean geometry, the first great example of what the modern mathematical philosopher calls an autonomous doctrine, that is, a body of propositions all derived by pure deduction from a relatively small and logically compatible set of propositions known as postulates. It is important for our purposes to note two things: (1) That Euclidean geometry was regarded as a set of factually true propositions about the properties of the physical space in which we live. Geometry was thus thought of as the science of physical space. (2) That the postulates were regarded as self-evident truths. This was the view even in Kant's day, and made it possible for him and his predecessors to take the position that we can have an *a priori* knowledge of nature, since by deduction from self-evident truths new truths can be arrived at. By the middle of the last century we find a change. Under the influence of nineteenth century scientific thought we find John Stuart Mill arguing that the postulates are not self-evident truths. He insists that while they are truths they are proved by the logical process of induction. It does not occur to him to deny that they are truths about physical space; he merely insists that the proof of their truth is by means of inductive logic. That is, he still has his general and his particular truths which he knows to be objectively true of the physical world; and from these he can deduce new truths. Deduction is thus still recognized as a legitimate tool to use in gaining new truths about the world without further resort to observation and induction. The only change in point of view is as to the method of arriving at the premises of syllogisms; that they are objective truths from which new truths can be deduced is not questioned. Would it be untrue to say that this view is still held today by many people who commonly regard themselves as educated? Most of us learned in high school to prove that the square on the hypotenuse of a right triangle is equal to the sum of the squares on the other two sides. As Bertrand Russell recently said, the only difficulty is that the proof proved nothing, and the only way to prove it is not by logic but by experiment. To this I would add, we need to find out what we mean by proof of the factual truth of a proposition before we conclude that it can be done even by experiment.

Be this as it may, men's notions of the validity of Euclid's geometry as the science of physical space were challenged when in the first half of the nineteenth century the Hungarian Bolyai and the Russian Lobachevski almost simultaneously but independently created non-Euclidean geometries, which were soon followed by that of Riemann. This was accomplished merely by substituting a different postulate for the celebrated parallel postulate of Euclid. Mathematicians, physicists, and philosophers were then compelled as never before to scrutinize the methods of science and indeed the concept of scientific truth itself. For, if two or more doctrines about the properties of physical space exist, each logically autonomous, but differing from the others as to at least one of its postulates, men are bound sooner or later to ask, which one is the true geometry of the physical space of our world; and this in turn leads ultimately to the more fundamental question, by what tests do we decide whether a proposition or doctrine is factually true?

As many of us know, the development of these new types of geometry, each one of which was developed by deduction from its set of postulates, has played an important part in bringing about a revolution in our ideas as to the scope of mathematics and of the function of deductive logic in the search for scientific truth. In seeking the answer to the question, Which one of these geometries is true, factually true, important discoveries were made. Let us note those of them which are important for our purposes. One is that as a branch of pure mathematics geometry has nothing to do with space. Apparently Euclid is from his postulates deducing the properties of space. These postulates all talk ostensibly of space. Any two points determine a straight line; any three points not in the same straight line determine a plane; etc., etc. Note now, as any book on modern mathematical philosophy will show, that we can replace the words, point, line, plane, etc., with any meaningless vocables whatever, and yet deduction can go on as before. If, following Keyser, we say that any two *loigs* determine a *boig*, that any two *loigs* not in the same *boig* determine a *ploig*, etc., we certainly do not know what we are talking about; nevertheless we can still deduce all the propositions with exactly the same logical rigor as before, only we shall not be able to associate with them concepts of space. As Keyser says, "The fact which thus leaps naked to view is that logical deduction depends entirely upon the form of the premises or postulates and not at all upon any specific meanings which we assign to their terms."

Suppose we say:
All gostaks are doshes,
All doshes are galloons:

again we do not know what we are talking about, but if we assume that these mysterious terms stand for classes of things, we can by the strictest of logic draw the inference that

All gostaks are galloons.

And so it comes about that the mathematicians tell us that mathematics is but the details of the tree of formal logic, and that it is the science in which we never know what we are talking about or whether what we are saying is true (Russell). As a branch of pure mathematics, then, geometry has nothing to do with space. If you examine any rigorous treatise on plane geometry you will find, as Morris Cohen puts it, that "it will make no difference in the form and sequence of the propositions if the indefinable points are replaced by complex numbers or if 'distance between points is replaced by differences of holiness in a multidimensional series of saints.'" To be clearly distinguished is geometry as a branch of experimental physics; and this brings us back again to the problem. Is Euclidean geometry as a branch of physics true of the space in which we live?

Perhaps we can best answer this question by asking another: Is arithmetic true—true, that is, as applied to our world? Is it true that 50 plus 50 equals 100? If we are counting, say apples, the answer is obviously, Yes. If however we know that the temperature yesterday was fifty degrees Fahrenheit, and that today it is one hundred, obviously we do not draw the conclusion that it is twice as hot today as it was yesterday. So, if we grade student A 50 and student B 100, we do not conclude that the latter knows twice as much as the former. If we add one liter of water to one liter of alcohol, do we have two liters of fluid? No; we have little more than one liter and nine tenths. So also if four hydrogen atoms are put together to form one helium atom, we can not say four times one is four, for the helium atom weighs measurably less than the four separate hydrogen atoms.

The result is, as Gilbert Lewis puts it, that we reach the conclusion that the method of counting can only be applied to things which can be counted. What can and what can not be counted can be determined only by trial and error; by experiment. Our answer thus is, that as a branch of pure mathematics arithmetic is true; but that as applied to the physical world a given arithmetical formula is in the abstract neither true nor false; it is useful for some purposes and not for others; applicable to some situations and not to others. We are then not surprised to have so eminent a physical scientist as Gilbert Lewis write as follows: "Are these non-Euclidean geometries true and is Euclid's false? This is a question which no longer conveys any meaning to our minds. Is chess true? Provided that a geometry contains within itself no inconsistencies or absurdities, then we regard it as true just in so far as it is interesting or useful." "All branches of mathematics [as branches of physical science] are but dummies upon which we attempt to fit our observations. To the scientist whose life is spent in trial and error it seems a natural thing to try one kind of mathematics after another in order to find one that fits his immediate problem." Note that Lewis himself—a chemist, not a mathematician—has had a part in developing a new type of geometry which he calls the geometry of asymptotic rotation, and that he believes this system will soon rival in importance, that is, in usefulness for some scientific purposes, that of Euclid itself. Apparently today, therefore, no mathematician believes that by induction we can prove the geometry of Euclid factually true of our world, in the sense that this would also prove non-Euclidean systems factually false. Scientists differ as to the extent to which Euclidean geometry is useful in scientific work; none deny its utility for many purposes, especially those of daily life. At the same time all apparently admit that other systems may well be more useful for other purposes, and that the only basis for choice lies in trial and error.

Noteworthy is it that almost contemporaneously with this development in mathematics came the work of Charles Darwin in the field of biology. His great work on the *Origin of Species* added its influence to the undermining of the belief which had ruled men's thoughts for over two thousand years that it was possible to arrive at "universals" in the Aristotelian sense, i.e., at factually true propositions which could be applied by syllogistic reasoning to the demonstration of new truths about the world without further observation and experiment. Underlying that belief is the idea of classes; that the objects in the universe can be classified in a mode which is objectively valid. Darwinism carries with it a denial that genera and species in biology are more than subjective conveniences. If we adopt the Darwinian hypothesis of the evolution of species, then, as Schiller puts it, "if the course of events could be recalled to life, we should watch each species gradually fusing with its congeners, the genera coalescing with their families, individuals exhibiting the qualities of what have since become divergent kinds, and at last learn that all the various forms of life have had a common ancestry, and are never realized except in individuals. . . . Thus a species is merely a temporary grouping of individuals. . . . We happen to snapshot them in that stage of their racial development at which they may conveniently be grouped together." Moreover, today's observations in many fields show one species gradually fading off into another through all the intermediate stages, so that the line between them must be drawn more or less arbitrarily, the only test being that of convenience for the purpose in view. To be sure, in strict logic this work in biology does not apply to inorganic things; nevertheless when added to developments in other fields it has had a tremendous influence in altering men's views of logic and of what we call the "laws of nature."

The significance of these developments in mathematics and biology was not fully apparent until the discovery of a whole series of new phenomena in the field of the inorganic sciences of physics and chemistry. X-rays, radium, radio-activity, the disintegration of atoms, the transmutation of one chemical element into another, electrons and protons, the Michelson-Morley experiment, the abandonment of the doctrines of the conservation of mass, of matter, and of energy as principles of universal applicability, the refusal of electrons to obey the accepted laws of mechanics; the quantum theory—all these and others have left modern physical science gasping for breath. Leading scientists admit that at present no one consistent scheme for the interpretation of physical phenomena is feasible, and many would perhaps hesitate to assert that it is to be expected. We have reached the era of relativity. By this is not meant the specific theories of Einstein and others, commonly associated with that term, but a point of view which, whatever may happen to specific doctrines, seems destined to remain as a permanent achievement in human thought. With much diffidence I venture to suggest what seem to me to be some of the characteristics of this point of view.

First and foremost, we find a frank and clear recognition of the extent to which all our thinking is based upon underlying postulates of which frequently we are entirely unaware but which color all our mental processes and in particular often give to those generalizations which we are in the habit of calling "natural laws" the form which they assume. Discard the postulates, and this form is altered. Frequently when we drag these postulates out into the light of day we find on examination that they are not in accord with anything in our experience. Striking examples are the assumptions underlying Newtonian mechanics that we have absolute measures of lapse of time and of spatial distance, and the concept that bodies move only when acted upon by some mysterious entity called "force." This latter assumption is apparently itself partly due to the assumption that Euclidean geometry is applicable to our physical universe. Subjected to a reexamination of this kind many of our immutable laws of nature turn out to consist in large part of conventions as to measurement, so that we are told by some writers that they are strictly analogous to the great scientific law that there are three feet in a yard.

A second feature of the newer point of view is the surrender of the hypothesis that the universe can be fully described or explained in terms of matter in motion, i. e., in terms of the changing configurations of particles of matter, the patterns altering in accordance with the classical laws of mechanics. This does not mean that the laws of mechanics have been discarded, thrown away, as of no further use; far from it. They still hold, i.e., are useful, in dealing with phenomena within a given range. Beyond that range, they do not apply. As one of our most eminent physicists, Robert A. Millikan, puts it, "The most strikingly revolutionary of the discoveries of twentieth century physics is that the very foundations of mechanics when looked at microscopically are unsound. We know now that the childish mechanical conceptions of the nineteenth century are grotesquely inadequate" as an explanation or description of the totality of our observations. Some scientists even go so far today as to suggest that the concept of matter itself can not be applied to the electron. In any event it seems to be recognized generally that it is not possible to form any purely mechanical picture of what goes on inside the atom.

As a third element in what I have called the relativity point of view is the recognition of the limitations of the process of deductive and inductive logic. In the first place, it is coming to be recognized that this "big blooming buzzing confusion" of a universe with which we are confronted does not present itself to us in classes, or so that it can be handled merely by a class logic. As William James has put it:

"The real world as it is given objectively at this moment is the sum total of all its beings and events now. But can we think of such sum? Can we realize for an instant what a cross-section of all existence at a definite point of time would be? While I talk and the flies buzz, a sea-gull catches a fish at the mouth of the Amazon, a tree falls in the Adirondack wilderness, a man sneezes in Germany, a horse dies in Tartary, and twins are born in France. What does that mean? Does the contemporaneity of these events with one another, and with a million others as disjointed, form a rational bond between them, and unite them into anything that means for us a world? Yet such a collateral contemporaneity, and nothing else, is the real order of the world. It is an order with which we have nothing to do but to get away from it as fast as possible. As I said, we break it: we break it into histories, and we break it into arts, and we break it into sciences; and then we begin to feel at home."

Apparently what we are entitled to say is this. By experience we find that we may for a particular purpose group together into a class a larger or smaller number of situations, each to some extent unlike the others, conceiving that their differences are irrelevant for the purpose in view. The essential characteristic chosen as the basis of our classification will vary with our purpose and must be relevant to it. An essential nature of water is that it quenches thirst; another, that it floats boats; another, that it cleanses; another, that it puts out fires. When we wish to put water into categories that will include other things, that is, to classify it, we must select some one of its essential natures that is material to the particular category we are at the moment interested in. The essential nature of the moon is one thing to an astronomer and another to a lover. Any grouping of this kind thus appears as at most a working hypothesis, to be tested by its consequences, and subject to revision in the light of further experience. Classification thus disappears as the statement of objectively valid and final truths about the world, and reappears as the adoption of working hypotheses, mental devices to which we resort in order to deal more effectively with our experiences. Classification is thus to be tested by its results and to be altered if those results are not satisfactory. When confronted by a new situation, i.e., one which is apparently different from any previously dealt with, so that we are in doubt what to do with it and are led to reflect upon the matter, we find that we can not deal with it merely as a new specimen of a given class. Our real task is to determine whether the differences involved which make us think of it as new, are as a practical matter, i.e., as tested by their consequences, important for the purpose we have in view; and so whether or not we can safely enlarge our class so that when we have finished our thinking it will include the new situation. Only after we have done this can we frame our syllogism, which thus appears rather as a way of stating the results of our thinking than as the mode by which those results are reached. "Universals," general rules, "natural laws," thus appear as working hypotheses or postulates; general ways of stating that for a given purpose we have in the past found by experience that it worked satisfactorily to group together a number of situations, no two of which are exactly alike; the validity of the grouping depending on whether it leads to desired results. Theoretically, all such working hypotheses are subject to revision in the light of further experience. In the case of many generalizations, however, this probability of revision is very slight; in others it is greater. And thus it is, as Keyser has so strikingly put it, that "the old cosmic absolutes—absolute space, absolute time, absolute matter, absolute natural law, absolute truth—are gone. The reign of relativity thus inaugurated by the basic sciences, is destined to work a corresponding revolution, deep, noiseless it may be, but inevitable, in all the views and institutions of man."

Statements of this kind recognize that we have expected too much from the process known as "induction." No subject has given the thoughtful scientist more trouble. Mill, as we have noted, regarded it as a method of proving the objective truth of general laws. Today we are told by some that what passes for induction is either disguised deduction or merely more or less methodical guesswork. Perhaps we need not go quite so far. Perhaps we can agree with Whitehead when he says: "I do not hold Induction to be in its essence the derivation of general laws. It is the divination of some characteristics of a particular future from the known characteristics of a particular past. The wider assumption of general laws holding for all cognizable occasions appears a very unsafe addendum to attach to this limited knowledge." The following allegory taken from *The New Astronomy* of Langley illustrates this point of view.

"We have read somewhere of a race of ephemeral insects who live but an hour. To those who are born in the early morning the sunrise is the time of youth. They die of old age while the sun's beams are yet gathering force, and only their descendants live on to midday; while it is another race which sees the sun's decline from that which saw it rise. Imagine the sun about to set, and the whole nation of mites gathered under the shadow of some mushroom (to them ancient as the sun itself) to hear what their wisest philosopher had to say of the gloomy prospect.

"If I remember aright, he first told them that, incredible at it might seem, there was not once a time in the world's youth when the mushroom itself was young, but that the sun in those early ages was in the eastern, not in the western sky. Since then, he explained, the eyes of the scientific ephemera had followed it, and established by induction from vast experience the great 'law of nature' that it moved only westward; and he showed that since it was now nearing the western horizon, science pointed herself to the conclusion that it was about to disappear forever, together with the great race of ephemera for whom it was created. What his hearers thought of this discussion I do not remember, but I have heard that the sun rose again the next morning."

In our reaction from the excesses of the older view we must not suppose that we can entirely discard the deductive process. Far from it. It plays a necessary and indeed indispensable part in all our thinking. By it we work out the consequences of rival hypotheses, and are thereby led to institute experiments or to make observations which would otherwise not be undertaken, and so discover phenomena which might have gone undiscovered for centuries. It has other functions. It enables us to arrange our knowledge in an orderly way, and so makes it more accessible for use in studying new situations. Without the logical dummies which by its means we construct we should be lost in the multiplicities of our empirical experiences. In addition, the arrangement of our knowledge in this orderly way satisfies the aesthetic side of our natures; our craving for symmetry and order. We must however be constantly on our guard lest we lose sight of its limitations and mistake the deduction of conclusions from premises for the ascertainment of factual truth about the external world.

Apparently I have wandered far from my field. What, doubtless many of you are asking, has all this to do with law. More than may at first sight appear, I venture to say. For, in spite of these developments which we have been considering, the naïve belief that men think in syllogisms and that new truth about the world can be deduced from general laws arrived at by induction, still persists in much of the thinking that goes on in the field of the social sciences. It is a curious paradox that when men are confronted with situations still more complex than those found in the physical and biological sciences, as is the case in economics, sociology, ethics, and law — situations which therefore are more difficult to deal with by scientific technique—the more insistent do they become as to the prior existence of fixed and universal principles or laws which can be discovered and directly applied and followed. Instead of thinking of principles as "methods of inquiry," as "instrumentalities for the investigation" of new situations, by means of which the "net value of past experience is rendered available for the scrutiny of new perplexities," they are prone to assimilate the problems in these fields to those of mathematics. As a result they either fail to discover what their problems are or to deal adequately with them if they do.

It may seem incredible, but it is still possible for eminent members of the bar to assert that all a court does in deciding doubtful cases is to deduce conclusions from fixed premises, the law; or what comes to the same thing, to assert that all the Supreme Court of the United States does in holding a statute of Congress unconstitutional is to apply by logic a preexisting rule found in the constitution. Let me quote the relatively recent utterance of an eminent member of the bar, a well known student of legal history and jurisprudence.

"Every judicial act resulting in a judgment consists of a pure deduction. The figure of its reasoning is the stating of a rule applicable to certain facts, a finding that the facts of the particular case are those certain facts, and the application of the rule is a logical necessity. The old syllogism. 'All men are mortal, Socrates is a man, therefore he is mortal,' states the exact form of a judicial judgment. . . . It must be perfectly apparent to any one who is willing to admit the rules governing rational mental action that unless the rule of the major premise exists as antecedent to the ascertainment of the fact or facts put into the minor premise, there is no judicial act in stating the judgment. The man who claims that under our system courts make law is asserting that the courts habitually act unconstitutionally."

Prominent teachers of law still tell us that we must preserve what they call the logical symmetry of the law, that after all the law is logical; and talk about deducing the rule to be applied to a new situation by logic from some "fundamental principle." Back of all this, it is submitted, is nothing but the old logic; the assumption that in some way or other we can discover general "laws," general "principles," Aristotelian "universals," which by means of logical, that is, syllogistic reasoning, we can use in dealing with new cases as they arise as merely new samples of preexisting classes. The nineteenth century notion of science as the ascertainment of all-embracing laws of nature, holding for all cognizable occasions, which we have seen disappearing from physical science in the twentieth century, still underlies apparently the thinking of the eminent law teacher and writer who is at present restating for The American Law Institute an important branch of our law and who not many years ago wrote as follows:

"The common law . . . is surely a philosophical system, a body of scientific principle, which has been adopted in each of the common law jurisdictions in this country as the basis of its law. Courts of each jurisdiction, in attempting to apply this general body of principles in its own jurisdiction, have sometimes misconceived it and misstated it, and this misstatement is apt to lead to a local peculiarity in the particular common law of the jurisdiction in question. But the general scientific law remains unchanged in spite of these errors; the same throughout all common law jurisdictions."

It would be safe to assert that essentially the same ideas underlie nearly all the teaching in our law schools. Consider what is done. Substantially the only materials placed in the hands of students are collections of cases, containing selected decisions of the courts and the opinions purporting to explain why the decisions were reached. By a process which the average law teacher would probably describe as "induction," the students under the guidance of the instructor formulate a series of generalizations which are supposed to state "the law" on the given topic. Where, as is frequently the case, the decisions in the half-hundred independent jurisdictions vary, in some way or other which is never made entirely clear to the student, the "better" view is supposed to be detected and the "unsound" view rejected. With the resulting "rules" and "principles" students are supposed to be equipped to decide new cases that may be presented to them. All of this is understandable if and only if one still believes in the efficacy of the old logic and in the notions of induction current in the last century.

Is is not obvious that from the point of view of present day ideas of logic and of scientific method this "traditional and known technique of the common law," as Dean Pound calls it, is as grotesquely inadequate for legal purposes as the childish mechanical notions of the nineteenth century have shown themselves to be in the field of physics? If we approach the problems which confront the lawyer and the judge in the light of what we may call the newer logic, what do we find? First of all, we discover that the practicing lawyer, as much as, let us say, an engineer or a doctor, is engaged in trying to forecast future events. What he wishes to know is, not how electrons, atoms, or bricks will behave in a given situation, but what a number of more or less elderly men who compose some court of last resort will do when confronted with the facts of his client's case. He knows how they or their predecessors have acted in the past in many more or less similar situations. He knows that if without reflection the given situation appears to them as not differing substantially from those previously dealt with, they will, as lawyers say, follow precedent. This past behavior of the judges can be described in terms of certain generalizations which we call rules and principles of law. If now the given situation appears to the court as new, i.e., as one which calls for reflective thinking, the lawyer ought to know, but usually does not because of his unscientific training, that his case is "new" because these rules and principles of law do not as yet cover the situation. If they did, the case would be disposed of more or less automatically. As it is, the lawyer finds competing analogies and so competing rules or principles which are possibly applicable. A familiarity with modern studies of human thinking would reveal to him that his job is, not to find the preexisting meaning of the terms in the rules and principles which he wishes the court to apply, but rather to induce the court to give to those terms for the first time a meaning which will reach the desired result.

If we shift our point of view from that of the practicing lawyer to that of the judge who has to decide a new case, the same type of logical problem presents itself. The case is by hypothesis new. This means that there is no compelling reason of pure logic which forces the judge to apply any one of the competing rules urged on him by opposing counsel. His task is not to find the prexisting but previously hidden meaning of the terms in these rules: it is to give them a meaning. A few judges are fully aware of this, men of the type of Holmes and Cardozo; others see it dimly; and still others apparently not at all.

The logical situation confronting the judge in a new case being what it is, it is obvious that he must legislate, whether he will or no. By this is meant that since he is free so far as compelling logical reasons are concerned to choose which way to decide the case, his choice will turn out upon analysis to be based upon considerations of social or economic policy. An intelligent choice can be made only by estimating as far as that is possible the consequences of a decision one way or the other. To do this, however, the judge will need to know two things: (1) what social consequences or results are to be aimed at; and (2) how a decision one way or other will affect the attainment of those results. This knowledge he will as a rule not have; to acquire it he will need to call upon the other social sciences, such as economics. Note now that our traditional technique makes no adequate provision whereby counsel can furnish the court with the needed data; neither does it provide the court itself with the machinery to acquire it. Why? I take it, because the assumption is that with nothing but his experience as a man and a judge he can by reasoning, by logic, decide the case—it is purely a question of law, and no evidence is required after the facts of the situation have been ascertained.

Underlying any scientific study of the law, it is submitted, will lie one fundamental postulate, viz., that human laws are devices, tools which society uses as one of its methods to regulate human conduct and to promote those types of it which are regarded as desirable. If so, it follows that the worth or value of a given rule of law can be determined only by finding out how it works, that is, by ascertaining, so far as that can be done, whether it promotes or retards the attainment of desired ends. If this is to be done, quite clearly we must know what at any given period these ends are and also whether the means selected, the given rules of law, are indeed adapted to securing them. In the light of this postulate and of the foregoing discussion of logic and scientific method, let us attempt to sketch in rough outline a university school of law or jurisprudence as it might be organized for the attainment of the end described by Huxley, as distinguished from a professional school for the training of practitioners. Such a school I visualize as a community of scholars, devoted to the scientific study of law as a social institution and to the training of other scholars for the same pursuit.

In the first place, it is obvious that what is demanded is not merely a broadening of the present vocational curriculum, organized as that is on the basis of the old logic, or the addition of a graduate school of law to the vocational school, but rather an entirely new and different approach to legal problems. First and foremost, the members of such a group would need to have and to give to their students a clear conception of what the scientific study of anything involves, and of the available tools for pursuing it in the legal field. This would require them to take account of modern investigations into logic and human reasoning, and to survey in general outline at least the development of science and scientific method. Only in this way, it is believed, can there be formulated an adequate conception of the technique involved in the scientific study of legal phenomena, and of the limitations of the technique; only in this way can there be secured the necessary degree of objectivity required for the study of legal problems.

In the second place, a scientific approach to the study of law will demand observation and study of the actual structure and functioning of modern social, economic, and political life, so that in dealing with what are in the last analysis problems of social and economic policy those working in their difficult field will not rely upon hit-or-miss information which has been picked up accidentally.

In the third place, studies will need to be made of the existing rules of law, so as to ascertain just what they are. Before we can improve anything, we must know what it is. This will demand for its successful attainment a careful analysis of the prevailing concepts and terminology now used by the legal profession, and a restatement of existing law in a simpler and more accurate terminology. One who has not worked in the field can hardly realize the extent to which muddy concepts and ambiguous phraseology abound. No adequate analytical studies of these concepts and of the verbal symbols in which they are expressed has ever been made. Studies of this kind would do much to clarify and simplify our law.

In the fourth place, in a school of the kind we are considering there would be carried on studies in the actual operation of our law. This would involve research into the conflicts of interest which arise in the community and into the adjustments of these which we seek to bring about by legal means. In this connection would be made studies in legal history, and comparative law, so that we may take advantage of the experience of other times and other peoples in solving similar problems. Here also would be required the study of present day social, economic, and political relations affected by particular bodies of law. The cooperation of students in the other social sciences would be needed —of students of economics in the field of commercial law; of students of the family in what lawyers call the law of domestic relations; of psychologists, in the field of evidence; of psychologists, psychiatrists, criminologists, and others in the criminal law, etc., etc. Time fails in which to go into details; I content myself with mere suggestions of the possibilities.

The time is ripe for the establishment of such a school. Its primary purpose would be the non-professional study of law, in order that the function of law may be more clearly understood, its limitations appreciated, its results evaluated, and its future development kept more nearly in touch with the complexities of modern life. It would demand critical and creative work by the faculty and the development of students capable of the same type of work. The student body would necessarily be small and carefully selected. There would doubtless be few classes in the usual sense of the term, their place being taken by discussion groups, conferences and individual work. Students would be expected not so much to take courses and acquire information as to undertake to educate themselves under the guidance of the faculty by engaging in the solution of problems and the carrying on of research. Results of their work would appear later in teaching and writing, but also in other ways. Without doubt some of the graduates of the school would go into practice, and perhaps become leaders of the bar, judges, members of the legislature, or members of administrative commissions or other public bodies. Very possibly those graduates who desired to go into practice would find it necessary to prepare for state bar examinations by spending a few months in acquiring the necessary information. That this would be entirely possible is clear. However, the aim of the school would be not the production of practitioners but the development of the scientific study of law. All else would be incidental.

This study might, nevertheless, include research which would have an important bearing upon professional legal education. If what I have said this morning is sound, it is obvious that the professional curriculum of existing law schools is inadequate for its purposes. Surely these schools should regard their function as something more than the training of practitioners. Lawyers should and do perform many functions in addition to acting as technical experts in carrying on litigation for others. They assist in the prevention of litigation by aiding in the adoption of the proper legal devices in the organization of industry.

They frequently act as advisers in the formulation of business policies not primarily legal in character; they advise their clients upon many problems of a social or personal nature. As governmental executives, members of legislative bodies, members of administrative commissions, heads of legislative reference bureaus, diplomatists, and so on, they play a leading part in the political life of the nation. They are often called upon to conduct investigations which cut across many diverse fields of specialized knowledge. As members of bar association committees upon legal reform they are called upon to perform services which demand a broad social vision and a knowledge of how law functions in society. If we bear these things in mind, the inadequacy of the training now offered in our law schools is evident. It may well be that a research school of the type under consideration could conduct needed research into legal education, such as a careful study of the present materials in the curriculum and of the methods of instruction and the preparation of new materials for the study of law with these broader purposes in view. It could perhaps carry on experimentation with the new materials and try out the new methods, attempting to measure the results so as to indicate the feasibility of their use by the professional schools. Thus without itself becoming a training school for practitioners or losing sight of its primary aim, the school might contribute much in the way of aiding the professional schools in developing adequate scientific training in law, so that their graduates would become not merely practitioners but socially minded members of a truly learned profession.

Millions have been given by the great foundations and by public spirited citizens for the promotion of medical research. Thus far little has been given for legal research, for the obvious reason that no institution offered itself as both willing and prepared to undertake the task of truly scientific work in the legal field. The opportunity is clear; the need is urgent. To be sure, the results will not be so obvious as in the field of medicine. The effects of faulty laws are obscure and difficult to measure, and still more difficult to correct. Nevertheless I venture to believe that much can be done if we put our minds to the task; that there is work worthy of being done if only it can be done worthily.

Officers of Association 1926-1927
President
Charles S. Whitman.....................New York City
120 Broadway
Secretary
William P. MacCracken, Jr....................Chicago, Ill.
209 S. LaSalle St.
Assistant Secretary
Richard Bentley...........................Chicago, Ill.
209 S. LaSalle St.
Treasurer
John H. Voorhees.................Sioux Falls, S. D.
Treasurer's Office, Room 1119, No. 209 S. LaSalle St.
Chicago, Ill.
Executive Committee
Chester I. Long (Ex of.).....................Wichita, Kan.
Edward A. Armstrong (Ex of.).............Newark, N. J.
Edgar B. Tolman (Ex of.)....................Chicago, Ill.
Jesse A. Miller..........................Des Moines, Ia.
William M. Hargest.....................Harrisburg, Pa.
Amasa C. Paul........................Minneapolis, Minn.
William C. Kinkead.....................Cheyenne, Wyo.
Henry Upson Sims.....................Birmingham, Ala.
J. Weston Allen.........................Boston, Mass.
James F. Ailshie....................Coeur d'Alene, Idaho
Frank Pace...........................Little Rock, Ark.

THE
UNIVERSITY OF CHICAGO LAW REVIEW

THE AUTOBIOGRAPHY OF AN EX-LAW STUDENT*
ROBERT MAYNARD HUTCHINS**

WHEN I began to study law in 1920 we were chiefly concerned with two things: one, our definition of law, and two, our desire to be scientific. We knew what we wanted in both cases. The law was what the courts and other governmental officers would do. If we were scientific we could predict what they would do. The task of lawyers, law teachers, and law students was therefore clear. It was to learn how to predict what the courts and other governmental agencies would do.

To acquire facility in this mode of prophecy we turned, as Langdell had turned, to what the courts had done. Since what they had done last was what they were most likely to do next, we kept up with the recent cases, and even studied accounts of them in newspapers and mimeographed sheets. Since what the courts had said shed some light on what they would do, we devoted a good deal of attention to analyzing and reconciling the language of learned judges. What they had said and done, carefully noted item by item, made up the vast collection of items which at the end constituted our legal information.

You will observe that we were thoroughly Baconian as to science and thoroughly behavioristic as to psychology. It was scientific to collect and examine a multitude of particular items, which gradually arranged themselves into rules the courts had followed. We knew that the courts would follow these rules in the future as they had in the past because courts were people, and people behaved as they were in the habit of behaving. Our scheme was very simple and quite complete.

Yet even in those remote days we had some qualms about it. Since we were a university law school, we could not limit ourselves to what the courts had done. Our function was to improve the law, not merely to learn it. We had to decide, therefore, whether the courts had done right. We could not content ourselves with the weight of authority; that was too

* An address delivered before the Association of American Law Schools at Chicago, December, 1933.
** President, University of Chicago.

much like counting noses. We could not test the cases by their conformity to principle. There were no such things as principles in our definition or our science. How were we to tell whether the cases were "sound"? Fortunately at this juncture pragmatism came to our aid. It told us that we could test the rules of law by discovering whether or not they worked.

This helped us a great deal. For a long time we sat and speculated about how the rules worked. In public utility law, for example, we decided that Mr. Justice Brandeis was right about the rate base and Mr. Justice Butler was wrong, because Mr. Justice Brandeis' rule would work better than Mr. Justice Butler's. Whether this was really because we were in favor of lower rates and thought the Brandeis rule would lower them, though today it would raise them, whether it was because we liked liberals and therefore preferred Mr. Justice Brandeis to Mr. Justice Butler, I do not care to say. In attempting to decide which rule worked better we had to assume a social order and the aims thereof, and then try to determine which rule did more to achieve the aims we favored. What made this difficult was that we didn't know much about the social order; we didn't have any special competence in the matter of social aims; and we didn't have the slightest idea how to go about finding out whether a given rule helped to accomplish them or not.

Suddenly we discovered that there were people who knew all these things, people who could tell us how the law worked and why. They were the social scientists. We had every reason to resort to them. The courts were social agencies; their conclusions must be conditioned by society. The social scientists could help us to predict what the courts would do. The psychologists would help us understand the behavior of judges. The psychiatrists could help us there, too, and could also assist us in comprehending criminals. Hand in hand with these other scientists we could become scientific.

Therefore we added to law school faculties men who had no legal training, but who were experts in these other sciences. Where such additions were impossible because of penury or prejudice, we took co-operation for our watchword and began to work with scholars in other departments of our universities. The social contacts we developed were very pleasant. Imagine our confusion, however, when we discovered that from their disciplines as such the social scientists added little or nothing. They taught us to reverence our own subject; it was more interesting to them than their own. With the enthusiasm of converts they showed us the masses of social, political, economic, and psychological data which lay hidden in the cases. They then proceeded to teach the cases better than we could teach them, not because they had been nurtured in the social sciences, but because they were good teachers.

The fact was that though the social scientists seemed to have a great deal of information, we could not see and they could not tell us how to use it. It did not seem to show us what the courts would do or whether what they had done was right. For example, the law of evidence is obviously full of assumptions about how people behave. We understood that the psychologists knew how people behave. We hoped to discover whether an evidence case was "sound" by finding out whether the decision was in harmony with psychological doctrine. What we actually discovered was that psychology had dealt with very few of the points raised by the law of evidence; and that the basic psychological problem of the law of evidence, what will affect juries, and in what way, was one psychology had never touched at all. Thus psychologists could teach you that the rule on spontaneous exclamations was based on false notions about the truth-compelling qualities of a blow on the head. They could not say that the evidence should be excluded for that reason. They did not know enough about juries to tell you that; nor could they suggest any method of finding out enough about juries to give you an answer to the question.

We decided, then, that it was nice to have met the social scientists and that we should continue to associate with them in the hope of some day striking some mutual sparks. If, for the moment, they could not help us to tell whether the rules worked, we could at least see for ourselves what the courts were doing. Since the law was what the courts would do and since all the courts do is not in books, we decided to observe the law in action. We collected tremendous numbers of facts about the operation of procedural rules and set about getting them in other fields. We thus added greatly to our accumulated data about what the courts had done. It was data of another kind than cases. But like the cases it was data absolutely raw. We did not know what facts to look for, or why we wanted them, or what to do with them after we got them. We were simply after facts. These facts did not help us to understand the law, the social order, or the relation between the two.

Nevertheless this new interest in facts had some effect on the curriculum. It culminated in what was known as the Functional Approach. The Functional Approach was based on the Fact-Situation. The Fact-Situation became the center of our educational attention. We knew that we were supposed to train young people to practice law. We knew that cases do not present themselves to the lawyer labeled Torts, Contracts, Equity I, or Constitutional Law. The lawyer is faced with a Fact-Situation. The

Fact-Situation may involve five or six of the traditional law school disciplines. We could see that this was wrong. We could see that if we could organize a curriculum of Fact-Situations we could by passing the young man through it prepare him to meet these facts or these situations in after-life. He would recognize a familiar Fact-Situation that he had known in law school and could deal with it as an old friend. So we shifted our courses around and renamed them in the hope that we might sooner or later find out how to introduce the student to those Fact-Situations he was most likely to encounter in the practice.

The trouble with the Functional Approach was that it threatened us with a reductio ad absurdum. If the best way to prepare students for the practice was to put them through the experiences they would have in practice, clearly we should abolish law schools at once. I challenge you to find the least excuse for one in the latest manifesto of Mr. Jerome Frank. We could not successfully imitate experience in the classroom. Even moot courts were probably a waste of time. The place to get experience is in life. The place to get legal experience is in a law office. Since there were already too many law offices, we saw no reason for turning the law schools into law offices, too. The Functional Approach seemed likely to remove the last vestige of excuse for the maintenance of law schools in universities.

By another route this general program led us toward another absurdity. The law is what the courts will do. Courts are people. What people do largely depends on their visceral reactions. The law may thus depend on what the judge has had for breakfast. The conclusion is that legal scholars, adopting the slogan of Shredded Wheat, "Tell me what you eat and I'll tell you what you are," should devote themselves to studying the domestic larders of judicial wives. The prospect of a life of such investigation might well put an end to legal scholarship altogether. Digestive Jurisprudence and the Functional Approach were on the verge of destroying the two characteristic activities of the university law school.

At the time when I stopped studying law these horrid possibilities were just appearing on the horizon. They struck terror to the heart of at least one law teacher. And there were other fears that daunted me. Had we not engaged in a hopeless task? There were thirty thousand cases and eight thousand statutes a year. In addition we had taken up the burden of discovering and studying a lot of facts outside the cases. In addition we had decided to master the data of the social sciences. We had to do all these things if the law was what the courts would do and our job was to predict what they would do next. How could we hope to make the slightest impression on all this material in one short life-time? Of course we could break the field down into smaller and smaller compartments, narrowing our individual vision to our individual capacity. But this would mean adding to the faculty every year until the number approached infinity.

Another thing bothered me. Suppose the legislatures should repeal everything we ever knew. Mastery of all the facts about the Sherman Act painstakingly acquired in the course in Trade Regulation might be a positive disservice under the N.R.A. Could it be that in presenting our students with Fact-Situations of the present or immediate past we were actually handicapping them in their battle with the Fact-Situations of the future? We had given them no weapons but our advice about these good old Fact-Situations. But suppose the foe was a brand new one, the product of a New Deal.

Finally I was haunted by the notion that our duty to our students was to educate them. We knew of course that they came to us without education. We had learned not to expect any from the colleges of liberal arts. When we got through with them we might flatter ourselves that we had trained them to be good technicians, competent craftsmen, or as Mr. Beale has put it, to make a noise like a lawyer. I could not see that we had done anything about their education. Education, I had supposed, was chiefly an affair of the intellect. Our curriculum was anti-intellectual from beginning to end. It involved not a single idea, not a single great book, not a single contact with the tremendous intellectual heritage of the law. We did not even expect intellectual exercise. We discussed the logic of the cases, it is true; but none of us knew any logic. We could not engage in intellectual exercise because we were not competent in the intellectual techniques which it requires.

I found myself therefore at the end of my legal career facing a series of dilemmas. We must educate students, but we couldn't do it because the law is what the courts will do and our students must become able prophets. This requires them to know all about what the courts have done and are doing. There is no time to do more than train them, even if we knew how to educate them.

We must, then, train students. This is a vain hope because the law offices can do it better, and because just when we get them trained new legislation which we cannot foresee may make the habits we have given them the worst they can possibly have.

We must, then, devote ourselves to legal research. But if the law is what the courts will do and we are going to be scientific we must get the cases, and the facts outside the cases, and the data of the social sciences. But when we get this material it is useless because we don't know what to do with it. It is a hopeless job, anyway, because there is so much material that we can't possibly accumulate it all, and we have no basis for selection and discrimination.

Now I put it to you that these dilemmas are the inevitable consequence of our notion of law and our conception of science. I do not deny that our definition of law and our conception of science are possible. I do assert that they are not complete and not fruitful for the study of the law.

I suggest that the essential constituent of a science is the analysis of its basic concepts. The proper immediate subject matter of a science is its abstractions, as can be seen as soon as the question is asked, What is the basis of the division, classification, and selection of the concrete material? The answer, contrary to the Baconian dogma, is that the basis must be found in the rational analysis, which is logically prior to the empirical operations involved.

Empirical operations do not make a science. Facts do not organize themselves. Let me emphasize as strongly as I can that we must accumulate cases, facts, and data. I simply insist that we must have a scheme into which to fit them. The law school that ignores the cases, the facts, or the social sciences will be a poor law school. The legal scholar who ignores these things will be a poor legal scholar. What I am suggesting is not to be taken as consolation or encouragement to those lazy, unimaginative, or irresolute souls who have opposed going beyond the language of judges into the facts of the law and of social science. I am not proposing that we discontinue those activities which have characterized the progressive law school in the past ten years; I am proposing an addition to them. To understand this addition we may refer with profit to the words of the great physiologist, Claude Bernard. "By simply noting facts," he said, "we can never succeed in establishing a science. Pile up facts and observations as we may, we shall be none the wiser. Endless accumulation of observations leads nowhere." Experiments and observations are employed to assist in formulating and to exemplify rational analysis, not as a substitute for it. It is rational analysis which finds and orders abstractions which can be organized into systems; and it is by the development or application of these systems in concrete material that we understand facts and data. One aim of science is to understand. This the law schools have neglected for the sake of another and an inferior aim, the prediction and control of behavior. Since a university is primarily concerned with understanding, a university law school might be primarily concerned with understanding the law. This is scientific in the highest sense.

Now I suggest that if we are to understand the law we shall have to get another definition of it. I suggest that the law is a body of principles and rules developed in the light of the rational sciences of Ethics and Politics. The aim of Ethics and Politics is the good life. The aim of the Law is the same. Decisions of courts may be tested by their conformity to the rules of law. The rules may be tested by their conformity to legal principles. The principles may be tested by their consistency with one another and with the principles of Ethics and Politics.

The duty of the legal scholar, therefore, is to develop the principles and rules which constitute the law. It is in short to formulate legal theory. Cases, facts outside the cases, the data of the social sciences will illustrate and confirm this theoretical construction. Where formerly they were worthless because we had no theoretical construction; where formerly we did not know what facts to look for or what to do with them when we got them; where formerly we could make no use of social scientists because neither they nor we had any mutual frame of reference which made material transferable, we may now see how all these things will assist our attempt to understand the law. We can even see how to tell whether cases are "sound."

The concern of the law teacher and of the law student, as well as the legal scholar, is with principles. The leading philosopher in America, Alfred North Whitehead, once addressed himself to the problem of the university school of business. His conclusions are applicable to the university law school, too. He said, "The way in which a university should function in preparation for an intellectual career, such as modern business or one of the older professions, is by promoting the imaginative consideration of the various general principles underlying that career. Its students thus pass into their period of technical apprenticeship with their imaginations already practised in connecting details with general principles." The general principles of the law are derived from Politics and Ethics. The student and teacher should understand the principles of those sciences. Since they are concerned with ideas, they must read books that contain them. To assist in understanding them they should be trained in those intellectual techniques which have been developed to promote the comprehension and statement of principles. They will not ignore the cases, the facts, or the social sciences. At last they will understand them. They will be educated.

I take it that an educated man knows what he is doing and why. I believe that an educated lawyer will be more successful in practising law as well as in improving it than one who is merely habituated to Fact-Situations. His training will rest not on his recollection of a mass of specific items, but on a grasp of fundamental ideas. The importance of these ideas cannot be diminished by the whims of legislatures or the vagaries of practical politics.

You will say that even if all this is true, it is utterly impractical: the students, the bar, and the public would never tolerate a law school organized to formulate and expound legal principles, even though such formulation and exposition must take account of the cases and the facts of the law and of social science. They believe these schools are founded to train students in the art of practising law and that facility in this art is best acquired through homeopathic doses of experience in law school. I think you are right. Therefore I suggest that in every university where there is a law school a department of jurisprudence be established. The object of such a department would be to formulate and expound legal principles. Gradually its efforts would be reflected in the curriculum and studies of the law school. Gradually it would be discovered that its students were more successful at the bar and even in predicting what the courts would do than the progeny of the law school. Gradually we might come to realize that the best practical education is the most theoretical one. And gradually, very gradually, the law might become once more a learned profession.

Journal of Legal Education

The Study of Law as an Intellectual Activity

James B. White

Others have recently spoken to you about the social and psychological conditions of law-school life, and no doubt conversations on that intriguing topic will command your attention for some time to come. What I want to talk to you about today is a different subject. My concern is with what you will be doing in law school intellectually speaking, that is, what we are asking you to do with your minds as you do the work of law school: reading your cases; preparing for class; asking and responding to questions in the classroom; and thinking and talking about legal questions with each other over coffee or lunch. The process may well seem new and strange to you, very different from what you have done in college, and I hope that I can make some remarks that will help to prepare you for it.

I don't want to attribute to any of you the sort of ignorance I once had, but it is possible that some of you think—as many non-lawyers do—that the law is at bottom very simple. I once thought that what the word "law" referred to was, obviously enough, the laws themselves. And I naturally expected that the laws were all written down somewhere to be looked up and applied to life. The rules, once found, were simple: the mystery of the law had to do with their location. What mainly distinguished me from the lawyer, I thought, was that he knew where to find the rules and how to be sure he had found all of them. What I conceived of as the "application" of the rules was easy. You move to a new state and you need to obtain a new driver's license and automobile registration. You send for or pick up the appropriate information and follow the directions until the process is completed. Or take traffic regulations: it is easy to understand that you should stop at a stop sign, yield at a yield sign, and the like. The rules are clear: you either follow or disobey them.

It is true that the law often works in this simple way, perhaps most of the time; for in many situations the law is sufficiently intelligible for

---

James B. White is Professor of Law, The University of Chicago. This talk was first given to the class that entered The University of Chicago Law School in the fall of 1976. It was later published in revised form as an "Occasional Paper" by The University of Chicago Law School, 1977. The author acknowledges the helpful criticism of his colleagues Walter Blum, Edmund Kitch, Edward Levi, Bernard Meltzer, Phil Neal, Geoffrey Stone, Hans Zeisel, and Franklin Zimring.

people to use it easily and sufficiently fair to occasion no feeling that there is something deeply wrong that calls out for correction. What is more, strongly held values support this simple view of the law: to one raised in a democratic system it seems that this is how the law *must* work. The rules are for my guidance, after all, and they must be intelligible to me. I vote for candidates on the "issues," which are frequently stated in the form of proposed legislation or regulation; to be competent as a voter, which my political system no doubt rightly assumes I am, I must be able to understand the laws. If they are unclear, it is certainly not through any necessity but because they have been made so by lawyers, eager to maintain the profitable mystique of their profession.

But this simple view does not account for all the ways in which the law works, and it omits entirely what is most interesting, difficult, and important in what we do. Think for a moment what would follow if it were true that the activity of law consisted of nothing more than memorizing certain clear rules and learning where to find the others. First, both law school and the practice of law would be intolerably boring. On the face of it, few things could be more dull than simply memorizing large numbers of rules or learning one's way about a bibliographical system. But the fact is that for many people the study and practice of law are both difficult and fascinating.

Second, since the rules that must be memorized are not invented at the law schools but exist outside of them, generally available to the world at large, there would be no substantial or interesting difference between a good legal education and a poor one. (Indeed, it would not be plain under these circumstances why we should have law schools or formal legal training at all. We could publish lists of rules and examine students on their "knowledge" of them at a bar examination.) And if this view of the law were accurate, there would be little to distinguish a good lawyer from a poor one. But there is general agreement, among those who claim to know, that a good legal education is something important and special, something very difficult to attain; that a good lawyer has capacities and powers the poor one lacks; and that in this field as in others excellence is rare and valuable.

The third consequence of this simple view of the law would be that the case method—"learning the law by reading cases"—would seem bizarre and perhaps sadistic. Why should one read these complicated and difficult cases simply to discover the general propositions for which they stand? But a great many lawyers regard their experience of learning how to read a case as a step of huge importance in their education as minds and as people, involving much more than learning to discover and repeat rules. Some, at least, would say that this training has helped them to find in the material of their daily professional existence a set of puzzles and difficulties that can interest them for life.

Law as an Intellectual Activity 3

In my view, and I think in that of my colleagues here, the simple model of the law with which I began is right only in the sense that it describes how the law sometimes works in the world; it is wholly wrong as a conception of the field of study and practice with which you are about to become engaged. For it is in the main only when things seem or threaten not to work in such easy and direct ways that lawyers are called upon to act. Our primary field of concern is the problematic and complex in the law, not the simple and orderly. Let me suggest that you regard the law, not as a set of rules to be memorized, but as an activity, something that people do with their minds and with each other as they act in relation to a body of authoritative legal material and to the circumstances and events of the actual world. The law is a set of social and intellectual practices that defines a universe or culture in which you will learn to function. Like other important activities, law offers its practitioner the opportunity to make a life, to work out a character for himself. What you will learn in law school, in this view, is not information in the usual sense, not a set of repeatable propositions, but how to do something. Our primary aim is not to transmit information to you but to help you learn how to do what it is that lawyers do with the problems that come to them. In the course of all this you must necessarily acquire a great deal of information, much of it essential to your training, and some of it will come from your teachers. But the acquisition of such information is incidental, not central. As a professor once said, "I am not a data bank; what I hope to be is a teacher."

Of course the law as an activity can and should be studied—and is studied at this law school—from the point of view of other disciplines. The operations of lawyers and the legal system can be studied by the anthropologist, the economist, the historian, the literary or rhetorical critic, the psychiatrist, the philosopher, the social theorist, and many other specialists. But in studying the law in such ways one is functioning, not as a lawyer, but as an anthropologist, as an historian, and so forth. What is peculiar and central to your experience in law school and beyond is learning how to participate in this activity, not as an academic, but as a legal mind.*

It might help if you were to compare the process of learning law not so much with your other experiences of the classroom as with your experiences of learning in ordinary life: learning to swim, to sail, to ski, to fly-fish, to understand music or art, to play poker or bridge, or to carry on a conversation at a lunch counter or a cocktail party. How would you describe what learning to engage in such activities involved for you? To what extent does it make sense to say that what you did was to "acquire

---

*I do not mean to suggest that all of you will or should choose to become lawyers by career. Some of you may have very different goals. But I assume that you all want to learn the law. And what I am saying for all of you is that the most important thing that you can learn here is, not what the rules say, but what it is that the lawyers and judges do and should do with the materials of the law.

information" in the usual sense? What did you do beyond that?

Let me address one of these analogies. Suppose that you were asked to teach a person how to sail a boat, and that you proceeded by explaining the names of the parts of the boat, how the various parts operated, and the principles on which they functioned. Suppose your student learned to repeat perfectly what you had said. What would he or she know about *sailing*? One summer I tried to teach people to sail that way, and what I found was that even those who could repeat what I said did not understand it; when they got into a boat and felt it move and shift on the water, the sails shake and fill in the wind, they had no real idea of what to do. Of course the information I offered was useful to one who wished to sail, but it could only begin to be meaningful after he understood something about sailing. I am suggesting that knowing the rules of the law is like knowing the names for the parts of the boat; it is useful information which teaches little about the enterprise itself. Or consider fly-fishing or a golf swing: what do you know when you can explain the structure of the equipment and the principles upon which it is used, when a cast or a swing has been described to you, but before you yourself have tried it? To learn law, one must do law. It is the function of our classes to help you learn how to do law.

A more complete analogy may be learning a language. One must know the rules of grammar and the meaning of terms, but to know those things is not to know how to speak the language. Such knowledge comes only with use. The real difficulties and pleasures lie, not in knowing the rules of French or of law, but in knowing how to speak the language, how to make sense of it, how to use it to serve your purposes in life. One's knowledge of a language, like one's knowledge of the law, is never complete. Again and again one hears new sentences and new terms; one sees, with surprise and pleasure, new operations and new moves. The speaker of ordinary competence constantly invents new ways to use the language. It is said that the most effective way to teach a language is to immerse the student in the culture, to start him speaking and talking and reading the language before he "knows" anything about it. Then it is always a language and not a scheme, not a subject, that he is learning. It is a similar perception which underlies the way we teach law.

In both language and law, learning has a double focus: if one is to live and act competently in a particular culture, one must learn how the language—or the law—is in fact spoken by others, by those whom one wishes to address, to persuade, to learn from, and to live with. But one also wishes to learn how to turn the language, or the law, to one's own purposes: to invent new sentences, to have new ideas, to do new things, perhaps to change the nature of the language itself. Your concern in law school is thus a double one: to learn as completely as you can how the legal culture functions; and to establish a place for yourself in relation to it from which you can attempt to use it in your own ways—in ways that increase your capacities and powers, ways that enable you to speak truthfully to the conditions of the world and to take positions (and offer them to others) which seem to you to be right. In doing all this you will subject your own views and inclinations to the discipline of the inherited culture and the conditions of the world; and you will have a chance, sometimes, not only to maintain but to improve the culture of which you become a part.

What I have said may suggest an explanation of what we call the "case method" of learning law, that is, by studying actual cases in which the law can be seen in action rather than by memorizing general principles or rules. It is true that the cases you will read in your courses can usually be said to stand for one or more propositions of law, and cases are often referred to that way by a lawyer writing a brief or by a judge in his opinion. But it is not primarily to learn those propositions of law (which may indeed be, in your view or that of others, erroneous) that you read those cases. Cases in your casebooks are offered to you as the occasion for individual and collective thought, as genuine problems for the mind and heart. Each opinion is the final stage of a complicated series of legal events. You are asked to reconstruct these events in your imagination so that you can participate in them second hand—pretending now that you are the seller, now the buyer, now one of the lawyers, now the other, now a judge, now a legislator. "What would I have done here, and why?" is your constant question and test.

This experience can be regarded as an idealized apprenticeship, as an intellectual training in the experience of the law, and it has its roots in our traditions. As you may know, it was once the custom in this country for a lawyer to learn the law by doing it as a clerk or apprentice to an established lawyer. One can, of course, learn to do the law that way, and such a training has many merits for one who wishes to learn the language of the law. But the material which comes into any one lawyer's office is not selected or structured to train the student in a wide range of activities, and one is stuck with an early and necessarily untutored choice of a single instructor. The idealized or imaginary apprentice system which the case method entails thus has the advantages of coverage, structure, and—may it also be said—unreality. The mistakes you make as you first try to do law are, under this system, harmless ones.

Your apprenticeship is idealized in another, perhaps to you less attractive, way, for your teachers are not themselves primarily engaged in the busy life of clients and cases—though most of them once were—but are people who think about and participate in the law in a different way, as writers or scholars. We cannot, as a group, pretend to offer you what seasoned and experienced practitioners would, and perhaps it is appropriate to say something of what we think we can offer. What our position gives us is the chance to stand back from the world of detail and practice and try to see something in it, to find something to say about it of a more general nature than would likely emerge from the press of a life in practice. At this school it is widely felt that good teaching requires a critical and creative engagement with the subject taught, for it is only when the teacher can regard the material as meaning or exemplifying something, as a field for the operation of his or her independent intelligence, that it becomes in any but a mechanical way teachable. Our writing is, among other things, the record of our engagement with the law, an engagment of a more general and reflective kind than we enjoyed in practice. We hope that this engagement will deepen our engagement with you.

We do not purport to be able to teach you everything you want to know, as lawyers or as people. It is of course true that, if you apply yourself, there are many things you will be able to do and do well when you graduate. But our function cannot be to create maturely competent, practicing lawyers, for no one has figured out how to do that in three years. Perhaps our object in this respect could be said to be to prepare you to make the most of your actual experience of the law at work in the world when the time comes, to see more and to learn more than you otherwise would. If you go into law practice in a firm after law school, you will find that the apprenticeship system continues, for a good law office puts a very high priority on teaching its young, and a recent law graduate has a great deal to learn.

To return to your present situation: what does the conception of the process of law school I have outlined above mean for you? What should you do, for example, when you read a case? What sorts of questions should you expect your teacher to ask of you, and how should you prepare to respond to them?

The first thing to understand is that the judicial opinion that you read in your casebook is the last stage of a long and complicated process. This kind of literature, which will form the bulk of your first-year reading, is the cultural deposit or artifact left behind by weeks or months or years of work by actual people in the real world, from which it is your task to learn—to figure out—as much as you can about the activity of law. It is a little as if you were given the last chapter of a novel and asked to imagine what went before. A prodigious task.

In my view, the best way to proceed is chronologically. Begin by trying to reconstruct from the opinion, so far as you can, the facts that occurred in the real world before any lawyer was brought into play. Tell the story chronologically, without any terms of legal conclusion. You should try to create a movie of life, a story of the experience of ordinary people in the ordinary world. Reflect in your story how each of the participants would characterize the events in his ordinary language. This is the experience upon which the law will be asked to act in its peculiar and powerful ways and for which the various people of the law will claim particular—and competing—legal meanings.

You will probably discover that your knowledge of the facts is less than complete. Ask yourself what additional facts you would like to know, and why. Here you can pretend that you are a lawyer representing one of the clients: ask yourself what questions you would put to him about what happened. This is, after all, what a lawyer does when a client comes into his office and tells his story. The client believes he has told the whole thing. The lawyer examines and reexamines the story, asking questions and more questions until he is satisfied that he has "enough" to enable him to turn to his books; what he reads there will suggest new questions, to which the answers will suggest new lines of legal inquiry, and so it goes, a jostling between the facts and the law throughout the life of the case. You can at least begin this process with every case you read.

The next stage of reconstruction is to ask (so far as you can determine from the opinion that you read) what each lawyer did, why you think he did so, and what you would have done in his place. One lawyer, for example, initiated the judicial process by filing a complaint, which necessarily rests upon one or more legal theories. What were the legal theories? Are these the legal theories that you would have asserted? Is he properly in this court rather than another, and why, if he had a choice of courts, did he choose this one? What relief does he seek and why? How else might you have acted on behalf of the plaintiff in the case? After the first lawyer acted, the second lawyer responded by filing an answer or motion in response to the complaint. How did the second lawyer respond? What would you have considered doing and why? Could the lawyers have anticipated their difficulties by sound planning or more skillful drafting? Is there a negotiated solution they seem to have overlooked? You are asked to put yourself in the place of each of the parties and each of the lawyers and ask yourself how you would have behaved, how you would have interpreted and responded to the events that underlie the case.

Almost all of the judicial opinions in your casebook are explanations of decisions reached in appellate proceedings. An appellate court is asked to approve or disapprove the decisions made by a judge at the trial of the case (or at some stage prior to trial). The evidence available to you on these matters is often skimpy, but you should try, so far as you can, to reconstruct the course of the proceeding the result of which is in question or in appeal. Can you figure out what each lawyer did? How would you have acted in his place? What actions of the trial court are claimed by the appellant to be erroneous, and why? Can you see other actions which you would have designated as error on appeal? On what theory would you have done so?

The appellant's designations of error usually define the issue or issues on appeal. Frequently the issues so defined will be stated by the court and the arguments of counsel summarized, explicitly or implicitly. At this stage ask yourself: What arguments would you have advanced for each side? Why? How do you evaluate the arguments you would make?

At the end you read an opinion that explains the judgment in the case, and here you face the hardest questions of all: How would you decide this case? How would you explain and defend your judgment? At this stage, the process of the law is no longer, if it ever was, a matter of rhetorical skill and intellectual deftness. It is a matter of judging right and wrong, better and worse, of coming to terms with the necessity and difficulty of judgment. The simple question—"How should this case be decided?"—presents a puzzle and a challenge that can occupy a life.

You can take it, then, that part of your training in this school is a training in a special kind of reading: not "reading for the main idea," as you may have learned in high school, and certainly not reading for maximum content acquisition in the minimum time, but reading as a species of thought, with a reconstructive and critical imagination. What can you see here, we ask, and what can you make of it? What seems at first easy enough becomes, as you study it, perplexing; simplicity becomes complicated. This should not surprise you. A football game—or a single move in it, say a block or a tackle—is simple enough to the mere fan, complex indeed to the coach or scout; beauty in music is one thing to the ordinary listener, quite another to the critic or performer or composer. So it is with a case, read, not as an exemplification of a rule, but as a deposit of the processes of the world in which experience continually frustrates expectation, in which facts and arguments seem inexhaustible and inconclusive. So it is with a statute or regulation, read, not as the statement of a general idea, but with a critical and inventive eye for the problematic case which will expose uncertainty or incoherence in what may at first seem a plain and clear statement.

In your classes you can expect your teachers to ask you to describe as accurately as the materials permit what happened at each stage of the process by which a case was made, how the lawyers behaved, and what you would have done in their place. It is especially important for you to understand and to be able to state clearly the arguments made by each lawyer on appeal, and to see where each could be said to be defective.

The truth is that there are no experts in the law, in the sense that there are no persons upon whose judgment you may as a lawyer rely without understanding it. Each of us is responsible for what he thinks and says, and it is no discharge of your duty to repeat to your professor what he has told you he thinks. You must make your own way.

It may or may not be comforting to hear this, but the sense of inadequacy and isolation which you should have as you now contemplate this process will always, in one form or another, be with you. One never knows all the law; one never feels wholly confident about any step taken in the law. The lawyer lives in an uncertain and indeterminate world, and his profession is to survive and flourish in it. To return to the sailing analogy, while you are sailing you can no longer plant your feet firmly on the ground and proceed by certain steps in a certain direction; but you can sail a boat on the water.

There is another way to put my point. The sense of isolation you now have is in large part the burden of acknowledged responsibility for what you do with the law. That sense of responsibility—which will be most acute when you find yourself making real decisions which actually affect the property, lives, and interests of other people—is central to the experience of the lawyer. I hope you feel it now. One way to state what I urge upon you is this: take the view that you have now spent the last day of your life as a "student of a subject" in the ordinary sense, as a student whose education is the responsibility of a school. Put your school days behind you. From this day on, you are a professional person, responsible alone for your own education, for the improvement of your mind, and for the judgments that you make in the world you will inhabit. What this means in practical terms for you as a new law student is that you should work hard on your cases, in the way suggested above, rather than looking for answers elsewhere. You should participate in class, both directly and imaginatively; if you are not asked to respond to a question, pretend that you are. When another person speaks, ask yourself how you would respond to him. Don't be afraid to be foolish or to be wrong; when your concern is how you can function in the law, there is nothing to be gained by hiding what you are. When you talk with other students about the law outside of class, try to talk as colleagues, teaching each other outside of class as you learn in it.

I would now like to make a general remark about the view of legal education I have offered you. On the one hand it is, as I have just suggested, a genuinely professional education, in which you are asked to function as a professional from the first day you begin. You are asked not only to do what a professional does but to have the attitude a professional has and to meet professional standards. In order to survive and succeed in the world defined by what lawyers do, you must learn how to do those things well. In that sense, you are all asked to learn the same thing: the conventions of that branch of our culture which consist of the activity of law. But, as I have defined it, your legal education is not merely a professional education. It is also a liberal education in the deepest sense. Our ultimate concern is not with your competence at imitating what others do, at learning the moves the lawyer must know, but with the development of your own capacities, sensitivities, and styles, based on a just recognition of the powers and limits of the human mind. As you work through the material of the law, now and later, you make judgments and choices, you write and say sentences that fashion a character for you out of your experience. You will learn both how to function in an inherited culture, as a member of it, and how to function at the same time as an individual. How you do this, as I have said, is your responsibility; our task is to offer you a world in which you can begin to work out your own double identity, as lawyer and as mind.

Searching For Archimedes—Legal Education, Legal Scholarship, and Liberal Ideology

John Henry Schlegel

One can say without fear of serious contradiction that legal education taken as a whole is best described as a craft that has been dead in the water since the late fifties. Changes there have been—clinical education has grown, seminars have appeared at the smallest schools, women have appeared everywhere in great numbers—but the fundamental structure of legal education remains essentially as it was at the elite schools in the immediate post-war years. And this is not because everyone is satisfied with legal education. Precisely the opposite is the case. The countryside is littered with complaints about legal education and, faded, failed proposals to improve it. There are even places like Wisconsin and Buffalo, Antioch and Northeastern where serious long-term effort has been made to institutionalize substantial attempts to improve legal education. However successful such attempts have been at the individual schools, they have caught on generally like bad breath—everyone talks about it, but no one seems to want some.

Similiarly legal scholarship can best be described as an open scandal, again since the late fifties. There have been flutters in the academy from time to time—law and economics and critical legal studies are the latest—but the boring sameness of the doctrinal policy analysis that has been the stable product of the law reviews for 25 years can be seen by even the most unwilling observer simply by staring carefully at the wonders assembled on racks in any faculty library. And this condition remains despite frequent, though more often private, calls for the improvement of scholarship and some object lessons, particularly the relative, if fragile, growth of the law-and-society movement.

Why is legal education and legal scholarship at a standstill? Most explanations emphasize large faculty-student ratios, a traditional commit-

---

John Henry Schlegel is Associate Dean and Professor, State University of New York at Buffalo, Faculty of Law and Jurisprudence.

This paper was originally written for presentation at a faculty seminar at the University of Wisconsin Law School. It condenses, indeed steals shamelessly, arguments developed at length in two forthcoming pieces: John Henry Schlegel, Between the Harvard of the Founders and the American Legal Realists: The Professionalization of the American Law Professor, to be published in a forthcoming issue of the J. Legal Educ. [hereinafter referred to as Between Harvard and the Realists]; and John Henry Schlegel, Langdell's Legacy, or The Case of the Empty Envelope, 36 Stan. L. Rev. (1984) (forthcoming) [hereinafter referred to as Langdell's Legacy]. Thanks are due to the faculty at Wisconsin who listened to me and tried to help me learn from the experience, especially Bill, Dirk, and David; and to Fred, who, as always, patiently read and helpfully commented on this and the prior pieces. Special thanks are due to David Trubek who originally agreed to publish this manuscript in his wonderful Working Papers series, but later suggested that it was more appropriate that it appear here.

© 1984 by the Association of American Law Schools. Cite as 34 J. Legal Educ. 103 (1984).

ment to teaching, the intellectual insularity of law schools, early tenure, lack of research support, and similar structural impediments to reform.[1] Though these factors should not be ignored, they are symptomatic of a much more fundamental problem: the relationship of the subject matter of law teaching and law scholarship—legal doctrine, the rules of law—to the professional identity of the law professor and the deep cultural commitment to the ideology of the rule of law. Thus, any attempt at a more than cosmetic improvement in either legal education or legal scholarship must of necessity confront both the problems it makes for the professional identity of the law professor and the challenge it poses to the centrality of the rule of law in liberal ideology. A brief sketch of the development of various academic professions around the turn of the century provides a basis for understanding why this is so.

The modern university, a distinctively American institution, did not become a recognizable entity until the founding of Johns Hopkins and Cornell in the 1870s, and of Clark, Stanford, and the University of Chicago about ten years later when the first graduate schools began to appear.[2] With these first modern universities and graduate schools came a whole new world of academic scholarship—the social sciences as we know them.

Each of these new disciplines followed a roughly similar pattern of development. Each was intellectually a part of an older tradition: Psychology came out of philosophy, economics and sociology out of a generalized mugwump reformist social science, history out of genteel amateur historiography, anthropology out of exploration. In each a figure or group of almost mythic proportions—G. Stanley Hall in psychology, Richard T. Ely and E. A. Ross in economics, Albion Small and Lester Ward in sociology, Henry Baxter Adams and J. Franklin Jamison in history, John W. Burgess in political science, and Franz Boaz in anthropology—is said to have founded a discipline that seems to have grown up over night in many different places. Often the most important contribution of the founder appears to have been not to the substance of the intellectual life of the discipline but to the form of its organization by serving as the head of an old-boy network that oversaw career development. In each field learned journals and professional associations appeared between 1890 and 1900. And at about the same time the Ph.D., once a degree available only in German universities, became for the younger generation the only way into a respectable academic position. Hours in public meetings and pages in the journals were spent in an attempt to delimit the field of inquiry in each discipline. Occasionally, for example in Ross's firing at Stanford or Ely's "trial" at Wisconsin, the question of the appropriateness of public comment, and thus the limits of academic study, became a public issue on which members of the profession pontificated, all in the name of "academic freedom." Similarly, questions of method, both of how to teach—the proper way to run the "historical seminary," the place of laboratory or field work in

---

1. For the most detailed of such explanations see Robert B. Stevens, Law School: Legal Education in America from the 1850s to the 1980s, 204 et seq. (Chapel Hill, 1983).

2. Support for the story told in this and the succeeding two paragraphs is provided by Schlegel, Between Harvard and the Realists.

the curriculm—and of how to research filled the time of otherwise well occupied people and thus generated journal articles and public debate. Occasionally such questions even defined a discipline as was the case with introspection versus experimentalism in psychology. And from time to time leaders of the profession, actual or hopeful, suggested various "missions" that the group could or had undertaken, seemingly in answer to the adolescent taunt to "justify your existence."

The parallel between this generalizable story and that of the development of academic legal education is striking. As the story is usually told,[3] in 1870 Christopher Columbus Langdell came to Harvard, the quintessence of the American college supported by the local gentry, and announced that henceforth law was to be taught from cases, largely old English cases assembled in chronological order, and by means of class discussion. Simultaneously he uttered some generalities about law being a science, proceeded to toss out of the law course almost everything except private law, and set to the task of lengthening the curriculum to three years and restricting admittance to it to college graduates. For twenty years he labored silently with only the intellectual comfort of the youthful, unpracticed Ames pouring through volume after volume of the yearbooks. Then, through the fortuity of a dispute with the Harvard Corporation over his salary, William Keener, a young teacher of Contracts, left Harvard to become Dean at Columbia, thereby securing the major bastion of the opposition for the Langdellian revolution.

After this first great victory others came swift and sure: Cornell, Stanford, Western Reserve, Northwestern, then finally Chicago, where the principle that nothing but "pure law" was established when Ernest Freund's heretical espousal of such courses as administrative law was finally suppressed. Meanwhile, law reviews, patterned after Harvard's, but never quite measuring up, swept the country. Finally, unable to get sufficient attention in the forums of the American Bar Association, the better law schools organized the Association of American Law Schools to carry on the fight for higher standards and, after twenty years of work, emerged triumphant, though unfortunately they were forced into a compromise that permitted night schools with their obviously second-rate, part-time programs to continue to exist. *Exeunt omnies* flags waving.

Debunking this story is easy and to some extent fun. But after all the debunking is done, the crucial parallel remains. During the last years of the nineteenth century each group created a professional discipline where before there was none.

To identify this phenomenon is of course not to explain it. When it comes to explanation Magali Larson's analysis of professionalization fits the data very well.[4] She argues that professionalization is an attempt by a part of the middle class to improve its social and economic position through a strategy of market control. In order to make this strategy work each such group of individuals has to create an identifiable product in a recognizable market.

3. The best retelling is Stevens, *supra* note 1.
4. Magali Larson, The Rise of Professionalism (Berkeley, 1977).

Because the product is an intangible, the traditional tasks of product standardization and differentiation, so dear to the heart of toothpaste, detergent, or margarine manufacturers, present a nascent professional group with a particular problem: the providers of service have to be controlled in order to thus indirectly standardize and identify the product.

Control of the providers of service is acquired in two ways: through state-sanctioned exclusion of potential competitors and through control of the production of producers. Together they perform the usual function of limiting supply in order to raise price. At the same time, exclusion of others and control of production permits another kind of control, that over the production of knowledge in the profession. The modern university, historically the key to the development of the academic social science disciplines, provides the proper setting. Obtaining control over the production of knowledge is important to a professional group because by so doing the group can supplement the force of state-established exclusions of potential competitors and also aid product differentiation through the standardization of the knowledge of its members who then shared a common cognitive base, a distinctive kind of knowledge leading to an exclusive possession of tools and techniques of the thus defined trade. In short, to establish a modern profession one needs state sanction for exclusive possession of distinct knowledge based on university production of certified professionals.

The key social institutions for professional advance are thus the state and the university, especially since the justification for the professional privilege flows directly from the assertion that university educational practices are meritocratic and indirectly from the service of the university to the state. But these two institutions are only necessary, they are not sufficient; to them must be added the standardized, differentiated product—the cognitively delimited and unified field of knowledge to be possessed by all members of the profession.

The academic lawyer, nestled as he is within a larger profession, faces problems that are in large measure the same as those of other professions: creation of an identifiable product, exclusion of others from the market for that product, and the justification of the market control acquired thereby. I will discuss only the first of these—product definition and standardization—because the others are rather fully discussed elsewhere.[5]

Around the turn of the century much effort went into the job of developing the law school's equivalent of Mr. Ford's Model-T, available in any color as long as it was black. This standardized product was only possible if the head of the standardized law student was filled with a standarized unit of knowledge and a unit that was somehow dispensed nowhere else in the intellectual universe. And here we must confront Christopher Columbus Langdell, for what Langdell had to offer was an intellectual Model-T, a wholly complete, conceptually unified universe to put in the mind of the standard student and thus with which to define the identity of both lawyer and professor.

5. Exclusion of others from the market is a story exhaustively documented in Stevens, *supra* note 1 and Jerold Auerbach, Unequal Justice (Oxford, 1976). The justification of market control is discussed in Schlegel, Between Harvard and the Realists.

Langdell's decision to chase public law out of the lawyer's world and to justify private-law doctrine internally, as a matter of logic and not as a matter of ends, may have been a stroke of genius. For the resulting curriculum of "pure law," though perhaps boring, was utterly without potential adverse claimants in the late nineteenth century world. Stripped of the political and economic theory that once was a part of the study of law, and thus intellectually impoverished, Langdell's curriculum nevertheless left the law professors in large measure as masters of their own turf who could profit therefrom. This then is a central aspect of our problem. The professional identity of the law professor is deeply wrapped up in the world of the Langdellian law professor for it is that world, the world of doctrinal law and its manipulation, that allows the law professor to claim a special spot in the academic division of labor. And that fact is not without important consequences, especially for scholarship.

Langdell's world, the world of rules, was an exciting one in those early years.[6] There was the enormous job of systematically stating the law, a job that was carried out not just in treatises but also in casebooks. But by World War I, when that job was done, legal academics faced a terrible problem. There really wasn't much more to do. The notion of law as a definable body of knowledge that was at the root of the Langdellian program meant what the task scholars were left with was to monitor the small changes in the law: a new development in eminent domain, a new wrinkle in consideration. Some did (and do) this necessary and time-consuming work patiently and lovingly, but for most the task has become less than exciting. Alternative tasks, be they historical or sociological, were theoretically unavailable because of the assumption that law was a definable body of knowledge and practically unavailable because the law teachers by training knew little about law beyond how to parse a case and organize a body of rules. For most teachers, scholarship became an episodic endeavor at best and in its place was substituted the preparation of teaching materials, a task that at least might simplify the job of teaching and in addition might provide a place to bury scholarship that is too mundane to publish. Teachers could, of course, restate the law, and they did, twice now, but the intellectual excitement of such an endeavor was limited, hence how well known were the occasional fighting issues that turned up in the process: Section 90 or Section 402A for example.

From time to time law professors have tired of the Langdellian program and tried to institute another. Realism attempted that with somewhat less than total success. Others did so later. Yet the monumental record of failure of innovation in law schools since World War II ought to suggest that something more fundamental is at stake here. Consider again Langdell's legacy. It was centered in the notion that the knowledge to be gathered by scholars and taught to students was about rules. This notion of law as rule, of the rule of law, is deeply bred in American culture. Consider for a moment the following thoroughly commonplace observations on the practice of law.

---

6. This and the succeeding three paragraphs are adapted from Schlegel, Langdell's Legacy.

> [K]nowledge of 'the law' may not help lawyers very much in practice. Many lawyers are involved in only a few fields of law and do not need to know 'the law' in all fields (although they must be able to find it and use it on occasion). And in any given field of law, much of what has to be done on a daily basis involves following forms or routines, with little recourse to the legal rules from which they are derived, or it involves the exercise of skills of negotiation, interviewing or advocacy, rather than of legal analysis. This is not to deny that some lawyers spend much of their time dealing with 'the law' or that most lawyers spend some time doing so. But the assumption that 'the law' of the textbook or the classroom preoccupies practitioners is illfounded...[7]

Then consider what gets taught, and especially what gets learned *because it is tested*, in classrooms throughout the land. How many times have you heard a colleague say, "No matter how hard I try to teach the theory they never learn it?" Or consider what actually gets written about in the journals. Indeed, I suspect that however fraudulent it may be, however implausible it is as a principle of action for a sensible lawyer, still the notion of law as a rule is as deep in our culture as motherhood and apple pie. And, if you wish to know how keep that is, check the reaction of individuals fresh from that culture. Take any group of middle-class, first-year law students and try any other approach than a doctrinal, rule-focused one. They hate the alternatives because the alternatives undercut the notion of law as specialized knowledge available only to, and for sale by, the professional lawyer. That is the identity, a part of the professional identity of the lawyer as Larson would see it, that they bring with them to law school for that is what the culture tells them law is about.

Legal education supports that notion of law as rule in the classroom and in the journals, in our bones as it were, just as it supports the notion that the rules as they are are on the whole justified, a comforting notion to the bar as well as to the neophytes we train. A detailed look at American law schools since World War II reveals that, but for clinical approaches—even today so poor a graft that they would surely be sloughed off if the academics thought that the bar wouldn't mind—innovations have been successful in direct proportion to how deeply they undercut the Landgellian legacy: the notion that law is rules to be found in books, ordered for easy reference, and, not, incidentally, for sale.

All of this gets us back almost to square one. The legal academic is trapped. The species is committed to teaching and scholarship dominated by the notion of law as rule and yet at the same time that scholarship is a largely completed task and both teaching and scholarship are bound to an intellectual anachronism. Or, to put it slightly differently, the academic legal professional needs a distinctive subject matter in order to complete the project of professionalization. The distinctive subject matter chosen—legal doctrine—has deep roots in liberal culture for it resonates well with the notion that law is rules, preferably neutral rules, but at least rules neutrally applied. Yet, commitment to that ideology, however well it reinforces professional identity, dooms any improvement in either legal education or legal scholarship for it means that rules must be the central subject matter of both, even though all concerned recognize that teaching the rules is essentially a pointless exercise and writing about them as exciting an

---

7. Consultative Group on Research and Education in Law, Law and Learning (Ottawa, 1983).

intellectual endeavor as straightening or occasionally rearranging pictures in an art gallery. The circle, if not the seemless web, is thus complete.

If you believe that I have now reached the point where it is incumbent on the writer to propose and to defend a grand solution so that the reader may be sent home happy, you will be disappointed. That is the point of my title. I am searching for Archimedes, for it is not obvious that there are levers or places to stand. The best I can do is to suggest the plausibility of certain strategies currently bandied about for leading us out of awfulness.

Four strategies come immediately to mind and seem instructive: The two wings of the law-and-economics movement and the two wings of the critical legal studies movement. Richard Posner, who touts the great accomplishments of one branch of law and economics,[8] speaks with arresting style but his view of law and economics points nowhere. The importance of his success in understanding the congruence between nineteenth century legal doctrine and classical economics is somewhat moderated once one recognizes that both bodies of thought were taught side by side as political economy. It would be quite surprising if these two bodies of knowledge were sharply divergent. More intellectually promising, for law at least, is George Priest's delightfully daffy 1930s vision of economics as an empirical science.[9] At least it is a clean alternative view of the subject matter of an academic discipline. The relative success of one vision of legal scholarship as against the other is not wholly a matter of whose tongue is more silvered.

One of the reasons for this conclusion is the way I see the relative success of Duncan Kennedy's brand of critical legal studies.[10] The radical critique of doctrine is catching on all over. Lefties are coming out of the closet in real numbers. In contrast, the social historical critique of law associated with Fred Konefsky and others,[11] while virtually identical in political content, seems to be going nowhere, though it has the potential for redefining the subject matter of legal scholarship. The old is somehow better even in radical dress.

The law and society movement in the law schools seems to suffer from the same problem. The more it fulfills its potential to recenter the study of law away from doctrine, for example in anthropological studies, the less the lawyers want to hear about it. Court studies have their market, even in the popular press,[12] as does jury behavior, but, as one can see from the recurrent,

---

8. Richard Posner, The Economic Approach to Law, 53 Tex. L. Rev. 757 (1975), makes the grandest claims.
9. See George L. Priest, Social Science Theory and Legal Education: The Law School as University, 33 J. Legal Educ. 437 (1983); George L. Priest, The New Scientism in Legal Scholarship: A Comment on Clark and Posner, 90 Yale L.J. 1284 (1981).
10. See, e.g., Duncan Kennedy, Form and Substance in Private Law Adjudication, 89 Harv. L. Rev. 1685 (1976).
11. See, e.g., Alfred S. Konefsky & Andrew J. King, eds., The Papers of Daniel Webster: Legal Papers, 3 vols. (1982–1983); David Engel, The Oven Bird's Song, Law & Society Rev. (1984) (forthcoming).
12. See David M. Trubek, et al., The Costs of Ordinary Litigation, 31 U.C.L.A. L. Rev. 1 (1983); Marc Galanter, Reading the Landscape of Disputes: What We Know and Don't Know (And Think We Know) About Our Allegedly Contentious and Litigious Society, 31 U.C.L.A. L. Rev. 4 (1983); Debunking Litigation Magic, Newsweek 98 (November 21, 1983).

unfulfilled vision of the unification of psychology and the law of evidence, acquisition of fundamental knowledge "about law," to steal Rick Abel's phrase,[13] has little attractiveness, divorced as it is from debates about law reform. This problem is not a new one. I described it in great detail when recounting Charlie Clark's and Bill Douglas's attempts to do empirical research at Yale in the late twenties and early thirties.[14] But I didn't understand the problem very well then. Attaching "law and" research to reform is necessary because without such an attachment the research is outside of the bounds of the professional identity of the law professor, without a sea anchor, the anchor that keeps the rule-against-perpetuities scholarship sailing along.

From all of this one can draw at least one conclusion. To the extent that one believes as I do that legal scholarship has got to be improved, if only to remove an embarrassment from the University, one needs carefully to protect and encourage all efforts in that direction. The analogy of hot houses for fragile plants is clearly appropriate. Fundamental research "about law" cannot be encouraged too much, even in the classroom. If it is sheltered, well watered, carefully cultivated, and fertilized, it may have a chance to grow. Without such care we will surely see the continuing cycle of discovery of "law and," high hopes, over ambitious projects, and slow decline into relative quiescence.

What I do not know is whether serious scholarship and teaching is bound to be a hot house plant forever. I would like to think not. I would like to think one might rebuild a legal academic's professional identity around theory about the practice of law—another scrap no one in the academy cares about. But the reception of feeble attempts in that direction does not give me great faith. Students for all their palaver about the narrowness of the curricular focsu on doctrine are often openly hostile and colleagues are bewildered even when not obviously threatened.

I bring no Archimedian solutions. Indeed, as Richard Rorty seems to be teaching,[15] there is no lever and no place to stand. If so, if all progress is really bootstrapping with the aid of mirrors, then I guess my message is that as far as we seem to have gone, at a number of law schools that are making an effort, is but a small fraction of how far we have to go. And the only resource on the journey other than a supportive University is a mutually supportive faculty and student body.

---

13. Richard Abel, Law Books and Books About Law, 26 Stan. L. Rev. 175 (1973).
14. John Henry Schlegel, American Legal Realism and Empirical Social Science: From the Yale Experience, 28 Buffalo L. Rev. 459 (1980).
15. Richard Rorty, Philosophy and the Mirror of Nature (Princeton, 1979).

The Dangers of the Graduate School Model

Paul D. Carrington

Roger Cramton has asked for my comments on his article for the reason that I have been the only voice on the Executive Committee of the Association of American Law Schools to question the creation of a faculty-edited scholarly journal of the Association.

My position is not entrenched. It rests not at all on admiration of the traditions of the student-run journal. While many such publications have seen many good days, one can reasonably doubt that it is important to preserve them in their traditional modes. If they cannot survive fair competition, so be it.

My different concerns are based on the same factual assumptions that Cramton advances in support of faculty editing. He and I agree that fashions in legal scholarship and teaching have changed as law schools have become more academic, more deeply and more intricately involved with other disciplines and with the universities of which most law schools are a part. Our difference lies in our assessments of the degree to which this evolution is inevitable or benign in all its aspects.

To be sure, I do not regret the affair of law with social science or of law with economics, or the revival of interest in legal history, in jurisprudence, nor even of the effort to apply the insights of contemporary literary criticism to law. All these developments unquestionably have been beneficial to the quality of law study; all have helped to lift us from an intellectual environment that was for too long too sterile.

But, just as the clinical studies movement has mistakenly perceived medical education as a proper model for making legal education more practical, so we may now be in danger of mistaking graduate schools as the model for elevating legal education intellectually. Perhaps it was inevitable that these obvious models be placed before us, but it is my continuing hope that we may be wise enough to resist both models, to develop patterns of professional education in law which are more intellectually liberal than clinical medicine, and more functional than contemporary graduate training. Such an independent course will require, I acknowledge, greater imagination than legal educators have been accustomed to apply to the problems confronting us. I fear that the attraction of the juried journal is, at least in part, an impulse to adhere to the model of the graduate school faculty.

Paul D. Carrington is Dean and Professor of Law, Duke Law School.

© 1986 by the Association of American Law Schools. Cite as 35 J. Legal Educ. 11 (1986).

I am not allowed space, nor am I now prepared, to identify all the benefits or all the costs of the ongoing process of the academization (or graduatization) of law schools. But one risk lies in the tendency of legal scholarship to address ever smaller audiences of ever narrower experts. One need not demean the worth of such highly elevated or advanced efforts in order to suggest concern for the efficacy of institutions whose scholarship is of little or no interest to their alumni. It is helpful to remember that the graduate school model rests on the assumption that the students are training to do what the professors do; in such a context, the deepening probe into a narrowing horizon may be a necessary and desirable process, beneficial to teachers and students alike. But a professional faculty that has lost interest in most of the work of its alumni has also lost interest in its students, and forfeited the legitimacy of its claim for their support.

One concern for the juried journal is that it will lead us precisely over that brink. Tenure and professional advancement even now are heavily dependent on the way in which the candidate's work is appraised by a narrowing audience of fellow academics, and diminishing value is assigned to work that might be useful to students and lawyers. I would not wish to return to a time when advancement depended not at all on scholarly attainments as appraised by one's peers, but perhaps enough of a good thing may be enough, even in this sphere. If one could advance only with the approval of specialized jurors selecting works to be published in faculty journals, we may jeopardize what little systemic incentive remains for legal academics to engage their minds on matters of importance to their students and alumni. There is an unfortunate tension between the consequential and the intellectually gratifying in legal scholarship; academic jurors seem likely to proclaim the worth of intellectual novelty and to deny recognition to work that may be more significant to the benign development of the law.

Also a concern is the equally ineffable effect of a system of specialist-jurors on the quality of academic freedom in law schools. It is well in considering this matter to recognize the highly political nature of almost everything in which law professors are rightly concerned. Even those matters that do not engage traditional political dichotomies are laden with debatable assumptions about the nature of law, the appropriate fashion in legal scholarship, and the role of intellect in professional life. One strength of contemporary American law schools in the degree to which some have come to shelter widely divergent views on questions such as, for example, whether medical schools or graduate schools are proper models. Although I am not prepared to cite examples in other fields where the juried journals are entrenched, there is at least a risk that, over time, a system of juried journals will rigidify by imposing generally accepted standards of scholarship that will exclude some divergent views or fashions. Most at risk, I have suggested, are those who would be inclined to write for professional audiences or on current issues of law reform, but there is no reason to suppose that the risk is limited to such groups. While the present structure tends to impose upon us the unwelcome requirement that we try to make ourselves understandable by students and lawyers, that regulation may be a more harmless orthodoxy than others we might impose upon ourselves.

All this is assuredly speculation. Maybe it would be as well for law to become a graduate school discipline, with the universities abandoning professional education to the profession itself, in the manner prevalent in every country outside North America. Whether so is a very large question, one which I am unprepared to answer. Acknowledging such doubts, I am too diffident even to vote against the faculty-edited journal. I am content to rest here with the always reassuring thought that a member of some future generation may say, he told them so.

Challenges to Legal Education: The "Two Cultures" Phenomenon

Harry H. Wellington

Few things are clear about legal education, but there is at least one feature of our noble calling that is a truth universally acknowledged. As a group, law teachers today are more academically oriented than they were 25 to 30 years ago. The converse of this truth is that they are less professionally oriented. My colleagues today care more about intellectual movements in faculties of arts and sciences than they used to; they care less about the activities of the bar, and, perhaps, even the output of the bench.

I worried about this "two cultures" phenomenon during much of my deanship at Yale, that is from 1975 to 1985. It seemed to me that our noble calling would be in trouble if law teachers failed to communicate with their former students. And this trouble, I thought, was a complicated one made up of many factors. One factor is the substantive agenda of the academic and whether, in constructing it, she or he has enough of a feel for the legal and institutional problems of the profession.

A second factor concerns the methodology of the academic. On the one hand, that methodology is apt to mirror the style of political and moral philosophy, and accordingly, appear to the practitioner as overly general and abstract, insufficiently particularistic and attentive to institutional considerations. (An example is some of the current writing on law as interpretation). On the other hand, the academic's approach may follow the model-building social sciences which, in their quest for a manageable number of variables, exclude others that may seem of major significance to the working lawyer. (An example is the economics of politics—a branch of social choice theory—where the fiduciary responsibility of elected representatives, is, as such, generally ignored).

A third factor is vocabulary: law teachers talk differently from practicing lawyers. In the Sterling Law Buildings and elsewhere one hears heated conversations about hermeneutics, externalities and deconstruction.

Today, I find this two culture problem less troubling than I did a year ago. Perhaps this is because I am no longer in academic administration. And, let me tell you, perspectives shift quickly when one has the great good fortune of being provided with the liberty of choice, a liberty that is the

---

Harry H. Wellington is Sterling Professor of Law, Yale Law School. This paper was given in a seminar on the future of legal education at Harvard Law School on the occasion of the 350th celebration of the founding of Harvard College.

©1987 by the Association of American Law Schools. Cite as 37 J. Legal Educ. 327 (1987).

prerogative of the senior academic at good universities. But I think there is a more objective reason for my diminished anxiety over the bifurcated nature of our profession. The legal academic has not lost his influence with the judges and the bar. This is the case at least where scholarship can be used by the rest of the profession to support ideology.

The legal scholarship of 25 or 30 years ago that could be used ideologically was used by those practitioners on the bench and at the bar who were liberals or who represented liberal causes. As examples, I would point to constitutional scholarship and the civil rights movement or to writings in torts and contracts and the growth of product liability law. The former scholarship emphasized the norm of racial equality in our atlas of national values; the latter insisted upon equality of bargaining power and the desirability of risk spreading in a liberal state. At Yale, in the constitutional area I think of Tom Emerson and Charles Black; in contracts, Fritz Kessler, and in torts, Fleming James. Each spoke, of course, in a language that is directly accessible to lawyers and judges and each employed a methodology that is familiar.

Today, lawyers who represent conservative causes (or who have clients with a case that might profit from a conservative perspective), along with conservative judges, use the work of academics that supports *their* ideology. Parenthetically, I know that it is risky to throw around words like ideology, liberal and conservative. They are to be understood as generalizations that disregard institutional considerations and that, for the purpose of this talk, have no normative implications.

With this disclaimer in mind, consider the influence of conservative law and economics scholarship on antitrust law and the influence it is beginning to have on tort and insurance law reform. Much of this scholarship is esoteric in method and vocabulary.

My point then is the simple one that, in their quest to win, lawyers will not allow the strangeness of the academic culture to deter them from using the academics' insights. Moreover the hegemony of law and economics in private law studies at universities suggests that more than a few law teachers still hunger for influence and adjust their agenda to the problems of that other real world, the one outside the ivy-covered walls.

But while the two cultures do feed and nourish each other, their separation does have unfortunate consequences for both. I have two such consequences in mind.

First, in mastering an aspect or two of one or more disciplines in arts and sciences, the law teacher may not have time to remember things she should never forget.

Consider constitutional law. Recently there has been an extraordinary amount of sophisticated scholarship addressing fundamental issues of constitutional method. The problem itself is almost as old as the Constitution. It used to be called strict and loose construction. It is related in practice, but not in theory, to another couple of old-fashioned terms—judicial restraint and judicial activism. The Attorney General has been instrumental in calling the public's attention to the subject by speaking about the importance in constitutional adjudication of the intention of the founding fathers. Constitutional interpretation is a hot subject and legal scholars have discovered a rich literature on interpretation in such sister disciplines as philosophy, religion, and literary criticism. One can find wonderfully interesting articles written on such things as comparative, normative hermeneutics, and written by professors of law.

But there is a striking fact about much of this interesting and important legal literature: it is noncontextual. It does not come to grips with the stuff of adjudication; that is, jurisdiction (or procedure in the large sense), power (or, as Robert Cover calls it in his posthumously published article, "violence"). Nor does it come to grips with the fact that lawyers argue cases to win, not to establish true principles of interpretation, and that majority opinions are desperately negotiated documents and not the carefully crafted work of a philosopher.

This means that much useful academic work has less impact than it should and it means that too few are doing the applied work that should be an important part of the mission of law schools. If we ask what the reason is we may find at least a partial answer; and this is my second point.

Too many very able academic lawyers who, for whatever reasons, do not venture outside the ivy-covered walls, scorn the practicing lawyer and his work (deprecate it) and look for rewards only from within the universities. This is an established phenomenon. It is now visible in a second generation of law teachers.

This phenomenon would not matter too much if it were not for the inescapable fact that the overwhelming majority of law students go into practice. They do not go into teaching. These students find themselves—or at least many do—much less interested than their instructors in the subject of their courses and worried, as a result of their mentor's disdain, about their own professional future. I believe that this is one of the factors that contributes to the extensive—but perhaps not intensive—unhappiness of law students. It is very difficult to do much about this. The attitudes of law professors cannot easily be changed. And thank God—or at least the Association of University Professors—for tenure.

Yet it may be possible to improve the educational experience of law students by taking professors as one finds them. They are, even as I have described them, a diverse lot. And of course some who teach live comfortably in both legal cultures and some are more at home with the bar than with their university colleagues.

Now at Yale we have, more or less, exploited this diversity through market mechanisms. With the exception of criminal law and some clinical requirements, all courses and seminars are elective after the first semester, although we do, to be sure, demand a considerable amount of writing before graduation. But the system is not as good as it should be because electives, open to all, or on a first-come basis, tend to make all courses more introductory than is appropriate. Indeed, this is becoming increasingly unfortunate. The practice of law is more technical than it used to be and the law teacher's enlarged grip on relevant (and irrelevant) social science and humanistic theory makes the subject matter of law school courses much more complex than it seemed to be when we were all much younger. Evidence of this phenomenon may be found in the diminishing regard of the academic for the student run law reviews and the growth of faculty edited journals.

Accordingly, I think it is time for us at Yale to have a more structured curriculum. I think this not because I have any clear ideas about how better to prepare students for the work lawyers will be doing in the next century, but because I believe that the educational experience of students will be improved, their intellectual horizons lifted, if they progress from the introductory to the intermediate to the advanced.

Nor do I care all that much what the subject matter of this progression is—at least for Yale students. Both they and their instructors operate at a level of intellectual competence and responsibility that is reassuring. Whether a student does the bulk of her work in an esoteric-academic or conventional-professional area, she will, when she graduates be ready to begin the practice of law. This is one of the great joys of teaching at Yale. We on the faculty have long taken advantage of it. It is time we turned it more directly to our students' benefit.

There are several ways to do this. The one I prefer requires a very favorable faculty-student ratio. What I would like for Yale—and it is related to an experiment, the Divisional Program, we tried some years ago—is to have each student in the second half of her law school career set forth, with a small band of other students and faculty, on a journey of increasing intellectual complexity, a journey that culminates in a serious effort at original scholarship. Even if students do not want to be academics, they are capable, with guidance, of performing useful, and sometimes exceptional work. How professionally or academically oriented that work will be depends on the student and her group. But that matters little if I am right about the intellectual quality of the community I live in. Whatever direction the journey takes, the travelers will emerge ready to begin law practice. And those new practitioners, who have learned the contribution to law of the arts and sciences, will help close the gap between the schools and the bench and bar; so too will those who have learned the limitations of our sister disciplines.

You're right if you are thinking that I want to have my cake and eat it too. But the happy fact is that it's a very big cake.

Public Policy

THE FUTURE OF LEGAL EDUCATION

Problems Growing Out of the Development of Two Distinct Types of Law Schools in the United States—Difficulties Due to Traditional Attitude Toward the Law as a Body of Technical Doctrine More or Less Detached From the Social Forces It Regulates—Possible Recasting of Curricula

By Hon. Harlan F. Stone
Former Dean of Columbia University Law School, Member of the New York Bar, and Attorney General of the United States

ALL of scholarship and of professional training are not embraced within the old fashioned virtue of thoroughness and fidelity to the day's task and the inspiration which the practice of them brings, but certain it is that there can be no real scholarship and no sound professional training without them and they are far more important to the development of the professional law school than most of the educational plans and procedures which engage the attention of those who are responsible for the progress of legal education in America.

Professional training, especially in law, is in very real danger from a kind of competitive zeal which has for some years adversely affected undergraduate education in colleges and universities. The desire to do something distinctive, to give some evidence of originality, to attract public attention, or to secure patronage, has led from time to time to the presentation to the public of numerous educational nostrums, as improvements upon the old educational fundamentals or as dispensing with them as relatively unimportant. "Point of view" on the part of the student or the callow instructor, on occasion, seems to be more important than the foundation of educational experience and intellectual capacity on which one may build the superstructure from which with years and experience he may hope to have a "point of view." "Openness of mind," it would appear, is more to be desired than the development of the mind's capacity to lay hold of the fundamentals of human knowledge and experience, and to organize and use them with discriminating intelligence.

Too often the organization of new courses and the rearrangement of old ones engage the attention rather than the mastery of the old and recognized fields of intellectual experience, for there is always a presumption in certain minds that the new and untried is an improvement upon the old and established mode of procedure. Recently we have been told authoritatively that the true solution of the problem of legal education in America is to be found, not in a more thorough and exacting study of legal science or in better standards of education and bar admission, but in so organizing our system of legal training as to bring the bar within the reach of the great and increasing number of applicants whose training, both liberal and professional, is of the most superficial character.

These new educational "discoveries" are not wanting in novel and dramatic qualities which are lacking to the ancient educational procedure of hard work inspired and guided by competent teaching. Nor are they so difficult of application. They are often the more attractive to students, especially to that growing class of students in America who are seeking some painless and effortless route to professional efficiency and success.

By these observations I do not mean, of course, that the last word on legal education has been spoken. There will undoubtedly be, from time to time, new ways of looking at law and new developments in the law itself which will affect the teaching and study of it. Nevertheless the constant search for the new and dramatic merely because they attract attention or have advertising value tends to shift emphasis from the essential and fundamental to the more superficial aspects of the educational process and to that extent it is a serious menace to the stability and orderly progress of professional education.

Whatever may be done therefore to improve and strengthen the type of legal education which is being developed, it ought to be steadily borne in mind that there can be no substitute for exacting standards of scholarly performance on the part of its students and inspiring and devoted service on the part of its teachers and that ultimately the reputation and public service of our schools of law will depend more on these factors than on any others or all others combined.

There are in fact two very distinct problems of legal education in America, neither of which has any very close relationship to the other, which must continue to invite our attention. The first and more important problem, one often alluded to in these reports, has grown out of the development in the United States of two distinct types of law school. One type is represented by a relatively small group of university law schools having high entrance requirements and exacting educational standards; the remaining 120 or more schools constitute a distinct class with low admission requirements, low educational standards and on the whole low professional ideals. Most of them give their courses at night or on a part time basis, their students' principal time and energies being devoted to activities other than the study or practice of law. The very existence of these Schools is made possible (*a*) by our traditional policy of low bar admission requirements which are less exacting than the standards of admission to other professions and (*b*) by the fact that, by providing instruction largely or wholly by part time instructors and with inadequate libraries and equipment, it has been possible to maintain such schools on a financially profitable basis.

This second group of schools has created the problem with which the American Bar Association has sought to deal in its campaign for raising bar admission standards by requiring that all candidates for the bar must have pursued a minimum period of liberal and professional study greater than that now required by the majority of law schools and requiring the schools themselves to be adequately equipped with teaching staff and library.

The problem raised by these schools can ultimately be solved only by insistence on what I have characterized as the old fashioned virtues of thoroughness and fidelity to the task of training men for membership in the bar and fitting them to perform the functions of a difficult and exacting profession.

That the bar has taken upon itself the reform of this phase of legal education is a hopeful sign of the times and that it has set its hand to the task in the right and only way to accomplish it is, I believe, not open to serious question.

The other important problem of legal education is suggested by the history and development of those schools which I have included in the first class. No one looking fairly and intelligently at the work of these schools can maintain that their problem arises from their methods of instruction or from any want of zeal for scholarship, or thoroughness or devotion to the educational enterprise. In all these respects they have set an example which might well be emulated by educational institutions of other types, and in all of them they have gained an educational leadership which they must under no circumstances relinquish by subordinating these fundamental things to the fads and fancies of an educational opportunism.

Present day problems of legal education, for schools of this type, arise, rather, from our traditional attitude toward the law as a body of technical doctrine more or less detached from those social forces which it regulates. We have failed to recognize as clearly as we might that law is nothing more than a form of social control intimately related to those social functions which are the subject matter of economics and the social sciences generally.

Twenty years or more ago this failure was most apparent in law school teaching for the very obvious reason that the common law itself is technically more highly developed than any other system of law and the law teacher not unnaturally directed his energies principally toward the exposition of its more technical aspects.

In the last fifty years, too, the law has expanded enormously both in the field it covers and in its content. It is not surprising therefore that lawyers and teachers of law in the effort to master the intricacies of the common law should have become absorbed in its technique to such an extent that they have to some degree lost sight of its true relationship to what I have referred to as social functions, and have come too much to regard it as a body of learning quite distinct and apart from those social forces which create it, much as the scientist regards the body of natural law which he studies and investigates as something apart from social organization and development. In recent years there has come a clearer understanding of this relationship and a noticeable tendency on the part of the most successful and distinguished teachers of law to direct attention more and more to those causal elements in legal science which are the more fundamental in the development of technical doctrine, instead of dissipating their energies in the vain attempt to cover, in the brief period of law school training, the entire technique of their subjects.

This change of attitude has not, however, up to the present time produced any noticeable effect upon the organization of law school work. For more than thirty years the only substantial change in law school curricula has been the addition from time to time of new courses to cover some new field into which law has expanded with the growing complexity of modern business and economic life. Starting with the fundamental courses in Contracts, Torts, Property and Equity, we have added courses in Insurance Law, Public Service Companies, Unfair Competition, Restrictions on Trade, Industrial Relations, Bankruptcy, Statutes, Damages, to mention only a few of the many new courses which adorn modern law school curricula, and withal every instructor continuously and persistenty presses for an increase in the time allotted to his subject in order that he may treat adequately its ever expanding technique. This is the process which has steadily been going on until at last we are beginning to realize that the logical outcome of it must be that ultimately students who come to us to be trained as lawyers must remain with us for most of their natural lives in order to be trained properly to begin the practice of their profession.

The only solutions that have been proposed are mere mechanical solutions. Some courses of lesser importance, it is suggested, may be taken superficially; overlapping of courses must be definitely located and eliminated; the law school course must be increased from three to four years, notwithstanding the fact that the changes in our law which require a four years course will by the same logic ultimately require a five or six or ten year course. There can be no mechanical solution for a problem which is created by the endeavor to force a continually increasing volume into a fixed space and we are being brought to the realization that we must seek other methods to adapt the law school course to the growing technique of the law.

Instead of dissipating our energies in the vain attempt to master in the brief period of three years the vast and growing mass of technical learning of our profession as an independent and detached system, we must seek a simplification of educational methods by coming closer to those energizing forces which are producing the technical doctrine of the law. We may hope to do this by reaching a clearer and more accurate understanding of the relation of law to those social functions which it endeavors to control and by studying its rules and doctrines as tools or devices created and placed in the hands of the lawyer as means of effecting that control.

That is, I think, the heart of our problem and it naturally divides itself into two subsidiary problems. The first is the problem of so re-arranging and organizing the subjects of law school study as to make more apparent the relationship of the various technical devices of the law to the particular social or economic function with which they are concerned, so as to present them in their true perspective with respect to the social enterprise and at the same time save the dissipation of energy and effort which goes on when not perceiving that relationship, we treat various technical doctrines related to the same social or economic function in widely separated and apparently unrelated parts of our curriculum.

The legal concepts of property and contracts are familiar devices for effecting social control. The first year student very properly begins his law study with a consideration of these subjects and of torts which deals with the legal control of acts which affect either persons or things, accompanied by an introductory study of pleading and procedure. Later his notions of the range of control of human action through the contract and property concepts is expanded by study of the doctrines of equity. In general most other courses in law school deal with various phases of the application of these concepts to particular social or economic functions but without any attempt at classification of the function involved or at bringing together in single courses the various devices applicable to a particular function.

For example, the undertaking of a lawyer to secure satisfaction of a judgment in favor of his client presents itself to him as a single problem to be solved by resort to a variety of legal devices, the particular device to be selected depending on the particular circumstances of the case.

But how does the law school deal with the problem? It treats of execution and levy in a course on procedure; of creditors' bills and equitable execution in courses on equity; so also of equity receiverships, whereas proceedings supplementary to judgment and receiverships in such proceedings are usually dealt with in practice courses. Assignments for the benefit of creditors, if dealt with at all, are likely to be dealt with in the course on trusts, whereas the subject of bankruptcy and the rights of creditors in bankruptcy proceedings are usually dealt with in a separate course.

In the same way in text books and law school curricula it is customary to treat independently the law of pledge, of mortgage, of conditional sales and suretyship as well as such specialized forms of security as endorsed bills of lading, warehouse receipts, trust receipts, equipment trusts and the various modern devices for the financing of marketing operations which have had a rapid development in recent years.

These various subjects are distinct branches of technical law, often having different origins and history, nevertheless they exist and have practical utility solely to make effective a single important business function, namely, ensuring to the creditor a hold upon a particular piece of property or the obligation of a surety, in addition to the personal obligation of the debtor, as security for the payment of his debt. All this is indeed but a phase of the business man's problem of administering his credit risks if he is a creditor and his problem of administering his credit resources if he is a debtor.

Many other examples might be given of our tendency to make isolated studies of various legal devices without reference to the more significant social functions which they serve, but these will suffice if they make it apparent that there is not only a waste of time and effort in dealing with separate legal devices having a similar use, at different times and in different courses, but there is a loss of educational opportunity in the failure to make a comparative study of them in the light and with clear understanding of the economic function which is being facilitated or controlled.

It is quite possible that, if for example, we brought into a single course a consideration of all the devices to which the creditor may resort to ensure payment of his judgment or if we brought into another, a study of all the devices by which the creditor might obtain security for the payment of his debt, the central idea in each being a consideration of the various legal methods by which law controls and effectuates the social function concerned, we would go far toward finding a solution of the difficulties in which the present day law school curriculum is involved.

There would certainly be some saving of time and energy and a more adequate and satisfactory treatment of the subjects concerned, than is possible with the present arrangement. What is more important, this proposal suggests the possibility of a reorganization of the law school curriculum with reference to the social and economic functions with which law deals in something more than a mere mechanical way and holds out the hope that it will be possible to continue the work of professional law schools without the continual multiplication of courses, which have characterized their curricula for the past twenty years.

With this purpose in mind we have been engaged during the past year in making an extensive analysis and survey of all the courses offered in the law school. Each instructor has prepared a complete descriptive memorandum of his course, giving in detail the subjects discussed and the method of treatment. These memoranda have been referred to a special committee of the Faculty for analysis and classification and with the report of this committee we should be possessed of the data on the basis of which a really scientific revision of the curriculum may be begun.

The successful carrying out of such a plan is a matter of years rather than of months, not only because of the necessary studies which must be carried on and adjustments made, but because it ultimately will require the preparation of new case books in which the material will be selected with reference to the functional approach to the study of legal devices.

The second part of the problem affecting what I may call the more scholarly type of law schools is related to the training in social sciences which students have received before they begin their study of law. It is, I think, quite obvious that if law is a study of a method of social and economic control, then the student in order to be adequately prepared for its study ought, not only to have good mental discipline, but he ought to have a thorough-going knowledge of the social functions with which the law deals. While the undergraduate departments of colleges and universities are offering a great variety of courses in economics and the so-called social sciences, few of them indicate that any effort is made at any systematic approach to the problem from this view-point.

It is rare to find among the students of entering classes in the law school, who are graduates of colleges and universities, any well developed knowledge of our social structure and how it functions. Their economic training is too often based on *a priori* assumptions and a kind of closet philosophizing which unfits them to deal objectively with the type of economic problem with which he must deal in law school and later on as a lawyer. Where his training has been objective it seems too often to have been concerned with the description of the minutiae of more or less unrelated phases of social development without dealing with fundamentals. Too often he knows little or nothing of economic functions of property, contract, commerce, credit, of distribution and of money and banking.

There is important work to be done by those responsible for the development of undergraduate studies in America in the preparation of courses of study in economics and social science organized along the lines here suggested. Such a program of study, properly organized and once established, would add greatly to the value of training in those fields for the liberally educated man, whatever lifework he may take up, and would be far more valuable than the present type of training to the student planning to take graduate courses in law or business. Such a readjustment with respect to the method and objective of the study of social sciences should give a new trend to training in that field which would strengthen liberal education and prove of inestimable benefit in carrying on the work of law schools.

[12]

SOCIAL OBJECTIVES IN LEGAL EDUCATION*

There is nothing new in the proposition that law should change to meet new developments in our social and economic life. For over fifty years, one man alone has been busy writing pages of surpassing brilliance to show that his calling is "forever adopting new principles from life";[1] and his disciples constantly multiply. But today the tempo of change in society is faster than ever. If the law is to be an implement rather than an impediment to progress, it must respond rapidly and sensitively to the needs upon which it touches. And the law's field is ever widening. The lawyer is the shock trooper in court, legislature, and executive mansion, where many of the battles of peaceful societal reconstruction are finally resolved.[2] Somewhat less dramatically, the broader and more significant policies of "big business" are framed with marked deference to legal advice.[3]

As the ramifications of the lawyer's functions become increasingly manifest, the demand becomes more insistent that he be equipped to deal

---

* This paper discusses chiefly the Harvard, Columbia and Yale law schools. The writer has chosen Harvard because, as a recent graduate of that school, he is more familiar with it than with any other. There is additional justification for this choice. Harvard for a long time overshadowed legal education in America, and is regarded abroad as our representative law school. During 1932 the writer visited a majority of the widely known law schools in the United States, and as a result of discussions with teachers and students, visits to classrooms, and examination of written materials, found them overwhelmingly patterned after the Harvard system. Columbia and Yale have been selected because they are the leading exponents of recent experiments in legal education.

The reader will notice that Harvard is described and evaluated herein in terms of classroom work, while the other schools seem to be measured in terms of the written materials which they use. These materials are referred to because they have been prepared recently for the specific purpose of introducing certain experiments, and therefore are the most concrete indicia of their scope and objectives. The writer, from attending classes and from intimate fellowship with numerous students at these schools, is confident that the nature of the written materials honestly reflects the character of the classroom work. A few of the teachers at Columbia and Yale affirm that the proper place to present non-legal materials is in class and not in books. To an extent, this may be so. But it is not unfair to judge the *capacity* of these teachers to handle non-legal materials by examining the quality of the materials which do appear in their books. Hopkins may have been a university when sitting upon a log. But he did not fashion the log, nor did he use it as a teaching weapon.

The writer deems it fair to state explicitly that neither the initiative nor the contents of this paper derive from anyone connected with the faculty of any law school.

[1] HOLMES, THE COMMON LAW (1881) 36.
[2] Thus Pound says that "the legal order is the most conspicuous and the most effective form of social control." LAW AND MORALS (1926) 25.
[3] The intensifying relationship between law and business is noted by Hanna, *A Modern Approach to Legal Education* (1930) 6 AM. LAW SCHOOL REV. 745, 749; Turner, *Changing Objectives in Legal Education* (1931) 40 YALE L. J. 576, 578.

with the social and economic perplexities which are at the center of the congeries of problems known as "legal."[4] And as the law school is the basic institution for training lawyers, it has been subjected to experiments of various sorts having this end in view. The purpose of this paper is to evaluate certain recent trends in this field.

I

In all the branches of private law as it is taught in the majority of American law schools, there is adherence to the methods of the analytical jurisprudence of the nineteenth century. Chief interest lies in formulating general legal "first principles" in order to rationalize decisions and to provide handy categories under which to docket new sets of facts. This emphasis on doctrine fixes attention upon problems the sole significance of which may be the difficulty of fitting them into a supposedly inflexible deductive system. There is no necessary or even customary identity between such problems and those which are of current social importance.[5]

(1) The study of the law as a "body of technical doctrines more or less detached from those social forces which it regulates"[6] prevents

---

[4] Pound was an early petitioner. See *The Scope and Purpose of Sociological Jurisprudence* (1911) 24 HARV. L. REV. 591; (1911) 25 *id.* 140; (1912) 25 *id.* 489. Later Pound wrote: "the problems of the law are social because the legal order is a social institution, a highly specialized form of social control. They are economic because the task of social control is one of governing human activities in the satisfaction of unlimited wants out of a limited stock of goods." *Social and Economic Problems of the Law* (1928) ANN. AM. ACAD. POL. AND SOC. SCI. 1. The law is "but one strand in the fabric of community life." Mack, Introduction to FRANK, LAW AND THE MODERN MIND (1930).

[5] W. R. Vance has noted the tendency of the law teacher "to exhaust his intellectual energy in formulating them [rules] and dexterously showing their logical relationship one to the other, and in making fine and hairsplitting distinctions of what may at first appear to be conflicting rules." *The University and Jurisprudence*, in UNIVERSITY AND COMMONWEALTH (1921) 144-5. At Harvard: In torts, cases involving liability without fault, which certainly represent one of the more vital questions in tort law today, are hurried over in a few days toward the end of the course. On the other hand, months are spent earlier in the year discussing hypothetical and highly improbable fact situations which test the consistency of a series of irreconcilable cases in negligence. In contracts, Hochster v. De La Tour, 2 El. & Bl. 678 (1853) is the most celebrated case in the course, not (*e.g.*) because it is shown that a substantial number of people sue for anticipatory breach, but because the problem interests the master of the law of contracts, and because he disagrees with the decision. But standard contracts, an important modern development, are largely neglected.—Now I do not deny the value of cultivating rigorous analytical techniques. The question is, what emphases direct the trend of legal study?

[6] Stone, *The Future of Legal Education* (1925) 5 AM. LAW SCHOOL REV. 330-331. The narrow technique of the law was the whole subject of law teaching in the "grand manner" years ago. *Cf.* HOLMES, *The Use of Law Schools* in COLLECTED LEGAL PAPERS (1921) 35, 37, 39, 41: "For all lawyers are specialists. Not in the narrow sense of persons who confine themselves to a particular branch of practice . . . but specialists who have taken all law to be their province . . . a law school should be at once the workshop and the nursery of specialists in the sense which I have explained."

students from grasping the actual workings of law in society. Verbal manipulation of the disembodied rule does not reveal either the original setting which called it forth, or the profound alterations in the societal structure upon which the rule may now be operating. The objection goes further: a lawyer so trained, far from comprehending the broader economic and social results of the law, is unlikely to understand its effect even upon the client whom he serves.

(2) The analytical study of an inflexible system of rules does not disclose the nature of the judicial process by which courts operate upon the law. The discretionary element in decisions, with its delicate and often tardy response to novel social situations, is blinked in favor of an unreal picture of judges as mere automatons dealing with a consistent body of changeless generalizations.[7]

(3) In this connection, it is interesting to note the function of legal history in the traditional system.[8] It might be supposed that historical study would serve in some measure to correct the shortcomings just mentioned. On the contrary, it is employed to explain seeming inconsistencies in doctrine by showing how separate branches stem off from a central root. Or it is used to supplement the analytical method by tracing the growth of doctrines up to the point at which they have somehow matured and worked their way into the closed *corpus*.[9] Historical study, instead of receiving its impetus and direction from felt contem-

---

[7] While I do not agree with Frank's central thesis as to the basis of the desire for legal certainty, he does dispel admirably the notion that any high degree of certainty is obtainable. *Op. cit. supra* note 4, *passim*, esp. c. 1. Somewhat more moderate is Llewellyn, who writes: "there is less possibility of accurate prediction of what courts will do than the traditional rules would lead us to suppose." *Some Realism about Realism* (1931) 44 HARV. L. REV. 1222, 1241. Pound, however, cautions that the true picture of how judges act must be based upon the ideal elements in the law as well as on the alogical, subjective elements. Of course Pound's ideal elements encompass more than those of the analytical jurisprudents. *The Call for a Realist Jurisprudence* (1931) 44 HARV. L. REV. 697, 699; *Ideal Elements in American Judicial Decisions* (1931) 44 HARV. L. REV. 136. Cardozo expresses "a mounting sense of wonder that with all our centuries of common law development . . . there are so many questions, elementary in the sense of being primary and basic, that remain unsettled even now." THE PARADOXES OF LEGAL SCIENCE (1927) 76. Holmes says that "certainty generally is illusory, and repose is not the destiny of man." *The Path of the Law* in COLLECTED LEGAL PAPERS, 167, 181.

[8] Harvard has no course in legal history for undergraduates, and the same is true of most schools. I refer rather to the part played by historical study within individual courses in private law.

[9] This is particularly true because the analytical approach regards the development of the law as completed at the point where the form of the rule becomes fixed. Thus if a rule attained its present form in 1890, an 1890 case is the "leading case" and may be used as a satisfactory basis for study. But the facts of the 1890 case may involve business practices which no longer exist, and the rule may be governing totally different situations today.

porary needs, is used as a tool to negate the possibility of future growth.[10]

(4) A course of study which neglects to describe adequately how the law actually works today fails to provide the groundwork necessary for an examination of whether the law works as well as it should. The historical and analytical jurisprudents, by conveniently setting the law off in isolation from the rest of life, have banished all consideration of social and economic problems.[11] This is reflected in the antithesis made between logic and experience, the setting up of "public policy" as a special doctrine in the law, and the dichotomy elaborated between law and morality.

(a) No rapier thrust of Mr. Justice Holmes has gained wider acclaim than the one he delivered half a century ago: "The life of the law has not been logic; it has been experience."[12] He goes on to explain that the felt needs of the time have weighed more than the "syllogism" in marking the path of the law.[13] If we take these words at their face value, as purporting to set up an antithesis between logic and experience, they involve a misconception of the nature of logic in the law or too delimited a statement of the postulates upon which law should be based. For logic does not limit our choice of premises, and that the law should be responsive to the experiences of man is certainly a premise that rational men may accept.[14] When Mr. Justice Cardozo, echoing his predecessor,

---

[10] Pound has pointed out that the analytical and the historical schools walk hand in hand, and that the historical theory denies "growth and progress in any effective sense through its belief that it had discovered finally the immutable lines of growth or had calculated once for all the fixed orbit of progress outside of which no movement could possibly take place." INTERPRETATIONS OF LEGAL HISTORY (1923) 12.

[11] Pound writes: "The historical and analytical jurisprudence of the last century sought to exclude all social and economic problems, as such, from the domain of the science of law. They sought to set up a self sufficient jurisprudence in which only authoritative legal materials, regarded as such, should come into consideration." *Social and Economic Problems of the Law, supra* note 4, at 1. By law the analytical jurist means the aggregate of authoritative legal principles that are applied as such by tribunals in a given time and place. See POUND, LAW AND MORALS, 22. An example of analytical jurisprudence in practice is the course in Equity II at Harvard. In discussing the real and personal theories in connection with cases involving attempts of successive owners of lands to secure for these lands benefits derived from adjoining parcels held by other persons, many weeks are spent in efforts to fit each case under one theory or the other, accompanied by ingenious logical sorties to test each situation by comparison with analogous legal maxims. Hardly an attempt is made to weigh the economic arguments for and against allowing such incidents of land ownership. As a result, while it is true that the student gains skill above the average at playing a well defined game, and consequently is in demand by large offices, it is not true that he has been encouraged to grasp the larger social implications of his sport.

[12] THE COMMON LAW, 1.

[13] *Id.*, at 36.

[14] In so far as Holmes' statements equate logic with the philosophy of the syllogism, he is correct in his strictures upon logic. This philosophy asserted that thought or reason had fixed forms independent of and anterior to concrete subject

SOCIAL OBJECTIVES IN LEGAL EDUCATION 441

writes: "If I am seeking logical consistency, the symmetry of the legal structure, how far shall I seek it?,"[15] he slips into a similar confusion. What he means is that, given a set of facts, he tries to reach a result by deduction from certain postulates, and when he finds that he is getting a conclusion socially undesirable, he abandons some of the postulates or substitutes others, provided that the precedents are not too compelling. But this interruption is caused, not by a departure from logic, but by the intrusion *in medias res* of a principle which should never have been lost sight of. The protest is not against logic, but against the tendency of those who use logic to neglect a revision of their postulates.[16]

It is extremely likely that Holmes' phrase is merely a *caveat* against the excesses and shortcomings of the analytical jurisprudents.[17] If this is the case, it is ironical that the phrase, accepted eagerly and uncritically by many law teachers, has encouraged the very approach against which Holmes inveighed. Of course logic must be used by every science to test the adequacy of any asserted proposition; and the law must aim to form as coherent and generalized a system as possible. But if logic and experience are regarded as antithetical, there is danger that experience be shunted into a corner as "anomalous," to be forgotten entirely or called into play only when the "law" falls down. In the curious conflict

---

matter. It implied that for every possible case there is a fixed anterior rule. See DEWEY, PHILOSOPHY AND CIVILIZATION (1931) 132. It has been suggested also that Holmes' strictures are justified if we equate logic with aesthetic symmetry, or if we regard logic as forcing one to accept along with a premise all that a person devoid of logical subtlety would suppose followed. F. S. Cohen, *The Ethical Basis of Legal Criticism* (1931) 41 YALE L. J. 201. Today we do not take these views of logic. Cook says that there is no universal principle ready to serve as the unique major premise by which a particular case may be decided, and that we are forced to note the economic and social consequences of superimposing any one of a multitude of relevant premises. Book Review (1929) 38 YALE L. J. 405, 406. *Cf.* M. R. Cohen, *The Place of Logic in the Law* (1916) 29 HARV. L. REV. 622, 630: "from the point of view of logic, the existence of men in society . . . is just as brute an empirical fact as that water expands when cooled near the freezing point."

[15] THE NATURE OF THE JUDICIAL PROCESS (1921) 10.

[16] M. R. Cohen writes: "Those who distrust formal logic . . . are expressing in a confused way a distrust not of logic but of what I have called the jural premise. . . . There is no justification for restricting the scope of logic to deduction from rules already established or realized." *Philosophy and Legal Science* (1932) 32 COLUMBIA LAW REV. 1103, 1113, 1115. Pound says: "We no longer hold anything scientific merely because it exhibits a rigorous scheme of deductions from *a priori* conceptions." *Mechanical Jurisprudence* (1908) 8 COLUMBIA LAW REV. 605, 608. For a recent discussion of the problem, see Llewellyn, Adler, and Cook, *Law and the Modern Mind: A Symposium* (1931) 31 COLUMBIA LAW REV. 82.

[17] It is interesting to note that Holmes' statement that "other tools are needed besides logic," THE COMMON LAW, 1, is infinitely better than the more famous epigram. He is better yet when he says, "The law schools pursue an inspirational combined with a logical method, that is, the postulates are taken for granted upon authority without inquiry into their worth, and then logic is used as the only tool to develop the result." *Law in Science and Science in Law*, in COLLECTED LEGAL PAPERS, 210, 238.

between "logic" and "experience" the latter runs a poor second: this is the significant failing of modern legal education. It is evidenced further in the treatment of "public policy" as a special or auxiliary doctrine in the law.

(b) In almost every branch of private law, as it is taught traditionally, those few cases which are decided on so-called "public policy" are segregated for special consideration. In the vast majority of cases, no mention is made of "public policy." One reason for this prevailing neglect is that by mixing fewer ingredients into the brew of the average case, the decision is simplified. The "logical symmetry," which should always float on top like an opaque cream, is not disturbed. Justification for this approach is often stated in terms of a doctrine of precedents, and in the name of "public policy" itself; *i.e.*, it is argued that "public policy" favors certainty and stability in the legal order, and that these objects are best served by a system narrow enough to make its results predictable in most cases. This argument is buttressed by pleas of administrative necessity. Such an approach overemphasizes the virtues of stability. In failing to question the wisdom of whole branches of "settled law," it leaves students profoundly unconcerned about their validity from the social point of view.[18]

Further, that which is categorized tends to crystallize. By handling only a few situations on grounds of "public policy," the contours of the doctrine become sharply defined; the solvent becomes a solid. "Public policy" should be a method of approach aimed at meliorating the arbitrary fixation of rules. Instead, it has developed a separate rigidity of its own. Somewhat analogously, rules of equity tend to become as hard and fast as those of law. The result has been that the student ceases to scrutinize the underlying social implications of the "public policy" cases any more carefully than he does the central legal framework. "Public policy," instead of being the pervasive spirit, becomes a tag to tie upon anomalies, or a *modus operandi* when there are no precedents.[19]

---

[18] *Cf.* F. S. Cohen, *supra* note 14, at 214-5. He argues that the separation of "public policy" from the body of the law reflects an attempt to exclude moral judgments from the judicial process. He criticizes the emphasis upon certainty as "attempts to set up as a standard of legal criticism truth or consistency rather than goodness." He is correct in pointing out that certainty must be evaluated in ethical terms. But it seems unfair to say that those whom he censures do not openly defend certainty in ethical terms. It is rather that they regard certainty as "goodness" because they want to stabilize the present social order in many respects. *Cf. infra* pp. 451-2.

[19] The traditional treatment of the law of contracts illustrates the evil referred to in this discussion. The central assumption, never brought to the surface, is that parties by agreement should be able to create obligations which the law will enforce. Situations where the law should not enforce agreements are generally overlooked, and circumstances in which the law does not enforce them are treated as "public policy" anomalies. If it were recognized, instead, that all obligations

SOCIAL OBJECTIVES IN LEGAL EDUCATION 443

(c) The dichotomy between law and morality[20] plays a large part in analytical jurisprudence. Considered non-moral are, first, those rules (*e.g.* commercial law) which satisfy a need for definiteness but which, it is said, might just as well be the reverse of what they are.[21] What is overlooked is that the mere recognition that it is important for reasons of social expediency to establish some rule is verily a moral judgment.[22]

enforced at law are created by the law in response to social needs, and that the duty to keep one's word for consideration is merely one such obligation, much would be gained. It would then be feasible to discuss the wisdom of creating obligations in a wide variety of situations.

Bentham recognized this, and put contracts last in the list of enforceable obligations. See 1 THE WORKS OF JEREMY BENTHAM (1843) 338-41. The law today ignores Bentham's utilitarian test, while it clings to the specific grounds enumerated by Bentham for invalidating those agreements which he thought inconsistent with a *laissez faire* society. See *id.*, at 331-3. The tacit assumption that social welfare will be best served by maintaining "freedom" of transactions may not meet the demands of economic life today. Note the law's preoccupation with physical, as contrasted with economic, duress or inequality of bargaining power. If it were once recognized to what an extent economic duress of one sort or another furnishes the background of "free consensual transactions," the entire traditional approach might be revamped. *Cf.* COMMONS, THE LEGAL FOUNDATIONS OF CAPITALISM (1924) esp. c. 3; M. R. Cohen, *The Basis of Contract* (1933) 46 HARV. L. REV. 553, 558-65; Hale, *Coercion and Distribution in a Supposedly Non-coercive State* (1923) 38 POL. SCI. Q. 470.

Pound's thesis in INTERPRETATIONS OF LEGAL HISTORY, c. 3, that the progress of the law since 1910 has been from contract to status may be accepted without denying that the progression has been hampered by the persistence of *laissez faire* dogma. Besides, some of Pound's examples are mere wishfulness. He cites the tendency of the courts not to enforce contracts not to compete. But it is submitted that "freedom of contract" was a desideratum subserving a scheme of individualistic enterprise. Contracts not to compete limit the very type of "freedom" that the *laissez faire* school valued, and the law's hostility to such contracts does not evidence any departure from the basic economic assumptions behind "freedom of contract" in general. And Pound's assurance of the expansion of the public interest concept as another sign of the trend toward status must be qualified in the light of Wolfe Packing Co. v. Court of Industrial Relations, 262 U. S. 522, 43 Sup. Ct. 630 (1923); Tyson v. Banton, 273 U. S. 418, 47 Sup. Ct. 426 (1927); Ribnik v. McBride, 277 U. S. 250, 48 Sup. Ct. 614 (1928); New State Ice Co. v. Liebman, 285 U. S. 262, 52 Sup. Ct. 371 (1932). *Cf.* O'Gorman & Young v. Hartford Insurance Co., 282 U. S. 251, 51 Sup. Ct. 130 (1931).

[20] The use of the terms "morality" and "ethics" always calls for some definition. One school, following Kant, says that acts have no ethical quality apart from the will of the actor, and that law and morality are independent domains. See Stammler, *The Theory of Justice* in MODERN LEGAL PHILOSOPHY SERIES (1925) 40-71. On the other side, the followers of Spencer maintain that ethics is concerned with conduct considered objectively as producing good or bad results. SPENCER, PRINCIPLES OF ETHICS, Pt. 2, Justice, § 246. The analytical jurisprudents completely separated law and morals: "law was for courts, moral principles were for legislators; legal precepts were for jurisprudence, moral principles were for ethics." POUND, LAW AND MORALS, 44. Pound himself takes the view that in so far as the dichotomy is "more than historical anomalies that ought to be pruned away, they arise from inherent practical limitations . . . which make it inexpedient in a wise social engineering to attempt to secure certain claims or enforce certain duties to the extent that might be desirable from a purely ethical standpoint." *Id.*, at 38-39. And see CARDOZO, PARADOXES OF LEGAL SCIENCE, 35. In this paper, I express the position maintained by Pound and Cardozo.

[21] For a concise statement of this posture, see MORGAN, INTRODUCTION TO THE STUDY OF LAW (1926) 32-33. For an excellent criticism of Morgan, see F. S. Cohen, *supra* note 14.

[22] Pound says that in these "indeterminate" fields, the only moral element is the duty to obey the law once it is made. LAW AND MORALS, 73-78.

Moreover, the realm of law in which one rule is as good as another is probably narrower than the analytical jurisprudent would have us believe. As certainty is exalted above all competing objectives, critical evaluation has been practically exiled from the field of commercial law. Though it is abundantly clear that considerations of social desirability should penetrate every part of commercial law, the impingement becomes particularly manifest where the relative protection to be accorded the creditor and debtor classes—poignantly emphasized by current talk about moratory legislation—is in issue. And he who runs may read the problem of static as opposed to dynamic society implicit in our rules of alienability.[23]

Laws are also said to have no relation to morals when they make criminal a course of conduct not thought morally reprehensible before the laws were passed, or when they impose tort liability without fault. But in the criminal law the decision to punish a certain course of action which is unaccompanied by *mens rea* is no different in principle from a decision to make *mens rea* an element of the crime. Either must draw its justification from the needs of the community. Likewise in tort law, the determination that a loss should fall on a particular person is ultimately an ethical question. This is true whether or not the individual's subjective blamelessness enters into consideration. In fact, whether or not his state of mind should be considered is certainly an ethical problem.[24]

Finally, it is sought to deny the relationship between law and morals either on the ground that the law fails to prohibit some conduct which

---

[23] Cardozo admits that in those fields where the finality of the rule is a jural end, logic "very likely has been too remorseless." PARADOXES OF LEGAL SCIENCE, 67-68.
The aim of a stable law would seem to be, not a rule that does not change its form, but a rule that stabilizes a given set of social relationships. Thus even if we accept the notion that in some branches of the law stability is the chief objective, we must nevertheless subject it to constant scrutiny to see whether it is accomplishing the aims which gave it origin. *Cf.* Demogue, *Analysis of Fundamental Notions* in MODERN PHILOSOPHY SERIES (1916) 352, 418-45.

[24] Holmes seems to have taken the strictly analytical position. He writes: "Morals deal with the actual internal state of the defendant's mind," and he banishes morality from the law of contracts by pointing out that contracts depend entirely upon external actions. *The Path of the Law*, in COLLECTED LEGAL PAPERS, 167, 168. He continues: "Nowhere is the confusion between legal and moral ideas more manifest than in the law of contract. . . . The duty to keep a contract at common law means that you must pay damages if you do not keep to it—and nothing else. If you commit a tort you are liable to pay a compensatory sum. But such a mode of looking at the matter stinks in the nostrils of those who think it advantageous to get as much ethics into the law as they can. It was good enough for Lord Coke, however, and here, as in many other cases, I am content to abide with him." (At 175.) He also excludes morals from tort law by showing that one may be liable in defamation although he erroneously thought he spoke the truth, and had no malice. At 176.

everyone regards as immoral[25] or on the opposite ground that the law forbids certain moral conduct.[26] As to the first claim, it is indeed true that since individual morality is not limited by the practicability of regulating conduct by the forcible exercise of the social will, its standards may transcend those of the law. But this involves a moral judgment as to how far the law should go, which in turn involves a consideration of how far the law can go. As to the second claim, its very nature implies a moral judgment passed upon the law.

It would be unjust not to admit that even those who divorce law from morality do at times test one in the light of the other. Also, in so far as the analytical jurisprudents slough off the narrow connotations of "morality" and recognize that the law should act where there is no element of subjective misconduct, they reach a result with which few would disagree. But the chief fruit of the dichotomy is a process of legal education which directs young men's minds for three years toward the uncritical scrutiny of an inflexible and symbolic system, and then sends lawyers out into the larger society.[27]

---

[25] The separation of law and morals on this ground has had its effect upon the teaching of torts. In Professor Bohlen's casebook, used widely, an attempt is made to classify certain cases under the heading "Moral Obligation and Legal Duty," and to urge that the former be made the basis for the latter in situations where today the law does not impose duties which every decent person recognizes. See also BOHLEN, *The Moral Duty to Aid Others as the Basis for Tort Liability* in STUDIES IN THE LAW OF TORTS (1926) 291. But this analysis emphasizes rather than minimizes the false separation between morals and law. By devoting one-tenth of the torts course to "moral obligations," the other nine-tenths is left supremely free from what should be a major concern.

[26] Holmes argues that "there is some plausibility to the proposition that the law, if not part of morality, is limited by it. But this limit of power is not coexistent with any system of morals. No one will deny that wrong statutes can be and are enforced, and we would not all agree as to which were the wrong ones." *Path of the Law* in COLLECTED LEGAL PAPERS, 172. Surely the fact that "wrong" statutes are enforced does not deny either the proposition that laws are passed to satisfy supposed ethical judgments, or the proposition that law should be appraised in accordance with a coherent ethic. In fact Holmes' statement that a statute is "wrong" implies an ethical judgment. Finally, Holmes writes, "You can see very plainly that a bad man has as much reason as a good one for wishing to avoid an encounter with the public force, and therefore, you can see the practical importance of the distinction between morality and law." (At 170.) Certainly this is not a distinction between morality and law, but rather a recognition of the most effective means of imposing certain moral standards upon bad men. On the whole, Holmes' position is not very clear. Certainly, in the third and fourth chapters of THE COMMON LAW, there are passages which show him swinging over to the opposing camp. And he has said that "the law is the witness and external deposit of our moral life." COLLECTED LEGAL PAPERS, 170.

[27] Pound has indicated how the analytical jurists have tended to bring about the non-enforcement of moral goodness even where enforcement would be desirable. LAW AND MORALS, 67. From a slightly different angle, Cardozo writes that "the analytical jurists . . .in stressing verbal niceties of definition, made a corresponding sacrifice of emphasis upon the deeper and finer realities. . . . The constant insistence that morality and justice are not law, has tended to breed distrust and contempt of law as something to which morality and justice are not merely alien, but hostile." NATURE OF THE JUDICIAL PROCESS, 134.

II

The foregoing consideration of traditional private law teaching indicates that it neither describes adequately the operation of law in society nor presents any kind of sociological critique. We have now to examine what is being accomplished in the same schools in courses in public law, legislation and jurisprudence.

The first named offers particular opportunities for the interplay of sociological technique. While not all of the teachers in this field are adequately equipped in the social sciences, a greater number[28] seek to set the law in the context of life. This may be partially due to the fact that the concepts in public law are relatively vague, so that only by the methods of sociology can any rationale be reached.

Even if the public law courses were conducted on the highest level, however, there is slight ground for believing that this would remedy the unfortunate outlook inculcated by the purely analytical techniques employed in private law courses. One suspects that the sociological materials and skills required in handling constitutional problems will vary from those required to resolve private law questions. The issue presented by a due process case does not necessarily penetrate to the ultimate desirability of a statute so much as it involves raising the doubt of a reasonable man against a particular judge. But the evaluation of a decision in private law is unlikely to escape the task of final social judgment. Again, the very classification of public as against private law, accentuated by the curriculum and the marked difference in professorial attitudes, prevents the social awareness which accompanies the study of the one from extending to the other.[29] Most important, the vast majority of students hardly become initiated into the public law field during their three years in law school.[30]

---

[28] At Harvard, for example, Frankfurter in federal jurisdiction and public utilities, Landis in labor law and legislation, McLaughlin in federal anti-trust laws, Powell in constitutional law and Sayre in criminal law are all thoroughly imbued with the sociological approach. At the same time, they have not perfected the technique of presenting pertinent non-legal materials; consequently they rely at times on the purely analytical technique quite as much as their associates. Constitutional law offers a good example. While Beale, with the consummate skill of the master analyst, shows that cases are all consistent, Powell uses an equally analytical technique to demonstrate that they are all inconsistent and that there is no "law." The latter method is more realistic; it shows that behind the face of a decision there is a court "wiser than they talk." But the student gets little insight into how tax statutes work, or how taxation fits into the scheme of national economy.

[29] The classification itself involves obvious difficulties. For example, workmen's compensation acts are private law so far as traditional methodology is concerned. Certainly an Englishman, familiar with the social effects of the Property Acts and the abolition of primogeniture, would smile at the attempt to consider the law of property as "private" in any sense.

[30] At Harvard all of the courses open to first and second year men are in private law. The following public law courses are open to all third year men:

SOCIAL OBJECTIVES IN LEGAL EDUCATION

The common law aversion to legislation is definitely established in the law schools, and the neglect of the subject takes a number of forms. Few schools present as a part of each course the relevant legislative materials, and bare mention is the most that they get in any event.[31] Nor is attention directed toward considering proposed remedial legislation, codification, and the supplementing of the common law by statute. Analysis may reveal that the cases are "wrong." But if the law is "settled," the door to speculation is closed. There is almost complete lack of opportunity to study the technique of legislation and legislative problems in general.[32]

The prevailing neglect of legislation may arise in part from the belief that most lawyers will not be legislators. The more important reason, however, is a cheerful confidence in the adequacy of the case method. Langdell said that the law schools could do no more than teach principles and methods, and how to look at a case. This insistence that the schools train in techniques and not in subject matter lies behind much of the objection to the study of legislation. But in fact subject matter is admitted to be of importance, as is indicated by how much of the law most teachers attempt to cover. It is argued also that most legis-

---

constitutional law, international law, public utilities, taxation, federal anti-trust laws and labor law. While practically the whole class elects constitutional law, not more than thirty per cent take public utilities, and hardly more than ten per cent elect any particular one of the other four courses. In law schools where a greater range of election is allowed, the public law courses are slighted. The 1930 REPORT OF THE COMMITTEE ON CURRICULUM OF THE ASS'N OF AMERICAN LAW SCHOOLS indicates that the most popular courses, taken by over three-fourths of the students, are bills and notes, code pleading, corporations, equity, evidence, real property, trial practice, and wills. Only a very small percentage of law schools offer public law courses during the first year. And it is probable that the first year is the most critical one in so far as developing attitudes toward the law is concerned. Though almost every school requires three or more specified private law courses—generally, contracts, property and torts—during the first year, very few require any public law work at any time during the three years. Yale prescribes constitutional law for the first year; Minnesota requires it during the second. See UNIVERSITY OF CHICAGO ANNOUNCEMENTS, ANNUAL REGISTER (1932-1933); COLUMBIA UNIVERSITY BULLETIN OF INFORMATION, SCHOOL OF LAW (1932-1933); OFFICIAL REGISTER OF HARVARD UNIVERSITY, THE LAW SCHOOL (1932-1933); BULLETIN UNIVERSITY OF MINNESOTA, THE LAW SCHOOL ANNOUNCEMENT (1930-1932); BULLETIN UNIVERSITY OF WISCONSIN LAW SCHOOL (1932-1933); BULLETIN, YALE UNIVERSITY, GENERAL CATALOGUE NUMBER (1932-1933).

[31] Of course, such documents as the Uniform Negotiable Instruments Law and the Uniform Sales Act are not neglected anywhere. And courses such as bankruptcy, public utilities and taxation deal largely with statutory problems. But torts is an excellent example of the sin by omission. Although the workmen's compensation acts have changed fundamentally not only the subject matter but also the underlying theories of an important branch of the law of torts, the course at Harvard deals with the common law materials only. The same is true of most other schools, including Chicago, Michigan, Minnesota, Wisconsin and Columbia. At Columbia, however, the acts are studied in the course in legislation. Yale includes the acts in its course in torts.

[32] At Harvard there is a graduate course in legislation which admits a handful of third year students, and at Michigan, Chicago and Yale there are similar limited facilities. Neither Minnesota nor Wisconsin offers a course of any kind. Columbia presents a required course for all first year students.

lation is a mere codification of the common law. This is becoming less and less the fact, and in so far as it is correct, it may be a manifestation of the failure to educate lawyers in the technique of change. It is claimed that legislation exhibits such differences in the forty-nine jurisdictions that it is hardly susceptible of treatment. But this, in itself, is merely an argument against national law schools. And in point of fact, it appears to be quite as possible to generalize the principles and problems of legislation as those of the common law.

The crux of the matter, however, is that the difference between legislation and the common law is not simply a matter of the materials involved. The theory of legislation is the theory of change. The study of legislation emphasizes social and economic elements, and tests the responsiveness of the law to public needs. The case system, which never purported to introduce scientific inductive method, and which was regarded from the outset merely as a pedagogical device,[33] has acquired at its maturity "the sterility of a fully developed system."[34] Those teachers most famous in its use do not construct the law from the cases, but fit new cases into the pattern of their conception of a preordained law. The study of case law is the method of analytical jurisprudence. It does not lead students to evaluate the law except in terms of its inner consistency.

Our thesis has been that it is not sufficient to train lawyers in the narrower legal technique. They should deal with the law as a social instrument. Accordingly, they must be initiated into problems involving the nature and purpose of law. The answers to these questions can hardly be found within the *corpus* itself. They must be sought in the study of jurisprudence and allied subjects. The argument in favor of neglecting such study until legal education is completed is founded upon the idea that one must know law before one can talk about it understandingly. Persons on the other side say that one must know in what spirit to study the law before one can study it properly. This methodological problem arises in every field. But the truth about most law professors is that they believe it to be unnecessary for a majority of the students to study the subject of jurisprudence at all.[35]

---

[33] See M. R. Cohen, *The Place of Logic In The Law* (1916) 29 HARV. L. REV. 622, 627. Redlich, in his criticism of the case method, indicates that its pretensions are merely pedagogic; his objection to it is that it fails to give a rounded conception of the law. See *Weaknesses of the Case Method In American Law Schools* (1925) 4 AM. LAW SCHOOL REV. 1-7.

[34] *Mechanical Jurisprudence, supra* note 16, at 605, 614. Pound cites "abundant examples of its failure to respond to vital needs of present day life."

[35] At Harvard, jurisprudence and comparative law are graduate courses open to only a very few third year honor men. The same is true at Yale. Chicago and Minnesota offer courses which reach only a few of the third year students lost in a barrage of electives. Wisconsin is experimenting with an undergraduate course. Columbia offers a course in comparative law to a select group of second and third year men. The general neglect must be regarded as unfortunate if one agrees with Laski that: "the study of jurisprudence is integral to the intellectual discipline

III

There have been voiced several clearly defined objections to widening the scope of traditional legal education. The first of these is that the undergraduate college, by training in the social sciences and by promoting the essentials of citizenship, can give the pre-law student all he needs in a non-technical way. Despite the charm of this picture of coordination between college and professional school, there are reasons to believe that the claim is unfounded. It seems clear that the social and economic implications of legal problems can be understood only after an intimacy with their precise nature. The legal rule must be known intimately before it can be tested in the light of broader social wants. Conversely, the practicability of achieving these social wants can be comprehended fully only when one sees what scope they are already given by the legal order. Therefore attention should be focused simultaneously upon the two. Further, the gap between college and the professional school is too wide. The typical student who has gone to college to prepare for a professional school, to get culture, to while away his time, or for some other undefined reason, enters law school to learn a money making trade, to prepare for his life work. He feels that he has put aside childish things. This attitude, more than increased maturity or the rigor of the subject matter, accounts for the fact that students work much harder in professional schools—particularly in the law schools—than in college. The sudden transition is accompanied by a tendency to forget whatever breadth of outlook college may have stimulated, and to revel in pure technicalities.

It results that a college education, even of the best sort, is not a sufficient preparation for a sociological critique of legal rules. And even if such preparation were adequate, the attitudes it provokes, as we have seen, are choked rather than nurtured in the law schools. The undergraduate school of law stands out as the proper place for training men, not only in the narrower workings of the legal system, but also in the sociological technique.[36]

Pound sets up three propositions in opposition to broader train-

---

I am advocating because without a knowledge of jurisprudence, . . . no lawyer . . . can really measure the meaning of the assumptions upon which his subject rests . . . the richer the jurisprudence of a given system . . . the nearer will be the law . . . to the needs of the times. The poverty of English jurisprudence since Austin is a measure of the inadequacy of our law to meet the swift changes of our social situation." A GRAMMAR OF POLITICS (1925) 577.

[36] For a concise statement of this viewpoint, see Oliphant, *The Future of Legal Education* (1928) 6 AM. LAW SCHOOL REV. 334-336. Dean Pound takes the stand that social science work should be done in college. REPORTS OF THE PRESIDENT OF HARVARD COLLEGE AND REPORTS OF DEPARTMENTS (1928) 202-203. Mr. Justice Stone supports our contention in *The Future of Legal Education* (1924) 5 AM. LAW SCHOOL REV., No. 6.

ing in the undergraduate law school. These are, (1) the work of law making and law reform does not depend largely upon the general body of practicing lawyers, but upon judge and legislator and administrator, (2) it is sufficient that the mass of law students be trained only as client caretakers, and (3) training in a purely legal technique is adequate preparation for the job of client caretaking. These propositions must be subjected to some criticism.[37]

It is not true that judge and legislator and administrator are the prime movers in reshaping the law. So much has been written recently about judge made law that the importance of the great body of the profession in molding the *corpus* has been neglected. For after all the judicial function remains a relatively narrow one. Mr. Justice Holmes, in dispelling the notion that judges are mere phonographs of the law, warns us in these terms: "I recognize without hesitation that judges must and do legislate, but they do so interstitially; they are confined from molar to molecular motions. A common law judge could not say, 'I think the doctrine of consideration a bit of historic nonsense, and will not enforce it in my court.'"[38] And Mr. Justice Cardozo has pointed out eloquently the limitations upon judges even within the interstices.[39]

---

[37] It must be insited that any argument as to whether Pound would subscribe definitely to these propositions is subsidiary to the fact that his administration at Harvard is predicated upon them. But that he does adhere to them expressly seems clear, for he has written: "we ought not to expect every graduate of a national law school to become a great law reformer . . . we should seek to turn out *well trained competent practitioners* . . . also we must seek to turn out from *time to time a chosen few, whom nature meant for such things, specially trained in the problems and methods of creative law making* . . . another chosen few . . . to become legal scholars and teachers." REPORT OF THE PRESIDENT OF HARVARD COLLEGE AND REPORTS OF DEPARTMENTS (1928) 202. Again he writes: "It is no longer held sufficient for law schools to produce competent well trained lawyers. Rightly the public looks to the national law schools to turn out legal scholars, lawmakers, law reformers, and legal and social engineers. . . . But the direct training for such purposes should be superimposed upon the professional training. . . . The demands of direct training for general public service, however, tend to push into the field of *training for the special public service of practicing law . . . we must be careful that the demands of training for lawmaking and law reform, pushing hard and continually upon the work of professional training, are not allowed to impair the latter, which is, after all, the primary function of the law school. . . . The best solution, as I see it, is to be found in a body of teachers devoted to teaching as their primary function, supplemented by a certain number of investigators, organized in institutes, whose primary work is not teaching, and whose energy may be given to public service and to special work . . . with graduate students and those training, not for practice, but for some particular public service.*" *Id.* (1930) 199. The undergraduate law school must train competent practitioners, and preparation for guiding public opinion *re* changes in the law must be left to the few in the graduate schools. *Id.* (1931) 203. Finally, he has written, "Our ultimate reliance must be upon education of judge and lawmaker and administrator." *Social and Economic Problems of the Law, supra* note 4, at 9. (Italics are all mine.)

[38] Southern Pacific Company v. Jensen, 242 U. S. 205, 221, 37 Sup. Ct. 524, 531 (1917).

[39] THE NATURE OF THE JUDICIAL PROCESS, 105-108, 115, 129.

SOCIAL OBJECTIVES IN LEGAL EDUCATION 451

Legislators are not limited in the same sense that judges are. But the pace of fundamental legislative change has not been rapid in a country where the spirit of the common law is strong. And administrators, despite their ever expanding activities, are by very definition fairly circumscribed in their actions.

Even if we could accept, which we cannot, the proposition that "law makers" (judges and legislators and administrators), as distinct from the practicing members of the bar, mold the law, it remains true that in the past the former have been recruited from the bar without reference to special graduate training. This condition will remain unchanged for some time. And it is well known that most judges, at least, bring to bear the knowledge, interests and predispositions gained during practice.[40]

It cannot be denied, then, and it seems superfluous to labor the point, that "the law is made by the Bar, even more than by the Bench."[41] This is true not only in the narrow sense that lawyers become judges, legislators and administrators, but, more significantly, in the sense that lawyers bring before courts and committees the basic facts upon which judgments rest. Thus judges even within the interstices, and legislators even when framing their measures, rely heavily upon materials presented before them by members of the bar.[42] Nor should the influence of leading lawyers exerted on the platform, at convention, and in print, be neglected. Thus the sort of basic facts the profession is trained to handle is of prime importance, and herein lies the task of the law school.[43]

The singling out of the judicial function, and legislation, as the sole media of legal reconstruction is not the work of simple minded men who overestimate the power of judge and legislator. In a more

---

[40] Volumes have been written on this subject alone, and the history of the Supreme Court in this century speaks above them all. A good treatment of the general proposition will be found in FITCH, THE CAUSES OF INDUSTRIAL UNREST (1924) 340-349.
[41] HOLMES, *The Law* in COLLECTED LEGAL PAPERS, 25.
[42] Even Pound at one point says that "the decisive factor in adapting our legal materials to the social and economic problems of the legal order of today will be found in the received ideas of the legal profession which . . . give the pattern to which authoritative precepts are shaped in the process of judicial theorizing." *Social and Economic Problems of the Law, supra* note 4, at 91.
Compare the careers of Holmes and Brandeis. Holmes has succeeded by a process of judicial self-limitation coupled with understanding, in getting desirable results without a profound knowledge of twentieth century America. But this could never make one a great lawyer in the sense that Brandeis is, nor could it make one a great private law judge in the fashion of Lord Mansfield. Brandeis' technique is a lesson primarily to lawyers, not to judges; when lawyers have adopted his approach, the judges will take care of themselves. *Cf.* Stone, *Fifty Years of the U. S. Supreme Court* (1928) 53 REP. A. B. A. 259, 271-2.
[43] "The method by which lawyers are trained is at the root of the attitude they will take in their profession to legal reform." LASKI, A GRAMMAR OF POLITICS, 575.

important sense it is the work of men who feel that the scope of desirable change in the law is limited to the sort of changes judges and legislators have effected in the past. It is the work of men who see no need for revaluation of those basic areas of law which give contour to our individualistic, business man's society.

Once this point is clear, Pound's second proposition is understandable enough. For the conception of a good lawyer which is satisfied by the client caretaker fits beautifully into nineteenth century *laissez faire*. The good client caretaker can live within the marked lines of this system unvexed by a desire to erase some of the lines. He functions best when he secures stability, when he avoids change by advising his clients so well that there is no need to go to court. He is the servant of the individual, in a society which should be static except in so far as his clients' interests demand motion. This concept of the practitioner as a purely conservatizing force does not meet the demands of a transitional social order.[44]

Many will insist however that under our present social order, the average practitioner can do no more than serve his client. Even if this is true, we cannot support Pound's third proposition to the effect that the traditional legal training is adequate preparation for this purpose. We have said that the study of legal rules detached from their functioning does not equip the lawyer to comprehend even the interests of his clients. Again, those who defend individualistic services argue that these perform a social function by bringing the conflicting interests of mankind before appropriate forums where they are reconciled and resolved. Indeed this is what Pound means when he refers to "the special public service of practicing law." This process of resolution and recon-

[44] *Cf.* BEARD, THE MYTH OF RUGGED AMERICAN INDIVIDUALISM (1931). It would be grossly unjust to Pound not to admit that his writings have urged constantly the need of recognizing the changes of contemporary life. "But when we look at our common law individualism in the light of the social order as it now is, we must recognize that the adjustment of this traditional spirit of our law to a different organization of society is not the least of the problems of the legal order." *Social and Economic Elements in The Law, supra* note 4, at 10. But when we examine closely the actual content of his sociological jurisprudence and his concepts of legal education, we find that they are both closely articulated with a desire for stability under the present reign of business. "Rules of property, rules as to commercial transactions, the rules that maintain the security of transactions in a society of complex economic organization—such rules may be and ought to be of general and absolute application." LAW AND MORALS, 73. Pound seems to equate morality in the law with critical evaluation; he says that the fields for morality in the law are interpretation, application, administration and judicial discretion all operating within the confines of the spheres already marked out. *Id.,* at 44-46. Pound has been subjected to considerable criticism recently in regard to the points through which he has drawn the line between rest and motion in the law. See Frank's chapter on Pound in LAW AND THE MODERN MIND. When we turn to Pound's views on legal education, we find them closely coordinated with his jurisprudence. Undergraduate legal education is dedicated to training primarily for the vast segregated areas of business law which he exempts from change.

SOCIAL OBJECTIVES IN LEGAL EDUCATION 453

ciliation can be worth while only if the combatants lay bare before judges the real social and economic interests struggling for ascendancy.

Those who look upon the profession as mere client caretakers suggest a helpful approach. For an inquiry into broader social interests may commence with a careful observation of how the law works upon individual clients, and how far it affects and can affect their affairs. This means that we must study the manner in which the economic interests of individual clients shape their legal actions and through these actions the law; and conversely we must study the way in which the law affects these interests. We must build a consideration of how the law can and should function upon a knowledge of how it does function.[45] This is the stated objective of the new movement in legal education, and we turn now to examine it in operation.

IV

Columbia and Yale are the two schools which have been most prominent in the experimental movement, and it is their activities which we shall consider.[46] We may begin with courses in business and property law, and in equity. These have been regrouped on the basis of the activities involved as they are met in practice, rather than the traditional legal compartments.[47] In pursuance of this plan, some courses

---

[45] See LLEWELLYN, A MODERN LAW SCHOOL (1930), reprinted from (1930) 22 COLUMBIA UNIV. Q., No. 3; THE EFFECT OF LEGAL INSTITUTIONS UPON ECONOMICS (1925), reprinted from (1925) 15 AM. ECO. REV., No. 4.

[46] For the story of the new movements at Columbia and Yale, see SUMMARY OF STUDIES IN LEGAL EDUCATION BY THE FACULTY OF LAW OF COLUMBIA UNIVERSITY (1928); REPORTS OF THE DEAN OF THE COLUMBIA LAW SCHOOL for 1928, 1929, 1930, 1931, and 1932; REPORTS OF THE DEAN OF YALE LAW SCHOOL for 1929, 1930, 1931, and 1932. There have been radical changes at Northwestern, but it is too early to assess their worth. The new first year curriculum there includes (1) constitutional government, a study of constitutional law and of the functions of government, (2) agencies of business, similar to the new courses at Columbia and Yale, (3) the judicial process in contracts, in criminal law and in torts, (4) language facilities, a course in the usage of legal terms. See Green, *A New Program in Legal Education* (1931) 17 A. B. A. J. 299.

[47] At Columbia there are no courses in equity. First year procedure includes equity jurisdiction and specific performance. Trusts and estates combines future interests, trusts and wills. Vendor and purchaser includes equitable servitudes and conveyancing. Contracts II includes equitable relief against mistakes and quasi-contracts. Creditors' rights surveys the problems concerning unsecured creditors, including bankruptcy and receiverships, and security touches the problems relating to secured creditors, including suretyship and mortgages, pledges and trust receipts, *etc.* Business organization includes agency, business trusts, corporations and partnership. There is also a course in corporation finance. At Yale, administration of debtors' estates includes bankruptcy and receiverships. Credit transactions includes the problems of secured creditors. Four courses in business units (finance, losses, management and reorganization) include most of the law of business organizations. At both schools, new casebooks have been prepared to meet the reorganization. At Columbia, some of these are: HANNA, CASES AND MATERIALS ON THE LAW OF CREDITORS' RIGHTS (1931); HANDLER, CASES AND MATERIALS ON VENDOR AND PURCHASER (1933); R. B. POWELL, POSSESSORY

have been organized internally in such a way as to deal with the materials on a functional basis.[48]

The next steps have been to incorporate descriptions of the actual business conditions with which the practitioner has to deal, and to train the students in a technique of client caretaking. These aims have been accomplished partly by the use of recent, well selected cases, and to a greater extent by the inclusion in casebooks of non-legal accounts of business terms and transactions as they are thrown before the attorney.[49] The student is given problems requiring him to do original work responsive to given sets of facts.[50] Excerpts from law review articles and digests of cases are used extensively, and while this is not a new practice, it is stated that it has a new purpose—to bring out the importance which the factual set-up plays in the judicial process. For this reason, it is regarded as the final step in equipping the student for service. He is taught to work with business and law, to draft documents, and finally to understand courts.

The claim is made that the job of training better client caretakers is only a prelude to the job of setting up some method of evaluating

---

ESTATES (1932) (tentative print) and CASES AND MATERIALS ON THE LAW OF TRUSTS AND ESTATES (1932) (one volume published). At Yale: DOUGLAS AND SHANKS, CASES AND MATERIALS ON THE LAW OF MANAGEMENT OF BUSINESS UNITS (1931) and CASES AND MATERIALS ON THE LAW OF FINANCING OF BUSINESS UNITS (1931); STURGES, CASES AND MATERIALS ON THE LAW OF CREDIT TRANSACTIONS (1931).

[48] For example, the Columbia course in sales treats express and implied warranties not merely on an historical basis, but especially as these two types of warranties arise out of present-day sales transactions at a distance. It also insists that modern practice necessitates initial emphasis on the contract of sale rather than on the transfer of title. The Yale courses on business units arrange the materials on the basis of a classification of business problems: hence the division is management, finance, losses and reorganization.

[49] Llewellyn's CASES AND OTHER MATERIALS ON THE LAW OF SALES (1930) contains a surprisingly recent array of cases and a splendid account of the newer forms of contracts. Douglas and Shanks in CASES AND MATERIALS ON THE LAW OF MANAGEMENT OF BUSINESS UNITS present admirably the new developments in corporation practice, especially the complications arising out of control by voting; the increasingly contractual nature of the shareholders' rights; holding companies; managerial powers under new forms of contracts, practices and by-laws. Their book contains also an elementary demonstration of business accounting, in connection with the treatment of dividend questions. For the extreme effort along this line, see BERLE, CASES AND MATERIALS ON THE LAW OF CORPORATE FINANCE, (1930); esp., definitions of capital as used in economics, in business and in accounting, at 204-206, 207-211; descriptions of functions of limited participation contracts, 425-426; of preferred stocks, 438; of purchase, retirement and reduction, 477-478. The book contains a complete account of the legal and financial process of forming a corporation, from the initial steps through the public issuance of securities.

[50] Extreme stress upon draftsmanship is shown in Pt. 3 of Powell's CASES AND MATERIALS IN THE LAW OF TRUSTS AND ESTATES. The inclusion of legal forms in casebooks is not novel, but there is a strong tendency now to use more of these, to distribute them throughout the book, and even to build the texts around them. Nor do the more traditional schools neglect draftsmanship entirely. At Harvard, examination questions frequently call for the construction of an instrument. But there is very little practice of this sort during the year.

SOCIAL OBJECTIVES IN LEGAL EDUCATION

the law in social terms. But the functional approach has not been fruitful in regard to this second task, especially in the fields of business and property law. In the first instance, most of the new work has not been done by lawyers who are social economists; it has been carried on by lawyers who know from practice the needs of the practicing lawyer. *As a result, the real rapprochement has been between the law school and the business school.*[51] And for many years the business schools have failed to integrate business and social economics, and have graduated men no more competent than lawyers to act in a public profession.[52] Another reason for the slow progress toward inviting social judgments from students has been that evaluative processes, even in the "new" schools, are conceived to have less place in business law than in torts or public law. Most important, even those who have tried to formulate social criteria are just beginning to fight.[53] The alliance between business

---

[51] Berle's CASES AND MATERIALS ON THE LAW OF CORPORATE FINANCE illustrates this point. It is a marvelous service manual for business lawyers. The references it contains to outside source books are of the type that would be helpful to this class of persons alone. See, for example, the references to books or articles on non-par stock, 282; preemptive rights, 354; dividends, 356; various types of bonds, 501. Pound has pointed out that the functional approach has been largely a union between business and law, and that there is danger of its making lawyers more skillful in helping clients avoid the law than in furthering social welfare. *The Call for a Realist Jurisprudence* (1931) 44 HARV. L. REV. 697, 708-9. Llewellyn denies the charge that the so-called realists are interested in business rather than in society at large. *Some Realism about Realism* (1931) 44 HARV. L. REV. 1222, 1233. But it seems that the range of inquiry, the social assumptions and the judgments of some of the functionalists are influenced by their prior experience as practicing lawyers. The original aim of the reorganization at Columbia was merely to integrate various subjects more nearly in accordance with business practices today. There was no desire to commence a social evaluation of these areas of the law. See Oliphant, *The Future of Legal Education* (1928) 6 AM. LAW SCHOOL REV. 329.

[52] There is here a striking similarity between current developments in law and in economics. Economics has revolted from the analytical system of the classicists, and swung over to descriptive study which reflects on the one hand an aimless eclecticism and on the other an interest confined to serving the narrow needs of business. There is great need for the reconstruction of economic theory to give direction to descriptive study and to widen its social range. See Mitchell, *The Prospect of Economics in* THE TREND OF ECONOMICS (Tugwell, editor, 1924) 3; Clark, *The Socializing of Theoretical Economics*, id., 73; Tugwell, *Experimental Economics*, id., 371.

[53] Berle's CASES AND MATERIALS ON THE LAW OF CORPORATE FINANCE, despite its profusion of non-legal materials, has very little that would aid one in passing social judgments. Material of this latter sort is confined to a statistical summary of the share of the national wealth which is in the hands of corporations. At 122-125. R. B. Powell's POSSESSORY ESTATES (1932) has no economic materials, except in c. 6, § 2, which contains the American Experience Table of Mortality and a short essay on the theory and practice of valuation. His 1 CASES AND MATERIALS ON THE LAW OF TRUSTS AND ESTATES (1932) presents in the second chapter some economic data on the distribution of wealth in the United States and the growth of trust practices. This data does little more than show that trusts is an important subject. In the seventh chapter of the same book there are some general philosophical excerpts about the basis for allowing or regulating testamentary dispositions. Sturges' CASES AND MATERIALS ON THE LAW OF CREDIT TRANSACTIONS has good references to legal periodicals, but very little drawn from other sources. A central

practices and the law has indicated some of the effects of the law upon persons immediately subjected to it, but there has been a failure to reveal other no less important effects upon these persons.⁵⁴ Of course, there has been still less success in providing a basis of social evaluation wider than the interests of clients.⁵⁵

In fields such as torts and domestic relations the new school has advanced farther than in business law areas. The attempt to reconstruct the concepts of negligence, duty and liability in terms of an industrial society drifting toward social insurance, is significant. Likewise there is value in the work at Columbia in family law. However, this critical evaluation is still too limited. It suffers from the "public policy" concept which tends to evoke new judgments only where, as Cardozo says, "competitive analogies fail to supply a clew." There is failure to recognize that new evaluative techniques must be used, not

---

obstacle to a wider range of evaluation is that business law is still supposed by most people to bear down only upon the business man's interests. Beyond this, the law teacher has simply more to learn about the other social sciences. Such a book as BERLE AND MEANS, THE MODERN CORPORATION AND PRIVATE PROPERTY (1932) can not fail to be helpful in this connection. It shows the cooperative efforts of a lawyer and an economist. [Even this does not go far. The first third, which describes absentee ownership today, and the second, which discusses the present state of corporation law, are splendid. But the last section, which enunciating the thesis that the corporation is now a social agency which affects interests beyond those of directors and stockholders, is rather naive in its assumption that economics has not progressed beyond Adam Smith; and the book presents no discussion of the effects of absentee ownership upon business, workers, owners and society comparable to the work done by Veblen. Cf. the latter's ABSENTEE OWNERSHIP AND BUSINESS ENTERPRISE IN RECENT TIMES (1923)].

⁵⁴ For example, the sales course at Columbia has worked out fairly well the effect of laws and practices upon buyers and sellers. It has done this by taking the concept of risk as a unifying thesis. But the problem of risk is not all-embracing, and many economic issues are left untouched. There is much evidence of the questionable assumption that the only task is to measure risks and to evolve laws minimizing them,—an approach apparent as well in Moore and Hope, *An Institutional Approach to the Laws of Commercial Banking* (1929) 38 YALE L. J. 703. It has been well said that while the "risk" approach is better than "legal concepts which are based upon an abstraction of purely physical or other adventitious factors in the business relation in question . . . [yet] only when we have adequate data as to business practices and their social and economic consequences, will we be in a position to formulate new concepts and rules for the apportionment of risks." Patterson, *The Apportionment of Business Risks through Legal Devices* (1924) 24 COLUMBIA LAW REV. 335, 359.

⁵⁵ Many commercial courses do not attempt this broader evaluation. It is only because Llewellyn does attempt it so courageously, and gives such promise of eventual success, that his course is in the limelight for criticism. Some parts of the course have arrived at tangible criteria. For example, in treating the MacPherson v. Buick Co. [217 N. Y. 382, 111 N. E. 1050 (1916)] situation, it is shown that from the social point of view risks should be placed upon those able to bear them and upon those able to exercise care. In the discussion of the "guarantee against decline" stipulations, the interests of consumers, as well as those of manufacturers and other groups, are considered. But on the whole, the chief weakness of the course is the tacit assumption that the interests of litigants coincide with the interests of society.

SOCIAL OBJECTIVES IN LEGAL EDUCATION 457

merely as an aid where other crutches break, but over the whole field.[56]

There is slight need to discuss public law because the attitude of teachers in this field at the new schools does not differ from that at the more classical institutions. The task at all points is simply one of progressing more rapidly toward an integration of law and the social sciences.[57]

V

Columbia offers a course in legislation prescribed for all first year men. Its object is to discuss the problems that the growing body of enactments casts upon the practicing lawyer, rather than to describe the effect of legislation upon society or the law. The student is schooled

---

[56] What may be accomplished where there have been opportunities for social science research is illustrated by JACOBS, CASES AND MATERIALS ON FAMILY LAW (1931) (prepared for students at Columbia; not printed), which was preceded by a study supported by the Rockefeller Foundation. See RESEARCH IN FAMILY LAW (1930), Jacobs, editor. The case book includes excellent statistical materials. At the same time, there are great gaps which show the need for further economic study. The chief defect of the work seems to be the overemphasis on historical materials, including old cases and much extra-legal material which have no demonstrated present day relevance. In the field of torts, only the earliest beginnings have been made. To say that a torts case presents a problem of allocating risks does not go much further than to say that it presents a problem of who should win. The important thing is to bring to bear the pertinent economic materials on the question of risk incidence. Who should pay? To what extent can the cost of industrial risks be shifted by legal rules? What are the economic considerations in torts cases where there is no problem of allocating risks among various groups? Does liability without fault promote care or does it do the reverse? How do the basic assumptions of tort law fit into modern economic society? While the questions are raised, the answers are not found in Holmes, *Agency* (1891) 4 HARV. L. REV. 345; Laski, *The Basis of Vicarious Liability* (1916) 26 YALE L. J. 105; Smith, *Frolic and Detour* (1923) 23 COLUMBIA LAW REV. 444, 716; Douglas and Shanks, *Vicarious Liability and Administration of Risk* (1929) 38 YALE L. J. 584, 720. One completed study which shows promise is the REPORT OF THE COMMITTEE TO STUDY COMPENSATION FOR AUTOMOBILE ACCIDENTS (1932). This demonstrates conclusively the unworkability of the common law rules of negligence, as administered by the courts, in regard to traffic hazards. It suggests a plan of compensation without regard to fault, the funds to be supplied by insurance and administered by a commission. For a description and critique of the Report, see Smith, Lilly and Dowling, *Compensation for Automobile Accidents: A Symposium* (1932) 32 COLUMBIA LAW REV. 785.

[57] MCLAUGHLIN, CASES ON THE FEDERAL ANTI-TRUST LAWS (1930) contains probably as much relevant extra-legal materials as any other work of the same type. Nor would FRANKFURTER AND DAVISON, CASES AND OTHER MATERIALS ON ADMINISTRATIVE LAW (1932) or SAYRE, CASES ON CRIMINAL LAW (1927) suffer by comparison. In regard to specific courses, no lines can be drawn on the basis of schools. Most, however, have a long road to hoe. For example, the Columbia class in trade regulation begins with a survey of marketing problems. It describes the various marketing agencies and their functions. It weighs the economic pros and cons of advertising and the middleman. Its treatment of resale price maintenance and of exclusive dealing agreements is accompanied by really first rate presentation of economic source materials. But other phases of the course, just as well suited to treatment in the same terms, are handled in much narrower and more legalistic fashion: *e.g.*, trade boycotts and inducing breach of contract.

in how to present most effectively before courts those cases in which statutory materials are involved.[58] The course is infinitely better than no course. At least it shows the student that there is more to law than the common law. And dealing—in any fashion whatever—with the factual basis of due process cases, reveals the law as a resolution of vast social interests more clearly than do most private law subjects. But the major possibilities of the subject are neglected. The study of legislation should be the basis for a survey of the law in terms of its social and economic effects, for an assessment of what the law as a social instrumentality does, can do and should do, and for a stimulation of interest transcending the business of client serving.

Probably more important than a special course in problems of legislation is the extent to which legislative problems find a place in individual courses in private law. This is bound to be the case because a course in legislation must be generalized; while the pressing need is to consider the possibilities of legislation in regard to particular shortcomings in the various branches of private law. Such a need is not met appreciably better in the new schools than in the traditional institutions.[59]

VI

The pioneer step has been taken at Columbia of requiring first year students to pass a course in the development of legal institutions. The most general claim made for the genetic approach in the social sciences is that it helps us to understand "how we got to be what we are."[60] However, serious doubts may be raised as to whether this objective is largely obtainable. Of course, the events of the past can be ordered in an historic sequence culminating in the present. But it is of little value to know that we have arrived at our present state by an historic process. To possess significance, the chain of events must be woven into a pattern with a causative theme running through it. In many instances such thematic development is mere *ex post facto* specu-

---

[58] For this purpose, the due process cases are introduced as illustrative of how courts are influenced by the factual basis of legislation and by legislative procedure. For the same reason, the course stresses problems of statutory intent, legislative sanctions and subordinate legislation. The casebook used is PARKINSON, CASES AND MATERIALS ON LEGISLATION (1932).

[59] Again the uniform acts are not neglected. And in torts at both Columbia and Yale, the principle of risk distribution is illustrated by the workmen's compensation acts. In addition, the REPORT OF THE COMMITTEE TO STUDY COMPENSATION FOR AUTOMOBILE ACCIDENTS, *supra* note 56, was discussed in the torts course at Columbia during 1932-3. By neglect of legislative problems is meant that such study is confined to cases where (a) legislation has been enacted or (b) there are well known proposals for legislation to cover fields where the common law is unsettled or where the common law rule works a long recognized hardship.

[60] See BARNES, HISTORY AND PROSPECTS OF THE SOCIAL SCIENCES (1925) 3.

SOCIAL OBJECTIVES IN LEGAL EDUCATION 459

lation.[61] Even where history does help us fully to comprehend origins, there are innumerable instances where such knowledge has no utilitarian value. One need not always know the past to understand the present in the sense that one must know the joys or scars of childhood in order to appreciate the full grown man. For example, the social utility of a law must be tested in terms of how it works today; and on this point there is no help to be gained from discovering the origin of the rule. For even if it can be shown that the social needs which gave rise to the rule have disappeared, the decision as to whether the rule serves some other worth while purpose today can be answered only by examining the contemporary scene. Appeals to history must yield ground to faith in action.[62]

Of course, what has been said is a *caveat* rather than a prohibition. So long as we retain faith in the experimental method, we cannot discard entirely the trials and errors of the past. To know the effective limits of legal action, we must observe how the law has worked in particular situations. This involves historical study, but it should not be confined to a single plane of inquiry. It is not enough to trace the internal development of legal rules. It is necessary to pose the further questions: why were the rules made; did they accomplish the purposes for which they were created; did they frustrate their own ends, create new aims and refashion society along lines unanticipated by their formulators. Such an exploration of the interpenetration of law and society must draw heavily upon the other social sciences.

This dependence upon the other disciplines goes further. It is impossible to survey and interpret the limitless phenomena of the past. If historical research is to avoid the aimless eclecticism and the purely cultural connotations which characterize it today, and to serve purposes

---

[61] *Cf.* Pound's criticism of the legal historian's illusion of perspective, INTERPRETATIONS OF LEGAL HISTORY, 19-20: "For when we look at the rules or the decisions or the texts of the past, through a rationalized medium of legal analysis and system, in a different setting from that in which they took form and were applied, we look at them for the purposes of present problems and with the ideas and the setting of the present before us. It by no means follows that what we see thus through the spectacles of the present is anything that was applied actually to the decision of causes anywhere or at any time. It is more likely to be an idealized reflection upon the legal problems of the present in terms of the texts of the past." And see M. R. Cohen, *The Social Sciences and the Natural Sciences*, in OGBURN AND GOLDENWEISER, THE SOCIAL SCIENCES AND THEIR INTERRELATIONS (1927) 437, 449.

[62] Holmes has long predicted the declining position of history in the law. "The present has a right to govern itself so far as it can; and it ought always to be remembered that historic continuity with the past is not a duty, it is only a necessity. . . . I hope that the time is coming when this thought will bear fruit. An ideal system of law should draw its postulates and its legislative justification from science." *Learning and Science*, in COLLECTED LEGAL PAPERS, 139; *cf.* 187, 242. Pound writes in a similar vein. INTERPRETATIONS OF LEGAL HISTORY, 11.

suggested above, the course of inquiry must be responsive to important social problems. This means that until adequate familiarity with these problems and with more varied techniques is possessed by the law teacher, he will have no chart by which to guide the scope and direction of historical inquiry.

The Columbia course, while very informative, does not meet these criteria. The political motif runs through the first half of the course: this restriction to a single plane of inquiry seems calculated to mislead. The latter half deals generally with the development of law through custom, precedent and legislation, and concludes with a chapter tracing the effects of intellectual and social factors upon a single legal doctrine. But no effort is made to focus history on contemporary problems; and it is doubtful whether a sufficient basis is presented for evaluating the relative parts which can and should be played by the various factors in legal change.[63]

VII

The newer tradition in legal teaching wants to broaden its field of endeavor. But it is walking on stilts. Not having a sufficiently integrated knowledge of the social sciences to bring them before the student, it nevertheless seeks to do so. As a result, it builds a vast framework of generalities but covers it with inadequate or poorly selected or irrelevant concrete materials. If there is a bright future for legal education, it is because of the promise offered by the zealous pursuit of new techniques. This is evinced by the number of teachers from other fields who occupy positions in schools of law.[64] It is indicated by the amount of joint-research that is going on.[65] Something fruitful may develop

---

[63] GOEBEL, CASES AND MATERIALS ON THE DEVELOPMENT OF LEGAL INSTITUTIONS (3d ed. 1931).

In fact, historical inquiry is likely to be profitless unless it arises from some particular need. Much more valuable is the part which a proper sense of historical values can play within the confines of courses throughout the curriculum. The historical abuses of the analytical teachers have been mentioned. On the other hand, Llewellyn's course in sales affords a splendid example of the judicious treatment of history, partly through open introduction of historical data, but more importantly through an organization and selection of materials which attests a silent practice more encouraging than any mere vocalization.

[64] On the Columbia Law School faculty, there is one man from the School of Business, one from the department of economics of the University, two from the department of public law. In addition, numerous men not on the law faculty give instruction in the law school. These include one from the field of marketing, one from insurance, two from economics and one from philosophy. On the Yale Law School teaching staff in recent years have been two teachers of business, an economist, a psychologist, a statistician, a physician and an historian.

[65] At Columbia, joint-research by men from various fields has included work in corporate development, family law, the rules of evidence, compensation for automobile accidents, and the concept of taxable income. During 1932 three publications of significance in the field of law and the other social sciences ap-

SOCIAL OBJECTIVES IN LEGAL EDUCATION 461

from the numerous research projects carried on by students,[66] or from the activity directed toward widening the general sociological concepts of the student body.[67]

Progress must be slow because the teachers have to widen their own knowledge of the social sciences as they impinge on the law.[68] Among the dangers to be guarded against are those of turning out specialists in restricted though novel fields, or setting up graduate institutes far removed from contact with the student body. Another source of error is overenthusiasm for what may be supposed to be the one and only method of the social sciences. The lawyer's zest for certainty can no more be realized by reference to statistics than by deductions from *a priori* postulates. Students suddenly converted to the "new approach" must be warned that economics is as fallible as law; both may profit from a new fellowship.

LEON H. KEYSERLING

COLUMBIA UNIVERSITY

---

peared. These are BERLE AND MEANS, THE MODERN CORPORATION AND PRIVATE PROPERTY; MICHAEL AND ADLER (Chicago), CRIME, LAW AND SOCIAL SCIENCE (1933); REPORT OF THE COMMITTEE TO STUDY COMPENSATION FOR AUTOMOBILE ACCIDENTS, *supra* note 56, by a group of lawyers in collaboration with several members of the law faculties of Columbia and Yale. The Foundation for Research in American Legal History and the Legislative Drafting Research Fund are being continued. Symposia conducted by lawyers and economists are held occasionally. For a full report of research at Columbia, see REPORT OF THE DEAN OF THE LAW SCHOOL for the period ending June 30, 1932, COLUMBIA UNIVERSITY BULLETIN OF INFORMATION, 33rd series, No. 17 (Jan. 21, 1933).

[66] At Yale students in first year seminars frequently study legal problems in connection with the economic background.

[67] One instance of this is the list of readings which Columbia students must complete before the start of their second year. Another instance is the instruction in legal ethics given to first year students at Yale and the new course which Professor Cheatham is preparing at Columbia dealing with the place of the legal profession in American life.

[68] No one has been more candid than R. B. Powell in acknowledging the limitations of his group. *Modern Movements in Legal Education: A Symposium* (1929) 6 AM. L. REV. SER. 402, 406.

[13]

LAW AND SOCIAL SCIENCE: A REPORT ON MICHAEL AND WECHSLER'S CLASSBOOK ON CRIMINAL LAW AND ADMINISTRATION*

By DAVID RIESMAN, JR.†

"LAW and social science" has been shouted by enthusiasts for a quarter century with very little done about it. Legal education has suffered a plethora of programs, first from the school of "sociological jurisprudence" and then from the school of "legal realism." Many of our Benthamic expectations for social engineering through law have been millenarian. As in any area of living, great expectations are bound to create moods of frustration or disillusion, of tired admission that the tried and tested ways are best after all. What has been wanting has been someone who would tackle the job of social science integration, not in fitful law review articles or books, but in methodical and tangible material to be used in teaching in a particular field. Only in that way could permanent advance be made in training a new generation of students. Only in that way could the ambitious programs of the legal realists be given demonstrative substance. Professors Michael and Wechsler, in seven years' joint work at Columbia, have developed such a tool for teaching, now for the first time made available for general circulation as *Criminal Law and its Administration: Cases, Statutes and Commentaries*. This Article will attempt to review the reasons why an integration of law with the other social sciences is important for legal education, to examine the failure of the case-method to provide that integration, and to indicate some of the exceptional contributions of Michael and Wechsler's work to the future of legal education.

CASE-ANALYSIS, SOCIAL SCIENCE AND PROFESSIONAL TRAINING

The case-study of law is certainly not geared, nor should it be, to teach the student what the law is, in the sense of general principles or minor rules. Instead, cases are usually arranged to indicate the historical development of legal doctrine, or to test the extent and application of principles by borderline cases. The settled areas of law are not litigated, and the study of cases teaches the content of the law only as a by-product of teaching how to learn the law as needs arise in practice. Nonetheless, the case-method is often utilized as an inefficient vehicle for imparting settled

---

*CRIMINAL LAW AND ITS ADMINISTRATION: CASES, STATUTES AND COMMENTARIES. By Jerome Michael and Herbert Wechsler. Chicago: The Foundation Press, Inc., 1940. Pp. xi, 1410.

† Professor of Law, University of Buffalo Law School.

doctrine. Such teaching satisfies the poorer students and the poorer bar examinations. But it compares to case study which is scientific rather than dogmatic as memorizing of words and their declensions compares with the general study of language. Brilliant social inventions, which once pushed developments forward onto a new level, seem inevitably in their old age to have a retarding influence. The inventions come to be misused, or reverently modified in small particulars. This is as true of the minor invention of Langdell as of the major methodological innovations of Marx and Freud.

Much case-study is not devoid of import for social science. A well-chosen selection of cases in any field can illustrate the social problem of legal and judicial method. It can show how courts use words and how legal doctrines are developed. As compared with text or office study, the case system of teaching inculcates unusual semantic astuteness and — in recent casebooks — awareness of the complexity of the common law. The method has been criticized because the "facts" in an upper court opinion are pre-digested and selected, so that the student does not learn to marshal and relate events into the frame of legal controversy. But as extended by the study of records, by "problem" cases, by moot court work, by clinics and by legal aid, the case system can provide some analytical training. The results of that training are best exhibited by the lawyer's eye for relevance — an eye (and in the good trial lawyer, an ear) which comes to be almost instinctive. The lawyer can listen to his client's story, pick out the factors relevant to the legal doctrines he knows, and bring them out by questioning, just as a good diagnostician finds out what is wrong with his patient in large part by good history-taking. Anybody who has listened, without interrupting, to clients' stories or patients' histories knows that the average layman's instinct for relevance is feeble. That may be not for lack of training but for lack of mind; I wish to avoid here the psychological controversy of whether there is such a thing as mind-training. The study of law, if it does not develop, does attract the analytical mind, grades it highly, gives it law review advantages and a head start. Analogous to analytical training is the dialectical skill developed by repeated dissection of cases, distinguishing them, arguing with them. This skill is useful to advocates, whether in courts, legislatures, or directors' meetings. With it goes an articulateness, and an ability to bluff — skills fostered by class discussions and by examinations; both with obvious utility for the lawyer. But study of the judicial process aims chiefly at giving the student an informed and sensitive ability to predict what courts will do. Or rather, an ability to predict what they won't do and to estimate the probabilities of their choice among the limited alternatives. Success in business involves similar predictive vision of what competitors and customers may do; politicians' stock-in-trade is artful guessing about voters' choices. This predictive skill, the ability to persuade courts to follow one course rather than another, and the eye for relevance, are gifts of no mean sort.

Today these gifts are not enough for the law student about to enter practice. The lawyer is likely to need more social science than is afforded by case-study of how courts behave. At the time the case system was invented, the lawyer did not need more, or, if he did, more was not available. Moreover, in 1890 a college-educated lawyer did not possess a mental horizon vastly different from that of all but a handful of thinkers. In a more stable world, values were less questioned, and the lawyer, if he did not truly understand his world, thought that he did, and could rule his life according to a syncretistic, consistent, usually ethical, pattern. The triumphs of deflationary understanding of Sumner, Max Weber, Veblen, Marx, Brooks Adams, Freud had not yet burst open the old values, and were not to unsettle the average American until the World War of 1914 or the depression of 1929. Nor did the scientific elaboration of these insights and methodologies — permitting the construction of a revised scheme of values and understanding on a more complex and sophisticated level — get going with its present momentum until recent years. Even an expanded case system, which delves facts from trial records and from Brandeis briefs (both litigious rather than evaluative), and which provides a limited clinical experience in legal aid work, cannot give the student adequate orientation on this level. For neither facts nor experience have meaning without interpretation; and the interpretations worked out by social scientists, though usually controversial and often rudimentary, have become too ramified and systematic to be picked up without explicit study. By the same token, neither chance conditioning nor the smattering of argumentative information which filters through cases or case-records can be relied on to prepare lawyers for their life and work.

Today, the lawyer is counsel to large power-units in society: to government, business, labor, farm cooperatives. As such, he is called upon to organize social forces — in other words, to plan. No course of law studies which deals with cases alone can possibly train lawyers for planning, or for the draftsmanship which is both its symbol and its technique. The student has bent his efforts to constructing legal rules out of case-book cases by inductive reasoning. That is essentially an analytical job. He has used his imagination in extrapolating cases to cover hypothetical situations suggested by his teachers, but he has seldom invented such situations. The draftsman's job, on the other hand, is imaginative and synthetic. He must envisage the controversies of the future, and organize opposed social forces into harmony for the resolution of these controversies. In this kind of prediction, courts are only one of a congeries of institutions, and the case system gives knowledge only of upper courts. The case system's feeling for words is semantic, but the draftsman needs another feeling, creative as well as critical. Planning the future with words, he must compromise divergences with them; he must educate or manipulate congresses and courts and publics.

The social sciences which the lawyer should study for this kind of work are not simply informational; they are also normative. It might be thought that the lawyer need only be told the sort of future his clients desire, and that he can then plan it for them if given the proper tools as part of his professional social science training. If this were true, the lawyer could do without making up his mind about social issues and values. But he cannot. He is called upon constantly, whether he be judge, legislator, or practicing lawyer, to make "policy" judgments. Clients, business or government, don't know what kind of a future they want. They want, partly, what they should have, and turn to their counsel for guidance as men once turned to the clergy. But training in the making of value judgments is not simply useful for lawyers in becoming bigger success boys. The agreed aim of legal education is to turn students into better citizens and community leaders. Even as technicians, the means they use to carry out their clients' policies shape the ends which are achieved. In human affairs, there are no machine tools. The lawyer as technician plays a part in bringing about the future even when he may not wish to, even when he may be unconscious of his role. The historical study of cases can check pharasaical complacence over the present state of the law, and the analytical study can indicate the values which are now immanent in the cases themselves. But a course of studies which is to be responsible for future values must take a transcendental attitude towards past and present expositions of the law.

The difficulties of forecasting what training will be helpful to students five, ten, twenty, thirty years hence are obvious enough. Yet the difficulties are no excuse for not making the inquiry. The inquiry involves much the same kind of investigation that went into Alfred Weber's pathbreaking essay on the location of industry. What law school graduates are actually doing at present should be surveyed, not guessed at, as some indication of what law school graduates may be doing in the future. What they are doing and will be doing, of course, is in part a function of the training they get, though also a function of the opportunities and peculiarities of each locality. Professions do die. New professions arise and belatedly win academic recognition in the form of "schools." Unless the law schools trust in a laissez-faire which is discredited in other areas, they should survey the future's need for special types of trained lawyers to the extent that this can be foreseen. It might have been foretold some years ago, for example, that lawyers would be needed to act as counsel for housing authorities, and as members of housing administrations. A particular school might set itself the task of building a program that would fit men for that job and for related jobs. Its courses in real property and mortgages would be oriented towards the history and present and future extent of the legal control of land use. They would teach the relation between mortgage and conveyance law and land speculation, and the relation of speculation to rural erosion and urban blight. Landlord and tenant law, waste and nuisance and lateral support law, perpetuities and restraints on alienation — these doctrines would be related to the way men live and to current efforts at reform. Zoning, eminent domain, valuation, municipal corporations, taxation (including schemes of differential taxation), tort liability of public bodies, civil service law — all would appear where relevant to housing. The law school would call on the resources of the attached university for architects and city planners, for authorities on case-work and urban sociology. Articulate practitioners and experts in land assembly, real estate management and tenant selection would come in for consultation. The administrative law course might use problems of a housing administration as illustrative material, rather than those of the ICC. Students would, in some degree, come to the school because this program appealed to them, rather than because of tradition or similar irrelevant lure. The community would have a body of trained men who are now wanting. Another school in an agricultural region, attached to a university possessed of a good school of agriculture, might fill a crying need by training lawyers to act as counsel for farm cooperatives or for processors. Such schools and such courses would not only mean that new and important subjects would be explored, but also, necessarily, that new training would be given. Without surveys, our common sense tells us that method-training rather than subject-training will have more useful residue later on. Without surveys, we know that the future will probably see an increase of social controls, of "planning," and that in the American tradition, lawyers are likely to be called on to do the work. Rather than seek to salvage a declining profession by rear-guard attacks on trust companies, unauthorized practice of the law, and administrative agencies, schools can help to develop new fields for their graduates, as well as to expand existing fields to serve larger sections of the population. Only in that way will law schools continue to attract their present bulky share of able and alert young men and women who are seeking a constructive professional career.

Despite this variety of present and future functions performed by law school graduates, matched no doubt by a variety of faculty personnel and of student background and desires, most law schools aspire to be isomorphic. Schools which draw men from all over the country often aim to be all things to all men, rather than to specialize on turning out qualified men for unusual types of counsel-work. And what holds for schools holds as clearly for courses within schools. Not all courses have to be courses in draftsmanship or planning. But certainly three years are not required to teach judicial method through the study of upper court cases. Like the division of labor which should take place among schools, the division of labor among courses is a question of balancing personnel, library resources, community needs.

Theoretically, almost any course could serve as a vehicle for training lawyers in methods for present and future needs. But, for the initial experiment, criminal law has advantages (beside the absence of pressure for laying out the law) of which the classbook of Michael and Wechsler makes most striking use. In the first place, social science data, though inadequate, are more extensive here than in most other fields bounded by the course-concept. The "crime problem" has called forth a wealth of literature, of surveys, of journalism.[1] Some law students will have had courses in criminology, or will have dealt with it in survey courses in urban sociology. In the second place, criminal law is the law about which laymen mostly talk, and about which law students and their friends and families have vehement opinions, interest and, occasionally, first-hand experience. In the third place, criminal law raises the ultimate problems of social control more starkly, more inevitably, than do other subjects. It is obvious there that social pressures come to focus in administrative action by officials, and that bearing on the criminal law are ethics, politics, criminology, social science methodology, economics, and psychology. Similar pressures and problems are hidden in the interstices of all the substantive law courses. But capital punishment, the third degree, entrapment, the right to shoot fleeing felons — these, and a host of problems like them, must necessarily rouse controversy by their very statement. Finally, as a first year course, criminal law offers an opportunity to orient students at once in constitutional law, statutory interpretation, administrative law, labor and civil liberties problems. Postponement of these matters runs the risk of allowing common-law habits of thought to become irremovably fixed, weighted as they are with all the respectability of tradition and the skill of long-experienced teachers.

Members of the bar, as prominent citizens, have a responsibility for the "crime problem." The public's derogation of lawyers because of general mishandling of crime gives the bar special incentives towards improvement of criminal administration. Lawyers can assume a central position as public officials, as voluntary defenders, as vigilant and informed critics and reformers of criminal law, procedure, and administration, and as professional protectors of civil liberties.

---

1. A periodical, *The Journal of Criminal Law and Criminology*, is devoted to it exclusively, as are many European reviews, while there are no law journals devoted to contracts or torts, sales or agency — let alone to the social implications of these subjects. See the thoughtful article by Professor Cavers, *New Fields for the Legal Periodical* (1936) 23 VA. L. REV. 1.

The Organization of Courses and Curricula

It is training for this professional position, as well as orientation in the methodology of social control, that Michael and Wechsler's volume seeks to give. The book is divided into four parts. The first part is an introduction which outlines the contents and methods of the course, and broaches the basic philosophical problems of the criminal law. The second part is *The Prevention of Socially Undesirable Behavior;* the third, *The Problem of Criminal Responsibility*; the fourth, *The Problem of Conflicting Values*. These titles alone reveal a profound difference from orthodox casebooks, which arrange their cases in legal rather than social categories: offer and acceptance, presentation, last clear chance, or, in the criminal field, first by crimes: murder, larceny, rape, etc., and then by defenses: insanity, compulsion, mistake of fact, etc. Since Michael and Wechsler's part on *The Prevention of Socially Undesirable Behavior* contains the materials on the various crimes, and the part on *The Problem of Criminal Responsibility* contains materials on the various defenses, it may be asked what difference the label makes. There has been a good bit of ridicule of the now so popular renaming of courses: turning agency and corporations into "Business Organizations," and sales and bills and notes into "Contracts II." Moreover, any given material can logically or analogically be organized according to various schemes of equal inclusiveness, and any scheme struggles vainly against the necessity for understanding all of the material before any of it can be fully comprehended. And a teacher can pattern his own course differently from the consecutive plan suggested by the editor. Nonetheless, the label does make a difference, as any advertiser knows. The headings in a casebook are often the teacher's or student's only clue as to how the compiler viewed his field. It indicates which problems he deems to be central, and which peripheral. Whether we go all the way with Kant or not, the categories in which we view "reality" are obviously of vital importance. The categories "economics," "political science," "psychology," have limited, as well as directed, our thinking about social problems. A division of a criminal law course into categories of "larceny," "arson," and "insanity" will tend to engender one kind of attitude, and "prevention of socially undesirable behavior" and "the problem of conflicting values" another, preferable, point of view.

The problem of the organization of the body of law and related materials within a school curriculum is essentially no different from the problem of its organization within a course. If anything, the propagandistic need for a socially significant plan of organization is greater for the curriculum as a whole, since the area to be correlated is enormous and since the division into "courses" taught by different men imposes an initial obstacle. Students fail to relate their common-law courses despite the similarity of methods and materials. In crimes and torts, for example, in the face of the obvious overlapping of the objectives of what is called criminal law and what is called tort law, a coherent view of controls of deviant behavior through law is seldom achieved.[2]

Professors Michael and Wechsler do not feel themselves bound by prevailing curricular morphology. They follow the trail of their specialty, criminal law administration, whether or not it leads into the domains of other courses. From the course in personal property, they take what they need to present the history of larceny, making use of Jerome Hall's pioneering *Theft, Law and Society*. From the domain of legislation, they borrow cases like *McBoyle v. United States*[3] to indicate problems of construction. They treat the constitutional and legislative issue of uncertainty in statutory definition (the *Cohen Grocery* case,[4] the *Nash* case,[5] etc.) along with the debate over the creation of common law crimes, and with cross-reference to the extensive case material on conspiracy; a Hague Court case coming up from Danzig indicates the Nazi approach to the same problem. These questions lead on into the most complete collection yet made of civil liberty materials, comprising in addition to the leading Supreme Court decisions relevant matters which are not "constitutional law": criminal libel, civil rights laws (including the important *Powe v. United States*[6]), wire tapping, the third degree, and vigilantism. Adjective law appears as it bears on specific substantive issues: burden of proof appears in connection with the burden of showing justification for homicide, and again in connection with the insanity defense; presumptions turn up in connection with receiving stolen goods and "disorderly conduct" laws; testimonial issues are raised by hypothetical questions to insanity experts.

The usual curricular divisions have left obvious lacunae. Just as many casebook-makers have sought to fill gaps by a simple process of addition: adding statutes, or "fact" material, or footnote citations to other cases and to law journals; so the curriculum-makers have added subjects to the curriculum: writing courses to teach research and organization of material; courses in labor law, corporate reorganization, government control of business to bring in economic materials and relate law to public policy;

---

2. Even where the same concepts are employed, such as negligence or intent, students fail to draw either parallels or discriminations. Torts negligence is Mr. A's "negligence," Monday, Wednesday and Friday, at 2:00; crimes is Mr. B's "negligence," Tuesday and Thursday at 9:00. Personal experience in teaching both crimes and personal property to first year men demonstrates that the use of different books, different hours, and different names for the hours overbalances efforts to deal with the concepts of possession and property as a whole, running through theft as well as many of the problems in personal property.

3. 283 U. S. 25 (1931).
4. United States v. L. Cohen Grocery Co., 255 U. S. 81 (1921).
5. Nash v. United States, 229 U. S. 373 (1913).
6. 109 F. (2d) 147 (C. C. A. 5th, 1940).

courses in administrative law (where they are not concentrated on delegation and judicial review) to examine the problems and procedures of administrative agencies; courses in comparative law (where they are not surveys of continental systems) to broaden the critical base for understanding a segment of American law; courses in legislation to rub students' noses in statutes, and perhaps deal with drafting on a modest scale (though many legislation casebooks simply deal with the judicial process as it controls the legislative process or interprets statutes); courses in legal history to trace the development of earlier legal doctrines; courses in jurisprudence (where they are not taxonomic studies of what has been thought and said) to raise permanent ethical and epistemological issues in the law. Neither in casebooks nor curricula is there any systematic attempt to relate law and social science as a whole. All law is public law. The more "private" it seems, the more difficult, and therefore the more necessary, to display its public implications in the classroom. All law worth teaching involves legislative problems, which can be illumined by comparative examples and by economic, political, or psychological analysis. To label a series of elective courses as "comparative law," "legislation," "jurisprudence," etc., persuades students and faculty that these essential approaches to all law are remote, "cultural," frilly dressings to the main dish of cases.

The consequent hostility to comparative and legislative materials prolongs the parochialism of the common law. By limiting legal studies to a particular type of institution, it keeps those studies from having any universal quality. Mere description or classification is not science. The failure to generalize is perhaps the most important factor preventing law from assuming its full status as a social science, in addition to its special, non-generalized status as systematic, sovereign definition. This failure gives a truncated answer to the critical question: what is law? It confines law to the study of the past or predicted conduct of officials who are judges or jurymen within a particular jurisdiction, rather than making it include the regularized conduct of officials everywhere, no matter what they are called. In the second place, common law parochialism tends toward a positivistic definition of and attitude towards law. If law is considered to be merely what goes in a particular jurisdiction or system of jurisdictions, critical and even normative slants implicit in comparative studies are likely to be excluded. To be sure, the presence of some fifty American jurisdictions minimizes the evil and curbs the ever-present tendencies towards Blackstonian rationalism and smugness. But these systems spring from a common source, and by failure to compare (at least within the culturally relevant and linguistically feasible limits of Western civilization) we unnecessarily confine the available alternatives for the law's adjustment of pressing social problems.

CRIMINAL LAW AND ADMINISTRATION AS A SOCIAL SCIENCE

Michael and Wechsler make law a social science by being steadily comparative, legislative, and jurisprudential—drawing upon the resources of the other social sciences to explain comparisons, assist legislation, and give content to jurisprudence. Where other compilers use illustrative cases, Michael and Wechsler incline to the use of illustrative statutes; reports preparatory or supplementary to legislation, such as the Criminal Law Commissioners' Reports and Macauley's Notes on the Indian Code, are extensively excerpted and cited. Robbery, arson, burglary are presented by selected statutes, with cases as annotations. The procedural distinctions between larceny, embezzlement, and false pretenses are dealt with as a problem in statutory consolidation, exemplified by the New York, English, Massachusetts, and California statutes, with several leading cases indicating the techniques and problems of interpretation. Even the common-law rules as to homicide are illumined in part through American declaratory statutes or through the codifications of the Cyprus and British Indian codes. Italian and Soviet homicide statutes are included for comparison.[7] Thus comparative law is not taught simply by juxtaposition, but is made an integral part of the entire book.

The authors have drawn upon collaborators from other social sciences wherever possible. Such collaboration is essential for any far-reaching researches which cross the railroad tracks separating law from the other social sciences. Collaboration need not necessarily be personal; where the relevant studies have been published, they can be read. Michael and Wechsler have ransacked the literature with exceptional thoroughness and imagination. A glance at the 24-page table of articles, books, and other publications shows the inclusion of such recondite sources as Catherine II's instructions to Commissioners Appointed to Frame a New Russian Code; of such fugacious pieces as articles in *The Nation* or in various trade journals, and newspaper accounts of criminal trials and vigilante activities; of the seldom-cited but valuable reports of a century of efforts by reforming and investigatory bodies. By this unremitting attention to efforts at law reform, past and present, they give their book a sense of social movement, even hopefulness, lacking in casebooks whose sense of progress is confined to the decided cases. They reprint the writings of alienists like Singer and Zilboorg as well as those of Stephen and

---

7. The Italian penal code was chosen for comparison, here and elsewhere, rather than French or German codes, because it is the product of the "advanced" Italian criminological movement. Like the Soviet code, though less self-consciously, it marches under the banner of "measures of social defense" rather than the more traditional slogans common to the United States and the countries of Western Europe. Comments relating the Italian code to the Anglo-American materials, particularly useful in the tricky fields of attempts, conspiracy, and mistake, were written for inclusion in the volume by Professor Nino Levi, formerly of the University of Genoa.

Ferri for their bearing on insanity and feeblemindedness; psychoanalytic literature has influenced the authors' approach to questions of deterrence and motivation. In dealing with juveniles, they set forth, in addition to legislation in New York, Italy, and Russia, and several leading cases, the Youth Correction and Youth Correction Authority Acts of the American Law Institute and Professor Waite's comments thereon, extracts from *The Forgotten Adolescent,* and Michael's extended book review of the Gluecks' *One Thousand Juvenile Delinquents.*

But reading the literature is not enough where it is sought to get at unrecorded practice — unrecorded because unapproved, or recent, or taken for granted. Here, personal contacts have been made. The authors or their assistants have talked with policemen and fire marshals, with insurance officials and grandjurymen, with parole officers and district attorneys, with victims of theft and with reformers. In the field of theft, for example, the classbook indicates the crucial importance of fences; the use of the criminal law as a club to force civil recoveries, especially in embezzlement cases, and the administrative difficulties of law enforcement where restitution has been made; the dubious roles of insurance companies and "no questions asked" advertisements in condoning theft.

In reprinting such materials, Michael and Wechsler are not simply eclectic. Prevailing theories of liability are related to the authors' own analysis of the ways in which the criminal law can and should operate, that is, to the question of what behavior it is possible and desirable to deter. Nor do they include criminological data merely because interesting; where, for example, they reprint three case histories of thieves, they do not leave to chance the interpretation of these probation officers' reports. They write:

> "Whatever the significance of statutory penalty variation in marking extreme limits, the heart of the sentence process is the exercise of judicial and administrative discretion. This is especially true in dealing with non-violent theft where statutory minima are rare, the injury often reparable, the crime not commonly terrifying and the demand for severity frequently subdued. To picture the working of discretion with precision and detail is necessarily a task for special investigation. The following case reports do no more than illustrate typical problems of the sentencing judge and suggest the type of assistance that may be obtained from competent pre-sentence investigation."[8]

Thus, legislative, comparative, and sociological materials are organized insistently around the central questions of legal and social policy: how does one decide what behavior is socially undesirable; what sorts of behavior should be made criminal; and what should be done with per-

---

8. P. 569.

sons who engage in criminal behavior, or in behavior which is indicative of dangerousness? In demanding answers to these questions, Professors Michael and Wechsler do not view the criminal law anthropologically, as do the emancipated realists — as a question of folkways. They believe in evil, which is a necessary condition for achieving good. The question of what is good is raised at the outset, in presenting the argument between positivists and retributionists; and the authors never let the student forget that civil liberty problems are inherent in all criminal law administration. The folkways are to be studied, in addition to ethical theory — ancient, medieval, and modern — for suggesting, though not controlling, what is good; and for indicating the limits of effective legal action in the achievement of any particular goal.

The first goal discussed in the book is the prevention of homicide, the undesirability of which is not open to serious question. The extended discussion of homicide focuses around two related problems: legislative individualization and administrative individualization. The distinctions between the degrees of murder and manslaughter, the problems of intention and negligence, of the felony-murder and misdemeanor-manslaughter rules — these are viewed from the standpoint of the critic of present and the draftsman of future penal codes. These legislative problems are considered with deterrence and reformation as the objectives of treatment, and nullification and administrative convenience as limitations. Whereas case-by-case treatment fosters the pigeonholing of decisions, a process aided for lawyers by the careful but unimaginative indexing of their paid retainers, *Shepard's, Corpus Juris,* etc., the legislative approach broadens the range of analogy and the choice of alternative policies. The labels: murder, manslaughter, non-criminal homicide, are subordinated to comparisons, in terms of social undesirability and the limits of effective legal action, between, for instance, the intentional killer who unreasonably believes he is justified in self-defense; the negligent killer; the killer who makes a mistake of law.

The problem of administrative individualization within the limits permitted by legislation is especially pointed up by the homicide field because of the discontinuous gradation between capital punishment and imprisonment, even for life. The authors give English and American figures on the actual use of the death penalty, and quote prison officials on the deteriorating effect of long (over ten years) prison terms. The famous Romilly-Paley debate (1810) over rule versus discretion in capital punishment is reprinted, as are excerpts from the report and minutes of evidence of the Select Committee on Capital Punishment (1930). The authors, here as elsewhere, include textual comments of their own, many of them taken or developed from their article, "A Rationale of the Law of Homicide."[9] Executive clemency, judicial discretion, jury discretion (statu-

---

9. (1937) 37 COL. L. REV. 701, 1261.

tory) and jury nullification, and sentencing boards, are dealt with as agencies of mitigation, extant or possible. The offered materials include, for example, messages of the Governor of New York in pardon or commutation cases, the few court opinions on sentence, and statistics on probation or suspended sentence. The problem of sentencing is kept in the foreground not only by these separate materials devoted to it but by footnotes to the cases in other sections, calling attention to the penalty imposed and its relation to the maxima and minima provided by statute. But the administrative problem — what should be done in a particular case — is always subordinated to the legislative problem — what is the design of a just and administratively workable penal code?

THE RISKS AND REWARDS OF SOCIAL SCIENCE STUDY FOR LAWYERS

There is no denying that these problems are difficult to teach. The usual case-course either tests the extent of substantive law principles by borderline cases, or presents the historical development of the principles by a series of cases chronologically arranged. Class discussion runs usually to "stating the case," discussing the soundness of its reasoning within the doctrinal framework of the other cases, and distinguishing cases which resemble the stated case. Sometimes there is debate as to the merits of a "majority" or "minority" point of view, usually revolving around the two "leading" but opposed cases which follow each other in the casebook, each trailing its footnote citing the other decisions in accord. This debate is the form of exercise students are provided for developing their sense of justice and their sense for social problems. The usual hypothetical case question: should the conviction of defendant be affirmed or reversed on appeal, is simpler by far than the problem questions which Michael and Wechsler append to each section in the book, or utilize in the course examinations at Columbia. Take for example the questions following the materials on violation of property rights accompanied by danger to the person:

"(1) What is the nature of the evil or evils threatened by the various kinds of behavior comprehended within the categories of robbery, extortion and criminal coercion?

(2) What significance should be accorded to the following factors in distinguishing criminal from non-criminal coercion:
  a. The nature of the injury with which the victim is threatened?
  b. The immediacy of the injury?
  c. The nature of the act demanded as the price of avoiding the injury?
  d. If the person who will be injured and the person to whom the threat is directed are not the same, their relationship, if any?

e. The ends which the person making the threat seeks to achieve?
f. The means employed to express the threat?

To what extent are these considerations legally material (a) in New York and (b) in England?

(3) Viewing the New York robbery, extortion and related statutory provisions as a unit:

a. To what extent do the various sections overlap?
b. What treatment discriminations do they make?
c. To what extent are the treatment discriminations justifiable or unjustifiable?

To what extent are they significant?

(4) Is the statistical data with respect to the treatment of persons convicted of robbery in New York of any value (a) in evaluating the statutory provisions or (b) in guiding administrative policy? If so, in what respects?

(5) In what respects do the English and New York statutes differ? Which is preferable?"[10]

How can students be taught to answer questions like these? Some will fail. With others, the problem is, in part, one of making statutes teachable. The case method continues to hold sway partly because cases, though seldom "literature," make easy reading. They are discursive, concrete, and, especially in criminal law, dramatic.[11] Statutes are abstract, unliterary. They require imaginative and creative spelling out, not routine condensation. A statute cannot be skimmed, and does not appeal to most students, who become rigid common-law lawyers on the day they enter law school, sharing with their elders at the bar an unwarranted admiration for judges as compared with legislators and administrators. Michael and Wechsler have no panacea for this problem. Their homicide statutes are gathered in an appendix, and appendices, like footnotes, are "skipped." New York students will read New York statutes because that is their "law," but balk at Massachusetts or California, and ignore India or Italy. In other words, they will study cases comparatively but not statutes. This comparative law method is fashionable for cases, for it has behind it the prestige of the big Eastern "national" schools where most casebooks are manufactured. Moreover, you can sometimes cite an Indiana case as currency before a New York court, but not an Indiana statute. Statutes, however, reveal patterns: they can be compared as cases can for imitation (precedent) and innovation. The English criminal law commissioners made use of Livingstone's code, and Italian statutes have

---

10. P. 400.
11. The very practice of abstracting shows how much padding the usual case contains. (Abstracted cases make up the bulk of case material in the Michael and Wechsler collection, although many of the leading decisions are reprinted in full).

influenced American criminologists. But students habitually think of themselves as advocates-to-be, and not as participants in the legislative process, much less as persons whose views on legislative issues, on public policy, have any importance.

Clearly, however, a class using Michael and Wechsler's book have no reason to resort to case-stating and case-argument of the usual sort. Nor is there any point in searching out and comparing other cases, other text-book theories; the book itself is a reference work, and covers more ground than can possibly be handled in class in a year's two-hour course. Nor will it be profitable simply to ask questions about the material, as it is not possible to add much to the problem questions in the book. As the classbook is recent, the assumed need to keep the students up to date with the advance sheets will not appear for a year or so. How is the hour best to be spent, then? Only in discussion. Discussion on the basis of the concrete descriptive and questioning materials common to teacher and class. Discussion and criticism of the hierarchy of values which Michael and Wechsler set forth at the outset and assume as a frame of reference throughout. Undeniably, many of the student's first thoughts about public policy and ethics will be banal and unsophisticated. So are the first critical and creative thoughts of anyone. The teacher must take the student seriously as he fumbles and explores, and must also compel his classmates to do so. Otherwise, the student will not take himself seriously. He must be made to feel that what he has to say about social policy has weight, and will have weight. It is clear, moreover, that the relation of the book's stimulating scholarship to its pedagogic utility is not very different from the relation of research to teaching in the work of an individual professor. Professors actively engaged in research can acquaint students with how knowledge is gained, how scholars' judgments are formed — aiding the students to discover criteria for their own judgment, on the intellectual side, and showing them what responsible scholarship signifies in the way of investigation and decision, on the moral side. Thus, by example and experience in class, the student can gradually develop the habit of independent thinking about policy and learn to have confidence in his critical and integrated judgments about values. These are the habits essential for Democracy.

But these are not the habits which law students develop today, on the basis of case-training. Some first-year instructors, desirous of turning out hard-boiled professionals, indicate that debates about values and about law reform are "college stuff," and frown on the expression of lay ethical views. Where this teaching takes hold, it tends to turn out cynical relativists. Other teachers try to do more than study the judicial method "realistically." They try to raise social issues under one of the current slogans, such as "balancing the interests," "competing social policies," or "reasonableness." But many casebook cases are only fossils to remind us of departed vitality: "There are laws which are like old houses: they endure and stand upright but no one lives in them anymore." It is inevitable that, where the social problems dealt with in the cases are dead or insignificant, students will be driven again to a cynical conclusion: it doesn't matter how a case is decided: there are always cases either way; pay your money and take your choice. But even where the problems are obviously real and pressing, and even where the traditional over-valuation of common-law wisdom does not stultify criticism, class debate about what is "reasonable" and how the interests should be balanced turns into a bull session. Information and philosophy are lacking on which sophisticated discussion could proceed. Discussion is, therefore, ended at a question-begging phrase about "competing social policies" at the very point where it should properly begin. Consequently, many students tend to develop the opinion that the lawyer does not balance the interests; he merely reflects them. Lawyers are on the mechanical fringe of policy-determination. The law is thought to follow, rather than reflect, the progressive insights of science or the drives of class. The law is like a chaperone at a gay party who is shocked and turns her back on the goings-on but eventually, though covertly, approves them. The lawyer so chaperoned will not study social science — it is strange and different and too difficult. Law is easy, but even there you need a course for every subject on the bar exam. How, then, can you aspire to cope with marginal utility economics or the determination of probable error in statistics or the classification of symbol data in social psychology? Those higher domains where the important truths are examined and revealed are outside the province of a mere legal technician. Thus law, which is the keystone of the arch of public policy, is robbed of vitality and significance. Partly, this is the human foible of seeing the green pastures elsewhere, but partly it is the consequence of pedagogic failure which for three years drowns imagination in technique.

There are, of course, a few schools and a number of law teachers who have made an effort to look over departmental walls. We talk in torts about the distribution of economic risks, in trusts about the economic effect of limiting investment to "legals," in constitutional law about "the national market" or the beatitude of minimum wage laws. But these superficial doses are as dangerous as the proverbial short drink. Able law students are apt to emerge from this training with an alarming confidence in their ability to master any social science. They are jacks of all trades. They evince a genuine scorn for social science, feeling there is nothing they cannot learn in six weeks' time by talking to the experts and reading a few books. Their exceptional case-trained sophistication about the meaning of meaning leads them not only to contempt for social scientists whose use of words is less self-conscious but also to a habit of underrating ideas which are not authoritatively defined.

That this pervasive contempt may in large part be justified is immaterial. It is equally immaterial that a crop of young lawyers may be so able and industrious as to overcome remarkably their handicaps in training. The point is that training, which produces such attitudes, diminishes to some extent the potential ability of these lawyers to work understandingly and critically with what good people and materials there are in the social science fields. Moreover, these lawyers who, without theoretical orientation, rummage around in economics or political science or labor or city planning, run the danger of falling for the current plausible fad, unaware of the controversy in the field surrounding it. The lawyer may carry on the fad after the experts in the field have long abandoned it. Sometimes the lawyer takes an attitude designed to prevent such ensnarement: "It is all bunk. You can find experts on any side of a question; why look into it deeply? Nobody *knows* anything."

These are the dangers in the prevailing shy advances toward social science integration. There are dangers likewise in the traditional case-limited teaching, and this, too, sometimes produces a devastating contempt for the work of other social scientists. Moreover, the assumed incompetence of lawyers to act as responsible individuals is largely a convenient fiction; no one can be judgment-proof. The only solution, then, is to go forward towards the development of a conscious and sophisticated judgment based on the type of thoroughgoing work Professors Michael and Wechsler have exhibited in their chosen field. We must realize in the meantime, however, that failure on our part to take sides on social problems does not always rest on a venial ignorance of social data, or on the naive optimism that in the struggle of opposing counsel the issues will be clearly stated and the right will triumph. "Facts" never determine values. And so we cannot wait for the last word in social science before taking a position; such waiting often really springs from timidity or cynicism or the hypocrisy of "objectivity" — and these are not venial. For they leave a vacuum of good leadership in the community, and if daring and democratic leadership is not provided from within the educational system, destructive anti-democratic leadership is amply provided from without. It is the peculiarity of democratic teaching that while it presents positions candidly, it also asks for criticisms. A student may read the Michael and Wechsler chapter on Civil Liberties and conclude that they are a bad thing, that Sacco and Vanzetti were properly electrocuted, and that the maxim *nulla poena sine lege* is decadent or overcautious. But he cannot read the chapter carefully without knowing that the authors disagree with him and without having to consider as a problem what he may previously have unreflectingly assumed. Naivete and cynicism are the characteristic reactions of today's adolescents, and the law students who succumb to them in turn repeat the legal phylogeny that runs from the simple symmetries of analytical jurisprudence to the revolt from an emaciated logic of Freudian, Marxian, and mixed-breed determinists. Naivete unfits lawyers as practitioners; cynicism unfits them as democratic citizens. Michael and Wechsler are not only informed and critical; they are also ethically vigorous and mature. Their book is proof that the progressive elements in sociological jurisprudence and in legal realism have finally overcome the period of growing pains and can pass free and adult among men. As its pattern becomes a model for the organization of equally inclusive materials around similarly vital problems of social control, we may expect a major shift in teaching, and, consequently, an improvement in the character and competence of the bar.

[14]

THE LAW SCHOOL OF THE FUTURE: FROM LEGAL REALISM TO POLICY SCIENCE IN THE WORLD COMMUNITY

MYRES S. McDOUGAL*

(*The following address was delivered before the Yale Law School Association on June 17, 1947. In the first section, entitled* "From Legal Realism to Policy Science," *Professor McDougal summarizes a proposed reorientation of legal education. In the second section,* "Objectives at Yale," *Professor McDougal indicates the present impact of this proposed reorientation on the Yale Law School curriculum. The Editors of the* JOURNAL *wish to thank the Yale Law School Association for the opportunity of presenting to a wider audience Professor McDougal's views on the function of the law school.*)

FROM LEGAL REALISM TO POLICY SCIENCE

I

FOR several decades the Yale Law School, like a number of other schools, has been inspired by, and has offered effective leadership in a philosophic movement known as legal realism.

The chief contribution of this movement has been to establish the fact that the doctrines, the verbal propositions, commonly called law are meaningful only when located in the total context in which they are being used—in the community process in which people are using these doctrines to effect, or justify, some specific distribution of values.

I do not scorn this movement, though I submit, and expect to show, that, taken alone, its attitudes and methods are not adequate to the opportunities and obligations of our time.

II

To appreciate fully the contribution of legal realism, we must recall the tremendous confusion in legal thinking and action with which it has had, and still has to cope.

This confusion has its roots deep in the distinctive language of the law. This distinctive language has long confused three completely different references:

(1) references that are naturalistic—statements of fact;
(2) references that are preferential—statements of the preferred events, of the values, sought by the speaker;
(3) references that are syntactic—statements of the formal, internal relationship of legal symbols and propositions.

Because of this confusion of reference, the propositions of our dis-

---
* William K. Townsend Professor of Law, Yale School of Law.

tinctive legal language are still too often considered as, at once, a summary of what officials have done, of what they will do, and of what they should do. The more important symbols of this distinctive language, even when restated by the American Law Institute, make a hopelessly indiscriminating reference to the facts of a controversy, to the identifications and demands of the parties, to relevant and irrelevant policies, and to applicable or inapplicable authoritative pronouncements. In their references to facts, these symbols still, to add further confusion, too often commingle the very different perspectives of the parties, the officials, and disinterested observers.

In recent years, the attitudes of observers toward this distinctive language of the law have varied between two polar extremes. At one extreme the uncritical assume that this language has some peculiar, compulsive, autonomous control over social processes—over relations between people—independently of concrete power structures, personalities, and other aspects of the immediate context. At the other extreme cynics deride this language as meaningless. In such extremes of ignorance, it is not surprising that there has been little understanding of the role that authoritative doctrine does, and can be made to play, among other interdependent variables, in affecting individual behavior and social processes in the distribution of values. It is not surprising, further, that little effective effort has been made, in many of the most urgent problems of our time, to clarify community values and to identify the conditions and means of their achievement.

III

To pose in sharpest outline the opportunities and obligations of the law school of the future, it may be helpful now to recall the conditions under which all this confusion arose and to note how such conditions have changed.

It may need emphasis that this confusion has been inherited from a time when we had less highly developed intellectual skills, when we were living in a completely different world, a world of completely different interdependences, and when attitudes toward the proper role and function of law in a community were very different.

This confusion was inherited from a time when people had no realistic understanding of psychology and personality, of how the human mind works, of how it uses words and other symbols, of the basic impulses of the human organism and the patterns of adjustment it makes to differing external stimuli, of how values, demands, identifications, and expectations are structured, consciously and unconsciously, into personality.

From a time when people were unaware of how to clarify values, but labored rather with endless and circular derivations from a metaphysics which posed unanswerable questions and asked for their resolution by methods upon which no two observers could agree.

From a time when people had a minimal insight into group behaviour, social processes, and community institutions, and into the methods by which the conditions and trends, relevant to prediction and control, could be studied. When scientific study of social phenomena was sometimes conceived as a mere quantitative study of movements, without regard to the personalities of the observed and the communications they make to each other.

IV

This confusion in legal thinking and action was inherited from a time –to draw the broader context—when western European civilization was successfully expanding its colonization over the four corners of the globe, annihilating all who resisted or subordinating them as dependents to its imperial power.

It was a time when the way of life which we know as private enterprise, with a minimum of community coercion, was free of any deep concern for its own future.

When men could pursue, secure, and preserve *wealth*, and use private wealth as a base for affecting the distribution of other values in the community, without too much regard for their effects on the community or how the community was likely to respond.

When men could pursue *power* and take for granted the stability of the framework within which they worked, without too much concern for the continuation of the values which gave them their power.

When men could pursue *enlightenment* after their own bent, without regard for the consequences—when men could smash an atom without expecting to smash mankind.

When every intellectual and artistic skill could be concerned with itself and its own idiosyncrasies, with a minimal regard for the community process which produced it and which it in turn affected.

When men could demand *respect* for themselves, without too much sensitiveness to the claims of others.

When differing conceptions of *morality*, of right, were developing with a minimum of effort at harmonizing the differences.

It was a time, in still more general statement, of intellectual and moral specialization and atomization, of the pluralization of interests, when each interest made demands for itself with scant consideration of the social context—a time when there could be elaboration for elaboration's sake and specialization for specialization's sake.

When every person, as well as every group and nation, felt relatively secure in pursuit of its own special interests, unconcerned with the larger whole of society.

When people still felt—despite tremendous innovations and changes in technology, in institutions, and in values—no imperative need to assimilate and integrate the great transformations they were experiencing.

V

Turning now to attitudes toward law, it was a time when law was regarded as legal doctrine only, a peculiar set of technical symbols, and not as the whole of a community's institutions of government, both formal and real—the sum of all the *power* decisions of the community.

When people ascribed to law only the rather primitive function of maintaining order and did not think of it as a positive instrument for promoting and securing all the basic values of the community.

When the court was regarded as the principal and only proper instrument of legal control, without imaginative consideration of the whole range of institutions and practices that can be created, improved, or rearranged for securing community values.

When the full role of the lawyer in the community—his impact on policy-advising and policy-making and, hence, on the extent to which a community can achieve its values—was not clearly apparent.

VI

It needs no emphasis that this is a time which has gone forever.

We all sense today that a very profound change has come over the world. The safety of our country and of mankind as a whole is in greater peril than at any time in history. With this peril to safety, there is, of course, peril to all of our other values. Those of us who cherish a way of life which preserves a maximum of private volition, free from community coercion, can view the future only with the deepest concern.

For this country, the two problems of overwhelming urgency are, first, to preserve our domestic strength and prevent economic depression and, secondly, to preserve our power position and handle our power negotiations in the world community with such effectiveness that we can force a compromise with competing ways of life that will remove the anti-democratic elements, the elements that destroy human dignity, from all.

If there is anything clear today, it is that we cannot achieve our own goals by acting alone and in splendid isolation from our effects on the rest of the world, and the effects of the rest of the world on us. We all know today that there is "a clear planetary indivisibility" [1] of all peoples everywhere, not only as to the minimum value of physical safety, but as to all values—the sharing of power, the production and sharing of wealth, well-being, enlightenment, health, and respect. Men no

---

1. SCHERMAN, THE LAST BEST HOPE OF EARTH 15 (1941).

longer ask for whom the bell tolls. They know it tolls for one and all. They are coming more and more to identify themselves and their interests, demands, and expectations, with all the communities—from local to global—to which they belong. The age of specialization for specialization's sake, of atomization, of pluralization, of sublime indifference, has gone.

With this new appreciation of community and interdependence there is coming also a new appreciation of the role that law can play as a positive instrument of community values—an appreciation of what can be achieved by bringing the important power decisions of the community under real as well as formal community control, and of the rich potentialities that inhere in bringing the best skills and enlightenment of the community to bear on these decisions. People everywhere are beginning to demand more perfect community instruments. They are beginning to show also a necessary willingness to experiment and to give up sentimental attachments to outmoded institutions, practices, and doctrines. Their clear call is for the creation of a law appropriate to the atomic era.

VII

It is, therefore, the opportunity, and the obligation, of this law school, as of other schools, to emerge from the destructive phase of legal scholarship—indispensable though the destruction was—and to center its energies upon conscious efforts to create the institutions, doctrines and practices of the future.

The time has come for legal realism to yield predominant emphasis to policy science, in the world community and all its constituent communities. It is time for corrosive analysis and inspired destruction to be supplemented by purposeful, unremitting efforts to apply the best existing scientific knowledge to solving the policy problems of all our communities.

It is fortunate that today the necessary intellectual skills and enlightenment are at the disposal of any school that wishes to take advantage of its opportunities.

We have a psychology which is daily working new miracles in the understanding of the mind, in disclosing the secrets of personality formation, and in delineating the variables that affect behavior.

We know today how to clarify values into blue-prints for action, without either getting lost in the obsessive elaboration of meaningless absolutes or spending our energies in futile controversy over the relative merits of equivalent means.

We have today a social science that can achieve enough precision in the study of the environmental variables that affect human behavior to found wise policy judgment, without requiring impossible and interminable investigations and without frittering away resources and energies in concern over pedantic trivialities.

Objectives at Yale

It is no doubt superfluous to state that we in this school intend to take advantage of our opportunity and expect to bring to bear, upon the important problems of this new era, all the skills and enlightenment which our resources will permit. We are conscious of our obligation, we have the insight to know what we want and need, and we have confidence in our capacity to do significant work. Though our plans are just in their inception and we have only begun to assemble the necessary skills and staff, we are well beyond the blue-print stage. The level of our aspiration, the range of our interests, the skills we expect to bring to bear, and the energy we intend to spend, may be indicated by reference to a number of recent curricular announcements and proposals:

Beginning with the curriculum announcement for the 1947 Summer Term, I find:

> "RECENT SCIENTIFIC DEVELOPMENTS AND THE LAW.
>
> The scope and purpose of the course is to consider some of the major implications of the McMahon-Douglas Atomic Energy Act and general legal problems raised by this measure for the domestic control of atomic energy. The legislation raises issues of novelty, but, more important, issues of the broadest significance for our social, economic, and political systems.
>
> Among the topics to be considered in lectures and discussions are the following:
> 1. Effect of the release of atomic energy on established economic institutions.
> 2. Atomic energy as a "socialist island" in a free enterprise system.
> 3. The Atomic Energy Act in its relation to general administrative practice. The Atomic Energy Commission as a quasi-legislative and quasi-judicial agency.
> 4. Civil liberties and the control of information.
> 5. The general control problem.
> 6. Fissionables as a new legal entity.
> 7. Atomic energy and patents.
> 8. Federal research policies and science under government.
> 9. Relation between domestic and international control of atomic energy.
> 10. Industrial uses of atomic energy and their legal aspects."

Looking back through the document, I see such items as:

> "LEGAL PRINCIPLES OF COMPETITIVE ECONOMICS.
>
> A study of the operation of the economy and of business practices in the light of the legal principles and problems which are incident

thereto. Consideration will be given to general theories and specific practices which characterize our economy and which arise in the conduct of industrial and financial enterprises. The interrelationship of these theories and practices with legal theories and specific legislation and court decisions will be discussed."

"LEGAL ACCOUNTING AND FINANCIAL ANALYSIS.

The course is designed to integrate law and accounting by examining the areas of rapprochement and divergence in the context of legal issues. The first part of the course will acquaint the non-accountant with the techniques and disciplines of bookkeeping. The present applications of these techniques will then be reviewed principally in the fields of financial statement analysis, controls by and of the corporation, public utility regulation, and a general selection of litigation involving accounting concepts. Underlying the course will be an attempt to test the utility of 'generally accepted accounting principles' as a legal norm."

"CASE PRESENTATION AND NEGOTIATION.

Study and practice in presentation of cases before courts, administrative agencies, arbitration boards, and legislative committees. Special attention also is given to the techniques of negotiation with opposing counsel."

"FRENCH COMPARATIVE LAW.

The objective of the seminar will be to familiarize students trained in the common law with the approaches and techniques of a civil law jurisdiction."

"RIVER VALLEYS OF AMERICA.

A study of the legal problems arising out of the planning for and execution of a program to utilize the natural resources of a major river valley region. In addition to general discussion of the problems, students will undertake individual studies of particular valley projects. . . . It is hoped that eventually a symposium for publication will result."

"THE WORLD COMMUNITY AND LAW.

Law and science as instruments for maximizing representative values [well-being, (safety, health, character) wealth, shared power, respect, enlightenment, skill] in the world community. . . ."

Elsewhere, the speaker and his collaborator, Professor Lasswell, have described the latter course more fully as *The World Community and Law: International and Comparative Law to Promote the Policies of the World Community*, stating,

"We assume that there is today a world community in the fundamental sense that all peoples, whatever their location or function, are interdependent in achieving all the major values of our time—safety; the democratic sharing of power, respect and knowledge; the production and sharing of wealth; the promotion of congenial personal relationships; and the maintenance of standards of rectitude. We recognize, however, that this world community is imperfect in that peoples are not yet fully conscious of these interdependences and have not yet reshaped their institutions to conform to the imperative requirements of these interdependences, and so to release their full potentialities in the production of values.

"It is our purpose to investigate the conditions under which the peoples of the world can be brought to a fuller consciousness and understanding of these interdependences and hence to shape the appropriate institutions.

"The conditions to be studied include, formally stated, the predispositions and environments of peoples the world over. The predispositions of people include the structures of demands, expectations and identifications with which they approach environments. Their environments may be described in terms of a hierarchy of communities—from neighborhoods through metropolitan communities and regions to nations and the world community—in which the representative values are differently distributed and hence present differing degrees of interdependence.

"In investigating these conditions it is our purpose to bring to bear all of the resources of modern psychological and social insight and skill, including the techniques of the newer and critical approaches to the study of law.

"Imaginative exploration of alternatives must include appraisal of institutions and practices, both governmental and private, from global organizations to the personal programs of people who share the same preferences. The institutions, practices and doctrines traditionally known as international law will require a reassessment and a determination of the extent to which they promote or retard the world community, with suggestion of appropriate improvements and alternatives. The study of comparative law as an investigation of the distribution of power and other values in the component communities of the world community can be given a new meaning and fruitfulness."

To give authentic notion of the range and variety of work being undertaken, I read a page titled "Seminars and Honors Work" from the curriculum announcement for the Fall Term 1947. For sake of caution I interject that a previous page presents a series of courses attempting to place all the traditional vocational work of the school in appropriate functional contexts. The list of seminars reads:

Admiralty	*Case Presentation and Negotiation*
Air Transportation	*Communication and Law*

THE LAW SCHOOL OF THE FUTURE

Corporate Readjustments, Mergers, and Consolidations
Criminal Law and Public Order
Current Problems in Estates and Trust Administration in Connecticut
Declaratory Judgments
Fact-Finding
Labor Law II
Labor Relations
Law and the Arts
Law, Science, and Policy
Law and the Industrial Pattern
Legal Aspects of Public Health, and Welfare Administration
Legal History
Political and Civil Rights
Public Control of Business IV: The Control of Competition
River Valleys of America
Security Regulation
Theories of Law
Workshop in Public Control

The full description of the course on *Law, Science, and Policy* may give brief indication of one kind of inquiry which is deemed necessary to bring the best knowledge of the policy sciences to bear on contemporary legal problems. This reads:

> "Law and science as instruments of public and private policy, with reference to selected problems of property and politics. The seminar is designed to test and to apply an analysis of the legal process outlined in publications by the directors of the seminar. New problems are selected each term in order to avoid duplication.
>
> "In the fall term emphasis will be on legal semantics. The distinctive language of the lawyer will be studied in the perspective of what is now known about language as a whole and an effort will be made to relate this distinctive language to the other variables that affect official behavior. Methods of forecasting appellate court decisions and opinions will be evaluated. Basic literature includes the work done and inspired by I. A. Richards, Rudolf Carnap, Edward Sapir, Charles W. Morris, Alfred Korzybski, and others.
>
> "In the spring term emphasis will be on the interrelations of the decision-making process and the structure of personality and culture. The effect on official response of education, experience, temperament, and character will be explored. Basic literature includes the work done and inspired by Max Weber, Marx, Pareto, Malinowski, Freud, Hull, Warner, Dollard, Fromm, and others."

To continue our illustration, some of the most effective work of the school is being done in the field of national economic policy. The most ambitious undertaking in this field is a new *National Policy Seminar*, an interdepartmental faculty seminar, including representatives of the departments of Economics and Political Science, as well as of the Law School. This Seminar is sponsoring research and publication on a number of urgent issues of national policy. Its immediate concern is with appropriate policies for implementing the Employment Act of 1946.

The undergraduate courses in this field of national economic policy, styled *Public Control of Business*, continue to proliferate in an apparently infinite series. The comprehensive conception which underlies these courses may be gathered from a statement by Professor Rostow, before the Association of American Law Schools, of what he and his collaborators are trying to do in the first course:

> "The traditional orientation of those materials is to have some cases on covenants not to compete, passing off, and trademarks and trade names; going on briefly into the field of the Sherman Act. That area of law is one of very great importance to practitioners at all levels of practice, but it is only a segment of the total machinery of our public law for the control of economic life.
>
> "It seems to me essential that the study of such problems should be put in the wider framework of an analysis of our machinery for the control of economic life as a whole. The study of this branch of law should in my opinion give the student an understanding of the interrelationship of our various economic controls, and of the functions to which the banking system, the budget, the tax statutes, our wage policy, and the other branches of our public law for the control of economic life are being directed and should be directed, in order to produce an effective and stable economy.
>
> "To undertake that kind of reorientation of the study of the public control of business does not require either an abandonment or an adherence to the case system as such. It requires, however, the accumulation of materials for the study of new problems in a different perspective, some of which are adapted to study by means of the case method and some of which are not adapted to study by means of the case method." [2]

For final documentation I should like to refer to the program in *Criminal Law and Public Order* under Professor Dession's direction. This program is a striking example of what we mean by the policy-science approach to law and gives promise of becoming as richly creative as any work in the history of the School. It demonstrates, if demstration is still needed, that concern with policy and the utilization of related social science skills not only are not inconsistent with, but are actually indispensable to technical legal instruction on the highest professional level. The program includes a continuing project of research in the use of negative sanctions, in which Mr. Dession has enlisted the collaboration of a variety of social scientists and the support of a foundation interested primarily in anthropology. The viewpoint is as broad as possible, drawing on studies in comparative law and comparative history. The effort is to extend our knowledge of the use of criminal and other negative legal sanctions—the last resorts of any society against destructive order-disturbing tensions—so that they may

---

2. HANDBOOK, THE ASSOCIATION OF AMERICAN LAW SCHOOLS 35 (1946).

more effectively contribute to the promotion of our basic values. The effect is greatly to enrich instruction on the strictly professional level. Students in the various criminal law courses are introduced to the federal specialties in the field as well as the simpler criminal law of county administration. They are taught the procedure and the practice as well as the substantive law. For those who desire it advanced seminars on the graduate level in criminal legislative problems and in legal medicine are available. Once again concern with the larger aspects of a subject and a willingness to utilize allied skills result in the teaching of more, not less, law—and a law which effectively promotes basic community values.

These samples are enough, I hope, to show that our aspirations are not modest and that our emphasis is now primarily upon construction.

There is no reason why we cannot build in this Law School a great creative center for processing the best contemporary thought into programs for *action*, action to maximize the values of all our communities. (*Here Professor McDougal refers to the peculiar advantages which the School has in terms of its location, officers, students, and alumni.*)

With all of these advantages, we hope before too long to become a faculty which is worthy of its opportunities—a faculty which can draw upon the full experience of the past and which can bring the best methods of contemporary science, and the creative flash of insight, to the task of creating the law of the future.

This is what I mean when I suggest that the time has come to move from legal realism to policy science in the world community.

[15]

SOME COMMENTS ON LAW TEACHERS AND LAW TEACHING *..

Roscoe Pound†

WHEN in my fifty-first year of teaching law I look back over the half century, what strikes me chiefly is the entire change in the attitude both of the legal profession and of the public toward the full-time law teacher. In the stories of James Fenimore Cooper, read universally in nineteenth century America, the professor is always represented as a silly unpractical pedant. When I was a small boy an itinerant teacher of penmanship had the title of professor. It is not so long ago that itinerant peddlers of medicine were called professors. I remember a blacksmith in the Eighties who had a sign, "Professor of Pathological Horseshoeing." An oft repeated gibe was "Those who can do, those who can't teach." All this was characteristic of the attitude of the laity fifty years ago. The practicing lawyers had a like low estimate of us. I remember that when I had been in active practice some fifteen years and had sat for a time on the supreme bench of my native state, but came to the Conference of Commissioners on Uniform State Laws with the unhappy label of Dean of the State University Law School, a practitioner from one of the older states, in answer to my remarks upon an inaccurate and badly stated proposition before the meeting, explained that the Conference was not interested in the theories of professors. Law was a practical matter. Likewise forty years ago, when I was urging the need of thorough-going reform of civil procedure as it had come to be in the United States of that time, something which the generation of law teachers coming forward today can hardly realize, a veteran judge in one of our large cities dismissed the matter with the remark that the professor of law had nothing to do but write papers and read them to bar associations, and when he had read one this year he would turn up at the meeting next year and read another.

Today the practicing lawyers know better. They know what law teachers have done in promoting and bringing about better requirements for admission to the bar, what they achieved for reform of legal procedure, what they have done in the Conference of Commissioners on Uniform State Laws, in the American Law Institute, and in the everyday work of bar associations, for improving the administration of justice.

* Remarks before the Conference of California Law Teachers, at Los Angeles, October 4, 1950.
† Law School, University of California, Los Angeles.

519

Simeon E. Baldwin, Governor of Connecticut, Chief Justice of Connecticut, and one of the founders of the American Bar Association, spoke fifty years ago of the danger to the law in the full-time law teachers whom he saw multiplying and replacing the older apprentice-type law schools by the university law school of today. The victory of the university law school in the last generation has become complete and we may flatter ourselves that it has been achieved not merely without danger to the law but with conspicuous profit to it. Yet I fear there may prove to be some basis of truth in Judge Baldwin's prophecy, now that preparation for the bar has been put completely in our hands, if we forget that we are training for a profession and bring up a generation with no conscious responsibility to the law and no deep conviction of the profession as a group of men pursuing a learned art as a public service. The apprentice system of preparation for the bar ceased, under the conditions of practice in our urban industrial society of today, to do the work of handing down effectively the tradition of a profession as distinct from a money-making calling. I fear we law teachers have not found, nor even tried very hard to find, how to do this part of the task which has devolved upon us.

In Hegel's Phänomenologie there is a chapter the title of which might be translated, not inaptly, as "The Intellectual Zoo and its Humbug." Royce translates it, "The Intellectual Animals and Their Humbug." Hegel said that what scholars of a certain type really mean by devotion to reality and objective method in dealing with their subject is that "they are fond of displaying their wits to one another and of showing their paces and of winning applause, and with a touch of the old savagery about them are also fond of expressing contempt for the failures of other men." Academic promotion depended upon the notice a beginner could attract by strikingly original papers and by severe reviews of the writings of others. Much of research and publication was a species of exhibitionism. I do not for a moment suggest that I should be in any wise so hard on my colleagues and friends who are full-time teachers of law as Hegel was on his colleagues and contemporaries whom he mercilessly sketches. But his candid confession of only too natural defects of his calling leads one, as he looks back on half a century of law teaching, to suspect he may see something of the intellectual zoo in our own profession. One thinks, for instance, of the succession of fashions in legal thinking and writing, the "movements" to which everyone must for a time adhere and even carry to an extreme if he is not to be branded as outmoded, unintelligent, unoriginal. In 1890 I came to the bar in the heyday of historical jurisprudence. Every dabbler in jurisprudence took a fling at Austin. Holmes' *Common Law* eight years before had started a cult of the Year Books. Every law teacher who pretended to scholarship had to have a set of the Tottel Year Books whether he could read black-letter law French or not, and to trace the idea in the details of the law of today to its beginnings in oracular utterances of the fourteenth and fifteenth centuries. About 1900 this fashion was succeeded by the mechanical economic interpretation. Marx's economic interpretation of history and Spencer's mechanical sociology, ingredients about as easy to mix as oil and vinegar, could be made into an attractive dressing for legal theories explaining the doctrine of *Rylands v. Fletcher* by differences between the land owning class and the traders in the cities in Tudor and Stuart England, or items in the law of employer and employee by the industrial revolution. About the time of the first World War a new fashion was set by Hohfeld's Hegelian logical analysis of rights which in the hands of its extreme devotees became a universal solvent for every difficult question in the science of law. In the period after that war the fashion changed to Freudian psychological realism, and we got for a time a science of law based on abnormal psychology. Today new fashions are beginning to be set by new types of logical approach; by neo-Kantian methodology or more attractively by a rising cult of natural law and call for a trek back to Thomas Aquinas and Aristotle.

Please understand me. I would not disparage those who gave the impetus to any of the movements that led to these fashions. We owe much to the historical jurisprudence of the last century. Much that we had been taught from Blackstone was straightened out by study of the Year Books. The economic interpretation of Brooks Adams makes us look more critically at much which we had assumed from the *ex post facto* reasons traditionally taught as the basis of legal institutions and fashions. Hohfeld taught us to clear away much rubbish concealed by words with too many meanings. Psychological realism has compelled deeper thinking about and more thorough study of the judicial and the administrative processes. Neo-scholasticism is compelling more serious attention to the theory of values as basic in the science of law, even if some of us are no more than somewhat worried by the give-it-up philosophies which teach that values have no place in a science. What I am seeking to bring out is the enthusiastic eagerness with which law teachers have followed one after another of these fashions, substantially one every decade, and how little has come of the extreme original and striking expositions of detail in terms of one or another in its heyday. The intellectual animals have been kept stirred up in our time as the intellectual zoo was in Hegel's day.

Of the teachers under whom I have sat I must speak of one not a law teacher who had the most influence on me of anyone I have known. Charles Edwin Bessey, professor of botany in the University of Nebraska from 1883 till his death in the second decade of the present century, in a small institution, with meagre facilities outside of laboratory equipment and his private library, which he put at the service of students, in crowded quarters and with none of the clerical and mechanical assistance such as university teachers have today, turned out a generation of botanists and teachers of the natural sciences who took rank among the scientists of his time. He was always at the service of students. He was never so busy, and he was a very busy man, that a student could not see him. He would go through his laboratory and stop to talk with each student, asking what he was doing, why he was doing it, and whether he was finding what he had expected to find. He did not trouble to see whether the student was doing what was prescribed in the text. He assumed that would be done anyway. But he had a real interest in all that the student worked at. Any question or phenomenon or organism, animal or vegetable, would bring suggestions from him about where to look and what to read and how to make the student's temporary interest lead to something which would help develop him to a true scientist. It was a tradition he could not be fooled. He saw who were diligent plodders, who were full of intelligent zeal, and the occasional pretentious trifler. Treating them all with every consideration he easily made the pretender thoroughly ashamed and often turned him to serious honest work. For anyone whom he found at work on something that might prove worth while, he would go into the stacks, pull out a book, and lay it before the student open at a relevant page. Thus far more was learned in his laboratory and in his herbarium than was in the four corners of any course. A tireless worker, he worked with an enthusiasm that was infectious. He got more work out of students than they were conscious of. It was a joy to work for him and one felt that he was working with him. Many years after graduation I came back to the University, as dean of the Faculty of Law, and saw him as a colleague. Here, the same qualities which made him a great teacher stood out. He was always willing to do whatever the University asked of him, and it asked much of him. He was acting Chancellor more than once and was a main reliance of the institution in the struggle to maintain it in an agricultural state far from wealthy and in an era of drought and depression. Through his activities in the agricultural and horticultural societies, to which he was always extremely useful, he was able to persuade a legislature of farmers of the importance of sustaining by taxation an institution teaching the humanities.

Of the teachers under whom I studied law those who stand out are James Barr Ames, John Chipman Gray, and William Albert Keener. Ames had a prophet's eye for what the courts would come to hold, as compared with Gray's sense of what contemporary courts would hold and what arguments would appeal to common-law judges of that time. I did not fully appreciate what Ames had done for me as a student nor while in practice. But after I began to teach I understood better. He had an exceptional sense for the ethical side of the law without expecting to use it as a universal solvent. His quiet but firm insistence on fundamental honesty and good faith made a strong impression on a student which deepened after going into teaching. He was as well a truly great scholar who knew the true role of historical continuity and made us feel the idea in the old books living and growing in the books of today.

Gray was the only one of my law teachers with whom I had any personal contact as a student, although I came to know Keener well when in practice and Ames well later when in teaching. Gray was the embodiment of good sense and sound judgment. No teacher had a keener instinct for how Anglo-American courts would look at things. But what I owe to him chiefly is the interest in Roman law and the civil law in which he set me on the right track at the beginning. What I have been able to do since in comparative law I owe to the good start he gave me. The story is worth telling as an example of what a teacher can do outside of the classroom. In the first volume of his *Cases on Property*, which we were using in the first-year course on property, there were many extracts from the Institutes of Justinian in connection with subjects where the Roman law had come into the formative English law by way of Bracton. As I had had a classical education these attracted my attention and I went to the attendant at the delivery desk in the reading room and was given Lord Mackenzie's *Roman Law*—about as bad an introduction as could have been chosen. It was during the Christmas recess and I was the only student in the room. Professor Gray came in presently and, I suppose, was curious to know what I was doing there. Coming up behind me he saw what I was reading and said in his characteristic somewhat abrupt way, "Don't read *that*." I inquired, "What should I read?" He asked, "Do you read German?" I said I could, and he went into the stacks, took out Sohm's *Institutionen des Römischen Rechts*, which had not then been translated, put it down before me at the subject about which I had been trying to read in Lord Mackenzie, said "read that," and went off as abruptly as he had come. Mastering this book was the beginning of years of private reading and study of Roman law and its development in the modern world. My study of jurisprudence began in my sophomore year in college when my father gave me Holland's *Elements of Jurisprudence*. Hence I was prepared for the short lecture on jurisprudence with which Professor Gray used to begin his first-year course in property. He did not much influence my thinking on jurisprudence because when I began to teach that subject in 1899 I had turned to the historical school. But I can never be sufficiently grateful to him for setting me in the straight path in Roman law. It should be added that he was an all-round scholar. He left a fine private collection of books on jurisprudence, on Roman law, on comparative law, and on the history of English law to the Harvard Law School, and an exceptional library of the classics to the Harvard College Library. He was the finest type of the scholarly common-law lawyer of the last century.

Keener was a born teacher. He was at his best with first-year students, who began by hating him, came to admire him grudgingly, and by the middle of the year swore by him. Third-year students saw that he was no such legal scholar as Ames or Gray, with none of Ames' prophetic quality nor Gray's sure sense of how courts will look at doctrines and theories. But no one could have been better suited to teach beginners the technique of finding the law from decided cases. He had a remarkable power of forcing even the dullest to see a point or follow a train of reasoning by sheer weight of argument. He was a persistent and relentless cross-examiner, catching up everything a student said and compelling him to justify it, ruthlessly exposing fallacies, dragging the student out of all bypaths of argument, and making him tread the straight and narrow path of dialectic whether he would or not. No student of his who in his first month ventured to support an argument by saying that a certain court had said thus and so in a certain case will ever forget the retort: "But suppose the court had said the opposite?" I found that I owed a great deal to him when I had to stand up to some of the masterful federal judges of the last century who liked to put the younger lawyers through their paces.

Of the law teachers whom I have known as colleagues one must put first the dean of American teachers of law, who for substantially fifty years was acknowledged the conspicuous example to all of us of how law could be taught, if only any of us could approach his performance. There is, one need not say, no one method of teaching or kind of teacher. But so far as there can be, Samuel Williston must stand for the ideal. Where Keener drove a class through the sheer force of personality, Williston led it with infinite patience; and by versatility of illustration and transparent clearness of exposition, persuaded it into the paths of logical sequence of thought and reasoning. His entire mastery of the subjects he taught and a sense of what is practicable in the legal adjustment of relations no less than Gray's enabled him to impress what he taught upon his students as a permanent acquisition. What he did for students in the classroom he did no less for the practitioners in the Conference of

Commissioners on Uniform State Laws and in the work of the American Law Institute, and for the law in his great treatises on Contracts and on Sales. In his tenth decade he is still with us, an outstanding example of fruitful scholarship and productive achievement in writing and teaching and in making for the improvement of the law. It was a high privilege to have been associated with him as a colleague for a generation.

Along with Williston one must put his contemporary and colleague for forty-five years, Joseph Henry Beale. Beale was a master of classroom dialectic and his ability to organize a group of decisions on a particular point or in a whole field of the law by a principle or a well thought-out idea made him an exceptionally effective teacher. Ten casebooks, published between 1894 and 1929, more than one of which went through a number of editions, tell only something of his range of interest and ability to systematize. His *Cases on Criminal Law* is still the foundation of more than one significant book in daily use and his *Cases on the Conflict of Laws,* which was standard for a generation, is still the outstanding collection. Indeed he rescued the latter subject from long neglect and made it one of the most important subjects in the law school curriculum. More than one course which he organized bears the mark today of his ability to put a new subject in the order of reason. He was a productive writer and was long a leader in the advancement of legal education and improvement of the law. He was active in the Association of American Law Schools in its formative years. He had much to do with the organization of the American Law Institute, and was one of the founders and a trustee of the Ames Foundation and of the American Legal Historical Society. He was a member of the Massachusetts Commission for Simplying Criminal Pleadings, and had much to do with giving Massachusetts a modern system long before the movement for simplifying criminal procedure in the present century became significant in the country at large. Above all he was untiring in devotion to his life work as a law teacher. I can only repeat what I said of him years ago.

He was untiring in his devotion to the Law School. His resourcefulness and talent for planning were always at the service of the administration. He took on himself willingly whatever was to be done in any emergency, and his ability to organize new subjects and his skill in teaching them led to his being called upon to teach in almost every corner of the curriculum. In everything that he did his versatility, his energy, helpfulness, and good will stood out. He had faith in his fellows and was confident that even the most difficult problems admitted of reasonable and just solutions. He welcomed new ideas and yet held fast to the tried ideas of the past, and was able to combine the nineteenth century belief in historical continuity with the twentieth century belief in the efficacy of effort at improvement. Above all, he had a great heart. He was wholly unselfish and responded to every call and went out of his way to help with unflagging zeal all who applied to him.

Two others whom I had for colleagues in my formative years as a law teacher deserve to be spoken of, Walter Wheeler Cook and George Purcell Costigan.

When Cook, just out of law school, came to Nebraska as a teacher in the College of Arts, I soon saw he was to be a scholar and a teacher of the first magnitude and induced the authorities to put him over into the Law School where he belonged. When later I became Dean of the Law School, he was my right-hand man in reorganizing it. A pupil of Keener, he had Keener's faculty of exposing fallacies and indeed surpassed Keener in general analytical power, although stronger in destructive criticism than in constructive systematic thinking. Later, when I left Chicago to go to Harvard, I urged him upon Dean Hall to take my place and a significant career, well known to you, put him in the front rank of contemporary teachers of law. He did much to improve the level of analytical teaching of the first part of the century and his critical power would be invaluable in the welter of loose thinking of this time. His critique of Conflict of Laws is a living force in that subject today. Unhappily he took little interest in the practicing profession and was not inclined to work with bar associations toward improving everyday administration of justice.

When Cook left Nebraska to go to Missouri, I was fortunate in discovering Costigan then practicing in Denver but not pushing enough to achieve the success in practice which he deserved. He was an excellent all-round teacher, well read over the whole field of the law, and with a marked power of clear exposition and a quiet humor which enlivened critical abstract discussions. He had eminent good sense and was useful in relations with the Bar Association and helping gain for the Law School the confidence of the practitioners. When I left Northwestern to go to Chicago, I recommended him strongly to Dean Wigmore and he proved a valuable man at Northwestern and later at California. He had a strong influence for good in his relations with students, inculcating high ideals of professional conduct and giving them practical meaning. His book on mining law was a real achievement of application of legal theory to a highly practical subject.

I must speak also of two whom I met as colleagues only in summer teaching, who became fast and life-long friends, and had abiding influence upon law teaching.

In the death of Wesley Newcomb Hohfeld at the height of his great powers, while he had yet so much to accomplish with them, the science of law and law teaching suffered an irreparable loss. I came to know him while teaching in a summer quarter at Chicago. Later, when I went to Harvard, he used to come to see me in May, when the school year ended at

Stanford, and used to stay at my house where we had many long and to me profitable discussions; as my wife used to say, staying up most of the night arguing what she called "transcendental torts." For years he and I wrote letters back and forth. He was a prolific letter writer, sometimes covering as many as thirty-six pages of neat and meticulous handwriting. He was well trained in idealistic philosophy and Hegelian logic, and reveled in metaphysical logical controversy. His main interest was in system and his inclination was to treat law as a body of logically interrelated precepts. His work in untangling the meanings of the term "a right" and analyzing the juristic conceptions which had been included in that term was intended as the first step in a system of the law after the manner of the Pandectists, something we still lack in the common-law world. He did not like equity, which cut across systematic lines, and was concerned to force its doctrine into common-law compartments. In the last letter he wrote me, the only short one he ever wrote, he told how he planned to put his Fundamental Legal Conceptions in final form and go on from there to a system of the common law.

He did a great service to the law in bringing home to teachers of law, and through them to practitioners and judges, the importance of more exact terminology. No one has as yet come forward to do the much needed systematic work he planned. He and Cook had much in common. But Cook was primarily critical. Hohfeld was critical but primarily systematic. I once told Cook that I should like to umpire a discussion of equity between them. Cook's approach was positivist. Hohfeld's was idealist metaphysical. Each held to logic. But their logics were quite different.

Henry Moore Bates deserves to be remembered in the history of American legal education. He played a leading part in creating understanding by the bar of the professor of law who was not a retired judge or a retired practitioner or an active practitioner giving a fraction of his time and energy to teaching, and no less in making for understanding of the bar by the full-time teacher who had had no substantial experience in practice. Next to teaching his interests were in legal education, reform of procedure, and improvement of the administration of justice. I came to know him well when we both taught in the summer quarter at the University of Chicago in 1909 and we worked together for years in the American Bar Association, in the section on Legal Education of that Association, and in the Association of American Law Schools. Early in his teaching career he was turned to administrative work as Dean of the Law School of the University of Michigan at a turning point in its development. He was a power for good in the critical time when leadership in training for the bar passed from the law office and the apprentice type of school to the university law school of today. He was a natural leader, of sterling character and attractive but firm personality, a scholar without a scintilla of display, patient except as to trifling by those who should be at earnest work and as to pretense and pseudo-scholarship and wise-crackery; zealous to make the law effective toward the advancement of justice, while not neglecting his immediate task of turning out competent lawyers, forgetful of his own fame and putting aside the writing of which he was entirely capable in order to give first place in his energies to his task as teacher and administrator.

A few words as to three deans under whom I have taught law will complete the picture I am seeking to draw.

John Henry Wigmore was an acknowledged leader in legal scholarship, as a writer of law books, in activities for improving the administration of justice and in legal education. He was a pioneer in and continued among the foremost promoters of the movement for remaking American law and legal procedure to the needs of an urban, industrial society. He will be best and longest remembered for his monumental treatise on Evidence, which is standard throughout the English-speaking world. It has been more than an authoritative exposition for bench and bar. It has its place with the creative law books of the formative era of our law and has been a quarry for those who have been urging a more effective administration of justice. Other notable contributions were the National Conference on Criminal Law and Criminology, organized at his instance and under his guidance, out of which grew the American Institute of Criminal Law and Criminology, the *Journal of Criminal Law and Criminology,* and the Modern Criminal Science Series. Three notable series of translations on philosophy of law and legal history, the Modern Legal Philosophy Series, the Continental Legal History Series, and the Evolution of Law Series, due to his initiative, have had much influence upon the development of the science of law in America. Another monument to his intelligently directed zeal is the American Judicature Society in which he took a leading part from the beginning. Indeed his influence may be seen in every important movement for the improvement of our law in the present century. Above all, he was zealous to assist and encourage beginners in legal scholarship and law teaching. Many a young man who had diffidently published his first paper in a law review was encouraged to enter upon a fruitful career in law writing by an appreciative letter from Dean Wigmore. Not only those who were working for a better administration of justice in America, but those who were doing scholarly work in any field of the law, have owed much to the stimulus of his encouragement and example.

James Parker Hall, like Dean Bates, was called to administrative work early in his teaching career. After four years of full-time teaching, two at Stanford and two at Chicago, he was put at the head of the Law School of the University of Chicago and served as Dean from 1904 till his sudden and untimely death in 1928. He devoted himself to building up a great law school, a school of highest standards rigorously maintained, and brought the institution to a leading place among American law schools. He was the embodiment of high seriousness and conscientiousness, a wise administrator, an effective teacher, a master of the subjects he taught, and he taught many in the earlier years of his teaching, but more especially of the law of Torts and Constitutional Law, which he taught for twenty-five years. He too was active in improvement of legal education and in organizations working for improvement of the administration of justice. He took a leading part in the Association of American Law Schools, in the American Judicature Society, and in the organization and work of the American Law Institute. Much work in the general administration of the University of Chicago devolved upon him and was performed with the scrupulous attention to detail tempered with good sense and sound judgment, which he displayed in every connection. A casebook on Constitutional Law, a model of analysis and comprehensiveness, which held the ground for more than a generation, testified to what he might have done if he had not had the burden of administrative work to carry during all but four of his twenty-five years as a full-time teacher of law. It remains to say that he had a conspicuously good influence upon students because of his dignity, conscientiousness, thorough preparation of everything he did, and insistence upon a high standard of performance of everything. Withal he was the most considerate of leaders, under whom and with whom it was a pleasure to teach. His death at the relatively early age of 57 was a serious loss to law teaching.

Ezra Ripley Thayer, son of a great legal scholar and law teacher and brought up in an atmosphere of law, had scant opportunity to show his powers to the world. Coming to the work of a law teacher, and at the same time to the engrossing work of Dean of the Harvard Law School, at the age of 45, it was a remarkable achievement to meet the measure of his undertaking in five brief and heavily burdened years. He was severely critical and consistently applied his critical powers to his own work. He made repeated redrafts of everything he wrote and probably would never have written much in point of quantity. But he had a keen scent for the cases which were significant in the maze of contemporary law reports, a power of reducing situations to their lowest terms, and a faculty of seeing through a mass of legal materials and perceiving a principle by which the inert mass might be given life. Moreover, although he was a man of positive convictions, he was able to detach himself from presuppositions, to perceive and weigh all relevant considerations, and to look at the larger aspects of a question at a time when so many legal questions were becoming social questions also, without losing his footing upon the solid ground. To some extent his powers are witnessed by a mass of patiently elaborated notes of lectures, critically revised from year to year, which in time would have borne fruit in contributions no less significant than those of his father. Yet these are but feeble testimony, and only those whose fortune it was to listen to him as he discussed the subjects of his study with the grasp and assurance of a master can know how truly he was a great scholar. He had a high sense of the importance of the teaching function and set himself to master this part of his work. He studied a class as carefully as a trial lawyer studies a jury. He was wont to note upon the cover of each examination book, without knowing whose book it was, his impressions of the writer derived from reading it and he kept careful memoranda with respect to the work, the capacity, and the mental characteristics of his students. Also he devoted much time to consideration of methods of presentation, often recording after each lecture his impressions of what he had done and what he had left undone during the hour. This conscientious preparation joined to penetrating analysis, a merciless cross-examining elenchus developed in the forum, to which he submitted his own views no less than the views of others, and an intellectual honesty that shirked no difficulty and tolerated no pretense, made itself felt in steady gain in his hold upon classes from the beginning of his teaching. He had already become a teacher of the first order, and much of the result of his critical study of his vocation was yet to become manifest. What stands out permanently in one's memory of him is his conscientiousness, his loyalty, his devotion to duty, and his considerateness of others.

What characteristics stand out in the great law teachers of the last two generations of whom I have spoken? Above all a sense of their high calling as lawyers and as teachers of law, devotion to duty, and putting forth of their powers to the utmost in the work of the law school and the service of the students. Each set an example to students of unremitting hard work, knowing that students will not work more nor harder than their teachers. Each was marked by thorough-going honesty of purpose and of execution and scorn of all pretence, exhibitionism, or vain display. They all had a deep seated interest in the law itself. They did not seek to limit their teaching to subjects that interested them, although, after much teaching of what was at hand needing to be taught, when there was occasion, they might come ultimately to some subject which the particular teacher had made peculiarly his own, and made more effectively his own because he could bring to bear upon it the knowledge of other subjects he had gained by teaching them. They sought to teach the best they knew what their considered judgment pointed out as most profitable for students to be taught.

Ezra Thayer used to tell with amusement about the young lawyer who wished to go into law-teaching and suggested as what he was to teach "constitutional law and the higher aspects of torts." I can imagine what Ames or Wigmore, or Hall, or Bates, or Thayer would say to the beginner of today who expects to be set at once to teach detailed applications of public law and is impatient of the subjects upon which his mature legal scholarship must build and on which the making of a common-law lawyer must turn. Much less would quest of some novel subject upon which to put out a case book appeal to them.

Note what Ames and Williston and Beale along with the practitioners did in connection with the Conference of Commissioners on Uniform State Laws. Note the stout fight for improved legal education led by Keener and Hall and Bates, and what Wigmore and Beale and Bates did for improvement of legal procedure. All but two of those of whom I have spoken, and those two were great enough to be exceptions to any rule, worked zealously and effectively in cooperation with the bar for improving the administration of justice.

Eugene Wambaugh used to say that the law teacher should take monastic vows of poverty, chastity, and obedience.

It must be insisted that the law teacher is a member of two professions —the profession of law, and the profession of teaching, and owes a duty to each, calling on him to practice a learned art in the spirit of a public service, none the less a public service because it may be incidentally a means of livelihood.

But there are four sources of menace to the professional ideal in the society of today. One, the exigencies of the individual economic existence, has always been with us. It is simply magnified in the crowded world of the time. A second is the multiplication of detail in every branch of learning, and notably in the learned arts pursued by the members of professions. Nowadays those details are multiplied beyond what the individual practitioner may hope to master. There is consequent need of cooperation among practitioners leading to partnerships of many members and huge staffs of assistants, of whom it is easy to think as employees, a term not properly applicable to members of a profession. Cooperative activities of professors with like staffs of assistants are not unknown. If all callings are only money-making activities with making of a livelihood their primary concern, it follows in an economic order in which the great majority are on the payroll of either the government or of some corporation, public, public service, charitable or private, that most of us are in a sense employees and likely to be caught up in a régime of employees' organizations, collective bargaining over wages, and strikes. Organization of lawyers for advancement of the administration of justice and organization of teachers for the advancement of teaching must then give way to organization of employees of every grade and kind of employer for the advancement of wages and dictation of the conditions of employment. Teachers in the public schools have been unionized in more places than one and members of university faculties are now active in a teachers' union in some of our old historic institutions. Thus as things are coming to be, in an era of large-scale organization of all activities and strenuous competitive self-assertion, the professional idea must contend with the rise to power of organizers of an expanding class of employees. This third menace to the professional ideal points the way toward a fourth, namely, absorption of the professions in the service state. The medical profession is threatened with this already. The service state is jealous of public service being performed by any other agency. We may be next.

On another side, the law teacher is being increasingly taken from his work for all sorts of political and governmental tasks. This recognition of what a real, as distinguished from an *ex officio* expert can achieve for the public has a good side. But the teacher who goes into politics and seeks political and governmental positions is another story. He is as much an everyday phenomenon as was the preacher in politics in the Eighties of the last century. Law is a jealous mistress. Law teaching is a doubly jealous mistress. If one's main interest is in anything but his teaching he will be no teacher.

Finally let me say something about writing and research. The term "research" is on every tongue today. We may justly claim it as a function of the law teacher. But let us think of *research*, not merely of *search* for what is already known except to the searcher, and let us insist on quality, not quantity. Wigmore, Williston, Beale, and Scott have been better law teachers for being also great law writers. Yet one who is only a legal scholar and does not put his best foot forward in teaching, while he may acquire kudos for himself and add to the reputation of his school, will be failing in his primary function of law teacher. The law teacher should be a scholar *and* a teacher. The way of the beginner in law teaching is often hard with the teaching load put on him in many schools. But a determined man with zeal to do his whole task may rise to its full measure in spite of all discouragement. Ezra Thayer used to say that a full-time law teacher should write at least one good law review paper every two years. He should do that and teach effectively too, doing both the best that is in him.

[16]

Some Notes on Law Schools in the Present Day[*]

Charles L. Black, Jr.[†]

An area specialist who took for his province all knowledge about the United States would have much to say about the American law schools. A look at the *curricula vitae* of first-rank politicians, of relatively non-political officials (among them, of course, the judges), and even of high corporate and foundation people, would convince anyone that, while there is more than one way to influence and power, the law school way is of great importance in our culture. Many of the people who took this way would tell you that studying in law school was the most decisive of their intellectual experiences. What goes on in these schools deeply affects our society as it will be; their current state foretells, though delphically, the future. I am going to write—very briefly indeed, considering the magnitude of the topic—about the uneasiness that now infects the law school enterprise.

It is not surprising that some of the student unrest which has plagued campuses at the undergraduate level should spill over into graduate and professional schools. Unless one buys two propositions which to me are refuted by all experience—that young people are better and wiser than older people, and that a shifting student population is likely to glow with pertinacity in its warmths of today—one might simply conclude that this storm could and ought to be ridden out.

But the anxieties go deeper than what may be an ephemeral student discontent. There exists among law faculties a profound and troubled conviction that change ought to take place, and that great change of some sort impends and must be managed.

At this level of abstraction—at least if we strike the word "troubled" —I say no more than could have been said about any good American law school at any time within the last twenty-five years, at the very least. The feeling that sweeping change is imminent and desirable is (however paradoxically) a permanent characteristic of our law schools—as perhaps it is of American life. Unless one probes more deeply, one easily finds *la même chose* in 1938. And the call for change in law schools has always taken the same double form: We tell ourselves, as we

---

[*] Reprinted from *Ventures* (Magazine of the Yale Graduate School), Spring, 1969.
[†] Henry R. Luce Professor of Jurisprudence, Yale University. B.A. 1935, M.A. 1938, University of Texas; LL.B. 1943, Yale.

505

always have told ourselves, first, that law (through liaison with social science, or by developing its own means, or in both ways) badly needs to inform itself more fully about the facts of life on which it operates, and, secondly, that all legal ways of work, procedural and substantive, institutional and intellectual, must be remolded so as to do more good, more real good, in this more accurately explored world. These two propositions have so many times, over the decades, been put forward, and so much work has been done to implement them, that one may be a little bewildered by seeing them inscribed on the most lately unfurled banners.

Yet I think most of us feel that, while the words are the same, the accompanying anxiety goes deeper than it ever did before. When our law schools are measured against the world in which they are training people to work and often to lead, many teachers now seem to feel not so much discontent as panic. This has many symptoms, and I will not go into all of them here, but the most disturbing one, to me, is something that might with only a little uncharity be called anti-intellectualism—the feeling that hope is to be seen not in adaptation, however imaginative, of our traditions of clean thought and fine sifting of fact, but only in a mystique of "involvement," in action to which thought is poorly ancillary—or in something else which can be discovered only by feverishly random trial and error. I cannot participate in these feelings, but I think I can grasp a little of their genesis.

In the face of war and poverty, there has come on the law schools an uncertainty not only about the proper shape of law and about the proper way to do the work of law, but about law itself as a set of institutions apt for doing any useful work at all in those very areas where supremely good work must be done if our culture is to survive outside the madhouse.

I will illustrate this from two fields. First (and this is one surely familiar to all readers) let me instance the field of civil rights, or, to turn the coin around, the field of racism. The progression here is classic. The institutions of law travailed. From the school segregation cases forward, law by its only known means—judicial decisions, statutes, administrative rulings—washed out of its fabric every trace of racism—or as nearly as that is possible in human political action. Yet black discontent has only increased. And the reasons, if not fully known, include two in chief. First, there is poverty, a poverty connected with racism, and even with slavery, by the most easily visible causal links. Secondly, there is an inchoate and not always clearly expressed desire for something—"identity," "community"—which law is incapable of

Some Notes on Law Schools in the Present Day

giving. For my part, I think that in this field of racism it is unfair and even purblind to reject as quite worthless the part law has played. Things have gotten tangibly and intangibly better for many blacks in ways which can be traced to law as clearly as effect can be traced to cause in most social matters. But the fact of poverty massively remains, and surely there is a great deal in the assertion that law, having made so fair a start, has simply failed to solve the problem of a racism fatally linked by history with a poverty with which law knows not how to deal.

A less familiar example is in the field of contracts. This last semester I took a vacation from constitutional law, my special subject, to "teach" contracts to a group of exceedingly able first-year law students. I had a good time; I hope they did, and that they were not permanently harmed. My impressions of the subject, thus systematically revisited for the first time since my own far-off student days, were horrifying.

First of all, much of classic contract law is trivial and insipid. Results are justified on grounds having no relation to any intelligible policy. This is true not only of such peripheral questions as whether an "acceptance" of an "offer" takes hold on the mailing or on the receipt of the accepting letter. It is true, *par excellence*, of the all but sanctified "doctrine" of "consideration," which says, very roughly, that valuable exchange for a promise must be given or pledged before that promise is valid and enforceable. In the fine grain of this doctrine, judicial reasonings are inconclusively metaphysical; no relation to sound or even comprehensible policy is made to appear. The "doctrine of consideration" was said by its exponents in another generation to constitute our chief answer to the question, "Which contracts ought to be enforced and which ought not to be?" My own summary finding is that the "doctrine" serves only the function of deluding us into thinking this question has already been satisfactorily answered, with the consequence that we have never undertaken the hard work necessary to beginning the construction of a good answer.

So much for the pathology of "contracts." On the other side, the contract law system may be seen as helping to maintain the smooth working of the economic system. I don't think it contributes as much to this as some others think it does; at its best it may help some. But how much interest can you expect a law student or a citizen today to have in that function? If an economic system may be said to have failed when millions of people are in poverty, though goods are abundant, then the smooth maintenance of our system is the smooth maintenance of a failed system. Take this at its least: Insofar as it contributes to lubricating our economic system, considered as a set of bargains, the contract law system is contributing nothing whatever to the solution of our most pressing problem of economic justice.

But the plot thickens. For the contract law system actually serves yet another function, a baleful one indeed, yet one clearly visible on the face of hundreds of reported cases. It serves massively and systematically as an *intensifier* of economic advantage and disadvantage. It does this because people and businesses who are in strong bargaining positions, or who can afford expensive legal advice, can and epidemically do exact of necessitous and ignorant people contractual engagements which the general law never would impose. Let me give an example. If a poor woman wants a washing machine, and thinks she can pay for it in instalments, and it is delivered, and it turns out to be seriously defective and inoperable, then the general law says she does not have to pay for it. This is obviously just, and obviously inconvenient to the seller. The history of contract law in the field of consumer transactions is a horrible history of devices—some of them successful—to make the woman pay for the worthless washing machine. She may, for example, be required to sign a "negotiable" promissory note, which is speedily endorsed to a finance company. Unless she is a very unusual poverty-bracket housewife, she does not know that "negotiable" means, "You have to pay even though the machine is no good." *Ignorantia juris*, however, *haud excusat*.

Now judges are often compassionate men, and are almost never sympathetic to delinquent vendors or to finance companies. So, in a hard-fought lawsuit, the housewife may sometimes be relieved from so harsh a bargain. But how small an achievement that is, in the face of poverty! If the system succeeds, if it works at its imaginative best, it simply thwarts one overreaching unconscionability, and sets the finance company's lawyers to working on the next one.

Nor does the contract law system offer any serious compensating advantage to the poor, or even to the middle class. The mere expense of litigation will usually make it uneconomic for them to appeal to it, and when they do they will often find that its intricacies of doctrine, or its rules of damages, make the appeal unavailing. I could go on and on. The contract law system is for the "haves." It is for those who can afford lawyers, to draft and to sue. At its best, it harmlessly mediates deals between fairly large business men. At its worst, it is a weapon in the hands of business men, for them to use on the rest of us, and most destructively on the poor. The best one could say of it is that no amount of restudy of doctrine, no overhaul in the light of social fact,

Some Notes on Law Schools in the Present Day

could ever make this system *affirmatively* responsive to the needs which now cry out so loudly for relief that other social demands ought hardly to be heard.

I have mentioned two fields—civil rights and contracts—where law has failed to solve the chief problems that society has tendered to it for solution. Other fields could be mentioned. But for now let us assume—and I think on examination the assumption would turn out to be warranted—that this failure is general.

Now the older mode of thought, within whose field of force the older calls for "change" were heard, would have been likely to say, "Civil rights law has not done nearly enough? Contract law is futile when not worse? Very well then! Let us take another look at the cases, at the statutes, at the methods the judges use, at the way we select juries, at our modes of collecting evidence. And let us see if we cannot set this right!"

The trouble is that now everybody knows what we have run up against. We have run up against poverty. "Civil rights" law cannot help the poor, unless and until a decent living is seen as a "civil right." Contract law can have no meaning to the poor unless and until their poverty is relieved to the point where, with its associated ignorance, it no longer puts them at a fatal disadvantage with respect to the forming and the enforcing of any consensual arrangement.

Law teachers and law students like to work hard if they think that they are thereby indirectly advancing justice. But, as I have said in another place, poverty, in our rich society, is an impudent defiance of the very idea of distributive justice. And law people are filled with anxiety. They are anxious because they do not perceive in what direction their efforts may usefully flow. This is so for two reasons, rather opposite in tenor, though certainly not contradictory.

First, the lawyer can see that the culture in which he lives, and in which his law must grow or not grow at all, is light-years from being ready to put forth the kind of effort and sacrifice it would take to give relief against the injustice of poverty. I have implied that a decent living ought to be a civil right. With this concept, if the society workingly accepted it, lawyers could deal. But the society does not accept it, does not show signs of beginning to accept it, and the lawyer who would mold it into the shape of law feels no clay coming into his hands.

Secondly, it is well perceivable by law people now that, if by miracle the necessary social and political will could be massed, the early years of the process would have little work for lawyers as such. Copiousness, readiness to make mistakes as long as they are in the right direction, generous inattention to many fine points—these are the virtues needed if we are to transform our society, and these virtues are not lawyers' virtues, nor skill in their proper measurement lawyers' skill.[1]

Law teachers, then, are brought as never before to a sense both of the futility of what they are doing and of the hopelessness of finding within law, however amply conceived, the right thing to do.

Some of them are leaving law for now, to become propagandists, administrators, or other kinds of teachers. I would send them out with a blessing. They may well be the sagest among us.

I fear that some others, most understandably but in my view most unwisely, would slowly change our law schools into agencies of social action, with emphasis not so much on keen thought and research as on the present relief of misery. I have said enough to show why I consider this understandable; I will now say why I consider it unwise. The great law schools of America are the places where, to the highest degree possible in our culture, carefully chosen men think, write and teach about the rational governance of our polity, in all its interconnected aspects. Some of these schools are very good at this job; many are good enough to be of value. If we remake them radically into something else, however valuable that something else may seem, we shall have wiped out a national asset which cannot easily, or perhaps at all, be replaced. In the long run, and even in the rather short run, a nation can only lose, and that very disastrously, by wiping out an asset of this character. Those to whom such an asset does not seem all but supremely precious will hardly be convinced by anything else I can say.

In what ways (short of destroying these institutions as they now exist) can the rational thought, writing and teaching of the law schools be made responsive, in part, to our society's terrible needs?

I would mention first a function which will not be at all glamorous, or perhaps even appealing, but which will undoubtedly be performed whether we like it or not. We will continue, as we have always done, to train a good many people who will see the law in relatively traditional career terms. We will do this because we cannot exclude able applicants who will not sign a pledge to be concerned only with social justice. And our contribution as to them will be to make sure that they are fully aware, before they leave us, of all the social implications of law and of the lawyer's status. I do not think this to be a negligibly

---

1. On further reflection, I would substantially qualify this paragraph. A good lawyer can be of help in managing anything—even generosity. But a full development of the qualification would make another article—perhaps even another world.

Some Notes on Law Schools in the Present Day

beneficial function; the country is full of good lawyers, mostly making their own way, whose contributions in time and thought are valuable, perhaps sometimes crucial.

Others of our students will be wanting to be prepared to go more directly for the jugular of social injustice. As to them, we ought to help them sharpen the knife, if they believe, with us, that the most thorough possible understanding, the best possible training in thought, is the right whetstone. If, instead of that, they want present action, there are plenty of other places where they can find it. There is no reason to think either choice is mistaken.

There are many things, on the periphery of poverty, that law in its present state of readiness can do. Civil rights gains can be expanded. The harmful incidence of every kind of law upon the poor can at least be mitigated. "Due process" can gradually be extended to matters now thought to be mere favors, so that a boy, for example, who wants job training will not be at the mercy of an administrator's assistant's secretary's whim.

Above all, we should make a start toward applying the reason of the law, its highest and most inclusive reason, to the claim of the poor, analyzing out of existence all sham defenses against it, and beginning the work of projecting a rational system in which the claim not to be poor, in a rich society, shall seem as natural as the claim not to be beaten up in a society which has the means to keep order. We should go to this work coolly, without bias or preconception, except for the lawyer's bias in favor of that justice which must be done lest the heavens fall upon our children.

Lawyering Skills

University of Pennsylvania Law Review
And American Law Register
FOUNDED 1852

Published Monthly, November to June, by the University of Pennsylvania Law School.
Copyright 1933, by the University of Pennsylvania.

VOLUME 81	JUNE, 1933	No. 8

WHY NOT A CLINICAL LAWYER-SCHOOL? *

JEROME FRANK †

I

The method of teaching still used in some university law schools (and accepted by them as more or less sacrosanct) is founded upon the ideas of Christopher Columbus Langdell. It may be said, indeed, to be the expression of that man's peculiar temperament.

Langdell unequivocally stated as the fundamental tenet of his system of teaching *"that all the available materials . . . are contained in printed books"*. The printed opinions of judges are, he maintained, the *exclusive* repositories of the wisdom which law students must acquire to make them lawyers.

Now it is important to observe the manner of man who impressed those notions on American legal pedagogy for more than half a century:

When Langdell was himself a law student he was almost constantly in the law library. His fellow students said of him that he slept on the library table. At that time he served for several years as an assistant librarian. One of his friends found him one day in an alcove of the library absorbed in a black-letter folio, one of the year books. "As he drew near", we are told, "Langdell looked up and said, in a tone of mingled exhilaration and regret, and with an emphatic gesture, 'Oh, if only I could have lived in the time of the Plantaganets!'"[1]

---

* This paper is a report made by the writer, in June, 1932, to the Alumni Advisory Board of the University of Chicago Law School.

† Ph. B., J. D., 1912, University of Chicago; member of the New York and Illinois bars; Research Associate, Yale Law School; author, LAW AND THE MODERN MIND (1930), and contributor to legal periodicals.

[1] It is said that, when a law teacher, Langdell once referred to "a comparatively recent case decided by Lord Hardwicke".

He practiced law in New York City for sixteen years. But he seldom tried a case. He spent most of his time in the library of the New York Law Institute. He led a peculiarly secluded life. His biographer says of him: *"In the almost inaccessible retirement of his office, and in the library of the Law Institute, he did the greater part of his work. He went little into company."* His clients were mostly other lawyers for whom, after much lucubration, he wrote briefs or prepared pleadings.

Is it any wonder that such a man had an obsessive and almost exclusive interest in books? The raw material of law, he devoutly believed, was to be discovered in a library and nowhere else; it consisted, as he himself said, solely of what could be found in the pages of law reports. One of his biographers praises him because he sought *"the living founts"* of law in the works on the library shelves! Practicing law to Langdell meant the writing of briefs, examination of printed authorities. The lawyer-client relation, the numerous non-rational factors involved in persuasion of a judge at a trial, the face-to-face appeals to the emotions of juries, the elements that go to make up what is loosely known as the "atmosphere" of a case,—everything that is undisclosed in judicial opinions—was virtually unknown (and was therefore meaningless) to Langdell. A great part of the realities of the life of the average lawyer was unreal to him.

What was almost exclusively real to him he translated into the law-school curriculum when, in 1870, at the age of forty-four, he became a law teacher at Harvard. The so-called case system (the "Harvard system" which the university law schools adopted and by which some of them are still largely dominated) was the expression of the strange character of a cloistered, retiring bookish man. Due to Langdell's idiosyncracies, *law school law came to mean "library-law"*.

It was inevitable that those who have administerd those numerous university law schools which are shaped according to the Langdell pattern should, for the most part, seek as law teachers those who have had little or no contacts with or a positive distaste for the rough-and-tumble activities of the average lawyer's life. It is significant that an official historian of Harvard Law School wrote in 1918 that, for law teaching, *"previous experience in practice becomes unnecessary as is continuance in practice after teaching begins"*. For Langdell, the founder of the Harvard method, had said in vigorous fashion: "What qualifies a person to teach law is not experience in the work of a lawyer's office, not experience in dealing with men, not experience in the trial or argument of causes—not experience, in short, in using law, but experience in learning law. . . ."

Did not President Eliot of Harvard boast that Harvard Law School was revolutionary because its faculty consisted of a "body of men who have never been on the bench or at the bar"? Not long ago an official publication of the Harvard Law School stated that practice of law for any length of time has marked "intellectual disadvantages" and that "a school conducted chiefly by persons drawn from the bar after many years of practice would lack the scientific intellect" essential to a first-rate law teacher.

Unavoidably, then, the acceptance of the Langdell-Harvard method meant that the university law school teachers, with few exceptions, were those who had never practiced or practiced for only a brief interval. It is probably true that a majority of the teachers in some of our university law schools have never met or advised a client, consulted with witnesses, negotiated a settlement, drafted a complicated contract, lease or mortgage, tried a case or assisted in the trial of a case or even written a brief or argued a case in an upper court. Just the other day one of the most brilliant university law teachers (who is an exception to the rule in that he himself engaged in active practice in addition to teaching) commented to the writer that most of the professors in some of our university law schools have seldom, if ever, been inside a court room.

A brief outline of the history of legal education in American universities is helpful as a preliminary to some tentative suggestions for changes: [2]

It began with the apprentice system. The prospective lawyer "read law" in the office of a practicing lawyer. He saw daily what courts were doing. The first American law school, founded by Judge Reeves, in the 1780's was merely the apprentice system on a group basis. The students were still in intimate daily contact with the courts. Then (about 1830) came the college law school with teaching on the college pattern of lectures and text-books. This step is ordinarily pictured as progress. For the student now devoted full time to his books and lectures and the distractions of office and court work were removed. A more unpleasant story could be told: The student was cloistered; he learned of court doings from books and lectures only; the *false* aspects of theory could no longer be compared by him with the actualities of practice.

There followed the period when the leading law schools were dominated by the great systematic text-book writers, the makers of so-called (American) "substantive law", substantive law which was divorced and living apart from procedure. The rift widened between theory and practice.

Then came Langdell. Noting his plea for induction, his efforts to avoid the glib generalities of text-books, one cannot help feeling that he was seeking obliquely and fumblingly to return to some limited extent to court-room

---

[2] The next few pages contain matter taken, with slight modifications, from Frank, *What Courts Do in Fact* (1932) 26 ILL. L. REV. 645, 667.

The writer, more or less out of laziness, has used his own published writings. Other material more or less along the same line will be found in the writings of such men as Arnold, Green, Llewellyn, Radin, Bingham, Clark, Cook, Yntema, Frankfurter, Corbin, Douglas and Oliphant. See for partial bibliography Llewellyn, *Some Realism About Realism* (1931) 44 HARV. L. REV. 1222, 1257.

actualities. But he was patently thinking of the lawyer as brief-writer and nothing more. Consequently, the material on which he based his so-called "induction" was hopelessly limited.

Ostensibly, the students were to study cases. But they did not and *they do not study cases*. They do not even study the printed records of cases (although that would be little enough), let alone cases as living processes. Their attention is restricted to judicial *opinions*. *But an opinion is not a decision*. A decision is a specific judgment, or order or decree entered after a trial of a specific lawsuit between specific litigants. There are a multitude of factors which induce a jury to return a verdict, or a judge to enter a decree. Of those numerous factors, but few are set forth in judicial opinions. And those factors, not expressed in the opinions, frequently are the most important in the real causal explanation of the decisions.

As stated above, the Langdell system (even in its revised version) concentrates attention on the so-called legal rules and principles found in or spelled out of the printed opinions. Now no sane person will deny that a knowledge of those rules and principles, of how to "distinguish" cases, and of how to make an argument as to the true *ratio decidendi* of an opinion, is part of the indispensable equipment of the future lawyer. For such knowledge is of some limited aid in guessing what courts will do. And in arguments made to courts lawyers are required to employ terminology in accordance with the fictitious assumption that the rules and principles are the principal bases of all decisions.

But the tasks of the lawyer do not pivot around those rules and principles. The work of the lawyer revolves about specific decisions in definite pieces of litigation. When he draws a will or passes on a mortgage to secure a bond issue, organizes a corporation, negotiates the settlement of a controversy, reorganizes a railroad, or drafts a legislative bill, the lawyer is as truly concerned with how the courts will act in some concrete case as when he is trying such a case. A lawyer tries to answer these questions: "What will happen if these specific documents or transactions should hereafter become a part of the drama of a lawsuit? What will a court decide is their meaning and effect?" For the legal rights and duties of the client, Jones, under any given document (a promissory note, a deed, contract, etc.) or in connection with any given transaction, mean simply what some court, somewhere, some day in the future, will decide (not what it will say in its opinion) in a future concrete lawsuit relating to Jones' specific rights under that specific document or in connection with that specific transaction.[3]

---

[3] Occasionally, too, the lawyer when advising his client, Jones, must consider what some court somewhere has already actually decided (not what it said in its opinion) in a specific lawsuit, which has already terminated, relating to Jones' specific rights under a specific document or in connection with a specific transaction.

Accordingly, laymen turn to the lawyer because the acts of laymen may give rise to, or have already occasioned, litigation. What the courts will decide in specific cases involving the rights of specific clients under specific acts, documents or transactions must, therefore, be the center of the lawyer's thinking.

Roughly speaking, then, the task of the lawyer may be summarized thus:

(1) A lawyer tries to predict and anticipate a future enforceable court decision (*i. e.*, a judgment, order or decree) in a specific lawsuit relating to a definite client.

(2) A lawyer tries to win a specific lawsuit; that is, to induce a court in a specific case to render an enforceable decision (*i. e.*, judgment, order or decree) desired by a definite client.

For the practicing lawyer and his client, the specific decisions of actual specific cases are ultimates. Decisions, not opinions. What the lawyer and his client want are concrete judgments and decrees—regardless of the presence or absence of concomitant opinions, irrespective of the contents of the opinions, if there are any. Since the opinions—and the works of those commentators who discuss opinions—are emasculated explanations of decisions, they are of limited assistance to the practicing lawyer. Not only do they disclose merely a fractional part of how decisions come into being, but, if the lawyer takes them as adequate explanations of how decisions are reached, he will act with a treacherously false sense of certainty in advising clients, drafting instruments, writing briefs—or any other work he has to perform.

For the law student to learn whatever can be learned of (1) the means of guessing what courts will decide and (2) of how to induce courts to decide the way his clients want them to decide, he must observe carefully what actually goes on in court-rooms and law-offices. As noted above, the opinions of upper courts conceal or fail to disclose many of the most important factors which lead to decisions. The "hunches" that produce many judicial decisions,[4] the numerous stimuli that cause verdicts to be rendered by juries, cannot be discovered in the printed opinions of upper courts. For, as noted above, a judicial opinion is not only *ex post facto* with reference to the decision. It is a *censored exposition,* written by a judge, of what induced him to arrive at a decision which he has already reached. The conventions prevent the judges from reporting many of the influences that induce their de-

---

[4] See Hutcheson, *The Judgment Intuitive: the Function of the "Hunch" in Judicial Decision* (1929) 14 CORN. L. Q. 274; Douglas and Shanks, *Insulation From Liability Through Subsidiary Corporations* (1929) 39 YALE L. J. 193; Frank, *supra* note 2, at 761; Frank, *Are Judges Human?* (1931) 80 U. OF PA. L. REV. 17, 232; Arnold, *The Role of Substantive Law and Procedure* (1932) 45 HARV. L. REV. 617; FRANK, LAW AND THE MODERN MIND (1930) 100-159; Frank, *Mr. Justice Holmes and Non-Euclidean Legal Thinking* (1932) 18 CORN. L. Q. 568, 598-599.

cisions. To study those eviscerated judicial expositions as the principal bases of forecasts of future judicial action is to delude oneself. The lawyer will go wrong who believes that (in advising a client, drafting an instrument, trying a case or arguing before a court) he can rely on the so-called reasons found in or spelled out of opinions to guide him in guessing what courts will hereafter decide. To do so is far more unwise than it would be for a botanist to assume that plants are merely what appears above the ground, or for an anatomist to content himself with scrutinizing the outside of the body.

Students trained under the Langdell system are like future horticulturists confining their studies to cut flowers, like architects who study pictures of buildings and nothing else. They resemble prospective dog breeders who never see anything but stuffed dogs. And it is beginning to be suspected that there is some correlation between that kind of stuffed-dog study and the overproduction of stuffed shirts in the legal profession.

Where the Langdell system is most seriously at fault is in its naive assumption of the inviolability of the *stare decisis* doctrine and its corollaries, in its implied belief that in a study of the precedents and nowhere else is to be found the answer to the question, "How does a court arrive at its decisions?" It assumes that if a lawyer learns, from a study of judicial opinions, the legal rules and principles, he can ascertain his clients' "rights" and "duties". There are many reasons why *stare decisis* is of limited value in guessing what courts will decide. But the major reason is that already indicated, *viz.:* Before a suit has begun a lawyer cannot tell from a study of the precedents (1) whether or not a question of fact will be raised and, if so, (2) what conflicting testimony will be introduced, and (3) what will be the reactions to the conflicting testimony of the judge or jury that may happen to try the case.[4a]

[4a] As the writer has said elsewhere, "Before and until a specific enforceable judgment has been entered, every bit of advice a lawyer gives about any man's legal rights and duties, and all the rights and duties under every document a lawyer prepares, are subject to that unavoidable uncertainty which results from the fact that no specific rights or duties can be known until a specific enforceable judgment has been entered in a future lawsuit pertaining to those specific rights or duties—a judgment which, so far as anyone can tell, may turn on conflicting testimony, a judgment which is therefore unguessable. . . . The legal rules unquestionably have some effect on an honest judge while he is making up his mind how to decide a 'contested' case. (A 'contested' case here means a case in which a question of fact is raised and in which conflicting testimony is introduced with respect to that question of fact.) Many of the legal rules are so unsettled that their effect on the judge's thinking is vague; but, more important, the rules, however exact, are only one among the many kinds of influences which affect him while trying to reach his decision. The judge's knowledge of the rules combines with his reactions to the conflicting testimony, with the sense of fairness, with his background of economic and social views, and with that complicated compound loosely named his 'personality', to form an incalculable mixture out of which comes the court order we call his decision. It is future specific, enforceable decisions (judgments, orders and decrees) which determine all legal rights and duties. Enforceable decisions, not legal rules. But there is prevalent a gravely mistaken notion that legal rules control and cause decisions. This is partly due to the fact that the judges, when they are entering their judgments, sometimes publish little essays, called 'opinions' in which they quote the rules and write as if their judgments had been produced by the rules, as if the rules had been the only in-

WHY NOT A CLINICAL LAWYER-SCHOOL?

After the trial in the lower court has been concluded, then, on appeal, knowledge of the precedents, so far as they are crystallized and clear, sometimes becomes more important. If (as in some jurisdictions in many cases) the doctrine purports to prevail that the upper court will not disturb the fact-finding of the lower court, then the outcome of an appeal—if there is one—will appear (although appearances are deceiving) to turn on the precedents. But, even so, that does not mean that before suit was begun in the lower court, a lawyer can know, by the aid of *stare decisis,* what the decision will be. And in those cases where the upper courts are doctrinally free to disturb the fact-finding of the lower courts, the lawyer cannot know from the precedents what the upper court will find as "the facts" after reading the conflicting testimony in those numerous cases where there is conflicting testimony.

The trouble with much law school teaching is that, confining its attention to a study of upper court opinions, it is hopelessly oversimplified. Something important and of immense worth was given up when the legal apprentice system was abandoned as the basis of teaching in the leading American law schools. This does not mean that we should return to the old system in its old form, that we want mere apprentice-trained lawyers or law schools which are merely "expanded law offices". But is it not plain that, without giving up entirely the case-book system or the growing and valuable alliance with the so-called social sciences, the law schools should once more get in intimate contact with what clients need and with what courts and lawyers actually do? Must we not execute an about-face and return to Judge Reeves' 18th century [4b] apprentice method, but on a higher, more sophisticated level?

---

fluences affecting them. These opinions do not refer to the other kinds of stimuli which influenced them; but that does not mean that the other undisclosed factors were not as or more important in reducing their decisions. The uncertainty of most legal rights and duties is then due to their dependence on the decisions in future specific lawsuits which, in turn, are affected by at least these three elements of uncertainty: (1) Many of the legal rules are unsettled or vague. (2) Some legal rules are clear and precise. But the guess of the judge or jury as to the facts in a contested lawsuit is unguessable, even when the legal rules are exact. And no one can prophesy which lawsuits will be 'contested' or what conflicting testimony will be introduced in any lawsuit. (3) The reaction of the judge to his guess, or the jury to its guess about the facts of a 'contested' suit, is unpredictable. There is moderate uniformity in the way the judges quote the rules. But there is a lack of any known relation between the exactness of the rules (even when they are exact) and the predictability of any concrete future decision (*i. e.,* a court judgment or order) in a 'contested' case. While there may possibly be some certainties or uniformities in the predictions of decisions in 'contested' cases, they have not yet been discovered or formulated."

[4b] As the writer said *supra* note 2, at 779: "A few years ago we began to hear much of a great metaphysical problem in the law schools. It might be phrased this way: Why is 'Law' not like 'law'? Why is what law school teaches unlike 'law' as it is practiced? What was really in mind was this: Why is law-school law dissimilar to what courts and lawyers do? It had begun to be moderately evident that law-school law, restricted as it is to the so-called legal rules of so-called substantive law, had come unduly to dominate legal teaching. The law schools had a little too obviously impoverished the subject matter to be studied; they had focussed on the Rules; they had withdrawn from the gaze of the student, the complicated, shifting and changing material which the practicing lawyer must encounter. The movement once more to enrich the materials of study took the form of a demand for 'sociological jurisprudence': Law, it was said, must be recognized as one of the social sciences; the law

II

To be more specific, the following ideas are recommended for consideration:

1. *A considerable proportion of law teachers in any law school should be men with not less than five to ten years of varied experience in the actual practice of law.* They should have had work in the trial courts, appellate courts, in office work, in dealing with clients, in negotiation.[5] Their practical experience should not have been confined chiefly to a short period of paper work in a law office.

This does not mean that there are not some highly capable teachers with little or no practical experience. For some teachers are brilliantly intuitive and to some extent make up for their deficiencies in experience by imaginative insight.[6] No student who was taught by Ernst Freund needs to be told that much can be learned from men who have not practiced law. To sit at the feet of brilliant men such as Walter Wheeler Cook, Thomas Reed Powell, Underhill Moore, Herman Oliphant, or Arthur Corbin is an invaluable vital event in the life of any law student.

Nor is it intended to say that mere experience in practising law will make a man a good law teacher. By and large, teachers are born, not made.

Professor Thurman W. Arnold is an excellent illustration of the ideal law teacher. He practiced law in Illinois, Wyoming and West Virginia, where he enjoyed the most varied kind of experience. He is now Professor at the Yale Law School, where he is able, with wit and brilliance, to make the students feel and understand the relation of the work of the trial court to every aspect of the undertakings of the lawyer. Any law school in which the majority of the faculty consisted of men like Arnold or Frankfurter would speedily reorganize its methods of teaching so as to combine a profound knowledge of what is in the books with a thorough comprehension of what courts and lawyers do in fact.

Of course, there is room in any school for the mere book-teacher. Part of the job of the lawyers is to write briefs in which, according to current conventions, it must be made to appear—contrary to the truth—that the legal rules and principles and the precedents are the principal bases of courts' decisions. The lawyer must learn the jargon of the courts, the art of judicial

---

school must mesh with the departments of economics, political science, psychology, and history. Splendid, that notion. May it flourish. But it did not go far enough. Chesterton says that the Christian medieval ideal was not tried and found wanting; it was tried and found difficult—and given up. That is an observation worth pondering. It is wise to see that the older generations were sometimes sounder than we are. Change does not necessarily mean progress. It is sometimes possible to back and find valuable ideas in the past."

[5] It is not intended to suggest that this experience can be best obtained in large offices or in large cities.

[6] But they are few. And why should all teachers be asked to guess by brilliant intuition what they are far more likely to learn and know more accurately by direct experience?

WHY NOT A CLINICAL LAWYER-SCHOOL?

rhetoric. The exclusively book lawyer can perhaps best teach such "library-law". But the "library-law" teacher should cease to dominate the schools.[7]

Unfortunately, attempted reform of legal pedagogy is frequently in the hands of the "library-law" teacher. With the best will in the world, such a teacher often finds it almost impossible to warp over the old so-called case-system so as to adapt it to the needs of the future practicing lawyer. For, as above noted, that system is centered in books. So long as teachers who know nothing except what they learned from books under the old case-system are in control of a law-school, the actualities of the lawyer's life are likely in that school to be considered peripheral and as of secondary importance.

A medical school dominated by teachers who had seldom seen a patient or diagnosed the ailments of flesh-and-blood human beings or actually performed surgical operations, would not be likely to turn out doctors equipped with a fourth part of what doctors ought to know. But our law schools are not doing as much for law students.

Many of our law schools are so staffed that they are best equipped not to train lawyers but to graduate men able to become book-law teachers who can educate still other students to become book-law teachers—and so on ad infinitum. They are not lawyer-schools (as they should be primarily) but law-teacher schools.[8]

It is significant that Dean Clark and Dean Green (the respective chief executives of two of the three law schools most alive to the needs of revision of legal pedagogy) are men who were seasoned lawyers before they became law teachers.

What is here suggested is not that all law professors should have had first-hand contacts with courts, lawyers and clients, but that a very large proportion of the professors should be men with such records. The law schools need for men like Frankfurter, Clark, Green, Douglas, Sturges, Llewellyn, Arnold, Medina, Smith, Dickinson, Morgan, Magill, Mack, Michael, Handler and Berle.[9]

---

[7] More than that, some of the teaching of the art of persuasive "reasoning" in briefs might well be done by men who have written many real briefs for real courts. See Bacharach, *Reflections on Brief Writing* (1932) 27 ILL. L. REV. 374.

[8] The writer's associate, Mr. Lee Pressman, calls attention to the effect of the Langdell type of law school on even those few teachers who had previously been practitioners. The spirit of Langdell so dominates some of the university law schools that the practitioner who becomes a teacher in such a school often succumbs to that spirit and forgets the difference between the theory he is teaching and the actual practice which he had previously encountered. In some instances this forgetfulness is due to the character of the individual teacher; he may have found practice distasteful and lacking in that certainty which he craved, so that he shifts with delight to a system in which far greater (but illusory) certainty seems to be a reality.

In some notable instances this is not the case. Men like Llewellyn after but a few years of practice become teachers who transmit to their students a keen awareness of the difference between the contexts of the law reports and the practice of law.

[9] The mention of these names does not indicate any belief that there are not others of equal worth and ability in the university law schools.

2. *The case-system should be revised so that it will in truth and fact become a case-system and not a mere sham case-system.*

A few of the current type of so-called case-books should be retained to teach dialectic skill in brief-writing. But the study of cases which will lead to some small measure of real understanding of how cases are won, lost and decided, should be based to a very marked extent on reading and analysis of *complete records of cases*—beginning with the filing of the first papers, through the trial in the trial court and to and through the upper courts. *Six months properly spent on one or two elaborate court records, including the briefs (and supplemented by reading of text-books as well as upper court opinions) will teach a student more than two years spent on going through twenty of the case-books now in use.*

In medical schools, "case histories" are used for instruction. But they are far more complete than the alleged case-books used in law schools. *It is absurd that we should continue to call an upper court opinion a case.* It is at most an adjunct to the final step in a case (*i. e.*, an essay published by an upper court in justification of its decision).

3. But even if legal case-books were true case-books and as complete as medical case-histories, they would be insufficient as tools for study. What would we think of a medical school in which students studied no more than what was to be found in such written or printed case-histories and were deprived of all clinical experience until after they received their M. D. degrees? Our law schools must learn from our medical schools. *Law students should be given the opportunity to see legal operations.* Their study of cases should be supplemented by frequent visits, accompanied by law teachers, to both trial and appellate courts. The cooperation of judges could easily be enlisted. (In the days of the Year Books the judges apparently went out of their way, at times, to instruct law students who were present in the court room. If Langdell had but taken that hint when he was sighing for the days of the Plantagenets!)

The "up-stage" attitude of the bookish-trained teacher towards instruction in the actualities of trial-practice is prettily illustrated in the following excerpt from *The Centennial History of Harvard Law School:* [10]

"Efforts have been made from time to time to give students some experience in the trial of cases by substituting a trial of the facts before a jury for the argument of questions of law, whether in the law clubs or in the obsolete moot court. Interesting experiments have been made in acting out a legal injury and summoning the witnesses of the event to testify; and on the other hand in coaching witnesses on the points of actual testimony in their reported trial and having them reproduce the testimony in the Practice Court. *Such experiments have been more suc-*

---

[10] THE CENTENNIAL HISTORY OF HARVARD LAW SCHOOL (1918) 84.

WHY NOT A CLINICAL LAWYER-SCHOOL?

cessful, in affording amusement than in substantial benefit to the participants. A fact trial now and then is well worth while, but only as a relief to the tedium of serious work."

One cannot but agree, in part, with that writer. Such *fake trials* are poor substitutes for careful observation of trials. Would any medical school substitute pretend-surgical operations for real operations as means for instructing students? Obviously, as said by the writer just quoted, such sham law-school trials can do little more than "afford amusement" or serve "as a relief to tedium". They are, indeed, not the equivalent of serious work.

Is it not absurd that during his law-school career a student should not be encouraged frequently to visit court rooms? That absurdity is a direct product of Langdell's attitude; his biographer tells us that it was a fundamental part of Langdell's intentions completely to exclude the "methods of learning law by work in a lawyer's office, or attendance upon the proceedings of courts of justice". Consequently, some of our university law schools by their unspoken attitude encourage indifference on the part of students to the actual work of courts and lawyers.

4. And now we come to a point which the writer considers of major importance. It was stated above that law schools could learn much from the medical schools. The parallel cannot be carried too far. But a brief scrutiny of medical education suggests the use of a device which may be employed as an adequate method of obtaining apprentice work for law students:

Medical schools rely to a very large extent on the free medical clinics and dispensaries. There exist today legal clinics in the form of the Legal Aid Society. Today that agency is by no means the equivalent of the medical clinics and dispensaries. The ablest physicians devote a considerable portion of their time to medical clinics while the Legal Aid Society is, on the whole, staffed by men who are not outstanding in their profession. The leading lawyers of the community do not actively participate in its activities. The Society is limited in the kinds of cases it can take, and the law teachers have little, if any, direct contact with its efforts.

Suppose, however, that there were in each law school a legal clinic or dispensary.[11] As before indicated, a considerable part of the teaching staff of a law school should consist of lawyers who already had varied experience in practice. Some of these men could run the law school legal clinics assisted by (a) graduate students; (b) under-graduate students; and (c) leading members of the local bar.

The work of these clinics would be done for little or no charge. The teacher-clinicians would devote their full time to their teaching, including such clinical work, and would not engage in private practice.

---

[11] *Cf.* FLEXNER, MEDICAL EDUCATION (1925) 269.

The law school clinics would not confine their activities to such as are now undertaken by the Legal Aid Society. They could take on important work for governmental agencies or other quasi-public bodies. The professional work they would do would include virtually every kind of service rendered by law offices.

In this way, the students would learn to observe the true relation between the contents of upper court opinions and the work of the practising lawyers and the courts. *The student would be made to see, among other things, the human side of the administration of justice,* including the following:

(a) How juries decide cases. The factors that count in jury trials. The slight effect of the judges' instructions on verdicts. The hazards of a jury trial.

(b) The uncertain character of the "facts" of a case when it is "contested", *i. e.*, when conflicting testimony is introduced. The difference between what actually happened between the parties to the suit and the way those actual happenings can be made to appear to a judge or jury. The transcendent importance of the "facts" of a case. The inherent subjectivity of those "facts" in "contested cases".[12] The inability to guess future decisions (even when the "legal rules" seem clear) because it is impossible to guess, before a suit has been begun, whether there will be an issue of fact, and, if so, whether conflicting testimony will be introduced, what judge or jury will try the case and what the reaction of that unknown judge or jury will be to that unknown testimony.

The student should learn that "legal rights and duties" are inextricably intertwined with litigation,—that, for instance, there is no such thing as "the law of torts" as distinguished from decisions in lawsuits, and that the so-called rules and principles of torts are only some among the many implements employed by lawyers in their efforts to win lawsuits.

(c) How legal rights often turn on the faulty memory of witnesses, the bias of witnesses, the perjury of witnesses.

(d) The effects of fatigue, alertness, political pull, graft, laziness, conscientiousness, patience, impatience, prejudice and open-mindedness of judges. How legal rights may vary with the judge who tries the case and with that judge's varying and often unpredictable reactions to various kinds of cases and divers kinds of witnesses.

(e) The methods used in negotiating contracts and settlements of controversies.

---

[12] See Frank, *supra* note 2, at 658-663, 782-784; and *supra* note 4, 80 U. OF PA. L. REV. at 33-38, 46-49, 233-242.

(f) The nature of draftsmanship: How the lawyer tries to translate the wishes of a client (often inadequately expressed by the client) into wills, contracts or corporate instruments.[13]

What is intended is not that (as a scoffing neo-Langdellian recently suggested) the student should in his law-school days learn "the way to the post-office" or "the mechanics of the short-trial list". What is intended is that, almost at the beginning of and during his law-school days, the student should learn the very limited (although real) importance in the actual legal world of so-called substantive law and of so-called legal rules and principles. He should learn that "legal rights" and "duties" mean merely what may some day happen at the end of specific lawsuits. And that all so-called legal rules—including the so-called rules of substantive law—are "procedural"; *i. e.,* among the many implements to be used in the kind of fight, conducted in a court room, which we call "litigation". He should learn that judges are fallible human beings and that legal rights often depend on the unpredictable reactions of those fallible human beings to a multitude of stimuli, including the rules, but also including the fallible testimony of other human beings called witnesses. The student should become aware of the slippery character of "the facts" of a case, when there is conflicting testimony, and of the marked importance of what happens in trial courts.

Recently Judge Crane of the New York Court of Appeals thus characterized the graduates of many university law schools:

> "With the practical working of the law he has little or no familiarity. He may come to the bar almost ignorant of how the law should be applied and is applied in daily life. It is, therefore, not unusual to find the brightest student the most helpless practitioner, and the most learned surpassed in the profession by one who does not know half as much.
>
> "Strange as it may seem, there were some advantages in the older methods of preparation for the bar. As you know, the law school is relatively a matter of recent growth. Formerly, a student, working in the office of a practitioner, combined the study of law with its daily application to the troubles and business of clients. He had an opportunity of hearing the story at the beginning, of noticing how it was handled by his preceptor, of reading the papers prepared to obtain a remedy; he accompanied the lawyer to court and became acquainted with the manner of the presentation of the case to the judge or to the jury. . . .
>
> "You know much more law after coming out of a university like this than these former students ever knew, but you know less about the method of its application, and how to handle and use it."

---

[13] Even the Langdell-patterned law school can do something in the way of teaching draftsmanship, although it must confine itself to "dead" materials; that is, it can do something in the way of showing the students how to draft mortgages or deposit agreements, or the like, which have a more or less stereotyped form. But *"creative draftsmanship"—the use of fact-materials thrown at the lawyer by his client and worked out in negotiations with counsel representing the other party to the bargain—cannot be adequately taught in most university law schools as they are now conducted.*

Is that not a shocking state of affairs? Think of a medical school which would turn out graduates ignorant of how medicine "should be applied, and is applied, in daily life". In this connection it is important to note that, according to Flexner, in the best-equipped medical schools, the student *"makes and sees made through physical examinations, painstaking records, varied and thoroughgoing laboratory tests, at every stage in the study of the patient; the literature of the subject is utilized; at one and the same time medicine is practiced and studied—teachers and students mingling freely and naturally in both activities."* In this manner there has been "effected the fusion of bedside and laboratory procedures alike in the care of patients, in teaching, and in research. . . . It is obvious that teaching, thus closely intertwined with scientific investigation, must proceed by 'sampling'. It is neither necessary nor feasible to make the several clinics schematically complete. From the standpoint of research, as I have elsewhere pointed out, no single clinic, no single university can make itself responsible for total achievements; progress is made in the form of steps forward taken in many different places under as many different auspices, integration occurring in infinitely varied ways and under infinitely varied circumstances. From the standpoint of training, *fragmentariness, if stimulative and formative, is desirable rather than otherwise,* for the medical school, not undertaking to turn out a finished product, but rather to train the student in method and technique, would logically address itself to intensive and thorough study of relatively few patients rather than to extensive contact with many. *The student must at one and the same time learn the technique of scientific method, which he can acquire only through 'sampling', and he must acquire a vivid sense of the existence of breaks, gaps, and problems.* The clinics I am now discussing carry him from the patient in the bed to the point beyond which at the moment neither clinical observation nor laboratory investigation can carry him. There he is left, in possession, it is to be hoped, of an *acute realization of the relatively narrow limits of human knowledge and human skill, and of the pressing enigmas yet to be solved by intelligence and patience."* [13a] Here is much that law schools should ponder carefully.

5. As a temporary device and until such time as clinical law schools are established, students, early in their student days, under the direct and sustained supervision of their law professors, should be working at intervals as apprentices in carefully chosen law offices. The practicing lawyers who assist in such apprentice-training should be made associate members of the law school faculty—perhaps with some compensation. Between the regular members of the faculty and such associates a plan of instruction should be carefully worked out.

[13a] FLEXNER, *loc. cit. supra* note 11.

WHY NOT A CLINICAL LAWYER-SCHOOL?

Incidentally, the lawyers who, as associate faculty members, give the students apprentice-training, might be a source of supply for future law teachers. At the same time, many law teachers should be encouraged to some extent to continue in practice—to "keep their hands in". The notable careers of such outstanding teachers as John Chipman Gray, Albert Kales and Mr. Justice Harlan F. Stone indicate that such a plan is both feasible and highly desirable.

6. It may be argued that there is not time for either apprentice or clinical work. But the law schools admit that at the end of a year or two under the present system the best students are often bored. The reason is that the dialectics which are the chief product of the present case system can be learned in a comparatively short time.

7. And here it should be remarked that in three years all legal subjects cannot be taught by the use of so-called case-books. Far greater recourse should be had in the law schools to text-books and general lectures in order to give the students an orientation with respect to many branches of law.

8. It will doubtless be urged in answer to the foregoing that the Langdell-patterned law schools have turned out our most successful lawyers. But that may well be *in spite of and not because of their method of instruction.* The experiment has not been a controlled experiment. For the students who attend university law schools are usually the pick of the lot. And they are not only the brightest students; they are the wealthiest, best connected socially and the like. Also, the fact of having gone to a university law school such as Harvard gives them prestige. Indeed for some three decades it was almost impossible for a man to obtain a legal education in a law school that was not Langdellian. The Langdell method became the prevailing method and most lawyers, dull or stupid, successful or unsuccessful, necessarily were products of that method. Most sucessful lawyers today do not wear beards, but it will scarcely be contended that the current habits as to hirsute facial decoration explain their achievements. And just so the correlation of Langdellian training and legal success may be accidental. In the days before the modern law schools arose, it could have been said, "Most successful lawyers have been educated under the apprentice system of reading law in law offices". The point is that the two systems of legal education have never paralleled one another at a time when both were working with the same kind of student material. (Even today some of the ablest lawyers are products of the apprentice-system; ex-Federal Judge Hugh M. Morris of Delaware will serve as an example.)

9. As noted above, law teaching needs to be integrated with the social sciences. The law student should be taught to see the inter-actions of the conduct of society and the work of the courts and lawyers. The usual law

school curriculum largely omits such teaching. It relies on prelegal courses in the so-called social sciences. The result is that the law student is graduated with the vaguest recollections of his pre-legal work, an insufficient feeling of the inter-relation between law and the phenomena of daily living, and an artificial attitude towards "Law" as something totally distinct and apart from the facts. To avoid that unfortunate result, men who need not have first-hand experience in practicing law, but who are skilled economists, historians, political scientists, anthropologists or psychologists might well be made full-time or part-time members of the law faculty. The brilliant work of Walton Hamilton at Yale or of Max Radin at California is illustrative.[14]

Knowledge of the other social disciplines will help the lawyer to be useful to his clients. Moreover, it will enable him to take his place as a constructive member of the community. As draftsman of legislation, as lobbyist, as a member of a legislative body, as advocate, as judge, as statesman, the lawyer should be adequately "socialized".[15]

10. Professional ethics can be effectively taught only if the students while learning the canons of ethics have available some first-hand observation of the ways in which the ethical problems of the lawyer arise and of the actual habits (the "mores") of the bar.

11. First-rate courses in logic and psychology with specific references to legal thinking should form part of the curriculum. There the students can learn something of the importance of open-mindedness, of the folly of dogmatism, of the provisional, experimental and tentative nature of most conclusions—particularly those relating to the conduct of human beings.

12. And, too, factual studies of litigation and procedure such as those conducted by Yntema and Oliphant at Johns Hopkins could profitably be made part of student efforts, for they serve to disclose what courts and lawyers and clients are actually doing, how well they are doing it and how those doings can be improved.

13. The students in these and other ways should be encouraged to consider that an important part of their future task is to press for improvements of the judicial process and for social and economic changes through legislation, and wise administration, but, at the same time, that proposals for ade-

---

[14] In this connection, see the brilliant paper written by Leon Keyserling, *Social Objectives in Legal Education* (1933) 33 COL. L. REV. 437. As the present paper was written in 1932, the writer did not have Keyserling's article before him when the present paper was written. The one grave defect in Mr. Keyserling's article is his failure to make reference to the admirable work done by Walton Hamilton at Yale.

[15] On the other hand, heed should be given to Alvin Johnson's comment on "the cross-sterilization of the social sciences".

And it must not be assumed that the so-called social sciences are or are likely to be "scientific" in the sense of any high degree of precision or exactness. Perhaps they would better be called "social arts" than "social sciences". See Frank, *supra* note 4, 80 U. OF PA. L. REV. at 254-260.

quate improvements should be formulated on the basis of moderately accurate information as to how the judicial, legislative and administrative processes actually function.

14. Some considerable attention, too, should be given to the art of the judge. With the help of able judges, many of whom would be delighted to lend a hand, students can be taught something of how trials and decisions look from the bench. In that way those students who will later become judges can learn something about their future jobs.

15. A law school made more or less on the lines above suggested should not be and would not be a mere "trade-school"; its products would not be "mere technicians". Knowledge of what courts and lawyers do in fact would be coupled with visual demonstration of the possible values of a rich and well-rounded culture in the practice of law.

In the last analysis, of course, the kind of law school here pictured must depend on its teaching staff To acquire a group of teachers of the desired quality is not easy; it will take time. But there are many able lawyers, capable of becoming brilliant teachers, who would be unwilling to make the sacrifices of time and money necessary to participate in the elaborate futilities of a stereotyped Langdell law school, but who could far more easily be induced to take part in a realistic lawyer-school.

16. In sum, the practice of law and the deciding of cases constitute not sciences but arts—the art of the lawyer and the art of the judge.[16] Only a slight part of any art can be learned from books. Whether it be painting or writing or practicing law, the best kind of education in an art is usually through apprentice-training under the supervision of men some of whom have themselves become skilled in the actual practice of the art. That was once accepted wisdom in American legal education. It needs to be rediscovered.[17]

---

[16] For the sake of those students who may become teachers, there should be some courses in the art of teaching law.

[17] That law teachers should have experience in practicing law was vigorously asserted in 1912 by Mr. Justice Harlan F. Stone, now Mr. Justice Stone of the United States Supreme Court. See Stone, *The Importance of Actual Experience at the Bar as a Preparation for Law Teaching* (1912) 37 A. B. A. REP. 747.

Judging from the comments in that and other papers, Mr. Justice Stone would not have agreed in 1912 with most of the suggestions made in the above. In part his disagreement would then have been due to his belief that the time required by the case system left little room for additions to the curriculum. The clear indications are, however, that, since that time, Columbia University Law School, like the other leading law schools, has reached the conclusion that too much time is ordinarily spent in the traditional study of case-books. See also Kales, *Should the Law Teacher Practice Law?* (1912) 25 HARV. L. REV. 253. Kales, who confined his practice almost entirely to writing briefs and oral arguments in upper courts, wanted law-teachers to be men engaged in that limited kind of practice. He had a curious contempt (often expressed) for the "office-lawyer" and an implied lack of respect for the lower court trial lawyer. Doubtless this was due to the limited nature of his own practice. As the bar is made up of all kinds of lawyers, it would seem wise that the law schools should be geared up accordingly. Most law teachers should therefore have had experience in (1) trial courts, (2) office work, and (3) upper courts.

COLUMBIA LAW REVIEW

VOL. XXXV   MAY, 1935   NO. 5

ON WHAT IS WRONG WITH SO-CALLED LEGAL EDUCATION*

If a person both can see and will do, he is, sociologically a freak. If he either cannot see, or seeing, will not do a thing non-traditional, he is normal; he is sane. The argument will base on the proposition that the health of any university, and more particularly of any law school, rests in departure from normality and deadly sanity. Freak persons and freak policies are needed; needed in very considerable

---

*This presents the substance of a talk delivered at Phillips Brooks House, Cambridge, on Jan. 22, 1935. It has, as of course in the circumstances, been duly submitted to the HARV. L. REV.; but as on other occasions their editor's canons of taste and policy did not jibe with mine.

Reactions from platform and floor were various: The ideals suggested were Utopian. . . . There had been practically nothing said that bore at all on legal education. . . . Would not segregated classes for slow men slow up the slow men further? . . . One professor, at last, had appreciated the point of view of a young man. . . . The speaker had no idea of where to stop. . . . Existing training was for a static world. We needed training for a world in flux. . . . The job of a law school was after all to train technicians. . . . There did seem to have been one point of interest. . . . Students were entitled to have what they came for. . . . This combination of lousy thinking and confessed incompetence. . . . The aim of the law was certainty, and such proposals would hinder the accomplishment of that aim. . . . What was meant, anyhow, by functional approach? . . . If a man went after roundedness in his first year, he lost out on the law review. . . . Could a curriculum, rather than the man himself, develop a rounded personality? . . . Why did the speaker sneer when he mentioned Wall Street practice? . . . Law students needed not only social fact, but the scientific theory of the social scientist. . . .

The diapason throbbed to the belief that there is already too much Law to learn, whereas the suggestions here made call for further expenditure of needed time. No diapason could more adequately evidence the need for publishing the paper. Truly neither law students nor law professors, as masses, have begun to appreciate either their job, or what can be done with that job.

In the paper I am conscious of borrowing chiefly from Herman Oliphant, Young B. Smith, Robert M. Hutchins, Charles E. Clark, and Emma Corstvet. Details are hard to trace. There is included, somehow, a net impact of several hundred criticisms from students old and new, among them certainly and importantly Ralph Heymsfeld, Ambrose Doskow, Milton Handler, and Herbert Wechsler—these last, no less as colleagues. Handler, for instance, taught my sales book once—and I learned. The attempt has been to "revise and enlarge" my writings of five years back: *Über den Rechtsunterricht in den Vereinigten Staaten*, 79 IHERINGS JAHRB. (2. Folge Bd. 43) 233 (1929); the Introduction to CASES AND MATERIALS ON SALES (1930); *A Modern Law School*, 22 COLUMBIA UNIV. Q. 316 (1930); THE BRAMBLE BUSH (1930). Also to get some understanding of why performance tortoises so far behind desire.

measure. This is true always and everywhere. But it is peculiarly true in a discipline whose very essence is tradition; it is peculiarly true in a teaching profession at those epochs when their tradition of teaching has grown blind, and withers.

But, cries the Devil's Advocate, we cannot junk tradition, we need stability, we need continuity, tradition provides the skeleton, we must continue. Right, Sir. Precisely right, Sir. We *cannot* junk tradition. "Continuity with the past is not a duty; *it is only a necessity.*" There are a hundred odd men in American legal education who for some ten years have been striving to see new needed things, and do them. They stick in tradition as a body sticks in muck. They are tied hand, foot, and eyes. Five years of struggle gets one hand free, to wave for help. This is why freaks are not a danger: they are very few, they are so little freakish, they are so tradition-ridden in what freakishness they have.[1]

What, now, is the situation? If Adam, a Baby, or the Man from Mars, fresh-eyed and curious, should survey this scene of ours, what would he see?

(1) He could not talk or think of "American Legal Education in Law Schools"; variety overwhelms similarity. The training ranges from work which, year for year, cleanly surpasses any other system of university legal training in this world to work so wretched that I doubt the existence of a counterpart in other lands. Let us therefore talk only of what can be regarded as first-rate law school education. Let us, for science's sake and decency's, be concrete in our subject-matter. Let us choose a subject-matter we are acquainted with. I shall direct my comment at "legal education" as practiced at Columbia, Harvard, and Yale.[2] But I wish to make it clear that I am not attacking these three schools, as such, or any of them. *Shabby and silly as they are, I know of no schools less shabby or less silly.*

(2) For the second self-evidence is that American law school training at these, and all, institutions is, viewed in critical aloofness,

---

[1] Take certain course-books I happen to know, all currently regarded as freakish, more or less: R. R. B. Powell's, both of Hanna's, and Jervey and Deák's, Havighurst's, Morgan and Maguire's, Chafee and Simpson's, and my own. The slaving to tradition, in any of these, accounts for 99 per cent of more of stuff, arrangement, treatment, and idea-content. The Man from Mars would find trouble finding significant differences between these books, or between any of them and a case-book of Langdell or Beale, or Costigan. It is not merely that all butterflies have wings, but that within one species of butterfly, color and spots are much alike; and all lay eggs that hatch out after their own kind. You need a micrometer to measure the freak-component. *Yet that is the component which gives the books such value as they have.*

[2] It thus hardly needs to be made explicit that I am myself, with all my colleagues, on the receiving end of any bricks this paper heaves.

ON WHAT IS WRONG WITH EDUCATION

blind, inept, factory-ridden, wasteful, defective, and empty. If you prefer verbs: it blinds, it stumbles, it conveyor-belts, it wastes, it mutilates, and it empties.

(3) The objectives of that education are a product of historical conditioning and chance. They miss most of what needs doing. They do not know what they miss, nor greatly care. Often they are plain wrong, plain vicious. Regularly, they are so confusedly perceived that they tangle one another's legs.

(4) The methods show, line for line, the lineaments of the objectives. A ghastly twinship.

(5) The trouble is as with the law itself. An outmoded tradition. A personnel which, in the large, clings inertly and incuriously to that tradition, as such, instead of viewing the tradition as one available tool, useful here, wasteful or futile there. A personnel which allows its aims to be dictated and limited by the existing tool, instead of seeking better or further aims, and then measuring the tool against the needed aims, and then setting itself to new invention when hammer and chisel are needed to supplement ax or adze. Or which Greenwich Villages into shrieking, miles beyond performance. In a word, an incompetent personnel: the conservatives blind, the radicals stickily quarter-baked.

All of this is understandable enough. It is pardonable. Law teachers are people. But the question is what is wrong with the job. The job is, too, not to explain merely, but to wrestle with my own conscience as a teacher. I find I come out worsted in the wrestling.

* * * * *

Objectives: What Do Lawyers Do?

By objectives I mean both the explicit objectives verbalized in that class of literature called Deans' Reports (as amazing a combination of reporting, propagandizing and suppression of the significant as man has yet devised) and those objectives implicit in the real workings of a school.

Both are alike in this: no faculty, and, I believe, not one per cent of instructors, knows what it or they are really trying to educate for.

Before the great case-book pioneers there seems to have swum a blurred composite photograph of the country-plus-city lawyer of about 1870. The shift even then occurring within the city-component received from the beginning less emphasis than was its due. The grosser evil lay in the over-simplication—as if there were a single kind of lawyer, with a single kind of practice, for which a single kind of training would suffice—and as if case-method were that single kind of training. That initial objective was and is false. But it is the initial objective which poses the problem, which frames the issue, for the future. No wonder subsequent work groans on a bias.

Anon, in the middle '20's, another composite photograph, no less blurred, began to swim before some innovators: the legal factory-hand, dedicated to the upper reaches of the corporation-factory. This was a needed correction. It involved, as most revolt-corrections do, a belated but vital perception of living, breathing, fact. But it involved, too, as most revolt-corrections do, too strong a swing toward the aspect newly perceived. Attempting to compass the new, we have whizzed by the old.

It is true that the 300-page corporate indenture is a part of today's life; it does need attention in the law school. But the old homestead is still being mortgaged. That needs attention too. And it is the effects of the new styles of mortgage-finance upon the old (and *vice versa*) which present the truly fascinating problem. Ancient rules and concepts of mortgage complicate and hamper the provision of corporate security. Ancient rules and concepts of trusteeship rise and walk, to defeat exemption clauses which should never have been drawn. While modern financing and modern statute draw farm and petty real estate mortgages into the orbit of a remodelled banking system. Such interactions cannot even be seen as long as either new phases or old are emphasized *alone*. So, through the other fields: I know for example no book on Corporations, and none on Business Units, that has *with due consistency* attempted to explore the differences between what one may call the investment- and the family-corporation. We see beginnings. We do not see full performance. Because the Small and the Big are not sharply drawn as needing, *both*, attention. Nor as needing, *each*, its own regulation drawn to its own problems, its own needs.

Meantime, what pictures should we of today be making about the actual workings of "the" heterogeneous Bar?

Not rules, but doing, is what we seek to train men for. Rules our men need. Rules do in part control or shape, do in still greater part set limits to, their doing. But the thing remains the doing.

What *is* this doing of lawyers? Whither are we to head our students? We do not know. Haphazard personal observation, conditioned by fossil concepts: these are our eyes. It is, knowing this, a lovely and touching thing to watch our guildsmen in the classroom. They feel the needs, they grope for answer. Whenever experience suggests a concrete illustration, Property or Pleading lies neglected for five minutes, while "I had a case . . ." or "I once knew a lawyer . . ." (told with skill and care) makes the teller reawaken with his audience. The trouble is, that

ON WHAT IS WRONG WITH EDUCATION 655

it happens by accident: haphazard, wasteful, only sometimes . . . because we do not know enough to choose or plan.

What do we *know* of the distribution of lawyers, by localities? What do we *know* of their work, quantitatively or qualitatively, or of the differences among them in their work? What do we *know*, as to how many law-trained men (or of our own graduates) are in law, and in what kind of law, or in what else? What do we *know* of their income; of their incomes by localities, or by specialties—*i.e.*, of what men can earn support, and how, from this long drawn-out "education"?

Nor does one find much interest in that other set of crucial problems: is the Bar's work too expensive to the people whom the Bar should serve, but whom it too often makes into milch-cattle? Can certain types of business be standardized and cheapened, and so made available to all who need counsel? Is the work as done, adequate? Where is it adequate, where is it not? Where, and for whom, are there gaps in the tasks actually performed? One suspects a piteous range of undone legal business; between the Legal Aid and the willing, paying client lies an unexplored, unexploited, *unattended* range of legal need. But how great is that need, and where does it lie, and what is it concerned with? We do not know. Do we care?

Yet if, as I premise, we claim to train men for a Profession, such things we need to know—and care about. *Know*, not guess at. Our graduates are to be placed. They are to be trained for their places. They are to make a living. They are to do the work a Bar is there to do. They are to do it decently, and for a decent price. As befits a government-protected monopoly, they are to do this for *all*. As befits a Profession, they are to do this—granted that they get a living—for those who cannot pay, or can pay little, quite as well as for those who pay the overhead or the installments on the Chrysler.

Neither may legal educators continue to overlook a further and major phase of law-work which we so thoroughly do overlook. Critique of law we not only too much neglect in class; when we do envisage it, then (bound in our technical Anglo-American tradition) we insist on viewing it from the angle only of the *judge*. But must law schools stay blind to the importance of the lawyer in political life? Can law schools not realize that political officeholders must reckon on displacement—that only the lawyer can hope to make immediate professional utilization, when displaced, of the publicity he gained while holding office? Can law schools overlook that even an unsuccessful campaign for public office affords that legitimate advertizing available otherwise only to counsel in a feature murder-trial? To politics, by the nature of our institutions, a good percentage of our graduates are predestined. For decent politics, what training do our law schools offer? A course in Constitutional Law, perhaps a sketchy course in Legislation. Trade Regulation may be added, or some new venture say on federal legislation. But what of *sustained* work, *throughout* the course, on the wherewithal for judging *and shaping* policy intelligently?

Let me repeat also what I have said elsewhere: I do not claim the absence in the orthodox curriculum of *occasional* intervention of policy-considerations when an instructor by personal accident *happens* to have acquired information, insight, and excitement. What "innovators" urge is the substitution of *sustained and consistent* labor with policy-facts and policy-choices for *occasional* flashes even of more-than-earthly beauty. Men see better by arc-light than by lightning.

To round out these considerations, one must include the recent trend of our law school graduates into government administration. That trend may be impermanent. Still, it demands reflection. To disregard the trend is to gamble on an hypothetical impermanency, while children in office are reaching decisions on which industries depend. Let me be plain: I do not often quarrel with their decisions. Far greater blindness and folly—where there is folly—lies, as I read it, in the opponents of these children. But, with more adequate training, there would be even happier results. Whereas we still stoutly train, not only for the blurred practice of 1870 alone, but for the technical phases of that practice only; even there, we spend most of our class-time playing checkers with pure "substantive rules."—No. I apologize. Checkers is much too solid. We play a cobweb chess. The pieces, clients, are fungible impersonalities: good old A, B and C. Michael Moriarty, The United States Steel Corporation; Al Capone, Secretary Mellon: "A," "B," or "C." Our graduate, if he is lucky, has learned enough theory to plead a bastard Ruy Lopez. The defendant answers. Our man brings out his "substantive" pawns and knights. He castles; he engages. He makes an oversight, for lack of *facts*. Mate! The poor client. . . .

Objectives: What Can Law Schools Do?

It does *per se* little good to show what is needed. The problem is, in view of what is needed, what can be done? Our immediate tools are a school and three years of time. Our excuses have been that we are merely a law school; that we have merely three years of time. I have heard Pound and Beale dig themselves in behind these flimsies, and Clark and Douglas, and Smith and Richard Powell. I, too, have found silly comfort in such digging in. For all of us, for each of us, I say now, such hiding makes out emotional and intellectual cowardice. Faced with a challenge, we slink to cover.

When business or government is confronted with a *Must*, business or government invents and improves. Or it goes under.

For law schools, the *Must* has today become inescapable. Either we produce, or our existing bankruptcy becomes an open shame. Demands on us rise by the hour. Either we make new payment in proportion to the rise, or we are exposed. As frauds. We have taken coin, we have usurped status, under the pretense of training for the law. While eyes and efforts have been fixed, and still are fixed, not on what *can* be done in a school in three years, but purblindly on what our predecessors, or ourselves, happen to *have been* doing.

Again, ground-clearing may require to be stump-pulling, if it is to give us an acre that yields more, and yet costs less to plough.

Consider the European schemes of legal education. In particular, consider the German in those days before party had become prerogative. There were seven semesters, spread over three and a half years, of academic training. Despite repeated reforms directed at making it more concrete, the university work remained over-theoretical. Compared with our best, it remained second-rate, or third. But complementing it was a further three years of *directed, rounded, apprenticeship*. Directed: no haphazardness of what office you might chance to find a place in; *a lawyer's legal duty was to take and train the man assigned to him*. The duty was abused. All duties are. But even exploitation trains. Rounded: the apprentice wandered from petty-court judge to appellate court, from courts to administrative agencies, from these to work with a practicing lawyer's office. He was to get an inkling of legal work at large. Three years of this, and then a *second* bar examination. Only after the second one was he let loose upon the public. *Meanwhile, throughout the apprenticeship, he received a modest stipend from the government.*[3] The State's interest was in raising judges and administrators. But it raised counsel, too.

Our schools face the absence of any apprenticeship at all. Why do they have to? What have we done to plug the gap? Where do you find signs that the problem has even been examined? We might, for example, look into the German system for its faults. I find nothing in it that really trains for the advocate's (as distinct from the judge's) job of legal argument; nor anything that trains for the lawyer's life-necessity of dealing with a client—or of getting one. I think of a certain old practitioner and his advice on how to avoid the consequences

---

[3] This varied by States, and by need, in recent years.

of a horseback opinion which had proved wrong. "Call your client back. Ask him to tell it all again, and with no prompting. He's sure to give you *some* new fact. Then hop on him: 'Why didn't you tell me *that* yesterday?'" This is not legal art, but legal artifice. Take, for contrast, the counsel of a veteran adviser of corporations: "Officers come to you to cover their own tracks. They want to do what they want; they want to have you to blame if it goes wrong. Your advice turns on the facts they give. Your reputation depends, therefore, on the record. So opinions do well to begin: 'You state that . . .' and to proceed: '*On the above facts,* my opinion is . . .'" This is not artifice; it is sense, it is decency, it is a solid, standard rule of thumb. Artifice or art: we purvey neither—save by accident. Though of course the curriculum is paved with good intentions.

Either of these stories brings home to a student the emptiness of rules without the facts, brings home the problem of turning legal or human knowledge into action. Their difference in tendency brings home to the observer the value of the full-time law-teacher who can hope to build perspective about which "practical" matters a Professional school can soundly inculcate. My own belief is: to fight wolves, you have to know wolves. And that wolf-study is a proper part of legal training. Ideals that cannot survive such study are stillborn.

Now are the virtues of sound case-training and full time instructors, obvious though they be, to obscure the need for complementing and supplementing the prevalent "best" training for the law?

A second line of semi-analogy lies in the care the medics exercise with regard to clinical service and to interneship. They have a longer theoretical training than ours. But they insist on *ordered* practical experience, before their graduates are certified to the helpless layman. Is medicine then more complicated than the law? I say, no. It is only that the standards for the law are lower. I have in mind a tentative questionnaire circulated recently among fifty lawyers. The question was, as to a long list of legal activities: From the angle of a client, but as knowing what *you* know, would you entrust to a person "of your experience" any one of the following matters? . . . The lawyers tried to answer honestly, despite certain ambiguities in the question (no mention of general skill, or of time available for research, *etc.*) The highest item found, out of the 50 questionees, 37 positive responses. The great bulk of lines of inquiry found no single lawyer-answerer who was ready to risk turning a case over to his equal.—No. Law is not simple. Well, then, is it no part of a law *school's* job to wrestle with the complexity? Or with the troublesomeness of turning rules into sensible *action?*

ON WHAT IS WRONG WITH EDUCATION

In a word: what have we tried to *do,* to make up for our inherent lacks, uncomplemented as they are by anything but chance—chance, which fails to make the dice turn up as we would want them?

Objectives: Deficient Preliminary Training

We know little, then, of the Whither of our graduates. Of the Whence of our entrants, we know a little more. But the more we see of that, the less we like it. They come unprepared. We know it. But about it, we do nothing. When we try, vaguely, to move, we find ourselves involved in hopeless controversy among ourselves.

I speak for no orthodox view, be it past or future, in regard to what pre-law-school work should be. As will appear, my belief is that *whatever pre-law-school work may be, it will never lighten the load on law instructors* for more than a moment at a time. Inadequate pre-law-school training forces law school men toward doubling the work they now do, in the accepted three years. More adequate pre-law training will ease the burden of doing what we are *now* doing. But it will not remove the yoke: it will indeed make heavier the labor of invention. For whatever we manage to be accomplishing, at any given time, and with any given human material, will always lag behind the demands bar and community are entitled to make upon us. Each upward shift of entrant-quality or -training represents merely a new opportunity to take on an untouched piece of our own proper load. There will always be the obligation to strain toward doubling whatever, within the three years allotted us, we may happen to be turning out.

Yet at first glance it is disheartening that no agreement can yet be had, as to what pre-law-school work should be. Look at the records. The last report of the Committee of the Association reproduced three disparate opinions of non-members of the Committee. Then it abdicated. Again, a bankruptcy. The medics can agree. The lawmen cannot. They cannot even reach tentative compromise.

In part this rests on their inability to know whether they themselves would go. In part, on their ignorance of educational processes, a matter still to be discussed. Most of all, it rests on divergent views of what law school is for.

There is therefore only one immediate answer. Disruptive and unfortunate, it still is the only road of hope. School by school—if schools cannot agree—each faculty must lay down what *it* requires. And, as Oliphant and Handler have insisted, law schools must themselves take over a full share of the job of seeing that they get what they demand. Our own colleges, or those in our own cities, feed each of us in good part with our entrants. In good part enough to afford some test, as against students from other colleges, of whether our ideas on pre-law work, when tried out, will have the value we think they may have, toward *our* law study. The laboratory for experiment is clear, and open. Frame demands, enforce them as to our own colleges, and then, in our own schools, test the work of those who have fulfilled our demands against that of those from schools which have not. Five years will give light. . . . That is, it would give light if we did not scuttle past the laboratory door.

Of the matters to be developed before entrance into law school, each man, today, speaks purely for himself. I, for one, am for an entrance test that would go far beyond the "capacity-tests" in vogue at Columbia or Yale, and far beyond the college degree. *I want every law student to be able to read and write.* Half of my first-year students, more than a third of my second-year students, can do neither. I want any entrant to have a smattering of logic, American historical fact, descriptive economics, sociology of institutions, and psychology of human behavior; also some conception of organic evolution, and some conception of weighing statements of "fact" according to the "Authority" which has adduced the statement; finally some idea of quantitative, as opposed to purely qualitative thinking. Of none of these have 50% of my entrants, now, an inkling. Those that have one, lack another.

But larger than any such technique or knowledge looms the question of emotional and intellectual *interest,* or eagerness. In professional school we do profit by a certain stepping up of interest that depends on the entrant's perception that his living is at length at stake. Still, we miss out on half of them. They sit. Dough without yeast. If any law school teacher honestly doubts that, unhelped by circumstance (professional school) and ancient tradition (the case-book), he is a dub at teaching, let him tackle a college class (even of pre-law men), and try to bring out such eagerness as any capable teacher is able to produce. Experiment aids perception.

Meanwhile, I argue: pending reform of the college, we have to reform ourselves. Unless our men *go forth* equipped to read and write, and (leaving all else aside) with intellectual eagerness and with some grasp of policy-consideration, we fail in our duty to the community if *we* admit them to the LL.B. degree. We may shift the blame for not being able to graduate enough lawyers to serve the community (though on this I have yet to hear complaint from the community). *We can not shift blame for graduating incompetents. We can not shift blame for minting our incompetents as competent.* Are "best" schools to go on having graduates whom their professors will not recommend? Or, what is worse, whom their professors recommend with conscience qualms?

Law must have all the matters, all the skills, all the attitudes, in its lawmen, which we have been discussing. Else law's prestige will perish. Law *schools* must then provide these things—or get them provided. *Demands are rising.* The three creditors knock with the petition.

But we leave these things to chance. For comfort, we fix our telescope on graduates in high place, on the success of Law Review men, and the like. As gamblers chew over like a cud the one-time pleasure of four aces in a hand.

Objectives: Ideals, and the Full Life

This awful symbol Chance should neither drone nor whine in its reiterations. Rather should it be made Miltonian thunder down the pillared aisles, to blast our souls with organ-throbbing realization that we of the guild do but repeat the history of the race. Always Chance rules, until perception and invention come to serve and save. Always tradition smothers while she gives suck, fresh sacrifice eternal to a fresh spawn of Chance.

All of this is, I repeat, inevitably human. Almost the inevitability discourages. The sociological processes concerned are so clear. There is a tradition, at any given moment. Most of us, consequently, just fit in. Those that do not are freaks. But most freaks are crazy, and useless, even disruptive.[4] The tradition therefore goes on until it has been long outworn. Only a genius breaks through it, to living gain. Even such a genius as Langdell needed an Ames, a supplementary executing genius, and thirty years as well, to make his idea dent his guild. Even that great team dropped out much of the value or what they themselves had rebelled against, though they carried over (Ames, at least) into their own work the values of the earlier style of thinking. While the epigones, pygmies, lack both the balance and the tradition of the giants. Out of once succulent steak they make a hamburger that reeks its age.

It would, then, be discouraging if Students and Times did not squeeze upon that dog-wagon short-order man known as a law school teacher.

---

[4] As indicated, this seems to me highly exceptional, so far as concerns their work and thought. But their personalities may sometimes work disruptively, within a faculty. In this they resemble saner folk. The problem is the same, with both.

Students: they look around them, and rebel. They rebel no less (in the interest of the Grand Tradition) where they suspect themselves of being guinea-pigs, than in the centers of the Ancient Learning—where they suspect themselves of being sacrificed to idols. This is magnificent. One thing we overlook much too often is the value (in addition to the despair) that comes to us out of the stubborn resistance of our students. That resistance is not only magnificent, it is of course also often magnificently fallacious. Looking abroad, the student seizes on one or two Major Figures, and asks: "Why are not All of Ours as good as they?" While abroad, similar students are holding caucus on some similar question.—But, for all lacks in perspective, the students do stir. They stir not only in matters of the intellect. Students turn up, as well, persistently, insistently, consistently, with matters involving their souls, and their whole selves. And so awaken us.

Their souls: they have ideals. Surprising to one who has watched the Wall-Street-flocking over a decade and more is this number of youngsters who now show hunger to make law *do* something. The number who prefer a government job. The number who are pestered with the prospect of becoming prostitutes. The spontaneous gathering this year, at my school, for example, of boys who plan organized inquiry into what a lawyer *can* do, and still remain both a citizen and a person—and into how he can shape his work to be more of a person, and more of a citizen. (My guess is, their Report will jar their faculty.)

Now have we no obligation in the engendering, in the guiding, of such ideals? I do not refer to "teaching Legal Ethics," in a course. I refer to the setting up of every course to bear, *inter alia*, on what the job in society of that branch of law may really be, and on how well the job is being performed.

Again, let me avoid misconception. I hold that a lawyer's first job is to be a *lawyer*. I hold that we must teach him, first of all, to make a legal table or chair that will stand up without a wobble. Ideals without technique are a mess.

But technique without ideals is a menace. The boy must be hard-headed, with trained hands and brain. He must, as said above, be able to fight wolves. But is that all? I say, as well, that he must want to take wolves' pelts. The encouragement of that desire is a law school job. And if the man—as so many will—goes into legislation or administration, then it is the law school's job to give him, first, a decent fact-foundation from which to work; and second, understanding of the need of facts; and, third, a driving interest in their acquisition; and fourth, the first beginnings of the wherewithal to weigh them and their

ON WHAT IS WRONG WITH EDUCATION

implications for a People. Techniques and interests, not merely as to "law," but as to "fact," and "policy." Peculiarly as to those *socially* vital facts which practice as such, in civil cases, so quietly and insidiously drops beneath the table.[5]

Neither does the job stop with this. Above I spoke of the student's whole self. That whole self needs attention. From the angle of a lawyer's dealings with clients, witnesses, jury, judge, and bench of five or seven. No less from the angle of a lawyer's living with self or children, after forty. Till forty—sometimes even till fifty—he can make out, after a fashion, on hard work, and (if he achieves it) on success.

But as in so many things, our law schools presuppose here some sort of ectogenic Culture, sprouted at home or in college, and somehow to be automatically reintroduced into the system in harmonious combination with whatever it is we teach. Now first, this Culture mostly has not sprouted. And second, our methods are such as to kill it if we can. "Make him think like a lawyer!" Park Culture at the door! This would be fine, if, *after* making the boy think like a lawyer, we really did reintroduce the Culture. Do we?

Indeed, the more "progressive" the school, the less time is left the student for anything but reading cases and chasing references—all with an eye as good as single to The Law. I think (and hope) that the Columbia level for a C+ man has now risen to over fifty hours a week of work. As a measure of a full time job, fine. But how of the work itself? Rules, always rules—or decisions—in the forefront of attention. (Yet a brief, in due course, will call also for composition, poetry and style.) Clear, legally artificial, dehumanized thinking—a touch of policy; but how much? (Yet trial or appeal in due course, will call also for "atmosphere," and some attention to what legislatures may have ordered.) The "issue" in legalistically procedural terms. (Yet life, in due course, will call no less for understanding human conflict, and the drama of human conflict.) Meanwhile some kid regrets that he has no time for piano practice; another yearns to compare Millay and MacLeish; the third knows none of these, and cannot understand the conversation.

The need is, in some fashion, for an integration of the human and the artistic with the legal. Not an addition merely; an integration. Attempt at such integration finds response. This is not yet the place al-

---

[5] So many folk have acquired the idea that realists are not interested in ideals or ethical problems that I want to guard against any misconstruction that this passage evidences a conversion, or coming round. The fact is that any would-be innovator, or changer of things-as-they-are-at-the-moment, is of necessity interested in ideals and in ethical evaluations. In my own case, I think that demonstrable in every paper or book published, at least since 1925.

lotted to discussion of means, yet discussion of means may here help clarify objective. I cite instances:

There were six photographs of Konenkov's bust of Holmes (the bust now at Columbia and Harvard). There were an equal number of the anonymous Maria of Bamberg, and of the Uta of Naumburg, and of another modern head. The artist's chisel has reproduced the model for his Maria with tragic devotion. He loved her; he chose her as model for his Mary. He did not see or know, but he recorded, that she was venal, hard, treacherous, as well as lovely. So with the Uta. Though so idealized that the full face is ethereal, the profile shows up cat and shrew.—These photographs, then, spread before a group of law students, with comment on the differences that light and angle made —on walking around the whole, to see it whole—on how the subject had determined the job, despite all canons. Then suggestion on how the seemingly simple record of a case could change in the light of color and experience of the observer—how every time an instructor read his cases over he saw new facets and new form. Or on how a single opinion rounded out if one read it successively as a case in contracts, in waiver, in pleading, or in sales.—Or on how judges, like artists, can respond to facts their fingers notice, while their minds deny those facts.— One cannot easily catch faces or reactions into print. One simply knew that sculpture and cases had acquired, both, new meaning; *and new relation*. With similar pictures of the Winged Victory, what could be done!

There was that boy who had no time to practice music, and found his law antagonistic to piano. And who saw, then, how the Bach fugue was what an instructor might try his poor best to emulate in a casebook chapter, or a lawyer in a brief;—how the job of legal exposition might, and must, run upon the same lines as that of musical.

There was the attempt to study how to argue, with students turning back to all their college literature in search of style; and to their cases, in search of build-up and persuasiveness; and to novels (Sergeant Buzzfuzz' opening), and life, in search of keys to human nature.

So much for examples. But we need more than examples. The objective of a full life, though we starve it, is stubborn as a desert plant. We must not let law smother the man in his study of it, nor let it cut him off from what art has to offer for and in its practice. We must recapture, or find a substitute for, the old-time lawyer's Bible and his Shakespeare. But least of all must law cut its students off from living, from rich living, after they become lawyers. Professors who are sterile dissecting knives, *and are no more*, wreak tragedy. . . .

ON WHAT IS WRONG WITH EDUCATION

I said above, not only the students, but the Times, squeeze upon the comfort of our dog-wagon cook. But with a difference. The Students can in some measure be restrained by austerity, by authority, by their own ignorance, by their habit of submission. The Times cannot. Indeed, what we have by now in the way of semi-reform of the Ancient Routine, is directly a product of the Times. Those newer movements which strike toward reorganizing rules in terms of modern problems rest one and all on the discovery that some lawmen are no longer behaving along the lines presupposed by obsolescent legal formulae. *E.g.,* despite all talk of "no liability without fault," much liability simply has been happening in accordance with ideals about risk-distribution. So, despite all talk about "acceptance only in the terms dictated by the offer," some offerors are getting stuck before the terms dictated by the offer have been fulfilled. Thus run the cases, even in the courts. Much more does the pressure show, on counsel in the office. Most of all, outside either court or office.

Thus, in the mid-20 period of new courses, new case-books, curriculum revision, did the Times show their power upon the resistant shellfish of the schools. In these past few years, the power grows. When a Handler (who has been off New Dealing), reorganizes a course in Trade Regulation to build around the N.R.A., that is perhaps merely a pleasant sign of industry and of the effects of outside stimulus. But when a McLaughlin, though he regards the N.R.A. as "a joke, a tragedy, an abortion, and a fraud," devotes a semester to its study, and along original lines, we may see truly that the Times do press.

It seems, in short, as if Student and Times may yet jar even a Law School loose. If jarred, it must start fresh in some direction; and some of the directions we have canvassed. But are there *means*, to go?

Methods: Defenses and Excuses

Such a canvassing of objectives as the above may be relied on to meet with immediate evasion. The lines are familiar as Hamlet's soliloquies.

(1) Of course high ideals of education are lovely. Everybody likes them.

(2) But we are limited, we are hamstrung, by time
                                           and by student material
                                           and by personnel.

(3) We therefore render unto preliminary education the things that are preliminary education's.

(4) And unto practice the things that are practice's.

(5) Our own curriculum, meantime, is full. So are our hands.

(6) . . . We stay put. Q.E.D.

Now to this, and its ilk, several things need saying quickly. They will be dealt with more fully hereinafter.

(1) Necessity need not, of course, mother invention. Nobody can tell, until he courts necessity. But faint heart never won fair lady.

(2) Even on our present knowledge, waste of time in existing curricula is patent. The pure case-method—as fine a tool as teacher ever invented—completes its work with a quick student in a year; with even a slow student, it would do its work within two years, if the slow student, in the second year, were given sustained instruction sharply directed to *his* needs. Second year instruction, as practiced, falls between two stools: an attempt to keep the quicker man interested, and an attempt to bring the slower man along. The combination is wasteful. It is self-contradictory. The Law Review, as an expedient, helps a little, for some; but only a little, and only for some. Even for slow men, then, one year's time is available to try out something different, something that can uncork other techniques than pure analysis.

(3) Our teachers teach wastefully, and are content. They do not try to pool experience. Each knows that he is right. Despite this, the older men do not try to correct the mistakes or misguesses of those younger men who make up such a large proportion of our faculties. None cares to know any educational method but his own tradition. Moreover, in sublime conceit, we teachers attribute all failure to the student.—Here lies untapped possibility, thus far aborted, and interred.—The range of that possibility we have been forced to see in one faculty that has labored with selective admission. *The students being reasonably certified, a flunkage of 20% must rest in good part on defective teaching.* Yet I know no better faculty.

(4) Some existing experiments in reorganization of material have definitely proved their worth, in getting more done in less time. Take Powell's condensation of Wills, Trusts, and Future Interests. Every such experiment makes room for further experiment.

(5) The practical certainty that many "C" men, given more individual attention, would get the knack of case-study more quickly by a year, has hardly been considered. Nor has the use of special sections in the second year, devoted to the special case-study problems of the slower men.

(6) The use, where the knack of analysis has been learned, of text and lecture and *reference* to a case-book to accomplish the *in-*

formation part of an upper class course, has hardly been tapped. This would free time for really working *with* the material, the student checking his reading of cases not by cross-examination in first year style on the well-known fifteen pages per hour, but by cross-examination on his *use* of the cases in drafting, argument, or advice.

All this merely by way of indicating that we have to reckon here not with counsels of perfection blowing lazily across the trees, but with a challenge. We *do* have room to move in. All signs indicate that we can make more room; much more room. So, instead of moving, we sit. This is a sleeping dog that needs a kick.

Methods: What Lawyers Do

To train, we must know what we are training for. As will appear, there are many things we can turn to, even without more knowledge of this than we have already. But to provide either solid soundness or new vision, we must investigate the bar.

Can we, then, find out what lawyers are really doing? Already three lines of attack have been developed. The New York County Lawyers' Association has begun one opening canvass. Garrison has headed an illuminating and singularly canny survey of the Wisconsin Bar: a census of who is in practice, and where, and with what income, and with what type of academic record. Also an inquiry into how far, and where, true over-crowding seems to exist.[6] The next step in Wisconsin, already initiated for Illinois by the Illinois State Bar Association, is inquiry into the *what* of lawyers' doing: how much work, and how much specialization, and in what? How much competence for various lines of work among either general or highly specialized practitioners? Fees? All but the last are difficult to reach with any accuracy. But the mere presence of the movement is a heartening sign.

Beyond that, and as regards the jobs left undone by the bar, we have little definite information as yet save from the Legal Aid Societies and from such investigation as has given rise to Public or to Voluntary Defenders.

Nor have we clear information on what happens to our graduates. Yet an alumni law register could be made to yield some light on this last.

On cheapening and standardizing—and so developing—such types

---

[6] Garrison tapped FERA funds. This had not occurred to other law school men. Garrison's methods and interpretation, moreover, would make most sociologists envious. The lawyer who becomes a social scientist seems to profit by his law. This does not contravene what is said below about the use of social science data by lawyers who remain *pure* lawyers.

of business as lease-making or counselling on leases, or simple wills, we are in the realm of pure guesswork.

Taken as a whole: the field seems open for inquiry. The bar is interested as it has not been within our lifetimes; what lacks is imagination, initiative, interest. Methods are largely still to be developed, and the work is still to be done. But the need cries. Courses on The Legal Profession canvass chiefly the literature, which in turn is made up almost wholly of guess, or viewing with alarm, or prophecy. Whereas we need proved fact. We need proved information as to the typicality or non-typicality of what our haphazard experience suggests to us to be the fact. For instance, it has been objected: "Why worry in the schools about apprenticeship? The men get it." But how *many* get it? And with whom? And under what conditions favorable to learning? Do you *know?* Does anybody?

Personally, I suspect that when we do once discover what law-trained men are doing, we shall find that the objectives for which we are to train include much both from old-style and new-style teaching. But that they include much in addition to both. And therefore will require either expansion of the curriculum—which seems unfeasible—or new economy within it.

Methods: Background of Social Fact

This matter of new economy comes to bear directly on the introduction of the background of social fact and policy. Unfortunate and often violent misconceptions fare abroad:

(1) There is the notion that introducing fact background means introducing it raw; *e.g.*, as extracts, reprints, or references that swallow social science studies whole. In rare cases, this may pay.

In very rare cases. For social scientists have not gathered their data to our use, but to their own; their data are focussed on the problem for which they have been gathered, and on the angle of that problem which interests the gatherer. However good, sound, thorough, illuminating, such a line of work, it intersects our lawyers' line at but a single point. Reading lines, to gather points, breaks the back. It is therefore normally the job of the instructor, and trebly the job of one who puts out a Materials book, to gather the strayed mass of materials together, and to extract from the intersections, in brief form, his *own* line of information. This costs editor's time; it means editor's education. *It overloads neither the student nor the curriculum.*

(2) There is the notion that adding social facts to The Law as law-course material makes the job harder, or longer, *for the student.*

ON WHAT IS WRONG WITH EDUCATION 669

This is sheer nonsense. The fact is that legal rules mean, of themselves, next to nothing. They are verbal formulae, partly conveying a wished-for direction and ideal. But they are, to law students, empty. A brilliant student told me recently of the pleasure of his course in Bills and Notes, in which he had been doing algebraic tricks. *This student had, however, never seen a bill.* (I had similar pleasure, once, in Bills and Notes.) It would not have been tactful to enquire into what he knew of foreign exchange, or the trade acceptance movement, or the use of acceptances in place of notes in England, or the differences in function and use between bills and checks. He could, however, and with real excitement, manipulate the Rules of Bills and Notes. I was reminded of how I used, in high school, to substitute $\left\{\frac{\text{"sin a"}}{\cos a}\right\}$ for "tan a," successfully, to get the answer, but with no picture of a rectangled triangle, or of the relation of side to diagonal, or of a sine or tangent curve, or of the meaning of any of these things. It was fun; it was futile.

This type of manipulation, for all its values esthetic and sometimes practical, is vicious when left to itself. In a judge, it threatens us with the "strong decision" beloved of Parke, B. In an advocate, it leads to trusting gossamer to carry iron; it leads to disregarding the earthy sense of courts. But what is worse (for a brilliant man will in due course learn what else he needs to know) it leads to the slower student's groping in a three years' daze, with hold for neither right hand nor for left. The slower student, the concrete-minded student, does not even get to taste the fun.

Whereas to set rules into their social context, into the context of how men do things, and of what difference the rule makes to those men—this is to give body to a rule for any student. It has graphic value, it has movement value, it has memory value. Rules thus seen are not only more meaningful. *They are also easier to learn.* You *save* time, when you teach them thus. You also make *critique* of the rule take on its human content. You make critique inevitable, because the human content, once introduced, will never be denied.

Let me take an example. (1) No simple contract is valid without consideration. (2) Any bargained-for detriment to the promisee, but only a bargained-for detriment to the promisee, is adequate consideration.—I suppose these are rules. Certainly they are current formulae.

Now put some cases from life. (a) A laborer is negligently injured, and worried over job, rent and food. The claim adjuster beats the ambulance chaser in. The laborer signs a release of claim in consideration of "one dollar and reemployment." He gets the dollar, and gets employment for a week. (b) One foreign exchange dealer gives another a "firm" offer for five minutes, and revokes after four of them. Both belong to the Foreign Exchange Club. (c) A brewer (or was it a pork-packer?) promises to pay a fixed sum per annum to his daughter after marriage to the Italian Count to whom she is engaged. They marry next day. Suit, years later, is, not by daughter or Count, but by a money-lender who has discounted the annuity. (d) Old Family Friend promises father to pay newborn son $10,000 if son is named after Old Family Friend. (e) An auto manufacturer of established reputation appoints an agent for Keokuk, the agent agreeing to seventeen things, the manufacturer to nothing; the agent has "bought out" his predecessor for $10,000. All five cases are bargains. What happens to "the" rules as they pass through the five cases, and what happens to "the" facts as the courts manhandle them to get decent results *despite the rules?* I claim these happenings not only give meaning to the rules, but make them stick in the head. Even a modicum of common sense embroidery has its justification. But, no less valuable, any real understanding of the social background typified in such cases *forces* policy-judgment.

The net result is: more effect, for less effort, for more men.

(3) The third notion abroad is that displacement of study-book space by "non-legal" material depletes the room for "necessary" "legal" material. I hold this idea fallacious; but I recognize its power. Judgments as to balance of convenience will differ.

Against the idea is to be argued, in addition to the time-*saving* just described,

(a) That our curriculum is already (and of necessity) so little representative of "legal" law at large that twenty or thirty per cent more or less makes little difference, provided more *and better* method be inculcated.

(b) That much expansion of present courses has run in terms of merely adding, rather than of significant reselection. This development is a function of blindness (as to the whole), vision (as to the course), and vested interest (of the instructor), in triple combination.

(c) That digesting and shrinking of cases for use in course-books (always with an eye on *the whole case*) can save more space than technique has yet been evolved to prove. Shrinking is dangerous. But over the long haul, we all do it, one way or another. I hold it better, if conscientiously done, than mere excerpting. And I hold that casebooks still too largely overlook the discussion-value of a shrunk case.[7]

---

[7] There is one good by-product even of bad shrinking: students consult the original, and challenge.

(d) Finally, and as a lunge to the throat: that without the background material no case has any business to be used at all: *better less, with real understanding, than more of the ununderstood.*

The counter-arguments will occur to any reader. I shall not list them. The choice is a choice among values.

But room for one piece of personal testimony I must claim, making due advance allowance for bias and for idiosyncrasy. With a "standard" case-book, I spent *four* hours a week on Sales, and got poor results, on rules, on Act, on everything else. With a case-book and course built to set background for the rules, I get in *three* hours a reasonable understanding of the Act, the cases, and the business meaning of both. This may evidence personal incompetence in handling a standard casebook. But it certainly evidences that curriculum-time *need* not be sacrificed merely because the field of study is widened. Thus, Michael has added real logical training to his Evidence. He teaches the Law of Evidence as effectually as before. Little more time is called for; the excess heretofore called for is shrinking. The more light, the less time.

Method: Social Background: Conclusion

The upshot seems to be that, within our time-limitation, we either integrate the background of social and economic fact and policy, course by course, or fail of our job. The early urge, say about 1910, was to pile on such courses as Legal History, Legal Philosophy, Jurisprudence, Comparative Law, in a fourth year. I, for one, am glad the students refused to follow the suggestion. Merely added on behind, such matters are well-nigh as ectogenic as Economics from college, frozen into harmlessness in the law school refrigerator. The students' sabotage of the Fourth Year has had as its function to wake faculty-members up to the job of *integrating* background—social or philosophical—into *every* course. And I shall be greatly surprised if the new four-year curriculum projected by the Yale Law and Harvard Business Schools does not, after a few years of experience, reconcentrate into a new and better Three Years.

The trouble lies of course with the instructor.[8] He knows his tradi-

---

[8] The instructor has first of all to conquer inertia. It is hard to plough new ground, and one needs to plough around the field before he knows its nature and its possibilities. The instructor has, second, to keep his balance. I agree *in toto* with Goodrich's cautioning, *Our Black Ink Balance* (1932) 7 AM. L. SCHOOL REV. 385, at 394-5: The social sciences harbor both school-exaggeration and a lunatic fringe; nor can a man *master* (in one sense) many disciplines. Yet there is a chasm of difference between such "mastery" as means first-rate standing as a worker in neighboring ploughland, and such modest "mastery" as means only the ability to read critically, and to evaluate the findings read and the methods out of which they came. Only this last is called for. It is enough to rejog think-

tional technique. More than that, he values it as the center of his work. Other techniques are strange to him. Suppose, even, that he learns to deal with social science, or social science factual material: the job of building two things into a whole is, even for his *own* thinking, stiff to do. And after that, emerges a further job: extracting and shrinking the stuff *in its bearing on his course*. A gigantic task.

But, therefore, a task to be begun at once. Intensively. Again, and yet again, the argument is for *sustained* inquiry, along lines which every living law teacher indulges, which every living law teacher recognizes as needful. whenever fate happens to have thrown one golden apple into a passive lap.

Nor is it wholly apparent to the Man from Mars why all understanding must be had by way of Course or Class. Students, being Americans, do find the acquisition of knowledge or understanding apart from Courses somewhat hard to conceive. Students in large classes, being human, find it hard to labor when the chances of being called on are three to a hundred. Students, being practical, prefer courses that head directly for the bar exam.—But how much do *we* do, *for 100%* of the students, toward counteracting such herd-human drives?

Methods: Critique of Law

"My brother Gray," runs one garbled version of a story. "has taught you what the law Used to be; my brother Ames has taught you what the law Ought to be; I intend, with your indulgence, to give some attention to what the law Is." Such a goal, as *one* goal, no reformer will quarrel with. The first task of a law school is still to turn out as much

---

ing, and to awaken appetite. True, shifting vocabulary solves no legal problems; but the concepts a new vocabulary adds, and the information which comes packaged in those concepts, may raise or clarify dozens of legal problems at a time.

Where I differ utterly from the net effect of Goodrich's paper at 395 is in my certainty that "collateral investigation" by the student "of all the fields of knowledge" is not of the essence of the problem; and in my belief that rightly prepared background simplifies and shortens the process of learning even legal analysis of decisions.

May I add two further observations?

(1) A black-ink *balance* is not produced by totting up assets. Sane accounting calls for a totting up, no less, of liabilities. Goodrich demonstrates his own point as to the dangers of playing with an unfamiliar vocabulary. But he demonstrates no less the value of emerging from the old, as an exclusive frame of thought. May there be more of him! May he go further!

(2) In no Continental country is there the hope our law education affords. *Our men specialize.* Whereas a Continental professor must be prepared, say, to teach all of Civil Law (Property, Estates, Obligation, Transactions, Representation, Family—and What Have You?), we have goodly numbers who teach Trusts and Torts, or Contracts and Sales, or such a combination plus but one or two other narrow courses. With such relative limitation of subject matter, the possibility of getting societal background becomes real.

of a lawyer as it can. Historians who do not eat do not continue long to understand. Nor do reformers who do not eat, reform.

Yet critique is of the essence, not only of understanding and reform, but of practice. Critique, intelligent critique, derives only from knowledge of effect. And again, rules must be sized up in the light of *doing:* laymen's doing, and the effect of such doing upon laymen. And yet again, isolated lightning-flashes do not do the work. *Day for day, week for week,* the background must be both provided and explored; and provided, and explored, not alongside, but as an inevitable part of, the rule-material studied. This, for understanding; this, for practical utilization; this, for criticism.

The social scientists make an interesting comment upon lawyers. "That rigid discipline," they say, "which lawyers take such pride in— that discipline shows sweetly in all purely *verbal* operations. [How an outsider can flatter!] In word-techniques, lawyers are admirable. Or on the facts of a particular case. [This compliment, now, is deserved— by any real lawyer.] But when it comes to broadly social facts, in their social bearings, lawyers are helpless—childish. They fall for the tripe that journalists talk to women's clubs, or politicians at a bankers' convention." The criticism is sound. Is there, for instance, anything sadder than the naiveté with which mere lawyers manhandle statistics? Say, on any aspect of crime, or on overcrowding of the bar?[9] Yet I think it demonstrated by work recently done in many schools on such topics as the N.R.A. that law students *can* learn to handle masses of social and economic fact, that they can learn this in law school, and that they can learn it with relatively small expenditure of curriculum hours. I do not refer in this connection to Law Review notes; those might show merely the ability of the chosen few. I rest my case on the work of the "C" man who, for a change, is given a chance.

It is patent, however, that personal investigation of social fact, or even personal canvass of the literature, is within a normal law curriculum a one-occasion business. It remains the faculty's job, course by course and case by case, to provide the material which will make it plain that judgment as to "the better rule" rests on more than ignorance and conceit. My experience is that "the better rule" is seldom either rule, but mostly an intelligent synthesis of the two, built in the light of the needs which each rule *partly* serves.

---

[9] Wickser and Garrison are notable exceptions. And a reasonable number of law school men have in recent years demonstrated their ability to do work more workmanlike. *Cf.* the Johns Hopkins studies, or the work of Warner, or Frankfurter and Greene.

Methods: Techniques Other Than Analytical

As things stand, an LL. B. tends to indicate that its possessor has had some training in telling dictum from decision, has some information not yet wholly forgotten about a few rules of law, and can, under examination pressure, avoid wholly blowing up.

It does not indicate that the possessor can use a law library, or find a case in point. It does not indicate that he can draft language that will cover a point, much less that he can see a point to cover. It does not indicate that he has any ability to devise a rule of thumb to get around a rule of law, or any information as to what useful rules of thumb have already been devised. It does not indicate that he can argue, or try a case, or even draw a pleading.

Some of these things a school cannot teach. Let us grant that. None of them, however, can a school neglect.

Still, the use of a law library is one thing that can be taught. Law Review men learn it. Moot courts give first aid to many more. The term-essay has proved its worth in making the learning universal. All one has to do, to prove this, is to match the third year term-essay of a "C" student with the one he wrote his second year. Compulsory essays in both years should be introduced into every school.

Drafting is a harder job to handle. It is not easy to learn. Background is hard to give; and on background intelligent drafting must depend. Interest is hard to awaken—that interest which alone produces the seven reworkings out of which skill to draft develops. Yet some things *can* be done. In every course there crop up rules which the instructor abominates. His business is to provide facts enough to make his abomination plausible. Why does this not set a statutory or a contract-drafting problem? Why cannot an hour then be devoted to critique of what students have drafted? Let me be brutal: the first effort will be a mess. Seven out of a class, at most, will have attempted real thinking; the rest is hogwash. And, on discussion, ninety per cent of a class, instead of either thinking or criticizing, will dully note down the result. But the third, and the fourth, and the fifth efforts, if decent underpinning has been provided, will *not* be messes. The esthetic pleasure of tailoring words to a situation has an appeal that three-quarters of a law class can get; they set the tone, and the one-quarter comes along. I argue that drafting is a part of *every* law course.

So, too, of counselling, in all fields but procedure. Day by day, the question must recur: "In view of this decision, what will you advise a man in the loser's position to *do*, next time?" I have no patience with the archaic objection that the student does not know enough about the situation to respond. *If he does not, he cannot understand the decision. If he does not, he does not know the rule.* Competent teaching of decisions and rules requires the building of enough fact-background to provide some basis for a counselling-question. Indeed, from the instructor's angle, nothing reveals so searchingly his own inadequacies in getting background over as the first silly answers to his questioning on what to do. For this alone, counselling-questions should be made obligatory.

The neglect of opportunity along this line appears nowhere better than in the use of forms in "modern" materials books. Campbell as early as 1925 did include in his Mortgages a form of corporate mortgage. It stands at the end, unannotated, wholly unregarded. Even in 1930, I put my forms at the end of the book. Neither they nor their annotations are ever looked at. Hanna, Douglas and Berle inserted forms where they belong; square in the text. Yet not even they have has really milked the forms for their teaching value, for their value as review materials, for their value as problem-setters. Tradition still binds imagination. Yet, clearly, the outlook brightens.

When we come to court-work, the European model offers hope. Let us concede that practice-courts have thus far been successes only in the hands of notable teachers. Let us concede that the artificiality of the atmosphere is too great for most instructors to overcome. What of that? There remains the fact that law school is needlessly abstract, and needlessly removed from life. There remains the fact that seeing-it-done gives reading-it-in-books new flavor, new perspective. If one afternoon a week, during one semester of one year, were free of other classes, and the students with an instructor should visit various courts; if written critiques of what had been observed were followed by the instructor's comment and criticism; if the lawyers concerned were invited to explain their own views on their strategy—

Or if law schools would deliberately set to work to plan an interstitial apprenticeship. Half of our students could afford to put in the first or second summer in a law office, for car fare and lunch money. There are enough lawyers who would cooperate, if anybody should go after them. Indeed, they could be induced to stretch a point; they could be induced to try to make the work rounded, for the student. But who tries to induce them? I do not believe, as Frank seems to, in the substitution of practice or clinic for theoretical instruction. But I believe with all my soul in the livening up, the making real, of theoretical work by practical complement.

Nor do I see reason why law schools should not deliberately set themselves to the job of planning and controlling a post-school apprenticeship. *And withhold the degree until that apprenticeship is served.*[10]

In 1919 Wigmore, stirred by Army method, built for law-students a "job-analysis." The aim was to take each of the operations a lawyer has to know, to devise a task which would test out or teach each of the necessary techniques, and then to put each student through each task. One of the most sweetly sparkling jewels yet cast before us.

Methods: Radical and Conservative

It has been argued above that the analytical technique in developing which the case-method is an incomparable tool can do its work for a quick student within a year, and, for any student who deserves to graduate, within two years. And it is ancient learning that as a purveyor of information the pure case-method is close to pure waste. To this one further observation should be added: with two exceptions, every superlative case-method class-room man I know of achieves his brilliance by so narrowing his base that only "law"-law is really under discussion. Once, or twice, or even three times, "law"-law, technically taught and consistently developed, is good training. Three times is enough. Four times is too many.

On the other hand, the innovators have proved little much worth proving. Man by man, almost all of them are quarter-baked. And where one of them does hit on something good, and useful, it remains his own. They build within so many schools, and in so many different directions, and with so little contact, that all they have in common is revolt. Yet the length and intensity of the fight to introduce the case-method itself evidences the inertia of the law-teacher. We need not only invention, but introduction. We need, then, not only creation, but transmission, and *machinery* for transmission. I look around in vain for any modern *transmissible* technique of teaching to supplement the one hydra-headed but limited tradition that we know.

Method: Towards a Theory of Teaching

We straddle, in a word, between regimentation and idiosyncrasy, both over-done. I think, because we have not taken thought. About the law, we have taken thought; and then about the judge. About the lawyer, we are beginning to. About our own procedures, no. Each man for himself. Teachers are born, not made. Selah!

Now as I marshal what I have seen, I find but one *born* teacher in my memories. The rest made themselves, and all but a few made

---

[10] I reserve here the possibility of some types of apprenticeship in business or finance, so far as demonstrable opening exists for specialization.

themselves slowly. Most borrowed something from their own teachers. They went ahead then by trial and error. The students paid. (As, through years, clients pay for turning into lawyers the misbranded product with which we dare to flood the market.)

Admit that true artistry comes only to him who is born to become an artist. Still—can we not speed the work? We recognize that we can. We put out course-books, which make one man's experience in part available to many other men. But as to *method* of teaching—there we balk at communication, we balk at analysis. This is idiocy, plain and drooling. Until the would-be innovators pool knowledge and experience, until they approach one another's teaching technique with sympathetic criticism, they will bubble each his personal bubble, and burst— perhaps loudly, but without effect. It would help, if schools started swapping teachers for a year at a time. It would help more, if schools started faculty seminars on how to teach: "Who was the best teacher I ever had, and why?" "My original theory of teaching, and why I had to change it." A report from last year's class: from a "C" student, a "B" student, and an "A" student, on whom they liked, and whom they didn't like—and why. *Etc.* Then analysis and synthesis. For there *are* techniques, as well as vaudevillian mannerisms.

Methods: Individualization

What with the case-book and the pseudo-Socratic monologue, we have grown sleepily comfortable among our conveyor-belts. And our Trustees have grown sleepily comfortable in the feeling that law schools are cheap. We can use an alarm-clock. It is time to challenge the régime of mass-production.

How do we teach? We rise and juggle balls before the class. Our more finished performers can juggle table, knife, and derby-hat. The class is supposed to learn by watching. It being mostly a simple type of juggling, the quicker men do learn it. The slower learn it partially, or not at all.

But these slower men are the crux of the problem. The slower men are the backbone of a graduate body. If they do not have eye and hand to get the juggling by mere watching, our job begins to be more than what we do. First, because we now squander their time and our own. Second, because without foundation there is no solid building. Experience shows that personal attention helps. Experience shows that three-quarters of those who need personal attention will not take the initiative in getting it. Experience shows that an awakened third-year class is more valuable than a corps of instructors, in giving personal attention to first-year men who still have not managed to get the knack.

Is all of this possibility to run off into the sewer, for mere lack of organization? Where is the best legal training in a law school? We all know: in the Law Review, *and under students.* Well?

In Sum

Law School education, even in the best schools, is, then, so inadequate, wasteful, blind and foul that it will take twenty years of unremitting effort to make it half-way equal to its job.

That seems no reason for not beginning. What matters it where we begin? To right, to left, in front, are materials crying out for use. Enlistment of the student body is one. The professor's job lies in such enlistment, and in the organization, for use in his own courses, of the fact-background necessary to give to a policy-inquiry interest; to a rule, meaningfulness; to a counselling-question, body; to a critical evaluation, hands and feet. The bar, meanwhile, has teaching and apprenticeship powers not tapped these seventy years.

Law School faculties, as distinct from single professors, need to set about discovering what it is they are training for, that joint action may be sanely guided. Pending that, there is much to be done already: especially the widening of the techniques taught. That defectively trained student-material comes to us is no excuse for *our* stamping legal illiterates with an LL. B. Proper limitation of pure case-method, proper subdivision of our groups into quick and slow, and decent individualization of instruction, can give us ample room to move in. Introduction of adequate fact materials speeds, and does not slow up, the teaching process.

Altogether it makes one think of Pilgrim's Progress. But whether the stage be Slough of Despond or Vanity Fair is hard to tell.

K. N. Llewellyn

Columbia University School of Law

[19]

THE LEGACY OF CLINICAL EDUCATION: THEORIES ABOUT LAWYERING

CARRIE MENKEL—MEADOW*

I. INTRODUCTION

THE DEVELOPING CLINICAL LEGAL EDUCATION MOVEMENT has been concerned with the central question "What is it that lawyers do?" This query has elicited a variety of answers that suggest some new theories about the role of the lawyer and the practice of law in contemporary society.

Some of these theories are closely associated with individual proponents or schools of law while others are the product of collaborative or anonymous effort. Clinicians have forged these new theories in an effort to incorporate the knowledge of those who have gone before them with explanations of their own experiences and observations of their own new reality. In order to fully understand the phenomenon of lawyering, clinicians must now join a discourse with each other and with other legal scholars and lawyers to enrich the inquiry into what lawyers do and to consider which theories will most usefully explain lawyering behavior.

In the hope of stimulating this discussion, this article will examine some of the various schools of thought about what lawyers do. It is offered as a commentary on the beginnning of a philosophy or sociology[1] of lawyering that is derived from the clinical movement which will survive long after the pedagogical and political disputes about clinical methodology have been resolved. This is a subjective study which incorporates my own interpretations of the concepts of the various schools of thought. I describe the approaches to or theories about lawyering and their "creators" as I know them, recognizing that some major theories, schools and people may not for one reason or another have come to my attention.[2] The schools of thought discussed may suffer from some distortion[3] both in their description and their attributions. Yet, even a

---

*Acting Professor of Law, University of California at Los Angeles. A.B., Barnard College, Columbia Univ.; J.D., University of Pennsylvania.

[1] One commentator has called this the phenomenonology of what lawyers do. See Simon, *Homo Psychologicus: Notes on a New Legal Formalism*, 32 STAN. L. REV. 487 (1980).

[2] This is one of the problems caused by the limited body of scholarly writing in the clinical field. The reader may note that many of the sources cited herein are "unpublished" or "forthcoming."

[3] This approach follows a now familiar tradition in legal scholarship—the discussion of models or "ideal types" in legal analysis which may be used at least for heuristic purposes, if not for total reliability of description. *See, e.g.,* R.

slightly distorted description of an approach to lawyering can help us to frame and to respond to questions about the lawyer's function in a legal system. Although there is controversy surrounding different views about the pedagogy or methodology of clinical legal education,[4] the focus of this discussion is on the theories of what it means to be a lawyer in our legal system, as they have developed from the clinical experience.

II. TOWARD MACRO AND MICRO THEORIES OF LAWYERING

Most clinicians would probably agree that the core subject of instruction and interest is the role of the lawyer in employing the skills and practices needed to advise and represent clients. Most clinicians would not hesitate to add that the lawyer employs these skills in a highly structured world commonly called "the legal system." Any inquiry into what lawyers do must necessarily consider what the legal system permits, demands, requires and provides. Thus, most theories,[5] explanations or descriptions of what lawyers do may be divided into two, somewhat arbitrary, categories — *micro* theories, which focus on the role and behaviors of the individual lawyer, and *macro* theories, which focus on the lawyer's interaction with the legal system, and the impact of lawyers on the larger world.

Obviously, long before the present clinical movement began, lawyers, legal scholars, anthropologists, sociologists, and political scientists examined these two aspects of lawyering.[6] But the clinical movement has spurred a variety of new approaches to our understanding about the role of the lawyer and the function of the legal system. Indeed, what has characterized the thinking of clinicians has been the systematic scrutiny of all aspects of the lawyering role and function — no matter how small or large a slice of the lawyering process to be examined. This reflection on and scrutiny of the lawyer's work has been undertaken out of necessity as well as out of interest, for in order to teach students how to

---

UNGER, KNOWLEDGE AND POLITICS (1975); Simon, *The Ideology of Advocacy: Procedural Justice and Professional Ethics*, 1978 WIS. L. REV. 29; R. Abel, Informal Alternatives to Courts as a Mode of Legalizing Conflict (forthcoming, on file with the author).

[4] There is, aside from the arguments about simulation versus client-centered clinical education and in-house versus out-of-house fieldwork programs, a bona fide dispute about the existence of a discrete clinical methodology in legal education. *See* Condlin, *The Myth of the Clinical Methodology*, 2 CLINICAL LEGAL EDUC. PERSPECTIVE 9 (1978).

[5] The words "theories about lawyering" are used cautiously. The models, explanations, conceptual frameworks or principles about lawyering described in this essay may not rise to the level of theories in the most abstract sense of the term. The reader may substitute any other term which more accurately reflects his or her sense of the subject matter.

[6] For a comprehensive guide to this literature, see Abel, *The Sociology of American Lawyers—A Bibliographic Guide*, 2 LAW & POLICY Q. 335 (1980).

be lawyers, clinicians have had to ask themselves what it is that lawyers do.

As more and increasingly diversified people have asked themselves questions about what lawyers do, certain theoretical patterns have emerged. Those who focus on the micro or individual level of lawyering emphasize the concepts of role and process, i.e., what does the lawyer do, for whom, in what context, and why? Thus, for those using the *micro*scope, the lawyer is decision-maker,[7] advisor,[8] fact developer,[9] advocate,[10] friend,[11] investigator,[12] and organizer.[13] Those who focus on the macro level of lawyering have emphasized the concepts of function and substance, i.e., what can law and lawyers accomplish? For them the lawyer is seen as an instrument of dispute resolution,[14] an agent of social change,[15] a medium for greater democratic participation,[16] and as a mechanism of social control[17] and symbol of stylized ritual.[18]

It is still too early to tell which theory or combination of theories best explains the purposes and functions of the lawyer, but these theories have stimulated some important questions. These common questions focus not only on what lawyers do, but also on how lawyers learn, make decisions, and interact with other participants in the legal system. Other questions which are implicated in this inquiry are how well does the lawyer perform her duties, how is the lawyer constrained by the larger system in which she operates, for whom does the lawyer work, by what rules or norms should the lawyer's work be governed and evaluated, how does the lawyer relate to the substantive law that is practiced and to what end does the lawyer work. Many clinicals have addressed these questions and offered interesting insights into the legal profes-

---

[7] Spiegel, *Lawyering and Client Decisionmaking: Informed Consent and the Legal Profession*, 128 U. PA. L. REV. 41 (1979); A. Amsterdam, Memorandum to Stanford Law School Faculty (July 27, 1973).

[8] D. BINDER & S. PRICE, LEGAL INTERVIEWING AND COUNSELING: A CLIENT-CENTERED APPROACH (1977); L. BROWN & E. DAUER, PLANNING BY LAWYERS: MATERIALS ON A NON-ADVERSARIAL LEGAL PROCESS (1978).

[9] See G. BELLOW & B. MOULTON, THE LAWYERING PROCESS: MATERIALS FOR CLINICAL INSTRUCTION IN ADVOCACY 304-05 (1978).

[10] *Id.* at 826-965.

[11] See Fried, *The Lawyer as Friend: The Moral Foundations of the Lawyer-Client Relation*, 85 YALE L.J. 1060 (1976).

[12] See G. BELLOW & B. MOULTON, *supra* note 9, at 339-407.

[13] See Wexler, *Practicing Law for Poor People*, 79 YALE L.J. 1049 (1970).

[14] See Abel, *A Comparative Theory of Dispute Institutions in Society*, 8 LAW & SOC. R. 217 (1973); R. Abel, *supra* note 3.

[15] See Bellow, *Turning Solutions Into Problems: The Legal Aid Experience*, 34 NLADA BRIEFCASE 106 (1977); Rabin, *Lawyers For Social Change: Perspectives on Public Interest Law*, 28 STAN. L. REV. 207 (1976).

[16] See Wexler, *supra* note 13; R. Abel, *supra* note 3.

[17] See Bellow, *supra* note 15; Wexler, *supra* note 13.

[18] See G. BELLOW & B. MOULTON, *supra* note 9 at 2-34.

sion. The following sections will examine *micro* and *macro* theories, though categorization will at times seem artificial, and offer some suggestions for further inquiry into the question of what lawyers do. We may ultimately have more questions than answers, but that is how theories are born and tested.

III. MICRO THEORIES: THE INDIVIDUAL LAWYER—PROFESSIONAL SKILLS AND INTERPERSONAL PROCESS

A. *The Notion of "Role" in Lawyering*

No discussion about theories of lawyering could begin without reference to Gary Bellow, generally regarded as the theoretical father of clinical education.[19] Although Bellow has written on many aspects of clinical education, including pedagogy,[20] course description[21] and lawyering process,[22] his writing on the individual lawyer level has been most notable for the attention it pays to the notion of role. In a text written with Beatrice Moulton, Bellow describes the effect of this notion on the lawyer's identity:

> In simple terms, a fully-socialized individual is one who is, does, and believes pretty much what society asks him or her to be, do and believe. The explanations focus on three key concepts: role—a socially generated set of expectations about one's behavior in specific situations; reference group—the audience (or audiences) to whom one looks for approval, support, acceptance, reward and sanction; and ideology—the constellation of beliefs, knowledge, and ideas which, in a given situation, serve to justify, legitimate and explain both role definitions and the allocation of reward and sanction power among reference groups. In the legal system (or any system of social relationships) role definitions, reference groups and ideology combine to produce a distinct legal subculture which powerfully influences the "professionalization" of young lawyers. Over time, professional roles become part (and sometimes a very large part) of one's identity.[23]

---

[19] William Pincus is generally credited with being the financial and instrumental father of clinical education.

[20] G. Bellow, *On Teaching the Teachers: Some Preliminary Reflections on Clinical Methodology* in CLINICAL EDUCATION FOR THE LAW STUDENT (CLEPR, 1973).

[21] Bellow & Johnson, *Reflections on the University of Southern California Clinical Semester*, 44 S. CAL. L. REV. 664 (1971).

[22] G. BELLOW & B. MOULTON, *supra* note 9.

[23] *Id.* at 11-12.

Thus, the individual attorney must locate herself within a professional context, examine the expectations of her role and choose whether or not to conform to those expectations. These role expectations are derived from the individual lawyer's functions and purpose as perceived by the lawyer herself, her peers, judges, clients and other members of the community who constitute the reference group.

The separation of professional functions into discrete areas or processes permits generalizations to be made about each of the functional "hats" or roles that a lawyer must perform. Bellow and Moulton liken the lawyer's roles to those of actors in a theatrical production.[24] By studying the character (i.e., the part or role of interviewer in the initial lawyer-client contact), the actor can master its constituent elements, its essence and its gestalt, and thereby learn to perform the role.[25] Thus, the lawyer's professional life can be divided into distinct roles such as the interviewer,[26] planner,[27] investigator,[28] negotiator,[29] examiner or interrogator,[30] advocate, debater[31] and counselor.[32] In this way, the particular skills or talents which are necessary for each role can be analyzed, conceptualized, practiced and mastered.

When the various roles are dissected, patterns begin to emerge. For example, as interviewer, investigator, negotiator and examiner, the lawyer must ask questions. Recognition of this particular skill requirement enables the lawyer to categorize the types and kinds of questions to ask in particular contexts. Thus, the "logic of question-framing" is born as a conceptual model of what lawyers do. When should an open-ended question be used? When is a leading question more appropriate? What are the effects of such questions on information acquisition? How does the form of question affect the client, the fact-finder and the lawyer's conceptualization of what she does?

The lawyer, thus, begins to learn about what she does by considering the roles she plays, examining what skills are necessary to play those roles, analyzing the constitutent elements of those skills and finally, evaluating which elements of each skill can be used for what purposes and with what effects. This model of examining what a lawyer does is simultaneously procedural, instrumental and evaluative. It causes the lawyer or clinician to ask a series of analytic questions about what the

---

[24] *Id.* at XIX-XXV.
[25] *Id.*
[26] *Id.* at 104-272.
[27] *Id.* at 273-429.
[28] *Id.*
[29] *Id.* at 430-606.
[30] *Id.* at 607-825.
[31] *Id.* at 826-965.
[32] *Id.* at 966-1104.

individual seeks to achieve, what is needed to accomplish these things and how well adapted the means chosen are for the ends desired. The Bellow and Moulton scheme of dividing the lawyering process into constitutent roles, skills, models and issues proceeds in similar fashion for all of the attorney functions.[33]

B. *Conceptualization of the Lawyer's Skills*

Perhaps the most sophisticated conceptualization of the lawyer's skills has been undertaken by one of the other "elder" statesmen of the clinical movement, David Binder, and his colleagues in the UCLA clinical program.[34] In their view, the lawyer's role is simply, but effectively to assist the client in the achievement of some client-defined goal.

Binder argues that the lawyer must develop the most effective skills to effectuate the client's purpose. Thus, in the initial interview with a client, the lawyer must provide the client with the opportunity to self-define her goals and concerns. The lawyer must then employ her professional skills to learn the relevant facts in the most efficient and logical manner.[35] When the clinician considers how best to acquire these facts in an initial client contact, she is conceptualizing about order, logic and purpose. In the litigation context, it is likely that a particular transaction, occurrence or event "caused" the litigation; therefore, the best way to proceed in such an interview is to undertake an exhaustive chronological exposition of the cause and its effects.[36] In the non-litigation context, the facts might better be acquired in topical order. For example, in estate planning the interview might focus first on family structures, then on assets and finally on dispositional desires.

Similarly, in counseling, Binder argues that the lawyer must facilitate the client's decision-making process[37] since the client must live most

---

[33] *See* notes 26-32 *supra* and accompanying text. In addition to this micro analysis, Bellow and Moulton view the lawyering process as including a view of the lawyer acting within a larger system, more specifically the profession's moral and ethical constraints. These constraints may affect the attorney's sense of her role, what skills will be used or not used and which means or ends will be permissible and which will not. Because this approach to the question of what a lawyer does includes macro analysis, discussion will be deferred to that section. *See* notes 82-92 *infra* and accompanying text.

Conversations I have had with Gary Bellow and Beatrice Moulton subsequent to the publication of their book have led me to believe they would prefer to be considered as expressing a more macro-societal and substance-oriented perspective and would now write a different book.

[34] The conception of and analysis for this article preceded my affiliation with the UCLA clinical program. I must confess, however, to a possible bias in discussing the contributions of the UCLA clinicians since this article was written in the shadow of the light of one year's influence.

[35] D. BINDER & S. PRICE, *supra* note 8, at 6-134.

[36] *Id.* at 53-75.

[37] *Id.* at 135-223.

closely with the decision. With this purpose in mind the attorney can use his or her skill and knowledge to assist the client in developing the best data base from which to choose and assess the available alternatives. Thus, the lawyer will present the possible legal and economic consequences of each alternative, while the client will present and assess the personal and social consequences of each alternative. This conceptualization of what the lawyer does and what she is trying to accomplish permits categorization of tasks, duties, information and the criteria for choosing from among the types of tasks, duties and information.

This analysis has also been applied to the lawyer's role as advocate in the decision-making process in which a fact-finder must choose between two competing versions of the facts.[38] By systematically exploring the fact-finding mechanism, the clinician considers the lawyer's role in the process. A close examination of this process reveals that the fact-finder assimilates the factual presentations of a case to his knowledge and experience of the world. Therefore, the lawyer must take care to present the facts in terms of the premises or generalizations on which she thinks the fact-finder bases his factual evaluations. If this is not possible, more proof, evidence or argument may be necessary to persuade the fact-finder to accept a version of the facts based on a different set of premises or generalizations, or the premises or generalizations may themselves have to be modified.

With a similar *modus operandi* Paul Bergman has suggested an approach to develop a sense of purpose in cross-examination.[39] Instead of learning through the folklore of the discipline, clinical students should be taught to think about their goals in cross-examination and to deduce the principles by which to achieve them.[40] Thus, if the purpose of a cross-examination is to develop evidence, proof, arguments or inferences that support one view of the world rather than another, the lawyer can begin to construct a logic of questioning that is informed by a measurement or calculus of risk. Although an adverse witness may be personally unknown to the cross-examiner, her relationship to one view of the world can be anticipated (i.e., the opposing side's version of the case). Thus, if the lawyer can rebut a "bad" answer by extrinsic evidence from her own factual perspective (i.e., another person or an inconsistent statement), a question to that witness will be relatively safe. Bergman uses this reasoning to create a "safety model" for cross-examination that helps the lawyer to understand her goals, and role as

---

[38] D. Binder & W. Graham, Deductive Reasoning in the Proof of Facts (1979) (on file with the author).

[39] Bergman, *A Practical Approach to Cross-Examination: Safety First*, 25 U.C.L.A. L. REV. 547 (1978).

[40] *Id.* at 548-49.

trial advocate, to conceptualize about a particular process, and to evaluate her choices and performance.[41]

The substantive principles described above are not nearly as significant as the process by which they are derived. The lawyer's purpose, role and skill—the components of her craft—are closely scrutinized, as if looked at through a microscope. By focusing intently on the elements of a particular role or skill, the clinician can frame concepts, generalizations and abstractions about that component of the lawyering process. By asking what the lawyer does, for what purpose and in what context, orienting models or conceptual frameworks can be developed for each of the lawyer's diverse skills and roles. Criteria can then be articulated to aid in making and evaluating behavioral choices.

These "models" of individual attorney skills are still in an early stage of conceptualization and development. Yet they offer great promise for explanations of lawyering behavior, not just for clinical instruction, but for our understanding of what, why and how lawyers do what they do.[42]

C. Lawyer Decision-Making

Other clinicians such as Anthony Amsterdam[43] have looked at the lawyer's decisions as the unit of analysis:

> What is the lawyer's role? What are the lawyer's goals? What are the available means for attaining those goals? What are the ingredients of judgment—of wise decision-making—in those choices? How are the lawyer's role, goals, means and decision-making processes affected by the structure of the legal institutions within which he works? And: how did you act or decide? What choices did that decision or action imply? What alternative courses were open? Why were they rejected, or not considered? In light of your objectives and resources, how could your process of decision making and responsive action be improved?[44]

This approach to studying lawyering behavior examines how choices are made in particular situations, evaluates the decision-making process

---

[41] *Id.* at 555-75.

[42] Other clinicians have also followed this method of analysis of the lawyer's tasks. *See, e.g.*, Schoenfield and Schoenfield, *Interviewing and Counseling Clients in A Legal Setting*, 11 AKRON L. REV. 313 (1977); G. Lowenthal, A General Theory of Negotiation Process, Strategy and Behavior (forthcoming, on file with the author).

[43] Anthony Amsterdam has written a number of articles concerning criminal law. *See generally* Amsterdam, *Perspectives on the Fourth Amendment*, 58 MINN. L. REV. 349 (1974). Beginning in 1972, while at Stanford, he undertook the responsiblity for updating TRIAL MANUAL FOR THE DEFENSE OF CRIMINAL CASES.

[44] A. Amsterdam, Memorandum to Stanford Law School Faculty (July 27, 1973).

and compares the decisions to alternative possibilities. This is similar to the analysis that is utilized when one evaluates how a court arrived at a particular result among competing choices as shaped by precedent, factual presentation, evidence and policy considerations.

The analysis of a lawyer's decisions can draw from the decision-making literature in other disciplines[45] as well as from the numerous accounts of legal strategies and choices in real cases.[46] Theories can then be formulated which tie together discernible patterns discovered in the decision-making process.

The potential for such analysis, given the clinician's rootedness in legal practice where scores of attorney decisions are made daily is enormous. Clinicians who employ simulation methodologies have an unparalleled opportunity to study and test the factors that affect lawyer decision-making under almost perfect laboratory conditions. Indeed, clinicians are in an excellent position to test theories about lawyer behavior that come closest to the scientific method Langdell envisioned for law study.[47] By observing simulated attorney interactions and tasks, clinicians can begin to deduce patterns, rules and explanatory models of lawyer decision-making. There is a possibility for a new empiricism about lawyering that, while borrowing heavily from the Legal Realists,[48] focuses more directly on lawyers who make millions of law-making, office[49] and litigation decisions every day rather than on judges, legislatures and agencies more commonly treated in the literature as legal decision-makers.

Indeed, this focus on lawyer decision-making broadens our understanding of how the legal system operates. If the analysis is to be meaningful, such studies must consider: the fluidity of facts and information at the lawyer's disposal; the impact of resource scarcity and allocation decisions on the lawyer's choices; the input of clients, opposing counsel and judges into the individual attorney's choices; as well as limitations based on substantive doctrine and professional norms. Thus, by focusing on the lawyer's decisions as a question of theoretical interest, clinicians can study not only how strategic choices are made, but also the behavioral models and implications of decisions in the broader context of the legal system. By closely examining the factors which influence an attorney in choosing between alternatives, such as whether

---

[45] *See, e.g.*, G. SCHUBERT, JUDICIAL DECISION MAKING (1963); T. SORENSON, DECISION MAKING IN THE WHITE HOUSE (1963); Simon, *Rational Decision Making in Business Organizations*, 69 AMERICAN ECON. R. 493 (1979).

[46] *See, e.g.*, Meltsner, *Litigating Against the Death Penalty: The Strategy Behind Furman*, 82 YALE L.J. 1111 (1973).

[47] *See, e.g.*, Wizner and Curtis, *Here's What We Do: Some Notes About Clinical Legal Education*, 29 CLEV. ST. L. REV. 673 (1980).

[48] Schlegel, *American Legal Realism and Empirical Social Science: From the Yale Experience*, 28 BUFFALO L. REV. 459 (1979).

[49] *See generally* L. BROWN & E. DAUER, *supra* note 8.

to litigate or settle, and by extending the scrutiny to aggregates of attorney decisions, it is possible to learn a great deal about why lawyers do what they do.

Working in this tradition of looking at attorneys as decision-makers, at least one clinical scholar has begun to formulate some normative ideas about how lawyers ought to make decisions.[50] Mark Spiegel has argued that if the nature of the lawyer's work is to make decisions for the client, the doctrine of informed consent, as applied to medical decision-making, must also be applied to legal decision-making.[51] Thus, if we focus on the content of the lawyer's decision it is too easy to designate some decisions as strategic and therefore must be left to the lawyer (such as the choice of forum, the proper legal claim to pursue, whether to demand a jury, whether to ask a particular question or call a particular witness) and others which involve the merits of the case and must be left to the client (such as decisions to litigate or settle).[52] If a client who participates in his case is more likely to achieve better results, as at least one study seems to indicate,[53] then there are instrumental and practical reasons to look more closely at the allocation of decision-making responsibility between lawyer and client. One can then examine the economic and normative implications of who should make what decisions in the lawyering context.

The importance of such theoretical inquires should not be underestimated. The theoretical questions or visions of each clinican can and have had a significant impact on the way law students and lawyers conceptualize and learn about the work and functions of a lawyer.[54] Given an emphasis on lawyer decision-making, students may learn to develop models for learning how to make, evaluate and critique their own decisions.[55] Thus, students, lawyers and clinicians will ask of themselves, throughout their careers, the questions posed in Amsterdam's memorandum.[56] From these inquiries, patterns and themes of attorney decision-making can be explored in the academy, the classroom and in the legal arena.

---

[50] *See* Spiegel, *supra* note 7.

[51] *Id.* at 49-67, 123-133.

[52] *See* ABA, CODE OF PROFESSIONAL RESPONSIBILITY EC7-7 (1978).

[53] D. ROSENTHAL, LAWYER AND CLIENT—WHO'S IN CHARGE? (1974).

[54] The ABA has recently attempted to adopt a clinical model for teaching young lawyers. *See* COMMITTEE ON PROFESSIONAL EDUCATION, ABA PILOT LAWYERING SKILLS INSTITUTE (1979-80).

[55] *See, e.g.*, the description of the University of Pennsylvania's clinical program in Spiegel, *The Penn Legal Assistance Office: Theory and Practice in Learning and Lawyering*, 13 THE LAW ALUMNI J. (1978-79) (University of Pennsylvania Law School).

[56] *See* note 44 *supra* and accompanying text.

D. *Lawyering As An Interpersonal Process*

When clinicians have asked the question, "What is it that lawyers do?", perhaps the most controversial answer has been that "lawyers interact with other people." In a growing body of literature, most clearly represented in the writings of the Columbia Law School's clinicians,[57] Thomas Shaffer,[58] Gary Goodpaster[59] and various psychiatrists and psychologists who have worked with clinicians,[60] the lawyer's roles have been described as interpersonal processes, characterized by interactions with lawyers, clients, judges and other actors in the legal system. At least one commentator has criticized this "psychologizing" of the lawyering process.[61] Yet this view of the lawyering process may also prove productive in analyzing reasons or explanations for what a lawyer does.

Many of these interpersonal theories of lawyering are derived from already existing theories of human and professional interaction developed in social psychology and sociology.[62] Indeed, the development of analogous theories in medical sociology[63] has far surpassed the formulation and acceptance of similar theories in the legal world. Whether

---

[57] I have identified the Columbia clinicians as Michael Meltsner, Philip Schrag, Holly Hartstone, and Jack Himmelstein, among others. *See* notes 69-70 *infra* and accompanying text for some of their writings.

[58] T. SHAFFER, LEGAL INTERVIEWING AND COUNSELLING (1976).

[59] Goodpaster, *The Human Arts of Lawyering*, 27 J. LEGAL EDUC. 5 (1975).

[60] *See, e.g.*, Redmount, *Attorney Personalities and Some Psychological Aspects of Legal Consultation*, 109 U. PA. L. REV. 972 (1961); Redmount, *Humanistic Law Through Legal Counseling*, 2 CONN. L. REV. 98 (1965); Watson, *Some Psychological Aspects of Teaching Professional Responsibility*, 16 J. LEGAL EDUC. 1 (1963).

[61] Simon, *supra* note 1. While I share some of Simon's views I believe he has committed the intellectual error of reductionism. As set forth, the "interpersonal process" theory of lawyering is only one of the theories being considered and developed by American clinicians. The impact of Rogerian therapeutic models of lawyering has been exaggerated by Simon. *Id.* at 51-52 n.93. It is my experience that to the extent such formulations are used at all, they are used in the interviewing segments of clinical courses. Yet, the more common model of clinical education is skills training as described in Section IB in the text. *See* notes 34-42 *supra* and accompanying text. Furthermore, the interpersonal school has been the most prolific in its writing, and thereby disproportionately represents the clinical theories about lawyering that have been published. *See, supra* note 2. This is not to deny or minimize the importance of this school of thought. The significance of caring for our fellow human beings in our service to them should never recede from the professional consciousness.

[62] *See, e.g.*, the symbolic interactionist school of sociology: E. GOFFMAN, THE PRESENTATION OF SELF IN EVERYDAY LIFE (1959); E. GOFFMAN, STRATEGIC INTERACTION (1968).

[63] *See, e.g.*, the works of Eliot Friedson: E. FRIEDSON, DOCTORING TOGETHER (1975); E. FRIEDSON, PROFESSIONAL DOMINANCE (1970).

derived from humanistic psychology,[64] more traditional Freudian psychology[65] or sociology,[66] the common themes in these theories about the human interaction in the lawyer-client relationship, are the recognition of human needs to be satisfied, both on the part of the lawyer and the client, the need for effective communication skills, acknowledgment and tolerance of values, goals and purposes held by others,[67] and the recognition of the role of feelings in what we otherwise think of as a "rational" legal system.[68]

In their written works concerning the Columbia Law School's clinical program, Meltsner and Schrag have described the use of group dynamics theory and practice as a means of focusing on the lawyer's interactions with others.[69] Their conviction that it is important for lawyers to step back and reflect on how they interact with others led them to test their theories by attempting replication or simulation of the human dynamics of the attorney-as-negotiator role in the student-teacher relationship.[70] The student is required to negotiate for instructor supervision and, in so doing, is expected to abstract and generalize from this experience in order to generate principles which will lead to a successful negotiation with opposing counsel. Thus, the student learns to share information, to express needs, to bargain for what the other side desires and to confirm agreements.

By focusing on the attorney-client interpersonal process, clinicians have developed theories about what motivates participants in the legal system,[71] what lawyers are able to do and what must or might be left to others. This focus on the interpersonal process of lawyering has obvious

---

[64] *See* C. ROGERS, ON BECOMING A PERSON (1961); Himmelstein, *Reassessing Law Schooling: An Inquiry Into The Application of Humanistic Educational Psychology to the Teaching of Law*, 53 N.Y.U.L. REV. 514 (1978).

[65] *See* Watson, *supra* note 50.

[66] *See* E. GOFFMAN, *supra* note 62; E. FRIEDSON, *supra* note 63.

[67] *See* D. BINDER & S. PRICE, *supra* note 8 at 6-7.

[68] I have always disliked the distinction between the rational mode (thought, idea) and the irrational or arational mode (emotion, feeling). If feelings are appropriate to the situation—*e.g.*, grief after death—then they are quite rational. Similarly, we have long had an emotional attachment to our ideas. For further discussion of these views see C. Menkel-Meadow, *Women As Law Teachers: Toward the Feminization of Legal Education*, in MONOGRAPH III HUMANISTIC EDUCATION IN LAW (Columbia Univ. 1980).

[69] M. MELTSNER & P. SCHRAG, PUBLIC INTEREST ADVOCACY: MATERIALS FOR CLINICAL LEGAL EDUCATION (1974); M. MELTSNER & P. SCHRAG, TOWARD SIMULATION IN LEGAL EDUCATION (1979); Meltsner and Schrag, *Report from a CLEPR Colony*, 76 COLUM. L. REV. 581 (1976); Meltsner and Schrag, *Scenes from a Clinic*, 127 U. PA. L. REV. 1 (1978).

[70] Meltsner and Schrag, *Scenes from a Clinic*, *supra* note 69 at 21-25.

[71] D. BINDER & S. PRICE, *supra* note 8; Goodpaster, *supra* note 59; T. SHAFFER, *supra* note 49.

implications for determining what is lawyer's work.[72] But, aside from the now trite question about whether a lawyer can or should be a social worker or psychiatrist, this aspect of the lawyer's work is in many ways most complex,[73] and very intimately related to questions not only of professional role or status but to issues of professional ethics and liability as well.[74] To what extent should lawyers be liable for their failures at interpersonal relations in the lawyer-client context, especially where such failures of communication have led to unsuccessful and perhaps preventable legal or judgmental errors? To what standard of care, training and expertise should lawyers be held in all of their interpersonal roles—advisor, counselor, negotiator, friend, etc. It is certainly important to look at these questions, speculate on the possibilities and ask other actors in the legal system—clients, judges, opposing counsel and adversary parties—what is expected or desired as clinicians formulate standards for professional conduct.[75] Examination of one's professional self-concept and behavioral standards both as teachers and as students can only result in more effective delivery of legal services by forcing more honest appraisals of our professional identities.[76]

Thus, as is the case with all of the questions posed by the microtheories of lawyering, when we examine the question of what a lawyer does, the answers are not really as limited, instrumental or individualistic as they might seem. In the interpersonal process school of clinical education, the questions asked are not only what will work best for this lawyer with this client, but also how should the attorney act with her clients and adversaries, and what are the implications for such theories of interaction for the legal profession at large. In short, when analyzing the means used by lawyers in interactions with others, we must inevitably come to grips with what ends will be served as individual attorney interactions aggregate and proliferate out into the larger system. Clinicians, by being in a position to critically observe a large and yet controlled number of interactions, have an ideal vantage point for reflection on the dynamics of the lawyering process and its implications for the legal system.

---

[72] Q. JOHNSTONE & D. HOPSON, LAWYERS AND THEIR WORK (1967).

[73] It is not unlike deciding when a lawyer ceases to be a lawyer, and begins to act as a business partner or advisor.

[74] G. HAZARD, ETHICS IN THE PRACTICE OF LAW 58-59 (1978).

[75] This seems particularly appropriate at this time since the proposed ABA Model Rules of Professional Conduct divide the lawyer's ethical obligations into categories, defined, in large part, by the interpersonal processes in which the lawyer is engaged. *See* ABA, PROPOSED MODEL RULES OF PROFESSIONAL CONDUCT (1980); Schwartz, *The Death and Regeneration of Ethics (1980)*, ABF. RESEARCH J. (1980).

[76] *See* L. DVORKIN, J. HIMMELSTEIN & H. LESNICK, BECOMING A LAWYER: A HUMANISTIC PERSPECTIVE ON LEGAL EDUCATION AND PROFESSIONAL IDENTITY (1980).

E. The Meta-Learning of Lawyering

The work of Robert Condlin and others at the Harvard clinical program, while associated with the Harvard School of Education,[77] while most often associated with the pedagogical and methodological theories and debates about clinical education, also contributes to the "micro" theories of lawyering. One of Condlin's major theories is that law students learn how to learn in the law school in a competitive and persuasive mode rather than in a collaborative and additive mode.[78] This learning mode replicates itself as law students learn each new aspect of their lawyering roles — how to brief and argue cases, how to argue with their professors and later their judges, how to communicate with their classmates and later their peers in the legal system, how to deal with more material than can possibly be absorbed and later how to handle cases that could fill up more than all of the available time.[79] Thus, if we look at the learning process of lawyering we will learn not only how to structure curricula but also how the socialization of the law school and its teaching is replicated and patterned in the socialization of the legal system and its participants. Clinicians, by examining their own processes as legal educators, can generalize and theorize about how their students will behave as lawyers. Learning becomes a metaphor for lawyering. Because the professional behavior of lawyers as practitioners is patterned on their prior learning experience, the present learning experience can be seen as establishing patterns for subsequent professional behavior as practitioners and educators. The practitioner acts as an educator when, for example, a counseling session becomes one in which the lawyer "educates" the client about available alternatives. This process contains the same manipulative potential that the teacher may use on the student for educational purposes. In similar fashion the lawyer may educate judges in court appearances, opposing counsel in negotiating sessions, and ultimately herself in general practice. Thus, this "school" of clinical thought looks at lawyering as a process within a system which, by its nature, structures learning and thereby shapes the behavioral repertoire.

F. Summary

From the above discussion, certain common themes that have emerged from the "micro" theories of lawyering can be identified. While micro theories focus on the individual lawyer's behavior and roles, they

---

[77] Described by Bolman, *Learning and Lawyering: An Approach to Education in Legal Practice* in ADVANCE IN EXPERIENTIAL SOCIAL PROCESSES (Cooper and Aldererfer eds. 1979).

[78] Condlin, *Socrates' New Clothes: Substituting Persuasion for Learning in Clinical Practice Instruction*, 40 MD. L. REV. 223 (1981).

[79] *Id.*

must of necessity confront the "macro" implications of how the legal system will be effected by aggregations and proliferations of individual attorney behavioral choices. Thus, if the unit of analysis is theories about how an individual attorney negotiates, one must account for the limitations of this particular role or function within the legal system. What skills the attorney will employ (making a first offer, making principled movements),[80] what interpersonal processes the attorney will employ (reasonable or unreasonable behavior, cooperative or competitive style), how the attorney will educate herself, and her opposing counsel about the case, what decisions the attorney will make and why, are decisions which will necessarily be affected by the legal context in which they are made.[81] Inevitably, the attorney must determine what she is trying to accomplish in the case, how the legal system permits or limits achievement of such goals, and what impact the choices made in this case will have on future choices to be made by other lawyers in other cases.

Whether the micro theorists address these latter questions directly or leave them to the macro theorists, it is useful to our understanding of what lawyers do that such questions be examined, tested, written about, and ultimately taught to our students. For as legal education and legal scholarship has thus far focused on theories of institutional decision-making and choices, the focus on individual lawyer choices, decisions and behaviors described by clinical micro theorists will add to our understanding of the legal system.

III. Macro Theories: The Legal Profession — Of Purposes, Power, Structure and Substance

In studying what lawyers do, some clinicians have begun to analyze the larger impact of the aggregate of attorney functions. What does the legal profession provide for society? What can a lawyer do for her client that cannot be done as well by the client himself? Once again, the clinician has an excellent vantage point from which to ask such questions and examine the answers. As both a working professional and a scholar or expert on the legal system, the clinician can view the aggregate impact of the individual lawyer on the legal system and, conversely, the legal system on the lawyer. Indeed, the clinician is ideally situated in time and place to develop a legal sociology or anthropology utilizing a combination of theoretical and empirical explorations in the fieldwork necessarily engaged in by most clinical programs. What then do clinicians have to say about the operation of the legal system from their perspective as philosophers-servants?

---

[80] C. Menkel-Meadow, Toward Another View of Legal Negotiation (unpublished, on file with author).

[81] Such as whether the negotiation is prelitigation or not. Schwartz, *The Professionalism and Accountability of Lawyers*, 66 CAL. L. REV. 669 (1978).

A. *Purpose—Resolving Disputes, Planning Transactions or Effecting Social Change?*

Those who have written about the appropriate function of the lawyer have argued that the lawyer is a loyal friend to her particular client, or a facilitator of the client's wishes, an agent of needed social change, a planner of transactions, or a dispute resolver. The arguments continue within the curricula of most clinical programs but without much edification by those who are best able to analyze lawyers' actions and comment on their effectiveness. The current trend in legal scholarship appears to be the comparison of the adversary system[82] with more participatory and less antagonistic systems of justice and dispute resolution.[83] Too little is heard about the purpose or functions of the legal system from those who have the best data base from having participated in, and have trained students to participate in, the legal system.

Bellow's clinical teaching, unlike that of other clinicians, has been inspired by a political vision. He has come from the legal services and public defender tradition[84] and views law as a means for promoting *more* justice in our world—economic, political and social—particularly on behalf of the poor and under-represented. Bellow's recent writing and work[85] has been devoted to maximizing the effectiveness of achieving these ends. In describing the patterns of legal service practice, Bellow finds that the practice has become routinized; clients are being manipulated[86] into accepting minimal results; settlements, acquiescence and conciliation are the norm rather than protest and contested lawsuits; and that lawyers fail to exercise their creative skills to engage in preventive law but rather focus exclusively on the initial problem presented to them.[87] Although Bellow is critical, he offers solutions for how lawyers might be more effective—solutions which come from a slightly broader and expanded notion of the skills he teaches clinical students. Lawyers must aggregate their clients, not necessarily in the legal class action form, but by analyzing patterns that exist in the legal problems they present.[88] Lawyers must adopt new strategies for select-

---

[82] *See* M. SCHWARTZ, LAWYERS AND THE LEGAL PROFESSION (1979); Simon, *supra* note 3.

[83] R. Abel, *supra* note 3.

[84] CLEPR, FOURTH BIENNIAL REPORT 1975-76 (1976).

[85] *See* G. Bellow, Proposal for Legal Services Institute (1978) (on file with author).

[86] Goffman terms this process of manipulation as being "cooled." *See* E. GOFFMAN, *supra* note 62.

[87] Bellow, *Turning Solutions Into Problems: The Legal Aid Experience*, 34 NLADA BRIEFCASE 106, 108-09 (1977).

[88] *Id.* at 119-22.

ing the cases they work on and what remedies they seek. They must ask themselves what they are trying to accomplish in larger terms for their clients rather than mechanistically apply their skills. They must perhaps learn new skills — organizing their clients, aggregating claims without using class actions — and reconsider their roles within the profession. Both in the Lawyering Process text,[89] co-authored with Beatrice Moulton, and in a subsequent article co-authored with Jeanne Kettleson,[90] Bellow explores how the contours and requirements of the Code of Professional Responsibility may affect such an expanded notion of the function of the legal services lawyer.

Bellow's focus on the political nature of lawyering and its direct relationship to the maldistribution of resources in this country, has been echoed by nonclinical authors writing on the connections between the social and legal structures.[91] Thus, Bellow's writings and thought forces one to step back from the micro view of an individual attorney in his role in solving client problems or planning transactions, and asks us to consider what purpose is served by what lawyers do. The lawyer's role and function in society must be vigorously debated as we develop theories and methods for teaching law students to be lawyers.[92]

B. *The Clinical Study of Legal Institutions and Substantive Law*

Many years ago, the Legal Realist movement attempted to close the gap between the law that is studied — appellate decisions — and the law that exists in actual practice — trial courts and law offices — by initiating studies of the legal system through both theoretical works[93] and empirical studies.[94] One might expect that clinicians would continue this tradition since it affords students of the legal system a unique opportunity to study the law, observe its application in action, and examine its impact on the protected classes, prohibited actors, enforcers and clientele affected by the laws.[95]

While some clinical programs have combined a study of substantive

---

[89] G. BELLOW & B. MOULTON, *supra*, note 9.

[90] Bellow & Kettleson, *From Ethics to Politics: Confronting Scarcity and Fairness in Public Interest Practice*, 1978 B.Y.U. L. REV. 337.

[91] Simon, *supra* note 1. *See also* J. AUERBACH, UNEQUAL JUSTICE: LAWYERS AND SOCIAL CHANGE IN MODERN AMERICA (1976); R. Abel, *supra* note 3.

[92] Other authors addressing the question of the appropriate function of the lawyer have argued that the lawyer is merely a facilitator of the client's wishes. *See* T. SHAFFER, *supra* note 58; Fried, *supra* note 11; Binder, *supra* note 8.

[93] J. FRANK, COURTS ON TRIAL (1969).

[94] Schlegel, *supra* note 48.

[95] For one suggestion of how this might work, see Sparer, *The Responsibility of Law Teachers*, 53 N.Y.U.L. REV. 602 (1978).

doctrine with field work experience,[96] few have utilized the opportunity to do more than study, in traditional fashion, the policy considerations implicated in legal doctrines.[97] Instead, the clinician's skills would be better employed by analyzing the impact particular rules have on the people involved with that body of law.[98] Thus, a discussion of the policy considerations connected with employer financed unemployment compensation programs might also consider the effects of such financing on the burden of proof, motivation to contest a determination, appearances at the hearings, control over the production of evidence and recovery rates.[99] In this way the clinician could bridge the gap between the law as written and the law as experienced by the actors in the legal system. Our understanding of the role of law and lawyer in society would be broadened by a sustained and rigorous analysis of the relationship of the different levels of the legal system to each other.

These suggestions have implications not only for the development of clinical themes in scholarship, but for the nature of clinical education as well. Most modern clinical programs will be forced to decide between two lines of development; to offer traditional process or skills courses, such as interviewing, negotiation, counselling and trial advocacy, or to develop substantive courses with clinical or fieldwork components, where the primary purpose is the study of the law and its doctrine in the context of the relevant legal institutions. Obviously, the two approaches are not mutually exclusive, but where resources are scarce and there is a desire for planned programatic and intellectual development, the choice may have to be made.

C. The Clinician as Empiricist

As an instructor and practitioner, the clinician has a unique opportunity to study the legal profession as an ethnomethodologist—that is, a participant observer.[100] The clinician, by observing and capturing thousands of data on the legal profession every year, has a rich opportunity for a systematic behavioral examination of the participants in and the structure of the legal system. The case study analysis of legal services work by Bellow and Kettleson is one example of such work.[101]

---

[96] Clinical courses at various law schools (i.e., New York University, University of California at Los Angeles, Rutgers, Ohio State, Columbia, Stanford) have been offered in the substantive areas of Criminal Law, Consumer Law, Welfare Law, Administrative Law, and Women's Rights, to name a few.

[97] See, e.g., Elson, *A Common Law Remedy for the Educational Harms Caused by Incompetent or Careless Teaching*, 73 Nw. L. REV. 641 (1978).

[98] See, e.g., J. NOONAN, PERSONS AND MASKS OF THE LAW 111-51 (1976).

[99] See Lesnick, *Reassessing Law Schooling: The Sterling Forest Group*, 53 N.Y.U.L. REV. 565 (1978).

[100] H. SCHWARTZ & J. JACOBS, QUALITATIVE METHODS IN SOCIOLOGY (1979).

[101] G. Bellow and J. Kettleson, Criteria for Case File Evaluation (on file with the author).

Evaluation studies of lawyer practice routines and alternative forms or types of practice is another example. In my own empirical work, I am studying how attorneys in a nonmarket context (legal services attorneys) allocate scarce legal resources.[102] There are a variety of such questions which could be subjected to this rigorous field and empirical analysis by clinicians with available data bases. Clinicians need only ask the right, i.e., most interesting questions, about lawyers and our legal system and then operationalize those questions in the field.

D. *Professional Norms: Ethical and Moral Codes*

Given the timeliness and significance of questions about our rules of legal ethics,[103] clinicians would seem to be particularly well qualified to offer analyses and suggestions for appropriate rules of conduct applicable to different kinds of lawyering situations. The work of Bellow and Moulton,[104] Bellow and Kettleson,[105] and Spiegel[106] seems to point us in this direction. Yet clinicians still need to consider whether the categories of lawyering functions and clientele served established by the present Code or the proposed Model Rules[107] adequately provides for the diversity of legal functions, professional services and client needs. At the very least, the subject matters and geographic areas we serve may reveal useful information about the allocation of legal services. Although clinicians can prepare law students to work in areas of greatest need this is only part of our function. Clinical teachers and scholars should also explore alternative methods of delivering legal services and of structuring our profession, particularly in controversial areas such as judicare,[108] mandatory pro bono work,[109] and lay or paralegal representation projects. There is no end to the policy issues effecting the practice of law that clinicians might profitably and intelligently address.

IV. CONCLUSIONS AND SUGGESTIONS FOR THE FUTURE

This essay has examined the contributions that have come from various clinical "schools of thought" to the theories about lawyering. These can be broadly categorized by their emphasis on the role of the

---

[102] Menkel-Meadow and Meadow, *The Allocation of Legal Resources in a Non-Market Context*, NSF Grant #SES-8020373 (July 1, 1980).

[103] New rules of professional conduct are presently being considered. *See* note 109 *infra* and accompanying text.

[104] G. BELLOW & B. MOULTON, *supra* note 9.

[105] G. BELLOW AND J. KETTLESON, *supra* note 101.

[106] Spiegel, *supra* note 7.

[107] *See* note 75 *supra* and accompanying text.

[108] S. BRAKEL, JUDICARE PUBLIC FUNDS, PRIVATE LAWYERS AND POOR PEOPLE (1974); LEGAL SERVICES CORPORATION, DELIVERY SYSTEMS STUDY (1980).

[109] ABA, PROPOSED MODEL RULES OF PROFESSIONAL CONDUCT (1980).

individual attorney or on the profession in general. Although the line of demarcation between "micro" and "macro" theories of lawyering is artificially drawn, it is useful for clinicians to identify the academic and practical issues the discipline raises, and thereby to determine which themes or disciplines the clinician can comfortably address.

While the exclusive focus on Maslowian survivial needs[110] may not be totally supplanted, the time has come for clinicians to address the serious issues of the process and substance of lawyering. The time has come to share what has been learned from clinical programs with both fellow clinicians and other members of the legal profession. Although the clinical movement has come of age as an educational medium, it remains in its infancy in legal scholarship. This is especially true of its potential contribution to a better understanding of the lawyer's role in contemporary society. If there is any legacy clinicians can offer to the future of legal education, it is to encourage the study of lawyering as a subject worthy of serious inquiry in our institutions of legal education. Although clinicians may on occasion disagree with one another and with non-clinical legal educators, the free exchange of ideas should foster a climate of experimentation and intellectual growth that will promote the development of more informed and effective teachers and practitioners.

---

[110] For too long clinicians have been focused on their "lower" survival needs, and have neglected the expression of their "higher" aspirations and values. A. MASLOW, THE FARTHER REACHES OF HUMAN NATURE (1971).

On Talking Tough to Each Other: Comments on Condlin

Gary Bellow

Allard Lowenstein, an old, special friend of mine, used to tell an interesting tale about a family with a lovely son who, for reasons that they could not fathom, never said a word. The son went through his early years, and then into his fifth year and sixth year, his seventh year, his eighth year and still never spoke, at least not to them. In all other respects the boy was just fine, but he never spoke when he was in the house. He spoke at school, but he never spoke at home. And then one morning, having sat down, as usual, for breakfast, he looked at his mother and father, and quietly said, "The toast is burnt." His mother and father looked at him with tears in their eyes. They couldn't believe what they had heard. After a few moments, they turned to him, and with great emotion, said, "Johnny, you finally said something! What made you finally speak?" He answered, "Well, up 'til now, everything was going alright."

I ask you to reflect on that tale as we try to sort through the intensity and emotion that surrounds the debate considered here and its implications for our work. For the debate seems to me to involve two separate but intertwined arguments—an argument among clinicians and another between clinicians and the rest of the faculty. In each, we are, perhaps, surprised at the degree of disagreement. Most of us have thought that things were pretty much going all right.

Let me start first with the critique Bob Condlin has leveled at his colleagues engaged, like him, in clinical teaching. As I understand him, his basic educational premise is that what we teach, in clinical programs or otherwise, is significantly affected by the way it is taught: that there is, in all educational processes, a meta-message contained in the way material is communicated. This seems obvious enough: Communication is inevitably a function of relationships, of interactions between people; this holds true whether the teacher is trying to demonstrate the importance of rigorous analysis or to show the ambiguities of the moral universe in which legal professionals work. Few of us fail to recognize that, if we expect students to become self-learners, the importance of mutuality, honesty, tolerance for other ideas, and self-awareness—all of which are basic to successful self-

---

Gary Bellow is Professor of Law, Harvard Law School.

© 1983 by the Association of American Law Schools. Cite as 33 J. Legal Educ. 619 (1983).

learning—have to be demonstrated and valued in our teaching. What I hear Condlin saying is that, as he looks at the work of clinicians around the country, these values are not being communicated. That is, clinical teachers find themselves—or, if they looked at themselves, they would find themselves—more unilateral, more controlling, less honest, less tolerant, and more judgmental than they would like to be. This is the meta-message concerning appropriate behavior that students are taking away from our instruction.

I have studied a great many such student-teacher dialogues over the years, including several that Condlin refers to in his paper, and I am now in the process of regularly taping my own work with students as a clinical instructor. By and large it seems to me that Condlin's insights are correct. He is right about me, and my hunch is that he is right about many people in this room. I find myself more controlling than I expected, less open and honest about the agendas that I am pursuing than I supposed, less tolerant and non-judgmental, in fact much less tolerant and non-judgmental, than I sometimes take myself to be. And I see my actions affecting the way my students learn, because students inevitably pick up, in addition to the material we teach, the patterns of action and models of behavior presented by those with authority over them. We might do well to deal more forthrightly with these weaknesses than perhaps we have.

On the other hand, Condlin portrays our weaknesses as moral failures rather than as gaps between what we would like to be and what we actually are. I agree that clinical professors turn out to be much more like regular law professors than they would like to be. But that fact does not warrant the condemnation that the article seems to communicate or the reactions Condlin's criticisms have generated. I support the main themes in his remarks, but express the following reservations.

First, we ought to be very careful about considering ourselves more central than we really are or taking ourselves more seriously than we deserve. My experience, in too many years of teaching, is that my students survive me extremely well, that they learn from lots of things besides and often in spite of the models and ideas I present. I will not deny that I want to improve at what I do. But it is not true, as I think Condlin implies, that there is a clear correlation between modeling and imitation, on the one hand, and indoctrination on the other. We ought to give our students more credit for their ability to judge for themselves.

Second, we ought to deal explicitly and, I think skeptically, with the implicit normative cast of what Condlin is saying. He says that resolution of some of the problems of professional responsibility in which he is interested requires that professionals explore more possibilities for collaborative behavior in their work—more mutuality, more honesty, more openness. I agree generally with that position although I think it needs far more elaboration and specification than it has thus far received. Not all mutuality depends on the absence of assertiveness; not all honesty is a function of full disclosure; openness is rarely possible without hard judgment and evaluation. In addition, there are many other values to be taken into consideration, in helping students think through problems relating to their professional roles, that are not encompassed in those three ideals: for example, kindness, social responsibility, fairness, loyalty. Condlin points to a number of norms against which we can measure our own behavior, but important though they are, they are in no sense, a complete guide for conduct.

Third, we might consider more carefully one aspect of legal education—its social setting—which I do not believe is dealt with adequately in Condlin's piece or in others drawing, as his is, on humanistic psychology, literature, or the more political writing of the Frankfurt school. Some of the problems with the way that teachers behave towards students are a function of the systems of privilege and hierarchy in which they operate. Some of the real world problems with which we want our students to deal are not going to be solved by a richer and more reasoned discourse, because they involve judgments about the way the world works and who is responsible for the consequences.

To open up these issues with our students requires a much more substantive and political orientation than Condlin articulates, both as to the character of the law-school world and as to the character of the social reality in which we function. If we are to engage in a process of self-evaluation of the sort he wants, we will inevitably have to confront our own politics. One of the most important insights of feminism is the degree to which it recognizes that politics are also personal, that is, that the way we treat each other expresses and, in fact, creates our political reality. Insofar as racism, class, and sexism are part of one's culture, they are also part of one's own behavior, and no substantive vision can emerge without some consciousness of their impact on each of us.

And so, I agree with what Condlin is saying to each of us as clinicians—we need to write more; we need to look harder at ourselves; we need to be less afraid of criticizing ourselves. But we also need to argue with each other in an atmosphere in which what is at stake goes beyond today's debate, yet does not constantly question the value of the entire enterprise in which we are engaged.

I also agree with the suggestions Condlin makes about the ways clinicians speak to nonclinicians. I agree that, insofar as we label faculty members too quickly, we do not find out what they really think; insofar as we become defensive, we miss opportunities for discussion and critique; insofar as we do not say honestly and explicitly what we think in ways that others will hear, we miss opportunities for changes and reforms that many of us support. But, in acknowledging those failures, it is also important to recognize how far reaching is the clinicians' critique of legal education in its present form and how much potential conflict is buried in the defense mechanisms that Condlin identifies.

Let me elaborate briefly on that observation. First consider the picture of the legal system that most clinicians convey. It is filled with people, relationships, and interpersonal dynamics. Indeed, I think that the basic jurisprudential insight of clinical education is the interpersonal character of legal institutions. Law is not seen as a set of rules or institutional structures; it is understood as a constant creation of human interaction. Clinicians present the world of law to students—from courts to administrative agencies, to what goes on in law practice—as not only affected but constituted by relationships between people. This is, of course, obvious, and yet a radical critique of legal education, as it currently exists. If we look hard at the way doctrine and policy are currently taught, I think we would admit that the images of the world that we project simply bear no relation to reality. Law-as-practiced is entirely different from the law-as-presented in the law-school classroom, and not simply a minor variance between the ideal and the actuality. We cannot begin to deal, either with the way the law world really works, or with ways in which it might be judged normatively, without more empirical knowledge and interest in the educational process. One of the radical impulses of clinical education was to bring the world back into the classroom, so that law schools had to deal with it, discuss it, confront its realities. That job, if carried forward, will create not only dialogue, but conflict.

The same is true of a second aspect of clinical education worth mentioning—its normative impulse. Clinicians invariably debate criteria and standards, whether we are dealing with the work done at Antioch on competency, or definitions of proper conduct in the morally ambiguous settings of practice. Most clinicians that I have worked with are deeply interested in substantive justice and substantive norms, whatever the failure of our own discourse on this subject. Again there is potential confrontation here. Most law is taught as if marshalling arguments on both sides of an issue were its end all and be all. There is very little closure around the question of right and wrong as the class moves from one case to the next. Indeed, justice as a criteria for decision is often dismissed in the first three days of classes as soft-headed and unrealistic. This is a very different mode of education than one that emphasizes judgment, decision-making criteria, and standards. A real dialogue initiated by clinicians and heard by faculty would be a dialogue about the content and pedagogy of the entire law school curriculum.

Finally, there is the question of the purposes of legal education itself. My own observation is that, contrary to the view of many law faculties, our present modes of education do not properly prepare students to practice law. I do not only mean that they do not have the requisite skills, although their incompetence is a part of the problem; I mean that they are left—in attitude, knowledge, and orientation—at the mercy of the environments in which they find themselves. If law schools were to take seriously its interest in teaching students to think like lawyers, in their ability to learn from their experience, they would have to adopt a much more sophisticated conception of what and how environments teach and a much more critical posture on its own failures and weaknesses. That no such inquiry seems in the offing does not bode well for the possibilities of a clinician-faculty dialogue.

All of this needs to be stated more carefully than I have just stated it, more rigorously, and more as an invitation to dialogue than perhaps I have expressed it. Al Sacks once said to me, "Well, it seems to me that what you're saying is that law school is empirically irrelevant, theoretically flawed, pedagogically dysfunctional, and expensive." And I am, of course, saying just that. When you add to these deficiencies, the incoherence of the second- and third-year course offerings, the amount of repetition in the curriculum, the degree to which unacknowledged ideology pervades the entire law school experience and the fact that no graduate of an American law school is able to practice when graduated, you have a system of education which, I believe, is simply indefensible. Clinicians have important things to say about these problems, in a form which invites dialogue and discussion, but which does not avoid conflict as well.

We need to demand of our colleagues that they be more empirically accurate, that their theories be more relevant, that their teaching be more likely to give students autonomy, and that our discourse be real discourse—concerned with normative values, not the justification of the system that currently exists. It may be that, as has been suggested, our concern with psychological models and our interest in empathy, communication, and feeling has made clinical studies a fundamentally conservative element of the very patterns and practices most in need of reform. Or it may be, as I think Condlin intends, that clinical education's concern for the psychology of conflict and consensus will be a resource for a deeper and more functional dialogue throughout the law school. I certainly hope that this is what the future holds.

If I Were Dean
Louis M. Brown

You have asked me to consider applying for the deanship of your school. During the course of that mutual exploration I have indicated some of my views. I appreciate that your school is a newcomer among approved schools. So that the record is clear, I prefer to summarize my vision of objectives that the school should strive to achieve.

Law schools are here for several purposes, but primarily to educate and train students to become members of the legal profession so that they can find a satisfactory way of life and contribute to society. Given a large lawyer population in your state, and nationally, and given the existing number of law schools, it is reasonable to ask: What can be the place of this school and its contribution? To this question there are optimistic answers and suggestions.

Every member of the law school faculty (and virtually every member of every law school faculty) has studied law, and teaches law. In a nutshell, very few I feel, have studied—or teach—lawyering. It is lawyering for which a professional school should educate and train most of its students. Such an objective means that the school is both a law school and a lawyering school. Lawyering includes law, but law does not necessarily include lawyering. So the law school that I envision must maintain its solid course work in law subjects. Several approaches can be taken to encompass lawyering within the educational institution.

Integration of Lawyering Within Existing Courses

This approach I have slightly demonstrated in a few of the classes you permitted me to conduct. The approach is described in "Teaching the Low Visible Decision Processes of the Lawyer."[1] The teaching material upon which that article is based is gathered in *Teaching Materials: Lawyer-Client Counseling and Decisions.*[2] Start with the notion that the appellate case in the case book is not really a case. It is more nearly an opinion. Make it approximate a case by filling in the life of the litigant, as client, and the lawyer. Pick out a time in the facts of the case when the client might have consulted a lawyer. Imagine a lawyer-client dialogue; write it. Students react energetically when class discussion concerns that dialogue. This is the Langdell case method extended to lawyering. I suggest selective occasional

---

Louis M. Brown is counsel with Sanders, Barnet, Goldsmith & Jacobson in Los Angeles, California and Professor of Law, Emeritus, University of Southern California.

1. 25 J. Legal Educ. 386 (1973).
2. Mimeographed. 1978, vii + 489 pp.

c 1985 by the Association of American Law Schools. Cite as 35 J. Legal Educ. 117 (1985).

use in classwork. One aspect of this teaching is the potential for direct involvement of a lawyer as a guest participant. The point briefly is the familiar observation that the study of law does not necessarily reveal how it functions and operates in the lawyer-client context, nor does the study of law necessarily reveal the role of the lawyer. Traditional study of law reveals, more nearly, the decisional process of an appellate court. Lawyering includes the decisional processes of the lawyer.

Course Work and Classes

The school now offers a course in counseling and negotiating; these are lawyering functions. Such a course is relatively new in law school curricula. It is a growing area of interest; now more that 25 percent of the approved law schools offer such a course. Its development needs constant attention. Participation in the Client Counseling Competition should, of course, be included.

Legal writing is a subject to which law schools have given attention in recent years. Mostly the legal writing course here, as elsewhere, concerns litigation writing. Law library research is taught for purposes of preparing briefs and pleadings. Law review offers writing experience probably for those students who least need it. All such writing is directed to the profession. Lawyers, however, also prepare transactional documents intended for nonlawyers. And much of the writing done by lawyers is directed solely to nonlawyers, their clients. Consideration should be given to the entire scope of legal writing from the writing of examinations in law school to the broad range of lawyer's writing. Some of this writing may be incorporated in regular course work without much more faculty effort. One such project I did with students is illustrated in "Information for Lawyers in Counseling Newlyweds."[3] In a preventive law course I taught we discussed premarital agreements. The Beverly Hills Bar was commencing a project through its Lawyer Reference Service to counsel persons who are, or were about to become, newlyweds. Students wrote segments of information as either a letter to a client or a memo to the lawyer who would counsel a client.

Several students work in law offices part time. The standards for the approval of law schools tend to discourage such activity, but it is common for students at this, and other law schools, to do this. In my opinion the law office is not only a place where law is; it is also a laboratory for learning. So let us take academic advantage of the experience of the students. Law office work of students can be made into fine seminar discussion and student projects. Assuming that permission of the employer can be obtained, consider these ideas. What, for example, is the work product of the law office? A law office exists to produce legal services. How is this accomplished? Look. See. Ask. Observe. Make a flow chart of the work performance of some item of legal services in the office. Come to class prepared to discuss aspects of the working of the office. What law? What nonlaw? What personnel? What is the division of work between lawyer and nonlawyer? Who decides? What do lawyers do? How much time is spent on the telephone, writing, reading,

---

3. 12 **Beverly Hills Bar J.** 59 (March-April 1978).

dictating, redrafting, in conference? How much of this is law? How much is fact gathering and organizing? How much is not directly related to a client's matter? Compare the litigation and nonadversarial work of the law office. How much time and effort for each? What is the source of the clients? How much time is face to face with clients? How is all this related to law school education, and law school courses? What are the professional responsibility problems, if any, in the observed activities of the law office? How are assignments made to you, as a law clerk? Is what you do law work? Fact work? Or what? Learn how to observe, analyze, and understand the law office. Compare your experiences with the experiences of other students. Students in traditional law school learning learn from books. Now learn how to learn from observation. Ultimately most students will practice law. Ability to reflect on practice is essential for the development and the improvement of methods of practice.

Clinic Segment

Clinical exposure in law schools generally is in the litigation (dispute) area of law practice. Fine. I do not know the extent of the school's present clinic program. Generally, however, clinical exposure is more doing than learning by finding and discussing the common elements in the lawyering process. What decisions are made by the lawyer for example? What decisions are client decisions? How are lawyer decisions made? What factors are taken into account? And now evaluated? Consider the alternatives to the court process as a means of resolving disputes.

There is little or no exposure in law school clinics to preventive law practice, an unfortunate omission in all legal education. Consider the experience described in "Periodic Check-Up: Report of a Law School Term Paper Project."[4] Have students perform a legal checkup on a "client." The client may be an average person with no apparent legal problems. Is that person in good legal health, or are there legal soft spots of which the client is unaware? In my opinion, this is a fine project for law schools, a splendid learning experience that includes law, client relations, as well as substantial segments of the fact world in which a person lives.

One recent surprise situation arose in my teaching. Instead of a checkup on an individual, a student made a checkup of a charitable organization. I call the review of corporate enterprise a legal audit.[5] The project was so worthwhile to the organization that the student and I received a flattering letter of thanks. The school could, on a systematic basis, undertake the performance of such legal reviews for any willing charitable organization. A student learning project can be first-rate education revealing the preventive law role of the lawyer. This sort of project fills a large gap in law school clinical work. It provides a means whereby students can do a lawyering task within a business context—the law of corporations, property ownership, flow of money, employment, contracts, insurance. At the same time the school would be performing highly beneficial legal work for the community.

4. 29 J. Legal Educ. 438 (1978).
5. See 38 S. Cal. L. Rev. 431 (1965).

Legal Autopsy Research

The technique of legal autopsy would be an interesting and exciting program to present to faculties and the law review.[6] I have performed several and so have students. My inability to spread this investigatory and learning technique beyond my own teaching is disappointing. I regard it as a significant "invention" of a research methodology. A student who is assigned to perform a legal autopsy of a decided dispute can learn enormous amounts about lawyering, the process by which the dispute is determined. Start with a decided controversy which may be an appellate case, a trial court judgment, or a settlement. With the cooperation of the lawyers (I have had excellent help from lawyers) review the case from its earliest beginnings before the lawsuit started. When was a lawyer first consulted or, even earlier, when might a lawyer have been consulted? Proceed through the whole matter, including conversation with the client with the lawyer's permission. Do the same for both sides. One major aspect is that the litigation process expressly excludes the lawyer-client relationship that this process makes available. It has the potential of being a fine methodology for exploring the settlement process—a process scarcely mentioned in traditional law school education. Costs of dispute resolution, another great omission in traditional legal education, can be explored. Every case study written up in the law review could embody, as one area of analysis, legal autopsy of some aspects of the case.

We should find ways to incorporate the settlement process in our course materials. Some, doubtless, is included in the teaching of negotiation. Some is included in the clinic program. Some can be developed from legal autopsy investigation. With a little imagination, settlement can be considered hypothetically in relation to appellate opinions in existing course books.

Law Office Classroom

The Law Office Classroom concept has yet to see its full use. More than ten law schools now have a facility identified as a law office classroom. Law exists in law offices with greater frequency than in the courts. Every approved law school is required to have a moot courtroom facility. Why not a law office facility used for teaching purposes? We could seek to have live depositions conducted in such a facility. Perhaps, also, such negotiations as settlement of litigation and property settlement agreement. Could we get a lawyer to conduct some real law office activities? I, once, had an assistant district attorney (Los Angeles) conduct an office conference with an investigator within earshot of a dozen students. The issue was the decision about prosecuting. Encourage lawyers to use your present courtroom/ auditorium to hold creditor's meetings where a debtor seeks to obtain composition with existing creditors. Maybe this school is the place to which lawyers will bring live bodies to illustrate law office activities in the view of students. A professor can lead discussions before and after the activity. If we can get lawyers to try it, they might like it. I know that students will like it, and learn.

---

6. 39 J. Am. Jud. Soc'y 47 (1955).

Law Office Operations

Very little is done in law schools about the operation and management of law offices. Law office management and the delivery of legal services ought not be the stepchild of legal education. We could use the help of lawyers to design a series of typical and teachable law office management problems. Some students may go straight from law school to open a law office. It would be better to learn and think about that before jumping into the swirling water.

Bar Examination

One deterrent to a lawyering school is the bar examination. That examiniation, good as it is in examining law, fails to examine lawyering. In the recent California Bar exam, some effort, I understand, was made along these lines, but I do not know the results. Some of my ideas were exposed in the article, "The Call of the Question."[7] Maybe—just maybe—this school can demonstrate that lawyering can be taught and tested. You might blaze a highly beneficial trail in improving the competence of lawyers in lawyering. Could this school become the center for the study of lawyering for lawyers in their early years of law practice? The relations with lawyers has been mentioned and partially described. Much involvement of lawyers need not be as course teachers but rather as resource people. Lawyers are remarkable. Their contributions in time and effort to the profession is unpurchaseable. Lawyers willingly, and freely, give a portion of their time to legal education; they would, if called upon, assist in much of the work I have described.

Involving Lawyers

Yet there is another—and somewhat different—lawyer involvment. Many law schools have an effective board of visitors, or overseers, or counselors—by whatever name. They meet at the call of their chairman or at the request of the dean. Their ideas and "sounding board" effect can be extremely helpful. Among other things, such a board can act to stimulate or caution the course of action of the school. Upon becoming familiar with the school, its faculty, and its students, they can become spokesmen, as well as critics, of the school. I wonder whether this school can go a step further. To what extent can lawyers be involved in any part of law school administration? Here are two examples: (1) placement; I can envision five or six retired lawyers or judges in this community who would be extremely helpful to our students in seeking placement, in counseling students regarding their approach to interviews, in preparing resumes, (2) recruiting for students; would lawyers interested in this school take some time to contact the college from which they graduated to inform the college counselor, or graduating students, about this institution? Next—a less likely prospect but worthy of consideration—have a lawyer attached, as ex-officio, to certain committees of the law school.

There might be come modification in the faculty recruiting policies. In

---

7. 4 Learning and the Law 56 (1974).

keeping with general practices of law schools, you ask for a curricula vitae which includes publications. "Publications" means law review articles and law books. You ought to welcome a bibliography that includes briefs in the litigation process, documents prepared by the applicant as lawyer, public issue prospectus, contracts, financial arrangements, identification of cases tried, letters to clients, memoranda to lawyers, and so on. The major problem in some schools with such bibliographies is that there are few faculty members equipped to evaluate them. Here are two suggestions: You might get help from your Board of Visitors; and, fortunately, you do have some members of your faculty with the law office experience that can enable them to judge.

Law Library

Your law library appears well operated. Like all law libraries it is largely limited to published litigation materials. You recall that Langdell said that the library is the laboratory for law study and research. If that is so, your "laboratory" could include law office materials. Such an undertaking is not easy but if accomplished, even modestly, what a wonderful source for research and enlargement of teaching materials.

I do not regard this as a complete statement of ideas for your law school. Nor do I think that it all can be done. I do believe that your faculty is intelligent, sincere, cooperative, energetic, and human. I believe that your school is in a position such that it can and should strive to accomplish educational objectives not performed elsewhere. These ideas, along with ideas by members of the faculty, should be part of curricula consideration. It might be fun to consider this and come up with workable developments in education for law and lawyering.

There is money, of course. Nothing in these ideas should cramp the effort to obtain funds. In fact, becoming a lawyering school might help. It gives the school a talking point that should attract the profession and the public. In all these ideas is the concept of the client as a human. Focus on the client should have a public appeal.

Your school can make its own contribution. It can be a fine example of the human aspects of lawyering. It can show its concern for the public our students will represent. It can be the school where lawyering, as well as law, is taught.

Part III
Looking for Answers Beyond Law

'Law And'

[22]

WHAT THE LAW SCHOOLS CAN CONTRIBUTE TO THE MAKING OF LAWYERS *

LON L. FULLER †

There are four competing conceptions of the objectives of legal education. The purpose of this paper is to examine the virtues, limitations, and dangers of each of these conceptions.

The four conceptions are:

First Conception. The object of legal education is to give the student *knowledge*. The faculty should study carefully what branches of law are most important today and arrange the curriculum so as to impart the knowledge most needed in modern law practice.

Second Conception. The object of legal education is to impart *skills*. We should survey the aptitudes and techniques demanded by modern law practice and devise teaching methods that will give the student these aptitudes and techniques. In terms of industrial management, we should conduct a job analysis or "skill-breakdown" of the legal profession, and then put our students through a conditioning process that will implant in their nervous systems the aptitudes that will make them successful lawyers.

Third Conception. True education, in law as in every other calling, consists in exposing the student to *Great Minds*.

Fourth Conception. The object of legal education should be to give the student an understanding of, and an insight into, the *processes* in which the lawyer participates.

Nothing compels us to treat any of these conceptions as an exclusive standard for the organization of legal education. Each could be viewed as supplementing the others. In actual discussions of educational policy this seldom happens. The polemical spirit generated by attempts to define ultimate aims tends to throw every point of view into polar opposition to every other point of view. Perhaps the present paper will illustrate this tendency in its advocacy of the fourth conception. In any event, in what follows each of the four conceptions will be analyzed both in terms of its capacity to furnish an exclusive standard and in terms of its capacity to furnish a corrective for the other points of view.

* This paper represents a revision of a talk given at the Inter-Professions Conference on Education for Professional Responsibility, held at Buck Hill Falls, Pennsylvania, April 12–14, 1948.

† Carter Professor of Jurisprudence, Harvard University.

189

First Conception

"Give the Student the Knowledge He Needs to be a Lawyer"

As a general standard for the organization of the curriculum, this conception enjoys a diminishing popularity. There are many reasons for this decline in favor. The changing demands of modern law practice make it impossible to predict what the student will need to know after his graduation. Successful attorneys generally ascribe a secondary importance to the content of the curriculum, and assert that the real service of the law school is to teach men to think like lawyers. A curricular organization directed toward conveying the most generally useful information would exclude highly specialized seminar courses of proved educational value.

The current preference for method over content should not blind us to the fact that those who talk content often have something important to say. Methodism, even in the non-ecclesiastical sense, can be carried to excess. There is need to recall that the slogan, "We teach men to think," has been the last refuge of every dying discipline from Latin and Greek to Mechanical Drawing and Common-Law Pleading.

It is a serious pedagogical error to select materials purely in terms of their capacity to inculcate method. Effective instruction in method cannot take place unless instructor and student believe (or share the delusion) that the problems they are considering are important and vital in the world as it exists today. If either pierces the veil of pretense and sees (or admits) that the game is being played for cardboard counters, instruction in method will fail of its own self-consciously formulated objective.

Content is important, not so much for itself as for its significance in the attainment of other objectives.

Second Conception

"Job Analysis or Skill-Breakdown"

This is probably the most fashionable conception today. The slogans are: skills, techniques, the art of advocacy, the art of counseling.

The conception that legal education should aim at imparting skills and techniques has performed a valuable service in opening the way for a reexamination of the traditional curriculum. It has stimulated proper doubts as to the real importance of some of the supposedly fundamental courses in private law. More usefully still, it has challenged the educational validity of the lines of division that conventionally separate the various law-school subjects—lines that actually had their origin not in educational considerations, but in the analytical needs of the text-writer.

Yet valuable as this conception has been in the razing of outworn structures, I believe that the greatest danger now confronting American legal education is that this conception will be taken too seriously and applied too literally. For so soon as an attempt is made to employ the skills-and-techniques conception as the exclusive standard for organizing legal education, the whole educational process is disoriented and cheapened.

When it is examined critically, it becomes apparent that the skills-and-techniques conception furnishes no real test of what or how men ought to be taught. Lawyers need every skill and aptitude that affects man's intellectual and moral life. They need to be able to reason logically, to reject irrelevancies, to detect unstated premises, to read and listen with understanding, to argue persuasively, to fathom motives, to write and speak good English—the list could be expanded indefinitely. There is nothing in the command, "Teach skills," that answers the inescapable problem of priorities, or that gives form and direction to the curriculum.

Not only does the skills-and-techniques conception fail to furnish any intelligible guide for organizing legal education, but the attempt to apply it seriously threatens to forfeit the most valuable feature of the American case method of instruction, namely, an impersonal absorption in problems. It converts what ought to be a disinterested exploration of issues into an exercise in self-improvement. It abandons the university tradition in legal training for something that smacks of Dale Carnegie or Charles Atlas.

Woodrow Wilson once observed that the man who sets about to achieve "character" makes himself ridiculous. Character is the by-product of a quest for other goals. In the same way, skills and techniques should be the by-product of an educational system that concentrates on problems rather than men.

Third Conception
"Exposure to Great Minds"

No juggling of courses, no curricular manipulations can take the place of good teaching. Nor is good teaching of any value if it is employed to convey trivialities. We must have good teachers, and teachers who have something good to teach. Beside these twin imperatives, all else is secondary. Those who speak of exposure to great minds perform a service in reminding us that this is so.

They do a disservice, however, when—as so often happens—they overstate their case to the point of asserting that the organization of the curriculum is of no importance at all. Indeed, the Mark-Hopkins-on-a-log theory is often advanced in a way which implies that in properly run law schools there has never been any conscious attention to the organization of the curriculum. This is of course fantasy. In American legal education we have inherited a curricular organization that was worked out through cooperative effort a good many decades ago. This constituted a coordinated program when it was devised. It is conceivable that it still constitutes the best way of arranging legal education. The conservatives who believe this should, however, assume the responsibilities appropriate to their position. They are not entitled to say, "Only little minds concern themselves with organizational problems," when what they mean is, "The inherited curriculum is right and should be preserved."

Anticipating the argument of the next heading, we may say that if specific knowledge and specific skills are relatively unimportant, an understanding of the lawyer's actual and potential contribution to society is not. The curriculum should be so arranged as to give the student that understanding in such broad terms that he will be able to perceive and relate to one another the various facets of the lawyer's work. This will not just happen; it must be planned.

Fourth Conception

"The Object of Legal Education is to Convey an Understanding of the Processes in which the Lawyer Participates"

The lawyer is a participant, and usually the most active and responsible participant, in two basic social processes: adjudication and legislation. Both terms are here used in a somewhat broader sense than is customary.

The adjudicative process has to do with the case-arguing and dispute-deciding aspect of the lawyer's work. As I use the term, it refers to all forensic methods of deciding disputes, including informal arbitration and the work of administrative tribunals as well as the traditional processes of our courts. Adjudication presents the lawyer in his rôle as advocate, or judge, or office counselor advising a client of the likely decision of a cause. All of these activities center about a single process, that by which controversies are argued and decided.

The legislative process, on the other hand, presents the lawyer in his rule-creating, structure-giving rôle. It presents him as a planner, negotiator, and draftsman. As I use the term "legislation" it refers not merely to the planning and drafting of statutes, but includes the negotiation and drafting of contracts and other private documents. Thus, the drafting of a will is, in this sense, legislation, since it establishes a legal framework within which the estate of the testator is administered after his death.

It is my contention that the purpose of legal education should be that of conveying an understanding of these two basic processes. If we take these processes as our point of orientation, I think we shall be able to make some progress toward solving the following problems of educational policy:

1. Is our present system of legal education satisfactory?
2. What branches of law should we include in the three-year course?
3. Where should the student's instruction begin?
4. How can we relate law to the life and theory beyond law without losing the sharp focus on specific issues that has been a cardinal virtue of traditional legal education?
5. How can we inculcate in our students a proper sense of professional responsibility toward client and public?

I shall begin with the first of these questions:

1. *Is our present system of legal education satisfactory?*

If we test our system by asking whether it conveys a sufficient insight into the two basic legal processes, I think the answer to this question is obvious. For reasons partly historical, and partly connected with the relative availability of materials, legal education in this country has almost totally neglected the legislative process, and has dealt with only one aspect of the adjudicative process, that of our appellate courts.

The isolation of a single phase of the adjudicative process from the process as a whole not only leaves many things untaught, but distorts and falsifies what it teaches. It conveys to the student almost no insight into the subtle issues involved in the proof of facts, for example. The appellate report usually presents a parched skeleton of the facts which lawyers connected with the case sometimes have difficulty in recognizing as a description of the situation with which they struggled for so many months. One of the permanent problems of the law and of advocacy has to do with that most perilous of human operations: attempting to transmit intact a set of facts from one human head to another. The appellate-case method gives little inkling of the existence of that problem, much less any understanding of the measures that may be taken toward solving it.

The almost total neglect of the legislative process is a more serious defect, which once again not merely leaves many things untaught, but distorts what it teaches, for the two processes of adjudication and legislation are themselves interrelated, so that neither can be fully understood without the other.

Legislation always looks forward in some degree toward adjudication. The careful draftsman legislating into existence the terms of a contract takes into account the possibility of trouble and seeks ways of protecting his client's interests in the event of litigation. On the other hand, most adjudication bears in some degree on someone's legislation. An understanding of the process by which contracts are negotiated and drafted is essential to the sound interpretation of a contract of disputed meaning. I have found in teaching Contracts that those of my students who have had some practical experience in what may be called generally "negotiation" bring to problems of interpretation a much more mature insight than those who lack this experience. Recently I tried the experiment of beginning my course with an exercise in negotiation and draftsmanship. My object was to convey, by a kind of vicarious or staged experience, the insight that comes from participation in the act of bringing an agreement into existence. While this educational venture has not been wholly successful, it demonstrates the close interrelation of the processes of legislation and adjudication. Students do actually draw on their experience in the drafting exercise in discussing judicial decisions that interpret agreements. The observable improvement in their insight and judgment tends to confirm a prejudice I have entertained for some time, namely, that no judge should sit on the interpretation of a contract who has himself never negotiated one.

Many law teachers affirm that what I have called the legislative process is taught as a natural by-product of ordinary case-method instruction. They point with pride to the fact that they frequently ask their students how the contract or testament involved in a particular case might have been drawn to avoid the difficulty that gave rise to the litigation, or how a statute should be amended to preserve the purpose of its draftsmen after a restrictive judicial interpretation.

I believe that this patchwork treatment of the problem is quite inadequate. Though, as I have said, the legislative and adjudicative processes are closely related, each of them represents a distinct set of problems and a distinct set of postures of the mind, so that neither can be taught as an unplanned by-product of teaching the other. The essential distinction between the two processes can be seen if we consider the different way each views facts.

Adjudication has to do with forensic facts. If we are dealing with appellate decisions, the facts reported have been filtered through the rules of evidence and purged of their natural ambiguities by presumptions and rules about the burden of proof. Even in the most informal administrative hearing or arbitration, however, facts assume a new character when presented in a context of litigation, being conveyed by self-conscious witnesses who—no matter how honest they may be—despair of conveying to the tribunal a full understanding of the situation as it appears to one living in it, and who, therefore, content themselves by relating only a segment of the truth, a segment which they think, more often wrongly than correctly, is the only aspect relevant to the decision.

Legislation, on the other hand, deals not with forensic facts, but with what may be called managerial facts. It is not the task of the lawyer acting as planner, negotiator, and draftsman to reduce the facts to a neat pattern, but to see them whole, in all their disorder, in all their ambiguity. He must gear his decision to a range of factual probability, and must devise a plan that will anticipate, and absorb without disruption, future changes in the facts.

Other differences between the processes of legislation and adjudication may be brought out by such a simple inquiry as: What is a contract? For the lawyer concerned with the adjudicative process a contract is a legally enforceable agreement, and its meaning is that which a court will give to it in the event of litigation. For the lawyer bringing a contract into existence it may be primarily a framework for co-operative effort, which performs its function without regard to its enforceability or the interpretations a judge would give to it. Often in phrasing the terms of an agreement the lawyer has to balance two desiderata against each other: (1) that of placing his client in a position to win any lawsuit that may grow out of the contract, and (2) that of creating an instrument of collaboration that will function effectively and not produce lawsuits. Iif he cannot have both these things, he may properly favor the second at some cost to the first, since his rôle as practical legislator for the situation may be more important than his rôle as advocate in a hypothetical future adjudication.

This analysis of the fundamental differences in the two processes might be continued, but I believe enough has been said to show how dangerous it is to assume that either teaches itself automatically when the other is taught.

I submit, therefore, that traditional legal education is not merely defective in detail, but in basic orientation, and that we must assume a responsibility for conveying to the student an understanding of both of the basic processes with which he will be concerned as a lawyer.

2. *What branches of law should we include in the three-year course?*

The remarks just concluded may suggest that I am proposing an impossible reform. A curriculum that deals by and large with only one phase of the adjudicative process is already dangerously overloaded. To add another whole facet of the lawyer's work would be not the straw, but the haystack that broke the camel's back.

On the contrary, I believe that the prescription I am urging would simplify the task of bringing our instruction within the limits of three school years.

Take, for example, the different ways in which a lawyer participates in the process of adjudication: as advocate, as judge, and as office counselor advising his client "what the law is"—that is, how real or hypothetical cases would probably be decided if they were litigated. In terms of a legal job analysis, these three tasks demand very different, almost antithetical skills and techniques. If our educational system is to be organized in terms of a skill "breakdown" then we are indeed on the verge of a curricular breakdown.

But I suggest that we need not take, as an explicit educational goal, teaching advocacy, or how to decide cases, or how to advise clients about what judges will decide. Rather, our task is to saturate the student with the adjudicative process, and let the skills and techniques develop as a by-product.

There are many things to learn about the adjudicative process. I have already spoken of the influence of a litigational context on facts. A full understanding of this influence can be obtained only by viewing adjudication as a process that makes its own peculiar demands on men's minds and attitudes, as a social relationship possessing unique qualities. Similarly, the tension that always exists between paper rules and the actual administration of justice is something that can be comprehended only if the student is immersed in the process of adjudication so that he comes to see its inherent limitations. All of this takes time, but it takes less time, and it uses time more effectively, than an attempt to train the student for each of the concrete tasks he may later be called upon to perform in connection with adjudication.

Again, the concept of the legislative process seems to me to furnish a standard that will simplify our problem of what to teach. As I have defined that process it covers a multitude of apparently disrelated activities—all the way from drafting a will in the quiet recesses of a five-name firm on State Street in Boston to negotiating a labor contract under threat of strike on the Galveston waterfront. And what a disparate set of skills and aptitudes this process demands of those who participate in it! The negotiator must have tact, an insight into others' motives, a sense of timing, a capacity for what may be called visceral decisions. The draftsman must have the capacity for painstaking logical analysis and clear, orderly English—and a horror of visceral decisions. Unless some common core can be found in these skills and activities we must despair of educating a lawyer in less than ten years.

But I believe there is such a common core, which I would define as the accommodation of opposed interests and the reduction of the pattern of that accommodation to clear verbal expression. I think we may even say that the man drafting a will is learning negotiation. He is considering how the interests of the widow can be accommodated to those of the children, and how the testator's desire to be generous toward his alma mater can be reconciled with his obligations toward his family. Such a draftsman is not like a man playing solitaire, but more like a player who plays in turn each of the hands in a bridge game. So that even the task of drafting a will may convey an insight useful in negotiating a contract. By the same token, negotiating and drafting a contract compels a man to perceive the demands contained in the task of drafting a statute and securing its passage.

I conclude that we do not need, and should not attempt, to teach men all the separate skills they will require to be successful negotiators, draftsmen, and planners. What we need to do is to convey to them, through selected problems, the core of the process by which conflicting interests are accommodated to one another. If we do that, we may trust the specific skills to develop, in those God intended to have them, as an unplanned by-product of insight.

In a similar way, I believe a focus on the two basic processes will simplify the problem of priority as to subject matter. We should not worry too much about turning the student out with a command over a particular set of legal rules. Rather, we should concentrate on the major ways in which legislation and adjudication function in our modern society, and let knowledge of rules become an unplanned by-product.

3. *Where should the student's instruction begin?*

This question may seem on a different level from those discussed so far and may appear as a descent to petty curricular details. I believe, however, that this matter of where you start is a fundamental problem, with premises that go to the root of educational policy.

I submit that we have had no defensible philosophy about how to open up a subject. There are a number of principles. One is to present legal doctrine historically, and some of the early casebooks presented the cases in an order corresponding to the years in which they were decided.

Another is to apply the test of chronology to the transaction under study. In Contracts, for example, you start with offers, because an offer is the first step toward making a contract. I submit that neither of these solutions is anything more than a default before the problem of a rational planning of the student's progress.

Another principle is to start with what is "simple and familiar." In Torts you begin with plain cases of A striking B, or of A striking at B; and the search in all courses is for the homely and commonplace as a starting point. This conception seems to offer a rational principle for opening up a subject, but in fact contains a serious fallacy. The simplicity of a legal problem is by no means guaranteed by the circumstance that its facts would make a good genre painting. One might almost assert the contrary. A neighborhood quarrel may seem a homely incident, yet one can hardly imagine a more subtle psychological process than that involved in determining legal liability for an event arising out of such a quarrel. On the other hand, proof in court of an elaborate legal document may be a very simple and routine matter. Nor is the fallacy of starting with the familiar merely a matter of procedural law. One reason for taking up early in the course in Contracts the question whether a posted acceptance is effective on dispatch or receipt is that this is supposed to be a problem that falls within the student's experience. Yet I know of no more difficult question of deciding what the substantive rule ought to be, if all of the implications of the problem are explored.

The prescription I am proposing would start not necessarily with simple facts, but with the processes of adjudication and legislation in their simplest form.

To illustrate: Courses in introductory procedure are generally organized on one of the principles I have previously described or a combination of them. You start historically with the common-law forms of action, or you start with the plaintiff's complaint because that is the first step in a lawsuit, or you start with lawsuits arising out of quarrels about the location of a fence, or some other allegedly "simple" controversy.

I believe the place to start is, rather, with the adjudicative process itself, presented in a context that reduces it to its most elementary form. I suggest that arbitration is, in modern times, that context. Here we have virtually no rules of pleading and usually no formal rules of substantive law at all. Yet we have problems—problems that pervade the whole adjudicative process.

One might start with a case in which the parties agree to submit an issue to arbitration, and where the award goes slightly outside the terms of the submission agreement. A labor arbitrator, for example, is asked to adjudicate five specified job rates, and sets a sixth rate because he considers it closely related to the rates submitted for his determination. The losing party refuses to accept the award as it affects the sixth job. I would discuss with the student whether anything was wrong with the procedure followed in this case. If the arbitrator, whose primary function is to bring peace between the parties, sees some tag-end that needs cleaning up, why should he be bound strictly by the agreement submitting the dispute to him? When the student has seen that there is another side to this question, he will have gained a fundamental insight into the purpose of pleadings.

The next series of cases would involve arbitration awards where the arbitrator, after hearing the arguments, makes an independent investigation of the facts. A labor arbitration involves the proper rate of pay for operating a particular machine, and neither party shows the machine to the arbitrator or even displays a picture of it. Discontent with abstract descriptions, the arbitrator visits the factory unaccompanied by the parties, looks at the machine, and then makes his award. Is there any legitimate objection to this course of action? If the losing party complains of this procedure, shall we treat him as an enemy of truth who wants cases decided in ignorance? Once again, when the student has seen what can be said on both sides of this question, he will have gained a fundamental insight into the whole adversary system, with its merits and its defects.

So, my suggestion is: teach processes, and start with the process in its most elementary form.

4. *How can we relate law to the life and theory beyond law without losing the sharp focus on specific issues that has been a cardinal virtue of traditional legal education?*

This is the issue suggested by the now fashionable question (too narrowly phrased, I think): How shall we bring about a synthesis of law with the related social sciences, such as economics, psychology, and sociology?

There are two schools of thought about this. One says, "Stick to law. You can't teach the student to be a lawyer in three years, so obviously you can't teach him also to be an economist, psychologist, accountant, sociologist, and personnel manager."

The other school says, "Law is related to these other subjects, so they must be brought somehow into the curriculum. We will assign extensive readings in psychology and economics. We will add psychologists and economists to our law faculties. It is true that we don't know now just what we will do with them, but their physical presence in the building will be a stimulus, and in time we shall work out together a program for using their special competences effectively."

I hold with neither of these views. As for the first, of course we haven't time in three years to make a man a lawyer. But that is not our task. Our task is to start him on a program of self-education, and to give him the fundamental insights and ways of thought that will enable him to draw the maximum profit from his later education in the school of experience.

If there is no time for economics in law school, you may be quite sure that the busy and successful lawyer will have no time for it. This does not mean that he will not make economic decisions. On the contrary, it is certain that he will participate in the making of many of them. It will merely mean that he will not understand as well as he should what it is that he and his fellow counselors are deciding.

The other school finds time in the curriculum for non-legal studies, but fails to integrate them effectively with instruction in law. Having been able to discover no other way to use the non-legal expert, it puts him to work teaching the student "skills and techniques." An outstanding example of this default is, to my mind, offered by a course given jointly by a psychologist and a group of lawyers which, in the words of its sponsors, is intended "to train the student more effectively to use his personality."[1] In this course it is the function of the psychologist (with the assistance of a Soundscriber) to teach the student the psychology of persuasion and to train him to use words that will evoke sympathetic responses on the part of judges and other "policy makers." With all deference to the able and imaginative men who conceived this course, in this aspect it seems to me the academic equivalent of boondoggling.

For about twenty years now American professors of law have been agreeing with one another that we ought to do something about the integration of law with the other social sciences. In view of this general agreement, it is remarkable how little of real significance has actually been accomplished in this direction. The explanation lies, I believe, in a failure to work out a conception of legal education that will make the integration something real and that will put it to work on tasks worthy of a university law school.

---

[1] James, *An Arbitration Laboratory in Law School*, 2 ARB. J. (N.S.) 79, 80 (1947). This reference is not intended as an unqualified condemnation of the course described in Professor James' article. The notion of trying the same moot case twice, first as an informal arbitration and then as a regular lawsuit, seems to me most ingenious and worth while. Indeed, I could hardly ask for a better practical application of the conceptions I am attempting to expound in this paper.

I suggest that we should take our orientation from the following considerations: The lawyer is today compelled to participate in decisions that represent a synthesis of many factors, of which legal rules are often only a part, and sometimes a very subsidiary part. This is obviously true of the lawyer in government service. Lawyers in private practice have put up a sort of rear-guard action against making what they call "business decisions," but they have lost the battle. Today nearly all lawyers have to make "business decisions," if for no other reason, in order to stay in business, for they have discovered that this is what clients demand.

These decisions are not arrived at by the lawyer independently, but in consultation with men of different training, who bring to the conference table distinct contributions that must somehow or other be fused into the final solution. Often, the lawyer is the man who presides over that process of fusion. Here, then, is a process into which he must be initiated and started off right in law school. He must learn what is involved in deciding not what legally can be done, or what action will be legally effective, but what should be done, all things considered, when all points of view have been drawn into account.

It is apparent that this process of synthesizing considerations that lie in different realms of human competence is one aspect of the larger process I have called legislation. Every important decision in some measure acts to impose pattern and structure, to create rules and precedents, to furnish a framework within which future decisions will be made.

I suggest that we take as our goal, therefore, not training the lawyer to be an economist, but training him to participate in a process of decision that brings law and economics into a common crucible. This means that he must know enough economics, and must have that kind of economic learning, that will enable him to utilize the economist effectively and appraise his contribution intelligently.

In more concrete educational terms, this means that an important part of the student's training in law school should be directed toward the solution of problems that involve a synthesis of legal and "extra-legal" considerations. Except in a few courses, problems suited to this purpose cannot be obtained directly from reported appellate cases. Something like the "cases" used in the Harvard Graduate School of Business Administration would seem to be in order. It is also in order to draw on the resources of the university as a whole and to enlist, wherever possible, the assistance of trained economists, psychologists, and other experts in fields outside the law, preferably those with some background of participation in practical affairs.

Experience in my own and other law schools indicates that the key to the successful use of experts in fields outside the law lies in the selection of problems for study that will give direction and legal relevance to the contributions of these experts. The devising or collecting of such problems is the primary responsibility of the law faculty. If the law faculty is unable to discharge this responsibility, it is a safe assumption that it will not profit greatly from the physical presence of an economist or psychologist on the law-school premises.

5. *How can we inculcate in our students a proper sense of professional responsibility toward client and public?*

The title of this conference expresses the widely held conviction that professional education has not been sufficiently conscious of the social responsibilities of the professions. In all of the lay callings—in law, engineering, medicine, and business administration—we are training men to make a good living for themselves, but we are not, it is said, doing enough to train them to advance the Good Life for all men.

Deeply as we may agree with this criticism, there arises the practical question of what to do about it. The problem of social and public responsibility has deep roots, that strike to the most intimate moral decisions a man may be called upon to make.

Merely telling students from time to time that they have undefined social responsibilities will accomplish little. Moral exhortation without content or direction is a futile thing. Indulged in widely enough, it is certain to arouse an irritation that will defeat its own end. On the other hand, shall we set about indoctrinating our students with the notion that they must advance certain definite social goals? If so, shall each teacher employ classroom time for the advancement of his personal political and ideological convictions? Or, to avoid the general canceling out that might result if this were done, shall the faculty agree on certain fundamental "values" and then seek to inculcate these in its students? The notion of a whole law faculty dedicated to a particular ideology is by no means unheard of in American educational history.[2] Yet for most of us there is something basically uncongenial about this kind of intellectual freemasonry.

I believe that the way out of this dilemma is to be found in a return to the Socratic conception that men find virtue best, not through

---

[2] CENTRALIZATION AND THE LAW; SCIENTIFIC LEGAL EDUCATION, a collection of essays by various authors published by Little, Brown and Company in 1906. To avoid misunderstanding, I should say that, so far as I can see, no trace of the ideological program outlined in this book is observable in the present administration of the school that once made it a matter of corporate adherence. The school today presents the wholesome variety of points of view characteristic of American law schools generally.

1 JOURNAL OF LEGAL ED.No.2

faith or exhortation, but through understanding. Because his paper seems to me to exemplify this conception, I believe we in law might well take Dr. Romano's [3] treatment of the physician's responsibility to his patient as a model for our own profession.

Dr. Romano sets about to explore the ethics of the physician-patient relationship. He finds that this relationship has its own peculiar demands, that cannot be met merely by good intentions or a sound upbringing. These demands require real understanding and insight before the physician can respond to them adequately, and it is the task of the medical school to convey this understanding and insight.

So I believe that we in the law schools should explore with our students the demands of the lawyer-client relationship as it arises in the two basic processes I have described in this paper. Certainly there is much here to study and understand. The successful negotiator almost inevitably finds himself from time to time cast in the rôle of mediator, a rôle that raises delicate questions of fidelity to client. The advocate finds himself under pressure to litigate cases that in his judgment ought to be settled out of court, and he must weigh in his own conscience the value of litigation as a release for bottled-up animosities against its wastes and hazards.

In this, as in other aspects of the student's education, I would begin with relationships or processes in their most elementary form. This means that attention should first be directed to the ethics of the lawyer-client relationship where the client is a single individual and no special problem is involved of the overlapping of the client's interests with those of the opponent. From there I would work gradually into more complex situations, until the lawyer has as his client the public as a whole, or where he can, without any question of propriety, regard himself, in Brandeis' words, as "attorney for the situation." The most effective way of placing the student in this kind of rôle would be to direct a substantial portion of his education toward legislative problems, in which his task would be to devise a scheme of statutory regulation that will adequately meet the public need, or that will achieve the most workable and just compromise of a complex set of overlapping and opposed interests.

I believe that this instruction should be conducted in the spirit of the case method, as an exploration of problems and an analysis of relevant factors, rather than with a view to securing open-and-shut answers. If this spirit is observed, I think it will be possible to discuss profitably

---

[3] John Romano, Professor of Psychiatry, University of Rochester School of Medicine and Dentistry; Psychiatrist in Chief, Strong Memorial Hospital, Rochester, New York, who spoke on "The Physician as a Comprehensive Human Biologist."

issues of "policy" that would otherwise be intractable to satisfactory treatment in class discussions.

For example, in questions like those of the reform of the divorce law, or of laws relating to contraception, it would be very difficult to obtain in any American law school a satisfactory and objective discussion of what the statutory rules ought to be. Here there are basic differences in men's conceptions of value, reinforced by the emotions of religious faith. On the other hand, we may take this very division itself as a problem. How can we in a democratic society arrive at satisfactory and just decisions about issues on which men are sharply divided by emotional and religious convictions? What processes or procedures are open to us? Here is a problem that men of different faiths and different philosophies of life can with profit study together. The secret is, in other words, to concentrate on the process, and not to try to determine in advance what results should emerge from the process in the form of specific solutions.

So in the field of labor law, we can discuss profitably such questions as: What are the respective merits of the following procedures for settling labor disputes: compelled negotiation, mediation, arbitration, administrative control, legislation, and court action? To be sure, since the results are going foreseeably to be influenced in some degree by our choice of method, some of the emotions and prejudices that plague this field will inevitably get into the discussion of procedures. But they will not usurp the discussion, as they are likely to do if we discuss such questions as what ought to be the minimum wage, or whether legislation should be passed to limit the amount of dues that can be assessed by unions.

I do not suggest a focus on process and procedures merely as a way of drawing off the fire. Rather, I believe, if I may say so, that this focus is metaphysically sound. Life is itself a process, and by making process the center of our attention we are getting closer to the most enduring part of reality. For that reason I believe that the recommended emphasis on procedures for solving conflicts will not tend simply to suppress those conflicts, but will promote their just solution. If we do things the right way, we are likely to do the right thing.

[23]

IN MEMORY OF HAROLD W. SOLOMON: COMMENTS ON SOUTHERN CALIFORNIA'S FLYER IN LEGAL EDUCATION

David Riesman*

A few years ago Christopher Jencks and I sought to get a sense of academic enterprise in the state of California, particularly the relation of the different levels of public higher education to each other (the Master Plan) and to the private colleges and universities. On the private side, we took brief account of such disparate enterprises as Stanford and Pepperdine, Mills and Cal Tech, the Claremont Group and Immaculate Heart, USC and the University of the Pacific. We gained a sense of USC's ambitions, its upward academic and intellectual mobility, its rising standards not only of affluence but of aspiration as it competed with latecomer UCLA, which in turn competed with Berkeley. We were dimly aware that USC had a law school, but that was all. Then the law school turned up again in another survey begun several years ago in preparation for an address given in September, 1967, at Harvard Law School's Sesquicentennial celebration, in the course of which I sought to discover what innovations had occurred in the teaching of law and in curricular organization during the last quarter century. In the absence of an opportunity to visit schools, I relied on catalogues and articles and on what could be learned by correspondence and conversation.

It was soon evident that one area of innovation lay in a great expansion of the more traditional legal and legal defender work, into a general concern with poverty—a concern that was extending beyond clinical practice on the poor (that has always been, till Medicare, a medical prerogative) to a concern for legal careers in this area. Indeed, especially in some of the distinguished national schools, students were responding to the prospect of providing legal services for the poor and disorganized as they once had responded to the hope of working for

---

* Henry Ford II Professor of Social Sciences, Harvard University. A.B., 1931, LL.B., 1934, Harvard; LL.D., 1954, Marlboro College, 1957, Grinnell College, 1962, Temple University; D.C.L., 1962, Lincoln University; Ed.D., 1959, Rhode Island College; D.Litt., 1960, Wesleyan University; law clerk to Mr. Justice Brandeis, United States Supreme Court, 1935-36; Late Professor of Law, University of Buffalo, 1937-41.

the affluent and well-integrated. Through the Western Center on Law and Poverty and the appointment of Gary Bellow to the faculty—he had carried a similar mandate out among the rural poor of California —the Southern California Law Center was making its bid in this area. So was the University of Detroit Law School, which had sought to reshape both its curriculum and its law journal to deal with urban problems. The catalogues also made clear that the law schools of national or would-be national recruitment, as well as some of the more provincial ones, have been orienting their second and third year optional courses toward the group of activist or exploratory students who today are seeking what they term engagement or relevance, and who are hoping to find some way of applying legal training to contemporary problems.

As a friend of Harold Solomon I had known of his career as an assistant district attorney in New York County, and had assumed after he joined the USC law faculty that the law school's course materials would reflect a similar preoccupation with social action. For example, in criminal law I expected to find legitimation for the law student's concern with raising the status of a branch of law that has been "contaminated" by its usually dubious clients and the modes by which they are conventionally defended or, for that matter, prosecuted.[1] In his last publication discussing "Justice and Poverty in an Affluent Society," Harold commented that the American attitude toward failure creates unconsciously intentional lacunae in our knowledge, especially on topics dealing with such "low company" as the subjects of criminal administration (and perhaps also when one must collaborate with such characters as psychiatrists, probation officers, social workers, and sometimes sociologists).[2] Presently, law students at USC can take part in the Harvard-USC Voluntary Defender Program for imprisoned convicts, and in other programs such as the Law Students Civil Rights Research Council and "house counsel for the poor."

The minority of law schools that recruits a minority of activist students has mostly handled the latter (and their faculty allies) through

---

[1] Until recently antitrust litigation and occasional civil liberties cases have been about the only instances where defending a man accused of crime has offered viability for a rewarding, non-precarious career. But there has been a recent effort in a number of schools to redeem the criminal law from the shyster defense attorneys and grandstand prosecutors who have helped make it seem uninviting—an impossible career or an absurd responsibility.

[2] See Solomon, *This New Fetish for Indigency: Justice and Poverty in an Affluent Society*, 66 COLUM. L. REV. 248, 268 (1966).

what Harold Lasswell has termed "restriction through partial incorporation": they have found room for them in extracurricular activities (which nowhere, to my knowledge, have the status of the Law Review), or in second and third year seminars. They have by and large left their first year programs relatively unchanged, offering the traditional staples principally geared to the supposed bread and butter of the practitioner. (Since a bright student gets the rhythm of the case method quickly, the third year is often enforced waiting time, heritage of an era when the law schools did not require any undergraduate preparation before entry.)

However, I found more than the activism I expected when I came to examine USC's first year teaching materials and corresponded with its faculty members—particularly with William R. Bishin, George Lefcoe, Martin Levine, and Christopher Stone. It dawned on me that the enterprise with which Harold Solomon had identified himself (as well as his own thought) went far beyond a critique of existing legal and other institutions, and of presentation—either academic or activist —of alternative social policy. What was being attempted was the renewal of legal education itself in more radical fashion, as ambitious as that which the legal realists at Yale and elsewhere had attempted in an earlier generation but had never carried through.[3]

Many of the law schools with good students seek in their first year courses to make a sharp break with the characteristic modes of undergraduate education. In part they do this by having dedicated teachers who have been but little influenced by the allergy in the best graduate schools and liberal arts colleges against academic showmen. Perhaps they do no more than play with energy the quasi-Socratic game of having students state cases and answer questions around them; but students often respond to this with their own desire to identify with the profession, and perhaps to put more speculative thought behind them, as a childish thing.[4] In contrast, the new faculty at Southern California— the generation of Harold Solomon—foster rather than reject speculative thought, employing it to attack the foundations of speculative thought itself. They lead students to question what they know and

---

[3] Most of the teaching materials from which I have profited are mimeographed (although George Lefcoe has a published volume), but some sense of the USC approach can be gathered from Stone, *Toward a Theory of Constitutional Law Casebooks*, 41 S. CAL. L. REV. 1 (1968).

[4] For discussion of the focus on teaching in the law schools, see Riesman, *Some Observations on Legal Education*, WIS. L. REV. (forthcoming); see also PROCEEDINGS OF HARVARD LAW SCHOOL SESQUICENTENNIAL (forthcoming).

whether, indeed, they know how they know anything. This is not the abrasiveness of parliamentary polemics, but the more demanding confrontation with basic epistemological questions. A course dealing with property as an idea and a process is designed, among other things, to undercut common sense ideas of what property is. For instance, it asks the students to read something by Norman O. Brown on property in the self and the boundaries of the body. This congeries of courses introduces students to the sociolinguistic vicissitudes of concept formation, abstraction, definition, and decision. It is a second chance at the liberal arts, not only for students with poor undergraduate preparation, but even for students who have gone through a good undergraduate college without such intellectual adventures.

These materials, it seems to me, are more speculative and playful, as well as more philosophically searching, than the usual first year bill of fare. But the new faculty at USC insists also on a more pragmatic orientation to the institutional worlds in which lawyers will eventually work: students explore the worlds of squad cars and station houses, savings and loan associations and zoning boards, corporate board rooms and mayors' offices. An enormous amount of law teaching at most schools, like other teaching in the area of the social sciences, operates on a plateau of low-level abstraction, neither concrete and detailed enough for reality-testing nor conceptual and detached enough for philosophical reorientation.

Contrary to what is often thought, most students, even at great universities, no matter how politically radical they may be, or how demanding of student power, are pedagogically pretty conservative; if they come to a place without awareness of its novelty, they may reject a demanding curriculum that does not provide a quick and ready professional identity. In tacit alliance with alumni much more conservative than they, they can wreck an innovation before it gets started, often without even realizing they have done so. Fortunately, the new departures at USC have had enough support from the incumbent faculty, from the University itself, and from the bench and bar of Southern California to have had by now a longer half-life than most efforts I have observed to remake existing academic institutions.

It may well be that the University of Southern California Law School avoids alienating and disorienting many of its students because it can provide them with a feeling that some of what they are learning they will use in day-to-day practice. At the same time, their conception of the life of practice may undergo mutation as the result of their whole experience.

The relative smallness of a law school faculty means that it is possible to recruit some new faculty, not one by one, or Noah's ark style, but in significant proportions. Efforts to remake academic institutions often suffer from the fact that intellectual interest groups cannot be bought off, being protected by tenure and rigidified by the understandable obduracy that people have about changing the commitments by which all of us live.[5] Newcomers, especially if they come as individuals, can also be undercut by what my mentor in these matters, Professor Everett C. Hughes, calls "side of the mouth" teaching by more established colleagues with their longer ties to the institution and its local supporters. Such colleagues can easily form an alliance with the complacent Philistinism among many entering students. This may often defeat a cosmopolitan itinerant faculty, especially if the latter do not have the patience to stick it out or to garner support from administrators and incumbents. But the new faculty at Southern California had the patience, and did in fact receive that support from the older faculty and the Administration.

Even in such relatively favorable circumstances, however, the eventual viability of innovations depends on attracting students who will be more than tolerant birds of passage. And here the educational systems tend to hinder the durability of reform when it does not occur near the very top of the academic procession. In general, upwardly mobile academic institutions seek to do things Michigan's way, or Yale's way or Harvard's way—of course with some inevitable lag and a somewhat greater rigidity. If to faculty members at such an institution one suggests a pedagogic novelty, their reaction is apt to be something like this: "Oh, you may be able to try that in the Ivy League where you have already arrived, but we cannot afford it, any more than in our graduate school of arts and sciences we can afford not to insist that everyone have the Ph.D." The University of Southern California is old for its region but new for America, facing severe competition from UCLA, Berkeley, and Stanford. Its law school has had an excellent local reputation, but only now is actively seeking a national recruit-

---

[5] A beautiful, brief account of some sources of resistance to change, which expresses unusual sympathy with these sources, appears in an article-review by William R. Bishin of Joseph H. Smith, *The Development of Legal Institutions*. Bishin, Book Review, 68 COLUM. L. REV. 175 (1968).

ment and a national impact. Since my own vicarious discovery of it, I have recommended it to undergraduates who, if they are not from the Southwest, would not otherwise have known or thought of it. This situation is changing, but in all such experiments the question is whether the change comes quickly enough to provide support for innovation in the face of the arduousness of the task.

I know from my own work as an undergraduate teacher that, while people speak glibly of interdisciplinary courses or experimental programs, to invent even one of these takes considerable effort, what seems like thousands of committee meetings, and the at least temporary surrender of serenity, visibility, and sleep. It requires some surrender of the narcissism so characteristic of a high proportion of creative men, at least in our kind of society. Saints excepted, if one has made such sacrifices one needs recognition by students and colleagues elsewhere.

Indeed, it seems clear from a distance that the new forms of legal education being pioneered at Southern California have been a collective enterprise, as few educational enterprises have been in the individualistic world of the law schools. Whether the casebooks (to give them an old-fashioned name) deal with property or with constitutional law, they convey a certain esprit de corps, which I hope carries over to a substantial number of the students. It would be perhaps even more unusual if that esprit de corps carried over to strengthen the ties of the Law Center with the rest of the University, for in most universities the law schools have remained autarchic, sharing only the most nominal connections with undergraduate and graduate education in the arts and sciences.

In the law school world as elsewhere, the best students are often dissatisfied. Many claim to want relevance, by which they mean something clinical, getting their hands on immediate problems of the city or of race, or both. As I mentioned above, some law schools are seeking to satisfy that hunger for relevance. Yet the newly-intense search for relevance among students runs the risk of anti-intellectualism: an all-too-American impatience toward philosophical and long-run perspectives. The faculty at Southern California Law Center, indeed, is rather quizzical about what relevance is and how to go about creating it.

One source of this skepticism may lie in the interest of a number of the new faculty in traditional philosophical and political thought, including its conservative variants. Thus, a review by William Bishin testifies to his awareness that social change always comes at a price in the lives of individuals, and that they generally do not understand the reasons for change that seem so self-evident to the enlightened.[6]

The danger of amoral relativism (perhaps preferable to ultra-moral fanaticism) is not absent from the shifting perspectives presented by the sophisticated Southern California faculty. There is a certain gaiety, and perhaps even mischief, in the willingness of the faculty to challenge liberal and radical pieties as well as more traditional ones. This approach, like any other, has its own risks. When I first studied the mimeographed materials, I thought that they might give students too ready an impression from various snippets that they could understand linguistic analysis, or psychoanalytic psychology, or existentialism, and thereby retain that unshakable sense of omnicompetence that is both the danger and the achievement of the leaders of the Bar. But on reflection I concluded that this danger of feeding the lawyer's ready vanity was overmatched by the sheer delight in the materials, the kaleidoscope of insights not easily assimilated, the awareness of the problems of cultural relativity without the easy gloss of cynicism.

Moreover, as is already implied in what I have said, the students at the University of Southern California Law Center are not exposed to any monotone of Young Turk irreverence; the Harold Solomon cadre does comprise a "critical mass" in the chemical sense, being large enough to perpetuate the reaction, and that is its hope; but it is not a monopoly, and teachers of more traditional topics and tones also have their chance with students. This prevents any development of a cult or a claustrophobic intellectual atmosphere such as one finds at some small, experimental undergradute colleges. Moreover, it should be clear that, while I have emphasized the philosophical sides of the pedagogic enterprise, these same men are also concerned with what the

---

[6] One political and social consequence of the press of faculty and student activism is to lead would-be Ombudsmen from the elite law schools to join forces with the Negro and white lower classes to harass the policemen, school teachers, social workers, and other white collar (and generally white) civil servants in the lower middle class, who are thus caught between the angry or fatalistic poor and their aristocratic and sometimes self-righteous defenders. In a letter I wrote Harold Solomon referring to his article in the *Columbia Law Review*, I spoke of his discussion of the role of the victim in evoking moral indignation from the educated middle class, and added that the students I myself teach "have a passionate hatred for police which they would regard as bigotry if it were addressed to any other minority group . . . and they lash out at the middlemen. . . ." I should add that the erstwhile romantic law students who go to serve and work with the poor will learn something about them (including the potentiality for paranoia from which most oppressed people suffer), while the complacent will neither learn or contribute to the solution of this particular form of class warfare in America.

late Karl Llewellyn called "law stuff" or what one might term decision-making (and decision-postponing) in everyday life. And it should also be clear that they have not gravitated toward the glamour subjects, such as international law, but want to redeem, for closer, more humane understanding, the day-to-day work of the lawyer. They are concerned with the tasks confronting the solo practitioner as well as the Poverty Program lawyer, the big firm corporate or government lawyer, and the future professor of law. All of these may in time carry the fire elsewhere.

Social Science Theory and Legal Education: The Law School as University

George L. Priest

I should like to address some implications of what I believe to be the most important development in legal scholarship of the past fifty years. Over this period, scholarship in the law, like scholarship in other intellectual fields, has undergone a tremendous specialization of interest. The direction this specialization has taken, however, is sharply different from the one that might have been expected fifty years ago. In 1930, prior to the realist revolution, future specialization in legal scholarship might have suggested increasingly detailed and narrow treatises addressing traditional legal subjects. Today, authorship of the legal treatise has been cast off to practitioners. The treatise is no longer even a credit to those competing on the leading edge of legal thought. Instead, legal scholarship has become specialized according to the separate social sciences. Specialization according to the social sciences has broken down older conceptions of distinctive legal categories. No modern scholar can usefully distinguish the various subjects of civil liability. The agency, corporations, and securities fields are only the most current subjects of this form of intellectual reorganization.

The most significant implication of this development is the change in the position that law and the legal system occupy as subjects of research. It is accepted today, virtually universally, that the legal system can be best understood with the methods and theories of the social sciences. It follows from this view, however, that one must abandon the notion that law is a subject that can be usefully studied by persons trained only in the law. Furthermore, it follows necessarily that one must reject the notion that the legal system is somehow self-contained or self-sufficient instead of simply another setting for the expression of whatever are the deeper determinants of human behavior. As a consequence, the importance of law and of the study of law is radically transformed.

The social sciences—more particularly, the behavioral sciences—challenge legal education substantively. They deny the importance of law as a subject.

George L. Priest is Professor of Law, Yale University. This article is the edited text of a presentation prepared for the Plenary Session, Annual Meetings of the Association of American Law Schools, Cincinnati, January 7, 1983. The author would like to thank the Center for Studies in Law, Economics, and Public Policy of Yale Law School for support.

© 1983 by the Association of American Law Schools. Cite as 33 J. Legal Educ. 437 (1983).

The phenomenon of interest to them is behavior. These sciences demonstrate refinement and sophistication by their increasingly complex understanding and explanation of behavior. As a result, a legal scholar with an interest in a behavioral science is torn between development of the implications of the behavior theory and mastery of the particular legal subject. As a legal scholar becomes serious about some behavioral science and sophisticated in its practice, he is pulled away from the law as a distinct subject and even as an interesting subject. Indeed, the more seriously the scholar takes the behavioral theory, the more difficult it becomes to justify why law is a subject worthy of study at all.

Let me offer a personal example. I am interested in economic theory. In economic theory, as in other behavioral theories, law is not a particularly important subject. Law as a phonomenon, of course, is socially omnipresent; it affects all of us one way or another, which gives it some claim on our attention. On this basis, to an economist, the study of law is of equivalent interest, say, to the study of the oil industry or, perhaps, of armament manufacture. From the standpoint of economic *theory*, law is much less important as a subject. There is no good economic theory of how individual, utility-mazimizing behavior generates a legal system. The legal system can be viewed as a consumption good of the society, suggesting a form of public choice analysis. But public choice approaches, for the most part, have not been successful empirically, and on subjects of much less complexity than the legal system. More typically, law is viewed in economics as a constraint on individual behavior. This is the approach of the many studies of the effects of specific laws or rules. Economic theory, of course, addresses behavior subject to constraint, but the study of behavior subject to constraint is different from the study of the constraint itself. In our current state of knowledge, law is a constraint on behavior in the way the need for eight hours of sleep is a constraint on the workday or as the molecular construction of nitrogen is a constraint on the effectiveness of fertilizer. Economic theory tells us very little about these constraints. In the most successful applications of economics, these constraints are taken as given. As a consequence, in this intellectual framework, law disappears.

Of course, as an ambitious science, economics aspires to explain these constraints, as it aspires to explain all social phenomena. But to date economic theory has explained the determinants of law about as fully as it has explained the determinants of the world's religious beliefs. Professor Posner's efficiency-of-the-law theory has attracted great attention to the intersection of law and economics, but his theory is of interest to legal scholars—as I have described elsewhere[1]—because it is essentially a legal theory, not an economic theory. Currently, there is no behavioral basis for the efficiency of the law.

The lack of theoretical interest in law is not peculiar to economics. I could describe similarly the relationship of law to any of the other behavioral sciences. In those fields associated with law that most closely resemble

---

1. George L. Priest, The New Scientism in Legal Scholarship: A Comment on Clark and Posner, 90 Yale L. J. 1284 (1981).

sciences—psychoanalysis, political science, sociology—there is an increasing distance between science and the law. The concern is less crucial, perhaps, in fields such as history—because much of the work in the field is essentially atheoretical. In addition, there are some forms of social theory in which law is a subject of particular interest—Unger's work is an example[2]—but again because the theory itself lacks rigor. Yet as even history and social theory become more precise and detailed and generalizing—that is, as they become more scientific—the systematic character of law loses relevance and is submersed in the particular historical or social explanation. Douglas Hay's work is illustrative.[3]

The demands of scientific theory create extraordinary internal conflict for the lawyer who develops an interest in social science. The lawyer-economist, -sociologist, -political scientist, -social theorist finds himself a modern-day Henry Adams, whose education teaches him that his training is obsolete and that the more he develops his scientific interest, the more obsolete his basic training—legal training—will become. The legal scholar may have been certain as he selected his career that the law and the legal system were subjects of central intellectual importance, but now theory tells him that he was wrong. Those with true intellectual courage would abandon the law and become full-time social scientists—but I know of none who have done so. Many convince themselves that extensive knowledge of the intricacies of legal doctrine and legal argument and legal tradition will perhaps make possible some deep theoretical discovery. This is a false hope. It is equivalent to the belief that Einstein would finally have discovered a unified force theory if only he had stayed a few more years in the patent office.

Most (including me) justify to themselves mining the intersection of the disciplines: employing behavioral theory to criticize the law. This approach makes possible rapid insights in comparison with ordinary legal scholarship, as should well be expected. A well-drafted set of rules will have anticipated most objections that derive from the ideas that dominate standard legal thought. But such rules will be as vulnerable as an alien who cannot speak the native language to the criticisms of a science with different presuppositions and organizing thoughts. The best evidence that the law is not uniformly efficient is that economists have so much to say about the legal system that seems truly novel.

Scholarship of this nature—the criticism of one language by another—is essentially shallow. Its relationship to the development of the theory itself is only the relationship between any translation and an original text. The scholar who takes theory seriously knows that such work is derivative and does not advance the theoretical enterprise. The lawyer-economist may seem powerful today, but only because of the undeveloped theoretical base of competing methods of legal thought. Furthermore, we can confidently expect that what passes today as sophisticated law and economics will be

---

2. Roberto M. Unger, Law in Modern Society (New York: Free Press, 1976).
3. See, for example, Douglas Hay, Poaching and the Game Laws on Connock Chase, in Albion's Fatal Tree, ed. Douglas Hay et al., at 189 (New York: Pantheon Books, 1975).

brushed away without reference once serious theorists begin to examine carefully the behavioral basis of legal phenomena.

The conflict between social science theory and the law is made particularly sharp by the demands of law teaching. There is always some tension between writing and teaching. For standard legal scholarship, it is most often the tension between the specific and the general. The scholar writes about a legal subject in a detail unsuitable for the classroom. Regardless, it is usually complementary to some degree, even to detailed work, to take another overview of a subject.

For the behavioral scientist, however, an overview of a *legal* subject as opposed to the *theory* itself is a diversion. Even where one can introduce theory into the classroom, the low level of theoretical training and interest of law students frequently makes one wonder whether the effort is worthwhile. In economics, for example, it is not helpful for one working on differential equations or econometrics in the morning to be exchanging hunches with students about least-cost avoiders in the afternoon. Thus, as the scholar becomes more theoretically sophisticated, law teaching in the standard form becomes increasingly remote from his work. The scholar serious about his teaching will strive to transform his course to make it theoretically challenging—that is, challenging to him. In our current state of theory, this objective often can be achieved within the bounds of the standard law curriculum. But the more sophisticated social science theory becomes, the stronger the pressures will be to alter the curriculum itself.

Behavioral science contradicts the primacy of law. As a greater proportion of law teachers become interested in the behavioral sciences, the structure of the law school will be forcibly changed. A law school, of course, could react to these developments by searching out a faculty devoted to the unique interest and importance of the legal system. But that will never do. Law-school curricula will always follow the most persuasive explanations of the law. And the best writing about the legal system *is* interdisciplinary. As a consequence, the structure of the law school and its curriculum must change. Currently, to the student, legal education resembles undergraduate education. The student takes a sampler of courses. The objective of the course of study is a liberal education: to expose the student to a broad set of different subjects. There is little writing and little specialization. From the standpoint of the instructor, however, legal education is more primitive than college education, and most closely resembles high school or perhaps junior high school education. Today, virtually every law-school faculty member is able to teach every subject in the curriculum. One might grouse if one were assigned a remote course. But most of us, I would guess, would pride ourselves on our ability, were it important enough to the institution, to teach any subject at all in the law-school curriculum. Indeed, the response of all but the junior faculty would be to engage in a challenge as to whether one needed one week's preparation or one day's. In contrast, the virtues of the generalist are foreign to college faculties and unknown in graduate departments. In this respect, faculties of modern law schools resemble faculties of medieval universities. We await the Enlightenment.

Social Science Theory and Legal Education

The Enlightenment is coming. Its source seems to be the increasing specialization of legal scholarship. If these intellectual trends continue—as I believe they will—the structure of the law school will change. The law school will of necessity become itself a university. The law school will be comprised of a set of miniature graduate departments in the various disciplines. Introductory courses may be retained (if not shunted to colleges). Even then, a wedge deeper than the one we see today will be driven between those faculty members with pretensions of scholarship and those without. The ambitious scholars on law-school faculties will insist on teaching subjects of increasingly narrow scope. The law-school curriculum will come to consist of graduate courses in applied economics, social theory, and political science. Specialization by students, which is to say, intensified study, follows necessarily.

It might be thought initially that the technical curriculum I have described is poorly suited for training *lawyers*. But our courts and legislatures are no less influenced than our curricula by current theories and ideas about the legal system. Indeed, my experience with practitioners suggests that they are desperate for new theories. A student trained in the law of torts by James Barr Ames would have a very hard time in today's legal regime. The law student of the future will be equally out-of-place without an education of increasingly greater sophistication in social science theory.

Humanism

[25]

TOWARD THE HUMANISTIC STUDY OF LAW
CHARLES A. REICH†

Law schools are in trouble with their students. They are not able to interest, inspire, or even hold on to many of their best college graduates. It is true that for most students the first year is exciting. The fresh incisiveness of approach, the active classroom, the impatience with fuzzy college ways are a great experience. But after the first year the excitement fades. Students cannot find courses they want to take. Having caught on to the classroom method, they drowse through increasingly obvious repetitions. They try to find new interest outside the classroom in legal aid, practice trials or law journal work. All too often law school ends with students merely marking time.

Law schools are also no longer attracting as many of the best and most imaginative college graduates. College students today value the intellectual life more than their predecessors. They like courses which are searching and speculative; law seems to them to require a narrow confinement of the intellect. College graduates are increasingly idealistic, and increasingly skeptical about the commercial society in which they have grown up. They regard the legal profession as an adjunct of business, and lawyers as hired special pleaders for the established values. Moreover, students reject a role as a gun for hire — a secondary being. Many come to law school with no real intention of practicing law, hoping that they can find a career in public service or teaching; some of the top students will not even interview the large firms.

Doubt and self-criticism are certainly not new to the law schools. But the doubt and self-criticism have not been deep enough, and the many attempts at reform have not succeeded. Law schools must keep seeking new answers, or see their position of leadership gradually lost.

I

Many of the ills of legal education are symptomatic of the fact that it is primarily professional in orientation, although it should also be preparing students for lives of public service and scholarship. This confusion of goals is tacitly recognized, and an appearance of unity is maintained by the theory that all three are accomplished by the law schools' special way of training the mind. But the unity rings false, and the schools do not accomplish all that they undertake.

The most important aspect of training for practice is methodology and approach. When the practitioner confronts a new problem, he rarely depends upon what he learned in law school. Subjects are too specialized and technical, too rapidly changing. The practitioner prides himself on his ability to become familiar with any area of law, no matter how new to him, in the course of working on a single case. His stock in trade consists of the ability to analyze and organize facts, the ability to communicate, argue and explain, knowledge of research and writing methods, and a free-wheeling mind. After about one

---
†Professor of Law, Yale University.

year, the law school has done almost all it can to equip the student in this style; the rest must be learned on the job. If the courses are to be of any value, they must offer something different.

But the courses in law school, although superbly adapted to the teaching of methodology, are far less effective when they try to accomplish other goals. In the first place, the materials of most courses — opinions of appellate courts — are well suited to logical analysis but inevitably have little depth or variety of outlook. Second, where modern casebooks have attempted to introduce materials from other disciplines, they have done so at a level that is so elementary and piecemeal that it has little value. Casebook social science usually consists of truncated excerpts from secondary sources, inserted into the notes in small type. Even where a law school offers courses dealing expressly with the social sciences and taught by experts in the field, the courses may turn out to be elementary at best. Third, the law school curriculum requires the student to consider a large number of complex issues in such haste that the result can only be superficial. Sixteen weeks of constitutional law allots only a few hours each to such immense questions as the limits of national power, federalism, the political role of courts, and the many problems of individual liberty. At best, such courses merely alert the practitioner to "where the issues are." Fourth, almost all these courses deal with their subjects at the same intellectual level of inquiry.

Law schools do little to encourage students to use initiative in educating themselves. Students are not really treated as adults. They are made to feel that they are beginning their education all over again, and the classes put very little emphasis upon individual work and thinking. The students get caught up in examinations, grades, and class ranking. In many ways the LL.B. program is undergraduate, not graduate education.

Even when law schools undertake to grant advanced degrees, the educational program remains at much the same level. Certainly there is no graduate training in law in the same sense that there is in the social sciences. Graduate degrees in law do not have the status of graduate degrees in other fields. The major law schools hire men for their own faculties without any concern for whether they have had graduate training in law, and a large number of the most respected professors of law have only a bachelor's degree.

In sum, despite many reforms, in spite of the language of expansive law school catalogues, in spite of widespread recognition of the need for further change, law school education in fact continues to reflect primarily the needs of the profession as the profession is now constituted. When these needs are met, there is little to hold even the professionally minded student. For the more uncommitted student, law school's procession of torts, contracts and procedure passes with little meaning.

II

What can the law schools do? I believe that their failure is primarily the result of the fact that they do not teach law as a subject matter. In other areas of graduate education, methodology is kept secondary to the subject matter itself. This is the law schools' missed opportunity. The underlying subject matter of law is as interesting and intellectually exciting as any branch of human knowledge. Legal institutions are among the most primitive and basic in any society. Law deals with human beings in their moments of greatest stress and in their most profound conflicts with each other and with society. The study of such institutions, and such questions, could have endless challenge. Surely the law schools can try to teach at least a few of their courses in this way.

In property, for example, a great question concerns the nature and functions of the concept or institution called ownership. This question is present, if not always articulated, in the discussion of the chief topics with which the course in property is now concerned: how much one person can limit another's rights of ownership by private volition; how much ownership can be split between different persons such as landlord and tenant; to what extent the state may take ownership for public use, and with what compensation; and what forms of wealth should be accorded legal protection as private property. If property were studied in depth, the problem of ownership would lead to a series of truly searching questions. What does "ownership" mean in our society? Ownership consists of a varying bundle of elements, and the problem is which of these go to the core of ownership, and which are only peripheral. What functions does the concept of "ownership" perform, and what values does it embody? Ownership can protect such diverse values as privacy, individual decision making, differences in taste, family succession, social status and pluralism in the political sense. Where should the line between the individual owner and the state be drawn, not in terms of vague constitutional formulas, but in terms of the underlying values at stake? It would be necessary to know the impact of the legal institution of "ownership" on individual human beings, and on society. Finally, how is the institution of property and ownership changing, and how ought it to change?

The study of ownership would necessarily have to draw on many fields. Among these might be anthropology, history — particularly the history of the institution of property, philosophy in general and political philosophy in particular, the ownership systems of other countries, social science information about the effects of ownership and non-ownership on character and behavior. The psychology of property would furnish both an explanation and a critique of much law; what men try to own and why; what needs they seek to satisfy through property; how these drives shape those who are possessed by them. Finally, in studying ownership students would encounter what is now regrettably omitted from most law schools: the richness, complexity, and imaginativeness of the common law, set in its historical background, with close attention to the infinite artistry of its detail. Such a course need not and should not become the watered down study of philosophy or history or social science. The focus and object of study would remain questions that are uniquely legal. But it would be law in greater depth, intensity and excitement.

A second course which needs greater depth is criminal law. Criminal law presents profound issues. How is blame to be divided between the person who commits an act and the persons and environment which laid the groundwork for the act? What is the meaning of free choice in light of the objectives of the criminal law and the knowledge supplied by psychiatry? Where shall "objective" standards of responsibility be set in terms of ability to resist temptation, ability to foresee risks, or ability to control the behavior of others? Such issues have long been the subject of intense thought and debate by philosophers, and in many ways their thinking about these problems is more advanced and sophisticated than that of lawyers. The basic issues of the criminal law are also treated with much insight in many works of literature. One could profitably read such diverse authors as Hawthorne, Melville, Dreiser, Kafka, Camus and Dostoyevsky, to say nothing of Shakespeare and the Bible, for their many different ways of looking at the law. Sartre's play "The Flies" is a more searching study of responsibility than any of the cases I have read. Criminal law is an area where the blackletter is relatively straightforward and easy, but the problems involved in the creation of standards are profound. This is a job which our society has assigned to lawyers. Philosophy and literature would aid the student lawyer to develop some part of the understanding needed for this almost superhuman task.

It hardly needs mention that criminal law also requires the insights of psychiatry and psychoanalysis. To a large extent law and psychiatry have talked past each other despite the growth of sophistication in both disciplines. In the sense of genuine communication, psychiatry and criminal law is still an untouched field.

Administrative law is a subject which is utterly unintelligible, even in the most narrowly "legal" terms, unless the student is able to see more than the cases. Agencies, and cases concerning them, are inseparable from history. Much legal doctrine can be judged only in economic terms. More important still, the whole object of the administrative process is to perform the vital and complex work (common to both the modern democratic and the socialist state) of planning and allocation. Our administrative agencies are our chief instruments of domestic social policy, more important even than Congress, and our chief distributors of wealth from public sources. When an agency decides where a highway is to be located, who shall be licensed to broadcast over a television channel, or whether a dam shall be built across a river, it is engaging in planning and allocation of major importance. In a democratic country, it is vital that all affected persons be heard, that all points of view be aired, that all competing interests be considered. How to accomplish this, and still get decisions made, is the great dilemma of planning and allocation. Unless this underlying process is studied in its own right, the judicial and agency opinions can only be wordy and baffling collections of formulas and criteria, signifying nothing.

If the curriculum were revised to permit study of the subject matter of law in greater depth, a school could offer several courses of unusual length and intensity — perhaps a two semester, ten hour course in property or criminal law. Readings would have to go far beyond casebooks. In part law schools stick to cases because the classroom method developed from cases is so effective; but that very effectiveness has now become a source of dependence and limitation. Ways must be found to be effective with other kinds of materials. Departure from cases would also mean that students would be compelled to do more original thinking. In the classroom they might be invited to criticize and contribute to the instructor's own ideas. On their own they might be asked to write papers requiring individual originality, rather than take examinations. Two short papers, each on a particular problem, would be far more worthwhile for student and professor than several standardized answers multiplied by fifty.

To teach such courses, law professors would need a broader education than most of them now have — not just a law degree plus a few years in practice, but some graduate study in the arts and sciences, or perhaps a new type of graduate course in law. An increasing number of young teachers are now seeking a broader education. Pending the millennium when such education is general on faculties, law schools could continue to appoint to their faculties scholars in fields other than law, and to permit students to take a wide variety of relevant courses in other branches of the university.

III

Law school education cannot exist for its own sake. It is not possible to talk about innovations in legal education without talking about them in relation to lawyers' work. And it is when we consider the changing nature of the legal profession that the real need for educational change becomes apparent.

The study of law in greater depth could, of course, be justified by even the narrowest view of the profession. It could be justified merely as a way to maintain interest during the second and third years which are now so barren. It could be justified as offering the practitioner greater insights and a wider ranging mind, without loss of anything now found in law school. It could be justified in terms of preparing teachers and scholars. And it would be particularly helpful in terms of lawyers going into public service. Government policymakers trained as lawyers are susceptible to becoming trapped in their own logic. They may operate wholly from within a logical system the basis of which (quite possibly mistaken) they do not question. And lawyers tend to be know-it-alls who believe no other branch of human knowledge is beyond their grasp. Men who "think like lawyers" can rigidify the operations and the thinking of government. Education which teaches the lawyer tight logic but then gives him enough spaciousness to free himself of that logic would in the long run greatly benefit a government dependent on lawyers to run its affairs.

But the most important reason for a new approach to the study of law is not simply to improve the present job of educating scholars, public servants, and practitioners as that job is now conceived. The ultimate justification for curricular revision, or rather the necessity, comes from the fact that the role of law in society has changed and is changing, and hence the role of lawyers must change.

Law now permeates every activity. This trend is inevitable as society rapidly becomes more institutional and bureaucratic. Today's social problems necessarily become legal problems. Thus, poverty is primarily a legal problem, since in a country of great wealth it is a problem of distribution, not a problem of producing more goods.

As a result of these changes, law in recent years has been called upon to serve many new causes. The civil rights movement used law as its primary instrument in a drive for fundamental social change. Many other groups concerned with protest or change have adapted civil rights techniques to their own objectives. The nation's awareness of the problems of poverty has revealed a need for lawyers in many new areas: defense of indigent criminals, protection of the poor in their dealings with private individuals (notably landlords), and assistance to the poor in confronting government (social welfare, public housing, education). The growth of governmental activity in economic affairs has brought law into many new areas of business and individual activity, and lawyers caught in the toils of the administrative process recognize the urgent need for a fresh approach to this unmanageable area.

Until very recently, the legal profession has narrowly limited its scope. Lawyers have traditionally concerned themselves with only one sector of the world in which law now operates, the sector of commerce. For most of them, day-to-day law has meant business law. Other problems have clustered around the business core, but these have also tended to be commercial in nature. Today, however, it is vitally necessary that lawyers actively participate in all of the areas of society in which law now plays a role. Their work may start with business, but it should range over criminal law, public housing, social welfare, unemployment, problems of the mentally ill, urban town and country planning, economic planning both local and national, civil rights, civil liberties, all forms of protest movements, and international law. In their private capacity they should be available to help all those individuals and groups who come in contact with law. They should learn to represent the various interest groups, constituencies and minorities in society — to help them develop points of view, speak for them, and interpret the world to them. That is the true scope of the practicing lawyer's calling.

In his public capacity, the lawyer's responsibilities are even greater. Every year government gets more vast and complex tasks to perform, and every year the government seems less able to cope with them. There are experienced men in the bureaucracy who believe that one day government will simply stop running altogether. That is almost what has happened with respect to decisions concerning television, dams, airline routes and highways. No profession has emerged to manage the affairs of government, which still remains the last great playground for amateurs, part timers and fortune seekers. Only lawyers can be the professionals of public life.

Moreover, policy making for public affairs must take on a new character. Most of our planning and policy making has been of the ad hoc, hand to mouth, empirical variety so congenial to lawyers. This has not been good enough. Planning must be based on a broader, more speculative philosophy, and keyed to longer range goals. Ultimately the role of the public lawyer must change very basically, so that he engages in a type of intellectual work far different from his usual day to day activism. It is for this that legal education must now equip him.

It is important to recognize explicitly that whether he is engaged publicly or privately, the lawyer will no longer be serving merely as the spokesman for others. As the law becomes more and more a determinative force in public and private affairs, the lawyer must carry the responsibility of his specialized knowledge, and formulate ideas as well as advocate them. In a society where law is a primary force, the lawyer must be a primary, not a secondary, being.

All of this leads to the law schools' greatest responsibility and opportunity. Today we lack — and desperately need — a profession concerned with the overall structuring of society. Where most areas, even philosophy and the social sciences, have become increasingly specialized, students of law have, of necessity, remained generalists. This is so because law touches all areas of life, and because it touches life in a prescriptive sense — by the setting of standards — and thus it unavoidably treats of society as it ought to be. Hence the study of law as a subject matter must be a study of society in the moral sense of ought and should. Herein lies law's true kinship with literature and with the other arts which seek a critique and an overview of society. Herein lies law's responsibility to be, not merely in apostrophe but in reality, the queen of the humanities.

Today's youth have high ideals for themselves and for their country. Their vision of a good life includes the life of the mind and the senses; it includes service to the oppressed and the disinherited; it includes a deep and abiding humanism.

Perhaps those idealistic students who now shun law schools and the legal profession are quite right; they would find little place for themselves in the present day profession. And it is not the object of this article to lead them to think otherwise. Change will be very slow in coming, and probably will not occur in time to offer careers to students now in college.

But ultimately the law does offer, more than any other way of life, what they are looking for. With only their idealism the new generation can have little impact. Law can arm them. Through law they can aid in the constant reform and adaptation of society. Through law they can help to keep impersonal organization from overwhelming the basic human values. And in law they can find a life that is richly creative. Law can be the intellect and the sword of this new generation, and through them, more than ever before, the servant of man.

Justice, Moral Theory and Philosophy

LEGAL EDUCATION IN A UNIFYING WORLD
ROSCOE POUND

I shan't undertake to consider the whole subject of legal education in all its phases in the unifying world of today. What I am moved to discuss is the place and the prospects of comparative law and of research in the American university law school.

In such a law school we must think of practice of law as a profession. We must think of the lawyer as one of an organized body of men pursuing a learned art in the spirit of a public service. But this learned art is also a practical art. The learning is directed ultimately to practical results. As I have argued elsewhere,[1] social control through law is a process of social engineering. We seek to order and adjust the realizings, and attempts to realize, human expectations in life in civilized society by a systematic process with a minimum of friction and a minimum of waste. Hence legal education has to make and maintain a balance between training learned men as well as men learned in their art, on the one hand, and, on the other hand, men practically equal to the task of aiding the courts in the administration of justice by proper and effective presentation of their clients' cases, and their other task of wise and effective advice to clients as to their rights and duties.

With his eye on one side of the balance, Mr. Justice Holmes told us to teach law in the grand manner. With his eye on the other side, Sir Edward Coke gave us for a motto *non multa sed multum*—not many things but much; not "everything a lawyer ought to know", for there is hardly anything that it may not be very convenient, if not necessary, for a lawyer to know in the course of his practice, but very thoroughly what he is taught. The popular lay fallacy, that no one may be expected to know anything unless he has had a formal course of instruction in it, has no place in the program of the university law school.

In view of this, what is the place of comparative law in the program of the university law school today? Much depends on what is meant by comparative law and to what ends its study and teaching are to be directed.

Roscoe Pound is former Dean of Harvard Law School, and Visiting Professor of Law at the University of California at Los Angeles.

[1] POUND, SOCIAL CONTROL THROUGH LAW (1942).

For a long time Roman law was regarded as a part of the foundation of the study of law. In Continental Europe it was not only the basis of systematic exposition, but as put in legislative form by Justinian, it had been received into the body of positive law of the more important states. In England and America in the nineteenth century we turned to the Continent for systematic ideas. Their law was a product of the universities, and from the sixteenth century had been highly systematized in great treatises, and had been codified at the end of the eighteenth century and at the beginning of the nineteenth century. Our law was a product of the courts, taught at first in the medieval societies of lawyers, which still control the upper branch of the profession in England, and from the sixteenth century till well into the present century studied by a sort of apprentice system of reading in the chambers or offices of practitioners. Hence when the need of system was felt we had little or nothing of our own and turned to the systematic treatises of Continental Europe. For a time we strove to shove the doctrines and precepts of our common law into modern Roman systematic categories where frequently they did not fit. But we had to abandon that endeavor a generation ago. The quest of system without, instead of finding system within our law, did some good in helping us work out systematic ideas and categories for our own institutions and doctrines. But it did harm in requiring distortion of doctrines and precepts in order to fit them into supposed universal systematic ideas worked out in the modern world from the Roman materials. Attempt to mold the common law to these alien systematic ideas often stood in the way of creative handling of our legal materials to the exigencies presented by the transition from a rural agricultural to an urban industrial society. Those of us who were teaching fifty years ago, or even forty years ago, can remember when our scientific text books expounded the law of public utilities on a theory of contract between utility and patron or of a legal transaction professing a public calling; insisted on contractual theories of agency and of partnership; urged a subjective theory of contract; opposed any ground of tort liability other than culpable causation.

Also we have had to give up an idea which had come to us from the law-of-nature school of the seventeenth and eighteenth centuries, which held that all positive law was simply declaratory of a natural law to be ascertained by pure reason. This theory was eked out by assuming that Roman law (meaning thereby the system of law in Continental Europe, built chiefly of the Roman law materials) was embodied reason. This idea played no mean role in the formative era of American law. In that era comparison of doctrines and precepts of the English common law with Roman and modern Roman doctrines on the same subjects was made use of notably by Kent and Story, who had made themselves learned civilians. But comparative law on that basis could not maintain itself as American law reached maturity.

Yet there is one idea of the law-of-nature jurists we have not wholly lost and we cannot afford to lose. I shall refer again to the idea of a universal law, in connection with the revival of natural-law thinking which is manifest today. Apart from that broad theory of all law as applied to morals and of an ideal law derived from reason, or from reason and revelation, as behind every detail of the adjustment of relations and ordering of conduct in a politically organized society of today, there does seem to be a universal element in the law having to do with certain fundamental expectations of men involved in life in civilized society, certain fundamental relations, and what one may call general jural postulates of civilization. The Greek philosophers had worked out an idea of what was just by nature and what was just by custom or convention and enactment. The Roman jurists held to a theoretical universal law of nature which, however, was not a body of precepts applicable to practical problems of adjustment of relations and ordering of conduct by the force of politically organized society, which were left to the positive law. Their law of nature was an ideal for creative juristic thinking and for criticism. The medieval idea of universality pervaded every institution and activity. Men held to conceptions of a universal church and a universal empire. Latin was a universal language for all official action. There was universal scholarship promoted by universities to which students resorted from all lands. There were the universal ethical precepts and ethical customs of chivalry, and we read in Froissart's *Chronicles* how knights came from many countries to take part in tournaments and how men passed freely from land to land, thought of as Christians rather than as subjects of some particular authority. The knight, the scholar, the merchant were, as one might put it in the secular political speech of today, citizens of Christendom. In the sixteenth century the Reformation, the division of Christendom into sects, the rise of strong central governments and growth of nationalism, and the rise of individualism on the breakdown of relationally organized medieval society, led to a decadence of universal thought and universal institutions. But the idea remained strong through the era of nationalism and individualism and is gaining new strength today in an economically unifying world in which men are coming to think once more of relations and associations, to value community interests as well as individual personality interests, and to seek to achieve human purposes through cooperation instead of through competitive free self-assertion. The idea of universality is the antidote to extravagant nationalism.

Perhaps if we contrast the law of marriage and the legal conception of marriage as creating status, which came into the law of all Christendom from the Middle Ages, with the diversity of divorce laws, which speak from the era of nationalism after the Reformation, the contrast will suffice to show something of the part which the ideal of a universal law has played in shaping the law of today. It might be added that the legal theory of marriage seems to be as stable and enduring as that of divorce is unstable and unsatisfactory. Such considerations must be in the domain of the revived comparative law of today. Beyond the mere comparison of particular precepts and institutions by Kent and Story we should have comparison of authoritative techniques and received ideals and of what lies behind them in different systems and bodies of law.

Only a few words are called for as to the place of the broader comparative law of today in the training of the lawyer for the everyday tasks of the general practitioner. As a member of a profession practising a learned art he must have not only a general culture but a culture in his own vocation which today calls for a learning beyond the system he is to practice. Certainly there is a minimum here which must find a place in his training. Also there will be a few who, in the course of general practice under the conditions of today, will have need of an intimate knowledge of the law of some country other than their own. Moreover, we must differentiate between the learning required by a general practitioner and that demanded of a teacher and law writer. The practitioner may well acquire what of comparative law is part of the learning of a learned lawyer from the competent teaching of his own system of law, which he is to practice, by well trained teachers who know how to use their knowledge of the rival system of law to make more effective the exposition of their own. The teacher, on the other hand, should have a thorough grounding in the law he teaches based on a sound understanding of the systematic, the technique, and the historical development of each of the two great systems which divide the civilized world. This knowledge, increasingly called for in the society of today, will bear fruit continually in discussion of newly pressing interests and new phases of old recognized interests.

Legal education is a part of the whole system of education, of training to make lawyers both all-round men, fitted and disposed to live understandingly and usefully with their fellow men in society, and also to make them proficient and effective in their chosen walk of life. Hence legal education must be thought of as part of a prime agency of promoting, maintaining, and furthering civilization. It must be thought of not only in relation to the urban industrial society of today as compared with the rural agricultural society of our formative era, but also in relation to a unified world of tomorrow as compared with the world divided into states, jealous of each other and always potentially hostile. Since the sixteenth century we have had a world of distinct, self-sufficient political units, conscious of their independence and ambitious of power. In contrast we are thinking of and endeavoring to establish a world order. But that order must be more than a world political regime with power to issue and enforce commands. "Without justice," said St. Augustine, "what are *regna* but large scale bands of robbers."[2] Organization directed solely to maintaining order, without regard to justice—a mere regime of force, defeats itself. A society which does not harmonize the expectations of those under its authority so as to fulfill them so far as it reasonably can, in the end breaks up or dissolves.

Daniel Webster said that justice was the chiefest interest of man on earth. Justice is a word of many meanings. If we think of it as the ideal relation among men, what we are concerned with in legal education is attaining and maintaining this ideal through a regime of adjusting relations among men and ordering men's conduct by systematic application of the force of a politically organized society. The universal social order of the future may not prove

---

[2] St. Augustine, de Civitate Dei Book Fourth, ¶ 4 (Welldon ed., 1924).

ultimately to be a universal regime maintained by a universal political organization. But experience thus far shows nothing else to which we may look forward. At any rate, in what must be a long period of a formative world order we shall have to rely on law as promulgated and applied by politically organized society as the agency of a world justice. So legal education shall realize the biblical prophecy as to those who educate many to justice.

A universal administration of justice raises problems beyond those of ethics and politics. Not all of them are entirely problems of ethics. They are not to be solved by reason alone. Nor are they entirely problems of political science, to be solved by application of reason to political experience. Law is experience of adjustment of relations and ordering of conduct developed by reason, and reason as to relations and conduct tested by experience. The experience and the development of it by reason and the testings of reason by experience are systematized and formulated for us in comparative law.

But there is no agreement as to this nowadays. At one extreme are those who urge that law is a pretence or an illusion or superstition. They hold that a political organization of society is only an organization of force; that those who wield the power of such an organization are governed wholly in what they do by the self interest of a dominant social or economic class or by personal individual prejudices or habits of thought reflecting their bringing up or their associations or their subconscious wishes. They do what the interest of their class or their personal interests or prejudices or wishes dictate and then clothe the result with an appearance of legal reasoning. At the other extreme are those who see in the administration of justice nothing but attempt to apply formulated reason. Law is nothing but formulated officially promulgated reason, or to some, a formulated combination of reason and revelation. From either point of view comparative law is a waste. From the one it possibly may reveal the self interest of a dominant class for the time being or the psychology of those in power for the time being, but beyond that is merely systematized illusion. From the other it can only show the gropings after reason of those who have sought to formulate its precepts in the past.

Apparently moribund in the last century, natural law has had a marked revival in the present century. It has a certain validity as a way of putting a universal element of a regime of justice, which, whether it may be referred to reason or to experience, is becoming apparent as we study the efforts in Soviet law to dispense with it. But natural law as a complete and self-sufficient solvent of all the problems of a legal order has not maintained itself.

Two distinct things have gone by the name of natural law. One I call natural natural law. It is an ideal of a universal body of fundamental principles derived by pure reason or from revelation supplemented by pure reason. The other I call positive natural law—that which is so universally established among men, at least in a time in the greater part of the civilized world, that an ideal is drawn from it instead of drawing it from the ideal. It is an ideal formulation of the principles in which the jurist has been brought up. Natural natural law is drawn from outside of the law of the time and place. Positive natural law is an idealizing of the institutions, doctrines and precepts of the time and place, more or less under the influence of the first, but often replacing the first entirely.

Positive natural law led in the eighteenth and nineteenth centuries to faith in a body of rigid, immutable dogmas. Taking an ideal form of the positive law, in which the jurist or legislator was trained, for a universal, immutable natural law had much to do with bringing philosophy of law into disrepute, especially in the English-speaking world. The attempt in the eighteenth century to formulate natural law as a body of detailed precepts good for all men in all times in all places has discredited all recognition of a universal element in law.

It was the worst feature of positive natural law that it made the principles and institutions of the positive law a critique of that law. It was held that natural law was the criterion of the validity of positive law. But this easily came to mean that an ideal form of the positive law for the time being was the basis of its validity. Acollas, professor at Paris in the last quarter of the nineteenth century, put it thus: "Natural law is identical with ideal law; it is the ideal law in itself, ideal law in all the divisions of the science of law and in all its details. Translated into formulas by competent authority it becomes positive law."[3] When positive law was taken to be declaratory of natural law it could readily happen that pre-

---

[3] ACOLLAS, L'IDEE DU DROIT 29 (1889).

cepts and institutions of positive law came to be taken as declaratory of natural law and hence must stand fast forever. American constitutional law suffered from this in the last half of the nineteenth century.

Natural natural law is not equal to many of the more difficult problems of a legal order. If they were purely moral problems they would give the jurist little or no difficulty. But there are questions which have troubled jurists and lawgivers from the classical Roman lawyers to the present, for which a variety of solutions have been proposed and tried, which have never been given a wholly satisfactory answer because the most of which they admit is a practical compromise of competing expectations. A universal legal order will raise many more such questions. Experience of practical solutions developed by reason is all that we can use for them. Here is the kernel of truth in the teaching of the historical jurists. As Mr. Justice Holmes put it, historical continuity is not a duty, it is a necessity. We must work with, we must apply reason to, what we have learned as to adjustment of relations and ordering of conduct in the history of civilization.

As the theory of natural law led in the last century to attempt to impose doctrines formulated in our formative era to the conditions of pioneer, rural agricultural America, to those of the urban industrial America of today as being eternal and immutable, in like manner there is danger of seeking to impose on other parts of the world a positive law of the world in the form of an ideal of the positive law in which we have been trained and with which we are familiar. A true comparative law is the best corrective of this. There is need of distinguishing what is universal in the problems of a world legal order and what is local because of geographical, economic, and historical social and political conditions. The comparative law which will show us those distinctions and correct attempts to impose details of positive law of one part of the world upon others is one organized not merely on analysis and legal history but on geographical, economic, and historical understanding of sociology and politics.

There is need, then, of effective understanding of comparative law behind the plans of world organization and world adjudication. International law as we have known it since the seventeenth century is not enough. But an effective understanding of comparative law involves much more than knowledge of legal precepts established or received in different bodies of law and of their derivation and historical development. It requires knowledge of the social and social-psychological and economic background on which the precepts must operate in their interpretation and application.

We may take as a basic fact a growing economic and cultural unification of the world. Such a unification had long been an ideal. A religious unification of Christendom in the church and political unification in a postulated empire was a fundamental academic tenet of the later Middle Ages. Classical Greece, a polity of independent and warring city-states, had an idea of Pan Hellenism. Alexander achieved a large scale political unification of the Hellenistic world and a cultural unification went with it and extended beyond his empire. The Romans achieved a political unification of the civilized world as a world of Hellenistic culture. The revival of learning brought back a cultural unification of Western Europe, and following the rise of the modern independent states in the sixteenth century, the seventeenth century saw the development of an international law which served well for three centuries. Jhering has pointed out how the growth of trade and commerce has been a powerful unifying agency in all times. With the development of industry in the modern world this agency has been increasingly effective and in the present century it has been supplemented by means of wide and speedy communication which make every part of the world the near neighbor of every other. The nineteenth century saw a cultural unification of the Western World and economic unification went on steadily in that century. The present century has seen two ambitious attempts at a world political unity and a world administration of justice. In spite of deep-seated traditional jealousies and lack of understanding and differences of political and economic ideas, there is a strong and increasing urge for world unity and world justice.

In particular there is a growing recognition of the idea of guaranteeing by law universal reasonable expectations involved in life in civilized society. This is shown in recent provisions in many parts of the world for strengthening and enforcing bills or declarations of rights and in increasing formulation of such expectations not only in newly set up states and in new constitutions for old states, but notably in proposed world constitutions. It is significant that the Soviet Civil Code of 1921 and the Soviet Constitution of 1936 purport to guarantee some of these universally recognized individual expectations. This tells a story even if they lack any effective enforcing agency and arbitrary powers of suspending, amending, or abrogating the guarantees by administrative action reduce them to mere window dressing.

There are three requisites of world justice according to law. One is an international law adapted to the world as it is, or as we seek to make it, that is, a world of democratic politically organized societies, a world of peoples rather than of sovereigns, in which the social interest in the individual life is increasingly valued and the social interest in the general security is kept in balance with it. Second is an effective political organization equal to making a system of world justice according to law possible. Third is sufficient cultural unification to bring about an ideal universal background of universally received ideals of right and justice behind the world legal order.

On more than one former occasion I have urged the need of a reconstruction of what we have known as international law for the purposes of a world legal order today. Not the least obstacle to an effective legal regime of universal justice is lack of an international law adapted to the world it is to govern. An international law framed for individual absolute rulers, and thinking of democratically organized peoples in terms of such personal rulers, is out of touch with the relations it must adjust and the conduct it is to order.

International law or the law of nations, as we know it from the seventeenth century to the world wars of the present century, was based on a theory of the law of nature, a postulated ideal law of universal validity and applicability, governing the conduct of all men at all times and in all places, derived from and demonstrated by reason. Its immediate origin was in the jurist-theologians of the sixteenth century. A cardinal proposition was that law in the lawyer's sense was an authoritative promulgation of moral precepts. Hence international law was a system of moral norms for international relations. International law so conceived of encountered two difficulties. One was the lack of any effective machinery of compulsion. In practice, whenever called upon to solve any conflict of pressing interests its precepts proved to be mere preachments. Hobbes put the matter epigrammatically: "Covenants without the sword are but words."[4] The second difficulty was that morals are not equal to covering the whole domain of human controversy. The clashing or overlapping of human desires or claims or demands, which call for adjustment with a minimum of friction and waste if society is to endure, requires more than moral precepts for solution. Much of the dissatisfaction with adjustment of the relations of individuals by the law of the state arises from a broad area of relation and conduct in which morals offer no solution or no clear solution where nevertheless, there must be a clear and authoritative body of precepts if the legal order is to attain its end. Law has struggled with problems in this area and still struggles with some for which numerous solutions have been argued for from the time of Augustus to the German Civil Code none of which has proved wholly satisfactory from the standpoint of morals. We have had to do the best we could with such questions through experience of what comes nearest to a practical solution. For, I repeat, law, in the sense in which we are using the term here, is experience developed by reason and reason tested by experience. The attempt from the seventeenth century to the nineteenth to treat this area of controversy by theories of morals worked out by pure reason has proved futile.

For three centuries we proceeded on the basis of the classical work of Grotius published in 1625. In his time the main theoretical reliance of jurists was reason. The relations and conduct of men, and so of nations, were to be governed by natural law and natural law was discoverable and to be discovered by revelation and by reason. Beyond a few broad and generally recognized precepts of justice revelation was silent. It did not touch the wide area where morals afford no adequate precepts and fell short of covering adequately the domain where the domain of law and that of morals coincide. Hence the real guide of the jurists of Grotius' time and of the time of his successors was reason. But Grotius took Roman law to be embodied reason, and so his system was one of adjusting the relations and ordering the conduct of nations by idealizing the precepts of Roman law as to the relations and con-

---

[4] HOBBES, LEVIATHAN 85 (original ed. 1651).

duct of individuals and applying them so idealized to the relations and conduct of states.

This was not difficult when Grotius wrote. The seventeenth century was an era of absolute, personal sovereigns. The monarch of the seventeenth century, the Spanish King after Charles V, the French King of the old regime, the Stuart King in England, and the Hapsburg ruler in Austria, was analogous to the masterful head of a Roman household. The relations of Philip and Louis and James and Ferdinand with each other were enough like those of the Roman *paterfamilias* to his neighbor to make the precept worked out by Roman jurists for the latter give useful analogies for the former. So long as the political organization of society remained what it was in the days of absolute rulers, and later when political ideas remained much what they had been, the law of nations worked out by Grotius and developed by his successors served the purpose sufficiently. But with changed political ideas it became increasingly inadequate to its tasks. Its fundamental idea is out of line with the democratic organization of societies of today. It has, therefore, conspicuously failed in the present century. If a regime of legal adjustment of the relations and ordering of the conduct of nations is to achieve its task competently in the world of today, it must proceed on a different theoretical basis from that of the international law of the past.

Undoubtedly the law which is to govern the relations and the conduct of peoples of the future will be able to and must use the experience of three and three quarter centuries under the Grotian system. But it should be able to and should use the experience of the law in adjusting private individual relations, and relations of individuals with the state in the same period. It is not that all this is to be taken over whole and in detail. It may be used just as Grotius used the experience of Roman jurists in the classical era of Roman law as set forth in Justinian's Digest. It is true Grotius did not use this as experience. He purported to use it as reason, postulating that the Roman texts were declared reason. They were, however, opinions upon actual controverted cases and commentaries upon them.

This experience upon which we must in part proceed in the building of an adequate international law should be worked over well by the method of an all-around comparative law in order to identify and bring out the universal element in experience of administering justice which will be usable for a world justice. Here is one function which of itself justifies a great, well-endowed center for comparative law.

No less should the center for comparative law be at work upon an ideal universal background for world organization and for a world law. The legal order operates on a background of religion, ethical custom, received morality and public opinion, much of it taking form in codes of professional ethics, rules of trade and labor organizations, enforced by professional and trade organizations and by household discipline, and inculcated by home and school training. When these several agencies of social control are in reasonable accord, when they give a homogeneous background to the legal order, the law is effective. But at times of transition or of reorganization of ideas, when doctrines of the ideal relation among men become seriously divergent and general conceptions of justice clash as well as individual interests, claims and demands, even in communities long accustomed to justice according to law, the legal order is less effective and may even fail. How much more, then, must we bring about a harmonious background of a world legal order before we can have much more than a paper organization and paper regime of world justice.

Today the law of the state suffers from increasing weakening of the authority of the received ideal element of the body of norms by which the courts administer justice. The old jural postulates, the old presuppositions of right and wrong to which legal precepts have been shaped have been losing something of their hold, and new ones are formative and are pressing, some of them in crude form, upon lawmakers, courts and law teachers. Until we can formulate an assured set of jural postulates of a world order, we cannot expect our world legal order to come up to what we demand of it.

Mere machinery of political and judicial organization of the world and a world code of international law cannot of themselves achieve what is sought. Laws, courts to apply them, and a political organization behind them will not of themselves, however well conceived, secure a world legal order. Even in the everyday law of the state dead-letter laws are a well known phenomenon. The world must be well prepared for the universal legal order before it can become effective.

To fulfill its task in an era of economic and cultural unification a broader comparative law than that of the nineteenth century is called for. There must be a comparative law grounded in philosophy of law, in analytical system, and in jurisprudence as one of the social sciences. Hence the law school of a university is the appropriate place in which to develop it. A body of legal scholars, in close touch with an actual legal system, but trained in the system of the rest of the world, and applying philosophy of law and the science of law as shaped by appreciation of the other social sciences, may be assembled in or about the law faculty of a university and work there under assured conditions of effectiveness and of gaining public confidence. In such an institution there is assurance of security of tenure, adequate facilities, competent investigators, and scientific spirit and method. Such things cannot be relied upon from governmental bureaus. It is true they are fairly assured in the case of endowed foundations. But there is manifest advantage where teaching and research go on together, each with fruitful results for the other. We cannot overestimate the value of a group of specialists in many lines working together in a community of scholars such as a great university affords.

But, you will say, why try to do all this in or in immediate connection with a law school, immediately training for practice of the legal profession rather than in a wholly separate institution? It may be admitted that a multiplicity of detailed aims and undertakings may involve a certain danger of dissipation of energy of teachers and students even if only through contacts with or proximity to much beyond their immediate tasks. Undoubtedly wise and firm, even if liberal, direction will be called for. Yet there is a great advantage in having each part of the wide plan integrated in a plan of study, teaching and research directed toward universal justice in which each benefits from close association of those working immediately at it with those working immediately at the others.

I have urged chiefly the significance of a center for comparative law in relation to the establishment of world unity and a world law. But it has significance for legal education generally and for promoting the advancement of law and of justice through law on every side through legal education. If research in law were endowed as is every other form of research in American universities, if it were possible for legal scholars to devote themselves to the furtherance of justice according to law by conducting the investigations upon which effective development of the law must proceed, the results would be hardly less far reaching and salutary than those which have flowed so abundantly from lavish endowment of medical research. What research has done for prevention and cure of disease, what it has done for engineering and the technical arts, and for business administration, it may yet do for social control through law. In no way may we be so sure of achieving the legal task of making straight the paths of justice as by assuring to our law schools the means of effective carrying on of the scientific investigations on which the development of law in the complex social order and unified world of the future must depend.

LAW, LANGUAGE AND ETHICS*

William Robert Bishin†

The problems lawyers must solve are not different from those that have occupied philosophers. Law is concerned with stating problems, asking questions, determining "facts," developing theories, defining values. These have always been the subject matter of philosophical dispute. Yet discussions of legal problems have been curiously devoid of citation to relevant philosophical treatments. To be sure, there is a Philosophy of Law; there are courses in Jurisprudence. Yet these offerings have been especially concerned with their own compartmentalized subject matter: What is law? What is justice? What is the nature of the judicial function? And, strange to say, even these courses fail to use much of the great philosophical works. When Aristotle, Plato, Aquinas, or Kant are considered, it is usually in their jurisprudential aspect. Otherwise, an indigenous group of thinkers is drawn upon — Austin, Holmes, Cardozo, Hohfeld, Kelsen, Llewellyn, Frank, Fuller, H.L.A. Hart — all concerned with "Law": as institution, process, idea or system of power relationships.

"Law, Language and Ethics" evinces this law school's determination to offer a course dramatizing the relevance and utility of significant philosophical thought in the solution of problems faced every day by lawyers, judges, legislators. Its animus is the conviction that every legal controversy — whether it concern Offer and Acceptance, Last Clear Chance, or the Rights of Prior Possession — has its analog in the realm of philosophical controversy. Strip away the technical legal terms, plumb the debate's assumptions and you will find that the disputants are really arguing about the nature of reality, the problem of knowledge, the functions of language, the requisites of morality, the meaning of the good life, the ends of society.

To make this point is not merely to remark an interesting phenomenon of the intellectual landscape. It is to reveal an insight which, if

---

*EDITOR'S NOTE: The article presented below is a discussion of a required first-year course to be offered here for the first time in the fall term. Professor Bishin's statement deserves prominence for we believe it not only describes a new course but also an entirely new approach to our legal education.

†Assistant Professor of Law, University of Southern California.

learned and exploited, adds immeasurably to the quality and effectiveness of legal performance. The lawyer counsels, plans, devises, directs, contends. These are functions of mind of the highest order. The greater his powers of analysis, the more extensive his resources for creation, the better will he perform these tasks. If his training does not emphasize the need to get beyond categories postulated by common sense and everyday life, the lawyer cannot expect to carry them out well.

The great institutions of American legal education have relied upon the case method and the socratic dialogue to encourage skepticism and inquiry, and to foster a certain versatility of mental function. These pedagogical techniques remain invaluable. But they are not enough. For the skepticism developed achieves at best the status of a useful tool, to be used sporadically and irregularly. Few assumptions are ever tested and these are usually intermediate, not first, principles.

There are no more fundamental problems than those of mind, of thought, of knowledge, of language, and of art. Every act of mind rests on some implicit resolution of these problems. What better way, therefore, to engender the desired skeptical attitude than to study the resolutions implicit in the acts of the legal mind. All bodies of thought, it has been said, are sub-categories of epistemology. And so of law. The *raison d'etre* of Law, Language and Ethics is to impart an awareness that what we "know" is not part of the natural order, but merely organizations of experience devised by men. In common parlance what we "know" we call "facts." And once we have decided that something is a fact it becomes a citizen in the democracy of unquestioned assumptions. But if we insist that facts are merely creations of mind, constructed from the rawest, unorganized sensations, they will lose their impermeability to skepticism. Then facts will not be "believed" because they seem descriptively "accurate" — because they conform to feelings one may have about the nature of life (of society, of the universe). Facts will be believed only when they further the purposes of man attempting to live by the use of his mind. They will not be viewed as *given*, but as *accepted*, and as rational beings we will demand *reasons* to accept them.

To many who distrust intellect and fear philosophy this will seem novel, if not subversive doctrine. Subversive it surely is; for it strikes at the root of mechanical and conceptualistic attitudes of mind. Novel it is not; for it represents but an interpretation of what has been the received epistemology for many years. It is, of course, only another manmade organization of experience, but — judged by its own test of legitimacy — it seems to be the most useful one yet devised.

To those who cry that law school should teach "law" and not philosophy, candor requires the admission that the derelictions of Law, Language and Ethics will not be confined by the boundaries of epistemology and ethics. A subordinate, but significant, aim of the new course is to suggest the relevance of all areas of human thought to typical legal problems. Sociology, anthropology, economics, science, mathematics: all have much of information and insight to offer the twentieth century lawyer. Law, Language and Ethics intends to make him aware of their availability.

For a law course to draw so much upon "non-legal" thought may seem a gross violation of current conceptions of legal education. Many grant that philosophy — or "something of the sort" — must be administered to those who would be lawyers. "A liberal education is essential," they agree, "but it is provided in the undergraduate school." The question is apparently one of economics, of allocation; and the allocation has been made.

This is not always a good faith objection. Sometimes it merely masks the judgment that a "liberal education" is somehow a frivolous education; if it must be given, let it be in the frivolous, not the get-down-to-business, years. Sometimes the objection is an indirect way of suggesting that exposure to the broad range of intellectual endeavor is irrelevant to the needs of lawyer *qua* lawyer. It may make the *man* more cultivated, more wise, more humane, but its bearing on legal problems remains obscure. Since college molds the man and law school fashions the lawyer it is clear where the interdisciplinary approach belongs.

For some, of course, the insistence on a division of educational labor is perfectly candid. The relevance of other disciplines to the solution of legal problems is admitted. But, it is urged, a mass of law material must be learned and time is short. There is little room for subject matter which should have been covered before.

The positions expressed by the contention that "liberal education" is an undergraduate affair cannot be dismissed summarily. They raise fundamental issues. The tendency to view philosophy as frivolous, as of the ivory — or, if you will, ivy — tower is the tendency which prizes the simple, and distrusts the complex, solution. It is the anti-intellectual tendency with its naive empiricism and its narrow conception of practicality.

The conclusion that philosophy is irrelevant to legal problems also has anti-intellectual roots. But it raises the further question of what the lawyer's social task is. If law is concerned with all of man's problems in society — precisely because the lawyer, in one capacity or another, may be asked to solve them — then all of our intellectual resources will seem relevant. If law is something less than this, then another conclusion may be in order.

Those who are truly concerned with the problem of time raise a fundamental issue of their own — an issue of educational policy. Implicit in the contention that law schools must confine themselves to "legal" matters is the assumption that the student, by himself, can achieve the necessary integration of his undergraduate and legal learning. Application of the teachings of one discipline to the problems of another might be considered a relatively simple job of importation, since the operative ideas have already been supplied by the first discipline. But this is to forget that the perceived "connection" between the two disciplines is itself an idea. If it turns out to serve some good purpose it will soon be considered a good or, even, a brilliant idea. It is an analogy and analogy is the method of intellectual progress. To act on the assumption that students can find the analogies of philosophy and law is to repose in them an unbounded and unrealistic confidence.

Law, Language and Ethics manifests deep confidence in the student — in his commitment, his integrity — his desire for an education, not merely a license. It assumes, however, that the anti-intellectual bias is an impediment to the lawyer's development as wise counselor, social engineer and statesman in the politics of human conduct. It builds upon the belief that every device of thought, every piece of information has meaning to the lawyer — *qua* lawyer. It views a training in the integration and coordination of different disciplines as invaluable preparation for the feats of generalship which society will demand of him. And, finally, Law, Language and Ethics insists that we must make formal provision to teach the student to make the analogies, to perceive fundamental fallacies, and to view law as both instrument and embodiment of man's progress in society.

TOWARDS A THEORY OF CONSTITUTIONAL LAW CASEBOOKS

*Christopher D. Stone**

I

Every fall the producers of constitutional law casebooks unveil an array of new models, each predictably a little longer and a little less manageable than the previous year's, but not significantly different from their predecessors or from each other. Yet, wondrously, we are embarrassed into a changeover and given a feeling that it will make a difference which text we choose. How is it that we customers have come to expect the energies of competition to produce little more than some diversity of notes and questions and a race to bind into hardcover the latest stylistic wrinkles from Washington?

Part of the answer to why we do not insist upon a rethinking of the entire *theory* of constitutional law casebooks is that no one is acknowledging that theory has anything to do with it. How else is it possible to explain that the most popular model—Lockhart, Kamisar and Choper's *Constitutional Law*[1]—still does not see fit to give over even one of its now 1500 pages to an earnest introduction? In any other field, a 1500 page undertaking would be expected to begin, after a word or two of apology, by assuring us that the materials were gathered in response to some theory (here: of education; of the Supreme Court) and then proceed at lengths to bare the criteria which are thought to fashion it into a teaching aid superior to its rivals. But not so, apparently, with constitutional law casebooks. In their market, Lockhart, Kamisar and Choper's silence is not even awkward. Consider the aggregate lack of conceptual worry in the prefaces to Freund, Sutherland, Howe and

---

* Associate Professor of Law, University of Southern California. A.B. 1959, Harvard University; LL.B. 1962, Yale University.
[1] W. Lockhart, Y. Kamisar & J. Choper, Constitutional Law: Cases-Comments-Questions, ch. 10, § 11 (2d ed. 1967) [hereinafter cited as Lockhart].
[2] P. Freund, A. Sutherland, M. Howe & E. Brown, Constitutional Law: Cases & Other Problems (3d ed. 1967).
[3] W. Dowling & G. Gunther, Cases and Materials on Constitutional Law (7th ed. 1965).

Brown;[2] Dowling and Gunther;[3] and Barrett, Bruton and Honnold.[4]

Now, I hold no illusion that an extensive introduction would, in itself, be able to contribute substantially to anyone's understanding of what was to follow (students are apt to skim such materials, at best). But by failing to submit to the discipline of coming to grips with a justification for their product, the various authors are reinforcing a sense of inevitability about what is currently being produced. It is an impression that well ought to be dispelled. Several of the casebooks, perhaps preeminently the one that is the immediate occasion of this piece, are so clearly the products of good hard work that each, in itself, demands our approbation. But there are underlying premises shared by the entire range of available casebooks that must be brought to the surface and examined before we satisfy ourselves that the market considered as a whole is making available an adequate sampling of alternatives. Perhaps, in the final analysis, the reader will feel that it is. But I intend to brief the case for a book organized around principles considerably different from those that currently prevail. And while the proposal I set forth is detailed too sketchily to warrant assurance that it could be carried beyond the drawing board, I hope at least to demonstrate that significant reassessments are both called for and feasible.

II

Lacking express statement as to what consensus guided the authors of the present texts, we are left to inference, and by inference one implicit area of agreement appears that is both widespread and peculiar: the authors are very largely resigned to remaining much less obtrusive with their own ideas than law professors usually feel constrained to be in articles or discourse. Forays are made with note and question but, in terms of the larger organizational issues, traditional treatment roams largely undisturbed. This is a treatment which presupposes by default that the authors' job is not so much to lead as to be led—by any traditional handle that appears convenient.

The Lockhart materials illustrate this reticence. From time to time the headings track the constitutional language—"Cruel and Unusual Punishment,"[4a] "The Nature of Due Process"[5]—as if to suggest that

---

[4] E. BARRETT, P. BRUTON & J. HONNOLD, CONSTITUTIONAL LAW: CASES AND MATERIALS (2d ed. 1963).

The introductions to these constitutional law casebooks should be compared to introductions in other casebooks. See, e.g., G. LEFCOE, LAND DEVELOPMENT LAW v-xii (1966); R. DONNELLY, A. GOLDSTEIN & R. SCHWARTZ, CRIMINAL LAW 1-4 (1962). But see P. KAUPER, CONSTITUTIONAL LAW ix-xii (1966).

[4a] LOCKHART, supra note 1 at ch. 10, § 11.

[5] Id., at ch. 10.

the authors' organizational task had been preempted by the Founding Fathers. Elsewhere, established judicial labels like "Prior Restraint"[6] and "Obscenity"[7] take the lead in deciding how problems are to be cast. Even where materials have not been gathered by reference to headings so blatantly deferential to constitutional "key phrases" or other traditional pigeonholes, the underlying assumptions are often the same. Reference to "sources of national power,"[8] for example, might suggest that the authors intended to present some of their materials in such fashion as to generate debate on theoretical justifications of federal activity, using various political science models. But a closer inspection reveals that even under such headings the authors' primary concern is still with the words in the constitution from which (I am not sure how one says it) the sources of power spring, *e.g.*, the war power, the treaty power, and the presidential power. The many moods, the sheer enormity of the Court's function, undoubtedly contribute to the perpetuation of these conservative organizational principles. No one is going to tame the cases into cages that will exhibit them to everyone's satisfaction—a sentiment that is part of what is reflected in the opening plea of the Freund casebook: "To prepare a casebook in constitutional law is, of course, an impossible task."[9] But there must be *best* ways to approach even "impossible" tasks. I doubt that we are finding them so long as the authors preoccupy themselves with current constitutional labels instead of invoking as organizational guides the concepts that their own analyses tell them are most dominant in reaching decisions.

How seriously the passivity of the authors may limit the vitality of their book is illustrated by Lockhart's Chapter 2, "Limitations on Judicial Power and Review." Here, for nearly 100 pages, the authors opt to classify the cases by the jurisdictional doctrines of the Court: "Advisory Opinions," "Mootness and Collusiveness," "Standing," "Ripeness for Adjudication," "Discretionary Review," "Abstention," "Political Questions." There may be reasons why, on balance, it is defensible to perpetuate such an organizational scheme. After all, students should learn the vocabulary of concepts into which important "jurisdictional" problems tend to be shelved. But it is not necessary,

---

[6] *Id.*, at ch. 12, § 8.

[7] *Id.*

[8] *See* LOCKHART, *supra* note 1, especially at ch. 4 ("The National Commerce Power and Related Sources of Regulation: Taxing and Spending") and ch. 5 ("Other Sources of National Power"), which include sections on "Civil War Amendments as Sources of Legislative Power," "Treaty and Foreign Relations Power," "The War Power," and "The Presidential Power."

[9] P. FREUND, A. SUTHERLAND, M. HOWE & E. BROWN, *supra* note 2 at vii (3d ed. 1967).

in order to teach those categories, to subordinate the materials to them. Nor does it follow from their presence in opinions that they represent the *concepts* which have been most dominant in structuring the Court's deliberative processes, or which will raise the questions that best enable us to evaluate the Court's functioning. Surely the authors are aware that there is a root level at which the controversies producing all these decisions—whether ultimately cast in the "advisory opinion" mold or the "political question" mold—share a common syntax: the Court's desire to conserve its fund of good will; an idea of the just state as one preserving for its citizens "rule by law"; calculations as to the probability that petitioners denied review will manage to get redress in some other manner; desire to spread the base of power. I agree that any teacher worth his salt will lead his class to these and other factors tugging the Court at the deeper levels where the really dispositive issues are formulated. But such a response neglects one of the prime purposes a casebook can serve: to direct our attentions in such fashion as to expose and bring into dialogue unexpected relationships from which one may produce a cloth of meaning from otherwise loose strands.

The authors' notes and questions (which are excellent throughout the book) play some of this role, of course. But why should not the questions be resolved by tentative answers, and the tentative answers be translated into organizational hypotheses to generate further thinking? How far removed this sort of leadership is from contemporary concepts of a constitutional law casebook's function is indicated by the authors' reluctance to test out even the hypotheses that have currency in academic debate. For example, I wonder whether the Lockhart book, whose inclusion of materials from scholars (legal) is rather broad, could not have used in its chapter on jurisdiction some of Bickel's "Passive Virtues" and the subsequent controversy.[10] And by "use" I do not mean merely to reprint and bind, but rather to employ as inspiration for organizational ideas. The authors may have declined to do so because the implications would have been too disruptive of the traditional structure. To channel materials towards a discussion of whether the Court has decided and ought to decide its jurisdiction according to principles other than those by which it disposes of cases on the merits would entail blurring the handy and universal (but

---

[10] A. BICKEL, THE LEAST DANGEROUS BRANCH, ch. 4 (1962); Bickel, *The Passive Virtues*, 75 HARV. L. REV. 40 (1961). *But see* Gunther, *The Subtle Vices of the Passive Virtues—A Comment on Principle and Expediency in Judicial Review*, 64 COLUM. L. REV. 1 (1964).

obviously restive) dichotomy between jurisdiction and other matters. Opinions formally declining jurisdiction and opinions reaching "the merits" in cases involving comparable issues (somehow conceived) would have to be brought into a single chapter to search one another's souls; and I assume, if Bickel's analysis were to be used as a guide, one would want to augment the cases with materials such as contemporary public opinion polls and political statements indicating the likely consequences of the Court's deciding not to decide one case, deciding to decide the other.

To ask of our casebooks either leadership in the formulation of approaches to constitutional law or even a testing of the theories that underlie contemporary debate would be to ask that they become truly creative ventures. It would entail so thoroughgoing a reassessment of possible materials as to bring forward almost no benefit from the experiences of other casebook compilers. And it would be a risky business—financially and professionally. The venture could flop, either because there is not enough of a market for plumbing to the conceptual bottom of things, or because our present low expectations of what constitutional law casebooks ought to achieve reflects a sober and valid judgment that an aspiringly creative set of materials would collapse under the weight of its own grand designs.

Still, we have yet to try it.

III

Undoubtedly, a constitutional law casebook could be considered a venture "about" many things. I suggest that a casebook would help us to guide students to a more sophisticated view of the constitutional law-making process if from its very conception its authors thought of it as a book "about" the problems of language and epistemology that underlie communication and understanding in general. After all, the Court's most significant functions are as an interpreter of language and as a thinking process, as is evidenced by the importance legal scholarship attaches to the debates generated under the headings of "formalism," "neutral principles," "core meanings" and "penumbras;" "balancing" and "absolutism;" "judicial activism" and "judicial restraint." These labels connote more or less commonsensical ways of dealing with problems that have been in the traditional province of systematic philosophy where, indeed, constitutional scholars have chosen to leave them untouched. There probably have been at least two reasons for this unfortunate insularity. The first is the lawyer's confidence that he can work his way to any solution starting from scratch—a heady state of mind that seems to be an occupational hazard of a profession generally exposed to other people's abilities only when the latter have so botched their affairs as to need some bailing out. The second is that to take stock of the various philosophical "solutions" would uncover how much the law is founded on elaborate and super-rational schemata that defy an easy and confident grasp.

But the alternative to striking out boldly is to surrender to a syntax of simple distortions, a syntax that defeats any hope of elevating the conceptual analyses of constitutional law to a meaningful level. Common sense may make a student feel uneasy at Justice Black's statement that the first amendment means what it says[11] and at Justice Robert's description of the judicial duty as one "to lay the article of the constitution . . . beside the statute which is challenged and decide whether the latter squares with the former."[12] But from what source does the student—or anyone—get the stuff to go beyond a feeling of anxiety and to put forth an articulate rebuttal grounded on a firm appreciation of how language works? "It just can't be that simple" hardly discharges the intellectual task that is posed. Not only will common sense fail to advance an understanding of the language problems that are expressly raised; it may fail to reveal, as being problems of language, the various implicit resolutions of meaning, such as Justice Douglas' opinion in *Griswold* that the Connecticut birth control law violated "penumbras" and "emanations" of the first, third, fourth, fifth, ninth, and perhaps all the amendments.[13]

How, too, short of an excursion into epistemology, are we going to make significant inroads into an understanding of the judgmental process? Only common sense will be satisfied that the facile dichotomy between judicial activism and judicial restraint is comprehended when described as one of basic attitudes towards Court power. What do these "attitudes" mean when translated into the dynamics of decision? Is the variance one in the "facts" that are considered? Or in the propositions that are deemed "factual"? Are different results reached because different values are mentally strung out in neat serial hierarchies? Or do the different views represent incommensurable world views—different "paradigms"[14]—each with its own special methodological insights that contain the germs of how problems shall be conceived, which proposi-

---

[11] Black, *The Bill of Rights*, 35 N.Y.U.L. REV. 865 (1960).
[12] United States v. Butler, 297 U.S. 1, 62 (1936).
[13] *See* Griswold v. Connecticut, 381 U.S. 479 (1965).
[14] *See* T. KUHN, THE STRUCTURE OF SCIENTIFIC REVOLUTIONS (1962).

tions shall be deemed immune from review, which shall remain unconsidered, and which shall demand what quantum and quality of support? One may rightly be skeptical that such analysis will lay a foundation for the discovery of neat formulae that will reduce the judgmental process to its atoms. But to adopt any other approach is to let the student flounder in the opinions, which will show him little but the poverty of self-consciousness of which Justice Frankfurter's opinion in *Rochin* is typical:

> In each case "due process of law" requires an evaluation based on a disinterested inquiry pursued in the spirit of science, on a balanced order of facts exactly and fairly stated, on the detached consideration of conflicting claims . . . on a judgment not *ad hoc* and episodic but duly mindful of reconciling the needs both of continuity and of change in a progressive society.
>
> Applying these general considerations to the circumstances of the present case, we are compelled to conclude . . . .[15]

The importance of laying bare the epistemological roots of how judges decide cases has more significance than merely to reveal how judges decide. It has consequences in dealing with the lasting controversies about the Court's institutional role. For example, I do not see how one can very fruitfully discuss separation of powers without laying a foundation in semantic analysis and epistemology: our estimate of the feasibility of separating the legislative and constitutional law drafting functions from the judicial function depends upon how adequately we believe printed symbols can transmit from draftsman to judge the directions that the former wants the latter to be bound by.

A model "legal system" may serve to illustrate this. Consider a government that consists for simplicity only of a legislative and a judicial branch. The officials set up among themselves a language L by agreeing on a set of symbols and on rules for manipulating them ("+" is "defined" by agreement that $2 + 2 = 4$). They further "agree" (and here not mere covenant but shared psychological conditioning would be required) on the set of perceptions that are to be associated with each of L's symbols. Then, if the perception experienced on reading *Eros* were not one of the perceptions programmed to win *Eros* the "connotation" of the symbol "freedom of speech," *Eros* would not be accorded the benefits of L's counterpart of our first amendment.

Now, let me put aside for a moment whether such a government

---

[15] Rochin v. California, 342 U.S. 165, 172 (1952).

would be desirable (or even whether we would be warranted in calling its "judicial" branch by that term). What I want to emphasize is the relevance to constitutional debate of the assumption that such a language system (including the implicit assumptions about how the mind categorizes) *could* be brought about. If we believe that language could be designed which transmitted complete instructions for all the decisions with which the system was to be presented, then we could go on to debate the desirability of setting up a government in which all the utilitarian and moral considerations were to be vested exclusively in the legislative (and constitutional law making) branch. If such a language *could* exist, then we could have a political system in which there would be no excuse for judges to orient their decisions by reference to their own maps of what ought to be. But if we do not believe that a language system could operate so as to allow so pure a separation of functions, a fortiori, we cannot expect such a performance in our present system. We emerge from these considerations with altered expectations of the judicial methodology. Our perspective on the problem of "separation of powers" shifts to be viewed only secondarily as a problem for political science, with its concern for, *e.g.*, life tenure and electoral base. Primarily—at its source—the question of how interpreters can be bound to a limited function is seen as a quandary of language and epistemology.[16]

So far I have tried to indicate how the traditional problems with which we expect constitutional law students to come to grips are rooted in problems of epistemology and language; that students should be guided to see this; and that they should be equipped to bring to bear on these problems a better than commonsensical analysis of the dynamics of interpretation. It might fairly be remarked that such a view, in itself, does not call for casting so fishy an eye on the state of constitutional law casebooks. No one has ever doubted that the juice of a constitutional law course is in the interpreting. And if my complaint were merely that some philosophy would prepare the student to approach constitutional law with a little more system, one might well respond by asking whether the materials prescribed could not better

---

[16] *See* K. POPPER, CONJECTURES AND REFUTATIONS 5 (2d ed. 1965):

The belief of a liberal—the belief in the possibility of a rule of law, of equal justice, of fundamental rights, and a free society—can easily survive the recognition that judges are not omniscient and may make mistakes about facts and that, in practice, absolute justice is hardly ever realized in any particular legal case. But this belief in the possibility of a rule of law, of justice, and of freedom, cannot well survive the acceptance of an epistemology which teaches that there are no objective facts; not merely in this particular case, but in any other case; and that the judge cannot have made a factual mistake because he can no more be wrong than he can be right.

be tested out elsewhere in the curriculum. For the past few years here at USC, my colleague William R. Bishin and I have taught, in the semester preceding Constitutional Law, a course called Law, Language and Ethics, which, among its several stubborn undertakings, exposes students to systematic epistemology. We have used materials which include excerpts from Ayer,[17] Carnap,[18] Cassirer,[19] Fuller,[20] Kuhn,[21] Langer,[22] Quine,[23] Peirce,[24] Russell,[25] Whitehead,[26] Wisdom,[27] and Wittgenstein,[28] and have found them valuable as a foundation for the study of constitutional law. But constitutional law casebook authors ought to take into account that such a background generally is not made available to law students elsewhere. Indeed, many schools expose their students to constitutional law before even a traditional legal process course. And even where students have had prior philosophy training, they are not prone to see the relevance of their learning without continued guidance and prodding. Thus, the value of coupling constitutional law on to prior, separate philosophy materials is considerably less than what could be achieved if these materials were thoroughly integrated, making themselves felt in appropriately placed selections, in questions raised, and in organizational ideas.

And let me emphasize that the changes I would anticipate are far reaching even where not limited to the addition of materials. For example, to put together as Lockhart, Kamisar and Choper have done, a chapter entitled "The Nature of Due Process,"[29] seems to me fraught with dangers a book that had gotten off to the "right start" would have avoided. For one thing, to organize one's thoughts about "the nature

---

[17] Ayer, *On the Analysis of Moral Judgments*, in A MODERN INTRODUCTION TO ETHICS (M. Munitz ed. 1958).

[18] Carnap, *The Elimination of Metaphysics Through Logical Analysis of Language*, in LOGICAL POSITIVISM (A. Ayer ed. 1959).

[19] E. CASSIRER, THE LOGIC OF THE HUMANITIES (1966); E. CASSIRER, LANGUAGE AND MYTH (1946).

[20] Fuller, *Positivism and Fidelity to Law—A Reply to Professor Hart*, 71 HARV. L. REV. 630 (1958).

[21] T. KUHN, THE STRUCTURE OF SCIENTIFIC REVOLUTIONS (1962); T. KUHN, THE COPERNICAN REVOLUTION (1959).

[22] S. LANGER, PHILOSOPHY IN A NEW KEY (1958).

[23] W. QUINE, FROM A LOGICAL POINT OF VIEW (2d ed. 1961).

[24] Peirce, *The Fixation of Belief*, in VALUES IN A UNIVERSE OF CHANCE (P. Wiener ed. 1958).

[25] B. RUSSELL, THE PROBLEMS OF PHILOSOPHY (1912).

[26] A. WHITEHEAD, THE FUNCTION OF REASON (1929).

[27] J. WISDOM, PHILOSOPHY AND PSYCHOANALYSIS (1953).

[28] L. WITTGENSTEIN, PHILOSOPHICAL INVESTIGATIONS (2d ed. 1958).

[29] LOCKHART, *supra* note 1, at ch. 10.

of . . ." involves an hypostatization that at best leaves a student directionless, at worst invites his inquiry away from trying to reconstruct a process of reasoning—a task that demands the total intellect—towards a vain search for some *thing*. From another perspective, such an approach seems to be based upon an implicit view of language that attributes to the connotation of the words "Due Process" a power over the judiciary's deliberations that I doubt they really have. At any rate, such a view of the interpretation process has important enough organizational consequences that casebook compilers ought not to adopt it without reflection. What makes it wise to gather under one heading *Rochin v. California*[30] (inadmissibility into evidence of heroin pumped from the accused's stomach) and *Murphy v. Waterfront Commission*[31] (state investigating commission could not, after grant of immunity from state prosecutions, compel testimony if possibility of federal prosecution was not foreclosed)? Why is there a more compelling reason to treat these two cases as "about" the same thing—the words "due process"—than as "about" different things? Why not treat the former as, for example, "about" a violation of the dignity of the human body, to be grouped with *Skinner v. Oklahoma*[32] (judicially ordered vasectomy on a multiple offender under state law, an "equal protection" case now hanging out under the bland and bankrupt heading of a chapter entitled "Other Personal Rights and Liberties, Section 1 Equality"). Why not treat the latter as, for example, "about" the effect of constitutional protections on the growth of organized crime, to be grouped with *Hoffa v. United States*[33] (admissibility of informer testimony under fourth amendment, now in a chapter called "Rights of the Accused"), or as "about" limitations on state investigatory power, to be discussed with *De Gregory v. Attorney General*[34] (time scope of legislative inquiry into communist subversion, now in a chapter entitled "Freedom of Expression and Association")?

Viewed from a perspective of language, the problem is this. There is a spectrum of competing views as to the extent to which words themselves transmit complete meanings and the extent to which meanings are supplied by context. Each view entails different ranges of casebook style. One who believed that the language of the law was one of "plain meaning"—that is, operated somewhat in the manner of language L

---

[30] 342 U.S. 165 (1952).
[31] 378 U.S. 52 (1964).
[32] 316 U.S. 535 (1942).
[33] 385 U.S. 293 (1966).
[34] 383 U.S. 825 (1966).

in my earlier example—would have little need for a book of constitutional law cases, except perhaps as an historical record telling us something about the demand in society for the judicial service. But the need to instruct students on the technique of decision would be insignificant. Judicially proper dispositions would have been determined by the lawmakers at the drafting stage, although dissents might be collected to advance our understanding of the phenomenon of judicial ignorance of language, or of worse defects.

I think that present casebooks by and large reflect a view of language that runs something like this. Words that suggest categories, like "Due Process" or "vehicle," are considered foremost as denoting aggregates of things or events. To determine whether some candidate for "Due Process" or "vehicle" falls within the category, one has first to assemble the aggregate of instances that "Due Process" or "vehicle" has denoted in past judicial usage. He then searches for characteristics common to both the candidate and the members of the assembled group. If a "compelling" similarity is found among the characteristics of the assembled group and those of the candidate, then the label is properly applicable. Such a view of meaning is consistent with the gathering of cases by reference to the constitutional and judicial words and phrases under which, in the terms of the unfortunate metaphor, they have arisen. The purpose of the gathering is seen as to make more convenient the search for common characteristics.

The problem with putting together a casebook in such a manner, however, is that complex and critical acts of judgment are masked when one facilely refers to the characteristics "compelling" a decision one way or the other. Before one can begin to match characteristics of the collected set and the candidate, he must have a procedure for establishing the set of characteristics to be noted. The possibilities are as diverse as the conceptual armament of the matcher. Suppose someone were to bring me an object (a wooden chair) and ask whether it was a table. Assembling all the things that had been identified as tables, how would I know my object was not one of *them*: the material (I may suppose) is the same; the color is the same; they have the same number of legs; they are used in the same room. True, there are characteristics with respect to which my object is different from any of the "tables"; but there are characteristics with respect to which all the "tables" are different from each other, too. Similarly, in the legal model, how the matcher decided which characteristics were to be noted (*e.g.*, the plaintiff's race, or prevailing economic conditions at the time of decision) would be crucial to the usefulness of his model, yet fall outside its claimed explanatory powers. Moreover, even when the task of selecting the characteristics to be noted—and determining whether they were present—had been somehow discharged, one would then be left to decide how the presence or absence of characteristics should be weighed in the event that some of the notable characteristics were shared, some unshared. How, for example, does one decide that the free speech characteristics of *Eastern Railroad Presidents Conference v. Noerr Motor Freight, Inc.*[35] are to dominate over the business regulation characteristics?

What is indicated is that the procedure of matching characteristics upon which such a view of meaning rests is illusory as a guide to how the mind actually invokes concepts, and insofar as a casebook's organization is implicitly predicated upon it, the book becomes suspect as a useful tool.

A loosened confidence in the power over judicial deliberations of "mere words" and their apparent past denotations should make a positive contribution to casebook compiling. It should liberate organization from the traditional mold, thus encouraging authors to assemble as dominant organizational principles those elements in the interpretative context which they believe have consistently been (or should be) more determinative in disposing of cases. Let me suggest, as one example, the problems facing the Supreme Court in wartime. Has wartime supplied an interpretative context so influential on decisions that wartime cases exhibit more cohesion, and are thus a more appropriate subject of study, than cases gathered with reference to the constitutional text? In *Ex Parte Milligan*, one will recall Justice Davis' admonition that "The Constitution of the United States is a law for rulers and people equally in war and in peace, and covers with the shield of its protection all classes of men, at all times, and under all circumstances."[36] But consider Justice Holmes' warning in *Schenck v. United States*: "When a nation is at war many things that might be said in time of peace . . . will not be endured so long as men fight and . . . no Court could regard them as protected by any constitutional right";[37] and Justice Burton's statement in *United States v. Central Eureka*

---

[35] 365 U.S. 127 (1961).

[36] 71 U.S. (4 Wall.) 2, 120 (1866) (on petition for habeas corpus, military commission held not to have jurisdiction to try and confine civilian newspaper editor in military district of Indiana, where there were no hostilities).

[37] 249 U.S. 47, 52 (1919) (sedition convictions of bolshevik sympathizers for obstructing draft held constitutional over first amendment objections).

Mining Co.: "[In] the context of war, we have been reluctant to find that degree of regulation which . . . requires compensation to be paid for resulting losses of income."[38] If it is thought valuable to have our students wonder about how the Supreme Court, as an institution, has responded in times of supreme crises such as war—to what extent have the justices ineluctably been influenced? to what extent have they consciously adjusted their decision? ought their decisions to take war "into account," so far as they have conscious control? how has the Court's response to wartime changed over the years?—then we ought to have a chapter which puts wartime cases together without regard to the constitutional pigeon holes into which the grievances were lodged; say, *Milligan*[39] from the Civil War, *Schenck*[40] and *Abrams*[41] from World War I, *Central Eureka*[42] and *Korematsu*[43] from World War II, *Youngstown Sheet and Tube v. Sawyer*[44] from the Korean War, *Abel v. United States*[45] from the "cold war," and *United States v. Miller*[46] from the Vietnam War. I should hope that anyone experimenting with such organization would find various approaches more fruitful than the chronological approach I have recommended as a start, and perhaps be able to uncover the traces of meaningful judgmental connection in wartime cases not ostensibly dealing with war activities.

Consider, too, the present casebook organization that gathers *Ginzburg*[47] (obscenity) and *Dennis*[48] (Smith Act) into one chapter. The student surely will not miss observing that the cases are not so much

---

[38] 357 U.S. 155, 168 (1958) (fifth amendment not violated by uncompensated government-ordered closing of gold mines in the interest of conserving equipment and manpower for more important war uses).

[39] Ex Parte Milligan, 71 U.S. (4 Wall.) 2 (1866).

[40] Schenck v. United States, 249 U.S. 47 (1919).

[41] Abrams v. United States, 250 U.S. 616 (1919) (sedition convictions of bolshevik sympathizers for conspiring to obstruct war production held constitutional over first amendment objections).

[42] United States v. Central Eureka Mining Co., 357 U.S. 155 (1958).

[43] Korematsu v. United States 323 U.S. 214 (1944) (exclusion by military order of all persons of Japanese ancestry from certain areas of California held constitutional).

[44] 343 U.S. 579 (1952) (President Truman's ordering government seizure of strike-threatened steel mills held unconstitutional).

[45] 362 U.S. 217 (1960) (evidence seized during a search, without search warrant, of the hotel room of an alleged Russian spy with rank of colonel held admissible in evidence by 5-4 vote).

[46] 367 F.2d 72, *cert. denied*, 386 U.S. 911 (1966) (conviction of draft card burner under Selective Service Act upheld over first amendment objections).

[47] Ginzburg v. United States, 383 U.S. 463 (1966) (federal conviction of publisher of erotic literature held constitutional over first amendment objections).

[48] Dennis v. United States, 341 U.S. 494 (1951) (federal conviction of communist leaders held constitutional over first and fifth amendment objections).

"about" the words "free speech" as "about" live problems—but how construed? In Lockhart, *Ginzburg* is in a subchapter called "Freedom of Expression and Association v. Standards of Decency, Morality."[49] But what is *that* play of values all about? I suggest that we could fruitfully plant thoughts at least one level deeper. Beginning with a selection from Freud,[50] or from a neo-freudian with institutional and cultural interests such as Marcuse[51] or Brown,[52] one could suggest that all societal agencies are under pressure to become instruments in a drive to mobilize human resources in such fashion that childhood polymorphously perverse sexuality is fashioned into a sexual organization that is socially more useful. How has the Supreme Court lent its power in *that* struggle? The answer will not emerge solely by reference to "free speech" cases. The issue so cast, one would have to bring together, at the very least, "free exercise" cases such as the anti-polygamy prosecutions of the Mormon leaders,[53] "cruel and unusual punishment" cases such as involve the death penalty for rape,[54] and cases involving procedural safeguards accorded sexual deviants.[55]

The more authors can overcome their uneasiness about experimenting beyond a "key phrase" generated text, the greater the influence such constructive substitutes will come to have. For one thing, I expect that the considerations of language and epistemology that I have recommended will come out as substantiating the legal realist position that the cases alone, no matter how imaginatively organized, will not equip students for dealing with the law. Old hat, true[56]—but isn't it interesting how little effort has been made to assimilate economic, social, philosophical, or psychological background into constitutional law texts? The possibilities of such incorporations are innumerable. Selections from Hofstadter's *Social Darwinism in American Thought*[57] would be useful to provide a bridge into presently under-represented debate, such as the extent to which the Court responds to adopt the philosophies of the times, and the extent to which, in turn, its "legitimating function" contributes to shape contemporary attitudes. Ma-

---

[49] LOCKHART, *supra* note 4, at ch. 12, § 8.
[50] *See* S. FREUD, CIVILIZATION AND ITS DISCONTENTS (1962).
[51] *See* H. MARCUSE, EROS AND CIVILIZATION (2d ed. 1966).
[52] *See* N. BROWN, LIFE AGAINST DEATH (1959).
[53] Davis v. Beason, 133 U.S. 333 (1890); Reynolds v. United States, 98 U.S. 145 (1878).
[54] Rudolph v. Alabama, 375 U.S. 889 (1963).
[55] *See, e.g.*, Rittenour v. District of Columbia, 163 A.2d 558 (1960); Guarro v. United States, 237 F.2d 578 (D.C. Cir. 1956).
[56] *See, e.g.*, Riesman, *Law and Social Science: A Report on Michael and Wechsler's Casebook on Criminal Law and Administration*, 50 YALE L.J. 636 (1941).
[57] R. HOFSTADTER, SOCIAL DARWINISM IN AMERICAN THOUGHT (rev. ed. 1958).

terials gathered from psychoanalytic literature would help us to construct a model of the Court as cultural analyst (or as cultural superego, for that matter) that would feed new life into our present stock of ways of viewing the supreme judicial function.

The failure to incorporate a substantial amount of non-legal material is certainly not owing to a failure of the authors to see its relevance; I do not think, however, that they are weighing its relevance appropriately. In part, the omissions may flow from a hope that the students' undergradute trainings will carry forward to do the job adequately; but, if so, the trust seems to me as far fetched as the estimate of the materials' usefulness is undervalued. Basically, I suppose the problem is seen as one of space, and there is no field in which one is inclined to have more sympathy for the authors, whose claimed needs in traditional material must already be causing unpleasant exchanges at the binderies. In response, let me first stress again that what is involved in my proposal (if it may be called that) is not so much that materials be added sufficient to make students experts on matters of which they are unaware as to suggest insights that will generate a greater variety of organizational approaches and will open minds to the possibility of assimilative thinking. The total amount of "extraneous" materials required would be a function of those more modest roles. Nonetheless, insofar as the changes proposed do entail additions to constitutional law casebooks, some other materials would have to give way, either traditional constitutional law selections, or, if constitutional law as a course were to be expanded, other materials elsewhere in the curriculum.

Obviously, estimates of the marginal utility of the recommended innovations will vary. Although I hold strongly for making the subsitutions, no amount of argument will carry the day until more thought is given to resolving the more fundamental question: what is it we want a constitutional law course—indeed, a legal education—to accomplish? Why should we assume that the casebooks have to swell under their present organizational guidelines, becoming obsolete with the close of each Court term? So long as the authors see their task as, for example, to survey the field of "sources of national power," they will feel it necessary to parade out the cases which trace development "under" the war power, etc. But are the judgmental considerations "under" any of these headings so different, so special, as to warrant the sacrifices in foregone alternatives? To the extent that one can find common threads of consideration underlying all these nominally separate powers, it seems to me that considerable economizing is justified. An organization that made those threads dominant would dispense with a good deal of essentially repetitious debate while gaining a power to organize thinking about the ideas that really have consequences for the decisional process and that point up vital areas of debate regarding the Court's institutional role. These, it seems to me, should be the essential concerns of an introductory constitutional law course. To the extent that subject matter essentially aimed at teaching constitutional doctrine is to be retained in the curriculum, it, and not constitutional theory (insofar as the two can be separated) should be deferred for subsequent study, when students who want so to specialize will be equipped to approach the specific problems with sophistication and sympathy. My impression is that in most curricula this order of study is reversed, with elective constitutional law seminars left to turn up the theoretical underpinnings as some sort of intellectual fringe pursuit.

We should also be alert to the possibility of transferring matter presently treated as in the province of constitutional law to other courses, except insofar as it has something unique to contribute to institutional controversies about the Court. For example, lengthy portions of the constitutional law books currently given over to laying out the standards of procedure in criminal cases could feasibly be shifted to the courses in criminal law and procedure. Conversely, we should also consider the worth of assimilating into the basic "constitutional law" course Supreme Court decisions rendered on non-constitutional grounds. Anomalies—and hence suggestive insights—will often thus be brought to light and contribute to theories of the Court as an institution (as opposed to theories of the constitution as a document). For example, reading a constitutional law casebook one learns how the Court in 1908 invoked the fifth amendment to strike down legislation that forbade railroads to discriminate against union employees.[58] Foremost in the Court's reasoning seems to be the need to preserve "liberty of contract." The student who felt that decision to be compelled by precedent might benefit from being made aware that the Court had previously refused on common law principles to uphold the "liberty" of a railroad to contract away damages resulting from its negligence.[59] Where was the "liberty of contract" there? Or, it may be worthwhile to note that at least as early as 1873, without express constitutional reliance, the Court carved out on behalf of a shareholder a sort of substantive due process to limit corporate recapitalizations

---

[58] Adair v. United States, 208 U.S. 161 (1908).
[59] Railway Co. v. Lockwood, 84 U.S. (17 Wall.) 35 (1873).

without shareholder consent—this on a theory that, "unless expressly authorized thereto," the directors could not effect a change "so organic and fundamental."[60] Surely such a selection adds a depth of consideration to the fact that it was not until 1935 that a suspect whose confession had been whipped out of him was able to induce supreme federal law that would get his state conviction overruled.[61] What was it about the institution that led it to invoke abstract principles of justice on behalf of an investor's interest in his capital position and voting privileges sixty-five years before it would invoke constitutional principles on behalf of a suspect's interest in his body? (Why did protection of the franchise to vote in corporate affairs become established so long before protection of the franchise in civic elections?) Both constitutional and non-constitutional cases may in such fashion have something to contribute to a book that really pays tribute to what I should think is obvious: that to study the constitution is to analyze an institutional process of decision.

I think that a constitutional law book that was the product of such a truly thorough reassessment would get closer to what is going on in our minds and on our streets. Reading a constitutional law book at present seems a trifle *unreal*. Cases are born in issues of drama and humanity. But in an effort to strain them through the legal mesh the juice somehow gets lost. This is regrettable when one considers how much of the material in the text deals with matters that occurred before the students (and often the teachers) were politically aware, and how necessary an understanding of the underlying spirit of the times is to an evaluation of the Court's ability to perform a unique function. The red hunt of the fifties is a good example. Cases that were left in its wake permeate the texts. Here there's a case about a "red" denied admission to the bar; there, one about loyalty oaths; here, one about the trial of the Communist leaders; and so on. But the issues are all so pulled into the shape the rubric requires, the cases so cast about, that when one has gone through the book he has only seen the traces of the "red hunt" and never its face. The seriousness of this loss can be appreciated by considering the Negro civil rights cases which are now being collected: today's students understand them—they can resupply from their own experience much of the fabulous life that the courts methodically extract—but in ten or fifteen years important elements in the context will be lost, and with it, much of what the cases *mean*. Some loss in

---

[60] Railway Company v. Allerton, 85 U.S. (18 Wall.) 233, 234 (1873).
[61] Brown v. Mississippi, 297 U.S. 278 (1935).

meaning is inevitable. But I do not doubt that, by exploring beyond the categories which structure our present casebooks, the authors will come up with materials that capture more of the life, more of what really matters when the Court is called upon to decide.

The benefits of developing such a book would not accrue merely to the student. It may be that much of the professional criticism owes to an undeservedly narrow way of viewing the Court's function, a way that is perpetuated by organizing our expectations around the pigeonholes of the texts we presently use.[62] This criticism, moreover, comes back to haunt us by exerting pressure upon the justices to express themselves in a rubric that does not conform to their thinking, a divergence that can last only so long before the rubric overwhelms the thinking, cutting it off from an independently tested "reality." The result is thus to foster a sort of institutional schizophrenia. What is needed is some "logotherapy"[63] that will encourage the Court to stock itself with fresh concepts more appropriate to its own self-conception and to a sensible formulation of the problems it must come to grips with. Further, only when the Court shall have so adopted a "vocabulary with which it can comfortably and openly express what is on its mind will we court analysts be able to join with the Court in a colloquy effective in working out the roles it might best serve. In this task, a truly ambitious casebook would have a good deal to contribute.

---

[62] *Cf.* Goldstein, *Book Review*, 44 COMMENTARY 103 (1967).

[63] The term is adapted from V. FRANKL, THE DOCTOR AND THE SOUL: AN INTRODUCTION TO LOGOTHERAPY (1953).

Economics and Law

The Intellectual Foundations of "Law and Economics"

Edmund W. Kitch

The principal intellectual foundation of "law and economics" has been its relative success in illuminating two fundamental questions: First, what effects do legal rules have upon society? And second, how do social forces shape and determine the law? Law and economics has enjoyed relatively greater success in addressing these questions in a provocative and illuminating manner than have other approaches to the study of the phenomenon of law.

Law and economics is not a set of analytic propositions that follow inexorably from first principles. It is a tradition of inquiry, analysis, and exploration of law that is as important for the questions it poses as the questions it answers. Critics who set law and economics, not against competitive methodologies and approaches, but against a standard of logical perfection miss this essential point. As scholars of the law, we have to work with the best we have. The continuing vitality of the law-and-economics tradition in the law schools is evidence, not of the perfection of law and economics, but of the fact that when the serious scholar of the law wishes to turn from the preliminaries and get on with intensive investigation of law and legal institutions, he can find tools and insights in the law-and-economics tradition that advance his work.

There are two distinguishable intellectual traditions present in modern law and economics. First is the venerable tradition of political economy, derived from the work of Adam Smith and a long line of distinguished writers and commentators. The interest of this tradition in law arises out of an interest in markets. Laws governing property rights, the enforceability of contracts, and the freedom of commercial activity play an important role in the way that markets behave. Thus an interest in market behavior leads naturally to an interest in law and the way in which law affects market behavior.

The second tradition is that of the law schools. In the law schools, law and economics evolved out of the agenda of legal realism. Legal realism taught that legal scholars should study the law as it works in practice by making use of the social sciences, and economics was one of the social sciences to which academic lawyers turned.

Edmund W. Kitch is Professor of Law and Member of the Center for Advanced Studies, University of Virginia.

© 1983 by the Association of American Law Schools. Cite as 33 J. Legal Educ. 184 (1983).

The scientific study of the social policy issues that inevitably lie within law and economics is a perilous and fragile enterprise, for the distance between investigator and subject is a self-imposed discipline at best. I will discuss these issues in the law-school context, but similar perils attend all work with obvious connotations for applied social policy.

There are three different functions that law-school faculty members perform: first, the exposition and transmission of the arts and traditions of the legal profession; second, the formulation and advocacy of reforms in the legal system; and third, the development and dissemination of scholarly truth about the legal system. Most full-time American law teachers now perform all three of these functions, albeit with varying emphasis.

The place of the first function in the life of a law school is easy enough to understand. Law schools exist in large part to prepare people for the practice of the law. This requires that faculty transmit to students the language, customs, received wisdom, and crafts of the law. Students must be taught to think and talk like lawyers so that upon graduation they will be able to perform their professional function.

There is a direct relationship between teaching about the law and issues of why, how, and with what effect. The task of organizing and explaining the law efficiently calls for organizing principles, and among the most convenient and powerful organizing principles are the purposes served by a rule or institution. To the extent that legal doctrine can be understood as serving specific ends, and the connection between that doctrine and that end can be clearly articulated, the task of communicating that doctrine has been simplified. It is much easier for a student to understand a body of law coherently related to some social purpose than to memorize a complex and apparently senseless body of rules. It is but a short step from the task of identifying and articulating the social purpose of legal rules to the next two functions: formulating and advocating reforms and pursuing the scientific study of law.

Any legal system that aspires to improve (or, more modestly, to offset deterioration) must have institutions that formulate and propose legal reforms. This is not an enterprise for which the academic has an exclusive franchise. In our republican system, an important function of the political process is to generate new ideas and proposals for reform and improvement of the law. The academic does offer some advantages to this process. The needs of teaching require the academic to think widely and systematically about areas of the law—to see the law whole, as an interrelated system. The academic's distance from practice means that he is not the servant of any immediate interest affected by law. A society could do worse than assign to men and women with the primary task of instructing the young, an interest in the law broadly viewed, and the time for patient reflection, the task of formulating and advocating ideas for the improvement of the legal system. It is an observable fact that most American law professors formulate and propose packages of reforms within their areas of special expertise—whether in the clarification and rationalization of judicial doctrine, the adoption of new legislation, or the alteration of constitutional rules. It is sometimes frightening—given how little we really know about the operation of legal rules and their effects—the speed with which the idea of an academic may be picked up, popularized by the media (often to the horror and astonishment of other academics), promoted by politicians, enacted into law, and then discredited. But it is unfair to blame this process on the academics, for it reveals as much about the demand for new ideas as it does about the foolishness of many of the ideas academics advance.

The scientific function comes naturally to any who aspire to make a basic contribution to the fund of knowledge to be taught and with particular ease to law teachers working within a university. "Scientific" is not used here in a methodologically restrictive sense and is meant to encompass all work of description, categorization, and analysis that is carried on with an open-minded spirit of inquiry and that attempts to test hypotheses about law and legal institutions against a factual record. It differs from the function of transmission in that the driving focus is not utility for practice—although the best preparation for practice is often fundamental scientific work; and it differs from the formulation and advocacy of reforms in that its moving spirit is not that of furthering change but that of understanding—although the soundest reforms are those based upon a deep and objective understanding of the law. In the scientific enterprise the academic lawyer has the advantage of his mastery of law and legal materials. But other fields such as history, psychology, political science, sociology, anthropology, and economics play an important role. The law as social phenomenon is not the preserve of any one department or discipline.

The coexistence of these three functions in the law school has many advantages. For the academic, they make life varied and provide an array of styles and work attractive to very different personalities. For the law student, they provide material for a wide-ranging and potentially profound legal education. For purposes of the topic here, however, they operate to confuse discussions about the nature, purpose, and intellectual integrity of legal scholarship.

One of the central crafts of the law is rhetoric, and law professors share with their colleagues at the bar an ability to clothe even the most absurd position in an aura of reasonableness. This rhetorical ability is most often deployed in the service of advocacy for proposed reforms, for it is clear that no small cachet attaches to the professor who not only advances but has adopted a proposal he has formulated. Although ideas that find a receptive climate may be adopted without extensive and profound analysis on the part of their originator, it is clear that at a minimum society requires that the person advancing them do so with vigor and confidence.

Further complicating the lines between the three functions is that in our culture a special weight is accorded to arguments supported by "scientific" authority. In the legal culture, this use of "scientific" argumentation dates at least from the Brandeis brief. Thus the vigorous and effective advocate of reform will deploy in its support whatever material of a "scientific" or seemingly scientific nature can be used. The advocate will, of course, downplay any weakness or insufficiencies in the "scientific" support for his proposal. Conversely, those who oppose the reform will be quick to seize upon any weakness in that support as a ground for opposing the reform.

I see no pressing need to give up these practices. I would prefer that more authors self-consciously attempt to signal the genre in which they are working, but I really do not expect advocates of reform to give up the rhetorical edge to be obtained by clothing their proposals in as much scientific attire as they can. An explicit understanding of the ends served by obscuring the lines between these different functions does help to explain the vehemence with which law and economics is sometimes criticized; for a critic's desire to "destroy" rather than learn from and strengthen what is positive about the law-and-economics tradition is often driven by the conclusion that law and economics has been too frequently associated with reform proposals distasteful to the critic. There is nothing quite as frustrating to such a critic as the appeal to "Pareto-optimality" with its complex, arcane, distracting, and ultimately inconclusive baggage. The principal rhetorical strategy of such critics is first, often with the assistance of the more enthusiastic partisans of law and economics, to blow law and economics up into an elaborate and imperial superstructure and then, the target well prepared for the kill, to show this superstructure to be fundamentally flawed on basic philosophical grounds.

This paper proceeds more modestly. It catalogues the analytic methods, factual insights, organizational contributions, and research agenda that law and economics has contributed to the scientific study of law. One objective of proceeding in this manner is simply to side-step as sterile all issues of what is or is not law and economics, and instead to identify and defend the basic contributions law and economics has made to the study and understanding of law. As the reader will quickly see, it is difficult to disentangle the unique contributions of law and economics from those of legal realism or even more generally from the tradition of thoughtful writing about law, which by its very nature has always been required to display sensitivity to the role of economic concerns in the practical affairs of everyday life.

I. Analytic Methods

The major analytic methods associated with law and economics are:

1. The subject to be studied is to be conceived of as a system of constraints and rewards interacting with individuals. A central objective of law-and-economics scholarship has been to analyze the interaction between a system of rules and the behavior of individuals in order to determine the effects of the rules. This conception of the agenda of legal scholarship was at the heart of legal realism, but economics, with its developed methods for thinking about the interaction between costs, returns, and individual profit-maximizing, provided an elegant analytic framework adaptable to this inquiry.[1]

2. The purpose of scientific analysis is to identify the systematic component of phenomena and separate that component from the random phenomena. A generalization is useful and worthwhile even if it can explain only a portion of the behavior examined. This insight is derived from social science generally and regression methodology specifically. It was a liberating

---

1. For an ambitious example—some have said "too ambitious"—see Richard A. Posner, Economic Analysis of Law, 2d ed. (Boston: Little, Brown, 1977).

insight for legal scholarship, because it freed scholars from the burden of explaining every case and problem and directed their attention to the identification of general tendencies. Many of the most interesting and provocative ideas about law advanced in recent years—ideas about the tendency of common law to further efficiency,[2] regularities in contractual relationships,[3] and the interrelationship between criminal behavior and the criminal law[4]—could not have been advanced and investigated without this underlying intellectual conception.

3. A strong regularity of human social behavior is behavior which serves the interests of the actor. This premise is drawn from the behavioral predicates of price theory, where its predictions have proven powerful and useful. It can be used to analyze responses to laws because it leads to the prediction that individuals will alter their behavior to avoid the costs of laws and to obtain their benefits. This prediction is a prolific generator of hypotheses for investigation—for instance, that laws that freeze rents will reduce the supply and increase the demand for rental housing;[5] that laws that restrict entry into an industry will reduce its output;[6] and that laws that tax or punish an activity will reduce its frequency.[7]

The emphasis on this premise in law-and-economics work has led to criticism of the work on the ground that it inculcates amoral habits of thought. But the premise that self-interest is a strong regularity of human behavior does not logically require the hypothesis that people will behave in antisocial ways. Rather, self-interest can explain precisely why people do conform to the moral and legal norms of the social community. The gains from trade can only exist if each individual is prepared to cooperate with others, and the moral and legal norms of society can be understood as the framework which makes such trade possible.

2. Paul H. Rubin, Why Is the Common Law Efficient?, 6 J. Legal Stud. 51 (1977); George L. Priest, The Common Law Process and the Selection of Efficient Rules, 6 J. Legal Stud. 65 (1977).
3. Anthony T. Kronman & Richard A. Posner, The Economics of Contract Law (Boston: Little, Brown, 1979). Richard A. Posner & Andrew M. Rosenfield, Impossibility and Related Doctrines in Contract Law: An Economic Analysis, 6 J. Legal Stud. 83 (1977); Charles J. Goetz & Robert E. Scott, Principles of Relational Contracts, 67 Va. L. Rev. 1089 (1981); Charles J. Goetz & Robert E. Scott, Enforcing Promises: An Examination of the Basis of Contract, 89 Yale L. J. 1261 (1980); Charles J. Goetz & Robert E. Scott, Measuring Sellers Damages: The Lost Profits Puzzle, 31 Stan. L. Rev. 323 (1979); Charles J. Goetz & Robert E. Scott, Liquidated Damages, Penalties and the Just Compensation Principle: Some Notes on an Enforcement Model and a Theory of Efficient Breach, 77 Colum. L. Rev. 554 (1977).
4. Gary S. Becker & William M. Landes, eds., Essays on the Economics of Crime and Punishment (New York: National Bureau of Economic Research, 1974).
5. Edgar O. Olsen, An Economist's Analysis of Rent Control, 80 J. Pol. Econ. 1081 (1972).
6. Because the restriction on entry reduces the potential competition. This point only holds if the restriction on entry effectively limits the entry of additional economic resources, rather than simply firms, or when the regulation restrains efficient methods of competition by those firms in the industry. The first effect was, for instance, documented in the taxicab industry. Edmund W. Kitch, Marc Isaacson & Daniel Kasper, The Regulation of Taxicabs in Chicago, 14 J. L. & Econ. 285 (1971). The second effect was documented in the airline industry. See the summary of the literature in Stephen G. Breyer, Regulation and Its Reform (Cambridge, Mass.: Harvard Univ. Press, 1982).
7. William M. Landes, An Economic Study of U.S. Aircraft Hijacking, 1961-1976, 21 J. L. & Econ. 1 (1978).

4. Marginal rather than gross or average effects are the important effects to analyze in understanding human response to law. This insight is also derived from price theory where it is used, for example, to prove the counterintuitive proposition that a business that loses money will continue to operate.[8] Past costs are sunk costs and have no bearing on decisions in the present. The cows-and-corn example in Coase's social-cost article is a notable example of the use of this insight:[9] once the liability system has been established, it is a nonmarginal cost which does not affect production decisions. Marginal analysis is critical to understanding the output effects of price discrimination and thus the effect of antitrust laws that proscribe price discrimination.[10] It is important for analyzing the effect of various transfer and tax programs, whose effect must be gauged in terms of how they affect marginal incentives.[11]

5. Observed stable behavior is an indicia of an equilibrium that serves the objectives of those who sustain it. There are many versions of this idea but it is presented here in the form that has been most important for legal scholarship: as a guide to inquiry. It is a useful counter to complex predictive models including those generated from price theory, for it guards against the theorist's tendency to disregard, as either abberrational or antisocial, behavior that does not fit his predictions. The richness of the best law-and-economics scholarship reflects the tension between the predictions of rigorous price-theory models and careful investigation and analysis of actual behavior by firms, courts, or legislatures. This guide was pioneered in the antitrust area, where business phenomena such as tie-in sales, restrictive distribution agreements, and long-term contracts that did not fit the predictions of simple spot-market-price theory had been explained as monopolistic. It turned out that by analysis of the actual practices reported in the cases in light of the question "how could the business benefit from this practice?," many of these practices could be understood in light of a multiperiod competitive model.[12] Similarly, phenomena such as the failure universally and uniformly to enforce criminal laws can be better understood if they are studied and analyzed in terms of the costs and benefits of criminal law enforcement rather than simply deplored as a failure of the system.[13]

6. Goods and services are multidimensional, and regulation of one dimension will affect the other dimensions of the good or service. This principle is important because laws frequently affect only one aspect of a complex set of interactions. For example, economic regulation often regulates only the price at which a good or service can be sold without regulating the quality and conditions under which it is sold. Sellers will

---

8. Because these losses are accounting losses on fixed capital that has no better use.
9. Ronald H. Coase, The Problem of Social Cost, 3 J. L. & Econ. 1, 2-6 (1960).
10. Richard A. Posner & Frank H. Easterbrook, Antitrust: Cases, Economic Notes, and Other Materials, 2d ed., 98, 144, 988-89 (St. Paul, Minn.: West Publishing Co., 1981).
11. See, e.g., Richard A. Musgrave & Peggy B. Musgrave, Public Finance in Theory and Practice, 3d ed., 301-23 (New York: McGraw-Hill, 1980).
12. See the discussion and literature cited in Robert H. Bork, The Antitrust Paradox: A Policy at War with Itself, 280-309 (New York: Basic Books, 1978).
13. George J. Stigler, The Optimum Enforcement of Law, 78 J. Pol. Econ. 526 (1970).

respond to a constraint on price by changing one of the quality parameters. Only if all parameters within the control of the seller are regulated, can these effects be controlled. When this principle is used in conjunction with the earlier principles, it can yield subtle hypotheses. For instance, safety regulation will not increase safety, because the existing amount of "safety" reflects a preexisting equilibrium and if one input to safety is increased by law, the participants will increase other inputs to risk in order to return toward the previous equilibrium.[14] In utility regulation, where many parameters of the service are regulated but price is based on a formula related to investment, this insight leads to predictions about the interaction between output regulation and investment decisions in the form of the Averch-Johnson-Wellisz hypothesis.[15] This insight also helps to explain why particular anticrime measures may have little impact on crime rates.

7. In evaluating the effects of laws, the multiparty, private transactional response is important. It is important to look beyond the reactions of a single individual to a rule of law and look at the systematic responses open to groups of individuals. If zero transaction costs are assumed, the Coase theorem comes into play and generates the corollary that law will not matter.[16] Although the zero-transaction-cost assumption is unrealistic, the theorem suggests that one should be wary of concluding that laws have large effects where the parties affected are in continuing and regular bargaining relationships with each other. Since they have already incurred the costs of bargaining, the marginal cost of adding a new topic—the new law—to their agenda is low, and it is plausible to expect complex multiparty arrangements to offset its effects. For example, one should expect that in response to a tax the parties involved in the taxed transaction will attempt to rearrange the transaction so as to reduce the amount of the tax. Workers and employers will respond to an income tax by converting what would otherwise be income into an expense. Or affected parties may cooperate in the operation of black markets or leave the jurisdiction.

8. In evaluating any market or regulatory arrangements, it is important to compare the arrangement being evaluated against other viable institutional alternatives. It is a simple intellectual matter to demonstrate the imperfections of markets and administration, but it is an intellectual exercise of little interest. Since perfection is not attainable, one should search for the best available.

9. Law reports and case records contain useful and carefully recorded information about private economic practices that is difficult to find

---

14. Sam Peltzman, The Effects of Automobile Safety Regulation, 83 J. Pol. Econ. 677 (1975).

15. The effect is the response of the firm to a constraint on its prices based upon rate of return where the firm responds by increasing its capital base. Harvey Averch & Leland L. Johnson, Behavior of the Firm under Regulatory Constraint, 52 Amer. Econ. Rev. 1052 (1962); Stanislaw H. Wellisz, Regulation of Natural Gas Pipeline Companies: An Economic Analysis, 71 J. Pol. Econ. 30 (1963).

16. Since the effects law has will be costlessly overcome by agreements among the affected parties, returning the arrangements to those they preferred in the first place. From the point of view of a legal scholar, it is unfortunate that most of the literature on the Coase theorem has focused on the hypothetical, tractable world where law does not matter rather than the actual world with which the law struggles.

elsewhere. The idea of going behind the opinion to use it and the associated record for the purpose of illuminating actual practices was pioneered in the antitrust area, but it has now spread to numerous fields.[17]

10. The study of legal history and comparative law is important, because significant differences in the structure of legal institutions will probably only appear where there are significant differences in the cost conditions facing the society. Thus fifty-state American studies may only identify differences that are so small that they do not matter—they are essentially the random component of the process output—while obscuring the dominant and important part of the process. If Massachusetts and Montana are alike in the things that matter, then we would expect them to disagree only on things that do not matter. To understand the really important aspects of our own legal system, we may need the comparative mirror of law generated by a very different culture. This leads to an agenda of study and analysis of institutions as diverse as the medieval commons,[18] property rights in primitive societies,[19] and the organization of socialist economics.[20]

Legal scholars have, of course, long realized the importance of historical and comparative studies. But these studies have been largely descriptive. Law and economics provides an analytic framework that can provide unifying direction to comparative and historical work. For instance: (a) Contractual relations have had varying scope within societies. What social variables account for the varying scope accorded to social ordering through contract? (b) What effects have different forms of economic ordering had on the productivity of societies? (c) Do legal institutions operate systematically to enhance human welfare; do they operate to protect and maintain the position of those in political power; do they have no effect; or should they be understood in some entirely different framework? If these questions should be answered differently in different societies, or at different times, what accounts for these differences?

II. Factual Insights

Law and economics has also been associated with a series of factual insights that have been important to contemporary American legal scholarship.

1. Markets have strong efficiency properties. Using only price theory it is possible to argue that markets are efficient, or, conversely, that they are beset by fatal imperfections. How well markets operate in practice is a question of fact. Are the theoretical imperfections important in practice or are they

---

17. John S. McGee, Predatory Price Cutting: The Standard Oil (N.J.) Case, 1 J. L. & Econ. 137 (1958); Gary T. Schwartz, Tort Law and the Economy in Nineteenth Century America: A Reinterpretation, 90 Yale L. J. 1717 (1981).

18. Donald N. McCloskey, The Persistence of English Common Fields, in European Peasants and Their Markets, ed. William N. Parker & Eric L. Jones (Princeton, N.J.: Princeton Univ. Press, 1975); Donald N. McCloskey, The Economics of Enclosure, in id.; Carl J. Dahlman, The Open Field System and Beyond (Cambridge: Cambridge Univ. Press, 1980).

19. Richard A. Posner, A Theory of Primitive Society, with Special Reference to Law, 23 J. L. & Econ. 1 (1980).

20. John H. Moore, Agency Costs, Technological Change, and Soviet Central Planning, 24 J. L. & Econ. 189 (1981).

relatively unimportant? The rise of law and economics has been correlated with a change in the intellectual climate, which has become more receptive to the view that markets are an effective form of social organization in many situations. This change in the general intellectual climate has made academic lawyers more interested in the private-law structures that support the operation of markets and more receptive to policy approaches that use private-market institutions. This has in turn made economics more relevant to law.

Law and economics has itself made only a small contribution to this change. The scholars of the 1930s who viewed markets as producing a situation in which millions were idle and hungry could hardly have been expected to have faith in the inevitable ordering properties of the "invisible hand." Nor did their background include any extensive experience with large-scale government economic management. The Interstate Commerce Commission, which was their most ambitious domestic precedent, was timid by modern standards of economic intervention. No wonder they said to themselves, "There must be a better way."

By contrast, the current generation of scholars has seen the power of markets to generate private production in the post-World War world and experienced first-hand the imperfections of bureaucratic management. On an intellectual level, it has been possible to place the Depression in historical perspective and to come to understand the role of the Federal Reserve Board in sustaining and extending the long downward economic spiral of the early '30s.[21]

Law and economics has played a role in this large and important transformation of perceptions in one respect. The antitrust-industrial-organization work has shown that many of the market failures attributed to barriers to entry, predatory practices, and monopoly extension are not in practice significant problems.[22]

It is this element of law and economics that probably accounts for the view of some that it is an intellectual movement hopelessly tainted by ideology. An appreciation of the power of markets to release human energies for public ends inevitably leads to nonsocialist prescriptions. The interesting thing is that the efficiency properties of markets are now so widely appreciated that this finding is seldom challenged. In the days of classic socialist theory, it was possible to argue that the emerging scale of production was so large that all markets would be dominated by monopolies. Ironically, the very technological progress that made large-scale production efficient also led to means of transportation and communication that vastly expanded the geographic scope of markets. This has forced socialist political theorists to abandon price theory to the liberals.

2. Much social behavior can be illuminated through rigorous use of self-

---

21. Milton Friedman & Anna Jacobson Schwartz, A Monetary History of the United States: 1867-1960, 299-419 (Princeton, N.J.: Princeton Univ. Press, 1963).

22. Phillip Areeda & Donald F. Turner, 3 Antitrust Law, passim and sec. 711b, at 152 (Boston: Little, Brown, 1978).

interest-maximization models, including such areas of noncommercial behavior as political behavior,[23] family behavior,[24] and criminal behavior.[25]

3. Private-law rules matter and involve policy issues as fundamental and important as public-law rules. One of the reasons that law and economics has been so well received in law schools is that it has addressed in an interesting way the concerns of the private-law lawyer—the rules of contracts, torts, and property.[26] For the preceding thirty years public law had been on the rise in American law schools and had attracted the most ambitious minds. In contrast, private law came to be viewed as narrow and technical. Law and economics placed private law in a larger policy context and generated vigorous literatures on liability rules and the nature and structure of contracting and property systems. Since private law does in fact matter, this more rigorous and systematic method of approaching issues of the significance of private-law rules was a useful corrective.

4. Economic regulation often has effects which are adverse to social welfare and is often imposed and maintained for the purpose of protecting the interest of the firms regulated. Law and economics, and particularly the industrial-organization literature associated with law and economics, documented a stunning series of failures in the structure of the economic regulation that lay at the heart of the New Deal's faith in economic management. These demonstrations focused on agencies tht restricted entry (airlines, trucks, communications common carriers), restricted pricing freedom (railroad, utility regulation, Robinson-Patman Act), or prevented the creation of private property rights (broadcast regulation).[27] In case after case it was possible to show, on the basis of rather elementary price theory and economic data, that these supposedly "scientific" regulatory regimes resulted in a social loss, protected politically powerful groups, and did not have the efficiency effects claimed for them.

---

23. Anthony Downs, An Economic Theory of Democracy (New York: Harper & Row, 1957).
24. Gary S. Becker, A Treatise on the Family (Cambridge, Mass.: Harvard Univ. Press, 1982).
25. Gary S. Becker, Crime and Punishment: An Economic Approach, 76 J. Pol. Econ. 169 (1968).
26. See Henry G. Manne, ed., The Economics of Legal Relationships: Readings in the Theory of Property Rights (St. Paul, Minn.: West Publishing Co., 1975); Kronman & Posner, *supra* note 3; Guido Calabresi, Some Thoughts on Risk Distribution and the Law of Torts, 70 Yale L. J. 499 (1961); John Prather Brown, Toward an Economic Theory of Liability, 2 J. Legal Stud. 323 (1973); Neil K. Komesar, Toward a General Theory of Personal Injury Law, 3 J. Legal Stud. 457 (1974); Guido Calabresi & A. Douglas Melamed, Property Rules, Liability Rules, and Inalienability: One View of the Cathedral, 85 Harv. L. Rev. 1089 (1975).
27. Much of this literature is to be found summarized in Breyer, *supra* note 6, and Alfred E. Kahn, The Economics of Regulation: Principles and Institutions (New York: John Wiley & Sons, 1970). Seminal studies include Richard E. Caves, Air Transport and its Regulators: An Industry Study (Cambridge, Mass.: Harvard Univ. Press, 1962); Paul W. MacAvoy, The Economic Effects of Regulation: The Trunkline Railroad Cartels and the Interstate Commerce Commission before 1900 (Cambridge, Mass.: M.I.T. Press, 1965); Paul W. MacAvoy, Price Formation in Natural Gas Fields (New Haven, Conn.: Yale Univ. Press, 1962); George J. Stigler, Public Regulation of the Securities Markets, 37 J. Bus. 117 (1964); Ronald H. Coase, The Federal Communications Commission, 2 J. L. & Econ. 1 (1959).

III. Institutional Innovations

Law and economics has also been associated with a set of institutional innovations that have had a significant impact on legal scholarship.

1. The introduction of unifying themes. Legal scholarship in its present state has many of the characteristics of descriptive botany. One legal scholar knows a great deal about corporations, and another knows about criminal laws. When they meet, they have little of professional interest to discuss for neither knows anything about the other's field. Each works alone and in isolation, except for recurrent and elaborate discussions of the sporting scene. Traditional jurisprudence, although supposedly the field of the philosophy and science of law, has been in practice a separate field of little relevance to legal scholarship. Law and economics introduced a set of methods and concerns that cut across fields and highlighted some of the central unities of the law. This has enabled people in different substantive fields to talk to one another and to identify and share common concerns.

2. Law and economics, largely through the conferences and programs run by Henry Manne, has provided occasions for legal scholars from different law schools who share common interests and concerns to meet and discuss topics of common interest. The importance of these types of formal and informal exchange has long been recognized in other fields, but they have come late to law. Many of the current generation of law teachers have obtained a sense of professional identity, knowledge of a larger community of interest, and access to enhanced professional skills through programs associated with law and economics.

3. Professionally edited journals have entered the law-school world through the example of the *Journal of Law and Economics* and the *Journal of Legal Studies*, published by the Law and Economics Program at the University of Chicago Law School. A system of student-edited journals had a strong and clear message about the importance of legal scholarship. The discontinuities and lack of consistency caused by ever-changing student editorial boards meant that law reviews could never acquire distinctive character or systematically develop and support a particular line of inquiry or style of work. No serious field of scholarship uses such a system of publication, and in this respect law and economics has brought higher standards of scholarship to the law schools.

IV. The Paradox of Efficient Markets

Law and economics has identified an important problem that is likely to remain at the center of the research agenda for a long time. In brief, it is the clarification and explanation of the paradox of efficient markets.

The standard explanation offered for the efficiency of markets is that they bring together in continuing interaction decision makers who will be rewarded in proportion to their correct decisions and who will lose in proportion to their errors. Each trader and investor deals in property rights which confer upon him the value of the future income stream of the property. To the extent he enhances the value of that stream, he benefits; to the extent he impairs it, he loses. This symmetry of reward and loss creates an environment that favors decisions that optimize the decider's wealth, and through an extended but elegant line of logic it can be demonstrated that these are the same decisions that optimize the wealth of the market participants as a group.

There are many problems with this story, and it is those problems that provide the agenda for frontier research in law and economics. For example: many market participants voluntarily enter into long-term institutional arrangements either through contracts or the creation of firms that put individuals in the position of making decisions whose consequences will be borne by others. When this is done, it is evidence that the firm or contract is more beneficial to the parties than the alternative market arrangement, but how can that be so? It can only be so if there are devices within the firm or contracting arrangement that control these "imperfections." What are those devices and how do they work?

1. If the "correct" decisions of market actors make markets efficient, then it is possible for third parties to free-ride on the efficiency of markets (for example, by buying an index fund).[28] Since "correct" decisions are the product of investment in the skills and information necessary to make them, this possibility—free-riding—suggests that there is underinvestment in information. But markets do have observable efficiency properties. How are these problems dealt with?

2. Political actors have power to make decisions free of market sanctions. Yet many legal systems, over long periods of time, have supported market systems. What pressures operate on the political system to cause this to happen; and what institutions and arrangements are used to sustain this outcome?

These kinds of questions have produced a vigorous, important, and uncertain literature on topics as varied as the economics of information,[29] the theory of the firm,[30] and public choice.[31] Work on these topics requires both careful theory and thoughtful empirical study. The inherent tensions of the paradox have attracted first-rate minds and resulted in much of the most interesting and insightful contemporary work in law.

The discussion so far has emphasized the significant methodological, empirical, and organizational contributions that law and economics has

---

28. George Foster, Financial Statement Analysis 406 (Englewood Cliffs, N.J.: Prentice-Hall, 1978).

29. See George J. Stigler, The Economics of Information, 69 J. Pol. Econ. 213 (1961), reprinted in The Organization of Industry 171 (Honewood, Ill.: Richard D. Irwin, 1968); Herbert A. Simon, Administrative Behavior, 3d ed. (New York: Macmillan, 1976); Oliver E. Williamson, Markets and Hierarchies: Analysis and Antitrust Implications, A Study in the Economics of Internal Organization (New York: Free Press, 1975); Edmund W. Kitch, The Law and Economics of Rights in Valuable Information, 9 J. Legal Stud. 683 (1980); Edmund W. Kitch, The Nature and Function of the Patent System, 20 J. L. & Econ. 265 (1977).

30. Ronald H. Coase, The Nature of the Firm, 4 Economica (n.s.) 86 (1937); Williamson, *supra* note 29; Michael C. Jensen & William H. Meckling, Theory of the Firm: Managerial Behavior, Agency Costs and Ownership Structure, 3 J. Fin. Econ. 35 (1976); Eugene F. Fama, Agency Problems and the Theory of the Firm, 88 J. Pol. Econ. 288 (1980); Oliver E. Williamson, The Modern Corporation: Origins, Evolution, Attributes, 19 J. Econ. Lit. 1537 (1981).

31. See Dennis C. Mueller, Public Choice (Cambridge: Cambridge Univ. Press, 1979).

made to the scholarship of law. Surely they are important enough to support the following conclusions: Scholars of the law can enrich their work by familiarity with its methods and its literature, and indeed most scholars now working in American law schools (and an increasing number abroad) do just that. There is nothing about law and economics to suggest that it is a short-run development that has run its course. The issues posed by law and economics are fundamental and interesting. The first fifty years—to age the activity generously—have largely consisted of a deck-clearing operation. It is not unreasonable to hope that the next fifty will witness significantly enhanced understanding of the institutions of the law built upon that foundation.

This essay opened with the suggestion that the principal "intellectual foundation" of law and economics was its success vis-a-vis the competition. Yet there has been no discussion of the competition. The reason is that there is none that offers anything like the range of methods, insights, and institutions that law and economics has, nor is there any competition that has been associated with a comparable quantity and quality of useful scholarly work on law. The treatise-restatement tradition that lies at the heart of the excellence of the traditional American law school involves work of systematic description, organization, and rationalization that is complementary to, but not competitive with, the concerns of law and economics. Members of the critical legal studies movement are eager to proclaim themselves an alternative, but even a sympathetic view has to concede that their alternative has yet to find even a clear self-definition—except, perhaps, a dissatisfaction with law and economics.

Much work in law and economics, of course, attempts to move beyond the core discussed here to expand the range and power of the enterprise. Quite properly so. The intellectual foundations of the core are sound. It is time to build.

Thoughts on the Future of Economics in Legal Education

Guido Calabresi

I will not spend much time on specific points in Summers and Schwartz, even though some of them are well worth discussing. For example, it seems to me that most of Summers's critique deals with lawyer-economists who follow economists in their narrowest ways. Summers argues that such narrow approaches and their practitioners are of limited use in the law curriculum of the future. This may be true but says little about the role of *economics* in that curriculum.

There is also nothing in Summers's critique to answer the puzzling question of why antitrust, but not, for example, an advanced course on the use of liability rules, should be laden with economics. His oral comment, stressing the importance of having judicial decisions stated in a language which the consumers of those decisions can understand, suggests an answer. Perhaps Summers believes an antitrust curriculum can use economics because the consumers of antitrust law know that language, while consumers of ordinary common-law decisions know the language of law but do not know the language of economics. I agree that most consumers do not know the language of economics. But we fool ourselves royally if we think that they know the language of law or are comforted by the fact that courts speak in terms of rights and other such things. All one needs to do is read critiques of our courts and of our system of justice to see how angry such consumers are because legal language is not their language any more than economics is their language. Still, Summers's distinction is an interesting one and would be worth exploring further.

I also do not want to spend much time on specific points in Schwartz's brilliant analysis, though I found his piece wonderful reading. I will mention, however, a couple of questions in passing. First, what distinguishes Schwartz's law school from a public-policy school, given that his course in law and culture is not at all a course in the legal culture? It is, instead, a course on taste-shaping. This is a crucial issue which ought to be discussed in a law curriculum. But taste-shaping is not "legal culture," and without a true course in legal culture there is nothing in the whole of Schwartz's curriculum that would not be at least as apt for a public-policy school as a law school.

Guido Calabresi is Sterling Professor of Law, Yale Law School.

© 1983 by the Association of American Law Schools. Cite as 33 J. Legal Educ. 359 (1983).

Second, what makes Schwartz think that one can teach allocation problems better across a series of factual areas but separate from, say, distributional problems than by teaching the interrelation of these two in one or two pseudo-subject areas? I say pseudo-subject because it is not the content of the subject that most of us teach at all. I can call something tort—or bananas or Thucydides or mustard plaster—and under that title I can bring in all four or five of the things that Schwartz wants to teach and discuss them not only singly but as they play off each other. Moreover, I see nothing in his presentation to suggest that one can teach the things he wants taught better separately than all together in various different legal contexts. Indeed, in his oral presentation he moved from one to the other in just such a way. Maybe we ought to do both, which, I think, is one of the things that Charles Goetz was suggesting a little bit earlier. I certainly am not saying that it *is* better to teach all five (or some of them) at once; I just say that Schwartz did not demonstrate the opposite in his discussion.

But I do not want to spend more time on these relatively narrow issues. Rather, I would like to make some more general comments on four interrelated matters that these papers and the conference brought to my mind. One is the relationship between "legal-process" thinking and "law-and" thinking. The second is "models" versus "laundry lists." The third is scientific policy-making languages and languages of justice. And the fourth is what the critics of law and economics require of us.

Legal scholarship in the last sixty or so years has alternated between two, and probably only two, major themes. One has been legal process: who ought to do what in law? (what ought courts to do? what ought legislatures to do? what ought administrative agencies to do?); and who *does* what in making legal decisions (which institutions are actually doing what)? The other theme has been "law and (some other discipline)." The two themes are not mutually exclusive. But one has tended to dominate legal scholarship just when the other has finished a period of dominance and growth.

Pound began as a sociologist of law. He was followed by and melded into the legal realists who in the beginning were essentially talking about "Who does what, don't fool anymore, who actually does what?" They, in turn, ended up in an orgy of law and social science in which not very good sociology was particularly dominant. (Some institutional economics was relevant at that time, as were some other social sciences; but by and large it was "law-and" bad sociology.) That petered out in the great flowering of that most extraordinary school, the Harvard Legal Process School, which dominated until the late fifties. Alexander Bickel was the last great blossom in that flowering. Then law and economics, the current law and economics, took over. I think it is interesting that in the very last few years there has again been significant writing on legal process. Ely's book, my book on the common law and statutes, and Ackerman's forthcoming book on constitutional theory are all "new" legal-process books. I could go on. I only mention these three because all three are written by close friends (especially me).

The law-school curriculum responds to these waves and it responds in two ways. First, it responds by giving rise to one or more courses explicitly on

Thoughts on the Future

topic. For instance, when we are in a legal-process period we inevitably have something which, whatever its name, is a legal-process course. (In the great flowering of the Harvard Legal Process School, it was usually even called Legal Process.) That course continues to be taught after the flowering, but enrollments diminish. It spreads out to more distant areas (to schools away from the original center of the movement). It becomes less significant. In the flowering times of "law-and" movements, instead, one gets "law-and" courses centrally in the curriculum, courses like "law and economic analysis." These courses become significant as legal-process courses fade. We are now beginning to get new courses which sound like legal-process courses even though they do not have that name. They are, however, doing the same sort of thing, and that suggests that something has happened, is happening, which indicates a decline in the latest "law-and" movement.

The curriculum responds to these waves in a second way as well. During the dominance of a particular approach there is a great deal of infusion of ways of thinking that reflect the dominant approach in ordinary courses. In the high days of a legal-process school, one gets legal-process types of questions in torts and in contracts: who is deciding what? what is really going on? etc. In my first-term torts course, I find myself teaching more and more about interrelationships between common law and statutes, something which ten years ago I did not do. In the high points of "law and," one finds "outside" disciplines being introduced in "traditional" courses. This infusion is often done badly, as Goetz has suggested, and serves to underline the need for the separate course. If one goes back and looks at the materials which were put together for common-law courses by the post-legal-realist, those who were part of *that* "law-and" movement, one finds exactly this.

There are two quite appropriate fears which are directed at all of the "law-and" periods, and they have both been brought up here. The first can be seen in the quite remarkable statement that Richard Stewart made. It is unfortunately true that the beginning of such a movement is heady stuff—heady stuff because we think we have answers. Now that is ridiculous. It should not be such heady stuff. We should not think we have answers when one of these movements begins. Yet each time the suggestion is made that if we can reduce the problem (and reductionism is the appropriate criticism) to the terms of a particular social science, then we can get "the" answer.

In Arthur Corbin's farewell address to the Yale Law School faculty, which I commend to you, you will find as good an answer to that illusion as you will find anywhere. He was speaking at the end of the last "law-and" movement and he said: "You look for answers and they're not there. They're not there in law, and they're certainly not there in these other disciplines. Examine them if you want, but you're not going to get very far."[1] Corbin's criticism (a very conservative man he was) in fact sounded very like the criticisms we have heard here from another quarter, but they are still the same thing.

The second fear is the one which I tried to bring up in answer to Steven Breyer. Too often, when one tries to introduce these other materials in law

1. This quotation is a paraphrase of Corbin's remarks, which are on file in the Yale Law School Library.

courses, one brings them in badly. The job is not done at a sufficiently sophisticated level, so we only succeed in teaching our students simple rules from these disciplines. Frank Michelman's criticism of such simple rules is not only appropriate but devastating. That was Grant Gilmore's great fear, and it is why, throughout the time that we were colleagues, he opposed social science in law. It was not that he thought social sciences irrelevant; rather, he thought we could not possibly teach them at a sophisticated enough level.

One can properly question Schwartz's curriculum on both counts. Will it work to avoid each of these problems? I am doubtful.

My second point deals with "models" versus "laundry lists." Traditional legal scholarship was often based on experience of part of a legal system, that is, cases. That type of scholarship tends to give rise to a laundry list of relevant values. It is no accident that that is what Summers's paper in some ways seems to be, and it is also no accident that the list is incomplete. After going through the whole thing, he tells us that it is tedious and that it is incomplete. It would still be tedious and incomplete if it were reduced or lengthened.

The alternative is to try to stand outside "experience" and make a model. Models create boxes and the boxes may be empty or they may be full. They give us a way of abstracting from our experience and looking for other things, other patterns. Both approaches can be useful ways of dealing with legal issues. My experience suggests that even the simplest kind of model building may prove useful.

Michelman, in his review of my book *The Costs of Accidents*, applied the analysis in the book to nuisance law and described three categories of rules with respect to nuisance. It was a classic list of rules derived from nuisance cases. Soon after, Doug Melamed and I developed the simplest kind of model in an article (it does not even qualify as a "law-and-economics" model).[2] The model suggested that there had to be a fourth rule, at least that there was a fourth box. Did that box mean anything, or was it just an empty box? Was the suggested rule useful? It turned out that it was. First, a case came out almost immediately after the article and (independently of it) "filled the box."[3] Second, it became obvious that the box had never been empty. Indeed, the box, the fourth rule, had been applied in thousands of eminent-domain cases by administrative agencies across all of the legal framework. Yet that fourth rule was not easily visible without the model because we were deriving our laundry list from court cases only. Even someone as sophisticated as Michelman did not see what was missing, and even a model as simplistic as the one we used helped!

What does that tell us? That the model is good? Not necessarily, because no model envelops the universe. Indeed, that is my problem with Schwartz's curriculum—it does not cover the legal universe. One can say of it what Mill said of Bentham: that he dismissed everything that did not fit his model as

---

2. See Guido Calabresi & A. Douglas Melamed, Property Rules, Liability Rules, and Inalienability: One View of the Cathedral, 85 Harv. L. Rev. 1089 (1972).

3. Spur Industries v. Del E. Webb Devel. Co., 108 Ariz. 178, 494 P.2d 700 (1972).

Thoughts on the Future

"vague generalities"; and that what he did not realize was that in those vague generalities lay the whole unanalyzed experience of the human race.[4] And that is a fair amount!

But Mill was also a utilitarian and believed that one should use models as well, because through models one sees some things that the laundry list of experience does not show and because models help explain that laundry list. What we have done at this conference has been a lot of playing back and forth between the advantages of doing one kind of modeling (that is, economic modeling) and the dangers of doing only that.

I had Professor C. E. Lindblom come to my law-and-economics class years and years ago. He told the class that modeling was terrible because at the time he was criticizing economics in those terms. The students were furious because everything that Lindblom was telling them to do instead of modeling was just traditional legal analysis under another name. They were dissatisfied with that and were looking for other answers. They hoped modeling was going to lead to such answers. The point of the story is that both the students (who thought that Lindblom was wrong and that modeling was going to give them the answer) and Lindblom (who was arguing that one could do without modeling) were overreacting to to weaknesses in the approaches they knew, in the approaches that had been dominant in their disciplines. As a result they were both too ready to buy as full answers what in other disciplines had already been shown to be flawed and incomplete.

My third comment has to do with ways of speaking about law. We could speak about all that we do in law using only "justice" or "rights" language. We could instead speak of all that we do using only "scientific policy-making" language, as if everything involved costs and benefits. Or we could use both languages and subsets of such languages, like primary accident costs (or efficiency) over here, and something else (distribution) over there. We could talk about distributional problems as if they involved "costs," and we could talk about "spreading" as if it involves some types of costs "in-between" efficiency and distribution costs. We *can* do any of these things.

The question is, which language highlights the similarity among those things which we tend to trade off against each other readily (or which are based on analogous kinds of data) and separates out those things as to which we wish to make trade-offs only more rarely, or perhaps not at all? (I do not believe the category "not at all" is very significant, though we may want to *say* that we do not make some trade-offs ever at all.)[5] In other words, we should use the language which allows us to put together those things which we want to talk about together.

An appropriate analogy might be that of currency exchanges. There are different kinds of trade-offs. There are trades which we can make in the same currency. There are trades which we can make only if we obtain another

---

4. John Stuart Mill, Essay on Bentham, *in* The Philosophy of John Stuart Mill: Ethical, Political, and Religious, ed. Marshall Cohen, 20 (New York: Modern Library, 1961).
5. See Charles L. Black, Jr., Mr. Justice Black, The Supreme Court, and the Bill of Rights, Harper's Magazine, Feb. 1961, p. 63, and discussion of it in Guido Calabresi, A Common Law for the Age of Statutes 173-77 (Cambridge, Mass.: Harvard Univ. Press, 1982).

currency before we make the trade. And there are situations in which we say that no trades, no exchanges of currency, are permissible, even if in fact black-market exchanges occur all the time because in a "hidden" way we want them to. Languages, and translation between languages, perform an analogous task. That is why it may be useful to use languages of rights, languages of absolutes which are not absolutes, and languages of costs and benefits, which only translate into each other with difficulty.

To translate from one language to another is to betray. That is the translation, and the betrayal, of an Italian saying: *"Traduttore, traditore."* Anybody who knows Italian knows that my translation of the saying inevitably does not state the saying precisely. And that is both the problem and the advantage of using different languages.

What I am suggesting to you is that the use of economic language to describe part of law is terribly useful. And it is even useful, occasionally, to play as if one could use economic language across all of law, but only so long as one does not get confused about the fact that the real trade-offs in meaningful areas are not on a one to one basis. And that is why, most of the time, it is better to limit the use of economic language to those issues in law where simple trade-offs *are* likely.

I still want to say a few words about our critics. It seems to me that the critics are rather like Goetz's description of Keynes. They act as if they are outside the system of law and economics, but they are in it, just as Keynes was in Pigou's world. What the critics require of us is an awareness that how we talk shapes what we become. And, hence, that a discussion of taste-shaping is essential to a law curriculum, and especially to a law curriculum influenced by economics. They also require us to concede that the fact that economics will not deal easily with some issues and traditionally tends to ignore others does not eliminate those issues or justify their being ignored.

For years economists did not discuss distribution because it was not easy to talk about, and yet we have to talk about it. Similarly today many act as though shaping of tastes is not to be talked about because it is difficult. And yet we have to talk about shaping of tastes, if we are going to talk seriously about other things in law and economics.

It is significant that Schwartz's curriculum focuses on shaping of taste and that Trebilcock told us that the most interesting parts of his law-and-economics course are those dealing with the limits, the fringes, of economics. I would conclude that some of the "easy kills" may actually lie in these areas (nominally the most difficult), precisely because we have not used even the most simple-minded tools with respect to them, since we thought that we could not. One of the ironies is that while we may not get all that far, we will get further in these areas by using simple-minded tools of economics than in other areas which by now have been overworked! And with that, I had better stop.

Part IV
Questions and Challenges

Feminist Theory

Women's Work: The Place of Women in Law Schools

Ruth Bader Ginsburg

For seventeen years of my life in the law, I served as a law teacher. When I started in the law-teaching business in 1963, few women appeared on my seating charts, perhaps 5 or 6 in a class of over 100. By 1980, across the country, women comprised over one-third of total law-school enrollment, up from 3.6 percent in 1963 and 9.5 percent in 1971.[1] In more than a few law schools today, 50 percent or more of the students are women. It is an appropriate time to indulge in a few memories of things past and to express the exhilaration I feel about the alterations that have occurred.

A matching change is in sight on the other side of the podium. The change was documented a year ago in an American Bar Foundation report.[2] In 1950, in all ABA-accredited law schools, 5 women were engaged as full-time tenure-track teachers.[3] Literally, women who worked as law teachers could be counted on the fingers of one hand. When the women numbered 5, the male count was over 1200. By 1967, when women neared 4 percent of all lawyers, they were only 1.7 percent of all tenure-track law teachers.[4] A dozen years later, in 1979, the 1.7 percent had increased to 15 percent and the numbers, from 39 in 1967 to 516 on the verge of the 1980s.[5]

The five women teaching law in 1950 were assigned to courses in three areas: family law, trusts and estates, and legal research and writing. Today, women and men teach in remarkably similar proportions in core first-year courses: civil procedure, contracts, criminal law, property, and torts. In those subjects, many law schools strive to field their first string team.

When I visit law schools nowadays, students, both male and female,

---

Ruth Bader Ginsburg is a United States Circuit Judge of the United States Court of Appeals for the District of Columbia Circuit. Before her appointment to the bench, she was Professor of Law at Columbia University. This article is excerpted from remarks delivered to a conference on legal education at New York University on November 3, 1981.

1. See ABA Section on Legal Education and Admissions to the Bar, Law Schools and Bar Admission Requirements: A Review of Legal Education in the United States (1980–1981).
2. Donna Fossum, Women Law Professors, 1980 A.B.F. Research J. 903.
3. *Id.* at 905.
4. *Id.* at 905.
5. *Id.* at 914.

sometimes volunteer that they have neither witnessed nor personally encountered sex-based discrimination in the classroom or in pursuing job opportunitites. Occasionally, a male student will venture his suspicion that women sometimes have an edge on an opportunity, simply because of their gender. I think back to the way it was barely a dozen years ago when complaints from women students abounded. Two textbook examples illustrate the altered climate.

A widely used first-year property casebook, published in 1968 and authored by a distinguished Columbia Law School professor, attempted to explain why the hiatus problem that can arise in connection with a life estate *per autre vie* must not go without solution. After all, the casebook author commented, "land, like woman, was meant to be possessed."[6]

Another illustration is a case of instruction students gave to a dear colleague of mine at Rutgers Law School. He was preparing a casebook on land transfer and finance in 1970. One of the topics was real-estate brokerage; one of the questions, what explains the high incidence of litigation involving brokers? In a draft tried out in a seminar, this comment appeared: "In forming your own theory as to why there is so much litigation, it may be useful to note that 40 percent of all real-estate brokers are women." When the material was distributed, the students who used it suggested that the conjecture betrayed a certain bias or insensitivity. The professor conceded he had not checked for correlations with religious affiliation, national origin, race, height, or hair color. He deleted the remark. It was a poor attempt at humor, he said, a distraction that did not advance study of the topic.

As to the job market for women law graduates, a 1963 survey of placement facilities at sixty-three law schools tells a story common in those pre-Title VII days.[7] Fifty-seven of the schools ranked discrimination against women law students by legal employers as overt and either "extensive" or "significant." Although women were long accepted as criminal defenders at legal aid offices, where salaries tended to be low, U.S. Attorneys' offices would not assign women to the criminal division. Pace-setting law firms wanted no women lawyers; prestigious clerkships were off-limits to women. Up until 1971, only three women in the Supreme Court's entire history had ever served as a Justice's law clerk. As of July 1972 there had never been a woman member of the legal staff at the Solicitor General's office.

All that now lies on history's scrap heap, and I am confident there will be no return to the old ways. The brightest signal of the changed complexion of our profession is the appointment of Sandra Day O'Connor

---

6. Curtis J. Berger, Land Ownership and Use: Cases, Statutes, and Other Materials (Boston: Little, Brown, 1968).

7. James J. White, Women in the Law, 65 Mich. L. Rev. 1051 (1967).

to the Supreme Court. Even on that highest court, I predict that within the decade women's place will no longer be singular.

With women at the bar (and even on the bench) no longer curiosities, bar associations, law schools, law firms, and other organizations are beginning to consider the question, does that development have any ramifications for our operations? Is women's participation in the legal profession in numbers affecting the way law business is conducted? It may be too soon for definitive answers. Early conjecture, I think, was short-sighted.

My first encounter with the question—what will women's participation mean?—occurred at the Association of American Law Schools' Annual Meeting in 1971. Conversation was stimulated by the prediction that a law school populated by as many women as men was not very far down the road. One of the participants in the discussion, after a moment of apparent insecurity, smiled, confident again as law professors often are, and said with assurance, business would go on as usual, nothing significant would change. What were women lawyers after all? Simply soft men.

A colleague added the following view. Women lawyers come in two varieties. First, there are the social workers, the ones that devote themselves to the poor and the oppressed, the truly needy. That type was not cause for concern. The social workers do not figure at all in the real world of legal business, the professor said. Second, there are the backstagers, women who would find congenial work in drafting wills and contracts, and research and brief writing. The rough-and-tumble, knock-down-drag-out adversary confrontations would continue, as always, he concluded, with hard men center stage.

As I see it, the social-worker stereotype of women earning law degrees in the 1950s and 1960s does hold up to this extent: many of those women are sympathetic to and active in humanitarian causes. But so are many men who have experienced discrimination or sensed the injustice of subordinate status, assigned without regard to one's ability or individual potential to achieve.

I would like to close by borrowing some lines from sociologist Cynthia Fuchs Epstein's book just off the press, titled *Women in Law*.[8] Professor Epstein documents how women have succeeded in making their way into law schools and the legal profession, despite the fact that they were not wanted. That women lawyers have done well, Professor Epstein concludes, is not surprising to any but the prejudiced. She predicts, and I share her view, that not only will women at the bar continue to do well, they will do so with a certain idealism and humanity, simply because those qualities are expected from them. But Professor Epstein urges, and

---

8. Cynthia Fuchs Epstein, Women in Law (New York: Basic Books, 1981).

again I agree, that society not assign to women, simply because they are women, the role of guardian of social consciousness. Humane concern, she writes, ought not be labeled "women's work"; it should be the work of all. And law schools, as I see it, have an important role in encouraging students to pursue that concern throughout their careers at the bar.

[32]

Kingsfield and Kennedy: Reappraising the Male Models of Law School Teaching

Catharine W. Hantzis

Many of us have struggled with the difficult and complex question of how best to teach our students. On one level, we ask: What are the best ways to convey information and skills to our students? How can we do it effectively in classes of fifty, eighty, one hundred, or more? On another level, we ask: What do our students need to know in order to become good lawyers? On yet a deeper level, the issue is political. Do we as women teachers make law school productive and rewarding for our women students? Do we promote nonsexist values that make it harder for the lawyers we train to dismiss the achievements of their female colleagues? Do we lead students to thoughtful questions about the larger society or are we simply one cog in a wheel that transforms a group of idealistic young people into fodder for large firms?

There is nothing inherently gendered about aspiring to good teaching. The same problems trouble many of our male colleagues. Nevertheless, the prevailing styles of classroom teaching and the sexism of many law students create special problems for us as women teachers. Sexism in the classroom is real, and it poses a genuine obstacle to the realization of educational goals. Sexism will not disappear from the classroom as long as it is pervasive in the surrounding society. It will create dilemmas for women teachers as long as our institutions remain only weakly committed to confronting it. Despite the unfairness of a gender handicap, our commitment as teachers requires that we creatively seek ways to prevent sexism from interfering with effective communication and effective teaching. This article seeks to further the analysis of gender in the law classroom by directly confronting and reappraising two paradigms of legal instruction that have had an influential role in constructing the classroom experience. The first is the popular image of Professor Kingsfield as the ultimate first-year law teacher.[1] The second is Duncan Kennedy's image of the law teacher as social revolutionary.[2] It is my hope that the reappraisal of both images will lead to further debate about classroom issues and that it will facilitate a distinctively feminist approach to these issues.

Catharine W. Hantzis is Associate Professor of Law, University of Southern California Law Center. This paper was given at the October 1987 meeting of the AALS Section on Women in Legal Education in Washington, D.C.

1. John J. Osborne, The Paper Chase (Boston, 1971).
2. This image stems from Kennedy's critique of legal education in Legal Education and the Reproduction of Hierarchy, *infra* note 3.

I. Kingsfield

Law students learn about law school teaching long before they enter their first law school class. Books, movies, and even television shows have shaped their expectations of what should occur in their classes. Typically such sources portray the professor as a rather distinguished-looking older gentleman who stands at the center of a large amphitheater armed only with his trusted casebook. He begins the class by calling on a student to recite the facts of the day's case. If the student can manage an adequate response, the professor proceeds with a series of questions about the reasoning of the case that inevitably leads the student towards a question to which there is no possible answer. At this point, the professor tries another student (usually one who has volunteered), who resolves the problem by rejecting one or more of the first student's assumptions. As the semester progresses, the competition intensifies as aggressive students actively seek the ultimate prize—the public esteem (or, for some, the lack of public disdain) of the eminent professor himself.

Notably lacking from these fictional accounts of the law school classroom are women professors or even women law students. While female students sit passively in the classroom in substantial numbers, their contribution to the plot mostly consists of hesitant, frightened answers when (infrequently) they are called upon, and supportive statements to their fellow male students who have been humiliated publicly by the "brilliant" professor.

The Kingsfield image is, one hopes, frightfully out of date. It is not just that the picture is exclusively male but that his classroom is awash with silent tension. Kingsfield is both boorish and pompous. He repeatedly affirms values of the highest intellectual excellence, yet he accepts from his students as correct the most question-begging doctrinal responses. Surely legal education has better teachers than Kingsfield—teachers who favor humor over tension, policy over doctrine, and encouragement and instruction over competition and ridicule.

Although Kingsfield is most certainly not the norm of law school teaching, he is, even in his absence, a dominant figure in student expectations. For many students, his central place in the popular conception of legal education legitimates his classroom style and renders marginal and suspect efforts by others to adopt different instructional techniques. The problem this poses for many thoughtful law school teachers is especially acute for women because the Kingsfield image is so exclusively male. If a man who resembles Kingsfield leaves a student confused and suffering from low self-esteem, *that* is to be expected. If, on the other hand, a woman teacher fails to make confusing material crystal clear, the student's confusion is the result of *her* bad teaching. The Kingsfield image excuses and legitimates failures of communication and instruction for any law school teacher who has enough in common with Kingsfield to be perceived as Kingsfield. It places a heavy burden on the non-Kingsfields among us to insure that our teaching is effective, since our failures may be seen *as failures* precisely because we have deviated from the perceived norm.

It is true that many of our students are grateful for the deviation. They are happy not to be bored or scared; they like experimenting with new ideas in an atmosphere in which the price of failure is not too high. Yet some part of them will feel that this is not the *real* law school experience, that they are not receiving sufficiently rigorous instruction, and that their desire to compete for the professor's esteem cannot be sufficiently rewarded by a teacher who has not enhanced the value of praise by humiliating other students. With these grumblings and dissatisfactions on the periphery of our classrooms, it is often difficult to focus on the instructional task as we ourselves have defined it.

Although many of us would be happy if Kingsfield had never been invented, we should not skip too quickly over the educational advantages his form of instruction offers. It is probably the fear of Kingsfield—real or imagined—that makes first-year law students among the most highly motivated students in the university. The kinds of effort that command respect from Kingsfield are clear. Students know that cases must be read carefully, that the "gist" of the legal rule is never sufficient, and that all the details must be mastered. The court's decision can never be taken at face value; it must be compared with other cases in the book and even with cases the student must invent. To the extent that good lawyering involves such skills, teachers who reject the Kingsfield approach must find an acceptable alternative.

I make this point because there is a tendency for beginning women teachers to be a sort of "Kingsfield in a Different Voice." In the process we may replicate all the bad parts of Kingsfield—the unvaried case method, the rigid classroom style—and lose all the things Kingsfield does right. Thus we may not tell students they are wrong. We may be reluctant and uncertain in revealing our own point of view. We may try to run the class democratically by putting important matters up to a vote. We may fail to give a clear message to students about what is expected and to encourage them to extra effort. This halfway approach is certainly not an improvement on the original. Nor is it sound educational technique.

II. Kennedy

The Kennedy paradigm of law school teaching does not arise out of popular culture, but instead finds its home specifically within the legal educational community. Kennedy's views on the law school classroom and its effect on students are described in several versions of his essay "Legal Education and the Reproduction of Hierarchy."[3] In addition, some version of this paradigm has been taught in his first-year classes at Harvard Law School since the early seventies. Because many of the younger generation of law school teachers encountered Kennedy or someone similar in their first year, the critique of legal education Kennedy espouses has become, even for those of us who do not agree with it, part of the shared vocabulary and symbolism with which we think and talk about our roles as law school teachers. Thus, Kennedy's paradigm is part of the raw material from which we construct our vision of the possibilities and limitations of our professional role.

3. I am relying on the text in 32 J. Legal Educ. 591 (1982).

Kennedy's critique has three main points. First, the law school classroom is marked by a disparity of power (a "hierarchy") between teacher and students. The law professor uses ineffective and even needlessly mystifying educational techniques that, when combined with the professor's gratuitous aggression and didactic assaultiveness, produce an oppressive atmosphere. Second, the oppression and mystification in the classroom are not random, but are aimed at influencing or coercing students to accept their place in the real-world hierarchy and at teaching proper hierarchical behavior. Finally, piecemeal reform of legal education will never do. The only appropriate response is to organize against hierarchy in the law school community and to form a left-wing bourgeois intellectual community that might ally itself with a mass movement aimed at liberating all people from oppression.

There is a great deal of common sense at the heart of Kennedy's vision. Kingsfield is not a good teacher nor is there much in his teaching style that encourages students to develop independent minds or make sensitive ethical choices. There is, however, much in Kennedy's critique of legal education that is not just false but disempowering (indeed silencing and coercive) to law students and faculty alike.

A. *Kennedy's Descriptive Claims*

Much of what Kennedy describes in his "typical" law school classroom does not resonate with my experiences either as a student or as a teacher. I do not teach cold cases (boring legalistic cases) and hot cases (cases in which "overriding" legal reasons lead to a grossly unfair result) in the way he describes.[4] I believe that courts should always strive to do justice between the parties. I do not teach what Kennedy terms the "intellectual core of the ideology"[5]—that there is a split between law and policy. Indeed, it is necessary to remind students frequently that law and policy are not distinct and that traditional examples of "legal" arguments are really appeals to policy. Students, Kennedy charges, are bullied into accepting bad arguments:

> Teachers convince students that legal reasoning exists, and is different from policy analysis, by bullying them into accepting as valid in particular cases arguments about legal correctness that are circular, question begging, incoherent, or so vague as to be meaningless. Sometimes these are just arguments from authority, with the validity of the authoritative premise put outside discussion by professorial fiat. Sometimes they are policy arguments (e.g. security of transactions, business certainty) that are treated in a particular situation as though they were rules that everyone accepts but that will be ignored in the next case when they would suggest that the decision was wrong. Sometimes they are exercises in formal logic that wouldn't stand up for a minute between equals.[6]

I am certain that I have occasionally fallen into errors of this kind. I regard such practices as intellectually lazy and poor teaching and strive in my class preparation to eliminate them. Although I am willing to acknowl-

---

4. *Id.* at 594.
5. *Id.* at 596.
6. *Id.* at 596-7.

edge that these things do happen in my classroom, I regard them not as the central and legitimate practice but rather as mistakes in urgent need of improvement.

I do not want to overstate the importance of the factual discrepancies between Kennedy's experience and my own. Theories of oppression and social change do not necessarily have to be based upon descriptive claims that are accurate for everyone or even statistically accurate for the oppressed group. All social theories, to some degree, center attention upon certain kinds of experience and marginalize the remainder. This does not mean that such theories are immune from questions concerning their factual bases. If the elimination of oppression is the aim, certainly some deference must be paid to the experience of oppressed persons. A theory of racism based entirely upon the experience of white people would be woefully incomplete. Similarly, a description of classroom oppression that fails to take seriously the experience of students within the classroom will not provide a meaningful foundation either for educational reform or for radical change. Perhaps for this reason, Kennedy attempts to describe legal education from the perspective of two "left" students.

The first such student is a liberal idealist who came to law school believing that social justice can be obtained by "guaranteeing people their rights and bringing about the triumph of human rights over mere property rights."[7] This student is entirely confused and defused by the law school experience. Once (s)he believed that the assertion of rights could remedy oppression. Now (s)he sadly realizes that the enforcement of rights will not transform society. It is not just that "rights" talk is ineffective, it is that rights are an inherent part of the legal reality that oppresses. Rights discourse contributes to the problem by legitimating irrational choices and by silencing certain demands for social reform. As Kennedy puts it: "Because [rights discourse] is logically incoherent and manipulable, traditionally individualist, and willfully blind to the realities of substantive inequality, rights discourse is a trap."[8] Thus, the liberal idealist confronts a depressing choice: either flounder in the rights discourse trap or give up his or her social agenda.

A second kind of student does not fare much better, even though equipped with Marxist ideology. This student adopts either "a conspiracy theory, in which judges deliberately subordinate 'justice' (usually just a left liberal-rights theory) to the short run financial interests of the ruling class, or a much more subtle thesis about the 'logic' or 'needs' or 'structural perquisites' of a particular 'stage of monopoly capitalism.'"[9] The difficulties the Marxist student faces in reinterpreting the law to fit this particular model are two-fold. First, there is too much law, too much doctrine (or—as Kennedy puts it—"too much drek") to be subsumed into the general theory. Second, such theories treat legal rules and doctrine as "window dressing" produced by the power alignments in a capitalist system, rather than acknowledging that the legal order is itself an integral part of the

7. *Id.* at 598.
8. *Id.*
9. *Id.* at 599.

"equation of power" in a capitalist system.[10] The Marxist student is stopped dead in the tracks of social revolution by the need to debunk and destroy the formal rules of capitalism. Since this is a task that can never be completed, the student becomes but one more paralyzed victim of the law school and the legal ideology it deploys.

The problem with these students, Kennedy argues, is that they possess "no base for the mastery of ambivalence"; their theories "provide no more than an emotional stance against the system."[11] Indeed it takes an "extraordinary student" to achieve the "theoretically critical attitude" necessary to avoid being paralyzed by the law school experience.[12] Common sense might suggest that it would be qualities such as maturity and a healthy sense of proportion that would save this student from the snare of legal ideology. Students who have some experience of the outside world and understand that formal law is but one element of social change should not be ideologically hogtied by the law school experience. But Kennedy's "extraordinary student" is not such a person. The "extraordinary" student must "know enough to figure out where the teacher is fudging, misrepresenting or otherwise distorting legal thinking and legal reality."[13] Such a student achieves what other more ordinary students do not— intellectual mastery of the entire legal system. By contrast, ordinary students possess only an emotional reaction against the system; they lack an objective intellectual position from which to speak their critique.

From a feminist perspective, Kennedy's vision contains some important kernels of truth. His description of the problem rings true. Idealistic students do experience much of what Kennedy describes. What is wrong is his purported solution. Liberation is not achieved by knowing everything or by obtaining an objective and exhaustive intellectual stance. Defending one's idealism means having the courage of one's convictions—listening to the intellect but understanding that questions of right and wrong are often questions of feeling and experience. The "extraordinary" student is elitist and male.[14] He represents the false hope that we can understand oppression from the point of view of a neutral observer and, in so doing, think our way out of it at last.

B. Kennedy's Normative Vision

One way to see what is wrong with Kennedy's vision is to look at who it marginalizes and who it centralizes, who speaks and who is silenced. Looking through Kennedy's glasses, we can see clearly only one kind of teacher: Kingsfield. We recognize him not only from his pomposity and brutality but also from his slavish devotion to doctrine and his rigid reluctance to engage in discussions of method or theory. The non-

---

10. *Id.*
11. *Id.* at 599.
12. *Id.* at 598.
13. *Id.*
14. Literally. When Kennedy speaks of the liberal idealist and Marxist students, the pronouns are female. With the "exceptional" student, however, the pronouns are male. See, e.g., *id.* at 598.

Kingsfields are totally marginalized. The "softies," with their "mushy" niceness and willingness to discuss policy, are dismissed as unpopular and ineffective teachers.[15] Minority professors and female professors are similarly marginalized: "Teachers are overwhelmingly white, male, and middle class, and most (by no means all) black and women law teachers give the impression of thorough assimilation to that style or of insecurity and unhappiness."[16] Thus, despite the presence of minorities, women, and "softies," Kingsfield is still the only member of the law school faculty who counts. It is no wonder that he dominates not only the classroom but also the students growing understanding of the professional world they are about to encounter.

The theory is not only marginalizing to nonwhite male faculty, it is also disempowering to students. At the CLS conference on racism, several minority scholars criticized the CLS critique of rights for failing to describe their experience.[17] To call rights talk empty rhetoric and to blame it for legitimating an oppressive ideology is to belittle the experience of people for whom rights have played an important role both in the transformation of their own consciousness and in their assertion of claims upon the system. I agree with this criticism and I also suggest that the critique of rights does not adequately describe my experience. In addition, it seems to me that students could make a similar point about Kennedy's vision of the classroom. In his vision, students have no right to good teaching, not just because they have no rights under the critique of rights but also because there is no such thing as good teaching because of the classroom hierarchy. Clearly, there is no surer way to disempower people than to tell them that nothing can improve their present situation short of total reorganization of the social structure.

Finally, Kennedy's essay is what I shall call "studentist." If professors oppress students in ways that are analogous to gender or racial oppression, then it should not surprise us that a professor writing about students should engage in a certain amount of negative stereotyping. The essay is replete with references to what "most students" believe, think, or feel. There are apparently no individual students in Kennedy's classroom. Kennedy can know what "most students" are feeling because he presumes that they are dominated by the oppression in the classroom. In fact, my own experience with students suggests an incredible diversity in how they experience law school. True, some students find it oppressive, but a significant number do not. Respect for students means that we should not so easily dismiss their actual thoughts and feelings as false consciousness.

---

15. *Id.* at 593.
16. *Id.* at 605.
17. Some of the papers from the January 7, 1987, conference are reprinted in 22 Harv. C.R.-C.L. L. Rev. 297–447 (1987): Richard Delgado, The Ethereal Scholar: Does Critical Legal Studies Have What Minorities Want?; Mari J. Matsuda, Looking to the Bottom: Critical Legal Studies and Reparations; Patricia J. Williams, Alchemical Notes: Reconstructed Ideals from Deconstructed Rights; Harlon L. Dalton, The Clouded Prism.

III. A Female Model of a Law School Teacher

It should be obvious that I believe that women are well advised to discard both Kingsfield and Kennedy as classroom role models. Beyond Kingsfield's intellectual rigidity and Kennedy's jeering cynicism lies a largely uncharted territory for feminist teachers, the outlines of which I would like to sketch. While it is true that too few of us have had the experience of being taught by women law teachers, most of us have had ample opportunities to observe both excellent women lawyers and excellent women teachers. My suggestion is that we draw a new and female picture of the law school teacher from these two images. The result is a teacher who is both practical and student centered. Her classes are aimed at teaching students and not at placing her own brilliance on display. She wants students to learn the material and to become mature, responsible, and reasonably happy human beings. While many of the details of her presence remain unclear, I think I see her well enough to know what she might suggest by way of practical advice.[18]

A. Spend Time with Your Students

Like Kennedy, many of us engage in "studentist" stereotyping. Discussions of teaching are frequently punctuated with such phrases as "students aren't interested in . . ." or "students want to be spoon fed." Such talk distances us from our students and distorts communication. Do not assume that you know what your students think or want. If you ask them, you may be surprised by the range of attitudes. Spending time with students does not mean that you must become best friends or an *ex officio* member of the student-hangout gang. Arriving in class a few minutes early and talking about the day's material is one way to find out where to pitch the class discussion. Having lunch with a colleague or friend in the student lunchroom also makes it possible to talk to students informally. Such conversations help you to replace names and faces with personalities and backgrounds, thus making communication more effective. By revealing how much students have understood and what they find difficult or confusing, informed conversations can also help you assess the class more accurately.

B. Show Your Students That You Care

If you ask students what they dislike about law school, many will say that it is the impersonal atmosphere generated by large classes and the traditional manner of instruction. Extra class-preparation hours spent mastering cases and law review articles may not be as helpful to students as a few extra hours spent on more direct methods of instruction. It is possible

---

18. The following suggestions are not original with me. They have arisen from many conversations with colleagues. Some of the suggestions come from a teaching workshop held on September 12, 1987, in San Francisco by West Coast Femcrits that featured presentations by Herma Hill Kay and Barbara Babcock. Others come from many sources, but I would particularly like to acknowledge Taunya Banks, Pat Cain, Tom Griffith, Jean Love, Chris Littleton, Frances Raday, Peggy Radin, and Judi Resnik.

to divide a large class into small sections of twenty for some of its meetings.[19] Written handouts are also useful. It takes very little time to convert a section of your class notes into a simple handout that will make the class discussion clearer to students in addition to giving them a format for recording the results. Written exercises and practice exams can demonstrate to students that you care and help you assess how the class is doing and where you need to focus your attention.

C. Find a New Experience for Your Students

Many legal issues require not only mastering the legal materials but also coming to an understanding of other people's viewpoints. Since many law students are somewhat inured to political rhetoric, no amount of mere talking will convey this understanding. Nothing moves students more effectively than a new experience or experiencing a familiar thing from a new perspective. For example, Taunya Banks requires her students in disability law to spend several hours at the law school trying to take care of business in a wheelchair. In my Women and the Law class, students play a game called "Starpower"[20] that teaches a powerful lesson about discrimination and oppression. It is worth considering for every class whether there are any experiences that would help your students understand not just the legal theory but the way in which that theory affects people's lives. Field trips for a large class may be hard to arrange, but the educational benefits are likely to outweigh the practical difficulties.

Conclusion

I am well aware of (and not entirely comfortable with) the reformist spirit that pervades this essay. There is real oppression in the world and, on balance, the American legal system works to further that oppression. All of us who participate in the world in a reformist way must continually ask ourselves whether we are making conditions less oppressive for some people at the expense of perpetuating and legitimating institutions that are truly the source of the problem. I am not always sanguine about the answer to this question, but neither am I able to come up with an acceptable alternative.

Kennedy's own suggested alternatives are hardly radical in nature. He suggests that we organize around issues of hierarchy in the workplace and that we build a "left bourgeois intelligentsia that might one day join with a mass movement for the radical transformation of American society."[21] What separates these proposals from reformist ones in Kennedy's opinion is that they are to be executed in a "rebellious" and "risk-taking" mode. In

---

19. One year, I did this once a week in my corporations class. The quality of the resulting discussions about corporate responsibility and the ethics of corporate life more than repaid the extra effort.
20. The game is distributed by Simile, P.O. Box 910, Del Mar, California 92014.
21. Kennedy, *supra* note 2, at 610.

general, I am skeptical about the modes of action he suggests and doubt that they effectively distinguish his proposals from reformism. With respect to teaching, I cannot agree with his analysis. I teach because I believe that human beings can learn things that will help them flourish and grow. I want my students to become strong enough to make their own way in an increasingly confusing world. It follows, for me, that there is good teaching and bad teaching despite the classroom hierarchy, and that a good teacher will stress the possibilities of social growth and change rather than the relentless character of oppression.

Critical Legal Theory

The Law-School Curriculum in the 1980s: What's Left?

Karl E. Klare

I. Introduction

A premise of this article is that there is, to borrow a phrase, a difference between the "curriculum-in-action" and the "curriculum-on-the-books." By "the books" I mean law-school catalogs, curriculum-committee memoranda, and the like. Behind the formal curriculum there is a "hidden curriculum"[1] consisting of a set of very powerful although usually unarticulated messages about substantive law, the definition of professional role and expertise, and the possibilities of and constraints upon human freedom. These messages are contained in the instructional methods, the emotional setting of the classroom, and the social hierarchy of the law school, and in the array of course offerings and requirements, the sequencing and pacing of courses, and indeed in the overall structure of the formal curriculum.

Based on this premise, and speaking now of the total curriculum—formal and hidden—the following are my primary claims:

1. Law-school education does not, by and large, train students either to practice law or to engage in serious legal scholarship. Rather, the law-school curriculum disenfranchises students intellectually and disables and incapacitates them professionally. The primary function of law schooling is to prepare and to socialize students for entry into a very narrow range of career lines.

Karl E. Klare is Professor of Law, Northeastern University School of Law; he was a member of the Visiting Faculty, Legal Sevices Institute, 1981–82. This article is the edited text of a presentation at the plenary session of the 1982 Annual Meeting, Association of American Law Schools, Philadelphia, PA.

1. After initially drafting this paper I learned that Prof. Cramton employs this concept. See Roger C. Cramton, The Ordinary Religion of the Law School Classroom, 29 J. Legal Educ. 247, 252–53 (1978):

   > The sources of the world view represented by "the ordinary religion of the law school classroom" [include] ... the informal or hidden curriculum that encompasses what students learn apart from the formal curriculum.... As in other educational settings, the "hidden curriculum" may be as important as the formal curriculum—the total learning environment influences what students learn.

   A colleague has called my attention to a book of that name. See Benson R. Snyder, The Hidden Curriculum (New York: Knopf, 1971).

●1982 by the Association of American Law Schools. Cite as 32 J. Legal Educ. 336 (1982).

2. Curriculum design operates on the assumption that training in the practice of law should occur *in* the practice of law. The economics of practice are such that for the most part only the large firms and some of the government agencies are set up to provide systematic on-the-job training. It is therefore a latent assumption of curriculum design that if the law schools have any responsibility at all to the consumers of legal services, it is only to those who are wealthy enough to afford big-firm counsel.[2]

3. The primary ways that the law-school curriculum disables and socializes students are: (a) by the systematic manufacturing of false consciousness; (b) by instilling a distinct set of social and moral attitudes in students; and (c) by ignoring or denigrating training in the intellectual and interpersonal capacities needed to practice and study law successfully.

4. Curriculum is designed to serve the needs, cater to the interests and abilities, and legitimate the power of law teachers, *not* to train law students.

After elaborating on these points, I will conclude by offering some brief prescriptions for curricular reform. My central thesis is that the law-school curriculum will not change very much until we—i.e., law teachers—change ourselves and our professional identities.

II. How the Law-School Curriculum Disables Students[3]

A. The Structure of the Curriculum[4]

What are the ideological and emotional messages in the contemporary curriculum? How does the curriculum disable students intellectually? To begin with, I would focus on the enormous significance of the overall structure of the curriculum. The key to that structure is the division and contrast between a tightly constructed first-year experience overwhelmingly focused on common-law doctrine, on the one hand, and, on the other, an upper-level experience loosely structured to the point of disintegration, consisting of a *mélange* or hodge-podge of public and private law

---

2. This is not to claim that poor people, unions, small enterprises, and other less-well-off clients never recieve first-rate legal services but only to assert that law schools are entitled to little credit if they do receive such service.

3. The stereotyped portrait of curriculum drawn here admittedly does not do justice to the diversity of American law schools, particularly those outside the most elite group. I believe the generalizations are useful and telling, however, because the instructional methods and curricular organization adopted by the elite law schools are widely copied and diffused throughout American legal education. Indeed, the vast majority of law teachers were trained at a remarkably small and homogeneous group of schools. See Roger C. Cramton, The Current State of the Law Curriculum, 32 J. Legal Educ. 321, 324 (1982); see also The Chronicle of Higher Education, Nov. 10, 1982, at 2, col. 3 (American Bar Foundation study shows that 20 top law schools produced 59 percent of all law professors in the United States in 1975-76).

4. The following argument draws heavily on Duncan Kennedy, The Political Significance of the Structure of the Law School Curriculum (unpublished paper delivered to the Faculty Seminar, University of Victoria Law School, Victoria, British Columbia, February 1980).

courses the only "unity" of which is their focus on doctrine, legal reasoning, and conventional modes of social policy analysis.

This structure sets up and constantly accentuates a set of contrasts between public and private law. The core of the curriculum (here I refer not to the number of hours allocated but to the way the curriculum is experienced by students), the portion that is presented as *hard, precise, lawyer-like, reasoned, judicious,* as the product of *"legal thinking,"* is the set of rules associated with the nineteenth-century vision of the market and private ordering as the central institutional basis for organizing social life. Real contemporary social problems, for example, the problems of occupational safety or of the poor consumers are not dealt with and cannot be dealt with in the first-year courses like torts or contracts. Such matters are "deferred" to advanced courses, and naturally so, because most significant social problems today are governed by statute or other complex legal institutions (like collective bargaining) and are therefore not suitable for the instructional mode common in the first year. The underlying message is that doctrine, particularly private law doctrine, is *rigorous.* Private law is governed by a technique of higher-order reasoning the mastery of which is the key to becoming a lawyer or at least the key to being rewarded in law school. Whatever particular instructors might say to the contrary, the curriculum presents the common law as containing a deep, inner rationality and coherence, or at least an adaptative potential. The legitimating aspects of the common law are ignored.

Since the 1930s at least, we have also accepted the public law courses into the curricular fold on a deferred and dispersed basis. Their deferred placement and smorgasbord treatment conveys the message that they are neither central to the definition of lawyers' skills (as opposed, perhaps, to their billing logs) nor are they coherent. Rather, they are *interstitial, mushy, political, ad hoc;* they are the courses in which major doctrinal developments turn on fortuities like the mustering of five votes in the Supreme Court.

These courses deal with a set of incremental government interventions in a market-centered regime, and the predominant discourse revolves around the appropriateness of such interventions, as though the market were not itself a regulatory system. The discourse does not revolve around the fundamental assumptions underlying public regulatory modes. For example, in labor law we discuss the appropriateness of this or that incursion on managerial prerogative. We do not ordinarily talk about who should own the means of production, or how work might be organized so as to make it a rewarding, developmental experience.[5]

---

5. This phenomenon cannot be explained on the grounds that such questions do not pose "legal issues." See, e.g., United Steel Workers of America, Local 1330 v. United States Steel Corp. 492 F. Supp. 1 (N.D. Ohio, 1980), aff'd. in part and vacated and remanded in part, 631 F. 2d 1264 (6th Cir. 1980) (ordinarily workers do not, by virtue of their labors, obtain a property right in the means of

The very structure of the law-school curriculum, then, is emblematic of the notion that the core of private property and private ordering arrangements constitutive of nineteenth-century capitalism is rational, structured, and central to the lawyering identity, and that to the extent that those arrangements need to be reconsidered, updated, or refashioned, the appropriate mode of doing so is through public law reform *via* interstitial, ad hoc adjustments, that is, chiefly through regulation of the type championed during the New Deal. From this powerful set of symbolic messages law students learn that the only lawyer-like way to view the world is *moderately,* through the window of moderate conservatism or liberal reformism. They learn that the only lawyer-like way to think about social change is in terms of atomized, marginal, incremental reform through governmental regulation of private conduct, i.e., that the New Deal represents the outer boundary of human wisdom in the art of politics. Finally, they learn that lawyers do not possess intellectual skills and preoccupations appropriate to discussion and analysis of fundamental issues of social and political organization and thoroughgoing social change. Inculcation of this one-sided array of political lessons inhibits students' intellectual progress.

B. The Emphasis On Doctrine

A second disabling feature of the law-school curriculum arises from the fact that almost the entire content of what we teach is doctrinal analysis. A typical criticism of this aspect of the law-school curriculum is that the overcommitment to doctrine prevents us from doing other valuable things, like "skills training." This is not my criticism. Indeed, properly understood, training in doctrinal analysis is a *form* of skills training which has an appropriate place in the law-school curriculum. My objection is on other grounds and has two interrelated components. First, we do not teach doctrinal analysis well because the curriculum takes the idea of legal reasoning seriously. Second, the purpose of stressing legal reasoning in the law-school curriculum is not to train students but to instill in them a certain ideological message that will be described below.

An inescapable signal is conveyed by the hidden curriculum, by the years of sitting through hierarchical classes in which the instructor guides students through doctrinal mazes toward correct answers. The message is that legal reasoning is a distinct mode of analysis that is in the possession of the legal profession and that it is the job of law students to master. The premise so carefully inculcated by our teaching is that this special mode of reasoning is capable of taking us from legal premises (e.g., precedents,

---

production); and NLRB v. Yeshiva University, 100 S. Ct. 856 (1980) (employees, like some university professors, whose work is at least in part a self-governed, developmental experience are not "employees" within the meaning of the National Labor Relations Act).

notions of rights or of social policy) to determinate answers, determinate solutions in particular cases, without resort to political or ethical choice.

This claim about legal reasoning—that it is autonomous from political and ethical choice—is a falsehood. It is a very important falsehood, because it legitimates the power of common-law judges and of the legal profession. But a falsehood it is nonetheless. To the extent that we induce our students by three years of doctrinal emphasis to believe in this vision of legal reasoning, we cripple them as legal thinkers.

Legal reasoning exists primarily as an array of highly stylized modes of justificatory rhetoric. From the standpoint of logic—as opposed, for example, to the perspectives of anthropology or hermeneutics—there simply is no necessity or determinacy to legal reasoning, no inner compulsion to its methods. Legal reasoning is a texture of openness, indeterminacy, and contradiction. Students need to know that in order to work creatively as advocates and analysts. To be *empowered* as legal thinkers our students must be totally freed from the tyranny of belief in the false coherence or compellingness of legal argument. But in fact our teaching leads ineluctably in the opposite direction, toward reinforcing the mistaken belief that legal reasoning accounts for legal results.

Intensive practice in doctrinal analysis would be a useful form of skills training if it were designed to accomplish the goal of acquainting students with the indeterminate character of legal reasoning. For example, a recurring law-school exercise is to identify the conflict between the respective advantages of "bright-line" rules and discretionary standards. Strict rules are thought to offer the desirable features of predictability, protection of settled expectations, promotion of judicial subordination to the legislature, and so on. Discretionary standards, on the other hand, are thought to be more amenable to appropriate application in the light of factual complexity and to the impulse to do equity in particular cases. It would be useful to train students to be able to take either plaintiff's or defendant's side of a case and to generate a persuasive argument on behalf of the client that tilts either toward a strict rule or toward a discretionary standard. But this is not the standard classroom fare. Rather, the typical outcome of the lesson is an overt suggestion or implicit innuendo that the case can be decided on the basis of the need for a rule or standard.[6] Likewise, in any case in which a right or a policy is asserted our students ought to be

---

6. Law teachers will often acknowledge that while the rule/standard distinction may be incapable of resolving a particular case, this conceptual apparatus does provide a compelling overall orientation to decision making in various areas of the law. (Thus, e.g., "strict rules foster the predictability needed in the law of sales, but open-ended standards are the appropriate guides for resolving child custody disputes.") The untenability of such a position is demonstrated in Duncan Kennedy, Form and Substance In Private Law Adjudication, 89 Harv. L. Rev. 1685, 1694-1713 (1976). This is not to say that it is impossible to observe judges and legal scholars formulating a consistent attitude toward the formal character of certain kinds of legal rules. It is to assert that such consistency derives not from the force of logic but from the ideological and symbolic cohesiveness of a particular legal world view.

trained to be able to articulate a countervailing right or social policy and to argue persuasively either to plaintiff's or to defendant's side of the case from each of the two rights or policy perspectives. But again, the usual outcome of the law-school class is the suggestion that analysis ("balancing") of conflicting rights and policy concerns is a process capable of resolving cases.

Although highly overrated, doctrinal manipulation of the kind I have described is demanded in the practice of law and is therefore entitled to a place in law training. Moreover, success at this type of doctrinal manipulation tends to emancipate students from belief in the false necessity of legal reasoning, and it is therefore valuable for that reason as well. But that is not what we teach. We teach legal reasoning as though doctrine had a determinate meaning, as though doctrinal analysis were capable of resolving cases without resort to political and moral choice. We teach legal reasoning as though enduring principles of social organization were embedded in the logic of the doctrines themselves (as opposed to the political and ethical meanings of the doctrines).

Imparting such beliefs in the autonomous necessity of legal reasoning denies our students access to the insight that they can only understand and they can only work creatively with legal rules by situating them in their cultural, moral, and political contexts. That is, they can only understand legal rules when they possess the tools of interdisciplinary social analysis.

C. The Emotional Content of and Silences in the Hidden Curriculum

A series of emotional messages is imparted and reinforced by the hidden curriculum. Particularly important is the intensity, confusion, and scariness of the first year, and the malaise and boredom of the upper-level program. Students learn from the emotional content of the law curriculum that they ought to distrust their own deepest moral sensibilities; that they ought to avoid global moral and political inquiry (because it is dangerous, simplistic, and unlawyer-like); that they ought to revere hierarchy; and that manipulating vulnerable people is an acceptable form of professional behavior.

What is left out of the law-school curriculum? Omitted is systematic training in how to learn from others; in how to criticize one's own work and the work of others; in how to learn about lawyering *from* practice, that is, in how to acquire the capacity for continuing self-development over the span of a career; and in how one might act in the central relationships that constitute the lawyering process: adversary, client, coworker relationships, and so on. Omitted also is systematic training in how to work closely and cooperatively with others in situations of high vulnerability and high risk and, finally, in how to think critically about morals and politics based on the best learning available from the social sciences and from ethical discourse.

III. Barriers to Change and Sources of Renewal

Why is the curriculum organized this way? Most fundamentally because curriculum is designed to justify the power of professors, not to serve students' needs. A doctrine-focused, case-method curriculum, structured around legal categories derived from common-law pleading and conventional definitions of public regulatory programs, is designed to base legal education on what law teachers do best and what they have been rewarded for doing well in the past. It is calculated to center legal education on what law teachers do with maximum authority, the least preparation, and the least exposure to the risk that students might have superior insight to theirs. The skills, capacities, and interests of most law teachers do not equip us to organize legal education in other ways, for example, upon a fieldwork-based, clinical model.

In this respect, not much has changed over the years from the time when Langdellian orthodoxy took hold. The Langdell model of a graduate program in pure law taught by the case method insulated the law professoriat from the rest of the academic community, justified its professional role, and, very important at the time, neatly tied in with nativist and class prejudice.[7] The legal realist revolution promised a great deal but was largely aborted in the area of curriculum reform, primarily because of the underdevelopment of the realists' social theory.[8]

The only truly seismic change in modern curriculum and law pedagogy came with the clinical education revolution of the past decade. A great promise of clinical legal education is that it poses fundamental challenges to the inadequacies of our curriculum. Precisely for that reason, clinical legal education has been disadvantaged and marginalized within the law-school hierarchy. As a result it also faces internal difficulties, such as the underdevelopment of its theoretical dimensions and, most recently, a tendency toward drift away from its initial political moorings.

What's left in the discussion of curriculum in the postrealist era? Many attempts to put back together the shattered myth that legal reasoning and legal education are apolitical, and many strategies of denial: denial that there is a problem, denial of the incalculable contribution of clinical legal education, and denial of the need for law teachers to become equipped with new theoretical and pedagogical capacities that they do not, by and large, presently possess.

---

7. On the rise and triumph of the Langdell model of legal education, see generally Alfred S. Konefsky & John H. Schlegel, Mirror, Mirror On the Wall: Histories of American Law Schools, 95 Harv. L. Rev. 833 (1982).

8. See Rand Rosenblatt, Legal Theory and Legal Education, 79 Yale L. J. 1153, 1172 (1970):

> [I]n education [the legal realists] realized that a new "method" of interpreting cases opened up large questions about how to study society and the legal system. But they tended to evade these questions through vague ideals of craft addressed primarily to pragmatic technique, and not directly to the difficult issues of what values the profession should support, how manpower should be allocated and paid for, and what kinds of intellectual, material, and political developments were required to realize their social and educational ideals.

Yet there are potential sources of change and renewal in the coming decade. Most important is the survival and growth of clinical models. The rapidly changing political climate in which we live—particularly the crisis into which liberalism has plunged—must prompt a rethinking of approaches to law and legal pedagogy. In this context, my hope is that the critical legal theory movement will offer positive contributions to legal education and, indeed, that it might show us that something is left.

IV. Proposals for Change

With that last hope in mind, the following proposals are offered for purposes of discussion. The law-school curriculum should be divided into three roughly equal components of (1) doctrinal analysis, (2) closely supervised, field-based clinical experience, and (3) advanced training in cultural and social analysis, that is, in political economy, anthropology, philosophy, and so on. Substantive law ought to be taught in each of the three settings, organized around inquiry into various social problems and relationships but without a separation between public law and private law learning.

Many others have defended the virtues of clinical training. Perhaps I should add a few words regarding the role of social theory in legal education. My proposal does not see theoretical training as a mere adjunct to law study or an opportunity to explore "higher" questions underplayed in the traditional curriculum. Rather, giving access to social theoretical tools is conceived as a way of helping students fundamentally to understand judicial action and other aspects of the legal process by cradling legal rules in their lived historical and cultural contexts. Only thus can we emancipate students from the mistaken belief that legal reasoning is capable of autonomously accounting for legal results. Emphasis on theoretical learning in the law-school curriculum would serve to bring a sense of totality and coherence to students' understanding of the common-law experience. Finally, it could empower students both by combating the frightening sense of disintegration, particularly in first-year legal education, and also by providing students intellectual tools they need in order to think with sophistication about the legal process.

Curriculum reform of the type advocated would obviously require massive changes in the law professoriate. Incumbent law teachers would be obliged to acquire new capabilities and capacities in practice and/or in social analysis. New teachers would be trained and recruited on a like basis. Change of the kind advocated or, indeed, any sort of serious curriculum reform, is simply impossible unless and until we retrain ourselves as a profession so that we would be in a position to deliver the types of intellectual and interpersonal training our students need. Education of the educators is therefore a necessary precursor of curricular progress.

Race and Critical Race Theory

[34]

BLACK LAW PROFESSORS AND THE INTEGRITY OF AMERICAN LEGAL EDUCATION

Henry J. Richardson, III*

INTRODUCTION

These reflections grow from a comment made by Professor James Jones** during a meeting of the AALS Section on Minority Groups, San Francisco, 1974, where he perceptively observed the need for Black law professors as a group to understand their relation to and role in American legal education, *even* where there are *no* minority law students in particular law schools.

I know of no writing on this particular issue, perhaps because of a tacit assumption among Black law professors and others that such issues are too crass to raise, and that the inquiries involved in thinking them through were somehow unneeded in the 'civilized' reaches of legal education. Such tacit assumptions are shortsighted, and to the extent that they forestall inquiry, over-optimistic in light of the history of Black people in the United States. In every field of endeavor, especially the more prestigious, Black people have arrived late over great opposition, and departed early during times of economic stress to cries of 'necessity.' Those who have remained have borne the twin burdens of being Black and being required to do a competitively superlative job, often against expectations to the contrary. Such situations have led Black people to ask, 'Why am I here?' or, more seriously, others to ask, 'Why is he/she here?' The imperative of inquiring into such questions in the context of legal education is already upon us, as was obvious in San Francisco.

The need to develop a principled vantage point relative to Black law professors may not yet be as dire as that implied by Samuel Yette in *The Choice is Survival*,[1] but events and problems have shown the desirability of doing so beyond any tacit or express assumption to the contrary. Further, since the profound impact of Black people on American history is now common wisdom, we may suspect that attempts to understand the role of Black law professors in American legal education cannot be confined to procedural arrangements and affirmative action statistics. Rather, such attempts must press on to examine the constitutive features of American legal process, as

---

* Associate Professor of Law, Indiana University (Bloomington): Visiting Associate Professor of Law, Northwestern U. Law School 1975-1976. My colleagues, Professors Julius Getman and Alan Schwartz, and Professor Derrick Bell, contributed useful comments on an earlier draft. With them is shared any credit for this essay, while whatever errors occurred despite their efforts.
** Professor Jones' remarks are reprinted in full at 488, *supra*.
1. New York, Putnam Press (1971).

well as those of the relationship of Black people to America. Hence, the reflections that follow.

The path of inquiry begins with identifying and clarifying three major premises that seem to undergird American Black/white relations:

(1) that one purported 'mission' of Black people is to be a redemptive force for the collective soul of white people;
(2) that Black-white social interaction is a dominant reality; and
(3) that (1) and (2) above convey a notion of a process of reciprocal enrichment between Blacks and whites, from which stems the core of the inquiry: the relationship of Black law professors to enrichment of legal process and legal education.

Enrichment must be considered relative to new obligations introduced into the law that are consonant with major goals of legal process and the wider community. A significant source of such obligations has been the confrontation between American legal process and the Black Experience; they extend across the entire scope of legal process, and enrich both sides of that clash. Evaluating these obligations from this source, for their meaning relative to enrichment, leads to their evaluation in light of four illustrative jurisprudential questions arising in this century. Discussing those questions in connection with enrichment highlights the dichotomy between the abolition of racism on the one hand, and causes of action at law on the other. It further illuminates contributions of the Black Experience directly to legal process by both introducing new obligations, and by stimulating new thinking on jurisprudential questions.

Black law professors are inevitably of the Black Experience as they are also legal scholars, and are therefore in the best position to systematically understand and communicate the conjunctions and disjunctions between Law and the Black Experience as they impact on legal process. This impact is of present and increasing significance: because of the intersection of social perspectives in the Black Community with selected issues in the majority white community; because obligations introduced into legal process by Black litigation are now being mobilized by other deprived American groups; because the jurisprudential questions raised by this introduction of new obligations go to the heart of American thinking about law and promise to recur in other contexts; and because the impact of the Black Experience on American law is now irrevocable. Thus the sum total of the foregoing must be incorporated within the training of all who would be lawyers because this is what the Law has become and is becoming. Not to do so would undermine the integrity of American legal education. Black law professors are essential as both scholars and conveyers of the Black Experience, to meet this need.

As noted above, some clarification of basic social premises in Black-white relationships in America as they affect Black law professors must precede any such inquiry.

CLARIFICATION OF PREMISES

The first premise concerns the purported "mission" of Black people to "save" - be a redemptive force for - the collective soul of white people. This premise has at least two facets: 1) Black people 'forgive' white people for past racist sins, and then join with them to sail off together into the sunset to build a new society. 2) Black people bring the Black Experience into the collective experience of white people, thus enriching it because (a) white people's lives are collectively sterile (technologically oriented to the suppression of the passions) while the Black Experience restores the passions through the African connection and its American derivations; and (b) change is the law of life and Black people are sources of new perspectives for change, and new demands the accommodation to which produces change. Inquiring into this premise is significant in that it underpins the notion of enrichment of American legal process, to which we return in a moment.

A second premise is that the moral arguments above, and indeed this entire essay, presuppose some ongoing social interaction of Black and white people, as contrasted with Black nationalist aspirations for the separation of Black and white societies. On the basis of past, present and projected realities such separation within the United States is impossible, and has been for quite some time, at least in important areas of power and wealth interactions. Thus proximity and intermingling are inevitable, and put in issue the factors involved in *regulating* this interaction. To state the obvious here intends to emphasize the interdependencies of American society among Blacks and whites, and to recall that these were intense even during slavery—the period of the most sustained and oppressive attempt at segregation—because of the common humanity of both groups locked into the same system on the same territory.[2] This is no less true now, in different forms, for legal education,[3] and the legal process as discussed hereafter.[4]

Redemptive forgiveness rationales do not seem key to inquiring into the role that Black law professors should play, for at least two reasons. First, they are not in a position to forgive white people for anything as representatives of Black people, because they are too elite as a group to be *that* representative. Secondly, redemptive forgiveness is a question *consciously* to be decided by

---

2. See generally Genovese's excellent ROLL, JORDAN, ROLL: THE WORLD THE SLAVES MADE (Pantheon, 1974), for example at 30-31, 47-49, 88-89.

3. The interdependency between a quality legal education and equal access under the law for all who would potentially walk into those classrooms was recognized by the Supreme Court as long ago as *Sweatt v. Painter*, 339 U.S. 629, 633-35 (1949). Recognition of this interdependency was implicitly continued in *DeFunis v. Odegaard* (Douglas, dissenting) 416 U.S. 312, 333, 336 (1974) in that the context was constantly recalled of there being only a limited number of places in *that* institution of legal education, and that equal protection issues must be resolved among interacting groups and individuals in *that particular* framework. In this connection, see also Redish, *Preferential Law School Admissions and the Equal Protection Clause: An Analysis of the Competing Argument*, 22 U.C.L.A. L. REV. 343, 361 et seq. (1974).

4. The first premise is not exclusive of "progressive" Marxist-oriented cutting-edge political thought in the Black community, which theoretically aims for unification of working class transracial groups for construction of a new political force to, *inter alia*, abolish racism. That is, socialism as an antidote to racism. This kind of thinking is encompassed by the forgiveness and enrichment issues in the first premise, *unless* racism can be eliminated by removing certain economic structural factors in the society. However, the alternative view is taken here: removal of those factors would not *guarantee* the abolition of racism. The argument here in part is that socialism-as-abrogating-racism still implies the validity of both enrichment and forgiveness issues, at least until the arrival of American socialism proves us wrong, *or* until the obligation on white America for past racism is discharged under some condition of forgiveness or recompense, for example, through effective payment of just reparations.

Black people, e.g. relative to reparations.[5] Black law professors, however, may well comprise an important group of brokers to help *ensure* that white people are not redeemed (vis-a-vis major attitudes among Black people) until Black people can know, understand and validly consent to terms and conditions of such forgiveness. This comprises, among other things, a question of law in its most profound sense,[6] and Black law professors should be in the forefront of formulating it.

Therefore, enrichment rationales emerge as most pertinent to the rest of our inquiry.

In this connection a third premise emerges. Enrichment is a two-way street. Black people have also arguably been "enriched" by white people, especially regarding modernization, industrialization, technology, all as part of a process again beginning with the slavery experience. One immediate question is whether the latter really constitutes enrichment, in terms of values most cherished in the Black community.[7] But no matter whether this gets an affirmative, negative or indecisive answer, the process certainly constitutes interchange incorporated into the Black Experience. Accordingly, our vantage point is not that of a separate group deciding upon assimilation, but of a partially assimilated group who are presumptively in the midst of a process of reciprocal though unequal and unfair interchange with white society.[8]

---

5. See Richardson, *Between Law and Justice: Professor Bittker's Case for Black Reparations*, INDIANA L.J. (forthcoming, Spring 1975).

6. It is such a question not only in the Hohfeldian sense that it deals with reciprocal rights and obligations on a broad scale, but equally because, with respect to two groups of participants in national social processes, the question of payment of Black reparations immediately focuses on community expectations about the authority of decision-makers within the general community to make decisions allocating resources among and within the two groups. *See* BITTKER, THE CASE FOR BLACK REPARATIONS (1973), at 71-86.

7. It is a commonplace that industrial social values, previously thought to convey only benefits, have not been called into question across the board not only from the suspicion that they may be too expensive in terms of other resources, but also that they may be fundamentally destructive to the human spirit. This suspicion is no less present on certain levels in the Black Community for various reasons. For example, the statistical indicators that tend to implement such industrial values have been inadequate at the least and oppressive at the most in their being used to regulate, among other things, the relationship between Black people and the majority American society. Cf. ROZAK, WHERE THE WASTELAND ENDS: POLITICS AND TRANSCENDANCE IN POSTINDUSTRIAL SOCIETY (Doubleday, 1972) at 33-40, 50-53, 58-59, 64-67.

8. It is clear to most if not all Black people that this life inter-change has been unequal and unfair on many levels. This clarity however has not been reflected in legal outcomes under the Equal Protection Clause, e.g. in the area of legal education. American legal process has had considerable difficulty responding to the ripple effects of white discrimination against Black people, and especially in finding rationales to justify educational policies that respond to those ripples for what they are, e.g. attacking such ripples in legal education as in *DeFunis*. The presumption *still* persists of the fairness of the interchange unless otherwise proved, and opportunities are taken on short notice to strengthen the presumption by pointing to superficial economic criteria to indicate a lack of unfairness and thus less need for corrective policies. E.g. in raising the issue of whether the offspring of Black upper middle class income parents should be eligible for minority admissions evaluation at a given law school. *See* REDISH, *supra*, at 395-96. Such economic criteria are almost totally beside the point because of the racism in the surrounding society pressing on both students and parents, including on the former in the supposedly advantageous educational institutions they attended. Such economic advantage as they enjoyed may well have gone mostly into ensuring psychic survival; this is vastly different from the Black student emerging from that institution on an equal footing with students who have never encountered such racism and who have even reaped its majority advantages. Yet, reference to these realities produces distinct scholarly, not to mention judicial, unease. *Id.* at 399.

The working assumption here is that this interchange has conveyed a mixture of enrichment and detriment both from white to Black, and from Black to white. For present purposes, the task is to identify Black to white enrichment factors in a defined area of interchange: the legal process, and particularly the scholarship, education, and appraisal mechanisms within legal process.

Stating the problem in this manner requires some definition of "enrichment," and then an exploration of the relationship of Black law professors to enrichment of legal process and legal education.

ENRICHMENT OF LAW AND THE BLACK EXPERIENCE

If we start from the proposition that the legal process must grow to remain consonant enough with social processes to be viable, that such growth necessitates change, and that such change has much to do with the aspirations, hopes and fears of the human participants in the processes of the law, then we might be at least halfway towards saying that all growth in the law constitutes enrichment of the law. But only halfway, because enrichment must refer also to the objectives of the major participants in the legal process relative to the values and goals they are seeking to enhance.

By way of fixing the outer limits, two crude examples illustrate legal change without enrichment. Refinements of legal procedures in Nazi Germany ultimately designed to move Jews more efficiently to concentration camps and gas chambers, or equally, refinements in Soviet law under Stalin in the late 1920's and early 1930's designed to easily obtain the process "confessions" of those victimized during the Communist Party purges, are not here considered to be either growth or enrichment because they grossly affront, in both their substance and procedures, values that mankind universally aspires to preserve and that are also inherently brutal. Even if the above may be argued as 'growth' in the law in terms of changes over time via an accumulation of new subject-matter and procedures, it still does not constitute 'enrichment.' It likely constitutes neither, but the distinction need not further disturb us here. Similarly, it need not do so relative to those principles and procedures facilitating American slavery.

Since enrichment is not a value-neutral concept but refers to the value-content of that which is introduced, we are on safer ground if we look for enrichment in the direction of new obligations incorporated within the law that are consonant with major goals of legal process of the facilitation of social change, the preservation of human dignity, and the maintenance of minimum public order. This direction points us towards the source of such new obligations. The late British international legal scholar, J. N. Brierly, has perceptively noted that the source of legal obligations lies outside of the legal process, deriving from the values, aspirations and plans in the wider community of human society.[9] This would seem not only the case for international law, but for law in national communities as well. In the United States, one source of legal obligations is the confrontation between the American (white-controlled) legal process and the Black Experience. This is even more apparent, and indeed self-evident, because the values, goals and objectives

---

9. BRIERLY, THE LAW OF NATIONS, 54-56 (6th ed. H. Waldock 1963).

that Black people have generally sought when utilizing the legal process are nowhere near the abyss of the above Soviet and Nazi examples, but are well within the goals, values and ideals of the Founding Fathers of the country and within the expressed goals of the international community.

The confrontation between the Black Experience and American Law is best conceived as an ongoing process. With significant exception, the strategy from the side of the former has generally been one of litigation.[10] Litigation is one of the primary pipelines by which outside influences are channeled into legal process in ways significant enough to alter it; indeed, we know this as the essence of the Common Law which incorporates the doctrine of *stare decisis*, on the one hand, a doctrine challenged in empirical form by the legal history of its frequent circumvention by the courts, on the other. Thus many litigants sue the court to impose a new obligation from their own perspectives on the respondent, or at least one not previously defined in the precise demanded form. And so it has been for the collective litigation of the Black Experience.

What new obligations has the Black Experience sought and to what extent has that litigation been successful? A complete answer to that question would come close to providing the jurisprudential meaning of civil rights litigation for American law: how has this widespread sustained attempt in the context of a social movement by ex-slaves, with the resulting judicial outcomes now being employed by other American groups' objects of deprivation to introduce *their* new obligations into the American legal process, changed the way of thinking about law in the United States, and arguably in the larger international community?

A full answer is impossible in the context of this essay, for it would literally require a history of Black people and the Law.[11] For present purposes, we may note that new obligations sought to be imposed by the Black Experience extend across a wide scope of legal process,[12] though certain general areas (e.g. school desegregation) have obviously attracted more attention than others. Black people further have framed, invoked and sought to have prescribed new legal obligations in doctrinal areas of the law not commonly associated with the Struggle, e.g. antitrust law as the basis of a claim to prevent real estate developers from conspiring to prohibit sales of property to Black people.[13] This wide scope only reflects the truism that the Black Experience has in some way reached into every corner of American life.

When a Black claim is successfully made out in an area of the law previously so "untouched," legal expectations are enhanced by the extension

---

10. The exceptions must include the 13th, 14th and 15th Amendments, and perhaps the following Congressionally enacted civil rights legislation: Voting Rights Act - 42 U.S.C. §§ 1971, 1973-1973p (1970); Civil Rights Act of 1964 - 42 U.S.C. §§ 1971, 1975a-1975d, 2000a-2000h-6; Public Accommodations Provisions - 42 U.S.C. § 2000a.

11. Derrick Bell, however, in RACE, RACISM AND AMERICAN LAW, (Little, Brown & Co., 1973) has come close enough to provide us with much valuable source material and food for thought along these lines.

12. *See e.g.* Bell, *supra* n.11, Table of Contents, pp. ix-xviii, and also L. MILLER, THE PETITIONERS: THE STORY OF THE SUPREME COURT OF THE UNITED STATES AND THE NEGRO (1966).

13. Bratcher v. Akron Area Board of Realtors, 381 F.2d 723 (6th Cir. 1967).

into that area of the principle of non-discrimination against Blacks, as subsequently applied to similar future problems. Such extension also enhances the Black Experience by providing, through a court order, leverage to enable Black people to more fully participate in or enjoy activities formerly encumbered by restrictions. It is a two-way street therefore, with enrichment arguably traveling in both directions. But this reciprocity also calls into question somewhat Brierly's original perception that the source of legal obligation necessarily lies *outside* of the legal process. Because where there are a few basic principles in a body of law of signal social impact, their subsequent *application* to future legal problems may be of significance in formulating new obligations equal to that from Brierly's crystallization of *social* expectations into a *new principle* and applied to the same problem. However, to understand whether a particular obligation introduced by a specific case derives from one source or the other requires an intimate and fundamental understanding of the social and economic process and progress of the Black Experience in this country. On this basis Brierly's conclusion retains some vigor, but there is still a question to be resolved.

This jurisprudential question as to the source of legal obligations that is raised by the Black Experience confronting American Law is the first of four such questions that will be noted here. That they are raised by this confrontation, and that a journey into the Black Experience is required for their resolution is indicative of the enrichment brought to American Law by Black-introduced obligations. We begin to see that enrichment is itself a process and, at least in part, conveys a notion of releasing potentially new answers from certain basic questions by reapproaching them from a fresh value direction. This seems a more accurate conception than a straight two-or-three-line-inclusive-definition, because the interaction between American Law and the Black Experience is itself a dynamic process. Accordingly, we move on to consider a second such question.

Part of the meaning of civil rights court decisions is that Black people using the federal courts have sometimes been able to gain at least temporary enforcement of their rights in communities where the majority of people were opposed. This has often involved flirtations with a breakdown of public order, as in Little Rock, Selma and Boston, and has required outside coercive force to prevent a complete breakdown. It further brings into view another jurisprudential dictum, Justice Holmes' observation that "A right is what a given crowd will fight for successfully."[14] But the confrontation between law and the Black Experience suggests that a right just might be something more, and thus raises our second jurisprudential question.

Holmes' dictum did point in the direction of the rise of the legal realism school of American jurisprudence. Part of the meaning of that advent was the shift of the basis of law as commands from some institutional or theologically-derived lawgiver, on the one hand, to the events, hopes, fears, and expectations of the people who are to be regulated by it. The substance of a right then, no longer depends upon the historical or theological validity of its formulations, but rather on procedures in the courts and in other arenas by

---

14. This general question has been well raised by Francis Biddle in JUSTICE HOLMES, NATURAL LAW AND THE SUPREME COURT (Macmillan, 1961).

which the right is invoked, prescribed and applied.[15] This philosophy can be said to be predominant today, especially in legal education.[16] For our purposes here it has produced several outcomes, among them vastly increased attention to the concept, details, enforceability, and integrity of procedural due process of law.

Again, this is no place to write a history of Black people and the Fourteenth Amendment, but the secularization of thinking about the law has put a premium on the dividing line between deprivations to people that the law will recognize - especially in subtle, relatively intimate contexts - and those deprivations that although very real to the people involved, will not be recognized and therefore not remedied. The subtleties and intimacies of illegitimate coercion by a state representative (for the purposes of 'state action') are ultimately defined by reference to principles still retaining much theological (natural law) content: 'fundamental fairness, due process, equal protection,' but are evaluated in a social context where legal process is increasingly thought of in terms of the expectations of the community. Where state officials are mostly white and defendants Black, 'fundamental fairness' relates directly to the detailed history of the interrelationship between the two groups, and therefore to the nature of racism.

As much of racism is subtle as crude: Black people and the Black Experience alone are experts on both. The overall legal question posed is not as Black people would generally want the law to define it: What is racism and once identified, how may legal process best eliminate it? Rather it is posed, "Is *this* manifestation of racism a violation of a legal principle (equal protection, due process, etc.) and accordingly what *partial* (*re* the abolition of racism) remedy is available? The result here is that even if a successful claim in litigation is made out and a new obligation created, procedural completeness will often be negatively compared with substantive completeness; this produces a further conclusion of substantive incompleteness in American law by some 23 million Black people in a nation of 202 million. This substantive incompleteness produces our third jurisprudential question, namely, the managing of the dichotomies in law between the realities of racism, on the one hand, and the generally more limited 'established' causes of action in legal process, on the other.

On its face, anyway, this Black Experience conclusion is consonant with both natural law and legal realism conceptions of legal process. The conflict between procedure and substance in this context bears much more reflection if the law is to be understood (and taught) as more than a system of naked control. Further, the ambiguity here produces our fourth jurisprudential question, namely, the meaning of legal realism for Black people and others who rely so heavily on certain constitutional rights of natural law origin.[17]

---

15. *See generally* H. Kantorowicz, *Some Rationalism About Realism*, 43 YALE L.J. 1240 (1934); M. Radin, *Legal Realism*, 31 COLUMBIA L.R. 824 (1931); Biddle, *supra*, 16-17.

16. *See* Lasswell and McDougal, "Legal Education and Public Policy: Professional Training in the Public Interest", (1943) reprinted in McDougal & Associates, *infra*; Brown, *Recent Trends in United States Legal Education*, 26 J. LEGAL ED. 283 (1974); cf. Richardson, *Reflections on Education in International Law in Africa*, 4 DENVER J. OF INT'L LAW AND POLICY 199, at 199-201 (1974).

17. *See* Biddle, *supra*, at 32. This issue as it directly relates to Black people was only raised by Biddle in a tangential reference to Little Rock (at 36) by way of differentiating Holmes'

Accordingly, while an all-inclusive definition of enrichment is not possible, these brief reflections do indicate that since the goals and objectives of Black people seeking legal redress are consonant with wider community goals, their introduction of certain new obligations into American law seems to constitute enrichment of that law because of the values underpinning those obligations, and because implementing such obligations has raised the distinct possibility of getting new answers from the above jurisprudential questions that could make American law more responsive to present and projected community-wide problems.

ENRICHMENT AND BLACK LAW PROFESSORS

Black law professors are irrevocably of the Black Experience, and relative to questions of jurisprudence and legal process such as the foregoing, bring a unique collection of both structured and inchoate insights. These insights collectively comprise a wellspring for the process of jurisprudential enrichment which must be understood by any lawyer purporting to comprehend and utilize American law. This is true for reasons that relate to *stare decisis*, but even more so to understanding law as a process of authoritative decision[18] in the immediate future of grinding decisions which must be made about social, political, economic and human priorities in the United States and throughout the world.

In the context of such decisions, the response of law schools and the legal profession— and ultimately the entire American and world community-to the above four jurisprudential questions illustrative of those born of the confrontation between the Black Experience and American Law, will loom large in the courts and other legal arenas.[19] Such questions are significant because the impact of the Black Experience on American Law is now historically irrevocable. Those early great Black litigators, especially Charles Houston and Thurgood Marshall,[20] have more than amply ensured this, as confirmed by the precedents now being cited in cases seeking to establish obligations of civil rights to Indians, women, and Chicanos. Those cases reveal the recitation of the early and recent cases confirming (or

---

"Right in the narrow legal sense" from "an activity to which men may believe they are entitled but which cannot be achieved through a court of law". The issue of course for us, Biddle, and Holmes is whether such a narrow conception of 'legal' right remains adequate and accurate in a society where (1) the legal process is much more than what courts do (as recognized by Biddle-Holmes, *id.*); (2) legal process is being called on to regulate an increasing number of social activities; (3) the idea of the *entire* executive apparatus of a society being wrong both morally and legally about virtually a universe of policies is now a familiar one; (4) the framers of the Constitution arguably anticipated (3) above in the notion of checks and balances; and (5) the concept of causes of action "in law" has now transcended national boundaries and arguably will increasingly do so, e.g. as an outcome of the incremental yet real growth of the international law of human rights. Arguably, one net effect of all of the above is to buttress our skepticism about a one-to-one identity between the existence of a legal right and its instant enforceability.

18. This concept of law (and this inquiry) has been substantially influenced by the work of Professors Myres McDougal and Harold Lasswell. *See generally* McDOUGAL AND ASSOCIATES, STUDIES IN WORLD PUBLIC ORDER (1960).

19. Some indication of this is gleaned by substituting "sexism" for racism, *mutatis mutandis*, in the discussion to this point.

20. *See* Burch, *The Brown Strategists*, 3 BLACK L.J. 115 (1974); McNeil, "Charles Hamilton Houston", *id.* at 123. An article useful for placing these and other Black lawyers in the concept of the Black Community is Tollett, *Black Lawyers, Their Education, and the Black Community*, 17 How. L.J. 326 (1972).

attempting to) the same or similar rights to Black people.[21] The choice is no longer open to judges, lawyers, scholars and others to reject the outcome of the Black Experience-cum-legal-expectations. Though such cases may be mis-cited, distinguished and limited, they must henceforth be dealt with via some variant of the same judicial and litigational principles and strategies which have built the common law. Further, this outcome has already begun to be felt, albeit incompletely, in concepts of legal education. There is some indication that *Brown v. Board* is emerging as a primary teaching tool in the constitutional law classroom, supplanting in this role such ancient stalwarts as *Marbury v. Madison*.[22]

Not only has the Black Experience had this major impact, but the future seems to promise more of the same, if only because issues raised by, and the perspectives of, various factions of the Black community intersect with similar though differently-motivated issues brought to the fore by white groups. For example, Black nationalistic desires for control over schools in Black ghettos intersect with white neighborhood school plans; Black desires for control over local police intersect with the wider question of urban decentralization; Black proposals for land-use cooperatives and land banks intersect with wider issues of regional planning, de-urbanization, and ecological conservation of land; Black distrust of white policemen intersects with the issue of the use of state coercion to suppress political dissidence. The list could be continued.[23]

In future decades the impact of the Black Experience - *in se* and as a legal stalking horse for other deprived American groups - is not likely to diminish. The perspectives introduced by Black-oriented litigation seem to have a continuing chance to be confirmed by the courts in some measure as new legal obligations, for two general reasons: (1) Because of probable alliances with selected sentiments and trends primarily white-inspired; and (2) the designation of legal issues, and therefore of significant court cases, as critical or survival issues vis-a-vis the Black community, is likely to continue to move upwards on the scale of subtlety following that of racist opposition— e.g., from the crude issues of having to desegregate drinking fountains and washrooms, to buses, to schools, to bussing, to employment in the context of layoffs in an economic depression, to compensation plans and affirmative

---

21. *See e.g., Reed v. Reed*, 404 U.S. 71 (1971); *Frontiero v. Richardson*, 411 U.S. 677 (1973); *In re Griffiths*, 413 U.S. 717 (1973).

22. I am grateful for Derrick Bell's confirmation of my intuition on this point, gleaned from general discussions with others in legal education.

23. The wide range of such issues generated by the Black Experience leads us to examine the converse proposition: that the relationship between Black law professors and the enrichment of legal process as discussed here, might well find close analogies in the relationship of Black academics to other disciplines, e.g., political science, sociology, philosophy, as has been suggested by Professor Jones. To anticipate the implications of this essay as completed, it would seem, *prima facie*, that similar truths could indeed be identified relative to enrichment in most if not all other disciplines. However, we focus here on law and legal education for two reasons, the first of which, briefly, is the personal preference and vantage point of the author. But secondly, law is unique as an intellectual discipline in that its inquiries, decisions, and students graduated from its schools tend, on a continuing basis, to have early consequences for the maintenace and quality of public order in the community. Further, there are substantial expectations throughout the society for these kinds of wide ordering and value-allocating decisions (in terms of e.g. power, wealth, and respect) to be made as a matter of legal process. In a context so significant, clarification of the legitimacy of Black participation in legal education might well influence the outcome of analogous issues in other disciplines, though this bears further investigation beyond the scope of this essay.

action, to the present need now to rid affirmative action programs of *their* discrimination against Black people. These are among the most passionate issues of American society because, among other reasons, Black people faced with racism of the most interlacing and subtle nature in "gatekeeper"[24] institutions, (e.g. Bar Examinations) are frequently forced into the strategy of advocating and working for the total abolition of such institutions (it being impossible to enforce their equitability), notwithstanding meritorious functions otherwise performed by them for both Blacks and whites (i.e. the enforcing of standards of professional competence in representing the interests of others).

Litigation against racism in all areas of the law, the new obligations it imports into legal process, and consequent modification and evolution of American law are now permanent features of the legal landscape and seem destined to remain so. This evolution therefore must be understood and taught in American law schools into the future, not to preserve a kind of intellectual Maginot line for the survival of Black people, but because this is what American Law has irrefutably become and continues in the process of becoming. Such a realization does not amount to charity to Black scholars, but rather an essential attempt to prevent a distortion of the education of all lawyers and to preserve the integrity of American legal education.

As the previous discussion has indicated, the confrontation between the Black Experience and American Law has not been one of two solid objects colliding on their outside surfaces, but rather that of the infusion of a dye throughout a cell. The jurisprudential questions already noted are only illustrative of a larger number that now doubtless arise and will arise throughout legal process.[25] The particular contributions which Black law professors can make relative to resolving these questions stem from their dual role as 1) carriers of the Black Experience, itself a sourcebook of non-legal influences incorporated into law; 2) legal scholars who understand both the Law and the Black Experience and can, in the most scholarly meaning of the term, 'make sense of' both the conjunctions and disjunctions between these two historical forces as they impact on legal process.

It is left for future inquiry, with regard to the unique contributions Black law professors have to make relative to *each* of these four questions, to spell out the substantial actual or theoretical impact of the Black Experience on understanding the particular issues involved. Such answers need not be awaited, however, to conclude that Black law professors approaching and contributing to legal scholarship, and teaching out of the Black Experience, clearly enrich American law and are essential, in vastly greater numbers than at present, to the minimum education of all lawyers in whatever law school.

---

24. This perceptive expression is that of Walter Leonard, Special Assistant to the President, Harvard University.

25. A fifth such question that could easily be added is that of the tort construct of the "reasonable man", when used as a supposedly neutral concept in a non-homogeneous society, emerging not as a touchstone of 'reasonableness' but as a technique of cultural and social majoritarian control. See in this connection Richardson, "Black People, Technocracy and Legal Process: Thoughts, Fears and Goals" in BARNETT AND STRICKLAND (eds.), POLITICAL AND ECONOMIC STRATEGIES FOR BLACK PEOPLE IN THE COMING DECADES, (forthcoming, 1975). coming, 1975).

[35]

It is Better to Speak[*]

Angela D. Gilmore[†]

I.

In September 1990 I attended a lecture given by a noted feminist scholar. Her topic was women's bodies as portrayed by the fashion industry. I cannot remember the lecturer's name; in fact, it is not even relevant to this discussion. What I do remember is that while I understood the lecturer's analysis of the fashion industry and how it depicted women's bodies, her lecture did not resonate personally for me. I had not had any of the experiences that the lecturer's "universal woman" had had with the fashion industry. I did not have the same reaction to pictures of thin, young, carefree models featured in fashion magazines as did the "universal woman." I began to wonder if there was something wrong with me since I could not personalize or relate to the experiences of this "universal woman," but could only conceptualize them as an onlooker, an outsider. An audience member's question clarified my confusion: "What woman are you talking about?" The questioner wanted to know if women of color, lesbians, overweight women, or poor women were included within the concept of the lecturer's "universal woman." When the lecturer admitted that she was talking about straight, white, middle-class women, I realized that it was no wonder that I, a Black lesbian from a working-class background, could not connect with the experiences of the lecturer's "universal woman."[1]

When I was a student in law school, I experienced this same sense of

---

[*] The title comes from the poem, "A Litany for Survival," by Audre Lorde. The poem reads in part: "and when we speak we are afraid/ our words will not be heard/ nor welcomed/ but when we are silent/ we are still afraid./ So it is better to speak/ remembering/ we were never meant to survive." Audre Lorde, *A Litany for Survival*, in Lorde, *The Black Unicorn* 31-32 (WW Norton, 1978).

[†] Faculty Fellow and Visiting Assistant Professor of Law, University of Iowa College of Law; B.A. Houghton College 1985; J.D. cum laude University of Pittsburgh School of Law 1988. I would like to thank Anita Allen, Rusty Barceló, Patricia Cain, Martha Chamallas, Mary Dudziak, Joe Knight, Jean Love, Amy Reynolds, Greg Williams and Adrien Wing for reading earlier drafts of this essay.

[1] Professor Angela Harris has labelled the lecturer's type of approach and perspective gender essentialism: "the notion that a unitary, 'essential' women's experience can be isolated and described independently of race, class, sexual orientation and other realities of experience." Angela Harris, *Race and Essentialism in Feminist Legal Theory*, 42 Stan L Rev 581, 585 (1990).

dissonance, of being an outsider, of not connecting. On one level, I was able to comprehend and learn the material that was presented in the 89 hours of class that I was required to take in order to graduate. On another level, a much deeper and personal level that I am only beginning to acknowledge and understand, I never truly felt that I totally belonged, that I was completely accepted in law school. While I may have done well academically, overall my law school experience was not positive. Looking back, I realize that I viewed law school as a means to some vague and unclear end. I tolerated the journey, in anticipation of the destination.

In class after class, a professor, almost always white, and almost always male, would spin hypothetical after hypothetical in which all of the actors with any power at all would almost universally be identified as male. When students questioned this practice, the professor's justification would be that "he" or "man" was used in the generic sense, meaning, he said, that the gendered terms "he" and "man" encompassed all individuals. I did not believe this explanation since the same professors would identify secretaries and victims and other less powerful individuals in the hypotheticals as females.

I often felt this same sense of dissonance and discomfort in law school when issues surrounding race were being considered. In my constitutional law course, Black students dreaded discussion of cases like *Bakke*[2] and *Weber*.[3] We were wary of having to defend race-conscious remedies or affirmative action plans; wary that our classmates would think that Blacks are unqualified on the merits and are only accepted into graduate school or only obtain jobs because of race-conscious plans; wary that our classmates would think that we were sitting in class with them or working in law firms beside them as a result of race-conscious plans. As a result, the participants in the discussions surrounding these issues were often exclusively white.

I can recall only three classes in my entire law school career where issues specifically related to lesbians or gay men were discussed. In constitutional law we discussed *Bowers v Hardwick*,[4] the case in which the Supreme Court held that consenting adults do not have a privacy right to engage in same-sex sexual activity. In family law I learned that two individuals of the same sex cannot marry because the traditional definition of marriage is a union of two people of opposite sexes.[5] In employment law I learned that employers may knowingly and willingly discriminate against lesbians and gay men without fear of liability under Title VII of

---

[2] *Regents of the U of California v Bakke*, 438 US 265 (1978).
[3] *United Steelworkers of America v Weber*, 443 US 193 (1978).
[4] 478 US 186 (1986).
[5] See, for example, *Baker v Nelson*, 291 Minn 310, 191 NW2d 185 (1971) (Minnesota marriage statute does not authorize marriage between two persons of the same sex).

the Civil Rights Act of 1964.[6] Thus, the only things that I learned in law school that had to do with a sexual orientation other than heterosexuality were that, as a result of my sexuality, I could be denied the right to marry, my sexual activity could be criminalized and employers could discriminate against me with impunity.[7]

This semester, Professor Jean Love is teaching a class at the University of Iowa College of Law entitled "Anti-Discrimination Law: The Intersections of Race, Sex and Sexual Orientation." The reading materials for a section of the class dealing with lesbian and gay issues included readings by Audre Lorde[8] and bell hooks,[9] Black female authors who write positively about lesbians and gay men. I think that if, along with reading cases about legalized discrimination against lesbians and gay men, I had also read articles that challenged homophobia, I would not have felt as invisible or legally insignificant.

By listing these experiences separately I do not mean to imply that I felt three different types of dissonance, that when I was confronted with racism only my "Black self" was affected, that my "female self" and my "lesbian self" felt safe. As a person who is Black and female and lesbian all of the time and all at the same time, I cannot always compartmentalize and distinguish either the oppression or the injury. When asked to do so I am reminded of what Audre Lorde has written: "As a Black lesbian feminist comfortable with the many different ingredients of my identity, and a woman committed to racial and sexual freedom from oppression, I find I am constantly being encouraged to pluck out some one aspect of myself and present this as the meaningful whole, eclipsing or denying the other parts of self."[10] Too many times, I've been confronted with racism at meetings of lesbians, and heterosexism[11] at meetings of Blacks. I think that the concept that one person could face both racism and heterosexism simultaneously escaped these individuals. I was, however, profoundly aware of the intersection of the oppressions. As a result, in law school I felt alone, different. I did not publicly identify myself as a lesbian when I was in law school. In fact, I worked very hard to establish an image that was heterosexual, but very progressive on issues of sexual-

---

[6] See, for example, *DeSantis v Pacific Tel. & Tel. Co.*, 608 F2d 327 (9th Cir 1979).

[7] I don't think that my law school experience was unusual. Conversations with friends who have studied and taught elsewhere lead me to believe that the curricula in most law schools do not adequately address and incorporate issues dealing with alternative sexualities.

[8] Audre Lorde is a Black, lesbian, feminist writer and the author of many books including *Zami: A New Spelling of My Name* (Crossing Press, 1982), her biomythography.

[9] bell hooks is the author of *Talking Back: thinking feminist, thinking black* (South End Press, 1989). Chapter 17 of her book is entitled "homophobia in black communities."

[10] Audre Lorde, *Age, Race, Class and Sex: Women Redefining Difference*, in Lorde, *Sister Outsider* 114, 120 (Crossing Press, 1984).

[11] Heterosexism can be defined as the system of beliefs that recognizes heterosexual roles and behaviors as the only acceptable ones. Heterosexism causes homophobia. Conversation with Papusa Molina, workshop leader, Women Against Racism Committee, Iowa City, Iowa (Mar 14, 1991).

ity. I now realize that the silencing I experienced in the classroom and my silence about my sexuality were intimately connected. At Black Law Students Association meetings I was sure that I was the only lesbian present, although then, and now, I have no idea if that was true. At the two events of the gay rights organization that I attended under the guise of being intellectually interested in the subject matter, I knew that I was the only Black. I did not personally know any other Black lesbians, in law school or elsewhere.

The discomfort and dissonance did not disappear upon my graduation from law school. I practiced law with a 140-lawyer firm in Baltimore, Maryland for approximately two years. During that time, the firm never had a Black partner, never had more than twelve female partners, and never had more than four Black associates. There weren't any identifiable gays or lesbians at the firm either. In fact, I was told by one of the female partners at the firm, when questioning her about the firm's attitude toward gay and lesbian associates, that it would be in my best interest to keep my personal life private. I was thus subject to a condition of employment that my heterosexual colleagues were not.

II.

In the November/December 1990 issue of *Ms.* magazine Barbara Smith[12] relates a conversation that she had with a Black woman graduate student as the student was driving her to the airport following a panel discussion at Yale University. The student asked "how she might survive as an out [of the closet] black lesbian artist in the decades that lay before her."[13] Smith's response inspired me to write this reflection piece: "You don't have many role models, do you?" she replied.[14] In the article Smith explains, "Just saying the words made me furious because it struck me how the black women writers, academics, and politicos who protect their closets never think about people like [the student] or about how their silences contribute to the silencing of others."[15]

Last month I found my high school yearbooks. It was the custom in my school to have classmates sign each other's yearbook. As I was reading through the yearbooks I was struck by a common theme found in almost all of the inscriptions. My high school classmates knew me to be an outgoing, talkative, confident individual. Two of my favorite inscriptions appeared next to one another. One read: "To Angela, a girl who always knows the right things to say." The second, obviously written by

---

[12] Barbara Smith is a Black, lesbian writer and activist. She is the editor of *Home Girls: A Black Feminist Anthology* (Kitchen Table: Women of Color Press, 1983), and is co-founder of Kitchen Table: Women of Color Press.
[13] Barbara Smith, *The NEA is the Least of It*, 1 Ms. 65, 67 (Nov/Dec 1990).
[14] Id.
[15] Id.

someone who knew me better, read: "To Angela, who may not always know the right things to say, but says something nonetheless." Somewhere along the way I stopped talking. I think that it happened in college. I left Chester, Pennsylvania, a city that is at least eighty percent African-American, and travelled nearly 400 miles to Houghton College in Houghton, New York. The school had approximately 1200 students, less than five percent of whom were African-American, and was situated in a rural western New York community, in which, as far as I could tell, no African-Americans resided. My method of coping with the situation was to take many of my aspects of self—my laughter, my speech, my poetry—place them in a box, secure the lid and store the box away.[16] Unfortunately, I forgot where I stored the box, and did not discover it until recently. It was not until after I completed college and law school and had practiced law for a while that I located my box of self. After I discovered a lesbian support group and an alliance of Black women attorneys, I was able to remove my box from its shelf, pry open the lid, put myself back together and experience the joy of being all that I am. Having recently found my own voice, I don't want to contribute to the silencing of others.

Audre Lorde writes beautifully about the effects of silencing on the silenced in her essay, "The Transformation of Silence Into Language and Action."[17] She tells a story about a conversation she had with her daughter in which her daughter captured the essence of the spirit-murdering[18] impact of silencing. In response to Lorde's concerns over delivering a paper on the topic of transforming silence into action and language, her daughter said: "Tell them about how you're never really a whole person if you remain silent because there's always that one little piece inside you that wants to be spoken out, and if you keep ignoring it, it gets madder and madder and hotter and hotter, and if you don't speak it out one day it will just up and punch you in the mouth from the inside."[19] There are still times when I am silent, most often because I am afraid, sometimes justifiably, sometimes not. Afraid, as Audre Lorde has written, of contempt, censure, judgment, recognition, challenge, annihi-

---

[16] Professor Charles Lawrence, at the 1991 annual meeting of the Association of American Law Schools, told of a similar experience his sister had upon matriculating at Swarthmore College. Statement to the Society of American Law Teachers Robert Cover Memorial Study Group (Jan 3, 1991).

[17] Lorde, *The Transformation of Silence Into Language and Action*, in Lorde, *Sister Outsider* at 40 (cited in note 10).

[18] Professor Patricia Williams, in her article *Spirit-Murdering the Messenger: The Discourse of Fingerpointing as the Law's Response to Racism*, describes spirit-murdering as "disregard for others whose lives qualitatively depend on our regard . . . . [I]ts product is a system of formalized distortions of thought, It produces social structures centered around fear and hate; it provides a tumorous outlet for feelings elsewhere unexpressed." 42 U Miami L Rev 127, 151-52 (1987).

[19] Lorde, *The Transformation of Silence Into Language and Action*, in Lorde, *Sister Outsider* at 42 (cited in note 10).

lation, visibility.[20] Yet usually I do not achieve anything as a result of my silence. Silence does not cause the fear to disappear. Silence does not make me feel more secure. Silence does not dispel ignorance.

III.

Thinking about my experiences as a law student and lawyer and about breaking through my silence has led me to think about my role as a law professor. I don't think that my status as a Black lesbian law professor limits me to being an effective role model only for Black or lesbian or Black and lesbian law students. My limited experience in the legal academy has shown me that students respond to and respect professors who genuinely care about them as people and as students of the law. I do think that the experiences that I've had as a Black lesbian and the multiple consciousness[21] that I've developed make me an especially effective role model for Black women and for lesbians, two groups of women who have been without very many role models in law teaching for a long time.[22] One of the things that I hope I am able to do, as a professor of the law who is committed to ensuring that students do not feel invisible or legally insignificant in my classroom, is reduce the level of dissonance that students who may not be white, or may not be male, or may not be straight often feel in the classroom.

I wrote this essay not long after I entered law teaching and not long after I discovered the legal scholarship of women of color such as Regina Austin,[23] Kimberle Crenshaw,[24] Angela Harris,[25] Mari Matsuda,[26] Judy Scales-Trent[27] and Patricia Williams,[28] and of lesbians such as Patricia

---

[20] Id.
[21] Mari Matsuda, *When the First Quail Calls: Multiple Consciousness as Jurisprudential Method*, 11 Women's Rts L Rptr 7 (1989). Professor Matsuda explains multiple consciousness as "not a random ability to see all points of view, but a deliberate choice to see the world from the standpoint of the oppressed." Id at 9.
[22] I have not had any Black female teachers since nursery school. I did, however, work as a research assistant with Professor Anita Allen at the University of Pittsburgh School of Law. I am not saying that I did not have any role models until that time, since that is not true. However, I can still remember the pride and excitement that I felt when Professor Allen was introduced to the class on orientation day, and my immediate adoption of her as a mentor and role model.
[23] Professor Austin is the author of *Sapphire Bound!*, 1989 Wis L Rev 539. Every time I read this article I am inspired by her declaration that "I simply refuse to be doubly or triply bound in the negative sense of the term by a racist, sexist, and class-stratified society without its hearing from me." Id at 549. I would add heterosexism to her list of oppressions operating in society.
[24] Professor Crenshaw is the author of *Demarginalizing the Intersection of Race and Sex: A Black Feminist Critique of Antidiscrimination Doctrine, Feminist Theory and Antiracist Policies*, 1989 U Chi Legal F 139. I met Professor Crenshaw at the Critical Race Theory conference in Madison, Wisconsin in November 1990. She is one of the first people who encouraged me to consider writing about the intersection of race, gender and sexuality.
[25] See note 1.
[26] See note 21.
[27] Professor Scales-Trent is the author of *Commonalities: On Being Black and White, Different and the Same*, 2 Yale J L & Feminism 305 (1990). Professor Scales-Trent, a Black woman

Cain[29] and Rhonda Rivera.[30] The writings of these women allowed me to see in a very tangible way that women of color and lesbians not only belong in law schools and on law school faculties, but that we also need to be vocal about the ways in which the law and law schools silence us and students. Reading the works of these women has helped me realize that a Black lesbian can and should contribute to law teaching and legal scholarship. Their scholarship has empowered me and helped me to break through my silence. The transformation of silence into language and action is an act of self-revelation, and is therefore dangerous;[31] however, the alternative, remaining silent, is more dangerous, and eventually on some level, deadly.[32]

Even as I was writing this essay I wondered if the risks of having it published in a national law journal would outweigh any possible benefits the article might reap. Would I lose friends, the respect of students and colleagues, employment opportunities? Did I want this much of my self in print? I found myself unable to discuss the contents of this essay with colleagues because it is so personal. Recognizing the irony of the situation in light of the theme of my essay, I realized that if I did not submit this essay for publication I would once again be placing bits of my self in a box, on a shelf, perhaps never to be rediscovered.

---

who appears white, writes about the intersection of race and color as well as about the intersection of gender and sexuality. She writes that just as she becomes more clear about who she is by "coming out" to people as a Black woman, her lesbian sisters "come out" as lesbians so that they can be honest with themselves and with other people. Id at 321-22. I feel that when I am silent about my sexuality, in situations where speaking out is called for (for instance, I am ashamed to number the conversations in which I've been a participant where anti-lesbian jokes and statements were made and I did not protest), I internalize and perpetuate the fallacy that silence is a suitable response.

[28] See note 18.

[29] Professor Cain is the author of *Feminist Jurisprudence: Grounding the Theories*, 4 Berk Women's L J 191 (1989-90).

[30] Professor Rivera is the author of *Queer Law: Sexual Orientation Law in the Mid-Eighties, Parts I and II*, 10 Dayton L Rev 459 (1985) and 11 Dayton L Rev 275 (1986).

[31] Lorde, *The Transformation of Silence Into Language and Action*, in Lorde, *Sister Outsider* at 42 (cited in note 10).

[32] ACT UP, the AIDS Coalition To Unleash Power, has shown the world in a powerful way through the slogan "Silence = Death" that the failure to transform silence into language and action, in this case to transform silence into research for a cure for AIDS, quite literally leads to death. The slogan is frequently printed in white, underneath a pink triangle on a black background. The pink triangle is the symbol used in Nazi concentration camps to identify gays. The emblem declares that "in the time of AIDS the death camps are not forgotten." Christopher Knight, *Art Review*, Los Angeles Times F1, col 2 (Jul 18, 1990).

Part V
The Debate in the Commonwealth

Modernism

[36]

PERICLES AND THE PLUMBER

Prolegomena to a working theory for lawyer education *

Miranda:	O brave new world,
That has such people in't!	
Prospero:	'Tis new to thee.
	(*Tempest*, Act V, scene I.)

To begin by clarifying some terms: the sub-title of this lecture is " Prolegomena to a working theory for lawyer education." " Education " is used here to cover the whole area that is sometimes divided into " education " and " training." The term " lawyer education," though ungainly, has the merit of separating off those aspects of legal education which are concerned with preparation for a career as a professional lawyer from those which have other objectives. The term " legal education " is retained in contexts where the distinction is blurred. This lecture is concerned first and foremost with the question: what is a desirable education for the prospective lawyer? Thus, for example, in this context it is a secondary consideration that a signficant proportion of undergraduate law students do not plan to or will not in fact take up the practice of law and that this proportion may well be increasing. Because most university law faculties do in practice try to make their undergraduate courses serve several objectives, such considerations are not irrelevant; but there are grounds for believing that a widespread ambivalence as regards objectives has been a fertile source of confusion of thought and of unsatisfactory compromises in our present system. If this is so, then it may be a sensible intellectual procedure to start by trying to develop separate theories for lawyer education and for education in law for non-lawyers, and only after this has been done, to examine to what extent their objectives and the best methods of attaining them are compatible. This lecture, then, proceeds on the basis that the problems of lawyer education are sufficiently complex in themselves to merit separate attention.

---

* An abbreviated version of the text of an inaugural lecture delivered as Professor of Jurisprudence at the Queen's University of Belfast on January 18, 1967. The complete text is to be published as a pamphlet in " The New Lecture Series " of the Queen's University. Professor Willard Hurst and Mr. M. J. Woods kindly read the lecture in manuscript and made some helpful comments.

As an academic jurist I am primarily concerned with that portion of lawyer education that does or might take place within universities. But these matters cannot be coherently treated in isolation from the context of the total process of preparation for practice. Accordingly I shall have to venture beyond the confines of the university campus, but I shall do so with the qualified diffidence of a dramatic critic who is not a professional actor. Finally, what is here offered is prolegomena, not a complete theory, still less a blueprint. That is to say, what is here offered is a collection of interrelated observations which, it is suggested, should be taken into account by any working theory of lawyer education purporting to give a coherent answer to the Lasswellian question: For what purposes should what be taught to whom by whom using what methods in what milieux with what resources?

The first step in developing such a theory is to clarify objectives. Just as our legal literature is peopled by such symbolic characters as John Doe and the " man on the Clapham omnibus," so the literature of legal education is dominated by a fictitious character, " the lawyer," who is used to symbolise the objectives, assumed or stated, of legal education. He seems to be even more Protean and elusive than the reasonable man; the only characteristic on which there appears to be general agreement is that he is a good fellow, not to be confused with the grasping shyster of the world of fiction.

Despite the bewildering variety of these images, generally speaking, they tend to approximate more or less to one of two polar images which, for the sake of alliteration, may be called respectively Pericles and the plumber. The image of the lawyer as a plumber is a simple one. " The lawyer " is essentially someone who is master of certain specialised knowledge, " the law," and certain technical skills. What he needs is a no-nonsense specialised training to make him a competent technician. A " liberal " education in law for such a functionary is at best wasteful; at worst it can be dangerous. Imagine the effect, it might be argued, on our drains and central heating systems if our plumbers had been made to study the history and philosophy of plumbing, the aesthetics of drains, housing policy, Roman baths, comparative plumbing, and a special subject in the water supply of the Houses of Parliament. When practitioners emphasise the value of a broad education for intending lawyers, they frequently also indicate that it is of secondary importance whether or not it is in law. Some go so far as to say that a subject other than law is to be preferred for university study. If plumbers are to study philosophy, it should not be the philosophy of plumbing.[1]

At the other extreme is the image of the lawyer as Pericles— the law-giver, the enlightened policy-maker, the wise judge. The Periclean image of " the lawyer " is not so distinct; this is perhaps due in no small part to the influence of our ideas of liberal education. In England three characters have regularly jostled for first position as the appropriate image of the liberally educated man: the cultured gentleman (education for leisure), the wise ruler (education for leadership) and the scholar researcher (education for scholarship).[2] Sometimes they are fused into a composite image, sometimes they are quite clearly differentiated; the differences between them reflect different strands within the liberal tradition; they tend, at least, to share a few attributes: intellectual discipline, detachment, breadth of perspective, an interest in human nature and a capacity for independent and critical thought. Although the three characters are most closely associated with the liberal arts, the pure scientist has been accommodated with relative ease in the guise of the scholar researcher. The social scientist, one suspects, has found it less easy to fit in. In recent times a fourth character, the applied scientist, sometimes in the guise of technocrat, sometimes more humbly as a technologist, has, in Sir Eric Ashby's words, been " tolerated, but not assimilated." [3] From outside the ivory tower there has nearly always been pressure, varying in intensity at different periods, to make university education more obviously useful and vocational. The " practical man," sometimes in the form of " business executive," sometimes as professional man, sometimes, more seductively, as " practical reformer," clamours for admission. He has often been resisted. Sometimes his demands have been ridiculed as being philistine, myopic, narrow-minded or trivial. He is most effectively repulsed when he is shown to have misconceived his own needs. Sometimes the line of resistance has verged on obscurantism: " a university education needs no justification," " a university has no purpose," or, as I heard someone assert recently, " we should take

---

[1] The Wilson Report (" A Survey of Legal Education in the United Kingdom," by J. F. Wilson (1966) 9 J.S.P.T.L.(N.S.) 1, 55–57) records 73·3 per cent. of barristers and 64 per cent. of solicitors as expressing a preference for graduates: " While the majority of practitioners, therefore, were in favour of the graduate entrant, views were more divided on the merits of a law degree " (62 per cent. of solicitors, but only 38 per cent. of barristers, definitely preferring law graduates to graduates in other subjects). It would be interesting to know how far these figures reflect a recent shift in opinion in favour of law degrees.

[2] See Ashby, *Technology and the Academics* (1963), *passim.*

[3] Ashby, *op. cit.* at p. 66.

a pride in being useless." In so far as such statements express a fear that concern with the vocational or the practical almost certainly involves a sacrifice of " liberal " values, they deserve to be taken seriously, though sceptically. In so far as they tend to glorify aimlessness, they are unacceptable, for one assumption upon which my argument is based is that education should as far as possible be treated as a purposive activity, at least at the level of discussions of strategy.

How to reconcile the liberal tradition with the demands of the world of affairs is one of the perennial problems of university education. Possibly of all university subjects law faces the basic dilemma in its most acute form. Other " professional " subjects such as medicine and engineering seem to an outsider to have been relatively uninhibited in their response to " vocational " pressures, perhaps because they have been relatively isolated from the liberal arts tradition. Our literature of legal education shows an almost pathological concern with trying to please our colleagues in the arts faculties and our brethren in the legal profession at the same time. It is small wonder that the Periclean image of the lawyer is something of a hybrid.

It is not here suggested that either the Periclean or the plumbing image bears much relationship to real lawyers, nor for that matter to the historical Pericles or real plumbers. Nor, when people articulate what they consider to be the proper objectives of legal education, are they often so modest as to equate lawyers with plumbers or so immodest as to suggest that every lawyer should aspire to be a Pericles. But much of our theory and practice about legal education proceeds on the basis of assumptions, hidden or only half-articulated, that are strongly influenced by these images.

While the plumbing image tends to identify " the lawyer " with a relatively humble small-town solicitor, the image of the lawyer as Pericles tends to identify him with a Law Commissioner or an appellate judge. In a delightfully revealing passage the Wilson Report tells us that " The general view of university teachers and practitioners alike was that law degree courses should be designed to provide the student with a liberal education and *to train him to think like a lawyer rather than to give him a vocational training*." [4] It is amusing to speculate on the implications of this contrast between " thinking like a lawyer " and " vocational training," but it is perhaps more revealing to substitute " Lord of Appeal " or even " Lord Chancellor " for " lawyer " in this context. In so far as university students, in the process of learning to think, are served

---

[4] *Op. cit.*, p. 92 (emphasis added).

appellate judgments as their staple diet, they are being taught to reason in a manner more suited to the work of appellate judges than to that of private practitioners, especially solicitors. When they are called on to evaluate the existing system, they are usually asked to adopt the posture of leaders of the profession. Our university curricula rarely, if ever, even descend to the level of courts of first instance to concern themselves with such matters as the reasoning processes involved in drawing inferences from evidence or the intellectual problems of sentencing, to take but two examples.[5] Even more rarely do they venture into processes that take place outside the courts. This surely is not because such topics are not suitable for teaching in a university, for many of them are as susceptible to " liberal " and rigorous treatment as many of the subjects included in conventional curricula. It can hardly be denied that the image of the lawyer that dominates law teaching in our universities is an elevated one.

Some of the complexities of the Periclean image may be explained in terms of the multiple objectives of university legal education and the consequent refusal to distinguish clearly between lawyer education and education in law for non-lawyers. But, it is suggested, more fundamental than this is a lack of consensus or clarity about what kind of end-product is required. This is confirmed if one looks to the United States, where for well over one hundred years their university law schools have unabashedly been concerned with lawyer education, yet similar strains between the Periclean and plumbing images have been apparent. The ways in which the Americans have tried to resolve these strains deserve consideration, for they have a close connection with some of the reasons for the high regard that many people have for the upper reaches of the American system. The development of their leading law schools may hold some clues for the future of ours.

The history of legal education in the United States still awaits a Rashdall or an Ashby. If there is any truth in the suggestion

---

[5] A good example of distortion is the attention paid in books and courses on " criminal law " to such matters as " insanity " and " diminished responsibility," which, as Dr. Nigel Walker has pointed out, " account for only an atypical minority of the detected offenders whose mental abnormality is recognized and taken into account." (" The Mentally Abnormal Offender in the English Penal System," Halmos (ed.) *Sociological Studies in the British Penal Services* at p. 133 (1965)). To what extent in our law courses is attention paid, for example, to mental abnormality in relation to post-conviction procedures under the Mental Health Act? To justify the exclusion of discussion of such topics on the ground that such procedures are not part of " the substantive criminal law," would merely raise the further question: " Why are students expected to restrict themselves to " criminal law," so defined? " I am grateful to my colleague, Mr. Kevin Boyle, for drawing my attention to this point.

that its law schools have made the greatest contribution of the United States to the general field of education,[6] then their story deserves an adequately equipped historian. There are some useful preliminary sketches; a wealth of detailed information and analysis is to be found in histories of individual law schools, in legal biographies and autobiographies, and in periodicals [7]; since the Second World War there has been a striking rise in the level of sophistication of discussions of legal education in the English-speaking world; in this development American law teachers have taken the lead. But two important ingredients still seem to be missing from most of the existing literature: first, a refined set of concepts adequate for the satisfactory discussion of complex issues and phenomena; and, secondly, the professionalism and the breadth of perspective that would be gained by setting the study of legal education firmly in the context of education as a whole. Even in the United States the literature of legal education is still in a relatively undeveloped state.

In the circumstances and in the course of a single lecture all that can be done is to draw a few brief sketches which may at least suggest potentially fruitful lines for further investigation and thought. In order to suggest some of the kinds of lessons that we in this country might learn from the American experience let us consider five phases in the development of their university law schools. The first two sketches are based largely on secondary accounts,[8] which tend to accept Carlyle's view of history as being but the biography of great men, and to tell the tale largely in terms of a few leading personalities and events. From this simplified treatment emerges a relatively simple picture of a long-drawn-out progress from haphazard apprenticeship and self-education to increasingly sophisticated instruction by full-time professional teachers in educational institutions.

Story

The first stage in this progress is commonly associated with the acceptance by Judge Joseph Story of the Dane Professorship of Law at Harvard in 1829. Up to that time nearly all professional

---

[6] Hurst, *The Growth of American Law* (1950), p. 275.
[7] Two useful bibliographies are Klein, *Judicial Administration and the Legal Profession* (1963), and Sullivan, *A Bibliography of Materials on Legal Education* (1961).
[8] Notably *The Centennial History of the Harvard Law School 1817–1917* (1918); Brown, *Lawyers and the Promotion of Justice* (1938); Harno, *Legal Education in the United States* (1953); Hurst, *The Growth of American Law: The Law Makers* (1950); Currie, " The Materials of Law Study " (1951) 3 Jo.Leg.Ed. 331; (1955) 8 Jo.Leg.Ed. 1; Reed, *Training for the Public Profession of the Law* (Carnegie, 1921).

training had taken place outside the universities, most commonly taking the form of apprenticeship supplemented by reading on one's own. Story's appointment to the Dane Professorship was a remarkable event. In the twelve years since its inception Harvard Law School had achieved very little and had a poor reputation. In 1828 there had been only four students. Story, by contrast, was one of the greatest judges to have graced the Supreme Court of the United States and his prestige was immense. Merely by accepting the appointment Story enhanced the status of law teaching. But he did much more than this. His mission was to assist in the establishment of an alternative system of legal training to the apprenticeship that had been his lot.[9] He was largely successful in his objective and by the time of his death Harvard Law School had been transformed. The school had achieved a national reputation, there were over 150 students, many of them attracted from outside Massachusetts, and Story had set an outstanding example to legal scholars by producing a remarkable series of eight treatises on different branches of law.

So great was Story's achievement that it may seem strange to hear that his influence on legal education has not always been regarded as salutary by his successors. When one bears in mind that Story was a man with lofty ideals and a high-minded attitude towards the profession of law, it seems almost paradoxical that he should be charged with fathering a narrow legalistic approach to legal education. The fact remains, however, that while his concept of the lawyer tended towards the Periclean, his educational ideas were in many respects better suited to the production of legal plumbers.

Story's conception of the vocation of the lawyer was noble and idealistic; he proclaimed it often, including in his inaugural lecture as Dane Professor.[10] Perhaps the most explicit statement is to be found in a letter to his son:

> " A lawyer, above all men, should seek to have various knowledge, for there is no department of human learning or human art which will not aid his powers of illustration and reasoning, and be useful in the discharge of his professional duties. It has been the reproach of our profession in former ages, and is, perhaps, true to a great extent in our own times,

---

[9] " The old mode of solitary, unassisted studies in the Inns of Court, or in the dry and uninviting drudgery of an office, is utterly inadequate to lay a just foundation for accurate knowledge in the learning of the law. It is for the most part a waste of time and effort, at once discouraging and repulsive ": letter to Principal of Dublin Law Institute, quoted by Harno, *op. cit.* at p. 43.

[10] " Value and Importance of Legal Studies," in *Miscellaneous Writings of Joseph Story* (1852), 503, discussed by Harno, p. 43 *et seq.*

that lawyers know little or nothing but the law, and *that*, not in its philosophy, but merely and exclusively in its details. There have been striking exceptions, such as Lord Hardwicke, Lord Mansfield, Lord Stowell, Lord Brougham and Mr. Justice Blackstone. But these are rare examples; and too few to do more than to establish the general reproach." [11]

Story's approach to legal education seems hard to reconcile with his picture of the good lawyer. He included in the curriculum only that which was solid law. " What we propose," he said, " is no more than plain, direct, familiar instruction," [12] and this is what his students got. It was highly desirable for the good lawyer to have studied philosophy, rhetoric, history and human nature, but it was not the function of the law professor to teach it to him. Liberal studies were an important part of the education of the lawyer, but they were separate from legal education. The study of law was essentially the study of established legal doctrines. When and how this liberal education was to be acquired is not clear, unless one takes at its face value Story's claim that " . . . in the elementary education, everywhere passed through before entering upon juridical studies, they were usually taught with sufficient fulness and accuracy." [13] This is a strange claim when one bears in mind that in Story's time there were no formal entry requirements for Harvard Law School and by no means all students had a college degree.

Story also appears to have accepted a fairly clear-cut distinction between " academic " and " practical " training. This does not mean that he saw the university study of law as having no vocational significance, far from it, but rather he saw its main function as being the learning of the general doctrines of the common law and little else. The development of the skills and arts of the practitioner were left to be acquired as an apprentice and in the early years of practice.

Thus in Story's educational programme one finds sharp distinctions between law and other disciplines and between legal doctrine and legal practice. Given the opportunity to lengthen the time spent in study and better resources generally, Story might have challenged this rigid segregation; perhaps it is not his fault that distinctions which were partly forced on him by circumstance

---

[11] Letter to W. W. Story, January 27, 1839: *Life and Letters of Joseph Story* (ed. William W. Story), Vol. 2 (1851), pp. 311–312.
[12] *Op. cit.*, n. 10 at p. 532.
[13] *Ibid*, p. 536.

should have persisted as gospel after the circumstances changed.[14]

This double isolation of the subject-matter of legal studies is, of course, very common indeed. In our own tradition, even today, rigid distinctions are often drawn between " law " and " not law " and between " academic " and " practical " legal studies. Criticism of these distinctions is at the base of the modern American rejection of Story's ideas; in so far as our ideas on legal education are similar to Story's, a study of the reaction against him may be suggestive.

Langdell

The appointment to Harvard Law School of Christopher Columbus Langdell in 1870 marks the next important development. Langdell, at the time of his appointment, was an obscure and somewhat retiring New York practitioner. What he brought to Harvard was a coherent theory of law teaching and a determination to apply it with consistency and rigour. A well-known passage from *A Selection of Cases on the Law of Contracts* (1871) is the classic formulation:

> " Law, considered as a science," said he, " consists of certain principles or doctrines. To have such a mastery of these as to be able to apply them with constant facility and certainty to the ever-tangled skein of human affairs is what constitutes a true lawyer; and hence to acquire that mastery should be the business of every earnest student of law. Each of these doctrines has arrived at its present state by slow degrees; in other words, it is a growth, extending in many cases through centuries. This growth is to be traced in the main through a series of cases; and much the shortest and best, if not the only way of mastering the doctrine effectually is by studying the cases in which it is embodied." [15]

Several points are worth making about Langdell's theory. He considered law to be capable of systematic study as a science, and if this were not so, " a university will best consult its own dignity in declining to teach it. If it be not a science, it is a species of handicraft, and may best be learned by serving an apprenticeship to one who practices it." [16] A university is not a trade school for the production of plumbers. Yet Langdell's image of the lawyer is too narrow to be Periclean; " the true lawyer " is someone who

---

[14] *Cf.* Harno: " Our criticism perhaps should be directed against those who followed Story for their tardiness, when circumstances were more favorable for the schools, in broadening the foundations he had laid ": *op. cit.*, p. 50.
[15] *A Selection of Cases on the Law of Contracts* (1871), Preface, p. viii.
[16] Address of 1886, quoted by Harno, p. 58.

has a mastery of legal doctrine and an ability to apply it; the law student must be fed on a strictly regulated diet of law, which for Langdell meant cases; non-legal matter was to be kept out of the curriculum. Since law was to be treated as a science, the most suitable kind of teacher was not necessarily an experienced practitioner. One of Langdell's innovations was to secure the appointment to a full-time teaching post of James Barr Ames, a young graduate with no experience of legal practice. The appointment was criticised, and Langdell's apology is revealing:

> " I wish to emphasize the fact that a teacher of law should be a person who accompanies his pupils on a road which is new to them, but with which he is well acquainted from having often travelled it before. What qualifies a person, therefore, to teach law is not experience in the work of a lawyer's office, not experience in dealing with men, not experience in the trial or argument of causes—not experience, in short, in using law, but experience in learning law; not the experience of the Roman advocate or of the Roman praetor, still less of the Roman procurator, but the experience of the juris-consult." [17]

In time Ames fully justified Langdell's faith in him and he became a noted legal historian. His appointment was significant, not only because of his qualifications, but also because, in the words of Hurst, it " inaugurated, as a new branch of the legal profession in the United States, the career of the scholar-teacher of law." [18] Up to that time nearly all law teaching had been done on a part-time basis; even Story had continued to serve on the Supreme Court after accepting the Dane Professorship. The histories of Harvard, Yale and Columbia law schools and many others tell the same tale: the rise to eminence of a law school is associated almost inevitably with the achievement of a strong faculty of full-time teachers.[19] Teaching, research, educational administration and intellectual leadership are functions that are nearly always best performed by people who are free to devote nearly all their time, energies and loyalties to them. The growth of this " other branch " of the legal profession was accompanied by repeated expressions of concern that a gulf was growing up between the academic and the

---

[17] Quoted by Hurst, *op. cit.*, n. 8 at p. 263.
[18] *Op. cit.*, p. 264.
[19] Two important differences between present patterns in the United States and the United Kingdom are that in the United States almost all law students have a college degree before embarking upon the study of law and almost all law teachers have had a substantial period in practice before they take up teaching.

practising lawyer. The Wilson Report reveals a similar concern at current trends in this country.[20] It has been one of the greatest achievements of American legal education that this danger has, on the whole, been averted. It is part of my thesis that this has been due not only to such obvious factors as the relative mobility of the American lawyer, who moves in and out of full-time teaching more easily than his U.K. counterpart, but also because of the predominance of a type of legal theory that has promoted a much healthier relationship between theory and practice than has been the case with English jurisprudence.

Langdell's contributions to Harvard were numerous: under his leadership the intellectual standards and the resources of the school improved immeasurably and a scholarly atmosphere was established which, *inter alia*, fostered a great series of legal treatises by Beale, Williston, Gray and Thayer. Langdell is, of course, best known for his introduction of a method of teaching—" the case method "— which was the main vehicle for implementing his theory of legal education. Langdell was not the first to emphasise the value of making students read cases in the original; nor was he the first American law teacher to employ the Socratic method; nor was he a born teacher—in fact his first efforts at Harvard provoked more opposition than support from his students.[21] His main contribution was to provide a rationale and a stimulus for introducing this method of teaching throughout the curriculum and, by producing a new style of teaching tool, his case-book on contracts, to provide a model vehicle for the method.

In the course of time with the help of brilliant teachers such as Ames and Keener the case method became established as the main method of instruction, first at Harvard, and later at nearly all leading law schools. It was not seriously challenged until the rise of the Realist Movement. In Langdell's version it had several obvious strengths: first, he insisted on the study of primary sources; secondly, he substituted participation for passivity on the part of students; and, thirdly, he established a tradition of scepticism, liveliness and rigour in lieu of dogmatic, dreary parrot-learning. The introduction of the case method also involved a crucial switch from emphasis on knowledge to emphasis on skill.

For the most part the mainstream of American legal education has been built upon these strengths. Langdell was later to become

---

[20] *Passim.* A well-known critique of relations between academic and practising lawyers is to be found in Gower, " English Legal Training " (1950) 13 M.L.R. 137 at 199–202; this is echoed by Abel-Smith and Stevens, *Lawyers and the Courts* (1967), pp. 183–184, 367, 375.

[21] A vivid account is given by Fessenden, " The Rebirth of Harvard Law School " (1920) 33 Harv.L.Rev. 493.

the target of criticism by Holmes,[22] Frank,[23] Llewellyn [24] and a number of others. But even his most virulent critics have not challenged these aspects of his contribution. What then was the weakness of his approach? Langdell, like Story, made a clear-cut distinction between law and other disciplines. Unlike Story he did not make a similar distinction between academic and practical training, but his picture of the " true lawyer " and his picture of the law teacher tended to produce the same sort of remoteness from life and from legal practice that the insistence on such rigid distinctions tends to promote in our system.

The Realist contribution

Langdell and his disciples set the pattern for nearly all the major law schools for the next fifty years. There were pockets of resistance from traditionalists in the law schools (for instance, at Yale), and his ideas were for some time viewed with scepticism on the part of practitioners. However, the most telling attack came from a different quarter. First Holmes and then Pound set the lead in advocating a jurisprudence that was broader in approach and closer to everyday life. The sceptical temper of the times, the philosophy of pragmatism and above all the extraordinarily rapid rate of economic and social change were some of the factors that drew increasing attention to what Pound termed the divorce between law in books and law in action.[25] But neither Holmes nor Pound really translated their jurisprudential ideas into concrete educational patterns.[26] Despite the fact that Harvard was the academic base of these two great pioneers of sociological jurisprudence, it did not become the headquarters of the movement for further reforms of legal education. The lead was taken in this respect first at Yale by Corbin, Hohfeld and Cook in the second decade of this century, and then during the 1920s by an extraordinarily brilliant group of young men of whom Herman Oliphant, Underhill Moore and Karl Llewellyn were the most prominent. Columbia in the 1920s was the headquarters of a concerted attempt

---

[22] Esp. 14 American L.Rev. 233 (a review of Langdell's case-book). *Inter alia* Holmes said: " Mr. Langdell's ideal in the law, the end of all his striving, is the *elegantia juris* or *logical* integrity of the system as a system. He is, perhaps, the greatest living legal theologian. But as a theologian he is less concerned with his postulates than to show that the conclusions from them hang together."

[23] Esp. " Why not a Clinical Lawyer-School? " (1933) 81 U.Pa.L.Rev. 907, *passim*; " A Plea for Lawyer-Schools " (1947) 56 Yale L.J. 1303, 1313.

[24] *e.g., The Common Law Tradition* (1960), pp. 38 *et seq.*, 360.

[25] (1910) 44 Am.L.Rev. 12.

[26] Llewellyn, *Jurisprudence: Realism in Theory and Practice*, p. 378.

to work out in detail the implications of sociological jurisprudence for legal research and legal education.

One of the most striking features of this ferment was the two-year-long study of the curriculum which took place at Columbia under the chairmanship of Leon C. Marshall, an economist. It has been rightly said by Brainerd Currie that these studies " constituted the most comprehensive and searching investigation of law school objectives and methods that has ever been undertaken." [27] It is worth quoting Currie's appraisal of their significance:

" Individuals and committees prepared for discussion at the faculty conferences approximately one hundred reports, covering eight hundred mimeographed pages, on various aspects of legal education. The result was a sweeping challenge to the adequacy of the organization, the materials and the rational basis of existing legal education. The fundamental thesis which emerged was this: Since law is a means of social control, it ought to be studied as such. Solutions to the problems of a changing social order are not implicit in the rules and principles which are formally elaborated on the basis of past decisions, to be evoked by merely formal logical processes; and effective legal education cannot proceed in disregard of this fact. If men are to be trained for intelligent and effective participation in legal processes, and if law schools are to perform their function of contributing through research to the improvement of law administration, the formalism which confines the understanding and criticism of law within limits fixed by history and authority must be abandoned, and every available resource of knowledge and judgment must be brought to the task.

" A drastic retooling would be required to convert the facilities of legal education to such an effort. Two basic requirements were announced to the law school world with seismic effect: First, the formal categories of the law, shaped by tradition and by accident, tend to obscure the social problems with which law deals, the purpose which is the vital element of principle, and the actual working of legal processes; they constitute a framework which forces artificiality in perspective and development; they must be revised along lines of correspondence with the types of human activity involved. Second, an understanding of the social structure in which law operates can no longer be taken for granted or regarded as irrelevant; law students—and hence law teachers—must acquire

---

[27] (1951) 3 Jo.Leg.Ed. at 333–334.

that understanding, and must somehow learn to take into account the contributions which other disciplines and sciences can make to the solution of social problems." [28]

Developments at Columbia in legal education preceded the rather unsatisfactory jurisprudential polemics of the early 1930s that have come to be known as the " Realist Controversy." A few provocative passages of a rather general nature have unfortunately given people in the United Kingdom a seriously distorted image of what these young scholars at Columbia and Yale were really trying to do.

Perhaps we can understand something of the significance of the Realist Movement for legal education if we compare the ideas of one of their number, Karl Llewellyn, with those of Langdell.

> " Langdell," says Llewellyn, " saw three deep truths. The first was that a university training in law, indeed a liberal arts study of anything . . . must be technically solid, technically reliable, in a word, craftsmanlike. . . . The second thing that Langdell saw was that history, carefully studied, is one good road to understanding. Depth is of the essence, and the time-dimension is one main road to depth."

And, thirdly, as was mentioned above, Langdell shifted the emphasis from acquisition of knowledge to development of proficiency in " legal analysis, legal reasoning, legal argument and legal synthesis." [29]

Llewellyn accepted these ideas, but he felt that as a theory for lawyer education Langdell's did not go nearly far enough. Llewellyn agreed with Langdell in putting considerable emphasis on training in legal method: " Technical skill is not *a* foundation only. It is *the necessary* foundation." [30] But whereas Langdell saw the group of skills that could be developed by his version of case analysis as being *the* skill that a university legal education should seek to develop, Llewellyn's conception of technical proficiency in this context was very much broader. For him the practice of law in a fused profession was the practice of a set of crafts.[31] Knowledge of legal rules and ability to extract doctrine from cases form only a part of these crafts. Lawyers in practice have to employ other skills, many of which are teachable, some of

---

[28] *Ibid.* pp. 334–335.
[29] " The Study of Law as a Liberal Art " (1960), reprinted in *Jurisprudence: Realism in Theory and Practice* (1962), pp. 375, 377.
[30] *Ibid.*
[31] This theme is developed at length by Llewellyn in some unpublished teaching materials: *Law in Our Society: A Horse Sense Theory of the Institution of Law* (1950 ed.), pp. 13–20.

which are teachable in a university. Llewellyn was chairman of a committee which in 1944 produced an influential report on the place of skills in legal education in which it was recommended that law schools should seek to foster not only the case-skills of the Langdell method, but also such matters as skill in interpretation of statutes, appellate advocacy, simple drafting and counselling (*i.e.*, the giving of advice), and the making of intelligent policy decisions.[32] Llewellyn himself pioneered a course in " Legal Argument " and in recent years a variety of other " skills courses " have been offered by American law schools, some of them making a relatively sophisticated use of clinical experience and simulation techniques. Llewellyn emphasised technical proficiency, but he was equally emphatic that technical proficiency was not enough. Langdell's skills, he said, " though sharp and well instilled, were narrow. The wherewithal for vision was not given." [33]

Llewellyn is best known as the exponent of a jurisprudential approach that emphasises the importance of observing the ordinary processes of the law in action in their social context. Doctrine must be seen in the context of legal process and legal processes must be seen in the context of the totality of social processes. Any lawyer, in this view, however humble, must be equipped to understand his environment; his perspective must be a broad one, preferably that of society as a whole. The message repeated again and again is that for practically any purpose law cannot be treated in isolation, and that any attempt to do so prejudices both understanding and efficiency. By concentrating on legal doctrine and by trying to set up an autonomous science of law, Langdell committed the cardinal sin from this point of view and he was branded as an apostle of formalism.[34]

This is not the place to give detailed consideration to the advantages and dangers of a contextual approach to law. The arguments will be familiar to many of you. Of course, Llewellyn and his fellow-realists were by no means unique in advocating this kind of approach. Perhaps their greatest contribution was in the direction of working out the implications of a sociological jurisprudence for detailed work of various kinds. The Uniform Commercial Code, the modern types of case-book, empirical research projects, such as the Chicago jury study—these and many other

---

[32] *Handbook of the American Association of Law Schools* (1944), 159–201; (1945) 75 Col. Law Rev. 345–391.
[33] *Op. cit.*, n. 29, p. 377.
[34] *The Common Law Tradition* (1960), pp. 38–39.

concrete achievements are the real monuments to the contribution of Llewellyn and his fellow-realists.[35]

Against this background it may be useful to consider Llewellyn's image of the end-product of lawyer education. From what has already been said, it should be clear that some of his ideas are compatible with the plumbing image. First, in discussions of legal education he nearly always identifies " the lawyer " with the private practitioner of law.[36] This, as we have seen, is closer to the plumbing pole than to the Periclean. Secondly, he emphasises the need for basic technical proficiency. But the lawyer, both to be effective and, more important in his view, to fulfil his responsibilities to his clients and to society, must be more than a competent technician, he must be more than a plumber. And if the plumbing image implies that a broad or liberal education is unnecessary for lawyers, then it must be rejected. In an address in Chicago he made the point with characteristic vigour:

> " The truth, the truth which cries out, is that the good work, the most effective work, of the lawyer in practice roots in and depends on vision, range, depth, balance and rich humanity—those things which it is the function, and frequently the fortune, of the liberal arts to introduce and indeed to induce. The truth is, therefore, that the best practical training a university can give to any lawyer who is not by choice or by unendowment doomed to be a hack or a shyster— the best *practical* training, along with the best human training—is the study of law, within the professional school itself, as a liberal art." [37]

Llewellyn's picture of the end-product of lawyer education shares something with both the plumbing and the Periclean images, but it is much more sophisticated and complex than either of them. It is, indeed, far too complex to receive full justice here. Before we leave Llewellyn, however, it is worth noting four points about his ideas that fit in with the themes of this lecture. First, he was one of the pioneers of the development of a systematic sociology of the legal profession, a subject that is currently receiving much attention in the United States.[38] Secondly, he was

---

[35] See the writer's forthcoming appreciation in *The Karl Llewellyn Papers* (University of Chicago). For a critique of the contribution of realism to the development of legal research, see Hurst, " Research Responsibilities of University Law Schools " (1957) 10 Jo.Leg.Ed.
[36] See especially *The Bramble Bush* (2nd ed., 1951). On the distorting effect of the private practitioner image in some contexts, see Twining, " Legal Education within East Africa," *East African Law Today* (1966), p. 139 *et seq.*
[37] *Op. cit.*, n. 29 at p. 376.
[38] *Op. cit.*, n. 36, Chap. II.

actively concerned with the problem of providing legal services to all classes of the population.[39] He was *inter alia* associated with law school legal aid clinics, those admirable institutions that marry clinical training and social service. These concerns of his were associated with the view that one function of lawyer education is to foster social consciousness, perhaps even a social conscience, in intending lawyers. Thirdly, shortly before his death he gave active encouragement to the individual who has made the most systematic attempt so far to relate a detailed job-analysis of lawyers' operations to problems of law teaching.[40] Finally, and perhaps most important, is the point that Llewellyn's jurisprudential themes and his ideas on legal education are so bound up together as to be almost indistinguishable; a concern with problems of legal education was a most important stimulus to the early development of his general juristic ideas, which ideas in turn had important implications for legal education. Many of those ideas had deep roots in the social sciences, notably anthropology, sociology, economics and psychology. In all of them lawyers' work was a central focus and it is fair to say that one of Llewellyn's achievements was to graft onto the traditional law-oriented jurisprudence a lawyer-oriented jurisprudence.

The Lasswell-McDougal plan

In 1943 Harold Lasswell and Myres McDougal published a notable paper entitled " Legal Education and Public Policy: Professional Training in the Public Interest," [41] which remains the nearest approach to date to a comprehensive theory for lawyer education. It is significant that the paper was also the vehicle for the first important statement of the Lasswell-McDougal intellectual system, which is commonly referred to as " Law, Science and Policy " or L.S.P. for short.[42] L.S.P. is currently the jurisprudential counterpart of L.S.D.: its effects on individuals vary from exhilaration, to deep depression, to indifference and nobody is quite sure to what extent it is habit-forming. There are some who would make it the basis of a religion. Bold, visionary, comprehensive, encased in a petrifying terminology, this neo-Benthamite theory has received in the United Kingdom far less

---

[39] *Ibid.*
[40] Irwin Rutter of the University of Cincinatti. See especially Rutter, " A Jurisprudence of Lawyers' Operations " (1961) 13 Jo.Leg.Ed. 301.
[41] (1943) 52 Yale L.Jo. 203, reprinted in McDougal, *et al.*, *Studies in Public Order.*
[42] The fullest treatment of " Law, Science and Policy " is to be found in a set of mimeographed materials used by the authors in a number of courses at Yale Law School.

attention than it deserves. The intellectual difficulties of the theory need not concern us here; for present purposes the paper is significant as representing the American viewpoint which goes furthest in the direction of the Periclean model. The authors take as their starting-point a bold statement of aim: " We submit this basic proposition: if legal education in the contemporary world is adequately to serve the needs of a free and productive commonwealth, it must be conscious, efficient, and systematic *training for policy-making*." [43]

Lasswell and McDougal justify this rather startling statement in terms of an image of " the lawyer " which even some American lawyers tend to find somewhat grandiose:

> " It should need no emphasis that the lawyer is today, even when not himself a maker of policy, the one indispensable adviser of every responsible policy-maker of our society— whether we speak of the head of a government department or agency, of the executive of a corporation or labor union, of the secretary of a trade or other private association, or even of the humble independent enterpriser or professional man. As such an adviser the lawyer, when informing his policy-maker of what he can or cannot *legally* do, is, as policy-makers often complain, in an unassailably strategic position to influence, if not create, policy." [44]

" Policy " in this context is defined as " the making of important decisions which affect the distribution of values." [45] In this usage the lawyer advising a potential petitioner for divorce, or a testator, is involved in " policy-making " almost as much as the participant in the decisions of appellate courts, administrative tribunals or legislatures. Nevertheless a perusal of the detailed proposals for the reform of lawyer education put forward by Lasswell and McDougal suggests that " the aggrandisement effect " [46] has been at work, for great stress is put on the higher levels of policy-making in the national (and the world) arenas and the operative images of their end-product seem to be the senior partner in the Wall Street law firm, the maker of American foreign policy and the world statesman. In short the Lasswell-McDougal plan for legal education seems to me to be a thinly disguised élitist programme for the training of national leaders, the sort of thing that

---

[43] *Op. cit.*, p. 206.
[44] pp. 208–209.
[45] p. 207.
[46] See Berelson and Steiner, *Human Behavior* (1964), p. 379.

might emerge if, in 1984, Plato's Academy were taken over by M.I.T. with Jeremy Bentham as director.

Apart from reservations that some people would have about the general theory of L.S.P., the specific proposals for lawyer education are open to criticism that they place far too little emphasis on the plumbing aspects of lawyers' work and that they are based on a serious underestimation of the difficulty of attaining minimum technical competence. However, in so far as nearly everyone's views of legal education aspire to some extent towards the Periclean image, the Lasswell-McDougal thesis is stimulating in its proposals for producing national leaders and devastating in its criticisms of traditional approaches and even of the piece-meal innovations that followed the Realist " revolution." [47]

It is not surprising that this extraordinarily stimulating exercise has been viewed somewhat sceptically by those whose ideas of lawyer education have been governed by a more humble image of the lawyer. Relatively few people have accepted the Las-Mac system *in toto*, and even at Yale, their headquarters, their ideas do not seem to have made as fundamental an impact on curriculum planning or teaching methods as might have been expected. Nevertheless there are signs that thinking similar to theirs is becoming increasingly influential. It is worth noting that in this analysis of the development of American legal education in terms of rough stages, each stage is marked by one or more notable departures in forms of student legal literature. The Story period is represented by Story's famous treatises; the Langdellian reforms by Langdell's case-book on contracts; the Realist " revolution " was launched by the publication of a series of case-books at Columbia Law School, of which Llewellyn's *Cases and Materials on the Law of Sales* is the outstanding representative [48]; the Asheville Conference, which will be discussed later, took place in the same year as the publication of Kelso's *Programmed Introduc-*

---

[47] For Llewellyn's assessment, see (1943) 43 Col.L.Rev. 476.

[48] (1930); others include Berle, *Cases and Materials on Corporation Finance* (1930), West Publishing Co.; Goebel, *Cases and Materials on the Development of Legal Institutions* (1931) Columbia; Magill and Maguire, *Cases and Materials on Taxation* (1931), Foundation Press; Hanna, *Cases and Materials on Creditors' Rights* (1931), Foundation Press; Hanna, *Cases and Materials on Security* (1932), Foundation Press; Magill, *Cases on Civil Procedure* (1932), Foundation Press; Patterson, *Cases and Materials on Insurance* (1932), Foundation Press; Jacobs, *Cases and Materials on Landlord and Tenant* (1932), West Publishing Co.; Powell, *Cases and Materials on Trusts and Estates*, 2 vols. (1933), West Publishing Co.; Powell, *Cases and Materials on Possessory Estates* (1933), West Publishing Co.; Handler, *Cases and Materials on Vendor and Purchaser* (1933), West Publishing Co.; Jacobs, *Cases and Materials on Domestic Relations* (1933), Foundation Press; Magill and Hamilton, *Cases and Materials on Business Organisation*, Vol. I (1933), West Publishing Co. (Report of Dean Young B. Smith, 1933, at pp 12–13.)

tion to the Study of Law, I, [49] a work which is notable both as being the first major application of programmed learning in legal education to have been published,[50] and also as being one of the most rigorous attempts to develop teaching of basic skills in a systematic manner; recently two books of materials [51] emanating from Yale Law School have been widely acclaimed as an important new departure in student legal literature; both show unmistakable signs of L.S.P.-type thinking. Do they mark the arrival of a Lasswellian era in some American law schools?

Asheville, 1965

So far in this brief tour of some high-lights of the history of American legal education we have glanced at a few of the operative ideas of leading thinkers—Story, Langdell, Llewellyn and Lasswell and McDougal. The last sketch is different: it is a conference rather than a thinker. I wish to treat it in personal terms, because it symbolises much of what to me, at least, is most admirable in American legal education. In September 1965 I was privileged to attend, as observer, a conference of law school deans at Asheville, Tennessee. The purpose of this conference was to consider reports on some twenty experimental projects in a general area designated as " Education for Professional Responsibility," [52] a title which, when I first heard it, carried associations of high-minded and vague sermons on professional ethics. The reality was quite different. In this context the term " professional responsibility " was used to cover not only matters relating to professional ethics, but also other aspects of the individual practitioner's relationship to his client (expressed in terms of " helping the whole client ") and the public responsibilities of individual lawyers and of the organised Bar. The projects ranged from variations on the well-known legal aid clinic to courses dealing with such matters as counselling in family law, to summer internships in correctional institutions or with organisations connected with the legal problems of the underprivileged.

In most of the projects class work was combined with first-hand experience of the law in action. In many of them there was

---

[49] Bobbs Merrill (1965).
[50] In the United Kingdom one of the first programmes for law was developed, significantly, by the Army Education Corps: Meyrick, *Military Law* (1964).
[51] Donnelly, Goldstein and Schwartz, *Criminal Law* (1962); Goldstein and Katz, *The Family and the Law* (1965); a third, Katz, Goldstein and Dershowitz, *Psychoanalysis, Psychiatry and Law*, has recently been published.
[52] See *Summaries of Law School Projects Supported by the National Council on Legal Clinics* (September 1965); the recently published *Proceedings of the Asheville Conference of Law School Deans on Education for Professional Responsibility* was not available at the time of writing.

a research element. All of them were done under the auspices of university law schools acting in co-operation with practitioners, judges and officials. Although many of the experiments were interesting in themselves, what struck me more was the general atmosphere of the conference. The stimulus behind this series of experiments and the spirit in which they were conducted was a deep and searching concern about the actual and potential role of lawyers in society. One could not but be impressed by the willingness to experiment, the fertility of ideas, the sophistication of the level of discussion and the hard-headed way in which experiments were evaluated. Academics and practitioners were talking on the same wavelength in a manner which presupposed a developing sociology of the legal profession and a shared professionalism about problems of education and training. It was also pleasing to an academic lawyer to find practitioners and judges looking to the law schools for intellectual leadership and to find the law schools responding.

One example may help to convey some sense of the occasion. During a discussion of the problems of teaching professional ethics there was a lively debate about a number of related issues. How far ought a teacher to go beyond posing for his students in as illuminating a way as possible some of the ethical dilemmas that confront practitioners? Should he abdicate all responsibility for moral propaganda? Are problems of professional responsibility best considered in a single course or are they more satisfactorily raised in the context of a large number of courses by what is known as " the pervasive approach"?[53] Can the ethical dilemmas of lawyers be discussed meaningfully without consideration of problems of professional loneliness and disillusionment and the whole psychology of lawyer-client relations? And so on. Some of these questions may be new to some of you, as they were to me; some raise perennial issues in a new context. In the course of discussion a fascinating range of methods of treating the subject was considered and a number of interesting ideas was aired. But even more striking was the amount of common ground that was taken for granted by people who were taking different stands on some of these issues. They assumed first of all that professional ethics is a suitable subject for discussion in a university course and that it poses problems that are as intellectually demanding as standard legal issues; they assumed that classroom time need not be expended on imparting elementary information about the content of

---

[53] See esp. Smedley, " The Pervasive Approach on a Larger Scale—' The Vanderbilt Experiment ' " (1963) 15 Jo.Leg.Ed. 435.

canons of ethics, because such information could easily be acquired by a student on his own; furthermore, they assumed that, even if indoctrination was a legitimate aim, sermonising would at the very least be an inefficient method of achieving this aim and it might well have an effect opposite to the intended one. Sometimes assumptions of this kind are indicative of shallow and thoughtless jumping to conclusions. But in this instance they appeared to represent a consensus that had been reached over a long period of trial and error and thoughtful discussion. This epitomises what I mean by sophistication in legal education.

The relevance of the American experience

The suggestion that there is much to be learned from American experience is not intended to carry with it the implication that the American system is wholly admirable or that there is nothing worthy of preservation in our own tradition. Nor is it suggested that the many significant differences between our respective situations should be ignored. Moreover, the ideas of Story, Langdell, Llewellyn and Lasswell and McDougal are, of course, the ideas of some intellectual leaders of a few élite institutions on the eastern seaboard—notably Harvard, Yale and Columbia. We have, in other words, been concentrating on only one small part of the total picture of American legal education; much of value was initiated in other places and in recent years the general excellence of the leading law schools has spread downwards to a large number of smaller and less well-known institutions. The fact that nearly all of the experimental projects under discussion at Asheville were based on smaller law schools is indicative of this. Nevertheless many thoughtful Americans are justifiably worried at the state of affairs in the lower reaches of the system. Carlin's notable study of *Lawyers on their Own* [54] in Chicago brings out in striking fashion how remote is the world of the national law school and the big law firm from that of the low-standard, despised, struggling and sometimes corrupt solo practitioner. It prompts the thought that perhaps the Americans might learn something from the British about the preservation of *minimum* standards of competence and ethicality.

Granted these caveats, I still firmly believe that we have much to learn from the Americans both in respect of general ideas and of specific techniques. At this moment of time the American experience of the 1920s and thirties seems to be particularly pertinent. Historically the American realist movement was as much

---

[54] *Op. cit.*, n. 56.

as anything a response to the joint stimuli of rapid change and increasing complexity in American life. There is perhaps something in the suggestion that there are quite remarkable parallels in the legal sphere between trends in the United Kingdom in the 1960s and trends in the United States in the 1920s and thirties; these parallels might be explained to some extent in terms of pressures resulting from social and technological change. If Professor Goldstein of Yale is correct in suggesting that we are due for " a realist revolution," [55] it can be expected to be less dramatic and less turbulent than the American one, not least because our problems of change and complexity are less acute. In a relatively homogeneous group of societies addicted to gradualism we may expect the " r " in " revolution " to be muted. Nevertheless, is it not fair to say that the pace of change is one of the most fertile sources of problems in our time and that, in the sphere of education, perhaps the most pressing problem is how to prepare students to cope with rapidly changing situations? Our legal system having lagged behind other institutions in adapting itself to modern conditions, the coming generation of lawyers may have to make extra adjustments. In short, adaptability must become a key concept of lawyer education for the future. Now it happens that circumstances have combined to make adaptability a central characteristic of the products of the national law schools in the United States. With students drawn from a large number of jurisdictions, it is practically impossible to concentrate on the law of any single jurisdiction, except in federal matters; the dominant place of law and lawyers in American society and, related to this, the great variety of types of lawyer within the legal profession; the ethnic and social heterogeneity; and the rapid pace of technological and economic advance are among the factors that have produced a concerted pressure to make legal education above all an investment in certain ideas and skills of wide application. In

---

[55] The context is a discussion of the prospects for development of empirical research into legal processes in the United Kingdom. The passage reads: " Though brave efforts are being made in a handful of places, it seems quite clear to me that research in the legal process of the kind and quality I have described can only come after the ideological spade-work has first been done. There must first be an extended period of inter-disciplinary fumbling; and that is likely to come only when English law teaching, and the conception of law which animates it, has had its ' legal realist ' revolution " Goldstein, " Research into the Administration of Criminal Law: A Report from the United States " (1966) 6 Brit.Jo. Criminology 27, 37. Compare the plea by G. P. Wilson of Cambridge for " a vigorous philosophy of law that will tie together the leading influences and motives behind the new developments and at the same time point the way to the future " [1966] C.L.J. 148–149. The interdependence of legal theory, legal education, legal research and legal literature is discussed briefly in the full version of this lecture.

trying to produce adaptable lawyers, whose stock-in-trade, it is sometimes said, is a creative problem-solving approach,[56] there have been two main shifts from the patterns of the Joseph Story tradition: first, a switch from emphasis on knowledge of rules of law to emphasis on the acquisition of skills [57]; secondly, a broadening of the focus of attention, so that legal doctrines are rarely studied without reference to the social situations, the problems, the policies and the processes which constitute the context of their operation.

American law schools have not had a monopoly of education for adaptability. Any contemporary institution concerned with the study of science or technology is faced with the same basic problem in a particularly acute form. Furthermore, it should not be forgotten that the notion of " transferability " has also been an important part of the " liberal " idea. Many would agree that the leading American law schools have recaptured much of what is worthy of preservation in the liberal tradition. Those who feel that the frenetic atmosphere of their law schools is inimical to quiet contemplation may also feel that the wine of Jowett and Newman (and of German vintage) was diluted while crossing the Atlantic. The bouquet was lost, perhaps, but fizz was added. Nevertheless, Llewellyn's perception that the liberal and the vocational could be wedded in a single institution was a sound one.

Four themes in need of development

Given time, many themes could be developed. Perhaps four should be singled out for brief treatment as having special potential significance:

(1) A systematic approach to the problems of lawyer education needs as a foundation a developed sociology of the legal profession. Before it is possible to formulate sound detailed objectives there is

---

[56] The idea has also reached Australia: " The essential task of the lawyer is problem-solving ": Preface to Maher, Waller and Derham, *Cases and Materials on the Legal Process* (1966), The Law Book Co. Ltd., Australia.

[57] There are those who would contend that the switch from acquisition of information has been carried too far in the United States, even having regard to the special conditions there; in the United Kingdom there would be considerable opposition, some of it justified, to the scrapping of all memory work (*e.g.*, see the Wilson Report at p. 52). My own position is that even in relatively stable times too much emphasis was put on " knowing the law," and in the present situation of enormous complexity and relatively rapid change, it is a poor investment to devote a great deal of effort to storing information in one's head. Nevertheless it is possible to carry this too far. In African contexts I have found myself disagreeing with compatriots who considered that there should be little or no time devoted to skills teaching in a university, whilst chiding those American teachers (not by any means all of them) who considered that the imparting of information was not included in their functions.

a need for a clear and differentiated picture of the kind of end-product desired. The simplistic images of " the lawyer " that have so often been hidden in people's assumptions about legal education have been a fertile source of confused and confusing controversy. Both the Periclean and the plumbing images are quite inadequate: they are crude, over-simplified and unrealistic.

In order to arrive at an adequate formulation of objectives there is a need to ask and re-ask the questions: What are lawyers for? What could lawyers be for? What should lawyers be for? A necessary foundation is a job-analysis of what lawyers do, a skills analysis of the operations involved and some reliable studies of the economics of the profession, the psychology of professionalism, and the many other fields of inquiry that fall under the general rubric " the sociology of the legal profession." [58] Of course, empirical research by itself will not provide all the answers. There will always be plenty of scope for variety and for disagreement about values, priorities and methods. Also, being concerned with the future, education must always involve a large element of faith, especially for the enlightened educator who looks on it as a long-term investment. Other ineffables will always be with us. Nevertheless much can be gained by starting from a solid base of reliable information about the present situation and current trends.

(2) There is a need to break free from the extraordinarily rigid stereotyped thinking that has come to dominate most discussions of legal education: that the cosmos is irrevocably divided into fields of law such as contract and torts; that the only mode of classification to be used in curriculum planning is that of fields of law; that examinations must be three hours in length; that examinations can only test knowledge of legal doctrines and ability to apply rules to hypothetical fact situations; that all courses must be given equal weight; that every course must have a textbook; that every textbook must conform to a standard pattern; that legal doctrine is *the* subject-matter of legal studies; that every lawyer is a private practitioner of law; that there should be a uniform pattern of qualifications for law teachers; that there are

---

[58] Following on the heels of the pioneering Survey of the Legal Profession summarised in Blaustein and Porter, *The American Lawyer* (1954), there have been some notable recent studies, especially Carlin, *Lawyers on their Own* (1962) and *Lawyers' Ethics* (1966); Smigel, *The Wall Street Lawyer* (1964); Weyrauch, *The Personality of Lawyers* (1964). Abel-Smith and Stevens, *Lawyers and the Courts* (1967), provide a most useful historical foundation for the development of the subject in England. A forthcoming study by Professors Johnstone and Hopson, *Lawyers and their Work*, promises to mark the rise of the comparative sociology of legal professions. The subject has potentially far-reaching implications for several areas of legal theory.

accepted and fixed criteria of the suitability of a subject for study in a university—and so on.[59] Such assumptions all need to be questioned. In particular some general working distinctions, which are admittedly useful in some contexts, have become frozen into rigid dichotomies; " education " and " training "[60]; " academic " and " practical "[61]; " theory " and " practice "; " liberal " and

---

[59] Several of these assumptions are to be found in the Wilson Report; examples of the others will almost inevitably be discoverable by anyone who cares to listen for a few hours to discussions of curriculum among academic lawyers.

[60] For a recent defence of the distinction between " professional education and vocational training," see Professor Kahn-Freund's stimulating lecture " Reflections on Legal Education," 29 M.L.R. 121. Contrast the following quotations from documents relating to industrial training: " The reason for this distinction between education and training [in the Industrial Training Act] is that in this country the provision of skilled training to meet the specific requirements of industry has always been accepted to be industry's responsibility, while the education service has been provided by education authorities. The Act makes no essential change in this position. It recognises the division of responsibility, but does not create it. Nonetheless, there is a danger that, in clarifying the position, the Act may tend to sharpen the distinction between education and training just at a time when that distinction is becoming less and less meaningful. We therefore think it important, at this early stage in the operation of the Act, to emphasise the point that, notwithstanding the formal division of responsibility between the boards and education authorities, further education and training are complementary aspects of a single process " (Central Training Council Memorandum No. 1, " Industrial Training and Further Education," Ministry of Labour (1965)).

A pamphlet of the City and Guilds of London Institute contains the following comment on this passage: " In particular, of course, the trainee will not find meaningful any distinction between the two concepts. There has, however, been much discussion on the relationships between further education and training; many attempts have been made to define them, but no generally accepted definition has so far emerged. Agreement may be reached as to what activities in technical colleges are ' training ' and which ' education ' for the purpose of determining who should pay for a given activity, but this is only a sensible and workable administrative arrangement which can be altered, as it was made, by the parties concerned. It is thus an insubstantial base on which to build any new philosophy of further education " (City and Guilds of London Institute, *First Year Certificate in Engineering Crafts, Regulations and Syllabuses valid for Examinations to be held in 1967* (1966) at p. 7).

[61] The worst example of this has been the division of fields of law into " academic " and " practical " subjects. Whereas torts, contract, equity and land law have been considered " academic," whatever that means in this context, civil and criminal procedure, conveyancing, company law, even interpretation of statutes and to a lesser extent evidence, have often been treated as " practical " subjects to be studied outside the universities or to be included within undergraduate curricula only grudgingly, as a concession to the profession. Analytically the distinction is difficult, if not impossible, to defend, except perhaps in terms of a question-begging differentiation between subjects suitable and unsuitable for undergraduate study. Two rules-of-thumb in determining suitability seem to have been that case-law should be preferred to statute-law and substantive law should take precedence over procedure. Dead or dying, both rules deserve burial. We have to a large extent rejected the old idea that legislation is not a fit study for gentlemen; we have yet to accept fully that it is unrealistic and often intellectually indefensible to study substantive law subjects in isolation from their procedural context. I would go further and say that civil and criminal procedure and the interpretation of statutes, cases and documents should be given a prominent place as foundation subjects in our university curricula. On this theme generally, see Abel-Smith and Stevens, *op. cit.*, Chap. XIII.

" vocational " [62]; " law " and " other disciplines." Over-reliance on such distinctions, it is suggested, has been the Achilles' heel of our present patterns of lawyer education. One suspects that some of them have been functionally important in the power struggle between the universities and the legal profession. If *rapprochement* is not practicable, then they may continue to serve a function. But are academics justified in assuming that the legal professions are doomed to perpetual and incurable unenlightenment in their attitudes to lawyer education? Are practitioners for ever to look on academics as inevitably destined either for effete and starry-eyed irrelevance or for the subservient status of plumbers' mates? If so, these distinctions will continue to be functionally important as artificial boundaries between spheres of influence.[63] There are signs, however, that the situation has become comparatively fluid recently and that there is an opportunity for a *rapprochement*. In particular the current dissatisfaction among practitioners about the provisions for lawyer education gives ground for optimism.[64] It is to be hoped that they will not be satisfied with what Riesman called " the reverent modification of small particulars." [65] If *rapprochement* is to be more than an uneasy patched-up affair it must be based on a measure of agreement about fundamentals at the level of theory. Otherwise the self-confirming element in these mutually hostile attitudes allied to other divisive factors

---

[62] American law schools have tended to adopt an openly vocational approach, yet the intellectual atmosphere of schools of my acquaintance compares very favourably indeed with that of their counterparts in other countries. This gives support to the view that there is no necessary incompatibility between a vocational approach and such values as free inquiry, intellectual rigour, independence of thought and breadth of perspective. In short, there is a false antithesis between " vocational " and " liberal " in this context. There is also no necessary incompatibility between a contextual approach to the study of law and a vocational approach to legal education. To contrast them is to make another false antithesis. Indeed, if the lawyer to be aimed for is to be a technologist rather than a technician, there is a high degree of compatibility between the two approaches; as Sir Eric Ashby says: " A student who can weave his technology into the fabric of society can claim to have a liberal education; a student who cannot weave his technology into the fabric of society cannot claim even to be a good technologist ": *Technology and the Academics* at p. 85. On false antitheses that have permeated our ideas on university education, see pp. 71–88.

[63] Gower, *op. cit.*, n. 20, at pp. 151–162, while acknowledging that the distinction between education and training can be pressed too far, favoured a clear separation between theoretical and practical training on the grounds of political expediency.

[64] According to a poll conducted by Wilson, only 22·5 per cent. of barristers and 29·5 per cent. of solicitors at that time considered that provisions were adequate; even more striking were the figures for practitioners of under five years' standing: 82·5 per cent. of barristers in this category and 68 per cent. of solicitors considered the provisions to be inadequate: *op. cit.* at pp. 73 and 83. Since then some changes have been introduced by the Council of Legal Education.

[65] " Law and Social Science " (1941) 50 Yale L.J. 636, 637.

(notably the growing tendency to recruit law teachers immediately on graduation and the increasing number of undergraduates who have little or no prospect of practising) will tend to widen the existing gap between the academic and practising branches of the profession.

(3) So far little has been said about method, because discussion of method is usually best done after the clarification of objectives. Much could be said. Clearly there is enormous scope for extension of the use of simulators, clinics, programmed learning and other devices. Perhaps the Asheville Conference marks the start of an era of systematic development of such techniques. A precondition for this is a faith in teachability. We may smile smugly, sometimes with justification, at the American tendency to believe that one can learn anything by taking a course in it; but in so far as this is occasioned by a persistent urge to make more communicable what man has had the opportunity to learn by experience, the impulse has much to commend it. An almost essential precondition for educational progress is a willingness to ask such questions as: Is it teachable? How might it be taught? Would expenditure of time and resources on teaching it be justified? What priority should it be given? The discipline of having to define " it " in this context can in itself be a substantial stimulus to thought and understanding.

In the United Kingdom a major obstacle to progress is likely to be the idea that the successful practice of law involves mastery of a mystical art that cannot be studied systematically, but can only be picked up in the course of practice. The Pickitup Theory of Training has a sound core of sense in it; but it is odd to find it still so predominant in law when in most other occupations haphazard apprenticeship and the cult of the gentleman amateur are both fast disappearing. Almost any sensible scheme of lawyer education would give a significant role to experience, especially planned experience, as a teacher; but there are almost certainly things at present left to be picked up which could be learned more efficiently or more economically or both by other methods; there are also instances in which it would be appropriate to try to capitalise on the lessons of experience by post-mortem discussions or more formal kinds of follow-up. Experience is often potentially the best teacher, but unaided the man of action is not always an equally good learner. In respect of such matters legal educators could probably learn much from the Armed Forces, from the medical schools and from those involved in industrial training, perhaps even from those connected with the training of real plumbers.

Of the various matters which might be treated under the heading of " method " there is one which deserves to be given very high priority indeed. There is surely an urgent need for a fundamental and rigorous re-examination of the whole system of law examinations. This exercise should be concerned not only with such obvious matters as defining with precision what is being tested and extending the range of techniques of testing, but also with some questions which may be of greater social importance: what are the effects of our present examination system on the behaviour of students, teachers, authors, publishers, curriculum planners, and the products of the process of legal education? To what extent are these effects compatible with desired objectives of the process? To what extent are these effects desirable and undesirable in other ways? It is a plausible hypothesis that the formal examination is the device which has more influence than any other on participants in the educational process, creating expectations, forming attitudes and channelling energies.[66] If this is so, those who are depressed by nutshells, parrot-learning, cram courses, stereotyped thinking and other features of the present scene would do well to ask some searching questions about the extent to which those who have most power over the examination system have been exercising their power with perception, enlightenment or responsibility. As a university examiner who has had a minute share of such power I confess that my conscience is troubled; it is a source of comfort that my responsibility has not been wider.

(4) A comprehensive working theory, based on a systematic study of the profession and using a developed terminology, would serve many purposes. One of the most important gains for lawyer education might be that proposals based on hard fact and systematic analysis might possibly make the most conservative of professions a little more amenable to innovation and experiment. The way might then be open for the belated injection of some educational professionalism into professional education. This will probably take a long time; while waiting, those who ought to be professional legal educators, we academic lawyers, might set an example by putting our own house in order. One suspects that our own educational amateurism has been a major factor in the ineffectiveness of criticisms of the traditional " system " of professional training. For surely many of its weaknesses have been primarily educational weaknesses: in formulation of objectives, in planning

---

[66] Megarry: " Under modern conditions, it is the examination that is the master of both the teacher and the author. If there are examinations on a subject, it will be taught, and books will be written on it; if there are no examinations on a subject, then probably, though not inevitably, there will be neither teaching nor students books ": *Lawyer and Litigant in England* (1962), p. 96.

of syllabuses, in teaching methods, in examinations, in administration, in the concepts and the thought patterns that have been dominant, and, in other respects, what has been lacking above all, or so it seems to an outsider, has been a willingness to learn from those who know something and care about education and training.

Envoi

These prolegomena fall far short of a comprehensive working theory. If the tone of this lecture has seemed in places to be radical, please remember that few, if any, of the ideas put forward are new. In fact my present position, as far as I am able to define it, seems to me to be somewhat conservative, or at least liberal-conservative. It would be good to see our idea of liberal education refurbished a little—in particular its associations with social and intellectual snobbery need to go, together with its proneness to defensive obscurantism—but the central values, such as free inquiry, interest in human nature, breadth of perspective, intellectual discipline, independence of thought and judgment and love of truth need to be preserved, indeed in legal education some need to be recaptured. This is hardly the creed of a revolutionary. Impatience with pre-Langdellian ideas is surely forgivable, if one remembers that in three years' time the centenary of Langdell's appointment to Harvard will be celebrated. Is there indecent haste in the suggestion that the lag behind the United States might be reduced to a decent thirty or thirty-five years? The Lasswell-McDougal plan for legal education, published in 1943, is still rather too *avant garde* for my taste. Let us by all means wait another ten or twenty years before introducing the first Lasswellian social planetarium into the United Kingdom. Is this hot-headed radicalism?

One final point: when this lecture was in a fairly advanced state of preparation it became apparent that it would bring together at least three potentially unpopular themes: I frequently encounter people who expect me to apologise for being a theorist; " legal education " is often sneered at as being a subject unworthy of the serious attention of legal educators; there are people who may think it unpatriotic to suggest that we might learn from the experience of others. Yet I have dared to suggest that we need a theory for lawyer education based in part on foreign ideas. I am unrepentant; and I hope at least to have communicated the idea that legal education as a subject is socially important and intellectually exacting and that as such it is worthy of sustained reflection, dispassionate inquiry and creative thought. Today I have merely flicked at a few cobwebs. A more disciplined treatment would require another medium and a better equipped exponent. As was recently suggested at a notable conference of younger law teachers, legal education is too serious a topic to be left to inaugural lectures.[67]

WILLIAM TWINING.

[67] J. P. W. B. McAuslan, " The Proper Relation between University Law Teaching and Training for the Legal Profession in England: Some Thoughts on our Present Discontents ": paper read at Conference on " The Concept of a Law Degree," Cambridge, September 1966.

Curricular Development in the 1980s: A Perspective
Roderick A. Macdonald

Discussions of the law-school curriculum typically highlight new courses, new methodologies, and new programs. Few examine curricular reform itself. In this paper the former themes are employed to investigate the latter. A primary goal is to illustrate how the insights of traditional speculative philosophy can facilitate a better understanding of fundamental issues in curricular reform. A second objective is to demonstrate that thoughtful curricular debate is a law school's primary heuristic device. The paper begins by considering several major trends in curricular innovation over the last thirty years; it then suggests ways in which each raises recurring problems in legal philosophy of which disputants may be only dimly aware; the essay concludes with several prescriptions tending to stimulate ongoing curricular debate.

When one assesses North American legal education in the immediate postwar period, certain elements emerge as characteristic. Law faculties offered a substantial number of compulsory courses, the majority of which covered the traditional common-law subjects; a few options in "esoteric" areas such as administrative law, labor law, or consumer law rounded out the curriculum. The boundaries of legal analysis were drawn narrowly; professors tended to characterize broader themes as policy analysis which operated on a different level than black-letter law. Most teaching was effected through the study of appellate decisions; even in courses given magisterially, the casebook served as the primary pedagogical instrument. Examinations invariably consisted of hypothetical fact situations which required students to predict the outcome of litigation; opportunities for drafting and overt theorizing rarely presented themselves. Finally, skills-and-tools courses tended to be the dominant, if not exclusive, nonsubstantive offerings; legal writing, trial and appellate advocacy, statute interpretation, case analysis, legal accounting, and law-office management held

---

Roderick A. Macdonald is Professor and Associate Dean, Faculty of Law, McGill University. This article is a revised version of a speech delivered on May 31, 1979, at the Annual Meeting of the Canadian Association of Law Teachers in Saskatoon, Saskatchewan, and published under the title Legal Education on the Threshold of the 1980s: Whatever Happened to the Great Ideas of the 60s?, 37 Sask. L. Rev. 39 (1979). It is republished here with the permission of that Review. At the request of the Editor, Professor Macdonald has redrafted the speech as a written essay, has attempted to use examples more familiar to an audience in the United States, and has provided occasional footnote references.

©1982 by the Association of American Law Schools. Cite as 32 J. Legal Educ. 569 (1982).

pride of place over jurisprudence, legal process, legal institutions, and sociology of law.

In the 1980s, a strikingly different landscape has emerged. Law schools have reduced the number of required courses; in principle, only first-year subjects survive as obligatory offerings. Professors now exhibit a more catholic concept of legal knowledge; "law and . . ." courses, supervised research programs, and interdisciplinary seminars have proliferated. Attachment to the study of appellate decisions has waned; the opportunity for thematic concentration through semester-long "special studies" programs and nonclassroom alternatives such as community legal clinics and corporate internships is a regular feature of law-school calendars. The litigation hypothetical set in the context of adversarial adjudication no longer dominates classroom and examination; teachers of tax planning, antenuptial settlements, contract negotiation, and sales and corporate financing frankly acknowledge the limited utility of studying only the "problem case" and judicial remedies. Renewed interest in the intellectual foundations and social functions of law has spawned courses in legal philosophy, judicial decision making, the legal process, law and society, comparative law, and legal history; doctrinal exegesis is being replaced as pedagogical orthodoxy by upstart approaches such as economic analysis and the "critical" perspective.

Of course, these patterns of curricular development were not inevitable. Nor was the erosion of received dogma necessarily the result of a well thought-out and widely shared concept of the mission of legal education. But it is not the purpose of this essay to suggest a historiography or a politics of curricular change. For the law-school program ultimately is the product of many influences: tradition, university politics, the expectations of the bar, government funding priorities, the wishes of students, materials of study available, and the views of professors about what law is and what part of it is capable of being taught. In this light, it is arguable that the developments highlighted here are not even the most significant changes in legal education. However, each points to at least one major issue in the philosophy of law and provokes inquiry into the educational significance of curricular debate.

Compulsory Courses and Optional Offerings: A Study in Classical Metaphysics

The dispute about the number and content of compulsory courses offers a first microcosm of the paradoxes facing legal educators. In the past, issue often was joined on the question whether law schools should dispense lawyer education or legal education. Those asserting the professional perspective justified curricular choices by recurring to data about how lawyers spent their time; not surprisingly, in addition to substantive subjects, they deemed courses in accounting, law-office management, and small business financing to be imperative. In this universe, almost all courses were compulsory, and those offerings thought necessary were also considered to be sufficient for a good legal education. Today, the ground of debate has shifted. Law is regarded as a university discipline, and this setting presupposes a conception of a law school's function different from that which prevailed even into the early 1950s. As the role of practitioners in legal education receded and as the number of career law teachers increased, the academic identity of law revealed itself in demands for greater diversity in course offerings. The volume of new courses alone shepherded the creation of an optional curricular framework. Moreover, the perceived need to prepare students for a variety of careers buttressed the movement towards fleshing out the curriculum and reducing the number of compulsory courses to a minimum. Consequently law schools were compelled for the first time to distinguish the optional from the obligatory among fundamental courses.

Either through inertia or as a result of administrative convenience this problem usually was approached by defining the compulsory in terms of first-year offerings. Yet, the first-year program did not change substantially when the number of compulsory courses was reduced: torts, contracts, property, criminal law, civil procedure, and constitutional law invariably remained obligatory. When faculties decided to permit optional courses to predominate in the upper years, they directed little attention to the content of the first-year program. Often it merely was assumed that the first-year courses appropriate to a wholly compulsory curriculum were equally appropriate as first-year offerings in an optional curriculum. Hence, analysis of this enigma of curricular reform profitably may begin with an assessment of the reasons given for teaching certain subjects in the first year of law school.

The common defense of standard first-year courses typically has two elements: it is said that these courses reflect the historical foundations and development of the common law; and it is asserted that their content remains fundamental to the contemporary practice of law. While this claim may have had elements of truth to it twenty years ago, it is indefensible in the early 1980s. Not only has recent scholarship suggested alternative conceptions of the common-law tradition, legislative activity has eroded much of the remaining common law. A few examples will illustrate how conventional mythology has deflected law teachers from grappling with either of these changes.

Property, contracts, and torts offer the best vehicles for uncovering assumptions about the content and methodology of first-year compulsory courses. Few would dispute that today the concept of property is more usefully rendered through studies of security interests, trademarks, subdivision control, condominiums, time-sharing agreements, and credit cards than by future interests, dower, and the fee-tail. But the depth of this idolatry only emerges when one considers the way in which historians now are reconceptualizing the common-law writs as exercises of administrative authority. From such a perspective Charles Reich's new property of franchises, licenses, monopolies, entitlements, and tax liability suddenly seems very old.[1] In the law of contracts a similar assessment is possible. Modern legislation effectively has confined the common law of contracts to the private sale of used typewriters and bicycles. Moreover, postclassical theorists claim that there never was a single common law of contracts, in that issues of offer and acceptance, consideration, and capacity always have been transaction specific. One wonders about the utility of postulating the discrete transaction as the archetypal contract in a world where even my barber knows that I refer to him as *my* barber.[2] The law of torts is also vulnerable to this kind of critical analysis. The subject as explored in the *Restatement* hardly merits the status of an obligatory offering in a world of medicare, pension plans, workman's compensation, compulsory auto insurance, and consumer-warranties statutes. It may be that certain common-law principles such as vicarious liability, occupiers' liability, defamation, interference with domestic relations, economic torts, and privacy retain much of their former vitality, but few of these topics receive detailed consideration in first-year torts courses. In a very real sense, ever since the days of Roscoe Pound, law professors have known that most emerging torts are taught more profitably as elements of corporate law, real-estate transactions, labor law, civil liberties, and family law.[3]

Similar comments might be made about criminal law, civil procedure, and constitutional law, which also typically are obligatory subjects in the first year. Collectively, the courses making up the compulsory curriculum imbue students with the view that relations between private citizens, as mediated by the courts in an adversarial adjudicative context on the basis of an uncodified law of precedents, continue to be today's predominant legal concerns.[4] Surely no law teacher seriously entertains this belief in 1980. Of course, the suggestion here is not that courses dealing with

---

1. Consider the thesis that judicial activity in the development of land law can be seen as an antecedent of modern administrative law; that the creation of a new writ was analogous to the awarding of a new monolopy, license, or franchise. See, e.g., S.F.C. Milsom, Historical Foundations of the Common Law, 2d ed., 1-239 (Toronto: Butterworths, 1981); Lawrence M. Friedman, A History of American Law 510 et seq. (New York: Simon & Schuster, 1973).

2. For a recent exposition, and footnote introduction to the literature, see Ian R. Macneil, The New Social Contract (New Haven: Yale Univ. Press, 1980); Patrick S. Atiyah, The Rise and Fall of Freedom of Contract (Oxford: Clarendon Press, 1979); Charles Fried, Contract as Promise: A Theory of Contractual Obligation (Cambridge, Mass.: Harvard Univ. Press, 1981).

3. The debate reviewed in and partly generated by G. Edward White, Tort Law in America: An Intellectual History (New York: Oxford Univ. Press, 1979), is instructive.

4. I have elaborated on this theme in a review of Stephen M. Waddams, Introduction to the Study of Law, 31 U. Toronto L. J. 436-50 (1981). A similar point is made in Harry W. Arthurs, Rethinking Administrative Law: A Slightly Dicey Business, 17 Osgoode Hall L. J. 1 (1979), and Jonah and the Whale: The Appearance, Disappearance, and Reappearance of Administrative Law, 30 U. Toronto L. J. 225 (1980).

Curricular Development in the 1980s

concepts such as property, covenants, compensation, coercion, decision-making models, or the constitutional process have no claim to be taught in the first year. Rather, it is that the mythological model of the common law depicted in the preceding paragraphs was invented for a political purpose in the late nineteenth century and that most first-year courses, as currently taught, appear as the centaurs of legal history.[5]

Freed from proselytizing parading as received tradition, law teachers now have an opportunity to confront directly the question of why certain courses and topics should be obligatory. Yet in spite of this freedom to speculate, a new dogmatism has emerged. Contemporary orthodoxy suggests that the preferred solution to this dilemma is neither to oblige students to enroll in newly conceived first-year courses nor to modify the content of existing courses but simply to make more courses obligatory. Support for a larger inventory of compulsory courses comes in some measure from members of the bench and bar, who feel that the increasing incidence of malpractice is evidence of incomplete legal education. Yet the coincidence of professional self-interest and professorial self-indulgence is hardly a satisfactory justification for curricular choices.

If law schools are to respond adequately to the ebb and flow of compulsory/optional pressures, they cannot avoid the issue by increasing obligatory offerings; rather they must discover or rediscover the values which underlie the selection of basic courses. This quest is tied less to issues of content and methodology (which most discussions seem to suggest) than to beliefs about how people learn and what kind of knowledge properly is acquired in a law school: the latter are questions of classical metaphysics which entail also asking what law schools are trying to teach. The oft-repeated claim that law school should provide students with substantive knowledge of fundamental legal rules and teach them to think like lawyers is an inadequate response since it explains neither which rules are fundamental nor what lawyers one should think like.

Two ways to pursue this inquiry have been suggested. The first is to argue that law is an empirical science: what the law is can be determined by counting statutes and tabulating the work of judges. Accordingly, basic subjects are those most frequently legislated or litigated. Yet few lawyers would argue that the volume of statutes and regulations generated in a given area reflect anything more than legislative preoccupation; nor would they claim that litigation volume acurately reflects settlement ratios. Neither all statutes nor all lawsuits are equally important. Those who cleave to the events of the real world invariably fail to appreciate the theory of reality which sustains their world so defined.[6]

---

5. In recent periodical literature, Robert W. Gordon, Historicism in Legal Scholarship, 90 Yale L. J. 1017 (1981), gives a good account of this problem.

6. Even the most persuasive modern empiricist, Willard V.O. Quine, falls victim in his celebrated essay Two Dogmas of Empiricism, *in* From a Logical Point of View (Cambridge, Mass.: Harvard Univ. Press, 1953).

Just as empiricism alone cannot provide a satisfactory answer to the question of what makes a course basic, neither can inquiry proceed entirely upon an *a priori* basis. It is true that theories about the content and elements of a subject must underlie law teaching, but brief reflection reveals the limitations of this criterion as a sole means for deciding why a course is basic. Rarely do judicial decisions reflect the strictures of received doctrine with much precision. Moreover, it is the proliferation of exceptions and undercurrents in deciding cases which stimulates the development of new theories. The constantly changing content of courses, as new offerings are spun out or collapsed, surely has more justification than the theoretical pecadillos of the legal Academy. Further, unless law is treated as more than an abstract theoretical enterprise, one has few standards by which to judge disputes among commentators or judges. The fate of esperanto counsels caution to those who would disregard the value of empiricism, for it is trite that the idea which is "good in theory yet bad in practice" is really bad in theory.[7]

There is an important lesson in the fact that law teachers typically advance, often inconsistently, a variety of reasons to justify their conclusion that a particular course should be compulsory. For example, one might say that the historical significance of common-law property renders it basic and also claim that family property law is basic because of recent legislative activity. By contrast, one might answer that the theory of intentional, nominate torts is fundamental because it introduces students to the interest-balancing function of law but deny that the theory of administrative law, which highlights the regulatory function of law, is basic. Lawyers assert both empirical and *a priori* arguments because both are necessarily deployed in deciding what is law. It follows that rejecting curricular proposals grounded exclusively in one or the other approach implies rejecting a theory of law which is ultimately reducible to one or the other. Yet seldom do curricular debates reflect an awareness that the concern over compulsory and optional courses implies asking and answering such fundamental questions.

Once these questions are brought to light, however, a professional commitment to legal education should compel law teachers to consider how they are conceived and disputed in modern speculative philosophy. An understanding of the concepts of causation, identity, unity, truth, interpretation, and history is presupposed in the determination of the obligatory in law-school curricula. One might hope that the discipline of justification in the classical tradition will provide a sufficient innoculation against continued superficiality in current disputes about compulsory courses.[8]

---

7. The best legal exposition of this truth is Lon Fuller's Introduction to the reprint of Legal Fictions (Stanford: Stanford Univ. Press, 1968).

8. This theme is persuasively argued by Martin Foss, The Idea of Perfection in the Western World (Princeton: Princeton Univ. Press, 1946).

"Law and . . ." Courses: A Problem of Epistemology

A second recurring item on the agenda of recent curricular development is the "law and . . ." course phenomenon. Thirty years ago such courses were practically unknown; today one hears that some schools teach so many "law and . . ." courses that students can graduate with a degree in "law and the bumble bee." While this kind of inarticulate carping does not merit serious reply, it is instructive to consider why "law and . . ." courses proliferated and why they have attracted criticism. Expanding notions about what materials are properly brought to the study of law account in considerable measure for this development. Thus, courses such as law and medicine, law and poverty, law and sociology, and law and the mass media can be viewed as an attempt to situate legal rules in their nonlegal context. But "law and . . ." courses also rest on alternative views about the unifying threads in our legal system. Intellectual coherence need not be generated exclusively by a legal concept applied across several discrete domains of human activity; it may flow from the subject matter itself as this is affected by discrete legal rules.[9]

The dispute about "law and . . ." courses reflects a deep-seated tension which is common to all pedagogies: given that everything cannot be taught at once, and given the limits of time and resources, should a curriculum be structured on the basis of factual subject-matter coherence or legal-concept coherence, each of which is equally the product of judgment? One might ask if law schools should teach courses entitled the Law of Beaches or the Law of Subdivisions, in which students examine elements of property, tort, contract, commercial law, and real estate as they relate to beaches or to subdivisions; or should beach torts be taught in a course about torts, the sale of beaches in a real-estate course, finders' rights on beaches in a property course, and exclusion clauses relating to beaches in a contracts course. Today a curriculum composed exclusively of courses on the law of beaches, subdivisions, forests, houses, and the automobile would have few proponents, although, paradoxically, the reverse might well have been true one hundred years ago.[10]

Presently most law teachers concede some courses of the "law and . . ." variety to be worthwhile: corporation law, consumer law, commercial law, and insurance—all spun out of the law of contracts on the basis of "law and . . ." factors—no longer fight for recognition. Nevertheless, professors invariably argue that courses integrating basic legal concepts as they are applied to a wide range of factual situations must predominate; they claim that pure legal concepts have a thematic coherence not found in the

---

9. See J. Anthony Jolowicz, ed., The Division and Classification of the Law (London: Butterworths, 1970).

10. One need only recur to journal and digest readings and the titles of various legal treatises or articles for a perspective on legal organization. See, e.g., R. Vashon Rogers, The Law of the Road or Wrongs and Rights of a Traveller (New York: Hurd & Houghton, 1876), George H. Oliphant, The Law Concerning Horses, Racing, Wagers, and Gaming (Philadelphia: Johnson, 1847).

unruly world of fact. However, this assertion leads to further questions to which few scholars have ready answers. For example, even if one assumes that torts is a course which integrates basic legal concepts, one may still have trouble finding its unifying conceptual thread: is it intention, fault, actual damage? Thematic coherence in so-called concept-based courses is as much an intellectual invention as legal coherence is in so-called fact-based courses.

"Law and . . ." courses also highlight conflicting attitudes about the importance of facts in the legal system. A generation ago law teachers began to realize that, contrary to the ethereal assumptions of text and casebook compilers, apparently irrelevant facts do make a difference in the application of legal doctrine. Yet most teaching proceeds at such a high level of abstraction that these differences can be glossed over. "Law and . . ." courses deny the teacher this comfortable escape and eliminate his ascendency over students to the extent that it is based solely on his superior knowledge of legal doctrine. A significant consequence of "law and . . ." courses, therefore, is that professors and students are compelled to account for both the major and the minor premise in the legal syllogism. It is one thing to say to a client: "I am not sure if the judge will find for you, but if he does, there is an 80 percent chance that he will invoke the rule in $X v. Y$." It is quite another to state: "I am 80 percent certain that the judge will find for you, but the basis on which he will do so is unclear. There are a number of possibilities that occur to me." The former assertion flows from the standard law-school exercise of issue identification, which is the stock-in-trade of courses organized by legal concept; the latter focuses on the intelligent evaluation of facts, which is most often a "law and . . ." exercise.

Today "law and . . ." courses are coming under increasing attack, and pure versions tend to have a short life in the curriculum. Either they die out or they become ". . . Law" courses such as Labor Law, Family Law, Consumer Law, and, most recently, Administrative Law. A course which starts life tied to a new social priority, touches other disciplines, and profits from the intellectual ferment of nonlawyers invariably survives only by evolving into a course which examines appropriately titled statutes and cases. In the end, one might say that criticism of "law and . . ." courses rarely is directed to their creation and elaboration but rather to recalcitrant offerings, or teachers, that resist their preordained evolution.

Two major themes, both tied to problems of epistemology, emerge from the above discussion: first, one must decide why certain topics are grouped together within a single course and what thesis sustains the structure of curricula; second, the basis upon which the boundaries of legally useful inquiry are determined must be clarified. Answering the first query requires an evaluation of the organizing capacity of legal concepts, for the argument that there is a subject called "Contracts" which should be taught implies that there is a recognizable legal coherence which can be explained in terms of the concept "contract." The absence of the course "Bumble Bees" suggests that the same unifying thread cannot be found in the term "bumble bee." Certain commentators claim that the difference is that contract is a legal concept while bumble bee is an object of experience. Yet this facile distinction does not withstand analysis: like bumble bee, the word contract can be and has been reified; moreover, at least in the *Bees Act* the word bumble bee, like the word contract, functions as a legal concept.

It is not immediately obvious that the term contracts, therefore, is a more meaningful organizing tool in the law than bumble bee. Indeed, most lawyers organize research around words such as bumble bee as well as contract. They appreciate that the meaning of legal concepts varies according to the situation in which they are invoked. They also know that human understanding of events usually originates with the familiar. It follows that the justification for preferring courses in contracts must be grounded on other claims about legal research and argument.

One such assertion is that traditional legal concepts facilitate the processes of integration and interrelation necessary for persuasive legal argument. But are the limits of, and connections between, legal concepts more easily drawn than those of nonlegal concepts? Surely it is as meaningful, and no more difficult, to teach the law of wasps in a bumble bee course as it is to teach unjust enrichment in a contracts course. The intellectual step by which the boundaries of a concept are drawn and by which analysis is extrapolated is identical, whatever the concept. Neither do legal concepts provide a more accurate understanding of the reality of a given social situation than other descriptions. Since the language of the law, like all language, depends on metaphorical abstraction, it is not necessarily more realistic to describe the purchase of food as a contract than as an incident of biological necessity or as the alienation of man from his labor. Moreover, it is far from clear that the legal description more effectively draws the attention of the lawyer or judge to relevant factors than does the nonlegal description. One need only think of the limited range of inquiry indicated by framing the abortion debate uniquely in terms of the Fourteenth Amendment.[11]

Epistemologists would claim that determining how course subject matter should be grouped involves deciding what kind of knowledge is necessary for effective participation in the legal process. In other words,

---

11. A useful technique for revealing tacit presuppositions which sustain our use of all organizing concepts is to take any Supreme Court case which generated a dissent and ask what the facts and issue are: some students will focus on the majority judgment; others will concur with the minority's view; still others, with prodding, will venture that problems to which the court did not even advert may have been the issue. Yet students are baffled as to how a lawyer goes about identifying the facts and issue to be argued. "Law and . . ." courses have the merit of making this inquiry crucial to legal education.

law teachers must address the fundamental philosophical concern, what can I, and what do I, know? If law teaching could be and sought to be primarily descriptive and were confined merely to informing students of statutes and judgments, without comment or explanation, it would be less necessary to ask this question. But since law teachers also purport to perform a synthetic function which includes sorting cases, developing interrelations, evaluating decisions, and predicting future legislative and judicial activity, they must inquire into what exactly they know about the law and where they learned it.

The alternative conceptual structure offered by "law and . . ." courses opens the door to this inquiry, and also compels law teachers to confront the limitations of intersubjective communication. For we all know that the verbal formulation of a legal conclusion conveys almost none of the knowledge brought to bear upon the development of that formulation. Accumulation of information is no guarantee of its efficient deployment.[12] A lawyer can recite Boyle's Law as well as any chemist, but his ability to use that formula to design equipment, isolate and solve system malfunctions, and derive corollaries is negligible. What the chemist knows that cannot be divined by the lawyer from a simple knowledge of the principle is when Boyle's Law provides reasonable counsel, and why.

Underlying the perennial development and transformation of "law and..." courses is the continuing rediscovery by law teachers, as some new segment of social reality enters public consciousness, that the traditional vocabulary of the law often obscures rather than clarifies understanding. Unfortunately, by failing to ask why legal vocabulary constantly shapes their pedagogical dilemma in terms of "law and . . ." courses, law teachers are unlikely to appreciate the cycle of creation and assimilation of new "law and . . ." offerings. Only an inquiry into the reasons for this pattern will lead law teachers to assert control over what they believe and teach.[13]

The Case Method of Teaching:
The Artificial Logic of the Common Law

Movement away from exclusive reliance on the case method of instruction constitutes a third major theme of postwar curricular development.[14] Traditionally, the case method was justified by the belief that the essential elements of legal reasoning were exemplified in judicial decisions. However, during the 1960s and 1970s, many law teachers came to ques-

12. Consider the arguments of Gilbert Ryle in respect of the "intellectualist fallacy" set out in The Concept of Mind (New York: Barnes & Noble, 1949).

13. See Owen Barfield, Poetic Diction and Legal Fiction, in Essays Presented to Charles Williams (Oxford: Oxford Univ. Press, 1947); Martin Foss, Symbol and Metaphor in Human Experience (Princeton: Princeton Univ. Press, 1949); and Erich Auerbach, Mimesis, trans. Willard R. Trask (Princeton: Princeton Univ. Press, 1953).

14. As used here, case method does not refer to Socratic teaching but only to the use of judicial decisions as teaching vehicles.

tion this orthodoxy. Today it is trite to note that cases present students with no more than still-life snapshots of complex social interactions; that, when edited for classroom use, cases reflect only a small part of the relationship between litigants; that cases decided by appellate courts tend to highlight the doctrinal reasons for decision and downplay the contextual aspects of decision making; that, when holdings are extracted by teachers and treatise writers, cases typically convey the impression of certainty and inexorability of judgments; and that, as they appear in casebooks, cases suggest that a legal rule is uninfected by its factual setting. For all these reasons, few teachers now would claim that the study of judicial decisions is analogous to the laboratory experiment or the business-school hypothetical.[15]

Law teachers also have come to recognize that reliance on cases as the primary source of law conceals alternative legal conceptions of the problem under investigation. If a judgment does not mention an issue or if an issue is edited out of the casebook, the student acquires a limited feeling for how the common-law decision-making process operates. The acts of understanding events, invoking concepts, establishing facts, framing issues, and applying linguistic rules cannot be explored adequately by studying cases as they are reported. Cases reflect a logic of justification and not a logic of discovery.[16] Moreover, the postwar era witnessed the rise of a general perception that the exclusive use of cases as teaching materials insulates students from legislative materials. Stock responses to questions about statutes such as "the law is not clear; there are no cases yet" began to assume an ironic flavor as bulging statute books and thousands of pages of regulations illustrated a changing recipe for legal effort. Once one acknowledges that law consists of more than cases decided by courts, modes of rationality other than that highlighted in judicial decisions must compete for equal curricular emphasis.[17]

Law schools recently have taken numerous initiatives to diversify the logical postulates of traditional teaching. First, certain faculties pioneered in the establishment of course clusters, criminal justice programs, business-law studies, family-law modules, and law-and-economics packages. Each was thought to highlight the psychological, sociological, and economic context of the law so as to counterbalance the myopia of the case method. For example, riding in police cars, working with probation officers, and visiting prisons permit students to see how little the reported

---

15. A century of legal educators have clung to this myth. Even teachers with views as divergent as Langdell, Llewellyn, Loevinger, and Walter Kennedy assumed that law could be transformed into a science, albeit their views on the nature of that science diverged.

16. For a detailed treatment of this point see Felix Cohen's exposition in Field Theory and Judicial Logic, 59 Yale L. J. 238 (1950); see also Abraham Harari, Negligence in the Law of Torts 1-11 (Sidney: Law Book Co., 1962).

17. A refusal to acknowledge this point seems to explain the impatience expressed by Geoffrey C. Hazard, Jr., Commentary on the "Fundamental Values" Controversy, 90 Yale L. J. 1110 (1981).

judicial-decision reflects of the criminal justice system; similarly, interning with corporations assists students in understanding the symbiosis of government regulation and corporate taxation. The creation of combined programs with other university faculties was a second curricular antidote which enabled students to acquire a broader perspective on legal reasoning. Business, social work, and environmental studies each present the student with alternative methodologies, explanations, and justificatory structures for decision and action. Both course clustering and combined programs assisted law schools in reducing the impact of appellate-court judgments on law teaching; by exposing lawyers to the perspectives and priorities of other disciplines, both also served to drive home the dangers of clumsily projecting the logic of judicial decisions beyond its effective limits.

Not surprisingly, these alternative approaches were soon perceived as a mixed blessing. They became so attractive that in some quarters the doctrinal approach to legal education was abandoned almost entirely.[18] Consequently the focus on problem-solving or problem-avoidance, which arguably is the central element of the lawyer's role, often became displaced. In addition, course clusters and combined degree programs tended to restrict unduly a student's course selection. By locking a student into a set program of studies over an entire semester, the benefits of diversity originally thought to justify a multi-disciplinary education frequently were compromised. Finally, professors began to have doubts that the most obvious defects of the case method could indeed be remedied by these alternative instructional vehicles. Issue-fractionation, concept development, social ordering through planning, and the legislative process do not immediately appear as primary goals of intensive programs and frequently received no more study than in regular courses.

While often advertised simply in terms of academic heterodoxy, the debate over clustering, internships, and combined programs raises philosophic problems of the first order. It invites professors to consider how the common-law methodology of appellate analysis transforms a lawyer's interpretation of events in the world; it also demands that teachers consider what effect, if any, appellate decisions have on these events.[19] Various assumptions about language and meaning sustain standard doctrinal evaluation of cases—assumptions that even the most accomplished practitioners of the art acknowledge to be indefensible. For example, teachers know that the case report does not completely reflect the human situation to which it relates; that all possible interpretations of

---

18. The exchange between Richard A. Posner and Bruce A. Ackerman in 90 Yale L.J. 1113, 1131 (1981), is instructive.

19. All great codification debates are essentially directed to this point. For a recent exposition, see Werner Stark, The Social Bond, 3 vols. (New York: Fordham Univ. Press, 1976) and the just-released volume by Northrop Frye, The Great Code (New York: Harcourt, Brace, Jovanovich, 1982).

this situation are not faithfully presented to the decision maker; and that the factors which influenced the judge are not all reported in his judgment. Yet by down-playing these assumptions teachers can talk as if, in any legal dispute, a clear rule fitting nicely into a larger principle or concept awaits the judge and screams for its correct application to the facts as they are presented to the court. In other words, these assumptions permit the creative and constitutive elements in law to be denied.

This need not be the case, and much of the problem with case teaching could be overcome were professors prepared to acknowledge and explain their sophistry. Imagine a course in which case recitation presupposed that facts were invented, not found; that the conceptual framework of a judgment was seen, not as a preexisting tool for structuring decision, but rather as a means for sustaining a particular explanation of that decision; that issues in dispute were manufactured by the parties and the judge to formulate events as a litigious problem; that the language of the rule invoked to justify a decision did not compel its own application. In such a classroom the logic of common-law decision making rightly would seem artificial. A request for the eviscerated holding of a case would appear as little more than an attempt to conceal beneath an unexplained theory of analogical reasoning the unboundedness of judgmental choice. Discussions of the materiality of facts would be seen as devices for avoiding the question of how any complex human event can be reduced to a mere fact. The invocation of the *stare decisis* principle and its mirror image, restrictive distinguishing, would be perceived as a means to deny subjectivity in any ascription of judicial intent.

When taught and understood as artifices, these elements of common-law reasoning serve an important pedagogical purpose. For if rules of law alone do not dictate legal decisions and if analogical reasoning is indeed *ex post facto,* one must look elsewhere for the underlying logic of the legal system. Inevitably this investigation leads to an examination of the decision maker himself as the key to authoritative decisions. What better way than course clustering and intensive programs to assist students in assimilating the role morality of the agencies of the law and the human dilemma of its principal actors? Riding with policemen, working on incorporation dossiers, and assisting a social worker in a child-custody case are situations where the student is exposed rudely to the variety of psycho-social factors which individuals use to organize and explain the choices delegated to them by the law.[20]

Skepticism about the case method of teaching does not spring simply from a view that much of the law occurs in public and private legislation, or that it takes place at lower levels in the great pyramid of the legal order. Rather, concern originates in an appreciation that the logic of the common

---

20. See Robert Samek, The Legal Point of View (New York: Philosophical Library, 1974) and The Meta Phenomenon (New York: Philosophical Library, 1981).

law is descriptive and not prescriptive. More generally one sees that traditional case teaching fails to deal adequately with important problems of choice and authority which are at the root of all human decision making. Thorough consideration of the divergent modes of reasoning and structures of rationality inherent in legal activity reveals acutely the peculiar logic of both the law and our curricular choices.[21]

Litigation Hypotheticals and the Problem Method: The Province of Political Theory

Until recently legal educators in North America tended to worship the problem-solving approach to learning. In examinations and in teaching the remedial aspects of the lawyer's role were emphasized. Contracts professors tolerated endless discussion of specific performance and damages for breach of contract, or of frustration, mistake, and misrepresentation; the shareholders' derivative action, insider trading, and preincorporation contracts dominated corporation law; problems of probate and disposition preoccupied teachers of wills and estates. During the 1960s and 1970s, however, this perspective fell into disrepute as broader conceptions of a lawyer's role gained ascendency.[22]

Faculties developed new courses and gave new direction to old courses in response to this perception. Typically the curriculum was enlarged to include courses such as tax planning, corporate finance, sales financing, antenuptial agreements, estate planning, contract negotiation, and collective bargaining. In each, emphasis was placed on litigation avoidance through private rule making or contract rather than upon the invocation of the legal rule itself in the framework of a dispute. Several existing courses also experienced a change in direction toward planning and problem avoidance. Even criminal law and torts, archtypes of courses whose thrust is predominantly the redress of wrongs, were not immune from reorientation: criminology was incorporated into basic criminal law courses as theories of punishment, deviancy, diversion, parole, and crime prevention invariably appeared on course syllabi; in tort, analysis of the deterrent, regulatory, and ombudsman functions of the law assumed almost cult status, with the study of alternative compensation schemes, insurance, preventive government regulation of dangerous activity, negotiated settlements, and mandatory inspection laws coming to preoccupy teachers.

As noted, a shift in emphasis from problem solving to problem avoidance implies a different conception of the role of a lawyer, but more importantly, it also signifies an evolution in the attitude of law schools

---

21. No one has captured this point better than John Dewey. See Art as Experience (New York: Minton, Balch & Co., 1934).

22. One should recall, however, that the seminal attempt to reargue the function of the lawyer was made by Myres S. McDougal and Harold D. Lasswell four decades ago. See Legal Education and Public Policy: Professional Training in the Public Interest, 52 Yale L. J. 203 (1943).

towards the courts. While law teachers always have paid lip service to the view that the courts are not the only source of legal rules, their symbiotic reverence for things judicial invariably engendered the belief that recourse to third-party adjudication constituted the essence of a lawyer's remedial function.[23] However, once the focus of teaching and learning is deflected from the litigation hypothetical, a more modest assessment of the role of courts emerges. Predictably, the past decade witnessed a renaissance of interest in a variety of dispute-settling processes. Numerous courses reflected this change, including the obvious candidates: administrative, criminal, and labor law. Class time in family law was devoted to negotiation of domestic agreements or to mediation as an alternative to judicial intervention in threatened marriage breakdown. Mercantile law courses typically included units on commercial custom as an ordering device. The proper deployment of bylaws and policy directives was incorporated into the teaching of municipal law and, more interestingly, of corporation law. Advanced administrative law courses such as Regulated Industries, Labor Arbitration, and Land Use Planning proved to be particularly useful vehicles for exploring the lawyer's role as architect of social institutions.[24]

A reexamination of legal methodology has emerged as a third consequence of downplaying the litigation hypothetical in the classroom. Once the importance of private rule making and nonadjudicative social ordering processes is confronted, three primordial commitments implicitly shared by most lawyers are exposed to direct challenge: first is the the traditional thesis which assigns to adversarial adjudication an indispensable legal function in social organization; second is the view that dispute resolution is the essence of law; and third is the identification of law with the political state. Again, the appearance of minor tinkering with litigation hypotheticals as a pedagogical tool implies a reality which points directly to an acknowledged province of philosophy—namely, political theory.

Adjudication is but one of an inventory of social ordering processes which includes negotiation, custom, mediation, voting, deference to imposed authority, and even deliberate resort to chance. The diversity of these devices reveals that the Montesquieuian construct of government is far from the only model of official conflict resolution presupposed by the concepts of law and state.[25] In fact, some argue that the assumptions necessary for meaningful adjudication cannot exist in legal matters, with the result that government by the judiciary is inevitable when a society

---

23. While few would go to the extremes of John C. Gray, The Nature and Sources of the Law (New York: Columbia Univ. Press, 1909), even analytical jurists such as Joseph Raz, The Concept of a Legal System (Oxford: Clarendon Press, 1970), place courts in the center of their legal universe.

24. See the models in Lon L. Fuller and Melvin A. Eisenberg, Basic Contract Law, 3d ed., 93 et seq. (St. Paul: West Publishing Co., 1972), and Lon L. Fuller, The Principles of Social Order (Durham, N.C.: Duke Univ. Press, 1981), for the implications of the view and a taxonomy of lawyering activity.

25. One may compare the version of law and authority offered by Philippe Nonet and Philip Selznick, Law and Society in Transition (New York: Octagon Books, 1978).

relies predominantly on adjudication as an ordering process. In many respects, the changing focus of teaching can be seen to flow from a perception that the political theory which elevates the judicial function to its exalted position may undermine other fundamental values of democratic society.[26]

In the challenge to the hegemony of adversarial adjudication one also sees the emergence of a more catholic view of the functions of legal institutions. Undoubtedly adjudication, mediation, and voting are, when properly deployed, excellent dispute-settling mechanisms, just as contract, custom, and imposed authority are effective rule-making institutions. Yet each really serves both functions simultaneously, as well as a third, namely, the production of disputes. In other words, one cannot evaluate the proper scope of these various ordering processes without noting how their divergent conceptions of the identity of persons in law actually creates the very disputes to be avoided or settled. In providing structures within which individuals attempt to orient their conduct, in authorizing sanctions to redress the disruption of expectations, in creating surrogates for defusing threatened disputes, and in channelling inarticulate grievances into defined issues, each of these processes fosters in its own way the necessary conditions under which individual autonomy is possible.[27] Dispute resolution, like pathology in medicine, may well be an important preoccupation, but it is neither the law's most frequent nor its most socially useful function.

Also implicit in any reevaluation of the role of official adjudication is a theory about the possibility of spontaneous order and the necessary domain of government: that is, every professor and lawyer makes judgments concerning the extent to which individuals are capable of arranging their own affairs and the extent to which the concept of law presupposes the existence of the political state. Fundamentally, litigation mania is a product of the view that the state has the duty to supervise almost all facets of life, to impose its policy priorities, and to dictate the structures and processes within which individuals are permitted to pursue their interests. By contrast, questioning excessive recourse to state-provided litigation facilities is the concomitant of a belief that private citizens are capable of developing their own decision-making institutions, deploying them justly, and finding meaningful commitments in communities other than the state. It is paradoxical that the lawyer, who portrays himself as protecting the individual from the state, long has advocated and embraced an

---

26. Though the lesson may be lost on constitutional lawyers other than William W. Crosskey, in my view the models of John H. Ely, Bruce Ackerman, Laurence Tribe, and Raoul Berger all presuppose the primacy of the judiciary. See the synopsis in Paul Brest, The Fundamental Rights Controversy, 90 Yale L. J. 1063 (1981).

27. On this point see Roderick A. Macdonald, A Theory of Procedural Fairness, 1 Windsor Y. B. Access to Just. 3 (1981).

approach to law which ultimately entrenches government as the mediator of all aspects of social life.[28]

An important part of legal education no doubt consists of understanding the remedial role of the lawyer as this role is reflected in the litigation hypothetical. Yet it should be far from a law faculty's exclusive concern. A curriculum which also recognizes the lawyer as planner inevitably invites careful rethinking of the purposes of litigation in courts, the respective province of various social ordering mechanisms, and the possibility of an autonomous order. Answers to the paradoxes thrown up by these inquiries ultimately rest on beliefs about coercion, trust, state, and community—the central concerns of political philosophy.[29]

Legal Skills and Tools in the Legal Process: Law and Ethics in Theory and Practice

The final theme in this survey of postwar curricular evolution is a development which primarily influenced courses not usually characterized as either substantive or procedural, that is, offerings which purport to teach about the law. Essentially, the debate fostered by this issue is a microcosm of a more recognizable problem: the perennial dispute about theory and practice. For present purposes, skills-and-tools courses are seen as those whose principal thrust is towards the teaching of technique. Legal writing, extracting the holding of a case, reading and interpreting statutes, drafting a pleading, and arguing a moot case are the intellectual inventory of such courses. In view of the traditional teaching locus of these matters, analysis of Introduction to Law courses is probably the most fruitful point of access to this issue.[30]

Legal skills courses of the early 1950s frequently were a devalued commodity, being given either by teaching assistants or as overload seminars by full-time faculty. Research and writing through the drafting of memoranda of law, the preparation of briefs, and the arguing of moot appeals were primary themes. Later, several schools created comprehensive Introduction to Law courses as a regular part of the first-year curriculum, although a divorce of legal writing from Introduction to Law offerings and a reorientation of the latter invariably followed shortly thereafter. This reorientation was not so much in the direction of the skills and tools of statute interpretation and case analysis but rather towards

---

28. This Burkean view of society may seem out of place in the liberal state of twentieth-century North America, but both Alexander Bickel and Christopher Stone have identified its elements and argued for its adoption. See, e.g., Christopher D. Stone, Existential Humanism and the Law, *in* Existential Humanistic Psychology, ed. Thomas C. Greening (Belmont, Calif.: Brooks/Cole Publishing Co., 1971). See, e.g., Alexander M. Bickel, The Morality of Consent (New Haven: Yale Univ. Press, 1975).

29. See Brayton Polka, Dialectic and Interpretation: A Theory of Interpretive Practice (5 vol., forthcoming).

30: A useful survey is Paul J. Brenner and Kathleen A. Lahey, Development and Shortcomings of First-Year Legal Skills Courses: Progress at Osgoode Hall, 14 Osgoode Hall L. J. 161 (1976).

jurisprudential problems such as the limits of law, the relationship of law and morals, the law in books and the law in action, functions of law, legal justification, the adversarial system, the institutions of law, and the legal process. Instead of the so-called practical skills of looking up cases in digests and statutes in citators, what became central to these second-generation courses were so-called theoretical concerns relating to the nature of the legal point of view.[31]

Several variations on the skills-and-tools theme were played out. Some faculties carried the Introduction to Law approach as far as developing broad-based and multi-credit first-year courses entitled The Private Law Process or The Public Law Process, in which substantive law was wedded to a critical examination of legal institutions and methodology. Here the apparent motivating factor was the belief that technique, method, and substance should not be studied independently.[32] In other faculties, Introduction to Law courses remained unchanged, but upper-year legal perspectives courses proliferated. Offerings such as comparative law, the legal process, law and philosophy, law and society, legal history, and judicial decision making took their place alongside jurisprudence as legal theory seminars. Frequently, the jurisprudence course itself underwent a change of content; lecture courses stressing definitions of law, sources of law, fundamental legal concepts, and schools of jurisprudence gave way to topical seminars organized around themes such as anarchy, freedom and responsibility, civil disobedience and justice. Many law professors came to rely less on legal writings and more on material drawn from traditional philosophical disciplines. For them, the epithet "positivist" inherited the same connotations as the label "natural lawyer" had a generation earlier.

By the mid-1970s, however, a new vision began to appear. Advocates of the skills-and-tools approach claimed that teaching was becoming too theoretical; that applied thinking was being overwhelmed by analytical abstraction or rhetorical mush; and that law schools were no longer providing adequate technical training for lawyers. The development of jurisprudence courses came to be seen as an impractical offspring of liberal ideology, and a neoconservative tendency led to demands for a return to a more traditional curriculum. Understandably, partisans rarely addressed the question of what makes a topic and approach theoretical and what makes it practical: those who raised the dichotomy invariably claimed that only courses which convey information such as black-letter rules of law are practical; those who resisted the bifurcation characterized much law teaching as irrelevant recent legal history. All agreed, however, that the issue is a perennial problem for legal education; for the debate

---

31. Karl Llewellyn's "Elements of Law" course at Chicago probably is the archetype.

32. One might cite Henry M. Hart and Albert M. Sacks, The Legal Process: Basic Problems in the Making and Application of Law (circulated in mimeographed form; Cambridge, Mass.: Harvard Law School, 1958) as the progenitor.

Curricular Development in the 1980s

about theory and practice necessarily raises every subtlety of the relationship between fact and value.

If discussions about the teaching of skills-and-tools courses and the place of jurisprudence in the law-school curriculum are typically undertaken without considering the fact/value dichotomy, it is hardly surprising that theories of justice receive almost no analysis in legal education. One can find various explanations for this omission. The moral theory which has been characterized as legalism—that ethical conduct consists of following rules—has long been predominant among lawyers.[33] A preoccupation with procedure and form has deflected the attention of legal scholars away from the perplexities of substantive justice. Extraction of case holdings and memorization of canons of statutory interpretation are elements of an approach which stresses the existence of a rule rather than its content. Key concepts such as the Rule of Law in constitutional law, due process in criminal law, and natural justice in judicial review of administrative action permit normative issues to be taught as factual postulates. While few professors may actually hold noncognitivist or skeptical views about moral discourse, most do teach as if the elaboration and application of legal rules were an ethically neutral enterprise.[34]

The axiology of legal positivism finds further reinforcement in the substantive curriculum of law faculties. Preoccupation with data generated by officials tacitly suggests that criticism of the law is an extralegal branch of study. When normativity in law is confined to the evaluation of legal rules, the separateness of law and morals is already presupposed. The analogy of law and science engenders the belief that lawyering can be a self-referential and technological phenomenon. Even scholastic and Aristotelian natural lawyers, existentialists, and neo-Kantians frequently teach rather traditional substantive courses. Paradoxically, the very dichotomy which the proliferation of courses in legal theory would seem to challenge is confirmed daily in the nonjurisprudential teaching of jurisprudence professors.

This litany illustrates that curricular evolution in the realm of legal theory ultimately is grounded in professorial conceptions of the relationship of law and ethics in everyday legal affairs. As courses which examine and evaluate competing legal procedures for achieving social goals flourish, scholars perceive the need to scrutinize both the internal integrity of these procedures and the goals in support of which they are invoked. For many the study of the alternative concepts of democracy and state postulated by Karl Marx, John Rawls, Robert Nozick, and Laurence Tribe has been the underlying theme of constitutional law. Bruce Ackerman, John Ely, and Paul Brest anguish over legitimation and judicial justification. Aristotle's

---

33. See Judith N. Shklar, Legalism (Cambridge, Mass: Harvard Univ. Press, 1964).

34. At bottom, was this not the complaint of Lon Fuller? See The Morality of Law, 2d ed., 187-242 (New Haven: Yale Univ. Press, 1969).

views on justice are called in aid of analysis in the resolution of tort, contract, and remedies problems. Michel de Montaigne, David Hume, Immanuel Kant, and Joseph Vining compete in illuminating the atomic structure of civil procedure and administrative law. Whatever may have been the case a decade ago, today law teachers are being pushed from the bedrock of simile to wallow in the mud flats of metaphor as they confront the nuances of the fact/value dichotomy.[35]

Both anxiety and self-righteousness have generated vitriolic denunciations of those who would interpolate moral philosophy into law. For once it is claimed that the justice of legal rules cannot be dissociated from their existence, it is no longer open to the lawyer or judge to disclaim responsibility for his actions by asserting that he was only following or applying the law. The realization that individual actors in the legal process are responsible for their decisions thus is an inevitable by-product of the reinjection of concern for justice into the teaching of law. How professors react to the demands of a nonpositivistic curricular structure probably will be the primordial question of the next decade. For unless an alternative to the dualistic vision of facts and values emerges, a retreat to either *a priori* other-defined authority or to *ex post facto* self-defined authority looms as the likely means for again avoiding the problem of justice.

Fundamentally, the creation of diverse courses in legal theory coupled with a change in focus of substantive and procedural offerings challenges law teachers to face up to their personal ethical theory and to justify the content and methodology they employ by reference to it. Like legal scientists in previous decades, the professoriate is learning that merely because it is ignorant of its philosophy does not mean that it does not exist; and like these scientists, law teachers have discovered that ethical choice pervades the very definition of objectivity.[36]

Conclusion

Implicit in this paper is a view that curricular reform is a continuing enterprise, beset by tensions which are perennial. Major issues tend to be neither paroxysmal nor discrete but reflect underlying problems which have been among the fundamental concerns of traditional speculative philosophy. The argument of this essay is thus sustained by a conviction that the seemingly ordinary developments in a law-school curriculum are only superficially ordinary, and a belief that these curricular issues reoccur approximately every generation because, in the spirit of the common law, law teachers are reluctant to decide more than is necessary or to address

---

35. I adopt here the suggestion of Susanne K. Langer, Philosophy in a New Key, 3d ed., 83–88 (Cambridge, Mass.: Harvard Univ. Press, 1957).

36. For two competing perspectives on this question, see Michael Polanyi, Personal Knowledge, (New York: Harper & Row, 1964) and Jurgen Habermas, Knowledge and Human Interests, trans. Jeremy Shapiro (Boston: Beacon Press, 1971).

Curricular Development in the 1980s

questions which do not immediately beg for responses. Of course, proposals for new courses or new directions in teaching will not cease because deeper concerns are addressed; they may become even more frequent. The benefit to be derived is that each law teacher will gain a better understanding of why he teaches as he does by being compelled to offer genuine justifications for his activity.

Three important and interrelated corollaries flow from this last observation. First, a satisfactory analysis of problems in curricular development cannot be undertaken in the absence of a general inquiry into the questions "What is law?" and "What is legal knowledge?" This is not to claim that each law school should define law *a priori* and then structure courses around that definition; rather, each law teacher must become self-consciously aware of the implications of what he is doing and be prepared to orient his teaching in consequence. Only rarely does the climate of an educational institution encourage professors to do so, even though most current law teaching unconsciously is derived from a theory about law propounded only a century ago. Since most curricular changes are implemented or retracted in the general spirit of tinkering, it is not surprising that the integration of new themes into existing programs has been difficult and frequently unsuccessful.

A second corollary is that curricular reform presupposes an intellectual context sympathetic to self-evaluation. In no university department are professors so wedded to the past by tradition and inclination as they are in law schools. Many new ideas have floundered because faculty members have been incapable of or unwilling to cease teaching as they were taught. Moreover, the external context of legal education is particularly unsympathetic to reform: no organization complains louder than the bar when the government attempts by legislation to overcome some long-standing travesty of justice; few professional groups regard their role as defenders of inherited values more jealously than the legally trained. Because law schools have been wary of carrying discussion to basic issues, they have permitted any genuine innovation to be undermined by self-interest parading as an inarticulate appeal to the status quo.

Finally, since curricular development is neither sporadic nor cataclysmic, its success depends on a professoriate with a well-thought-out philosophy of knowledge and reform. Law-school calendars, like civil codes, tend to become etched in stone. Monumental effort is required to change the scripture. When change does occur, the intellectual exhaustion it engenders usually inhibits repeat performances. Intent upon protecting current curricula, and not coincidentally the acquired knowledge of law teachers, law faculties overlook the fact that both law and legal knowledge are always in flux. The challenge for legal educators is to prepare students for change, not to hark back to the glorious past or to cling desperately to the somewhat less glorious present. Too often resistance to change is a self-serving defense of an already-mastered subject matter and a refusal to keep one's self well educated.

In view of these corollaries, four tentative prescriptions are offered by way of conclusion. Each is directed to the goal of consciously nurturing diversity in all aspects of law-school activity. First, curricula must become less standardized. There is no surer sign of intellectual bankruptcy than the fact that almost all law faculties are teaching the same courses, in the same way. Leading law schools, contrary to their presumptions, have no monopoly on wisdom; is it not a refusal to copy mediocrity that truly distinguishes the leader? Second, law schools must appeal to a more varied clientele. Revising admissions criteria will not itself radically change legal education, for almost all applicants still desire to be lawyers. If one is serious about creating a climate of curricular debate, one must attract students who will stimulate debate. Those students who have not, and do not, themselves contemplate a legal career are ideally situated to challenge the shibboleths of the legal Academy. Third, law schools must be more heterodox in hiring policies. Civilian-trained lawyers should be actively recruited by common-law faculties. Moreover, if anything will contribute to creative curriculum review, it is the infusion of nonlegally trained professors. Law teachers are neither good social scientists nor good economists nor good philosophers. Legal educators should profit from the experience of others rather than half-heartedly trying to emulate them. Fourth, law schools must reject professionalization. The bar and the attitude it engenders have but a small place in a university. Law teachers cannot abdicate to the market their sense of purpose.

A concerted effort in each of these directions will foster in the law faculty a climate of turmoil, experimentation, anxiety, and trust; a climate in which the process of curricular reform will itself perform a significant educational function; a climate in which justification of curricular choices (read: all choice) will take its place beside content and methodology in the teleology of legal education. In such a climate our efforts will lead, not to an intermittent, yet repetitive, rediscovery of the problem, but to a continual and creative rediscovery of ourselves. In the end, can there be a higher mission for legal education?

The Prospects of "Law and Economics": A Canadian Perspective

Michael J. Trebilcock

Gellhorn and Robinson paint a somewhat qualified picture of the impact of economic analysis on legal education in the United States, reporting less effect on teaching than on research. Meanwhile, the reception that has been accorded economic analysis in the better United States law schools (although perhaps only in the better schools) stands in some contrast to the very limited inroads it has made into Canadian legal education generally (and, one suspects, legal education in most other Western jurisdictions). What explains this difference in experience? If economic analysis of law yields such rich insights into the functioning of a legal system, why is it not selling better in Peoria (or, in this case, Canada, Oxford, Cambridge, or Sydney)? With respect to Canada, one can conjecture several explanations.

First, in most parts of Canada legal education as a full-blown, university-based discipline provided by full-time faculty to full-time students essentially dates back only to the early '50s. Prior to that time, legal education was mostly the preserve of provincial law societies who provided training through various combinations of apprenticeship requirements and practical (often part-time) instruction in proprietary schools run by the profession. Thus the shaking off of the shackles of a trade-school orientation towards legal education has been more recent than in the United States.

Second (a related point), a significantly higher percentage of law-school graduates enter the private practice of law in Canada (about 85 percent) than in the United States (about 65 percent), which creates additional pressures on the demand side from students and, through them, from prospective employers to eschew "irrelevant" emphasis on theory (of whatever kind) and to provide a concentrated emphasis on doctrine, coverage, and practical payoffs from education. The tightness of the current job market for lawyers exacerbates these pressures. Moreover, the quiescent state of Canadian antitrust law (probably for the most part an optimal state for a small, open economy) has largely removed a ready practical rationale for economic analysis of at least one major body of law. Perhaps the current rationalization of United States antitrust law towards a less interventionist orientation may imply a similar reduction in the practitioner-oriented demand for law and economics in the United States in the future.

Michael J. Trebilcock is Director of the Law and Economics Program, University of Toronto.

© 1983 by the Association of American Law Schools. Cite as 33 J. Legal Educ. 288 (1983).

Third, on the supply side, the enormous physical expansion of Canadian law-school capacity in the '60s and early '70s meant that many individuals with a conventional professional orientation were appointed to faculty positions, and the capacity or willingness of many of these appointees to pursue serious theoretical or interdisciplinary teaching or research has been limited. (It is a somewhat quaint irony that factors two and three raise the question of the justification for legal scholars attempting to propagate a greater emphasis on legal theory, especially law and economics, in defiance of forces of supply and demand to which neoclassical economic theory normally accords such high primacy! To some extent, law and economics in the law schools may take on the character of a consumption good for its proponents.)

Fourth, to be more speculative, the normative biases often perceived to be embedded in neoclassical economics are probably less congenial to many Canadian faculty and students than their United States counterparts. The political culture of Canada throughout its history has been much more accommodating to collective intervention in economic and social affairs than in the United States. The revolutionary origins of the latter have probably tended to lead historically to a measure of popular and intellectual skepticism about the role of government in American society, something of an adversarial relationship with government on the part of many groups and individuals in that society, and an emphasis on the primacy of individual preferences and freedom of choice as social values (i.e., a liberal, individualist ideology).

The historical evolution of Canada was in many ways quite different. To achieve and maintain a sense of nationhood involved an explicit decision, taken at the time of confederation, and reflected in the national policy debates precipitated by Canada's first prime minister and perpetuated until the present day, that the Canadian nation should be built on an east-west axis and be insulated to some extent from the strong north-south pulls in economic, social, cultural, and political affairs. Thus, early government involvement in the construction of an east-west railway line, the imposition of tariffs to encourage the development of domestic manufacturing industries, subsequent direct government involvement in the development of a domestic airline industry, government regulation of foreign investment, and government regulation of the communications industry and certain infrastructural industries such as banking all were designed to nuture, to some extent, this conception of Canada as a nation. Social attitudes in Canada towards collective intervention are necessarily conditioned by the much more accommodating environment between government and affected interest groups that has existed from the birth of the nation. The same historical distinctions between Canada and the United States also partly explain a much less ideologically hostile attitude in Canada to various social policies, such as regional development policies, universal health care ("socialized medicine" in the United States), unemployment insurance, state-supported education, old-age pensions, etc.

All of this is to say that many Canadian legal academics and law students are likely to be less sensitive or sympathetic to a framework of analysis that stresses the importance of individual preferences, the virtues of voluntary exchanges in freely functioning markets, and the alleged inefficiencies induced by many collective interventions in those markets. Allocative efficiency, as a single-value policy touchstone, is clearly far too narrow to capture central forces at play in Canadian policy making. However, a positive side to this environment is that the challenge of bringing an economic framework of analysis to bear on different aspects of the legal system has barely begun and the opportunities for significant scholarly endeavors are virtually limitless, although sensitivity to the political culture of the country is important if the risk of dismissal on grounds of marginality is to be avoided.

The Law and Economics Program at the University of Toronto Law School—the only serious law-school-based program in the field to date in Canada—has attempted, in modest ways, to respond to this challenge. Two full-time law professors, three economists with joint appointments, and several graduate students are involved in the Toronto program which regularly offers a substantial number of courses. Nearly one-half of the full-time faculty of thirty have participated in Henry Manne's summer economics course for law professors. A steady flow of research articles and monographs has resulted, and eight books are in the process of publication. An active law-and-economics workshop has assisted in expanding the base of interest in law and economics in the faculty as a whole and furthered rigorous collegial criticism of research work in progress. The strong emphasis on co-teaching in many courses in the program, complemented by active participation by members of both disciplines in workshops, has done much to establish a common currency among members of the two disciplines, give each a basic literacy in the other's discipline, and provide a stimulus to joint research.

Participants in the program, both lawyers and economists, have not only been tolerant of but have actively fostered competing perspectives with a view to establishing some common ground as to what the important theoretical questions are in legal scholarship today, whatever disagreements might arise as to how those questions should be addressed. We have attempted to avoid excessive intellectual imperialism, insularity, or condescension, which serve only to alienate rather than engage colleagues whose support might otherwise be enlisted. The long-term contribution of law and economics to legal scholarship may lie as much in the quality and significance of its attention to limits as in the sympathetic applications it stimulates.

Because economics offers so rigorous, coherent, and pervasive a set of analytical paradigms (in its own terms), it has challenged other legal theorists in ways that they have rarely been challenged before to develop and articulate competing paradigms of similar rigor and coherence. The recent revival of interest in legal philosophy, legal history, and critical legal studies can, to a significant extent, be viewed as a response to the challenges of law and economics. The role of law and economics as an intellectual *agent provocateur* should not be underestimated and should be seen as a strength to be nurtured. We intend to do more in the future consciously to promote this strength. Even our present course in Economic Analysis of Law is as much an exploration of the limits of the utility of economic analysis of law as it is an effort in promoting unlimited applications of the analysis to all legal relationships. This unifying jurisprudential orientation has made the course a popular and stimulating experience for students. I do not accept Gellhorn and Robinson's negative prognosis[1] for the future of such courses if they are properly and sensitively presented.

The prospects for law and economics in Canada seem to be brightening, with emerging indications of interest at a number of Canadian law schools. These prospects are to some extent linked to the prospects for the field of law and economics in the firmament of legal education generally. In that respect, I must register certain notes of disquiet.

Much of the recent law-and-economics scholarship (e.g., studies of liability rules in tort and contract) evinces extremely impressive technical rigor and sophistication. This work prompts two concerns. First, as Epstein has eloquently and persuasively argued,[2] the social consequences in any systemic sense of classical common-law rules, in either allocative or distributive terms, seem likely for a variety of reasons to be very limited compared to legislation or regulation. If this is so, one wonders whether economists, and lawyer-economists, in devoting so much attention to liability and related rules in the common law have fallen prey to the same delusion that has afflicted law professors for decades in overestimating the social importance of the common law and thus, to some extent, misallocating their time.[3] These are tendencies that we have tried to resist in our own programmatic priorities.

Several factors may explain such tendencies. First, at least for lawyers, economic analysis of the private law seems easier (cows and corn, trains and sparks, etc.) where interactions can be analyzed with simple, stylized numbers in miniature two-party "markets." Economists moving into these areas may simply have reacted to false cues. Analyzing the effects of many public laws (e.g., the impact of taxes and subsidies) from either allocative or distributive perspectives is infinitely more complicated. Second, the outcomes of collective legislative or regulatory interventions cannot be explained or justified purely in terms of efficiency given the incentive structures of our political system, whatever room there may be for debate about the efficiency of the common law, so that normative judgments about the optimality of outcomes will almost necessarily implicate noneconomic perspectives (e.g., distributive justice). Alternatively, economics must be content to confine itself to explaining (and perhaps predicting) in positive terms how different

---

1. Ernest Gellhorn & Glen O. Robinson, The Role of Economic Analysis in Legal Education, 33 J. Legal Educ. 247, 266 (1983).
2. Richard A. Epstein, The Social Consequence of Common Law Rules, 95 Harv. L. Rev. 1717 (1982).
3. "Falling down rabbit-holes," as Karl N. Llewellyn put it in On Our Case-Law of Contract: Offer and Acceptance, 48 Yale L. J. 1, 32 (1938); or "minute inspection of the entrails of a goose," as Ronald H. Coase has put it in Coase Theorem and the Empty Core: V. A. Aivazian & J. L. Caller: A Comment, 24 J. L. & Econ. 183, 187 (1981).

institutional arrangements in the collective domain create different incentive structures which are likely to influence policy outcomes in various ways (the focus of the field of public choice). While this is an exciting domain of inquiry, it is probably one of the most speculative areas of economic analysis and yields few firm conclusions or readily testable hypotheses.

A paradox is beginning to confront us. As economic analysis of liability rules and other private-law rules becomes increasingly refined, it becomes increasingly indeterminate with, for example, switching points on liability rules, choice of remedies, and formulation of defenses influenced by a host of variables, most of which are difficult to generalize about in the abstract or to measure in particular contexts. Two types of policy implications may well be drawn from this state of indeterminacy, neither necessarily congenial to many practitioners of law and economics. The first is that the extreme difficulties facing courts in framing and utilizing economically efficient rules in many settings, and therefore the improbability of their making economically correct decisions, may provide a justification for them making adjudications on some other basis, e.g., "fairness"[4] or ethical theories of rights.[5] To carry the point further, it can be and indeed has been argued that even in Coase's simple zero-transaction-cost world, if the law cannot affect the efficient allocation of entitlements, it might as well award them on some basis where it can have an effect, e.g., distributive justice between the parties. Economic analysis here can be viewed as offering an open invitation to be ignored.[6]

The second implication that may be drawn from this recent body of law-and-economics literature is that the demands placed on courts in many settings by economic analysis (e.g., nuisance cases involving multiple parties, subjective amenity values, and complex abatement options) are such as to make it unrealistic to expect them to undertake this role at all and that more "expert" centralized regulation may be necessary if economic analysis is to receive its due.[7] As we know too well, regulation is subject to its own set of frailties, failures, and biases, and the prospect of invoking economic analysis of law to make the case for more direct regulation is not unqualifiedly attractive. The point is a straightforward one: as the field of law and economics becomes more theoretically refined and technically rigorous, it increasingly overreaches the capacity of legal doctrine and legal institutions to utilize it. The challenge to lawyers (as opposed to economists) who are interested in law and economics and who are capable of drawing on the rich insights offered by this literature is to reassert their comparative

---

4. Gary T. Schwartz, Contributory and Comparative Negligence: A Reappraisal, 87 Yale L. J. 697 (1978).
5. Ernest J. Weinrib, Utilitarianism, Economics and Legal Theory, 30 U. Toronto L. J. 307 (1980); Richard A. Epstein, A Theory of Strict Liability—Toward a Reformulation of Tort Law (San Francisco: Cato Institute, 1980); Bruce Chapman, Ethical Issues in the Law of Torts, 20 U. Western Ontario L. R. 1 (1982).
6. See Weinrib, id.
7. Anthony I. Ogus, Social Costs in a Private Law Setting, Law and Economics Workshop Series, University of Toronto, Sept. 22, 1982; Lon L. Fuller, The Forms and Limits of Adjudication, 92 Harv. L. Rev. 353 (1978).

advantage in matters of institutional arrangements and design, while conceding to economists the value and importance of their comparative advantage in economic theory. This involves reclaiming enough influence in the field that problems of formulating and using manageable legal rules, assessing comparative institutional characteristics, capacities, and limitations, and designing workable institutional frameworks come to be recognized as central constraints in the application of economic analysis to the legal system.[8] In the absence of such a recognition, there is a danger that economic analysis of law will disappear into the wide blue yonder, while most of the major actors in the legal system remain back home in the trenches oblivious to its whereabouts.

---

8. Ronald H. Coase, Economics and Contiguous Disciplines, 7 J. Legal Stud. 201, 208 (1978).

The Democratic Intellect and the law

Neil MacCormick
Regius Professor of Public Law, University of Edinburgh

I

The occasion of the publication of a survey of jurisprudence teaching in the law schools of the United Kingdom is a good occasion for reflecting upon the point of jurisprudence teaching in a law school. There are indeed other good occasions for such reflection, and in fact this paper was initially prepared for such an other occasion.[1] By the invitation of the Editor, it now appears in this Journal in revised form as an outrider to Barnett and Yach's survey of jurisprudence teaching in the United Kingdom.

One cannot but compliment the authors on the thoroughness of their survey work and on the richness of detail of their report. This comment will not seek to rival that richness. Its first and primary point of contact with the report is the point revealed by the authors that a very substantial number of UK law schools treat jurisprudence, legal theory and cognate subjects as wholly optional within their curricula. Further, they disclose that the number of such schools is on the increase. This, it will be argued, is a disturbing, indeed a deplorable trend. So far from being properly optional, an element of theory seems essential to legal education both as liberal education and also, indeed, as vocational training fit to the vocation in question.

A second point of contact lies in the topic of ranges of coverage of jurisprudence courses. It is refreshing to notice the shifts in emphasis which have been going on since the last like survey, and fascinating to see the stock of some writers and schools of thought rise as that of others falls. Yet even in appreciating the fascination of such changes and in welcoming the changes of emphasis and opening of minds which they betoken, one may also question whether our traditional ways of listing authors studied and topics covered gets to the root of the matter of jurisprudence.

Here, it will be argued that we must try to conceptualise the point of philosophical theorising about law at a rather deeper level than that of such listings. In due course, certain fundamental questions will be proposed as fundamental both to the point and to the structure of all jurisprudence teaching. This should not, however, be taken as implying that other authors and historic traditions of thought should be ignored. Far from it. But what is essential is that the work of other authors and traditions be related to the fundamental questions of our

1. The original version of this paper was presented as the Presidential Address to the Society of Public Teachers of Law at its Annual Conference in Edinburgh on 19 September 1984. The present version has been substantially revised in style (though not much in substance) under the helpful, and gratefully received, advice of the Editor and of Professor William Twining and Mr Zenon Bankowski.

subject, and that their answers to our questions be taken seriously. By carefully correlating answers with questions, one can the more readily avoid fallacious and factitious oppositions of view as between schools of thought which actually have different foci of theoretical attention.

So far is this paper from dismissing the significance of intellectual traditions in academic enterprises that it deliberately advertises itself as working from a certain intellectual tradition, *viz* that of the 'Democratic Intellect', in the sense subsequently to be explained. This intellectual tradition has to do more with the theory of education than with the theory of law. I hope to show that it is a fruitful one in terms of which to think about legal education and, specifically, about the question whether and how far legal education is, or ought to be considered as, a philosophical enterprise in some significant sense of the term 'philosophy'. My case will be that law is indeed in its very nature a philosophical enterprise and that a proper legal education thus contains a substantial philosophical element.

The presentation of this case will proceed by: first, an explanation of what I understand by the tradition of the Democratic Intellect, and its relevance to legal study; and, secondly, an exposition of the questions which, in that light, I think fundamental for jurisprudence or legal theory as an essential element within a sound legal education.

II

*The Democratic Intellect*2 was the title Dr George Davie gave to his famously path-breaking and majestically polemical study of the persistence through the nineteenth century of the Scottish tradition in university education. It was also his name for the tradition itself. For Davie, the distinctive quality of the Scottish universities in their great days was a commitment to philosophical study and a philosophical approach to all topics of learning, taking the term 'philosophy' in a broad and generous understanding of it. This called for an openness and generalism of study, which was in turn paralleled by an openness of opportunity in higher education to the generality of the land. The tradition on its intellectual side gave pride of place to speculative philosophy; its democratic side was that of giving access to higher education to all who by talent showed themselves able to profit from it.

The main point of this paper is on the 'intellect' side of 'the democratic intellect'. As to that, it should not be thought that the only thing at issue was the status and position of philosophy, as but one, albeit central, subject within a curriculum. It was also a question how far other subjects in the curriculum should be taught with a strongly philosophical bias.

One illustration which Davie gives of this was a competition for a Chair in Edinburgh University in 1838.[3] It is surprising enough to learn that the competition was carried on in public before the Town

---

2. G. E. Davie *The Democratic Intellect* (Edinburgh, 1961).
3. Davie *Op cit*, pp 105–126; at p 120 for the quotation below from Hamilton.

Council as patrons of the Chair, and all the more surprising that this and other like competitions were matters of considerable public interest and comment; yet there is more of surprise to come, for it has to be added that mathematics was the subject of the Chair in question. The contest in particular was between Duncan Gregory, a representative of the philosophically based and biased Scottish tradition in mathematical training and study, and Philip Kelland, a representative of the more specialised and analytical approach to mathematics then current in Cambridge. When the contest and controversy were at a height, Sir William Hamilton, Professor of Logic and Rhetoric, weighed in with a pamphlet on the election to the Chair, in which he argued:

'If lectures in mathematics are to form a useful part of an academical system of liberal education, the Professor must possess so much literature and philosophy as will enable him to take a comprehensive view of the nature and relation of his subject so as to accommodate the matter taught and the means of teaching it to the intellectual improvement of his pupils.'

And he went on to point out that such previous holders of the Chair as:

'... Maclaurin, the two Stewarts, Leslie and Playfair ... would, even if they had been guiltless of geometry and algebra, have been otherwise celebrated for rare accomplishments.'

However that may be as to mathematics, it is no doubt the case that all academic lawyers would wish that even if they were guiltless of crime, delict and tort, they could be otherwise celebrated for rare accomplishments. And it is the pith and substance of the present thesis that they should seek to possess 'so much literature and philosophy as will enable them to take a comprehensive view of the nature of their subject'; for this is essential if lectures in law 'are to form a useful part of an academical system of liberal education'.

But are lectures in law to form a useful or indeed any part in an academical system of liberal education? Certainly, the great prophets of the democratic intellect at its high water mark around 1850 would have taken leave to doubt this – so far as concerns the undergraduate stage of education, anyway. Legal and other professional or technical studies were for the postgraduate phase of education. Only after successful completion of the staple Arts curriculum in humanity (Latin studied as literature rather than in a minutely textual or philological way), in mathematics and natural science, and in philosophy both speculative and practical, only after that should one proceed to take classes in law. The study of law, upon that view, should build upon, rather than of itself seek to constitute, the substance of a liberal education. So, certainly, would have argued – did argue – James Lorimer,[4] a hero of George Davie's book, author of *Scottish Universities*,

---

4. See Davie *op cit*, pp 47–55, 81–82 and compare MacCormick, 'The Idea of Liberty: Some Reflections on Lorimer's Institutes', in V. Hope (ed) *Philosophies of the Scottish Enlightenment* (Edinburgh, 1984), pp 233–248, for a view of Lorimer's contribution to legal philosophy.

Past, Present and Future, and for many years Regius Professor of Public Law at Edinburgh University. (Some of Lorimer's pet projects failed to reach fruition, but not all did. In stressing the need to build up in the Scottish universities research schools more along the lines of the German model he advocated policies which he could reasonably regard as to some extent fulfilled through more recent developments within law faculties.)

The Scots view of law as essentially and properly a postgraduate study was exported to the Universities of the United States and the older Commonwealth and has survived there rather better than it has in Scotland, where since 1962 the LLB degree has been available, and most commonly taken, as a first degree. There is much to regret in the passing of the old 'MA, LLB', but it is difficult to foresee circumstances in which the pattern of education could be restored.

Anyone who expresses such regret may be or seem to be selling the pass on the question whether law can at all or should be considered a fit subject matter for an 'academical system of liberal education'. All the law faculties in the UK have, however, recently (1984) argued that it can and should be so – they did so in a submission to the UGC offered in response to the Chairman Sir Peter Swinnerton-Dyer's Questionnaire about the future of higher education. The topic has also attained to the eminence of controversy in the letters page of The Times, involving counterblasts to Mr Roger Scruton's attack in that newspaper on the acceptability of law degree studies as adequate preparation for practice at the Bar or ultimately for elevation to the Bench.[5]

There is some point in recalling to memory what Mr Scruton argued in his piece in The Times newspaper. He suggested, rightly, that the role of judges in developing and refining common law (statute law, too, he might well have said) was a role which called for them to be persons of breadth and generosity of mind, not mere narrow technicians. For such a role, an education in literature or philosophy or history, he argued, must fit a man or woman better than immersion in the rebarbative detail of the law right from the beginnings of one's higher education. Wrongly, he suggested that the study of law at a University is and is only such an immersion.

Or was he wrong? There is one hard-nosed view around that law faculties are for teaching law and law students for learning it; that good lawyers are people who know well the law whatever else they know, and that indeed whether they know it well or ill, legal education therefore is and ought to be an immersion in the details of the law, nobody to be certified a graduate in law without success in grasping the detail of the law and committing it to memory. The day of the cultivated generalist is done, say the hard-nosed. Liberal education being the cultivation of generalisations, legal education neither is nor should be tainted with any taint of liberality.

5. See Roger Scruton, 'Laying Down the Law' The Times, 20 December 1983; also The Times (letters), 27 December 1983 (Lawton LJ), 18 January 1984 (N. MacCormick).

To say that this paper rejects that position would be to mislead by understatement. It is the kind of position which almost makes true such observations as M. J. Detmold's recent one that positivism is incompatible with legal education:[6]

'Legal positivism, and in particular the thesis of the separation of law and morals, is not able to accommodate the idea of legal education. Education is not the simple conveyance of information. Education and moral ability are logically connected concepts. Legal positivism sees law as something the existence of which can, in principle, be conveyed as a matter of information. The positivists, therefore, are committed to the view that there is no such thing as legal education.'

Perhaps there is a positivistic fallacy to match the naturalistic one. In truth, it is not a fallacy which has (as Detmold thinks) been committed by those legal theorists who have elaborated the doctrines of legal positivism. But it has certainly been picked up by some writers, teachers and practitioners of the law from a kind of crude version of these theorists' position. The fallacy is the one so masterfully castigated by Brian Simpson in his splendid essay 'The Common Law and Legal Theory', where he described it as the 'rule book' theory of the common law.[7] It is, in sum and substance, the theory that law is nothing more than an aggregate of learnable rules, a theory which, as Simpson well observed, no scholar of the common law can possibly accept without the gravest qualification.

A proper response to this fallacy must start from the thesis that legal education can be and ought to be a liberal education. This is the very thesis which the present paper aims to establish. It is to this end that arguments are advanced for the further thesis that a proper education in law contains a substantial philosophical element.

III

In putting the case that way, I risk committing a different fallacy, stigmatised as follows by William Twining, who says that we need:[8]

'. . . a safeguard against the error of treating one part as if it were the whole. The most common version of this error today is the tendency to treat Legal Philosophy as being co-extensive with Legal Theory. It is unduly narrow and impoverishes the discipline of law, to equate Jurisprudence with Legal Philosophy or to treat philosophical questions as being the only, or the primary, worthwhile concern of every serious jurist.'

To see whether one can avoid committing this philosophical fallacy, to see, perhaps, whether there is such a fallacy or merely a rivalship between wider and narrower conceptions of the philosophical, it is

---

6. See M. J. Detmold *The Unity of Law and Morality* (London, 1983), pp 89–90.
7. A. W. B. Simpson 'The Common Law and Legal Theory', in Simpson (ed) *Oxford Essays in Jurisprudence, Second Series* (Oxford, 1973), pp 77–100.
8. W. L. Twining 'Evidence and Legal Theory' (1984) 47 MLR, 261–283 at 266.

necessary now to explain the substance of the case. What is meant by the claim that legal education ought to be thoroughly imbued with philosophy?

What I mean is that there are six questions to which any serious approach to higher education ought to allow of some answer, preferably one reached after substantial reflection. In quick and summary form, the questions are: (1) What is there? (2) What is the structure of the things there are, and how do different kinds of existence interrelate? (3) How do we know what there is, and how do we have acquaintance with the things that exists? (4) By what method should we explain and expound the various matters open to our knowledge? (5) What is the place of human beings as rational agents in relation to whatever else there is? and (6) In the light of all this, how are we to live and conduct ourselves?

Now, at least if one allows to the term philosophy that broad and general sense which the tradition of the democratic intellect gave it, one has to concede that these questions are philosophical ones. And yet they have a bearing on all that is done by lawyers and legal educators. They also have a most significant bearing on the construction of a course in jurisprudence as part of a law degree curriculum.

So first of all, what is there? Are we to follow Hägerström and Olivecrona who tell us that only the material world is real, or shall we be materialists in some other, eg Marxist, sense?[9] If 'yes' to any form of materialism, what will become of the entities we so cheerfully admit to our property classes, such as rights of succession, liferents and fees, or floating charges? And what will become of laws themselves, and what of the consciousness of the subjects conscious of law? Legal studies reduced to strictly behavioural studies would be vastly different from what they are today. Nor is it plain that they would be better adjusted to their subject matter, to put it mildly.

It may therefore be that we have at least to entertain the possibility that there are other kinds of fact than the brute facts of material existence. Perhaps at least there have to be admitted such things as 'institutional facts', as Ota Weinberger and I have argued in development of ideas propounded in other contexts by Professors Anscombe and Searle.[10] After all, if it is not a fact that Lord Emslie is Lord President of the Court of Session, not a fact that Lord Hailsham is Lord High Chancellor of Great Britain, then there are fewer facts in being than most people think. But if these are facts, then there are facts beyond the reach of physics, physiology or dialectical materialism.

9. See A. Hägerström *Inquiries into the Nature of Law and Morals* (Stockholm, 1953); K. Olivecrona *Law as Fact* (especially 1st edn, London, 1939; 2nd edn, London, 1971); M. Cain and A. Hunt *Marx and Engels on Law* (London, 1979); H. Collins *Marxism and Law* (Oxford, 1982).
10. See D. N. MacCormick and O. Weinberger *Grundlagen des Institutionalistischen Rechtspositivismus* (Berlin, 1985), to be published next year in English as *An Institutional Theory of Law: New Approaches to Legal Positivism* (Dordrecht, 1986); MacCormick 'Law as Institutional Fact' (1974) 90 LQR 102–129; G. E. M. Anscombe, 'On Brute Facts', (1958) 18 Analysis 69–72; J. R. Searle *Speech Acts* (Cambridge, 1969) pp 50–53.

Once we go down this line of inquiry, however, we risk facing the inquiry – from David Lyons,[11] for example – why we should be hesitant to admit moral facts. Is it any less a fact that there are morally binding promises than that there are legally binding contracts? What is there to stop us thinking that the former is a fact about our moral obligations just as the latter is a fact about our legal ones? If it is not a fact that some things, like rape, are things we ought never to do, and others, like taking reasonable care for our neighbour, are things that we ought always to do, then the ordinary usage of 'a fact' is ontologically unsound.

Even so, that there are problems about ideal moral facts as well as about institutional facts is well known and widely acknowledged; it deserves to be added that there are more problems about so-called brute facts than we ordinarily acknowledge. What is of present moment, however, is neither to air such problems nor to suggest solutions to them. It is only to press home the point that neither the study of law nor the study of evidence in law can go forward without some at least implicit view of what there is and of how the kind of thing that law is fits in with whatever else there is.

This thought of how things fit together raises the second question on the list of six, the question of the structure and interrelation of the things that there are. If only material things are real then indeed consciousness of law has to be false consciousness mirroring an ideological superstructure rather than a real base; or it has to be some other form of fiction, whether in the Benthamite or the Scandinavian realist sense. And of course these hardest of hard-nosed materialist views go beyond even what was earlier stigmatised as the hard-nosed law teachers view that students should just learn the law – the rules of law – and never bother with metaphysical speculations. For the hard-nosed lawyer's approach must, however inarticulately, envisage as real the existence of non-material entities such as legal rules. And once we let in these non-material entities, how are we to exclude others such as moral facts and reasonable men; how are we to account for the structured interrelationship between material and non-material realities?

This unanswered second question drives me inexorably into the also-not-to-be-answered third question: the 'how do we know?' question. Materialistic and other monistic views on the matter of what there is – the ontological question, to be pompous about it – tend to rest on the supposition that sensory perceptions have privileged status as guarantors of real existence. What can be seen, heard, felt and smelt is real, and what can't isn't. Notoriously, however, such evidence alone is insufficient to generate any knowledge of causality or of causal laws and related ideas. Furthermore, the kind of empiricism which rests everything on the evidence of perception is actually an extremely weak basis on which to defend materalism, if not indeed fated to lead on into some kind of idealism, with primary reality

11. See David Lyons *Ethics and the Rule of Law* (Cambridge, 1984), chs 1–3.

ascribed to the idea directly present to the perceiving subject's consciousness.

In any event cognition of the world in any terms other than those of particular immediate sensory perception must be governed by some presupposed categories or principles. This essentially Kantian insight lies behind the standing ascribed by Kelsen and his contemporaries to the principles of causality as the structuring principle for a scientific cognition of the world. But if this is acceptable, then surely there may be other structuring principles, such as Kelsen's principle of imputation, governing our cognition or normative realms? Anyway, whether or not the Kelsenian is the correct view, it remains the case that any pluralism in our theory or opinion as to what exists is likely to have to be matched by a pluralism in our view as to our modes of acquaintance with what there is – to be matched by an epistemological pluralism, if I may again lapse into the pomposity of jargon.[12]

At all events, so long as anyone wishes to claim that legal knowledge is possible or that legal education is to do with the acquisition and transmission of such knowledge, it follows that there has to be some theory of legal knowledge. One crucial task of jurisprudence must be, as Richard Tur has put it, to provide such a theory of legal knowledge, an epistemology of law.[13]

This in turn leads on to the topic of method, that is to my fourth question, how we should explain and expound the various matters open to our knowledge. If laws are thought of in normative terms, as guides to human conduct and thus as connecting with the rational and intentional aspect of human conduct, it will follow that the appropriate method of study is what is sometimes termed a 'hermeneutic' one. That is, it will seek to expound law as meaningful to human beings in the terms in which it is meaningful.[14] But on other views of what there is and how it is knowable, this will be rejected in favour of more behaviouristic or structuralist approaches. Here the terrain of dispute is one common to all the social sciences. The question whether sociology of law is necessarily part of jurisprudence is accordingly answered with a speedy affirmative, the more urgent question being what is the right way in which to study law sociologically.

Finally, let me run together my last two questions, as to the place of human beings as rational agents in relation to whatever else there is and as to the way we should live and conduct ourselves. These mark the transition from speculative descriptive (including sociological) questions to practical reasoning and discourse. The general topic is that of the possibilities (if any) of giving some kind of objective justification for decisions how to live and to behave; in law more particularly, it has to do with the question how and how far objectively sound justifications can be offered for judicial and legislative decisions.

12. *Cf* Weinberger 'Facts and Fact-Descriptions' in MacCormick and Weinberger, *op cit* above n 10, ch 3.
13. See R. H. S. Tur 'What is Jurisprudence?' (1978) Philosophical Quarterly 149–161.
14. See MacCormick *H. L. A. Hart* (London, 1981), ch 2–4; and *cf* V. Villa 'Legal Science between Natural and Human Sciences' (1984) 4 LS, 251–273 at 264–268.

This concern with practical reason is of course at the forefront of all our concern in the law. Lawyers are above all else practical reasoners. And the main thrust of contemporary work in legal philosophy is into various aspects of the practical reasoning of lawyers.[15] There are two points to be stressed here: that our ideas about practical reasoning cannot be kept apart from the preceding speculative matters, but must necessarily build upon and fit together with our opinion on the right lines for answering the preceding questions; and that the practical reason element in legal philosophising is the point at which the liberal-educational and the vocational aspects of legal education overlap and fuse together.

The particular laws one learns as a student may change and change again at the whim of the legislator. The skill of weighing, evaluating and making arguments, once acquired, is never lost and is always at the centre of a lawyer's skills, as much those of the office- or chamber-practitioner, as those of the virtuoso of the courts. The critical evaluation of laws in their social context belongs integrally to this process of making and testing arguments at law. The extent to which such arguments belong within or outside legal deliberation is itself one of the questions with which the study of legal reasoning as a department of practical reasoning must deal. We go right back also to the question whether there are moral facts and whether law is among them, as I take it Ronald Dworkin argues; and we certainly pick up here the point of Detmold's earlier-quoted remarks.

This quick review of six questions for legal philosophy and of the considerations relevant to answering them indicates the kind of philosophy I think should imbue a law course, and the elements of this philosophical approach. What really matters is the range of questions, not a set of cut and dried answers. The questions are ones which ought to remain open and alive for every law teacher, law student and indeed legal practitioner of whatever rank and eminence. That they are fundamental for lawyering and for legal education is one reason why a jurisprudence course is of structural and vital importance to any law degree within the tradition of the Democratic Intellect; that they are so fundamental indicates why all those providing law degree courses should wish to bring them within that tradition.

Yet one would be claiming too much if claiming that all or any of the courses in jurisprudence surveyed by us have got it right. If the present six questions are well-framed, they could form the basis of a critique of any of these courses, the Edinburgh one certainly included. We perhaps approximate to showing the questions, and the reflections material to them, for what they are. But we do not show clearly enough, I suspect, why we lead our students through particular sets of ideas and texts and what we expect them to take out of these.

All the more would one be claiming too much for one course or class if the claim were that only in jurisprudence classes should these issues

---

15. See MacCormick 'Contemporary Legal Philosophy: the Rediscovery of Practical Reason' (1983) 10 JLS 1–18.

be broached and raised? As with mathematics in Sir William Hamilton's view a century ago, so too now with substantive law. Surely that can and should be taught in a reflective and philosophical spirit and with an eye to the six questions, or something like them?

Indeed, it is a dozen years since Zenon Bankowski and Geoff Mungham in their *Images of Law*[16] made the point that theoretical and critical studies of law can be emasculated precisely by being marginalised or hived off into separate courses. So far as a philosophical or sociological approach to law matters, it matters all the more in the main line professional subjects like contract and delict, property and commercial law. If theory courses and substantive law courses run on quite different tracks, the theory part can become a purely decorative fifth wheel. Moreover, theorists risk the criticism (which is in some cases more than amply justified) that they lack any real interest in real law. So theory and law are driven apart. This is one of the points that William Twining was making in the quotation given earlier from his London Inaugural Lecture. There are all sorts of middle-range theoretical questions about law and legal institutions which are devalued if we equate legal theory solely with the most abstract and general questions in legal philosophy as it is sometimes practised.

Twining's point is, quite simply, correct. But the conclusion to be drawn is that, all things considered, law as a discipline is in all its phases, not simply in the jurisprudence class, an intrinsically philosophical discipline. And of course this is true. No great doctrinal work in law, be it on crime or contract, property or taxation, company or trade union law, social security or succession, can be other than at the very least implicitly theoretical. Traditions in the development and exposition of legal doctrine are expressions of positions in practical philosophy. This is vividly shown by the great institutional writings of the century from Stair in Scotland to Blackstone in England and beyond. It is true of the masterworks which invented and systematised the English law on contract, on easements and on a host of other subjects in the nineteenth century, and the tradition goes on at least up to Goff and Jones on *Restitution*.[17] Such work, Nigel Simmonds has argued most convincingly, depended upon a coherent body of theoretical assumptions about law, and if there are to be successor works in a different paradigm, that will call for the articulation of new underpinning theories.[18] As I have put it myself, law can only be a rational discipline in so far as it is informed by a practical philosophy.[19]

On such grounds I do certainly as a law teacher commend the adoption or continued vigorous cultivation in our law schools of what I have suggested is the intellectual strand in the tradition of the Democratic Intellect. There are no doubt elements from its democratic strand which are of no less concern in the organisation of law schools and the distribution of places in them. But these would be for pursuit

16. (London, 1976), especially at pp 1–6, 49–72.
17. 2nd Edn, London, 1978.
18. See N. E. Simmonds *The Decline of Juridical Reason* (Manchester, 1984).
19. See MacCormick, 'The Rational Discipline of Law' (1981) Jur. Rev., 146–160.

on another occasion and in another context. Anyway, whether or not jurists should be democrats, it is surely past argument but that they should be intellectuals.

Jurisprudence, philosophy and legal education—against foundationalism
A response to Neil MacCormick

Alan Hunt
Reader in Law, Middlesex Polytechnic

I. Introduction

There are grounds for being optimistic about the future of legal education. Not least of these is that there is emerging a broad alliance, embracing a range of intellectual positions, which is increasingly outspoken in its criticism of the dominant vocationalism which characterises so much legal education. Neil McCormick has recently added his forceful voice to the criticism of the narrow and intellectually barren fetish of 'learning the rules' which constitutes the great bulk of the practice of law teaching.[1] The context of MacCormick's advocacy of the virtues of a broad philosophical orientation in legal education was the publication of Barnett and Yach's survey of jurisprudence teaching in the United Kingdom.[2] This report indicated a vigorous development within jurisprudence courses marked by an expansion and diversification of the issues and materials employed. MacCormick however draws attention to one trend which he sees as giving grounds for concern, namely, a trend towards removing the compulsory status that jurisprudence has traditionally occupied as a final year subject within the law curriculum.

I will argue that the demise of compulsory jurisprudence is not a cause for concern. In developing this argument I will contend that MacCormick's position is the product of his foundationalist view of philosophy. I will argue that we should abandon a foundationalist view of philosophy; a space is thereby created to argue against a privileged place for jurisprudence, and instead to mount a case for an elevation of the role of 'theory' within legal education. My defence of 'theory' involves an insistence that legal education must address the 'big' questions about the place and function of law and that this, in turn, involves arguments and differences about how those questions are to be posed. A concern with theory requires attention to the choice and selection of concepts and of methods of inquiry, and it also commits us to consider which levels of abstraction are pertinent in approaching these questions.

Before developing this argument I want to stress that my purpose is to strengthen, rather than undermine, MacCormick's case for the role of

---

1. D. N. MacCormick, 'The Democratic Intellect and the Law' (1985) 5 LS 172–182. All subsequent page references in the text are to this article unless indicated otherwise.
2. H. Barnett and D. Yach, 'The Teaching of Jurisprudence and Legal Theory in British Universities and Polytechnics' (1985) 5 *LS* 151–171.

what he refers to as 'the democratic intellect' in legal education. Briefly this stand for the capacity to take a broad and comprehensive view of one's discipline in its connections with the wider public concerns of the time. My claim will be that the case I make out, which, for the time being, can be called 'the case for theory' as against MacCormick's 'case for jurisprudence', provides a sound and intellectually defensible stragtegy for legal education.

The importance of the case for a theoretical and critical legal education has become increasingly important in late-Thatcher Britain. The enveloping cloud of vocationalist pressure from government, industry and many academic administrators has produced a common response in many law schools which to employ the inelegant language of the political Left, I shall call 'opportunism'. By opportunism I designate the tendency for legal academics to abandon their colleagues in the social sciences and the humanities to the cutting edge of Thatcherism, whilst pleading a 'special case' for law. Law is to be protected on the grounds of its 'vocational relevance'. There is impressionist evidence that law students are increasingly adopting this vocationalist rationale both in their decision to study law and in their expectations of legal education. Not only does the special pleading couched in the rhetoric of vocationalism desert colleagues in those disciplines most under attack, but, more immediately, it undercuts the progressive developments that have occurred within legal education since the 1960s which had made legal academics less subservient to the anti-intellectualism of the professional organisations. Making explicit this all too underdeveloped sketch of the politics of legal education is intended to reinforce Neil MacCormick's case for intellectual values in legal education as being both academically and politically timely.

II. The place of jurisprudence in the curriculum

MacCormick argues that the trend which can be detected from the Barnett and Yach survey is for jurisprudence to become an optional subject within the curriculum and such a development is 'a disturbing, indeed a deplorable trend' (p 172). As a teacher of jurisprudence in a law school which has only recently decided to abandon jurisprudence as the single compulsory final year course,[3] I would like to offer a defence of this strategy. I will go further and argue that it is fully compatible with his own educational objectives.

The most pervasive model for the legal curriculum is the one which locates jurisprudence as a final year compulsory subject. This orthodox

3. The re-submission of the LL.B offered at Middlesex Polytechnic submitted to and approved by the CNAA for introduction in the session 1985–86 contains no compulsory third year jurisprudence. (Jurisprudence is however still offered in a more specialist guise as an optinal subject). The most distinctive curriculum change in the new curriculum is the introduction of overtly theoretical course as compulsory features of the first two years of the course. A theoretically orientated 'Introduction to Law', replacing a traditional English legal system course, and is followed by a 'Law and Society' course in the second year. Within these courses theoretical, historical and inter-disciplinary issues and perspectives are progressively introduced.

model is not the source or guarantee of intellectual values nor does it necessarily create the space for their presence within the curriculum that MacCormick believes it provides. Rather it suffers from a set of interrelated deficiencies which I will sketch.

Compulsory jurisprudence suffers from the defiency which I will call the finishing school sydrome. Inserted at the end of the educational process it is both too little and too late. Jurisprudence plays the part of the intellectual icing on the otherwise stodgy cake that is legal education. It provides 'too little' because it offers the standard justification for excluding theoretical/philosophical issues from the standard diet of compartmentalised substantive law. It provides a rationalisation for a 'learning the rules' orientation towards substantive law by 'removing' or postponing theoretical issues that may arise in the context of substantive law. The classic expression of this is that now declining, according to Barnett and Yach, approach in which jurisprudence was preoccupied with 'legal concepts'. Any sustained treatment of concepts such as 'property' and 'possession' were removed from property law courses or 'personality' from company law. The jurisprudence course thus produced was a hybrid of miscellaneous concepts treated in isolation. More generally the presence of compulsory jurisprudence locates 'theoretical' or 'philosophical' issues as a special preserve separate and distinct from the real business of legal education.

Compulsory jurisprudence comes too late because by excluding theoretical/philosophical issues from the preceding years of study it ensures that staff and students alike become imbued with an antithoretical and empiricist perception of the project of legal education. The result is that jurisprudence is forced to stand in splendid and, all too often, arrogant isolation from the rest of the curriculum. The educational experience of jurisprudence is often unsatisfactory for both parties. Students often feel coerced into studying a subject whose concerns and methods are out of keeping with the students' acquired agenda for the study of law. At best jurisprudence becomes a safe haven for those students who are alienated from the massification of legal rules. Jurisprudence lecturers run the risk of facing students unsympathetic to their pedagogic objectives. They are confronted with the problem of having to undo the commonplace empiricist assumptions about the nature and function of law before they can adequately embark upon whatever substantive projects they wish to pursue through the medium of jurisprudence. Students, all too often, come to the study of jurisprudence firmly committed to a taken-for-granted version of what Ronald Dworkin calls 'the plain-fact view' of law.[4] I suggest that these problems contribute significantly to producing a widespread style of jurisprudence teaching as a more or less rapid chronological survey of jurisprudential 'big names' which makes little or no connection with issues and concerns generated elsewhere in the curriculum. Lest this view of the plight of the jurisprudence lecturer seem too pessimistic and stark I argue that the problems described are not inherent to the jurisprudential project but

4. R. Dworkin, *Law's Empire* (London, 1986).

are the result of the location of jurisprudence within the curriculum. Jurisprudence is doomed to failure in its role as the finishing school of legal education.

The apparently privileged status of jurisprudence as the final year compulsory subject does not attest to the importance of theoretical or philosophical issues within legal education. Paradoxically it is evidence of their marginalisation.[5] Jurisprudence is not only the odd subject out, being distinct in its method, style and content, but it lacks any prior grounding in the curriculum of most law schools such that most courses lack any preparation in theoretical or philosophical studies.

The separation of jurisprudence from substantive law subjects operates in much the same way as the pervasive separation of law and morals, consecrated by both jurisprudential and common-sense positivism. Within substantive law teaching evaluative or critical issues occupy an uncertain and unprepared terrain. It is a distinctive shift in modern legal education that evaluation and criticism are given some recognition. The problem is that little or no attention is given to the basis for such activity. Assessment of substantive law is all too often treated as a matter of personal taste or value. The criteria by which some facet of doctrine or a new piece of legislation is 'good' or 'bad' are generally undiscussed and undebated. A variety of evaluative strategies, for example judgements against policy considerations, against legal impact or legal effectiveness, against principles, or, most frequently, against a coherence test, are randomly deployed because consideration of the intellectual basis for such judgements does not form part of the curriculum. Students simply are not provided with the intellectual tools necessary to make considered judgements. And as a result not much weight or value is attached to this dimension.

The separation of law and values has its distinctive impact within jurisprudence itself which pervasively operates within the dichotomy of substantive law/legal theory. The result is that the critical or evaluative resources of jurisprudence are normally focussed upon the assessment of rival juristic theories. The critical capacity of jurisprudence is thus largely inward-looking. It is rarely directed towards the evaluation of legal institutions, rules and procedures. The separation between substantive law and legal theory operates to the detriment of both. It is an all too common experience that this separation results in legal academics working on either side of the divide unwittingly to reinforce this separation through their emphasis upon and perpetuation of a view that imposes two distinct sets of methods and preoccupations.

The paradoxical result of the separation between substantive law and legal theory is that far from the elevation of theoretical, evaluatory or critical intellectual concerns within legal education, it results in their marginalisation and subordination. Compulsory jurisprudence offers no guarantee of the place of the 'democratic intellect' in legal education. Rather its isolation from the mainstream of the intellectual experience of

---

5. MacCormick recognises the problem of the marginalisation of theoretical issues (p 181), yet strangely he does not pursue its implications.

law students renders the position of the broad intellectual concerns, which MacCormick so rightly seeks to defend, an endangered species within contemporary legal education.[6]

The defence of the trend away from compulsory jurisprudence is not a 'give it all up' philosophy of despair nor is it an abandonment of the intellectual values which MacCormick seeks to encompass within the idea of the democratic intellect. On the contrary it is a positive programme to ensure that broad intellectual objectives, which are dependent upon a theoretical orientation towards legal studies, achieve a central role within legal education. It insists that this cannot be achieved by granting an ambiguously privileged position to jurisprudence within the curriculum. Rather it suggests the need for a radical restructuring of the law curriculum.

It is not my present concern to advance a detailed programme of curriculum reform.[7] I do, however, want to argue for two principles which I suggest are central to such a project. First that an explicitly *theoretical* dimension should be introduced into all stages or levels of the law curriculum.[8] The objectives of such a theoretical core are compatible with the objectives which MacCormick elaborates in his defence of the centrality of philosophy for legal education. Second that the separation between theory and substantive law can only be overcome when the substantive law syllabi become more self-consciously theoretical and when theory takes substantive law as a major object of its attention. In the broadest terms this programme can be described as one advocating the diffusion of theoretical concerns throughout the curriculum. However it is important to recognise that the approach I defend has its risks. It does open up the danger that if compulsory jurisprudence is abandoned but nothing else in the curriculum changes then the dark-age of 'black-letter' law will becomes even more deeply entrenched. Put briefly my justification for a more ambitious strategy is that reforms that have not tackled the core of substantive law teaching have either failed or been marginalised.

III. The critique of philosophical foundationalism

The major thesis which MacCormick sets out to defend is that 'a proper education in law contains a substantial philosophical element' (p 176). He identifies six questions with which any 'serious' approach must grapple. What is distinctive about these central questions is the very high profile given to epistemological issues: 'What is there? How do we know what there is? What methods are available to explain what is there?'

---

6. A fuller discussion of the interaction between substantive law and legal theory would need to pay attention to the very considerable expansion, as measured by the volume of legislation and decided cases, of substantive law syllabi; a trend which generally reinforces and deepens the basic separation between legal theory and substantive law as the substantive law syllabi bulge at the seams.

7. An introduction to the project of curriculum reform is advanced in my article, 'The Case for Critical Legal Education' (1986). 20 The Law Teacher 10–20.

8. I will elaborate upon my concept of 'theory' in Part IV below.

I am not primarily concerned with the substantive answers which MacCormick proffers; rather I will direct my attention to the implications that flow from this selection. I will, however, make one comment about this substantive philosophical position. For reasons that are not explained a mock battle is joined against the rogue wolf 'materialism', with the passing inference that Marxism is the name of the beast. But on closer inspection the beast turns out to be a version of behaviouralism, so extreme in its dedication to 'brute facts' that not even a committed behaviouralist such as Donald Black[9] would subscribe to the position which MacCormick sets up. No issue is joined, least of all with Marxist materialism, as to whether it is a 'fact' that Lord Hailsham is the Lord Chancellor. Even within the canons of behaviouralism the fact that Hailsham sits on the woolsack, appoints judges and displays other distinctive behaviour which constitutes this politico-judicial role points to the unexciting conclusion that he is indeed the Lord Chancellor. A more challenging and relevant issue might be joined over whether the concept 'fact' is a helpful one for classifying the forms of human experience.

Once the beast of materialism/behaviouralism has been slain we are offered a commitment to epistemological pluralism coupled with a hermeneutic method. Epistemological pluralism stands for a declaration against monism but it offers little illumination about the substantive philosophical position which MacCormick would wish to defend. It is to MacCormick's credit that he has, through his reinterpretation of Hart,[10] exposed British jurisprudence to the hermeneutic tradition. He advances a distinctly moderate and uncontroversial hermeneutic position, one which 'will seek to expound law as meaningful to human beings in the terms in which it is meaningful' (p 179). The most orthodox Marxist would find little difficulty in assenting to hermeneutics in this form. Though he might well suggest that a concept such as 'ideology' provides a useful means for developing such a line of inquiry on the grounds that we need to go beyond the empiricist issue of establishing the content of what is 'meaningful' for each social agent or group to ask questions about the relationship perception and social position, standpoint or perspective. For example, the 'meaning' of law held by legal practitioners is highly significant for such an inquiry; but there are of course very significant differences between analyses which grant some privileged status to a practitioners' 'concept of law'[11] and those which treat such a standpoint as one among many which render law 'meaningful'.

I want to focus attention on the implications of the particular questions which MacCormick selects as having 'the most significant bearing on the construction of a course in jurisprudence' (p 177). The preponderant

---

9. D. Black, *The Behavior of Law* (New York, 1976). For a criticism see A. Hunt, 'Behavioral Sociology of Law' (1983) 10 JLS 19–46 and the recent defence from M. Cooney, 'Behavioural Sociology of Law: A Defence' (1986) 49 MLR 262–271.
10. D. N. MacCormick, *H. L. A. Hart* (London, 1981).
11. Without developing or supporting the contention I would suggest that pursuing the implications of MacCormick's hermeneutic reinterpretation of Hart yields the conclusion that Hart's 'concept' can be most usefully understood as an expression of the professional ideology of legal practitioners.

thrust of the core questions which he identifies is epistemological and involves an ever-present claim that philosophy is foundational. Even his opening question, 'What is there?' is treated as if it were epistemological rather than ontological. Philosophical foundationalism, in its strongest form, involves the claim that philosophy has the capacity to provide access to the conditions and requirements of human knowledge. In a somewhat weaker form philosophy is conceived as providing the means of checking the grounding and implications of knowledge claims generated within substantive disciplines. In either form philosophy is understood as a providing a more or less solid foundation for all other disciplines which makes it possible for them to proceed with some degree of confidence to the exploration of their particular disciplinary concerns.[12] MacCormick does not set out his own philosophical position in great detail but an explanation for his strongly epistemological focus may be that his strong commitment to the Scottish enlightenment, with its broad humanist and ontological conerns, has become tarnished with the narrower preoccupations of English (read Oxford) philosophy.

With respect to the present concern with the relationship between jurisprudence and legal education, MacCormick's foundationalism has problematic implications. Not only the questions which he poses but the order of their presentation import the implication that once an appropriate epistemological position has been adopted it is then possible to proceed with confidence to the selected object of inquiry, namely, 'law'. The danger is that this line of thought creates the illusion that the object of knowledge can be directly tackled once the epistemological undergrowth has been cleared. The result is to posit the existence of a taken-for-granted unitary and autonomous object of inquiry. This reproduces, in albeit more sophisticated form, precisely the same intellectual project as that of orthodox legal scholarship with its presupposition of the unitary character of 'law phenomena' which is most powerfully and pervasively captured in the concept 'the legal system'.

In MacCormick's case the force of this criticism is in no way weakened by the fact that his role in British jursprudence has been more open than others working within the tradition of analytical jurisprudence to the posing of questions about the relationship between law and society, and law and politics.[13] The problem of law as an autonomous object of inquiry persists because the form of MacCormick's rapprochment with sociology (and by implication with political science and economics) is that it takes the form of 'law *and* . . .' perspective within which 'law' remains an autonomous object of inquiry which has be to investigated in its connection with similarly unitary and autonomous objects of knowledge, 'society', 'politics', 'economy', etc. I concede without reservation

---

12. For a forceful critique of philosophical foundationalism see Richard Rorty, *Philosophy and the Mirror of Nature* (Princeton, 1980), and in condensed and consummate prose in 'The Contingency of Language' *London Review of Books*, 17 April 1986. For the implications of the critique of philosophical foundationalism for legal theory see Allan Hutchinson, 'From Cultural Construction to Historical Deconstruction', (1984). 94 Yale LJ 209.

13. For example, he gives a 'speedy affirmative' answer to 'the question of whether sociology is necessarily a part of jurisprudence' (p 179).

that 'law and . . .' talk has a self-evidence that is deeply imbedded in the discourse not only of legal scholarships but of the other disciplines referred to. Indeed it is an important feature of my case to note how difficult it is to escape from these linguistic habits; but it is their deep penetration of our common-sense linguistic practices which is itself part of the core intellectual problem which confronts legal scholarship.

The derivation of law as an autonomous object of inquiry via a foundationalist view of philosophy plays the role of validating a particular conception of the role of jurisprudence within legal education as the theoretical element within law-as-a-discipline. The implication of this view of jurisprudence as the theoretical or general part of an assumed disciplinary unity allocates to jurisprudence the role of providing the cement which ensures the cohesion of the increasingly differentiated and sub-divided edifice of law-as-a-discipline. The aspiration that jurisprudence can produce a unified project for legal scholarship overburdens jurisprudence by giving it a task which not only rests on a questionable assumption of disciplinary unity. But, additionally, it sets up an objective that is almost certainly doomed to failure; jurisprudence cannot provide a unification and integration which flies in the face of the reality of differentiation and sub-division within the various disparate projects which are the reality of the law enterprise.[14]

MacCormick's project for legal education and jurisprudence manifests this transition from a concern with constituting law-as-discipline to a legitimatory exercise. His sixth and widest philosophical question, 'How are we to live and conduct ourselves?' undergoes a very interesting transformation. He transposes it from the broadest ethical inquiry into a significantly different question: How can objectively sound justification be offered for judicial and legislative decisions? This question has increasingly become the central question of modern analytical jurisprudence.[15] What is significant is that to focus on the justification of legal decisions operates to marginalise, if not to exclude, other responses to the question of how we are to live and conduct ourselves which are less concerned with the legitimation of professional roles than with problematising those professional roles.

14. The quest for unity and integration within law-as-discipline involves complex motivations which takes us beyond my present concerns. I want to suggest, without elaboration, that there is a connection between a common feature of academe which to use functionalist terms is concerned with boundary maintenance. Each discipline is predisposed to maintain and reinforce its position within the academy by appeal to a unique homogeneity which constitutes its natural boundaries. At the same time the claim for the unique boundaries of law-as-discipline is closely associated with the requirements for the legitimation of the professional status of legal practice. The tension in the marriage between professionalisation of legal practice and the legal academy is partially concealed by a mutual interest between the two parties to sustain both public and academic confidence in the unity of law-as-system and law-as-discipline.
15. In its most contemporary form this question is the core of Ronald Dworkin's project despite his concern to distinguish himself from 'positivism'. It gives the question of transAtlantic inflexion which seeks to blend the traditional concerns of British analytical jurisprudence for the justification of judicial decisions within the common law with the American concern with the justification of judicial review. It is this project which explicitly informs *Law's Empire* (London, 1986).

In summary, MacCormick's rooting of jurisprudence within this particular philosophical tradition not only involves the unexamined problem of philosophy's claim as a foundational discipline but it also operates to reinforce the existing preoccupations of analytical jurisprudence. His programmatic construction of the field of inquiry of jurisprudence serves, even if unintentionally, as a form of closure which both naturalises the established preoccupations of the legal profession that assume that legal academics are and should play a subservient role and, more importantly, serves to exclude alternative sets of questions about law. This argument rests upon the contention, which I will not seek to defend here, that the 'questions about law' selected for discussion and debate by our leading jurisprudential writers revolve around issues generated within judicial and professional practice.

An alternative strategy for constructing the agenda of jurisprudence would, first, dispense with any foundational epistemological claims and instead ask: What questions about law are generated by our contemporary perception and experience of legal phenomena? This route leads to a more rigorous pluralism than that defended by MacCormick since it generates questions which embody the concerns and preoccupations of different constituencies:

(a) Can legal regulation provide a framework of social integration in increasingly pluralistic and fractured communities?
(b) Is it possible to articulate persuasive internal and external grounds for obedience as the forms of law become more varied and expand their regulatory fields?
(c) What capacity do legal mechanisms have as viable agencies of social change in the diverse struggles for human well-being and emancipation?
(d) How are legal mechanisms and institutions related to the persistent inequalities of social power and conditions of life?

These questions do not purport to be either exhaustive or systematic, but they do serve to mount a case for debate about the scope and purpose of legal education and the role of jurisprudence within it. First, they serve to stress that there is no privileged source of 'questions about law'. They emphasise that the questions we ask are generated from identifiable 'perspectives' (what ideological or political view do we take as our starting point?) or 'standpoints' (who am I, practitioner or activist, judge or accused, etc?).[16] This strategy does not seek to displace or exclude questions arising from legal professional contexts, but rather to make the point that should not need to be defended that the universe of legal scholarship is not bounded by the concerns of the legal profession.

Challenging privileged questions has not only an intellectual and pedagogic rationale but it also contributes to creating the space for a real and defensible pluralism within which a variety of different intellectual projects within legal scholarship can coexist. The exponents of contemporary liberal jurisprudence, despite their loud defence of pluralism, all

---

16. Twining and Meirs in *How To Do Things With Rules* (London, 1982), provide an interesting application of sensitivity to 'standpoint' for pedagogic strategies within legal education. They tend, however, to conflate 'standpoint' and 'perspective' and thereby endow standpoint with an unjustified objectivism.

too often act in such a way as to exclude or marginalise alternative perspectives. I make no judgement of whether this is an intentional strategy or merely the result of the privileged status given to professional preoccupations. In MacCormick's case this takes the form of the privileging of a jurisprudential perspective rooted in a foundationalist view of philosophy. Whilst he does not seek to subject his students to a single school within philosophy the very way in which he understands and defends the role of philosophy acts as a closure or exclusion of other positions. Put in its strongest form my contention is that today it is the radical intellect rather than the liberal intellect that can provide the surest defence of pluralism.

IV. The case for theory

My argument is nearly complete. It remains only to suggest that one of the ways to mark the supercession of the priviledged role of philosophically grounded jurisprudence as the core of legal education is to offer 'theory' as an alternative core. 'Theory' is self consciously neutral as between competing disciplinary traditions but allows the space within which to consider the potential contribution of alternative disciplines to the project of legal education. In other words I am anxious to repudiate a position for which I have argued previously, namely, that the salvation of legal scholarship is to be found in the displacement of legal philosophy by the sociology of law. The advocacy of the importance of theory in legal education and legal scholarship is intended to advance two rather unoriginal but nevertheless important claims. First as a counter to the naive empiricism which dominates much legal education which assumes that both the materials and the methods employed are self-evidently given and limited to statutes and law reports. Second, and more important, is the insistence that the concepts employed in legal discourse just as in any other are not natural or pre-given; but rather that the selection of concepts involves choices which have ramifications for both the method and the direction of all inquiries that take place under the auspices. 'Theory' as I seek to defend it involves nothing other than the insistence that the choice and selection of concepts is not innocent and should be subject to self-conscious scrutiny. My argument is that this modest defence of the centrality of 'theory' in legal education is not only to be preferred to the elevation of jurisprudence, but that it more adequately fufils the project of advancing the 'democratic intellect' which MacCormick espouses.

I will not say much about the implications of giving priority to 'theory' for the construction of curricula for legal education. Ideally there should be no necessity for the isolation of theory as a compartmentalised ingredient within the curriculum. But since the ramifications of espousing the central role of theory constitute an attack on the prevailing naive empiricism which dominates legal education it may, in the short term at least, be necessary to design and teach 'theory' courses as core elements within the curriculum. In so far as this is a necessary transitional stage before a theoretically self-conscious perspective becomes a

302 Legal Studies

universal feature of all the constituents of law courses I would merely wish to repeat the argument made earlier that theory should be injected at the beginning of courses and that we renounce the finishing school role that has so widely been given to jurisprudence.

Comments

Honourable Mr. Justice
Mark R. MacGuigan, P.C.*

The Public Dimension in Legal Education

If law be not a science, a university will best consult its dignity in declining to teach it. If it be not a science, it is a species of handicraft, and may best be learned by serving an apprenticeship to one who practices it. Christopher Columbus Langdell in 1887.[1]

I. Introduction

Legal education, while always a subject of fascination to law students and professors, only periodically becomes a matter of more general interest. But that is what I believe has happened in Canada in the mid-1980s as the result of three publishing events.

The first was the publication in 1983 of *Law and Learning,* the Report to the Social Sciences and Humanities Research Council of Canada by the Consultative Group on Research and Education in Law (hereinafter referred to as the *Arthurs Report).*[2]

The second was the National Conference on Legal Education held in Winnipeg, October 23-26, 1985, the proceedings of which were published in part in 1987 as *Legal Education in Canada.*[3]

The third was the 1987 publication by the Osgoode Society of a superb history of that turbulent period when legal education in Ontario became the subject of daily newspaper headlines: *The Fiercest Debate: Cecil A. Wright, The Benchers, and Legal Education in Ontario 1923-1957,* by C. Ian Kyer and Jerome E. Bickenbach.[4]

On the assumption that the fundamental purpose of the legal profession, as of the law itself, is to bring about a just society, I adopt in

---

*Of the Federal Court of Canada.
1. Christoper Columbus Langdell "Harvard Celebration Speech" (1887), 3 L.Q.R. 123, 124. Professor Francis A. Allen, "Humanistic Legal Education: the Quiet Crisis" in Neil Gold, ed., *Essays on Canadian Legal Education,* (Toronto, Butterworths, 1982) 9, at 10 says of this quotation:
> Dean Langdell's statement encompasses an assertion that retains a high relevance almost a century after it was made. It is that one cannot proclaim that law studies are appropriately included in the curricula of universities without accepting certain necessary implications about the nature and obligations of university-based legal education.
2. Ottawa, Minister of Supply and Services, Canada.
3. Montréal, Federation of Law Societies of Canada/Fédération des professions juridiques du Canada.
4. Toronto, Published for the Osgoode Society by University of Toronto Press.

this article the standpoint of the public and pose the question "What does the public have a right to expect of legal education?"[5] From this perspective nothing more will need to be said of the second publication above, since unfortunately it devotes small attention to this issue.[6]

II. The Background

The earliest formal instruction in the common law was provided at the Inns of Court in England, but, following Blackstone's first lectures at Oxford University in 1753 (leading to his appointment to the Vinerian Professorship in 1758), a number of other universities established chairs in the law. Finally, in 1826, Harvard established the first university law school. The next major advance in legal education came with the introduction of the case method by Dean Christopher Columbus Langdell at Harvard in 1870. Langdell's case method was based on the belief that law was a science which could be discovered by studying decided cases. If law was a science, the law library was its laboratory.

In Canada the first permanent common-law school was founded at Dalhousie University in 1883 by Richard Chapman Weldon, "a man who was clearly inspired by Harvard Law School."[7] From the beginning the University had the co-operation of the Nova Scotia Barristers' Society. The Society controlled the articles of clerkship and admission to the bar, but otherwise left it to the University to provide for legal education. Kyer and Bickenbach write that the result of this harmonious partnership was that, by 1921, the school's second dean, Donald A. MacRae, had "brought Dalhousie to a position of leadership in legal education in Canada";[8] its curriculum was recommended by the Canadian Bar Association and served as a model for law schools throughout the country.

Nevertheless, perhaps because it lacked financial resources, or perhaps because of the blind adherence of the Law Society of Upper Canada to the English system of office apprenticeship,[9] Dalhousie unfortunately

---

5. The public's attitude to the law in Canada was manifested at the People's Law Conferences in 1983 and 1984, the first of which was recorded and published as *The People's Law: What Canadians Want from the Law* (Ottawa, the People's Law Conference, 1984). These conferences were an attempt by the Federal Government "to move beyond the perspective of the legal profession and reach the basic concerns of those the law is intended to serve" (at 3). The Conferences did not, of course, focus on legal education as such.
6. I should note than an earlier draft of this paper was prepared for the National Conference on Legal Education and excerpts from it were published in *Legal Education in Canada, supra*, note 3, at 174-185.
7. Kyer and Bickenbach, *supra*, note 4, at 28.
8. *Id*, at 50.
9. The history is chronicled by Kyer and Bickenbach through the life of Dean C.A. Wright. In a recent review of the book, I wrote *(Canadian Historical Review)*: "At this remove it may

never actually set the pattern of legal education in Canada, and a succession of able deans — MacRae himself, John Read, Sidney Smith, and Vincent MacDonald were lured from the school to other positions. Dalhousie's approach was emulated in some other provinces, but it was only in 1957 that the most powerful of the law societies, the Law Society of Upper Canada, succumbed to progress. In that year, Osgoode Hall Law School, which had been run by the profession since its founding in 1889, became a university law school (though without a university until its affiliation with York University in 1968). As well, the Law Society signalled its acceptance of other university law schools in the province.

Since 1957 there has been an enormous growth in the number of law schools, law students and law professors in Canada. Including civil-law schools, there are now 21 university law schools in the country with about 9,500 students and over 600 law professors. The number of law students in fact more than tripled in the years 1962-63 to 1976-77. The increase in women law students has been particularly striking (from 5% of all students in 1962-63 to 37% in 1980-81). This remarkable growth levelled off in the late 1970s, though a steady demand for places has remained.

But has this expansion been a good thing? An American law dean, John Henry Schlegel, said of Canadian law schools in 1984:

> What seems to have happened is that in merely thirty-five years the Canadians have recapitulated American developments of over one hundred years . . . and [come to] the same dead end.[10]

That dead end is the notion that the law is a body of definable rules: a finite body of knowledge that is all too quickly exhausted, leaving a dispirited faculty and a student body oriented solely to practice. But that is running ahead of our story.

The public significance of legal education, as opposed to its significance for the profession, the students, and the schools, has never been a dominant theme in the assessment of legal education. An approach to it was, however, sketched by Alfred Z. Reed in a study for the American Bar Association in 1921, where he noted that the practice of law is a "a public function, in a sense that the practice of other

---

be hard for readers to comprehend the stubborness of the Benchers in the face of contemporary trends in legal education, particularly in the United States.... One has perhaps to analogize to the flag debate or to the more recent debate over the Charter to get some idea of the feelings in play — two other debates incidentally, with similar overtones of competing British and American influences."

10. John Henry Schlegel, "Langdell's Legacy Or, The Case of the Empty Envelope" (1984), 36 Stan. L.R. 1517, at 1527. Schlegel's chronology is a bit off — the time period in Canada was actually 27 years.

professions, such as medicine, is not. Practicing lawyers do not merely render to the community a social service ... They are part of the governing mechanism of the state. Their functions are in a broad sense political".[11]

Moreover, the public interest perspective was adopted in "a now classic 1943 law review article"[12] by Harold Lasswell and Myres McDougal. Lasswell and McDougal argued that previous efforts to integrate law and the social sciences had been largely unsuccessful because of a "lack of clarity about *what* is being integrated, and *how,* and *for what* purposes".[13] Their basic proposition was as follows:

> [I]f legal education in the contemporary world is adequately to serve the needs of a free and productive commonwealth, it must be conscious, efficient, and systematic *training for policy-making.* The proper function of our law schools is, in short, to contribute to the training of policy-makers for the ever more complete achievement of the democratic values that constitute the professed ends of American polity.[14]

Hence, in addition to the traditional emphasis on the mastery of legal technicalities, the Lasswell-McDougal law curriculum consisted of "thought skills" such as of goal-thinking, trend-thinking, and scientific-thinking. Furthermore, all these skills of thought needed to be supplemented by observation skills and management skills.

Goal-thinking for Lasswell and McDougal required the clarification of values, and had to relate general propositions to operational principles so as not to become, in their terminology, too philosophical. Implementation of values required trend-thinking, which looks to the future and is unswayed by current preferences. Implementation of values also required scientific-thinking in order to direct trends, where possible by the skillful management of the factors that condition them. Efficient training in scientific thinking required that students become familiar with the procedures by which facts are established through planned observation, mostly by various forms of inference. Finally, for Lasswell and McDougal acquaintance with methods of observation not only furnished a sound basis for policy planning but also contributed directly to skill in the practical management of human affairs.

---

11. Alfred Z. Reed, *Training for the Public Profession of the Law* (New York, Charles Scribner's Sons, 1921) at 3.
12. Harold D. Lasswell and Myres S. McDougal, "Legal Education and Public Policy: Professional Training in the Public Interest" (1943), 52 Yale L.J. 203. The description of their article is from Frances Kahn Zemans and Victor G. Rosenblum, *The Making of a Public Profession* (Chicago, American Bar Foundation, 1981) at 9.
13. Lasswell and McDougall, *id.,* at 204.
14. *Id.,* at 206.

In their 1974 report to the American Bar Foundation on American legal education, Boyer and Cramton provided a perspective on Lasswell and McDougal 30 years later:

> With the publication of the famous article by Lasswell and McDougal on legal education and public policy in the 1940's, thought about the nature and function of law entered the "post-Realist period". Despite the wide currency of the Lasswell-McDougal approach and the considerable discussion it provoked, the concept of the lawyer as policy maker and implementer of democratic values had only a modest influence on the total law curriculum. At best, more emphasis was given to the policy aspects of standard course content, and a sprinkling of seminars devoted to policy questions were added to the curriculum. These policy courses, however, were usually electives that were taken by only a small proportion of the eligible law students, and their introduction was largely confined to a handful of elite private schools until the rapid improvement of publicly-supported law schools in recent years.[15]

Boyer and Cramton expressed considerable frustration at this educational wheel-spinning:

> A striking as well as depressing aspect of current debates over the future shape of the law school curriculum is the ancient lineage of many of the major issues, and their cyclical reappearance in the literature on legal education. Indeed, the historians remind us that the effort to integrate law and the behavioral sciences has been going on for nearly half a century and that "[a]rticles could be lifted out of the Law School News of 1915 and passed off today as tolerably fresh ideas in the Journal of Legal Education".[16]

It is hard to avoid the conclusion that American legal education may have gone as far as the predominant jurisprudential schools of recent times allowed. Roscoe Pound and the American legal realists had their disagreements, but they shared a distrust of all legal American absolutes because of how they had seen them used by legal American courts to protect vested property interests. The realists, in addition, as Jerold Auerbach puts it "were simplemindedly devoted to empirical social science research as the methodological answer to all questions".[17] Auerbach concludes that:

---

15. Barry B. Boyer and Roger C. Cramton, "American Legal Education: An Agenda for Research and Reform" (1973-74), 59 Cornell L. Rev. 221, at 225-6. Another analysis of Lasswell and McDougal is found in Stewart Macaulay, "Law Schools and the World Outside their Doors: Notes on the Margins of Professional Training in the Public Interest" (1968), 54 Va. L. Rev. 617.
16. *Id*, at 227-8. The quotation is from Stolz, "Training for the Public Profession of the Law (1921): A Contemporary Review", in H. Packer and J. Ehrlich, *New Directions in Legal Education* (1972) 228.
17. Jerold S. Auerbach, "What Has the Teaching of Law to Do with Justice?" (1978), 53 New York U.L.R. 457, at 461. It is interesting to note that this perceptive article on legal education is written, not by a lawyer, but by a professional historian.

The idea of law as a public profession, with obligations that transcend client loyalty (which, after all, must be seen in *its* social context: loyalty to those who can pay the most), seems too strong to die but too weak to prevail.[18]

Canadians have fortunately not shared the extremes of behaviour, controversy, and ideology that have marked the Amercian experience in the law and legal education. Moreover, by being the better part of a century behind in the institution of widespread legal education in universities, we are better situated to take advantage of the perspective which historical reflection can offer. But the greatest advantage Canadian law schools have over those in the United States, and the reason the issues in university legal education differ so substantially in the two countries, is Canada's continuance of the apprenticeship tradition in articling and in profession-run Bar admission courses. Canadian university law schools are as a result freer to devote themselves to the more academic and intellectual aspects of the law.

We may therefore reasonably aspire to the conceptualization and development of a public perspective on legal education in a more supportive professional context. It is no doubt true in Canada as in the United States, as it was there pointed out by David Mellinkoff, that:

> Lawyers as a group are no more dedicated to justice or public service than a private public utility is dedicated to giving light. It just happens that for a variety of personal reasons laywers . . . have chosen to engage in an occupation that more than others is "affected with a public interest" . . . . The profession is a public profession because as a profession it exists to satisfy a public need. But individual lawyers are members of that public profession to satisfy private, personal needs. . .[19]

Whatever the personal motivations of individual members of the profession, the central truth for the profession as a whole must remain as stated by Zemans and Rosenblum in the introduction to their 1981 study for the American Bar Foundation:

> The enormous influence that lawyers wield in both the public and the private sectors makes their professional development of particular concern in a democratic society. There is little doubt that the legal profession is both ubiquitous and extremely influential in the life of the . . . polity. The prominence of lawyers in public elective and appointive office, even considering in addition the lawyers holding numerous other government jobs or serving as important policy advisors, represents only a part of the political role of the bar. More pervasive and potentially more important is

---

18. *Id.*, at 473.
19. David Mellinkoff, *The Conscience of a Lawyer* (St. Paul, West Publishing Co., 1973) at 9.

the public impact of the bar in its generally private role as counsellor and advocate of private interests.[20]

The public significance of legal education is thus not to be measured simply by the role of that minority of the profession which directly engages in public life or government administration, but rather by how well the profession as a whole serves the public interest. In other words, even the private-law role of the lawyer must be justified in terms of the common good and not merely by the standard of the client's interest.

What kind of legal education is needed to prepare members of the profession to serve the public interest? Because of the continuance of the apprenticeship system to which I have already referred, Canadian law schools cannot readily look to American schools for working ideals.

The *Arthurs Report* finds that the current ideal of legal education in Canada, one which it finds acceptable as an ideal, but not as presently applied, is humane professionalism. It consists of three elements: legal rules (doctrine), legal skills (interviewing, advocacy, negotiation), and developing a humane perspective on and a deeper understanding of the law as a social phenomenon and an intellectual discipline. These elements of humane professionalism are arranged in no fixed proportion or sequence, but are all contained within an eclectic, optional curriculum. Unfortunately, eclecticism has in the *Report's* view proved to be the wrong vehicle for humane professionalism, because it has resulted in the predominance of doctrinal teaching, which is identified with professional formation. In the *Report's* view, what Canadian law schools are doing today is not academic but professional. Despite good intentions in the law school the professional always overwhelms the academic, which the *Report* terms "the chosen vehicle of humane values".[21]

The *Report* argues that academic studies in law will occur only if a distinctive academic option is created at the LL.B. level within an overall structure of pluralism.[22] This scholarly option could take many forms, perhaps the simplest being the institution of a scholarly stream within existing law schools.

In a perceptive review, Judge Maxwell Cohen points that the *Arthurs Report* leaves unaddressed a number of difficulties. There is, first, the sheer difficulty of ensuring the emergence of a new scholarly perspective.

---

20. *Supra*, note 12, at 1.
21. *Supra*, note 2, at 54.
22. It is a historical irony that although Kyer and Bichenback can rightly chronicle "Caesar" Wright's career as a triumph of progress in legal education, they can also make the assertion that "in many respects ... Wright created a model for the type of legal teacher and scholar that was severely critized by the Arthurs Commission in the study *Law and Learning,*" *supra*, note 4, at 276.

Cohen notes that "even McDougal and Lasswell could not create a 'separate' stream programme within the entrenched teaching structures — however policy-oriented they were (and are) at Yale, in the law school generally"[23]. The more general difficulty he puts more broadly:

> In other words has the Arthurs *Report* really told us any part of the answer to the central question raised by the *Report* itself, namely, even if it is possible to define with more manageable precision what is meant by "fundamental", how shall law schools proceed to incorporate that definition into programmes that are credible both to the social scientist and humanist on the one side and that will be of some utility to the better understanding and running of the legal order in its daily operational life on the other.[24]

In my view, this is no more than to say that we cannot look to the *Arthurs Report* for all the answers. Personally, I find persuasive its arguments as to the necessity of a scholarly discipline of law and, concomitantly, of the creation of the requisite conditions for such an approach in law schools. But my concern here, the public significance of legal education, has less to do with the emergence of a new sub-profession of academic-minded lawyers (which is rightly the preoccupation of the *Arthurs Report)* and more with humanizing the professional study of law for the great majority of law students who will choose not to be legal scholars. My perspective is the totality of legal education viewed in the public interest.

III. Legal Education in the Public Interest

In this respect I start from a few key assumptions or postulates. First, to speak of society is to speak of law, since law is the principal means for the achievement of social ends; law cannot be defined apart from these ends, foremost among which is justice. Second, the importance to society of law means that the public has a unique stake in law-making. Third, the legal profession is the most influential law-making profession: even when lawyers are not themselves the actual legislators or administrators (as they still are in considerable part), they are the indispensable advisers of governments, legislatures, subordinate law-makers, and administrators of

---

23. Maxwell Cohen, (1983), 61 Can Bar Rev. 702, at 709. Mark Weisberg, "On the Relationship of *Law and Learning* to Law and Learning" (1983), 29 McGill L.J. 155, defends traditional legal exegesis against what he feels is its depreciation in the *Arthurs Report* and charges (at 160): "'The Report suggests, correctly, that we should reject the vision of law as an autonomous system to be studied in isolation from its connection with the world. But in its insistence on the privacy of 'law and' research it offers the opposite vision: law as totally merged with the world. Lost in this clash of opposites is any sense of law as a partially autonomous system."
24. *Id.,* at 709.

the law. They also make up the judiciary, which interprets the laws. They can also be said to be the single most important body of policy-makers in corporations, unions, associations, etc. in our society. Fourth, just as the importance of law means that the public has a unique stake in law-making, so the importance of lawyers means that the public has a unique stake in legal education. Fifth, the public interest demands that legal education relate to social goals or ends as well as to means, and particularly that it present law as the principal social means for achieving justice.

Let us turn first to an analysis of what it is that lawyers do. A comprehensive list of lawyers' tasks is provided by Lasswell and McDougal:

Drafting, promoting, interpreting, and amending contitutions.

Drafting, promoting, and interpreting executive orders, administrative rulings, municipal charters, and so on, and attacking or sustaining their constitutionality.

Drafting and interpreting corporate and private association charters, agreements, dispositive instruments, and so on, and attacking or sustaining their validity.

Deciding or otherwise resolving causes or controversies, and making other decisions which affect the distribution of values, as judges, executives administrators, arbitrators, referees, trial examiners, and so on.

Bringing to, or obscuring from the attention of decision-makers the facts and policies on which judgment should rest.

Advising clients on how to avoid litigation and controversies and on how to make the best possible use of legal doctrines, institutions, and practices for the promotion of their private purposes and long-term interest. (Clarifying, *inter alia*, intentions as to property disposition, business transactions, and family relations).

Consulting and negotiating with clients, businessmen, opposing counsel, and decision-makers of all kinds.

Reading, digesting, and reinterpreting the decisions and reasoning of past decision-makers of all kinds.

Guiding, conducting, and preparing for investigations and hearings (criminal, regulatory, legislative, social-scientific, administrative).

Preparing arguments, legal forms, witnesses (ordinary, expert), trial briefs, and so on.

Selecting courts, juries, arbitrators, negotiators, and other decision-makers.

Selecting clients.

Selecting clerks, associates and successors.

> Preparing or supervising press conferences, issuing news releases, preparing radio material, or newsreel material.
>
> Developing influence through participation in civic and other public activities (organizing and directing pressure groups, lobbying propaganda, and other control procedures) and private sociability.
>
> Participating in professional organizations (organizations engaged in selection, exclusion and training of members, and with the maintenance of standards of varying degrees of ambiguity).
>
> Contributing by investigation, writing and lecturing to legal and social science (publishing facts and analyses of the relationship between legal rules and human relations; reformulation of legal rules).[25]

Some would undoubtedly wish to add to such a list the handling of the emotional aspects of dealing with clients. Indeed, this is one of the reasons for instituting clinical legal education.[26]

Lawyers must learn to perform their legal tasks competently. There is therefore a great public interest in lawyers' behaviour and consequently in legal education, which is supposed to develop professional competence, by imparting to students the traditional knowledge and skills of the lawyer. As Lasswell and McDougal put it:

> It is the lawyer's mastery over constitutions, statutes, appellate opinions and textbooks of peculiar idiom, and his skill in operating the mechanics (procedure) of both governmental institutions (courts, legislatures, administrative boards, executive offices) and private associations (corporations, partnerships, trade associations, labour unions, consumers' cooperatives), that set him apart from, and give him a certain advantage over, such other skill groups in our society as diplomats, economists, social psychologists, social historians and biologists.[27]

The last thing society needs from legal education is a new class of well-intentioned but professionally unskilled social scientists. What the public prizes about the legal profession is its professionalism, its sure sense of craft. The public expects from lawyers such qualities as a sharp sense of relevance, a rigorous analysis of words and concepts, and a working-hypothesis approach to synthesis — in other words, all the action-oriented techniques appropriate to maximize the possibilities for success of any undertaking or enterprise. The lawyer is expected to be the facilitator *par excellence* of our society.

Such a point of view is not at odds with the *Arthurs Report,* which, I think it is fair to say, accepts the primacy of professional education, and

---

25. *Supra,* note 12, at 209-210.
26. On this point see Edward Veitch, "The Vocation of our Era for Legal Education" (1979), 44 Sask. L.R. 19 at 34.
27. *Supra,* note 12, at 215.

even insists that students in the proposed scholarly stream must "be assured that they are not forever excluding themselves from professional opportunities".[28] In fact, one of the subordinate, though important, themes of the *Report* is that professional objectives themselves "are not particularly well served by the present eclectic curriculum".[29] In particular, the *Report* argues that the example of medical education supports the desirability of establishing clinical studies in law. President Derek Bok of Harvard has recently developed the same theme of the inadequacy of legal education from the professional point of view:

> [L]aw schools train their students more for conflict than for the gentler arts of reconciliation and accommodation. This emphasis is likely to serve the profession poorly. In fact, lawyers devote more time to negotiating conflicts than they spend in the library or the courtroom, and studies show that their bargaining efforts accomplish more for their clients. Over the next generation, I predict, society's greatest opportunities will lie in tapping human inclinations towards collaboration and compromise rather than stirring our proclivities for competition and rivalry. If lawyers are not leaders in marshalling cooperation and designing mechanisms that allow it to flourish, they will not be at the center of the most creative social experiments of our times.[30]

This is a powerful plea for a more pluralistic legal education. While there is no need to pursue this theme here, because the profession's own interest in technical competence is not different from that of the public, I would observe in passing that the necessity of clinical education in university law schools would be made more striking if there was ever any lessening in the requirements for articling or admission to the bar, which at present provide superior clinical experience.

However, in this paper I want to focus rather on what I believe is unique about the public interest in legal education, i.e. that law is the social means to the achievement of justice. This is what I call the *public dimension* in legal education. It might be argued that even here, the professional interest, rightly understood, is the same as that of the public, but unfortunately this is not generally perceived by the Bar to be true.

Even the Holmesian "bad man" needs to know not only how to achieve his own goals, but whether they are legally acceptable and whether they are likely to be considered socially acceptable. A client who

---

28. *Supra*, note 2, at 142.
29. *Id.*, at 53.
30. Derek Bok, "A Flawed System of Law Practice and Training" (1983), 33 J. Legal Ed. 570, at 582-3. At the first People's Law Conference I had occasion to say, *supra*, note 5, at 16: "A legal system designed solely to regulate people's conduct is appropriate for the ideal of confrontation. A legal system designed to respond to and secure people's needs points beyond confrontation to cooperation."

wishes to purchase a property which for its best commercial exploitation requires a land use variation does not need to know merely how to go about obtaining the variation. He or she also needs guidance as to any foreseeable neighbourhood reaction which might either prevent his or her obtaining it or render it largely ineffective even if obtained.

In fact even the individual lawyer's duty to serve his or her client's interest is coupled in the very first Rule of the *Code of Professional Conduct* of the Canadian Bar Association with parallel duties to "the court, members of the public and his fellow members of the profession".[31] Once he or she has accepted a client, of course, he or she owes that person his or her best efforts, subject to a prior duty to the Court. He or she may act only "within the limits of the law", and so may not, for example, "abuse the process of the tribunal" or "knowingly assist or permit his client to do anything which the lawyer considers to be dishonest or dishonourable".[32]

However, between clients, as it were, and as measured in the totality of his or her professional life, the lawyer cannot shirk moral responsibility for the kind, variety, quantity, etc. of the clients he or she accepts. He or she is, after all, a free and responsible human being. The lawyer may choose to refuse a client either to spend more time with family or to avoid representing only a particular class of person. He or she may agree to represent a client for the regular fee or out of idealism (or for both reasons).

More important, the profession as a whole will not be seen to serve the public interest if it appears to look only to the sum total of interests of individual lawyers in their individual clients. The public interest requires lawyers to defend every class of defendant, to draft and interpret laws as well as to litigate them, to demand justice and equality for all and to effectively mobilize social forces to achieve these goals. Legal education

---

31. The Canadian Bar Association, *Code of Professional Conduct*, adopted by Council on August 25, 1974. The most elaborate statement of professional ethics in Canada is found in *Professional Conduct Handbook* (Toronto, Law Society of Upper Canada, 1978). The first Rule reads: "The lawyer must discharge his duties to his client, the court, members of the public and his fellow members with integrity."

32. The C.B.A. Rule on The Lawyer as Advocate, Chapter *VIII, id.,* reads as follows: "When acting as an advocate the lawyer must, while treating the tribunal with courtesy and respect, represent his client resolutely, honourably and within the limits of the law." The commentary on the Rule adds, *inter alia:*

The lawyer must not, for example:
(a) abuse the process of the tribunal by instituting or prosecuting proceedings which, although legal in themselves, are clearly motivated by malice on the part of his client and are brought solely for the purpose of injuring the other party;
(b) knowingly assist or permit his client to do anything which the lawyer considers to be dishonest or dishonourable...

must ensure that every lawyer understands these public responsibilities and that an adequate number of lawyers is motivated and indeed inspired to undertake them.[33]

I must admit that my own teaching experience has left me with a somewhat more modest view of the pedagogical possibilities with respect to individual students than Lasswell and McDougal appear to have. They write, for instance, that "a legitimate aim of education is to seek to promote the major values of a democratic society and to reduce the number of moral mavericks who do not share democratic preferences."[34] In my view, the proper aim of what I shall call perspective studies is cognitive rather than affective,[35] *i.e.*, to make law students aware of both social values (or ends) and legal means. If this also has the effect of eliciting from students socially desirable value choices all the better, but that is a happy result beyond pedagogical guarantee in the individual case.[36] Nevertheless, it is absolutely essential that the overall system of legal education be structured in such a way as to maximize the likelihood that the social value of justice will be served as well as understood by lawyers.

Professor Francis Allen puts the need for education in values strongly and I believe accurately:

> Law school education and research is or ought to be preoccupied with values. We ask or ought consciously to be asking not only "how to do it" but "why we do it" and "ought we to do it all all"? There are few departments of the university in which such questions are so much a part of the daily grist as the law schools. The reason why it is important that such questions be asked is not simply that we are under obligation to be critics of the law and its institutions. We are under that obligation, and the

---

33. In his monograph *Unequal Justice: Lawyers and Social Change in Modern America* (New York, Oxford University Press, 1976) at 12. Professor Jerold S. Auerbach defends the thesis that:
> In the United States justice has been distributed according to race, ethnicity, and wealth, rather than need. This is not equal justice. The professional elite bears a special responsibility for this maldistribution.

He defines the professional elite as corporation lawyers and law professors recruited from Anglo-Saxon Protestant stock. Law Professors had a *modus vivendi* with practitioners which "permitted them to speak their conscience on public issues while they prepared their best students for corporate practice" (at 155). In my view one could not analyze the role of the professional elite so negatively in Canada, if only because Canadian society itself is probably less economically motivated.

34. *Supra*, note 12, at 212.

35. On this point see Andrew Petter, "A Closet Within the House: Learning Objectives and the Law School Curriculum", in Gold, *supra*, note 1, at 77.

36. Of course, different considerations are in play in courses such as legal ethics and professional responsibility, where teachers should feel the need directly to affect each student's future behaviour. On this, see Boyer and Cramton, *supra*, note 15, at 267-8, and also on the general emotional climate of the law school, at 258-270.

law school's role as critic of the law, and, indeed at times of the legal profession, is one of its most important social functions. If it is inadequately performed by the law schools, it will be performed by others; and there is no assurance that the criticism of the others will be as informed or as relevant. There is another reason for legal education's concern with values, however: such concern is essential to the understanding of law. How can law be "known" in any fundamental sense apart from its purposes? And how can the future development of the law be anticipated except by reference to how well these purposes are being achieved and how acceptable they remain to the wider society as the community's needs and perceptions change? Concern with values is thus far from being merely of academic interest. On the contrary, it goes to the very essence of technical professional competence.[37]

It is important to have a teaching staff dedicated as a whole to teaching law with an awareness of its dimensions, beginning with legal method itself. There are those who think the contemporary law school is doing this badly. Basing his analysis on what he calls the total curriculum — not only the formal curriculum but the hidden curriculum consisting of the unarticulated views about law held by the faculty — Professor Karl Klare argues that law schools disable their students intellectually by overstressing both the inner rationality and coherence of the common law and the legal reasoning contained in doctrinal analysis:

> This claim about legal reasoning — that it is autonomous from political and ethical choice — is a falsehood...
>
> Legal reasoning exists primarily as an array of highly stylized modes of justificatory rhetoric. From the standpoint of logic — as opposed, for example, to the perspectives of anthropology or hermeneutics — there simply is no necessity or determinacy to legal reasoning, no inner compulsion to its methods. Legal reasoning is a texture of openness, indeterminacy, and contradiction. Students need to know that in order to work creatively as advocates and analysts. To be *empowered* as legal thinkers our students must be totally freed from the tyranny of belief in the false coherence or compellingness of legal argument. But in fact our teaching leads ineluctably in the opposite direction, toward reinforcing the mistaken belief that legal reasoning accounts for legal results...We teach legal reasoning as though doctrine had a determinate meaning, as though doctrinal analysis were capable of resolving cases without resort to political and moral choice. We teach legal reasoning as though enduring principles of social organization were embedded in the logic of the doctrines themselves (as opposed to the political and ethical meanings of the doctrines).[38]

As typically taught, legal reasoning endows with much legitimacy what Cardozo called the rule of analogy or the method of philosophy by

---
37. *Supra*, note 1, at 14-15.
38. Karl E. Klare, "The Law School Curriculum in the 1980's: What's Left?" (1982), 32 J. Legal Ed. 336, at 340-1.

which the directive force of a legal principle is exerted along the line of logical progression, of which he writes:

> It has the primacy that comes from natural and orderly and logical succession. . . . At least it is the heir presumptive. A pretender to the title will have to fight his way. . . . In default of other tests, the method of philosophy must remain the organon of the courts if chance and favor are to be excluded, and the affairs of men are to be governed with the serene and impartial uniformity which is of the essence of the idea of law.[39]

Unfortunately, this method often fails to exorcise what Cardozo termed "the demon of formalism"[40] or to deny what Holmes called "the fallacy of logical form",[41] which conceals the underlying "judgment as to the relative worth and importance of competing legislative grounds, . . . the very root and nerve of the whole proceeding".[42] Only a public perspective can achieve this ultimate realism.

IV. Perspective Courses for Values Perspective

In my view, law must be studied as a value science rather than as a value-free discipline. Law schools, therefore, should offer "perspective courses" in order to cultivate in students this view of law as inescapably public and social. Canadian law schools have improved in this respect from the mid-1960s onward, according to the *Arthurs Report:*

> Within the curriculum, courses offering perspectives on the legal system as a whole increased: legal history and philosophy, law and economics or law and society. Moreover, courses were introduced that demanded some understanding of social context, although they were ultimately professional in orientation: urban planning, labour relations, social welfare or civil liberties.[43]

What has occurred has been called "the law and . . .' course phenomenon",[44] which was intended to situate legal rules in their non-legal context. It introduces into the law a slice of real life, but a narrow one, and of course such offerings are entirely optional.

The picture as seen by the *Report* therefore remains a dark one:

---

39. Benjamin N. Cardozo, *the Nature of the Judicial Process* (New Haven, Yale University Press, 1960) at 31-6.
40. *Id.,* at 66.
41. O.W. Holmes, "The Path of the Law" in MacGuigan, *Jurisprudence: Readings and Cases,* 2nd ed. (Toronto, University of Toronto Press, 1966) at 55.
42. *Id.,* at 54. I set out my own views on the judicial process in "Sources of Judicial Decision Making and Judicial Activism," at 30-40, in Sheilah L. Martin and Kathleen E. Mahoney, ed., *Equality and Judicial Neutrality* (Toronto, Carswell, 1987).
43. *Supra,* note 2, at 48.
44. Rod Macdonald, "Legal Education on the Threshold of the 1980's: Whatever Happened to the Great Ideas of the 60's" (1979), 44 Sask. L.R. 39, at 44.

Yet our survey of teaching methods and curriculum shows that most students receive no exposure at all to scholarly subjects such as legal history or theory or interdisciplinary perspectives on law, and that few have anything more than minimal exposure...[45]

I can only think that this is truly an unfortunate state of affairs from the viewpoint of the public interest. On the whole, law students in Canada are receiving negligible exposure to perspective studies. In my opinion, the public interest demands that students be required to pursue a minimum number of perspective courses at law school so that they can fulfill their role as policy-makers and articulators when they become practising lawyers. In other words, law schools must make compulsory for every law student at least two or three perspective courses such as legal history, jurisprudence, judicial process, legal process, law and society, legal methods and research methods.

This is not an infallible way of assuring the protection or furthering of the public interest, any more than the rest of the law school curriculum provides an absolute guarantee of professional competence. But it seems to me to be the best available protection of the public interest in the achievement of justice.

V. Entrance Requirements

A supplementary — and complementary — means of protecting the public interest is ensuring that all law students are prepared to take full advantage of the more reflective part of the law school curriculum by having completed a more general course of studies before entering law school. It has been an unfortunate, in my thinking, characteristic of Canadian legal education (in comparison, say, with the U.S.) that law schools entrants have not been required to have obtained a first degree. Most in fact have done so, and indeed the strong preference of most admission committees has been in this direction, but a minority of law students even now do not have a first degree — and some law schools even allow law students to work on a first degree course (such as a Bachelor of Commerce degree) simultaneously. The lack of background of this minority of students inevitably colours both their own comprehension and that of the schools as a whole. In my view, every law student should be required to complete a first degree as a condition of admission.[46]

---

45. *Supra*, note 2, at 135.
46. I do not of course mean to suggest that students who have completed their first degree requirements but not yet formally received their degrees before the opening of the law school term should be denied admission. What matters is that they should have fulfilled the requirements for the degree. Given that the percentage of first-year law students without prior

The necessity for a first degree, which I derive from the need to serve the public interest, might also have an advantage for the law schools in relation to government funding. The *Arthurs Report*, recognizing that the scholarly option proposed will be expensive, refers to the realistic "fear that the professional Peter will be robbed to pay a scholarly Paul".[47] Additional resources will indeed have to be found.

With a new emphasis on academics, particularly if it were to become a second-degree program (in this respect like graduate studies), legal education would have a ready-made case for being more heavily "weighted" in the scheme of government funding. The present weighting for law in Ontario is 1.5, whereas in comparable U.S. systems it is often 2.5.[48] An improvment in quality in legal education must inevitably, it seems to me, lead to an increase in weighting and hence funding. Of course, there is no guarantee that increased funding made available to universities on behalf of law students would necessarily find its way to the law schools. However, given the political skills of the law faculties, it is probably safe to assume a reasonable proportionality between increased university funding resulting from increasing weighting for legal education and the actual availability of increased funding for legal education.

VI. Conclusion

I have not attempted in this discussion to be definitive with respect to the content of the perspective requirement in law schools. I have no doubt that there are in fact several approaches which might successfully be used. Each law school would undoubtedly develop its own approach.

What I do insist on is the right of the public to a legal education oriented to justice as well as to law, because democracy itself demands it.

Even apart from the *Charter* the day has disappeared when mere legislative fiat can confer legitimacy on law. Today the legitimacy of law

---

degrees seems to be no higher than about 25% of the class at any common-law school and is as low as about 3% at some schools (this is in stark contrast to civil-law schools where as many as 75% of the incoming students may lack first degrees), I do not believe any large number of students will be seriously inconvenienced. But even if they were, I believe the goal of a student body with a better preparation for a perspective approach is worth it, in terms of the overall good. The strongest case for not requiring prior degrees is with respect to mature students who are given special admission. Since they are in any event such a small proportion of entering students, their admission without prior degrees would perhaps be consistent with a general rule otherwise requiring such degrees, with their maturity constituting an acceptable substitute for the degree requirement.

47. *Supra*, note 2, at 149.
48. The weighting of law students by the Maritime Provinces Higher Education Commission is better than that in Ontario — 4.0, in comparison to 1.5 for arts and 3.0 for graduate studies — but only 25% of the university budget is affected by such course weighting, the rest being based on an entirely different kind of formula.

is measured by the public according to its perceived adequacy in expressing the public's conception of justice.

Justice itself is not objectively measurable, which is to say that it is a value-term bearing symbolic connotations as well as a more precise meaning. But it ought to be possible to find agreement at least on the minimal formulation of Professor Auerbach:

> Justice should be defined not only by process but by product: is the result, measured by the interests of clients and the needs of society, fair?[49]

Law is the principal means to attain justice, and society cannot accept a system of legal education, any more than it can tolerate a legal profession, which does not recognize its responsibility to have as its principal aim the achievement of justice. Such a perspective will define the public dimension of legal education.

---

49. *Supra*, note 33, at 308.

Post-Modernism

[42]

WHAT SHOULD BE CONSERVED?

By BRENDA BARRETT*

ANYONE who advocates conservation is likely to be accused of conservatism![1] However, conservation implies the selection of that which is worthy of being saved in the face of change; whereas conservatism has customarily meant aversion to all change.

Change is inevitable: frequently it is brought about by circumstances wholly or largely beyond the control of those who are affected by it. When experiencing change it is important to be aware of it and to respond to it in such a way as to get the maximum advantage, or minimum disadvantage, from it.

There are three possible responses to change: (a) resist it in order to delay or reduce its impact; (b) use it as the opportunity for review and stock-taking; (c) encourage it as the opportunity for a major revision of the existing order of things.

The present writer prefers, wherever possible, to adopt the middle course in the context of the development of law teaching, and ventured to suggest such an approach when writing in a previous issue of this Journal,[2] but it would seem thereby acquired the reputation of being an exponent of black-letter law.[3]

Five years have passed since that article was published, so it is perhaps worthwhile again to indulge in the process of review and stock-taking to try to identify what, from the law teaching of the 1980s, should be carried forward and strengthened in the years ahead.

In order to predict what lies ahead it is helpful to know how the present situation was reached. This is particularly so when the subjects under review are law and law teaching. The law itself is the product of evolution, and law teaching to some extent must reflect that evolution. The law syllabus has to change from year to year in order to accommodate new laws, and the evolutionary nature of their discipline tends to influence the character of the teachers themselves. Thus the way in which law is taught today is the result of an evolution whose stages have been marked by articles in this Journal over the past twenty years. The development of law teaching in the future is likely to flow from decisions made about teaching strategies at the present time.

HOW DID WE GET HERE?

No one can deny that law teaching, like higher education in general, has come through a period of great change. Twenty years ago graduate entry into the legal profession was by no means the norm and undergraduate teaching in law, apart from teaching for the London University External Degree, was exclusively confined to universities. The great expansion in law degree teaching, which occurred in the 1970s, was related to changes in the sort of student who enrolled, the sort of staff who taught and the sort of environment in which law was taught.

The expansion of higher education in the wake of the Robbins Report[4] gave opportunities for entry on to undergraduate courses of large numbers of British students from lower middle-class and working-class backgrounds and also of students from developing countries. A fair proportion of the newly-enfranchised students, both home and overseas, were mature students, who had not the conventional 'A' level entry qualifications, or, if they had, had obtained them many years previously.

*Middlesex Polytechnic

The expansion of law teaching was accommodated by the introduction of new courses, particularly—though not exclusively—in the public sector of the education system. The teachers for these new courses were, initially, largely drawn from those who had hitherto taught either on sub-degree courses or on the External London LL.B. Their ranks were swollen by heavy recruitment of new staff, many of whom were young, newly-graduated and without formal teacher training: these new recruits had to develop their teaching skills either from memory of how they themselves had been taught or by observation of how their colleagues were teaching. Indeed, for many this situation is little changed today. Thus what is taught by one generation is a development from, and sometimes a reaction against, the teaching practices of the preceding generation.

The curricula of law degree proposals submitted to the Council for National Academic Awards in the early 1970s were influenced by the environment and background of those who prepared them in at least three respects: firstly they consciously sought to escape from what was perceived as the strait-jacket into which the External London Degree was believed to have forced law teaching; secondly, the departmental structure, as it existed within the public sector at that time, encouraged multi-disciplinary teaching; and, thirdly, the undergraduate was perceived as requiring about 12 "contact hours" a week.

Most institutions unashamedly wanted their degrees to qualify their students for exemption from Part I of the professions' qualifying examinations: they were accordingly careful to submit courses which met the 'Ormrod criteria'[5] regarding the suitability of courses as foundations for the legal professions. In practice, most of the programmes were what Ormrod described as "mixed degrees"—that is to say, they included about 20 per cent of 'non-law' work. These non-law courses were normally prepared, and in due course taught, by staff who had graduated in the disciplines to be taught. In some institutions the non-law element was injected by expanding the law syllabuses themselves rather than by introducing discrete units of study.

THE 1980s

Barely had the C.N.A.A. considered, and in the main approved, the new law degree schemes in the public sector than, in the mid-1970s, a wind of change began to blow—a cold 'cutting' wind, curtailing all further expansion and bringing fear of what the future might have in store.

The climate was already becoming unfavourable by 1981 when the Association of Law Teachers held its Conference, "Law in Higher Education: Reform and Experiment in the Curriculum". The Conference coincided, for many institutions, with the phasing out of their original C.N.A.A. law degree schemes and the phasing in of the first revisions of those schemes. The delegates included representatives of two 'generations' of teachers. There were the 'father figures' from the early days—persons who had both served on the C.N.A.A. in its formative years and led their own working parties to the successful submission of the original C.N.A.A. degree schemes: they were, by then, for the most part, Heads of Department. Many of them have since retired. There were also present a younger generation who had entered the public sector to teach at, or after, the launching of the original C.N.A.A. law degrees.

WHAT SHOULD BE CONSERVED?

Whereas the older generation tended to have, in their youth, largely studied black-letter law with, possibly, a little Austinian jurisprudence, the younger generation had a firmer grasp of, and inclination towards, both legal theory and contextual studies. Many of the conference papers were presented by the younger generation. Their emphasis was on law as a social science. There was a desire to resist pressures, supposedly emanating from the legal profession, for curricula overly-full of detailed rules. No particular consideration was then given to structuring of curriculum content and teaching methods to the worsening economic climate.

At the time of this Conference it seemed to the present writer that, in relation to the LL.B. course, the position had been reached where:

(1) There was a danger of reducing the law input into the degree to an unacceptably low level because the 'mixed degree', which most institutions in the public sector were offering, contained subjects which were overtly 'non-law' while at the same time their law courses contained large amounts of contextual material;

(2) There was a danger of 'over-teaching' students by exposing them to many contact hours and thus leaving them little opportunity for personal development through private study.

These trends seemed to the writer to be dangerous because:

(1) There was such a volume of law that it was questionable whether undergraduates could obtain a mastery of it in combination with both contextual studies and complementary disciplines;

(2) The worsening economic climate cast doubt upon whether high contact hours could be maintained;

(3) The aging profile of the law teaching profession could render teachers insensitive to the needs of the young whom they taught.

With hindsight it seems to me that when I attempted to express my opinions five years ago I had two themes which, possibly because of the emphasis of the Conference, I failed sufficiently to distinguish and acknowledge. The first theme—that of the Conference—was the development of the law teacher's perception of his subject. The second concerned the nature of the environment in which the teacher exercised his profession. These themes ought to be closely related to, and interacting on, each other. Nevertheless, they are two separate themes and this ought to be clearly recognised. The initiative for the determination of what takes place in the classroom is largely with the teacher: changes in the external environment are largely outside his control.

When the teacher is in his classroom he has a choice: he may divorce himself from the outside environment or he may relate to it and adjust his teaching in response to it. Ultimately, if he ignores the fire alarm, he and his class may be burnt to death.

Interpreting the concerns which I previously expressed by reference to this imagery, what I was suggesting five years ago was that law teachers were in danger of becoming so isolated in their classrooms that they might fail to hear and respond to the alarm signals concerning the external environment, and that trends in the content and philosophy of curricula might fail to relate to developments in the external environment. What I now wish to attempt is to review the developments of the last five years and to consider whether this danger is still present. Following my new analytical framework I propose to consider firstly the 'external environment', then secondly, the trends in law teaching. Finally—and no doubt controversially—I shall venture some opinions about the responses which are demanded by changes in the external environment. Throughout I shall be focussing on the Polytechnics and drawing largely on this Journal as the principal channel of communication for law teachers employed in the public sector of legal education.

THE EXTERNAL ENVIRONMENT

The world beyond the classroom is so vast and complex that any selection of particular matters as relevant to what goes on in the classroom must inevitably run the risk of being considered either random or subjective. The following matters would nevertheless seem to be relevant in the period under review:

(1) *The volume and complexity of the law itself.* The output of new laws has not diminished. That we once may have supposed that the Law Commission might, like a latter-day Justinian, reduce English law to a relatively short code, now seems as unreal as a dream. The Court of Appeal has indicated that in its view the Employment Appeal Tribunal ought not to be multiplying precedents in employment protection laws,[6] but, even in that narrow area, judicial review and the European Court have provided new sources of case law. Across the spectrum of the subject-areas Parliament has been busy and the courts have, in their turn, similarly been active in creating precedents. There has therefore been a considerable increase in the volume of material available to teachers. Moreover, legal rules have tended to become more complex as anyone who has, for example, dealt with *Junior Books Ltd.* v. *Veitchi Co. Ltd.*[7] will readily concede.

(2) *The political scene.* The Conservative Government has enacted legislation making radical changes to the statutory framework and these changes have to be reflected in syllabus amendments: some of this legislation, like that concerning trade unions, has been expressly intended to alter the balance of power within society; some of it, like the Police and Criminal Evidence Act, has been capable of being interpreted as having this objective. At the least controversial assessment of the changes thus brought about, there have been alterations in the internal balances of syllabuses and in some instances the balances between subject-areas.

(3) *The 'crisis in education'.* The future of education is now a major political issue. Up till now the media have focussed on the two extremes of the teaching profession, schools and universities—particularly schools, as a result of the year-long industrial dispute. However, the plight of the Polytechnics is actually worse than that of the universities. The problem of inadequate funding in Polytechnics did feature on the front page of *The Times* newspaper on 8 April 1986, when it was suggested that student numbers would be reduced to prevent standards from falling yet further. Parliament's attention was thus momentarily attracted to the Polytechnics and Sir Keith Joseph, the then Secretary of State for Education, wrote to *The Times*[8] denying that there was a problem. Shortly afterwards attention reverted to the universities with the announcement that some universities would get small funding increases in the wake of a "Radical grants review" by the University Grants Committee.[9]

WHAT SHOULD BE CONSERVED?

The following are given as indicia of the gravity of the situation for Polytechnics and of its significance for law teaching in particular:

(a) *Staffing reductions.* In January 1984 the Committee of Polytechnic Directors stated that in 26 Polytechnics there had been reductions in posts which totalled 2,200 and that over half of these posts were teaching posts. Observation suggests that reductions have continued since that time as a result of early retirements and non-replacement of staff. Support services from administrative, secretarial and manual staff have also been reduced. The impact of these general reductions will not have fallen evenly across the disciplines, or evenly between law schools, but most law schools will have been affected by them to some extent.

(b) *Student numbers.* Student enrolment on C.N.A.A. law degree courses in Polytechnics apparently continued to rise between 1980 and 1983, when the C.N.A.A.'s Annual Report stated that first-year enrolments were 2,341.[10] Government policies, as interpreted at institutional level, may now be reducing these numbers in relation to demand, though the actual level of demand will not be known until the results of the first year of the P.C.A.S.[11] operation are known. However, a Polytechnic law teacher has recently published a paper suggesting that the true demand for lawyers will continue to increase.[12]

(c) *Library resources.* Few, if any, Polytechnics will have been able to maintain their expenditure on books because of the general reduction in resourcing. One account shows that, as far as the twelve largest Polytechnics are concerned, the average bookfund expenditure per 'full-time equivalent student' fell from £23.01 in 1983/84 to £21.80 in 1984/85.[13] This was at a time when the price of books was rising rapidly. While law libraries, in some institutions, may have been protected from the full force of these cuts, the situation can only be extremely serious for the future of a discipline which is so dependent on library facilities.

(d) *General Funding.* A D.E.S. Statistical Bulletin published in December 1985 showed that while *per capita* funding for Polytechnic students had been £3,655 in 1979 it had fallen to £2,990 by 1984: the comparable university figures showed a rise from £4,825 to £4,898. In real terms unit costs at Polytechnics have fallen by 18 per cent since 1979-80, mainly because of a growth in student numbers of 24 per cent. Unit costs in universities, where student numbers have been held back in order to protect the resources available for research, have risen slightly.[14]

In summary, in Polytechnics, fewer teachers have been teaching more students in a deteriorating environment. Even if this downward spiral were to stop it seems unlikely that conditions would significantly improve.

At this point relationships with the National Advisory Body, the C.N.A.A. and the legal profession ought to be considered.

The N.A.B. A major development of the 1980s has been the creation of the National Advisory Body for Local Authority Higher Education with the task of advising the Secretary of State on student numbers and on associated funding. This body has rapidly established a considerable control over the development of Polytechnics by its recommendations as to the size of the student body for which particular institutions should be funded and its recommendations as to funding of specific programme-areas. Some areas are marked for more favourable treatment than others. Social science is identified as an area where student numbers should be contained. Law is classified into this unfavourable area. This classification has not been accepted without protest by such bodies as The Committee of Heads of Polytechnic Law Schools, and the profession has lent them its support. It is too early to tell whether law will be re-classified. In the meanwhile, however, the Heads of Law Schools have no easy task when seeking to maintain their position within the resourcing and planning committees of the Polytechnics. Establishing that the law school is operating at student/staff ratios of 20:1 is not likely to persuade Directorates to sanction further law staff appointments.

The C.N.A.A. A crucial role was played by the C.N.A.A. in securing the development of law degree courses in the Polytechnic sector.[15] It determined the model for such degree courses and set the standards for their successful operation. It is undoubtedly helpful that the C.N.A.A. has recently published a paper on resources and the standards of C.N.A.A.-validated courses, in which it has stated that the Council believes that serious consequences will follow if there is further decline in the unit of resource. However, in the 'post-Lindop'[16] era the C.N.A.A.'s own role has still to be identified, and it is by no means clear that its voice will be so powerful as hitherto within the Government or even within Polytechnics.

The Profession. The careful distancing from the profession of the academic institutions which provide courses that qualify their graduates for exemption from Part I of the profession's own qualifying examinations, has traditionally been much advocated by law teachers, but it has correspondingly removed the profession from the problems which have recently faced the academic institutions. Although both branches of the profession have, most helpfully, questioned the classification of law as a social science, the price of the independence of the law schools from the profession has to be that, in the last instance, the battles of the law schools over the funding of undergraduate teaching must be fought by the law schools themselves rather than by the profession. Indeed, the profession is engaged in shaping its own future.[17]

THE LAW TEACHER

The model of today's practising law teacher can be constructed from what has been said concerning the environment in which he is operating. The 'typical' law teacher entered Polytechnic teaching between 1970 and 1975, is now aged 40-45, came to teaching with a law degree and obtained a higher degree, either before starting to teach or while in service. He taught at one other institution before taking up his present appointment. He has been in this appointment more than five years and he is currently receiving little or no staff development. He works longer hours than he used to do, teaches larger classes and has an increasing load of administrative work. His workload, combined with restricted library facilities, make it more difficult than formerly for him to keep up with his subject, which is getting more difficult to keep up with anyway. The increased price of books makes it more difficult for him to buy them.[18]

WHAT SHOULD BE CONSERVED? 193

The question now to be considered is how does this teacher perceive his subject? What does he consider as worthy of debate? In what directions does he see his subject developing? As was promised earlier, the answers to these questions will be sought through considering the materials published in his principal specialised publication—*The Law Teacher*.

A glance at the contents listed on the covers of the issues of *The Law Teacher* since 1981 is sufficient to demonstrate that the Journal has continued its tradition of featuring some major articles on developments in substantive law; at least one article in any issue is concerned with academic analysis of rules of law. That part of the Journal which is entitled Recent Developments also bears responsibility for keeping the Association of Law Teachers' members abreast of changes in the law. The Upjohn Lecture provides the occasion for a contribution from an eminent lawyer from the profession or from the university sector.[19]

Significantly, a large part of the Journal is always devoted to disseminating views about how law should be taught, and to whom it should be, or is being, taught. Somewhat surprisingly, however, relatively few articles emphasise that changes are taking place within the environment in which it is being taught.[20]

An awareness that good practice and external pressures suggested the law teacher ought not to devote his whole time to teaching undergraduates was shown when the Association organised a two-day Conference in May 1983 to discuss research and research degrees; subsequently a whole issue of the Journal[21] was devoted to the papers delivered at the Conference. Nevertheless this was somewhat disconcerting because it tended to demonstrate the difficulties which lawyers experience when trying to establish themselves in research as currently understood and evaluated.[22]

The emphasis in the Journal is, this research issue apart, heavily biassed towards undergraduate teaching, and within the realm of undergraduate teaching, the focus is on law degree teaching. Even though many of the members of the Association are not working in Polytechnics or Colleges of Higher Education, which have undergraduate teaching, it is somewhat unusual for the Journal to cater explicitly for this group.[23] The majority of the contributors come from the Polytechnic law schools and are normally concerned with the teaching of law on undergraduate courses,[24] although it is true that there are contributions from those who teach law in other parts of the world and who wish to share their experiences[25] or compare developments within their own jurisdiction with changes taking place in the United Kingdom.[26] Occasionally a contribution from the university sector will describe an unusual pattern of law teaching from within that sector for wider consideration and evaluation.[27] Some of the articles directed towards the undergraduate law degree's teachers cover a range of matters peripheral to the curriculum, such as a survey of the entry qualifications of students,[28] a discussion of the ways in which the student can be assisted in coping with the problems associated with learning[29] and evaluation of methods of assessment.[30]

However, analysis of the subject-matter covered by the Journal throughout its history and, perhaps even more especially in the last few years, reveals a hard core of contributions in which the authors are asking, in relation to the curriculum itself: What are we doing?, How are we doing it?, and For what purpose are we doing it?

The proposition stated in the Journal[31] that—

"... the two fundamental educational questions 'What should we teach?' and 'How should we teach it?' are to this day little addressed in published material in this country ..."

does not really seem justified when measured against the output of the Journal.

A recurrent theme is dissatisfaction with the present legal profession and an express or implied rejection of the hypothesis that law teaching at the undergraduate level should overtly be closely related to the legal profession as it at present functions.[32] The escalation of the debate, which has been reflected in the pages of the Journal concerning the relationship of law teaching to the profession, is encapsulated in the opening paragraph of an article by Dr. Alan Hunt:

"There is a growing feeling that all is not well in legal education. The distinctive location of legal studies astride the academic-vocational divide creates the concern that legal education suffers the same fate as all who sit upon the fence. The concern is that as presently practised legal education may fail to match up to either academic *or* vocational aspirations".[33]

The initial proposition is a statement with which few academics would be likely to disagree, and possibly many practitioners would also accept it. However, to agree that there is a problem is not necessarily to agree its treatment and Dr. Hunt's case for critical legal education need not be the accepted solution.[34]

Leighton and Sheinman identify three models of law teaching: clinical, sociological and black-letter.[35] The emphasis in the Journal in the last five years has undoubtedly been on the sociological, and on legal method which relates to the sociological approach.[36] It has been overtly theoretical rather than vocational; certainly more expressly so than had the emphasis been on either the clinical or the black-letter approach. The exponents of the current sociological movement frequently wish to incorporate the techniques and literature of legal theory into discrete areas of substantive law and use the conventional subject-areas as the basis for a "critical approach to society".[37]

Underlying much of this writing is an awareness of the danger, as one writer puts it,

"of rule-centredness, 'appellate courtitis', court room centredness, indifference to empirical enquiry, the consideration of reform essentially as the reform of the existing legal rules rather than starting from a consideration of the social problem".[38]

Many of these writers expressly advocate the rejection of the pathological model which "focusses on malfunctions, on disputes, on the breakdown of normal relationships".[39] It is, as Leighton and Sheinman point out, in many ways the antithesis of clinical legal education: it is the Kahn-Freund sociological model rather than the "lawyer-as-craftsman"—or Llewellyn—model which those authors label clinical.[40]

The identification of social norms by which to measure the law involves the teacher in making value judgments which can in turn lead to the question, "Can and should a law teacher be morally neutral?"[41] or could justify the statement that law teachers have an obligation to consider law and politics as two ways of looking at the same thing.[42]

ANALYSIS

How far, I ask myself, do the events of the last five years, both the developments within law teaching and changes in the environment in which it is taught, relate to the trends, and the inherent dangers in these trends, which I believed to be apparent in 1981?

The brief references made at that time to the likely consequences of the worsening economic environment were undoubtedly an underestimate of the severity of the reduction in resources, and the consequences of that reduction, which we have actually suffered.

The suggestion which I then made that lawyers ought to adopt a more "black-letter" approach to their teaching was based on the assumption that "mixed degrees", with contextual studies offered by colleagues from the social sciences, would remain the model for the C.N.A.A. degree. It is interesting to note that in the period under review only one author writing in the Journal appears to have advocated such an approach.[43] The theme of most of the contributors to the Journal has been that the sociological input should be part of the law syllabuses themselves rather than isolated and allocated to teachers from other disciplines. In this author's own institution, and possibly in others, the introduction of critical analysis into the law syllabuses has taken place to the chagrin of the sociologists albeit they do not relate to the lawyer's perception of sociology. However, it is not clear that the law input in the undergraduate curriculum is any greater than it was five years ago.

Indeed, not the least of the problems involved in writing about the present sociological movement is that it is difficult to identify exactly what is comprised in the present sociological model. There are seemingly as many explanations of it as there are contributors to the debate. The present writer empathises with the following comment about that aspect of the movement which describes itself as critical legal theory:

> "Critical scholars have yet to adopt a clear, common, ideology . . . while the open-ended nature of their methodology makes it difficult to regard critical scholarship as more than an analytical technique."[44]

A risk inherent in this analytical technique is that the teacher who introduces critical evaluation of laws must come close to inserting his own value-judgments into his teaching. Few are capable of even recognising when they do this. Personally, I subscribe to the ". . . unwritten rule that teachers should not attempt to commend any particular viewpoint to their pupils or students".[45] However, I am not sure that I always recognise when I am, as I am sure that I am at times breaking that rule, at least by a gloss on facts or an inflexion of the voice. At one level few would disagree that it is relevant and justifiable, even desirable, to put, say, a statute in the context of the government which brought it into being. If legislation had the avowed objective, in furtherance of a political party manifesto, of, for example, reducing the power of the trade union movement, the success of the legislation can only be judged by measuring the extent to which it achieves that objective. However, to go on to suggest whether the legislation's objective is socially good or bad is, in the present writer's view, to introduce one's own value-judgments and ought not to be done.

Moreover, the present debate about the nature and content of law syllabuses does not seem to extend to considerations as to the balance between contact hours and private study.

CONCLUSIONS

There are, in the present writer's opinion, a number of very disturbing features about the curriculum crisis which law teachers seem currently to be experiencing. Foremost among these is that the debate as to the curriculum is essentially introspective. In so far as it relates to the external environment at all it relates only to that part which consists of the body of law which must, in the final analysis, be the raw materials with which the law teacher works.[46]

A major anomaly in the sociological movement must be that it moves the teaching of law away from the vocational at a time when the political emphasis is on vocational studies. This disregard for the political climate seems strange considering that the majority of law students wish to be trained for the legal profession.

Unfortunately, the movement does nothing to alleviate the problem which we share with the profession: namely coping with the immense volume of law which even in a computer age has become quite unmanageable. To retreat from this practical problem into theory about the social function of law avoids, rather than resolves, this issue. Again this is somewhat unhelpful to the majority of law graduates who intend to enter the legal profession.

Initially the Polytechnics catered particularly well for those who came to undergraduate work with an unusual academic background: very often students who wanted a 'second chance' to make a career. Such students are usually very vocationally orientated. It is by no means clear that the somewhat theoretical approach to studying law which is currently advocated is best suited to their needs. Particularly urgent problems, which ought to be addressed, therefore, are the creation of teaching programmes, and the development of teaching methods, which will allow such students speedily to adapt to the rigours of learning the law in a regime of high student/staff ratios.

Arguably also, insufficient thought has been given to developing law inputs in the more favoured N.A.B. programme-areas.[47] The answer seems self-evident if the question is asked: Does the business studies or management student, who is predominantly concerned nowadays with cost-effectiveness and the flexible firm, really want a sociological approach to law?

Finally, while the debate rages about what sort of law courses law teachers would like to teach, no consideration is being given to the responses which ought to be made to the dramatic impact which changes in funding are having on the teaching environment. There seems to be an unspoken assumption, in discussions about curricula, that the C.N.A.A. model of the 1970s, in so far as it related to class sizes, teaching years, contact hours and library facilities, was based on immutable laws of nature. Thus while considerable attention has been directed, since the first C.N.A.A. law degree submissions, to the philosophy, content and methods of imparting the material covered by law syllabuses, no adequate consideration seems to be have been given to the question of how a sufficient understanding of the law may be imparted to students in larger tutorial groups, seen less frequently, and with less favourable library facilities than the original submissions envisaged. A possible reason why these problems have not been addressed is that no thought has been given to the training of law graduates in teaching. The result is that adaptation to change is more readily perceived as an academic

WHAT SHOULD BE CONSERVED?

debate concerned with the philosophy of curricula than as a practical questioning of how to adapt in order to maximise limited resources.

To conclude by reverting to the analogy with which this review of the last five years began: the reduction in teaching resources which has been experienced during the past five years represents a fire bell which has been ringing loudly outside the classroom door. It is high time that law teachers gave urgent consideration to what it is essential to conserve if law degree courses are to survive in the public sector. In the present writer's view our energies should be directed to:

(1) Emphasising the vocational aspects of law teaching;
(2) Strengthening our provision for mature students and ethnic groups;
(3) Devising ways of imparting knowledge with limited resources;
(4) Strengthening inputs into business studies and other vocational courses;
(5) Providing initial teacher-training and improved staff development.

If the debate inside the classroom continues for much longer the class may be engulfed in flames before the teacher responds to the real, rather than the academic, crisis which faces law teaching in the public sector at the present time.

---

1. See "The Law Teacher's Dilemma", Frank Bates, (1983) 17 *Law Teach.* 151.
2. "A Plea for Conservation", (1981) 15 *Law Teach.* 146.
3. See "Central Questions in Legal Education", Patricia Leighton and Leslie Sheinman, (1986) 20 *Law Teach.* 3, and "Curriculum Development in Legal Studies", Phil Harris (1986) 20 *Law Teach.* 110.
4. *Higher Education, Report of Committee,* Cmnd. 2154 of 1963 (H.M.S.O.).
5. *Report of the Committee on Legal Education,* Cmnd. 4595 of 1971. (H.M.S.O.).
6. E.g. *O'Kelly* v. *Trusthouse Forte p.l.c.* [1984] Q.B. 90.
7. [1983] 2 A.C. 520.
8. April 9th, 1986.
9. *The Times,* 21 May 1986. On the following day a response from the universities interpreted the proposals as imposing further cuts. See also "Crisis on the Campus", *The Observer,* 1 June 1986.
10. Compare *A Plea for Conservation* (n. 2 above), footnote 18, where it was noted that Polytechnic enrolments (admittedly not quite the same) were then 1430.
11. The Polytechnics' Centralised Admissions System.
12. "Probable Demand for Lawyers and Law Courses for the Next Ten Years", Alan Wharam, (1986) 20 Law Teach. 180.
13. Comparative Council of Polytechnic Librarians Statistics.
14. *Department of Education and Science Statistical Bulletin,* December 1985.
15. See, "The C.N.A.A. Law Degree", S. B. Marsh, (1983) 17 *Law Teach.* 73.
16. *Academic Validation in the Public Sector of Higher Education,* Report of Committee of Enquiry, Cmnd. 9501 of 1985 (H.M.S.O.).
17. See for example, "Charges against the fat cats", *Spectrum, The Times,* 26 May 1986.
18. See Dr. Marsh's researched profile, (1983) 17 *Law Teach.,* p. 94.
19. E.g. "The Teaching of Law and Politics", J. A. G. Griffith, (1982) 16 *Law Teach.* 1; "Reform of the Legislative Process in the Light of the Law Commissions' Work", Lord Hooson Q.C., (1983) 17 *Law Teach.* 67.
20. A valuable exception to this generalisation is Frank Sharman's "Computers Communications and the Future of Legal Education", (1981) 15 *Law Teach.* 139.
21. (1984) 18 *Law Teach.* No. 1.

22. Possibly too little emphasis was given to the amount of scholarly activity required of those who practise in the legal profession without professing to research.
23. But see "Law Teaching at Colleges of Further Education", J. S. Bailey and S. B. Marsh, (1981) 15 *Law Teach.* 83.
24. But see "Law, Law Staff and the C.N.A.A. Business Studies Degree Courses", N. A. Bastin, (1985) 19 *Law Teach.* 12. This paper was commended by C.N.A.A.
25. E.g., "Evaluating Class Participation: Some Reflections on the University of New South Wales and Macquarie University Experience" Razeen Sappideen, (1982) 16 *Law Teach.* 179.
26. E.g., "The British Response to Surrogate Motherhood: An American Critique", Thomas A. Eaton, (1985) 19 *Law Teach.* 163.
27. E.g., "Academic and Practical Legal Education: The Contribution of the Sandwich System", Martin Partington, (1984) 18 *Law Teach.* 110.
28. E.g., "A Survey of Law School Admissions", Robert G. Lee, (1984) 18 *Law Teach.* 165; "Admissions Policies in Law Schools", Nigel Duncan and Neil Wojciechowski-Kibble, (1986) 20 *Law Teach.* 36.
29. "Coping Strategies in Legal Education", James R. Elkins, (1982) 16 *Law Teach.* 195; "Games Law Teachers Play", Paul Bergman, Avrom Sherr and Roger Burridge, (1986) 20 *Law Teach.* 24; "Communicating the Law", Graham Viskovic, (1983) 17 *Law Teach.* 30; "In Video Veritas", Andrew Hart, (1983) *Law Teach.* 17; "The Paperchase Revisited: The Huddersfield Experiment", Diane M. R. Tribe and Tony Tribe, (1985) 19 *Law Teach.* 24; "The Baby and the Bathwater: Developing a Positive Socratic Method", Steven Alan Childress, (1984) 18 *Law Teach.* 95.
30. "Methods of Assessment in British Law Schools", T. A. Downes, P. R. Hopkins and W. M. Rees, (1982) 16 *Law Teach.* 77.
31. (1986) 20 *Law Teach.* at p. 4.
32. See, "The Responsibility of the Law School", Frank Bates, (1981) 15 *Law Teach.* 172; "The Provision of Legal Education and Services in Britain: A Tale of Two Systems, Robert C. Elliot, (1981) 15 *Law Teach.* 1; "The Quality of Professional Services", K. M. Stanton and A. M. Dugdale, (1983) 17 *Law Teach.* 166; "The Future of Legal Services: A Review", William M. Rees, (1983) 17 *Law Teach.* 42.
33. "The Case for Critical Legal Education", (1986) 20 *Law Teach.* 10.
34. See, "A Progressive Critique? The Contribution of Critical Legal Scholarship to a Marxist Theory of Law", Julian S. Webb, (1985) 19 *Law Teach.* 98.
35. (1986) 20 *Law Teach.* 6.
36. E.g., "Contract and Legal Method: An Attempt at Integration", Tony Downes, (1985) 19 *Law Teach.* 133; or advocates incorporating into the syllabus literature which may help ". . . to eliminate the pathetic contrast between the law of contract as it is taught in most text books and modern contract as it functions in society" W. Friedman, *Law in a Changing Society,* quoted in "Criticisms of the Traditional Contract Course", Richard Lewis, (1982) 16 *Law Teach.* 111 at 120.
37. "Land Law and Legal Education: Is There Any Justice or Morality in Blackacre". Ronnie Warrington, (1984) 18 *Law Teach.* 88; *cf.* "There Once Was an Ugly Duckling: Land Law in 1985", Kate Green, (1985) 19 *Law Teach.* 65.
38. "Legal Education and Reflection", Anthony Beck, (1985) 19 *Law Teach.* 193 at 204.
39. "Ignoring Complexity: Law, Law Schools and the Public Interest", Max Weaver, (1985) 19 *Law Teach.* 3.
40. (1986) 20 *Law Teach.* 3 at 5. It is therefore interesting to note that Max Weaver has also identified advantages in clinical education: "Clinical Legal Education—Competing Perspectives", (1983) 17 *Law Teach.* 1.
41. "Morality and the Law Teacher", Anthony Hofler, (1981) 15 *Law Teach.* 114. Cf. Warrington, note 37 above. Cf. also "The Moral Crisis in Modern Legal Education", Frank Bates, (1984) 18 *Law Teach.* 181. 42. J. A. G. Griffith, note 19 above.
43. "Why Teach Economics to Law Degree Students?", David Morris, (1985) 19 *Law Teach.* 76.
44. Webb, (1985) 19 *Law Teach.* 101. 45. Hofler, (1981) 15 *Law Teach.* 114.
46. One of the contradictions in critical legal theory is that it emphasises the need to study legal materials while not identifying either with the legal profession or the litigation process.
47. It seems unlikely however that Business Law degrees will be classified as business studies rather than law.

A LIB-LIB PACT: SILENCES IN LEGAL EDUCATION

By KATE GREEN* and HILARY LIM**

THE DEBATE about the form, content and method of legal education which has been conducted in this journal, and elsewhere, is far from new. Many articles have been written, apparently from a variety of perspectives. Thus far, discussion has primarily centred on the content of courses, largely at an individual subject level. This discussion has posed little threat to the underlying ethic of the system, but we would argue that the debate could, and should, be on a much wider and more profound level.

Most academics would defend the values of a liberal education, which has its roots in ancient Greece:

> "... the Greeks attained the concept of an education that was 'liberal' not simply because it was the education of free men rather than slaves, but also because they saw it as freeing the mind to function according to its true nature, freeing reason from error and illusion and freeing man's conduct from wrong".[1]

Without being aware of it, most academics would also defend the values of a liberal education rooted in European economic and political theory of the eighteenth and nineteenth centuries. It is hard to distinguish between the two, because this modern liberalism (as did other creeds[2]) adopted the Greek ideal—but it also introduced new values, thereby creating a hidden 'lib-lib' pact. In this article, we use the term liberalism to describe those values, which are an essential part of European thought over the last three hundred years; where necessary specific reference will be made to Graeco-liberal ethics. Our purpose is to uncover the influence of liberal values within legal education, in order to stimulate a more constructive debate about the ends and means of that education.[3]

To state that legal education is imbued with liberal ethics may seem a truism, but if so, it is surprising that this has not been examined in any coherent way. Even the critical legal studies movement, whose avowed aim is "... bringing to consciousness the taken for granted in and about law so that we can recognise what it means",[4] has failed to expose this, the most important "taken for granted" about legal education.

THE VALUES OF LIBERALISM

Liberalism is notoriously difficult to pin down. It is no longer the explicit manifesto of an eighteenth-century revolutionary movement, nor the tamed bourgeois common sense of the nineteenth century. Rather it is a diffusion of values which feed and inform social and political life. These values are based on the "engine" of liberalism—the individual and the development of the self. To achieve self-determination and self-realisation (in the Greek sense), all individuals must be free and are to be treated equally.

Liberal philosophy starts from a view of the individual in reality, reconstructs the equal individual in the abstract, and then re-applies it to reality[5]. The inevitable and paradoxical result is the production of real inequality between individuals. The epitome of this philosophy is the notion of freedom of contract: equal individuals competing in the market

*LL.B., Ph.D.
**LL.B., M.A. The authors are Lecturers in Law at North East London Polytechnic.

have—according to liberal orthodoxy—equal bargaining powers, but the actual result is unequal bargains. Free competition amongst abstract equals produces concrete inequality.

In liberalism, authority over the reified individual is justified wherever the needs of self-determination and self-realisation require it. For example, J. S. Mill wrote that the principle of liberty applies only to "human beings in the maturity of their faculties".[6] This predicates the position which can be illustrated by Hofler's remark that a teacher will need to "draw on his legal or traditional authority in order to defeat" challenges to it, "and thereby to establish that 'modicum of order'... [which] must be maintained if anything resembling a process of education is to take place".[7] Neutrality is the defining characteristic of liberal authority: under the rule of law, liberal "judges" preside as neutral arbiters over conflict between formally equal subjects.

LEGAL EDUCATION

The values of formal equality and neutrality, which are the institutional expression of liberalism, together with its defences of authority and competition, inform all areas of the law school, at every level. In order to demonstrate this, we analyse legal education through its avowed goals, utilising the recent survey of law lecturers' views which was undertaken by South Bank Polytechnic.[8] Respondents were asked to list in order of importance thirteen possible objectives.[9] These objectives may be divided into two sets: we term these the 'reflective' and the 'inspective'. The aim of the first is that the student is to develop her- or himself: the aim of the second is that the student satisfies the standards of the course.

(i) *The Reflective Goal*

A good example of this is:

"... teaching students ... to think for themselves, to have confidence in their own judgment, but to be aware and capable of the discipline needed to form judgments while conscious of their own and others' prejudices ... this in itself requires liberating the mind, at least temporarily, from bondage to the unconscious preconceptions of normal social life".[10]

In the South Bank survey, several of the objectives fall within the general heading of 'reflection', and all were ranked highly by respondents. They include "human relations skills, ... research ability" (ranked fifth), "Maturity, tolerance" (seventh), as well as a concern with "theory and philosophy" (second), "social context" (third), "criticism" (fourth) and "practical context" (eighth).

The student-teacher relationship is central to the reflective goal, for students must imitate their lecturers for it to be achieved. This relationship is more than simply classroom interaction. The tap on the shoulder in the library, the eye contact across the examination hall, the Law Society dinner, the implied reproach in a greeting after a missed class and the chance encounter in the supermarket are all aspects of this unequal partnership.

This inequality is not always immediately apparent from lecturers' styles, which of course vary infinitely, from teacher to teacher, from subject to subject, from class to class. Lecturers are formally "in charge" because of their place in the hierarchy of the institution. This position is strengthened by the physical environment; a teacher can abandon the lectern and walk around, or rearrange desks and chairs, but the familiar authoritarian architecture of the institution prevails.

The curriculum, which involves both knowledge and skill-acquisition, is the medium through which "reflection" is to be attained.[11] Ranked firmly in the middle of educational objectives by South Bank respondents was, "to ensure that the student acquires legal information". However, skill-acquisition was more attractive than the idea of acquiring "legal knowledge": the most highly favoured objective in the South Bank survey was, "to enable the student to develop general intellectual skills, *i.e.* comprehension, application, analysis and evaluation".[12]

Holding 'the knowledge' and facilitating skill-acquisition overtly invest power in the teacher; she or he has the authority of expertise, and the individual student is either an active or passive receptacle. This, and the other manifestations of authority, conceal the dynamic nature of the student-teacher relationship, within which power constantly shifts; it is exceedingly difficult to describe the subtleties, but one example familiar to most lecturers is the experience of facing a roomful of students who are unwilling to co-operate in the accepted 'seminar' mode—*i.e.* they will not speak.

However, it is not merely a question of the lecturer's perception of her or his role. Students expect that, after a minimum of eleven years of 'education', knowledge comes from "above". They sense that they cannot have an equal relationship with the possessors of this knowledge—and also that, even within this kingdom of the elect, there are some who fly higher than others. It is also understood that learning is not necessarily fun. Innovations in teaching method which reduce the role of the all-knowing teacher, or bring pleasure into the classroom, meet more resistance than lecturers' decisions over content, which remain relatively immune from student comment. Even the most unwilling member of the elect is thereby vested with the academic gown of the Master.

(ii) *The Inspective Goal*

The several authoritative roles of the teacher are linked together in the assessment process, for the collective silent scream of the examination hall echoes through the whole course; it affects the totality of student-teacher-institution relations. All students are keenly aware of it, and its influence continues beyond graduation.

One of the reasons for this is the fact that lecturers have the power of assessment over students. These inspectors constantly deny the fundamental importance of examination in legal education: for example, in the South Bank survey, the aim of passing assessment was rated twelfth out of thirteen! The absurd pretence that examinations are merely incidental to legal education is the result of its justification by reference to the reflective goal. It takes a great effort from both sides to see the gown of the Master for what it is, the Emperor's new clothes.

A review of methods of assessment in British law schools in 1982[13] revealed that by far the most prevalent method of assessment was the traditional unseen examination without materials. This is frequently combined with an element of coursework or a dissertation, and these *may* involve judging reflection, but examinations are proportionately much more important in final classification.[14]

Many lecturers would assert that this is because of the influence of the professional bodies, but it is not altogether clear why this should be so.[15] Reliance on unseen examinations has in fact permeated throughout degrees, well beyond the parameters of the 'core' subjects. Even those who have resented this external control over teaching have not openly struggled against it.

The defeatist line frequently adopted under the pressures from worsening staff-student ratios, conservative colleagues and professional bodies may be due to the assumption that There Is No Alternative. However, in the broad context of the debate about a national curriculum for school children, it seems extraordinary that The Law Society and Council for Legal Education have effectively imposed a national curriculum on all law students with so little resistance.

Why have highly intelligent and critical law teachers not seriously questioned the centrality of unseen examinations? Certainly, to investigate the examination system as it operates in practice is challenging and unsettling—far easier to continue with the old tradition. Unfortunately, this comfortable orthodoxy ensures that in practice the objective of reflection is not really assessed at all. If it were to be assessed, the *least* effective way to do so would be by means of a test conducted over a ludicrously short period of time, in a highly stressful and painful context.

However carefully one may draft and mark an exam paper, success in examinations is related directly to technique. In general, students are rated not according to how thoughtful they are, or how much more thoughtful they are now than they were six months ago, but according to whether they have displayed the required skills and knowledge. We may reward the achievement of reflection at the highest level—a first class degree—but this is extremely rare, and is gained despite the method of inspection.

LIBERAL VALUES IN LEGAL EDUCATION

We have asserted that liberal values underlie the entire structure of legal education. "Equal" individuals are set to develop themselves in competition with one another, measured by objective standards. It is for the individual student, by reflection, to develop her or his self-awareness within the area of autonomy awarded to her or him by liberalism. She or he must also display the requisite knowledge and skills before the neutral judge.

The judge of reflection does not merely represent the liberal ideal of ancient Greece, because it has been coloured by the modern liberal concepts of knowledge and skill. It is hard to appreciate this "tinting", since these concepts deny other possibilities. Liberalism is much easier to detect in the goal of inspection, but the paradox is that, while we constantly inspect student performance, any growth of self-awareness is, finally, irrelevant.

The pursuit of knowledge and skill lies behind the philosophy of reflection. In the liberal curriculum, knowledge is impersonal, scientific, balanced—and therefore neutral:

> "It is a necessary feature of knowledge as such that there be public criteria whereby the true is distinguishable from the false, the good from the bad, the right from the wrong. It is the existence of these criteria which gives objectivity to knowledge; and this in its turn gives objectivity to the concept of liberal education".[16]

The valued skills of analysis, comprehension and criticism are also liberal:

> "If ... the reflective approach is genuinely adopted it will result in a debate in which no viewpoint is promoted and every viewpoint is subjected to criticism ... [and] ... our basic principles assume that aloofness, independence and impartiality are capable of achievement" [17]

Within liberal education, every argument is and must be equal, every conclusion is and must be neutral.

The inspective goal is realised through examinations, which assess the individual work of the individual student in circumstances of total formal equality. However friendly the student/teacher relationship has been, the students hunch in silent rows; detached lecturers glide along the aisles like members of an enclosed religious order. Justification lies in:

> "... the fact that all candidates are subject to the same conditions of examination (barring individual illness) with few social factors intervening to favour one type of candidate over another at the actual time of the examination". [18]

The setting not only reinforces the appearance of inequality between staff and students, already noted, but also increases the distance between them. Revision periods are a strategy whereby all the players of the game— whatever their status —can map out their personal exclusion zone. This zone also operates to increase the distance between individual students. How often have we said to students," You're on your own in the exam"? This is not the solitude of calm reflection, but the solitude of the atomised individual in competition with her or his "equals" for the survival of the fittest.

There is a silence amongst lecturers about the competition in which students are engaged. The inspected, however, are not at all reluctant to talk about it. All success for them is—as it always has been—externally assessed. They compare 'A' level grades, essay and examination marks, and degree classifications as well as their relations with lecturers, job offers and, at a later stage, career development. They compete to enter college, to survive the first year, for their degrees, and—ten years later—they are still rivals for status and salary. The market-place may be relocated, but the competitive relationships endure.

This competition is judged by neutral authorities who claim to rank according to an abstract criterion. We may not overtly "mark on the curve",[19] or award a constant proportion of upper and lower seconds, but we do in fact compare one paper with another and rate them in a hierarchy. Further, we grade students not only against their cohort, but against ourselves and all students we have ever marked, or ever will mark. It is thus impossible for one institution ever to produce 100 per cent upper seconds; if this did ever happen, students—and others—would place no value upon their certificate.

The pretence of a "scientific" method of assessment pervades the inspection. So, an external examiner may award 46 per cent instead of 47 per cent, and lecturers marking scripts argue about the difference between 54 and 58, as if they were counting sheep. Nonetheless, the most self-conscious are silently aware that these sheep cannot be defined. Although there is general agreement about extreme cases, when examinations are marked completely independently by two lecturers, any illusion that there is an objective standard is hard to maintain. Examiners may comfort themselves, after comparison of their widely divergent marks, with, "Well, we agreed most of the time!", but they dare not enter into the quicksand of a real analysis.

This illusion of scientific assessment is the basis of neutral authority and the students' insecurity—producing the fragmented community of the inspected who become willing participants in that very fragmentation. Compelling evidence of the extent to which they have been brought into the system is found in their touching belief in arithmetical marks, and the reassurance found in double marking and external examiners.

Liberalism's formal equality and neutrality dictate that all scripts should be equal before the examination board, so that we should not even take into account "individual illness". In practice, markers and examination boards struggle in the exercise of their discretion—where to place the boundaries of the acceptable face of liberalism? The conflict is concealed behind the facade of the Court, rules are interpreted, precedents are cited, counsel for the defence "drools and drivels" over statements in mitigation.[20] Thus the ideal of liberal 'justice' is celebrated and the rule of law triumphs again. However, at the end of the "due process" all participants are confused about what they have done and why.

CONCLUSION

Liberal concepts of knowledge, skill and scientific standards imbue the present system, such that anyone teaching within it is implicitly teaching liberal values. Even the most radical statement of the aim of law lecturers:

> "To expose the sense in which law is a liberal institution by demonstrating the liberal assumptions and values not only in the idea of law itself but in legal institutions, concepts and forms of reasoning ... [providing] a way of relating often highly technical aspects of the law to the living experience of liberal capitalism and to the everyday political issues it generates"[21]

cannot be achieved within the framework of a liberal education. It is impossible fully to criticise such institutions when one's most immediate experience is, unwittingly, a liberal construct.

The failure of liberalism as a political philosophy is demonstrated again by its failure in education. The self-development of "equal" individuals is negated by the liberal form and content of the law school which inform the goals of reflection and inspection.

Liberalism creates a conflict between the various roles demanded of all the players. Lecturers are uneasy in the present system but have not seen that this is because of the liberal rules of the game. These rules demand silences—for example, on the traditional methods of assessment, on the need of students to pass their exams, on the competition between them and on non-existent scientific standards in marking. Until the cause of their unease is exposed, it cannot be assuaged.

The unquestioning acceptance of the liberal mode—of teaching, assessment, knowledge and skills— has led to a concentration on content at the expense of method, while in reality they are indivisible.[22] We must hear the silences and feel the ghostly presence of liberalism in our institutions.

The debate about legal education has to involve the whole process; the discussion about how, why, what and who we teach is incomplete so long as legal education indulges in this lib-lab pact.²³

1. Paul H. Hirst, *Knowledge and the Curriculum*, Routledge & Kegan Paul (1974) at p. 31.
2. *Ibid.* at p. 32.
3. Other influences of course exist alongside liberalism, but cannot be investigated here.
4. Alan Thompson, "Critical Legal Education in Britain", *Jo. Law & Soc.*, Vol. 14 (1987) 183 at p. 194.
5. Roberto Unger has stated that in liberalism "the legal person or moral agent are constructed as abstract and formal universals, out of individual lives, and then treated as if they were real and independent beings": *Knowledge and Politics*, The Free Press (1975) at p. 74.
6. *On Liberty*,Everyman Edition (1859) at p. 73.
7. Anthony Hofler, "Authority—Its Nature and Educational Manifestations", (1982) 16 *Law Teach.* 106 at p. 110.
8. Reported on by Julia Macfarlane at the "Learning Through Clinical Legal Education" Conference at the South Bank Polytechnic, 18-19 Sept. 1986.
9. The list is interesting in its own right, demonstrating the unconscious acceptance that certain values are incontrovertible in legal education.
10. Anthony Beck, "Legal Education and Reflection" (1985) 19 *Law Teach.* 193 at p. 197. In the context of legal education, Alan Thompson has said that it "provides a way in which students can recognise themselves in and, therefore, assume responsibility for legal doctrine" (note 4 above, at p. 196).
11. "The achievement of knowledge is necessarily the development of mind—that is, self-conscious rational mind of man—in its most fundamental aspect" (Hirst, note 1 above, at p. 39).
12. These are obviously based on Bloom's taxonomy discussed in T. A. Downes, P. R. Hopkins and W. M. Rees, "Methods of Assessment in British Law Schools" (1982) 16 *Law Teach.* 85 at pp. 91-96.
13. *Ibid.* An interesting history of the development of competitive examinations is contained in Robert Montgomery, *Examinations*, University of Pittsburgh Press (1965).
14. For example, the following quote is taken from the report of an external examiner, "I remain concerned about the purpose of assessed course work marks improving the result of weak candidates generally and not helping—indeed often hindering—the better candidates".
15. "Many academics are reluctant to take the time and trouble to apply to the professional bodies (and have their courses closely scrutinised by them) (Downes, Hopkins and Rees, note 12 above, at p. 100).
16. Hirst, note 1 above, at p. 43.
17. Beck, note 10 above, at pp. 201-202.
18. Downes, Hopkins and Rees, note 12 above, at p. 85.
19. For a recent discussion of the practice of marking on a curve, see J. Feinman and M. Feldman, "Pedagogy and Politics" (1985) 73 *Geo. L.J.* 875.
20. We criticise 'justice' academically, but practice it uncritically.
21. Thompson, note 4 above, at p. 196.
22. This will be discussed by us elsewhere.
23. With many thanks to our colleagues, Kate Harrison and Jonathan Hayes.

[44]

TRAINING FOR THE HIERARCHY? REFLECTIONS ON THE BRITISH EXPERIENCE OF LEGAL EDUCATION

By CHRISTOPHER STANLEY*

THE debate about legal education has, until relatively recently, been marginalised through being concerned either with detailed empirical and correlative studies on the form and content of the curriculum[1] or the worried reflections of legal scholars armed with the benefit of hindsight, who have paused to express muted discontent.[2] Occasionally individuals have addressed themselves to problems of educational instruction within their own specialisation.[3] But it is only with the advent of Critical Legal Studies (C.L.S.) that comprehensive examination and construction of critique of legal education has been attempted on any scale approaching academic seriousness. It is the purpose of this article to evaluate the effect of this literature and to assimilate it into an analysis of the situation in the British law school. The debate is causing some in this country, and also in North America and others in Europe, a period of introspection and reassessment of their position as teachers and scholars of law.

The title of this article is adopted from Kennedy's 1982 essay, *Legal Education as Training For The Hierarchy*[4] which provides the most accessible and straightforward account of legal education as yet available. It is also the most polemical (and amusing). The agenda of C.L.S., of which Kennedy is a leading exponent, is devoted to exploring the ways in which law constitutes and reinforces relations of domination, exploitation and subordination in a society.[5] It is not surprising that much of the work passing under the label C.L.S. is concerned with the development of radical critiques of the institutions and devices of the legal system including legal education.[6] Kennedy's work can be compared with that of Unger: 'If Kennedy is the Pope of C.L.S. then Unger is the Christ figure'.[7] Unger's importance as part of the C.L.S. project is reflected in his work, which has a profound philosophical significance for social theory and the role of law in modern society over and above the polemical left-politics concerns of Kennedy and others.[8] Finally, Mathiesen's work provides an interesting European contrast in his development of a model of legal education as part of the superstructure of law in capitalist society, drawing as it does upon a sophisticated Marxist analysis of capitalism and the theories of the Frankfurt school of Social Theory.[9]

Despite their disparate concerns the three authors arrive at similar conclusions with regard to the underlying political purpose of legal education, the constitutive factors of which, when applied in this country, appear to be grossly accentuated. All three present a clear need for examination of what they envisage as a necessary period of crisis. Legal education has ceased to be academic (if it ever was) and has become moribund as ideologically dominated with the most negative effects. Kennedy and Mathiesen identify the perpetuation of a capitalist power structure in which lawyers, in their maintenance of the Rule of Law as an inequitable device of legitimation, provide a foundation for the generation of hierarchical power relationships (relationships of domination, subordination and exploitation). Unger concurs in his identification of the reproduction of hierarchies but the ideological form of this process, no less concerned with the legitimation of oppression, is one of the continued

*Lecturer in Law, University of Lancaster.

bureaucratisation of society. The recurrent theme is the idea of educational socialisation within a formalist closed model of rationality and the provision of ideologically founded instruction in preparation for the perpetuation of roles within the hierarchy of the legal superstructure.

The task now is to apply these conclusions to the British experience of legal education. The expression of an ideologically founded hierarchy within the law school as a microcosm, and part of the generation of roles illustrates that, in the most highly evolved common law system, the conclusions which have been reached abroad merit serious consideration.

The analysis will proceed on the basis of examining the two interlinked components of the conditioning process for the hierarchy. First, the issue of educational socialisation through behavioural conditioning of societal attitudes during institutionalisation. Second, the ideological framework of the hierarchy built upon the education techniques of the curriculum and legal reasoning.

EDUCATIONAL SOCIALISATION

The law school's main concern is the production of suitably qualified lawyers. It provides an important passage into the legal profession. Even though this pre-vocational stage takes place within an academic educational institution, the fact that much of the process of the law school is dictated to by the legal profession signifies that attitudes of professionalism are introduced at a very early stage. The degree of external professional requirements on the law school has some initial effect on the social composition of the entrants.

1. *Social Composition*

Research has been carried out into the class origins of the legal profession. In 1981 McDonald came to the not unremarkable conclusion that law was an almost entirely graduate dominated profession. Although entry to higher education in this country is run on equitable lines, a system which depends on stringently applied examination grades for an over-subscribed course is going to favour those individuals coming from a domestic/educational environment in which preparation for both examinations and progression to higher education are stressed. Because of the recognition of the marketability of the law degree above many others in a free-market individualist enterprise culture of increasing self-dependence, the law school is dominated by the middle classes. The Benson Committee noted this prevalence in that the professional middle class is the major source of recruitment to the profession.[10] McDonald concludes that it was 'hard to resist the inference that the legal profession, far from undergoing any proletarian shift, remains unremarkably constant in the social composition of its intake'.[11]

The studies undertaken by Glennester and Pryke[12] establish that there is a startling narrowness in terms of professional recruitment which suggests a 'closed-shop' in operation, stemming from a circulation of elites between professions. In addition to tracing the obvious connections between the public schools and entry to the profession, there appeared to be correlative links between individual family histories and the profession.[13]

A number of initial conclusions can be drawn from this brief analysis of the potential pre-law school social composition of entrants. First, professional socialisation has already commenced in the home/school, the seeds of behavioural conditioning having been sown. Therefore, what may otherwise appear to be a very daunting prospect with regard to training will appear as a natural progression since the entrant is already an initiate to the hierarchies of the professions. Time spent in the law schools becomes merely a rite of passage. Second, this dominance of the professional middle class establishes an automatic collective consciousness and a subconscious recognition of the nature of the socialisation process as part of the equation of acceptance by the legal hierarchy. Finally, because the pre-vocational 'academic' stage of the process will be identified as being just that—'a stage', it becomes a necessary preliminary hurdle. Since the majority of entrants are destined to become lawyers in some capacity the evolution of the law school has largely been dictated by fulfilling professional entry standards. Time will be devoted to passing examinations in as painless a manner as possible, accumulating 'skills' perceived as appearing useful to the profession. These are in addition to those compulsorily required and establishing professional connections so as to ease passage to the vocational and apprenticeship stage.

2. *The Law School and the Institution*

It is enlightening to reflect on the relationship of the law school with the total institution of which it is a part. Law is most often bracketed with other 'prestigious' disciplines, such as medicine. Frequently law inhabits a Faculty in its own right, and it is from this faculty that, as Twining has pointed out, many of the key administrators in the institution emerge.[14] The law teachers are themselves political operators in a hierarchical power structure of institutional politics. As part of the collective consciousness of members of the law school, there appears to be an automatic elitism: they are not studying law, they are lawyers. There is a (sub)conscious recognition of the power potential of the discipline which other disciplines appear to lack. They are the 'trouble-shooters' and problem-solvers; the lawyer as the supreme generalist aligned to the profession which they feel to be of universal significance. The labelling of themselves as 'lawyers', other than being a convenient collective noun (for such nouns exist for the students of politics, economics and so forth—who would dare call oneself a philosopher?) operates as an exclusionary factor to separate out the law students from the general student body.

The law teacher working in an institution devoted to the pursuit of *academic* excellence has to deal with the problem of role. More so than any other academic the law teacher will face the unspoken accusation from the class that 'those who can, do; those who cannot, teach'. The law teacher is merely a necessary conduit of knowledge, a guardian to be approached during the passage of professional socialisation on the journey to the rightful place in the hierarchical structure. The fact that their purpose appears to be to guide students through the hurdles of the requirements laid down by the external validating body only serves to reinforce the contemptuous attitude toward the law teacher the he/she is an instrument. In addition, the parameters of student expectation with regard to knowledge are very narrow. He or she is not allowed to cross those parameters for fear of castigation that the adulteration of the discipline by the introduction of political or moral value-judgments (other than in the name of vaguest policy arguments of convenience) will somehow endanger the transition process. Students may have to think and transcend the boundaries of pre-formulated rationality and thus question the purpose. The problem of law teacher as academic has been discussed by Twining, who notes a paradox in the nature of the job.[15] First, the teaching programme is dominated by the need to fulfil external professional requirements and therefore much research time is filled by the production of textbooks on those subjects, or the production of practitioners texts. Neither can be considered purely academic in the classical sense, since it is a process of annotating and elucidating given knowledge. Second, the history of law as academic subject has been dominated by a naively positivist assumption concerning the nature of legal reasoning in legal science and the non-referential closed model of rationality which determines the extent of knowledge.[16] Thus the legal academic, no matter how dearly wanting to converse with colleagues in other faculties, is largely isolated in the ivory tower amid ivory towers.

3. *The Law School and the Legal Profession*

As part of the process of educational socialisation, the role of the profession is very significant. However, there exists a fundamental dichotomy between the law school experience and the practical realities of lawyering. That much of what is taught in the law school is dictated by the requirements of the professional validating bodies obviously reflects the apparent importance of the profession in relation to 'academic' law. But the arbitrary selection which constitutes the core subjects and the prevalent teaching methodology concerned with the bland exposition of rules through the techniques of legal reasoning has little relation to actual lawyering experience. A number of immediate examples are that even the professional vocational courses stress that facts are more important than law, negotiation more important the litigation, and if you do have to know the law in relation to 'x' you can look it up in a book. But the sanctity of the 'confidence trick' which is the core subject hurdle, provides a certain perverse camaraderie between the law students and the 'real' lawyers, a common bond through rigorous abstraction and absurd remove from reality. The actuality of lawyering can only be learnt through experience. The law school provides something more important than knowledge or skill in its provision of the initial introduction to professional socialisation as part of the ideological foundation of the hierarchical structure:

> "Professional socialisation provides the initiate with a knowledge (tacit or explicit) of the norms and values of the occupational community. Socialisation also serves as a source of formal and informal social control within the profession. Clearly, the formal system of education and training for law provide the recruit with a certain definition of this professional role."[17]

Thus the presence of the professional ethos, devoid of its practical experience within the corridors of the law school provides insight into the process of initiation through the ritual of professional socialisation.

4. Behavioural conditioning

Much of what I have said in the preceding three sections coalesces to form the collective student consiousness in relation to educational socialisation:

> "This training is a major factor in the hierarchical life of the law. It encodes the message of the legitimacy of the whole system into the smallest details of personal style, daily routine, gesture and tone ... and expression—a plethora of 'P's and 'Q's for everyone to mind. Hierarchical behaviour will come to express and realise the hierarchical selves of people who are initially only wearers of masks."[18]

Kairys's succinct statement reinforces the nature of the ideological programming inherent in the process in developing the collective consciousness. Freud writes of the study of law being part of a search for a surrogate father figure, a desire for authority and a will to defer. Weber would seem to concur when he comments on the authority of the legal superstructure resting upon patriarchialism.[19] Indeed there may be no respect for the law school and the institution of which it is a part and its constituent members or even the routine of academic legal study other than on a most superficial level of the need for absorption of the requisite degree of knowledge. What there is respect for is the activity of becoming a lawyer: the pursuit and achievement of the vocation of the pseudo-respectability of legal practice through ritualisation. Subconsciously this pursuit of vocation, 'the respectable face of law', is inherently linked to the fact that an understanding of the law is a key to exercise of power. Thus the atmosphere of the law school is one of a mixture of twisted camaraderie through the shared experience of the process of initiation and also of open peer pressure and competition. This combination provides the basis for the ethos which will later prevail in the barristers' robing room or between solicitors in the lobby of the magistrates' court preparing for the next 'fixture'. Both the student and the lawyer are playing to the authority of the hierarchy. All is part of a continuing initiation process conditioning through ideological process of method and social ritualisation:

> "The occupational culture of law cannot be reduced to a matter of formal education and training because the lawyer never simply learns law through the mechanism of formal instruction. The would-be lawyer is initiated into law; his definition of himself as a practitioner, his awareness of the formal and informal within the profession, the reference groups he adopts and his sensitivity to the system and partronage within the law ...".[20]

THE LEGAL CURRICULUM

In analysing the legal curriculum and classroom experience, what has to be understood is the tradition of ideologically founded doctrinalism. The legacy of legal education as abstract, ahistorical and pedestrian *neccessarily* encourages only a narrow cognitive sense of law. Doctrinalism is the outcome of the technique of legal reasoning based upon a formalist closed model of rationality which precludes (by definition) reference to critiques or methodologies other than its own:

> "Posed in terms of the social organisation of a discourse, the control over the selection and distribution of a knowledge, legal education is clearly an important facet to the highly restrictive process of institutionalism."[21]

Legal knowledge accumulated in a manner which is ideologically founded but which is denied the expression of its ideology constitutes educational indoctrination in the patterns of thought operated by the personnel of the legal hierarchy.

1. *The Scope of the Legal Curriculum*

An initial examination of the legal curriculum (without pursuing the nature of its contents) betrays a remarkable narrowness in terms of academic scope. First, taking the core course requirements as laid down by the professional bodies, the emphasis is placed upon private law (70%) as opposed to public law (30%). This dominance of rule based, procedural subjects which are of relevance only to certain sections of society ensures the continued individualist, free-market ethos. Public law accommodates existing social, political and economic problems and calls into uncertainty state legitimation devices. Since public law rule conflict is not so immediately distinguishable, the prospect of the introduction of referential policy arguments arises. Second, the influence of private law interest infects the selection of other courses, since it is, for instance, straightforward to perpetuate patterns of thought presented in the law of obligations and thus contract law gives rise to commercial law, consumer law and company law. Third, student demand will dictate the courses offered, either because of gaining exemption from further professional requirements or simply as a future possible source of income. Finally, any introduction to the theoretical analysis of law becomes marginalised within the curriculum. Similarly, 'skill courses' in addition to being marginalised may not exist at all save for the elementary introduction to research and the statutory moot. In conclusion, the legal curriculum, with its entrenched bias toward private law and the abstract complexities of superficial rule handling, spurns the practical and the theoretical and automatically operates to preclude all but the most basic of academic aspirations, as the ideological framework of the hierarchy requires it to do.

2. *The Ideological Content of the Legal Curriculum*

What is important is not necessarily the content and structure of a law degree but the methods employed to convey knowledge and to stimulate student reaction, preferably beyond student conceptions of what they perceive to be required. It is not *what* is taught but *how* it is taught, a concept which counters the cries from radical lawyers who demand that we should 'tear up Treitel'. Individual subjects and their related textbook traditions are merely tools, vehicles for the communication of ideas and techniques, values and assumptions. The traditional method of teaching law has been the expository technique of rule-based analysis. Two reasons can be suggested for the dominance of the black-letter expository tradition. First, there may be a positive benefit to be gained from the expository tradition in the development of the ability to be able to handle rules and interpret technical details in a logical and precise manner. Law as science may be a mental training which enhances the analytical faculties of the mind. But so what? As Shklar comments:

> "The urge to draw a clear line between law and non-law has led to the constituting of ever more refined systems of formal definitions. This procedure has served to isolate law completely from the social context within which it exists. Law is endowed with its own values, which are all

treated as a single unit sealed off from general social history, from general social theory, from politics, and from morality. The habits of mind appropriate, within narrow limits, to the procedure of law courts in the most stable legal systems have been expanded to provide legal theory and ideology with an entire system of thought and values. This procedure has served its own ends very well: it aims at preserving law from irrelevant thinking off from all contact with the rest of historical thought and experience."[22]

If the 'benefits' of the expository tradition enable students to develop the capability to analytically confront and attempt solutions to legal-factual problems, then the presumption of the technique must be that this is what is required when in practice. In applying legal techniques via reasoning, the student is prepared for later application of the 'correct' method in an actual rule-dispute situation. Being able to dissect a problem in the law of contract through analysing the nature of the contractual obligations, the form of the breach and the remedial options available is presumed to be a distinctive lawyering pursuit. But would a student faced with a similar problem in practice recognise the importance of placing facts above law, the techniques of negotiation, the ability to numerically calculate an out of court settlement and so forth? Would the same student be able to conduct a successful interview with an annoyed supplier of widgets, or search through the firm's data retrieval system for the most recent case law, and then, using a word processor, write an opinion? Are these 'skills' and techniques assumed to be picked up 'on the job' or should they be introduced during a degree course? Alternatively, to what extent would the student understand the why of contract and thus be able to formulate critical hypotheses of why this factual situation has arisen, understanding the conflicting theoretical foundations of contract law, the moral factor of contract as promise, the contract as an economic bargaining device, the nature of individualism or the theory of the commodity-exchange school? These references to competing rhetorics of description may be difficult to assimilate alongside the technicalities of offer, acceptance, consideration, but they provide an attempt towards understanding why contract has evolved as it has and constitute a justification for the doctrines of contract law. They also enable the possibility of the development of critiques of these otherwise seemingly isolated rules. The problems of practice cannot be coldly solved like a crossword puzzle on one piece of paper and with reference to one textbook. The expository tradition may be safe, comforting and inducive of security, but it can be argued that it kills thought, stops it dead in its tracks: there is merely allegiance to tradition without understanding and, more importantly, without anything more than merely superficial questioning.

The second reason for the dominance of the expository tradition method is cynically founded and lies once again with the hierarchy thesis and the social control over the distribution of knowledge. Superficially, since the tradition is not even particularly vocationally orientated, the method is argued for because it is simply a tradition based upon the glorious past of positivism. It is a way of studying law which has been passed on and which now provides a structure for the bulk of academic legal research and teaching methods. It is a method which provides the foundation for the sustained acceptance of the authority of the system.[23] By concentrating on the marginal complexities of the rule-based legalistic system *(apellate 'courtitus')* attention is drawn away from the broader study of the system as a whole and of an understanding of the theoretical foundations which lead to the formulation of critiques and criteria of effectiveness. There is a bias toward understanding how the system works, whilst not questioning its purpose or effectiveness. The black-letter lawyer must say that all is well with the whole so as to justify his or her existence, which depends on tinkering with the cosmetic complexities on the edges. To stand outside the whole means both a total re-orientation of perspective based upon the far more subtle and complex use of theoretical perspectives *and* the inherent threat of finding substantial fractures in the whole which cannot be so easily papered over as the superficial cracks. Existence is threatened. A blackletter lawyer:

"... will fight to the death to defend legal rights against persuasive arguments based upon expediency or the public interest or the social good ... (s/)he believes, as part of his(/her) mental habits, that they are dangerous and too easily used as cloaks for arbitrary action."[24]

But the black-letter lawyer is already a dodo. Law as science is isolationary, denied the existence of its social context. It is thus an academically prohibited frame of reference, severed from other academic disciplines. Teaching 'techniques' tend toward the acquisition of knowledge in a short period, the benefits of which are questionable: the technique of the application of knowledge is a useful skill, the mere acquisition and retention of knowledge is not.[25]

CONCLUSION

By concentrating upon the narrow mental pursuit of rule-handling techniques and the retention of largely irrelevant amounts of knowledge, students are orientated toward participation in the specialised hierarchical roles of lawyers. Ideologically, this method enforces the law and power relationship and thus inculcates students into the hierarchy. 'Responsible' jurists are produced who do not question: the power is theirs and they have become "zealous partisans and promoters, anxious to secure their moral empire".[26]

And the professional criteria for participating in the power game is student indoctrination and subservience through mental and social ritualisation processes. It is overtly ideological without reference: "For the learner, a way of seeing becomes a way of not seeing."[27] Once again, what occurs during the legal education process is professional socialisation, an acceptable product being manufactured. It is neither truly educational nor academic.

This situation is anathema. Legal education becomes merely part of a scheme of maintaining an unjust legal status quo. The alarm bells ring as the internal solidarity of the superstructure seems to be threatened. The traditionalists will retort that one ideology (if they accept its existence at all) is about to be replaced by another. No, the aim is to break the stranglehold of the prevailing hierarchical ideology. A start has been made in 'knowing thine enemy' in the analysis of the ideology of legal scholarship (as elitist, Establishment orientated, dynamically conservative) and not just in the sterile socio-legal 'spotting the gap' game but in a rigorously academic construction of critiques which is the agenda of Critical Legal Studies.[28] As legal educators, our responsibility is to develop *academic* teaching techniques.

1. For example, H. A. Barnett and D. M. York "The teaching of jurisprudence and legal theory in British Universities and Polytechnics" (1985) *Legal Studies* 151.
2. Some amusing examples are to be found amongst the annual presidential addresses of the President of the Society of Public Teachers of Law in the *Journal of the Society of Public Teachers of Law* (N.S. 1980-89).
3. Such as W. Twining "The Great Juristic Bazaar" (1978) *J.S.P.T.L.* (N.S.) Vol. 14 n. 3 p. 185.
4. In *The Politics of Law* (ed. D. Kairys, 1982) Pantheon. See also D. Kennedy "How the Law School Polemic Fails" 1 *Yale Review of Law and Social Action* (1970) 71. Kennedy has remained remarkably constant in his views in the two decades from being a student at Yale to becoming a Professor at Harvard.
5. On C.L.S. generally, see M. Kelman *A Guide to Critical Legal Studies* Harvard University Press.
6. An example of the level of discussion emanating from the Standing Conference on Critical Legal Studies can be found in the Symposium on Legal Scholarship (1981) 90 *Yale Law Journal*. For a synopsis of the history and agenda of C.L.S., see A. Hunt "The Theory of Critical Legal Studies" (1986) 6 *Oxford Journal of Legal Studies*, 1.1 and Hunt's useful bibliography of C.L.S. work (1984) 47 M.L.R. 369.
7. L. B. Schwartz "With Gun and Camera Through Darkest C.L.S. Land" 36 *Stanford Law Review* nos. 1 & 2 at p. 41.
8. Unger's reflections on C.L.S. and legal education are in R.M. Unger *The Critical Legal Studies Movement* (1987) Harvard University Press. But see also, Unger, *Law in Modern Society* (1976) Free Press.
9. T. Mathiesen *Law, Society and Political Action: Toward a Strategy Under Late Capitalism* (1980) The Academic Press, ch. 2, pp. 89-111.
10. *Report of the Royal Commission on Legal Services* (1974) Cmnd. 7648 (Sir Henry Benson) no. 7.1, 458.
11. P. McDonald "The Class of '81—A Glance At The Social Class Composition of Recruits to the Legal Profession" (1982) 9 *Journal of Law and Society* 2, 264. "As long as British social structure is such that the traditional ruling class can still command some deference, the law, to be sure of respect, must partake of the style of that class." M. Plowden in *What's Wrong With the Law?* (1970; ed. M. Zander) Weidenfeld and Nicholson.
12. M. Glennester and R. Pryke "The Contribution of Public Schools and Oxbridge 1: Born to Rule" *Power in Britain* (1973; eds. J. Urry and J. Wakeford) R.K.P.; see also J. Scott *The Upper Classes* (1986) Macmillan.
13. Scott above.
14. W. Twining "Goodbye to Lewis Eliot: The Academic Lawyer as Scholar" (1980) *J.S.P.T.L.* (N.S.) Vol. 16 n. 1.
15. Twining (1980) above.
16. D. Sugarman "Legal Theory, the Common Law Mind and the Making of the Textbook Tradition" in *Legal Theory and Common Law* (1986; ed. W. Twining) Oxford.
17. Z. Bankowski and G. Mungham *Images of Law* (1976) p. 82 R.K.P.
18. D. Kairys introductory essay in *The Politics of Law* above.
19. See P. Goodrich *Legal Discourse* (1987) p. 172, Blackwell.
20. Bankowski and Mungham above.
21. Goodrich above.
22. J. Shklar *Legalism* (1964) pp. 2-3., Harvard University Press.
23. C. Stanley "Activating the Differences: A Critical Analysis of the Artifice of Legal Scholarship" (unpublished paper given at Rijksuniversiteit, Limburg. The Netherlands. 1988).
24. J.A.G. Griffith "The Law of Property (Land)" in *Law and Opinion in England in the Twentieth Century* (1959; ed. M. Ginsberg) pp. 114-19 Oxford.
25. See A. Thompson "Critical Legal Education" in *Critical Legal Studies* (1987; eds. P. Fitzpatrick and A. Hunt) Blackwell.
26. Shklar above.
27. Bankowski and Mungham above.
28. One such critique is that of deconstruction: see J. M. Balkin "Deconstructive Practice and Legal Theory" (1987) 90 *Yale Law Journal* 742.

The author wishes to thank Anne Bottomley, Peter Goodrich, David Sugerman and Lynne Williams for their stimulating responses to his research into legal education. All errors are the author's.

The Future

EDUCATING LAWYERS FOR THE 21st CENTURY

The Rt. Hon. Sir Ivor Richardson

The topic for discussion today is educating lawyers for the 21st Century. To provide an answer we first need to ask what role lawyers should have in that society. That in turn conjures up a host of questions. What kind of society do we want to be in the 21st Century? How do we set about achieving the social and economic goals we seek? To what extent should we expect the education process to develop and change society as distinct from reacting to presently identified needs?

The next level of questions concerns the functioning of the legal system. If the goal is to have a workable system in which people have faith, how do we assess whether it meets that goal? By the criteria of access, process, standards and outcomes? And how are those qualities measured and to what extent is justice measurable on a cost benefit basis? What are the respective roles of the individual, the family, the state and other institutions of society in the justice system?

Associated with that is the role of lawyers in that society. When we speak of lawyers are we limiting the discussion to barristers and solicitors? Should we assume that the structure of the legal profession will or should remain frozen in the time warp of the 1980s? What are the irreducible functions for lawyers in society? To conduct litigation in the traditional courts? Or to be involved in any kind of dispute resolution? To advise on legal questions? To facilitate problem solving in commerce or in family and property affairs. To approach it another way how, if at all, is specialisation in various kinds of financial and business and property consultancy different when carried out under the badge of legal practice from where it is carried out separately or as part of other activities?

Then against that background we come at last to consider the education of lawyers. Again there is a series of questions. At the tertiary institutional level is law a multi-purpose course equally valuable for those expecting to be engaged in problem solving, negotiating and advising in business and government as it is for those intending to practice law? To what extent should the answer to that question affect the course content and the method of instruction? To what extent should legal education be available at a range of institutions and through a range of courses? How should it be funded? What is the future of para legal work and of para legal education? Where does responsibility for educating the judges lie and what form should it take? Whether or not tied to maintenance of credentials, what is the role and what is the content of continuing legal education? No doubt many further lines of enquiry could be opened. Questions in this are are much easier to pose than to answer.

Where then to start and to end? It would be presumptuous for me to pretend an understanding of Australian society on the basis of limited work experience there and social visits, and I shall be speaking from the perspective of a New Zealander. Clearly, however, there is a shared commitment to a democratic form of government; to the rule of law as a means of controlling the use of power and of providing for the orderly settlement of disputes between citizen and citizen or citizen and the state; to the operation of a mixed economy with private, co-operative and public activity; and to the balancing of individual, family and community responsibility. Clearly too the continuing development of the Closer Economic

Relations should lead to a greater harmonisation of our commercial laws and practices. Over time our shared heritage, geography and community of interests in the Pacific may lead to further economic and political institutional links.

I want now to answer some of my questions and in doing so to narrow the focus of the discussion today to a number of changes and challenges which I think those involved in legal education may be expected to face over the next decade and beyond. I shall begin by saying something about the objectives and principles underlying the justice system and then go on to discuss some of the challenges facing the next generation of lawyers and the place of legal education in meeting society's needs, both for professional training and as a multi-purpose education leading to other career choices in the private and the public sector.

Reporting in May of this year the New Zealand Royal Commission on Social Policy identified the objectives of a workable and credible system of justice as being:

1. to provide a fair and efficient means of dispute resolution;

2. to uphold the rule of law in a manner consistent with individual justice in the protection
of society; and

3. to provide a forum for the appropriate punishment of those who commit offences.

In a paper written for the Royal Commission by Dr Warren Young and Ms Caroline Bridge the authors identified five basic principles underlying the system of justice:

(a) it should be accessible and affordable to all citizens;

(b) it should protect the rights of minorities and disadvantaged groups;

(c) its decisions should be enforceable;

(d) it should be independent of direction political control; and

(e) it should provide a system of punishment which is humane, consistent and proportionate to the offence.

On their assessment they concluded that in many respects New Zealand's system of justice has not managed to observe these principles. There is a widespread perception, especially amongst some ethnic minorities and disadvantaged sections of the population but to some extent amongst all consumers of the legal system, that it is complex, alien and remote from the lives of ordinary people. There is also a perceived ethnocentric bias both in its procedure and in outcomes, and the feeling that the system is failing to provide an adequate service or adequate redress to significant sectors of the population, and is, therefore, failing to regulate relationships between citizens efficiently and effectively.

This takes me back to the question I asked earlier as to how a system of justice is to be assessed. Here, as in other areas of social provision, neither fairness nor efficiency should ever be lost sight of. Resources, material and human, are always limited. No one would suggest that access to justice requires that the state ensure unlimited provision of legal services to everyone in every situation on a demand driven basis. To do so would bear unfairly on others caught up in the process as well as diverting resources away from other uses. Rather it is a matter of ensuring that equal justice under law becomes a reality rather than being confined to those who can afford it. And here there is a real challenge for all of us. Not only are societies such as ours more litigious than previously - as reflected in the criminal and civil statistics, the case load of tribunals of all kinds and increasing reliance on alternative dispute resolution machinery - but the nature of the cases dealt with has also changed markedly. Changing social attitudes in an increasingly diverse and restless society and the greater willingness to challenge previously accepted norms and structures have contributed. Paradoxically the increased costs of delivery of legal services as the legal profession geared itself to handle better the increasingly complex and increasingly international corporate commercial work, and the limited availability of legal aid have both added to the problem.

Here then is a major challenge for lawyers and legal educators over the next twenty years. It is to ensure that in conformity with common standards of social justice in our respective countries adequate machinery is available for the fair, efficient and orderly resolution of disputes. That will, I think, require much more emphasis on public interest law in the law schools and on the part of the legal profession and the legislature. But it will need more than that. It is a matter of delivering adequate legal services to the full spectrum of society. Not just to the rich and the downtrodden, but also the the silent majority. Not just through a traditional focus on the adversary system in the general courts, but also through mediation, conciliation, arbitration and other alternative dispute resolution machinery. And no system can be regarded as either fair or efficient unless it provides for the orderly resolution of disputes within a reasonable time.

In considering the legal aspects of the great issues of our times we must recognise that litigation under the adversary system does not readily allow for an extensive social enquiry. The parties or their lawyers may lack any interest in exploring wider issues. The Courts have not developed the techniques of obtaining amicus curiae briefs from government and affected industry and citizens groups. Yet we can benefit from a much more rigorous analysis of the economic and social and administrative costs of the orders we are asked to make.

Let me give two examples. One concerns the development of the principles of natural justice and fairness in the administrative law context and potentially spreading into private law areas. I do not know of any research into the wider costs and benefits actually achieved but I suspect that a consideration of outcomes as well as processes might lead to a more cautious application of those principles. The other concerns the development of the modern law of negligence. Again it would be useful to have an analysis of the costs to society and how they are distributed. For example, in New Zealand the economic burden of careless advice and omissions on the part of employees of local bodies has to some extent been shifted from luckless plaintiffs to local bodies. However, that burden may not in the end rest on ratepayers as the Courts perhaps expected, but may have been shifted through increased permit fees to the construction industry and be ultimately reflected in building costs.

It is in consideration of all those wider issues where the system of legal education is so important. In a passage in his report on the reform of professional legal training in New Zealand, 1987, Dean Gold succinctly brings together various features of modern legal education. It is a lengthy passage, but I quote it in full because it bears on a number of matters I shall be discussing.

He said:

> As with all university education, the study of law, especially at the undergraduate level, seeks to assist students to develop intellectually and to acquire those cognitive skills and strategies which are more or less common to all higher level disciplines. In particular it seeks to hone and refine the skills of analysis, synthesis and evaluation, to aid both in expressing the value and utility of law and its future application. Problem-solving generally speaking, is an important skill set which the legally educated require in all their work settings. Beyond such intellectual skills development lies the desire to instil learning in the contexts, concepts, principles and theories of law. Law education is both deep and varied. Because law cannot helpfully be abstracted from its social, economic and political milieu, it cannot be truly understood except in the context of human aspiration and endeavour. Yet is is also a practical subject which seeks solutions to difficult problems of policy and justice. In the best of all possible worlds it is a general legal education which prepares graduates to face and adapt to change in all aspects of their lives, but especially throughout their legal careers. Law is anything but static: it is effective lawyers who can respond to the dynamic forces with which they are bound to be faced. Therefore, only those courses which serve as foundations of law study - its concepts, policies, values and theories need to be prescribed. If one adopts this 'building block' approach one assures a strong basis and myriad opportunities to ensure the acquisition and development of appropriate legal methodology, as well.

There are four points I would particularly emphasise. The first is that the rigorous training in analysis and evaluation of legal principles and underlying policies is now, we all like to think, at the heart of legal education. There is a healthy insistence in much of our legal education on the examination of social processes which legal rules now serve. That focus has extended the ability of law graduates to assess the wider considerations increasingly relevant to the resolution of controversies that call for an evaluation of economic and social values and goals.

The second of Dean Gold's points I want to emphasise is that only those courses which serve as foundations for legal study need to be prescribed. The review of legal education in New Zealand carried out under the aegis of the Council of Legal Education was instituted because of endemic concerns over professional and skills based training generally. The review committee and the Council soon realised that those concerns had to be considered in the context of the total programme, and so having regard to the degree requirements for admission purposes. Because of the dominating influence of the long lists of subjects prescribed for admission purposes there has in the past been relatively limited opportunity for New Zealand students to pursue elective areas and for New Zealand law schools to develop their own strengths and directions. Following a great deal of debate the Council reduced the core admission requirements down to six of the 17 courses required for degree purposes. They are basic courses in legal systems, contract, torts, property including equity, crimes and public law. We took the view that it is not necessary for every practising lawyer to have taken family law, commercial law, evidence and taxation. We considered there was much more to be gained by allowing greater flexibility and opportunities for some specialisation. Room must also be allowed for development of courses to meet or anticipate current needs. Several areas may be noted. One group involves minority rights, the Treaty of Waitangi, cultural influences in law and women's studies; another includes dispute resolution, professional responsibility and clinical education; and a third inter-departmental studies in law and economics and law and sociology.

Another quite differently focussed view of future needs for lawyers is reflected in the proposed LL.B. programme of Bond University which identifies communication skills, computing and data skills, management, and cultural and ethical values as core subjects.

Most of the law schools have already responded to the changes in curriculum requirements for admission purposes by modifying their own degree requirements. The resulting changes will provide both opportunities and challenges for law schools and students alike.

The third point is that lawyers obviously need to develop an understanding of the law in practice. Lawyers must be equipped to predict how the law will operate in actual fact situations. Facts may be messy. Their identification and the operation of legal rules must be assessed and reassessed in today's world and with regard to often unstated judicial attitudes. The academic rigour of the case method and the learning and critiquing of basic legal assumptions through analysing judicial decisions are a significant component of legal education. But Holme's aphorism that the life of the law has not been logic: it has been experience, remains true. Legal principles are given life and are given limits in their practical application, and theory and practice should be integrated right through the degree programme. But, and this is preaching to the converted, professional legal education needs to be the subject of special focus as in the skills based courses in Australia and now in New Zealand.

The fourth point to be emphasised is that law should be viewed as a multi-purpose course. As with all university graduates, lawyers receive a general education in the foundation of the discipline. They develop intellectually. They focus on concepts, values and principles. Law and public issues are increasingly enmeshed and lawyers are often operating at the focal point of controversy. Because of the content of many law courses and the range of teaching methods employed, law schools are exciting places to be. If law schools are achieving their objectives, those foundations and the skills of analysis, synthesis, evaluation and the making of judgments are just as important for those engaged in advising and decision making in business and government as for those working directly in the practice of law. A law degree may properly be regarded as an alternative education to an arts or commerce degree by those who never intend to practise law. And the systematic examination of judicial decisions through the case system where the library is the laboratory, provides some of the advantages of a scientist's training and at much less cost. If law is viewed as a multi-purpose degree that is all the more reason for the law programme to allow flexibility to students and above all to resist a narrow focus on the storing up of detailed knowledge of an ever expanding area of law subjects.

The fact that values need to be continually reassessed, modified and in some cases discarded and replaced creates a stronger society in the longer term. What is important is to recognise that society is pluralistic and that it has always been so. Pluralism always existed in the differences between different generations. It always existed in our two countries between indigenous peoples and settlers; and the values of settlers reflected the different places from which settlers came.

When looking forward as lawyers and educators to the 21st century, we can safely assume that society will be neither homogeneous nor static. The problem of identifying community values and reflecting them in our social processes and decision making is increased where there are different sets of values whether economic, moral, political or social which are strongly, even tenaciously held. This is unavoidable in a pluralistic society. The problem is compounded where society itself is in a process of marked change and the outcome is not clear. The barb directed at economics that the questions remain the same only the answers change, can be applied in other areas. Where different kinds of interests are involved they cannot be balanced without injecting the policy values of those doing the balancing. We should never be deluded into thinking that values difficult to balance should be ignored as externalities or that all values can be reduced to a common standard, any more than that apples and oranges can be compendiously and sensibly measured together as pieces of fruit.

Inevitably many lawyers and judges will at some time be involved in social change and in resolving conflicts between social values. Legal education should prepare for this. It should assist in providing a framework for recognising, articulating and testing alternatives and for shaping the profession and the law to meet the aspirations and necessities of the times. The essential object of all social policy is to seek policies and structures to reflect the values and goals of the people. I firmly believe that, inspired in part by their legal education, lawyers can and should play pivotal roles in expanding a national vision of a free and just society. Clearly they, that is lawyers and legal educators, must help to map out the directions in which society needs to move to answer the most troubling legal questions facing the profession and the nation.

Any list of such legal questions is bound to be arbitrary and to reflect the limitations of one's background. In adding that change and continuity sit uneasily together, no doubt I may be accused of exhibiting that limitation, but I am convinced that decision making in areas of legal and social change requires a balancing of policy, principle, precedent and pragmatism. My short list of crucial issues for New Zealand lawyers and for their education for the 21st century reflects that and accordingly includes :

1. redetermining what are the crucial features of legal practice and expanding the development of multi-disciplinary activities;

2. redefining the relationship between professional responsibility and commercial performance both within the megafirms and through the range of legal practices in the country;

3. responding to advances in technology and in such a way that legal services can be provided both for the affluent and the corporate sector on the one hand and for the great bulk of the population on a low cost basis on the other;

4. recognising and rectifying discrimination against women and minorities in the market place and in the corridors of power; and

5. valuing cultural diversity and recognising the unique character of New Zealand founded on the Treaty of Waitangi just as many other countries such as Canada and Belgium have given constitutional and social recognition to the circumstances of their founding and to their ethnic composition.

Part VI
Making Use of Competing Visions

[46]

Legal Education and Curriculum Innovation: Law and Aging as a New Field of Law

Martin Lyon Levine*

"There are few things more fascinating in our jurisprudence than the organization of what comes, almost immediately, to be perceived as a new 'field' of law."

--Grant Gilmore[1]

How does it happen that we come to perceive the existence of a new field[2] of law? To perceive is an act of decision[3] that might be made in many ways. The question of recognizing a new legal field invites attention for a number of reasons. *Classification*, the process of grouping items, and *division*, the reverse process of breaking down a larger class into subgroupings, are age-old concerns of philosophy.[4] As a matter of the organization of research, a scholar may seek criteria for treating a particular bundle of issues as an interrelated set forming a single whole, to be distinguished as a separate part of the broader discipline.

As a matter of curriculum, a faculty may seek criteria for recognizing one set of topics as a separate law course, rather than as part of a larger unit or as a topic to be scattered among other courses.[5] As law schools recognize a new field, publish-

---

* Professor of Law, and Professor of Psychiatry and the Behavioral Sciences, University of Southern California; President, National Senior Citizens Law Center, Inc. I wish to thank Louis N. Brown, Lawrence M. Friedman, Ronald A. Garet, Walter Gellhorn, Myres S. McDougall, Dr. Pauline K. Ragan, Dr. K. Warner Schaie, Larry Simon, Peter Strauss, and especially Dr. Ralph S. Levine, for their comments. Support for underlying research was provided through the generosity of the UPS Foundation with the aid of Dean Scott H. Bice and Dean James Birren.

1. G. GILMORE, THE DEATH OF CONTRACT 9 (1974).
2. As defined here, a "field" of study is a subdivision within a broader discipline, such as law. For criteria that might be used in recognizing a discipline, see Levine, *Does Gerontology Exist?*, 20 GERONTOLOGIST — (1980).
3. *See, e.g.*, Steinberg, *The Eye is a Part of the Mind*, in REFLECTIONS ON ART (S. Lange ed. 1961), *reprinted in* W. BISHIN & C. STONE, LAW, LANGUAGE, AND ETHICS 1101 (1972).
4. Curriculum classification is a mundane cousin of the great philosophical problem of classification, which has been analyzed in a long tradition stemming from Aristotle's *Categories*. See Thompson, *Categories*, in 2 ENCYCLOPEDIA OF PHILOSOPHY 46 (1967).
5. *See* Riesman, *Law and Social Science: A Report on Michael and*

ers of research tools for practitioners are likely to do so also, thus facilitating and promoting legal practice in the newly recognized area, as well as altering the analogies lawyers and judges are likely to draw.[6] Some law professors do not ask questions about curriculum[7] because they implicitly assume that the current classification is optimal or perhaps inherent in the law.[8] Others may think the current curriculum is adequate or that the questions of classification and division are not important enough to warrant attention. Still others may believe that curriculum change is best handled informally by the individual teacher.[9] Problems of classification and division, however, may confront any given faculty when there is an overall curriculum review or when it is suggested that there be a change in the list of required courses, electives, research institutes, or service programs.[10]

Wechsler's Classbook on Criminal Law and Administration, 50 YALE L.J 636, 642-44 (1941) (discussing the organization of courses and curricula). *See also* Gardner, *Specialization in the Law School Curriculum*, 81 U. PA. L. REV. 684, 687 (1933) ("Some [law school topics], like property and contracts, reflect popular notions about man's fundamental relations to his neighbor. Some, like torts, reflect what was once the judicial organization of Great Britain. Some like taxation, security transactions, or insurance, reflect a demand for instruction in some specialty."); Riesman, *In Memory of Harold S. Solomon: Comments on Southern California's Flyer in Legal Education*, 41 S. CAL. L. REV. 506 (1968) (discussing legal education reforms at U.S.C.); Riesman, *Some Observations on Legal Education*, 1968 WISC. L. REV. 63 (suggesting that law schools take an approach more closely oriented to social sciences); Stone, *Towards a Theory of Constitutional Law Casebooks*, 41 S. CAL. L. REV. 1, 8-11 (1968) (discussing the organization of casebooks).

6. This pattern is not intended to be exclusive. Certainly the needs of clients and practitioners may influence the adoption of a new legal field. *See* text accompanying notes 87-119 *infra*.

7. *But see* Kelso, *Curricular Reform for Law School; Needs of the Future*, 21 U. MIAMI L. REV. 526 (1967). "[B]y what criteria do our first year courses justify their continued required existence: frequency of application; social significance; doctrinal fundamentality?" *Id.* at 528. While Kelso supposed that fundamentality of doctrine is the usual answer, he questioned whether the property, torts, or contracts courses actually were fundamental, and suggested more topical courses. *Id.*

8. Plato, Aristotle, and philosophers typified by the "realists" of the Middle Ages believed that groups and classes of things are learned by reason or by observation; they are not simply mental conventions. *See* Hancock, *History of Metaphysics*, in 5 ENCYCLOPEDIA OF PHILOSOPHY 289, 292 (1967).

9. "[Alterations in content are] produced by the internal combustion of the professor in charge of the course, who, consulting his own notions of what was timely or, at any rate, what interested him, went ahead and changed the curriculum." Gellhorn, *Commentary*, 21 U. MIAMI L. REV. 536, 537 (1967). Similarly, another commentator maintains: "[T]he new 'area' is often recognized and articulated after the curricular change has already been established by the seepage of updated materials." Rutter, *Designing and Teaching the First Degree Law Curriculum*, 37 U. CIN. L. REV. 7, 11 (1968).

10. *See, e.g.*, Stevens, *Two Cheers for 1870: The American Law School*, in

There are manifest reasons why Law and Aging[11] should at least be considered a candidate for recognition as a new field for law practice, teaching, and research. The United States and other industrialized nations are experiencing an increase in the number and percentage of elderly in their populations[12] that is unprecedented in the history of the world. Although in 1900 there were fewer than five million Americans over the age of sixty, amounting to about 4% of the population, there are now approximately thirty-two million elderly, constituting almost 11% of the nation.[13] Demographic projections suggest that the percentage of elderly Americans will increase in the next half-century to perhaps as much as 17%.[14] By one estimate, 24% of the federal budget currently goes to support programs for older persons, and within half a century such programs may require 40% of the budget.[15]

Since differentiation among legal fields primarily affects legal teaching and scholarship, this Article derives criteria for the recognition of new legal fields from alternative visions of law schools—what they are and what they do. Applying these criteria to Law and Aging, the Article maintains that the time has come to recognize Law and Aging as a new field of law.

LAW IN AMERICAN HISTORY 403, 517-18 nn.52-54 (D. Fleming & B. Bailyn eds. 1971).

11. Law and Aging is not included in the standard lists of legal fields. *See, e.g.,* ASSOCIATION OF AMERICAN LAW SCHOOLS, DIRECTORY OF LAW TEACHERS 844-45 (1980). When the 7,877 teachers listed with the Association of American Law Schools were surveyed, 29 responded that they taught courses, seminars, or clinic programs in Law and Aging, 23 were involved in outside projects or programs, and 27 were doing research and writing in the field. Twenty-two professors listed themselves as using their own materials for teaching. (There are, no doubt, others in the field who did not respond to the survey.) *See* INSTITUTE OF LAW AND AGING, SURVEY OF NATIONAL LAW SCHOOL PROGRAMS AND MATERIALS IN LAW AND AGING 42-44 (1978). *See generally* Levine, *Research in Law and Aging,* 20 GERONTOLOGIST 163 (1980).

12. *See* Cowgill, *The Aging of Populations and Societies,* 415 ANNALS 1, 5 (1974). *See also* Eisele, *Preface* to *id.,* at ix.

13. U.S. BUREAU OF THE CENSUS, SERIES P-23, No. 59, CURRENT POPULATION REPORTS 3-4 (1978).

14. U.S. BUREAU OF THE CENSUS, SERIES P-23, No. 43, CURRENT POPULATION REPORTS at i (1973); *cf.* Bouvier, Atlee & McVeigh, *The Elderly in America,* 30 POPULATION BULL. 1, 7 (1974) (13 to 15% of the population will be elderly).

15. *See* Nelson, *Time of Trial: The Burdens of Old Age on the Family,* L.A. Times, Jan. 19, 1979, § 1, at 1, col. 1, at 22, col. 6. By another estimate, more than 30% of the Federal budget is spent on programs for the elderly. Samuelson, *Busting the U.S. Budget—The Costs of an Aging America,* 10 NAT'L J. 256 (1978). These estimates may be high.

I. FIVE VISIONS OF LAW SCHOOLS

Criteria for the recognition of new legal fields can be generated from different visions of legal education[16] that reflect differing assumptions about purposes[17] and methods.[18] In this section, five such visions will be presented: the Practice Model, the Rules Model, the Principles Model, the Policy Model, and what may be a new Fifth Model. These models of legal education[19] are based on historical epochs in the development of American law schools,[20] but are used here as ideal types.[21] In reality these models are not mutually exclusive; in the past,

---

16. *See generally* H. PACKER & T. EHRLICH, NEW DIRECTIONS IN LEGAL EDUCATION (1972); J. REDLICH, THE COMMON LAW AND THE CASE METHOD IN AMERICAN UNIVERSITY LAW SCHOOLS (1914); A. REED, TRAINING FOR THE PUBLIC PROFESSION OF THE LAW (1921); Stevens, *supra* note 10.

17. In response to the overall question, "What are the aims and objectives of legal education?," the 1947 Committee on Curriculum of the Association of American Law Schools considered six possibilities:

(1) To orient the student in relation to the problems, materials and methods of the law?
(2) To fortify the student with as much basic information as may be essential to a working knowledge of the law?
(3) To practice the student in the more important craft skills of the law?
(4) To instruct the student in the nature and scope of the law as a system?
(5) To inculcate an understanding of social background and of the law's relation to its purpose?
(6) To cultivate sensitivity to professional responsibilities and an appreciation of the lawyer's place in society?

Quoted in A. HARNO, LEGAL EDUCATION IN THE UNITED STATES 161-62 (1953).

18. Among the many competing methodologies in legal education today are: lecture-text, case, legislative-statutory, historical, problem, conceptual, functional, and transactional. *See* material cited by Del Duca, *Continuing Evaluation of Law School Curricula—An Initial Survey*, 20 J. LEGAL EDUC. 309, 310-11 (1978). In addition, law courses today may emphasize skills training, professional responsibility-values orientation, clinical exposure, integration of law and the social sciences, analysis of the judicial decision-making process, use of empirical methods, and use of electronic data processing. *Id.* at 311-13.

19. Law schools can be differentiated in many ways, such as by how they resolve the tension between the role of a professional school and that of a graduate school, *see* Goldstein, *Educational Planning at Yale*, 21 U. MIAMI L. REV. 520, 525 (1967); whether or not they accept the wider functions symbolized by the "law center" concept, *see* Vanderbilt, *The Mission of a Law Center*, 27 N.Y.U. L. REV. 20 (1952); and the modes of interaction among students, faculty, and administration, *see generally* Kennedy, *How the Law School Fails: A Polemic*, 1 YALE REV. L. & SOC. ACT. 71 (1970); Stone, *Legal Education on the Couch*, 85 HARV. L. REV. 392 (1971); Watson, *The Quest for Professional Competence: Psychological Aspects of Legal Education*, 37 U. CIN. L. REV. 91 (1968).

20. Others have classified the stages of the development of American legal education differently. *See, e.g.,* Pound, *Some Comments on Law, Teachers and Law Teaching*, 3 J. LEGAL EDUC. 519, 520-21 (1951); Woodard, *The Limits of Legal Realism: An Historical Perspective*, 54 VA. L. REV. 689, 709 (1968).

21. *See generally* M. WEBER, THE THEORY OF SOCIAL AND ECONOMIC ORGANIZATION (1947).

several visions were simultaneously represented, and this is true within the law school today.

A. THE PRACTICE MODEL

In the earliest era of American legal education, most aspiring lawyers learned on the job.[22] In the Practice Model, law is studied in a procedural and client-centered context. In apprenticeship training,[23] the usual mode of practice learning, subjects of study are generated by the flow of cases. Thus, concepts are often raised out of logical order, skipped over entirely, or combined in various patterns, as determined by the facts of the cases. The senior lawyer guiding an apprentice may attempt to supplement the limitations of the training method by raising logically related questions or by lecturing.[24] The mentor may also assign texts for study, or the student may choose a series of law texts to read.[25] To the extent that texts are employed, the Practice Model is combined with another approach, typically the Rules Model.[26]

---

22. This practice may have originated in England, where the Inns of Court dominated English legal education through about 1650; thereafter, lawyers either "read law" in law offices, or followed a well-known list of recommended books. P. SMITH, A HISTORY OF EDUCATION FOR THE ENGLISH BAR 38-40 (London 1860). One nineteenth-century English writer on legal education advised against beginning law study by reading texts or attending lectures, maintaining instead that one should begin as a pupil in the chambers of practitioners. S. WARREN, A POPULAR AND PRACTICAL INTRODUCTION TO LAW STUDIES 396-403 (Am. ed. 1846) (1st ed. London 1835).

23. Beginning with the Colonial period, most aspiring lawyers prepared for the bar through apprenticeships. *See* A. HARNO, *supra* note 17, at 19. A course of attendance in a law office was required in nearly all states. Clerke, *Appendix* to S. WARREN, *supra* note 22, at 627. Of course, some might try to educate themselves solely out of books. *See* L. FRIEDMAN, A HISTORY OF AMERICAN LAW 525 (1973). Lincoln wrote that the "cheapest, quickest and best way" to become a lawyer was to "read . . . , get a license, and go to practice, and still keep reading." Nortrup, *The Education of a Western Lawyer*, 12 AM. J. LEGAL HIST. 294, 294 (1968).

24. But the student "rarely receive[d] any kind of regular instruction" from the practitioner. Clerke, *Introduction* to S. WARREN, *supra* note 22, at vii.

25. *See, e.g.*, J. REDLICH, *supra* note 16, at 7-8.

26. In the Colonial period, the books available to students gave no comprehensive view of the law. *See* P. HAMLIN, LEGAL EDUCATION IN COLONIAL NEW YORK 65-66 (1939). Coke's work, "the main reliance of all students, [was] inveighed against [for] the obscurity of its passages and the complexity of its arrangement," *id.* at 70 n.35, and was deemed a "disorderly mass of crabbed pendantry." Thayer, *The Teaching of English Law at Universities*, 9 HARV. L. REV. 169, 179 (1895). By the late eighteenth and early nineteenth centuries, "Whatever else might be omitted, in any case, Blackstone's *Commentaries* never were." Baldwin, *The Study of Elementary Law, The Proper Beginning of a Legal Education*, 13 YALE L.J. 1, 3 (1903). Blackstone taught for the first time "the continuity, the unity, and the reason of the Common Law," C. WARREN, A HISTORY OF THE AMERICAN BAR 177 (1911), and thus was "the stimulus . . . for

B. THE RULES MODEL

The first American law schools that grew to supplement apprenticeship training provided their students with lectures and common law treatises or printed versions of the teachers' lecture notes. These presentations of legal doctrines were rule-oriented and often non-systematic. The early schools adopted the standard divisions of the common law as units for curriculum. These traditional titles did poor service as working classifications for fields of the law, however, since the topics bore little relation to each other, making it impossible to classify the law or apply logically consistent canons of distinction.[27]

The titles were grouped into "courses" in arbitrary fashion based on mere convenience.[28] In the early law schools, it became necessary to divide the curriculum when the schedule of instruction lasted more than one year, or when there was more than one teacher. The development of a schedule of courses at Harvard, for example, was determined originally "by the necessity of keeping two professors occupied."[29] Professor Greenleaf and Judge Story split the work between themselves, and then divided their own work into further compartments, each of which might combine two, three, or four texts. Although these original divisions were organized to suit the convenience of students and faculty, and not on the basis of the subjects taught, the courses nevertheless survived as the components of the Harvard curriculum.[30] Even after the creation of the modern law school curriculum, the trend through 1920 was based less on an idea of "legal science" than on the requirements of a rather rigid mechanical system. "Legal 'titles,' which never possessed much logical significance [had] become stereotyped divisions of the law, whose size [was] somewhat arbitrarily determined."[31]

C. THE PRINCIPLES MODEL

Christopher Columbus Langdell is regarded as the inventor

---

our own early attempts at systematic legal education," Thayer, *supra*, at 170. "[B]ut after all, his valuable work, without familiar explanations and practical systematic exercises, affords inadequate help to most minds." Clerke, *supra* note 24, at vii.

27. *See* A. REED, *supra* note 16, at 345.
28. Before Langdell, Harvard had "a curriculum without any rational sequence of subjects." J. AMES, *Christopher Columbus Langdell*, in LECTURES ON LEGAL HISTORY 467, 477 (1913).
29. A. REED, *supra* note 16, at 363.
30. *Id.* at 364-65.
31. *Id.* at 367.

of modern American legal instruction[32] by virtue of the changes he imposed in legal education after he became dean of the Harvard Law School in 1870. His conceptual ordering became the standard for law schools throughout the country.[33] The often quoted introduction to his 1871 casebook sets forth his analytical approach:

> Law, considered as a science, consists of certain principles or doctrines ... to be traced in the main through a series of cases .... If these doctrines could be so classified and arranged that each should be found in its proper place, and nowhere else, they would cease to be formidable from their number.[34]

Langdell viewed the law as a science and the library as its laboratory; law consisted of principles which were derived from the cases by inductive reasoning.[35] The task of legal scholarship was to state those principles. The content of each law course in a Langdellian model of legal education was determined by tracing legal principles through a line of cases; course boundaries were generated analytically from conceptual dividing lines.[36] The application of Langdell's model led to the definition of legal fields in terms of their supposed underlying principles. With

---

32. *See, e.g.*, J. REDLICH, *supra* note 16, at 9. Gilmore, for example, wrote that "Langdell's *Cases on Contracts* was the first casebook of all." G. GILMORE, THE AGES OF AMERICAN LAW 125 n.3 (1977). *But see* note 42 *infra*.

33. Langdell's method became predominant over time. *See* L. FRIEDMAN, *supra* note 23, at 534-35. At Notre Dame, for example, from 1869 through 1905 textbooks and lectures were the major instructional method; by 1905 the case method had been adopted and remained the dominant technique until 1953, when emphasis shifted to the problem method for second and third year students. *See* P. MOORE, A CENTURY OF LAW AT NOTRE DAME 112 (1969). As of 1902, twelve schools had adopted the Langdellian system for their entire curriculum; 48 had adopted it in part; 34 maintained either a text book system, or a textbook and lecture system. *See* Huffcut, *A Decade of Progress in Legal Education*, 25 REPORT OF THE TWENTY-FIFTH ANNUAL MEETING OF THE AMERICAN BAR ASSOCIATION 529, 541 (1902). By 1920, nearly every American law school had assimilated Harvard's basic curriculum. *See* J. SELIGMAN, THE HIGH CITADEL: THE INFLUENCE OF HARVARD LAW SCHOOL 42-44 (1978). There were some holdouts, however. The University of Virginia Law School, for example, used a lecture system until the 1930s. J. RITCHIE, THE FIRST HUNDRED YEARS: A SHORT HISTORY OF THE SCHOOL OF LAW OF THE UNIVERSITY OF VIRGINIA FOR THE PERIOD 1826-1926, at 56 (1978).

34. C. LANGDELL, A SELECTION OF CASES ON THE LAW OF CONTRACTS at viii, ix (1871).

35. *See* Langdell's 1886 address quoted in 2 C. WARREN, HISTORY OF THE HARVARD LAW SCHOOL AND OF EARLY LEGAL CONDITIONS IN AMERICA 374 (1908). Langdell's method suggested that "the legal process was principally adjudication by logical reasoning deriving from immutable general principles." A. SUTHERLAND, THE LAW AT HARVARD 177 (1967).

36. Thus, for example, it is not difficult to state the conceptual dichotomies by which contracts can be distinguished from torts, torts from criminal law, criminal law from criminal procedure, or criminal procedure from civil procedure.

respect to contract law, for example, Grant Gilmore observed that "the idea that there was such a thing as a general law—or theory—of contract seems never to have occurred to the legal mind until Langdell stumbled across it."[37]

Of course, Langdell's innovations did not spring full-blown from his brow. The idea that law is a "science" had occurred to many before him,[38] along with the idea that legal education should be based on a "scientific" version of law.[39] Even at Litchfield, the first American law school, Judge Gould preferred that law be taught in a manner similar to "other" sciences as a system of consistent and rational principles, and organized his own textbook accordingly.[40] Gould declared it unsatisfactory to treat law as the compilation of positive rules, taught in a way to test the "mechanical strength of the reader's memory."[41] Lang-

---

37. G. GILMORE, *supra* note 1, at 6. Of course, that contracts was a field of its own, with its own law, was hardly a novel idea. *See, e.g.*, T. PARSONS, THE LAW OF CONTRACTS (6th ed. 1873). *See generally* A. REED, *supra* note 16, at 349.

38. Blackstone, for example, had written of a "science" of law, reducible to principles. 1 W. BLACKSTONE, COMMENTARIES *4. He also called equity a "science" by analogy to law, 3 *id.* at *55, and regarded legal judgments as "flowing" from reasons or premises. 3 *id.* at *379. *See generally* D. BOORSTIN, THE MYSTERIOUS SCIENCE OF THE LAW 20-25 (1941).

39. In this tradition, in the pre-Langdellian era at Harvard, Greenleaf wrote of "instruction in the science of law," and Story of a "scientific system of legal education." A. HARNO, *supra* note 17, at 43.

40. *See* J. GOULD, A TREATISE ON THE PRINCIPLES OF PLEADINGS IN CIVIL ACTIONS, at vi-viii (2d ed. 1836). Hoffman, another early writer on legal education, recommended that the law student read certain books "in a progressive succession." D. HOFFMAN, COURSE OF LEGAL STUDY at vii (1817). Hoffman, like Gould, favored a systematic study based on principles, and referred to the statement of Sir William Jones in his *Essay on the Law of Bailments* (1796):

> The great science of jurisprudence, like that of the universe, consists of many subordinate systems, all of which are connected by nice links, and beautiful dependencies; and each of them, as I have fully persuaded myself, is reducible to a few plain elements, either the wise maxims of national policy and general convenience, or the positive rules of our forefathers, which are seldom deficient in wisdom or utility. If law be a science and really deserve so sublime a name, it must be founded on principle, and claim an exalted rank in the empire of reason; but if it be merely an unconnected series of decrees and ordinances, its use may remain, though its dignity be lessened, and he will become the greatest lawyer who has the strongest habitual or artificial memory.

D. HOFFMAN, *supra*, at x-xi. Thus, the Langdellian method of principles had been long foreshadowed, and without Langdell's repudiation of policy considerations.

41. J. GOULD, *supra* note 40, at ix. Judge Gould intended his treatise as instruction in "the science" of pleading. The doctrines were to be presented "not as a compilation of *positive rules*; but as a system of *consistent and rational principles*." *Id.* at viii. He considered "almost all our modern and most popular treatises, upon the various other titles of the common law" to be wanting as works of instruction in a "science" of law.

For while every other science is taught, by a detailed explication of its

dell was not the first to believe that law students should learn principles from cases,[42] nor were Langdell and James Ames the first to believe that the case method should be the basis of classroom teaching.[43] Langdell was, however, the first to shape

---

principles, the doctrines of the common law are usually exhibited, in our legal treatises, as if they were the insulated enactments of *positive* law—without reference to the *reasons* on which they rest. And thus the common law is presented in most of our books, rather as an *art*, than a *science*; and the acquisition of it made to depend, more upon the mechanical strength of the reader's *memory*, than upon the exercise of his *understanding*. But it has been left on record, by the highest legal authority, that 'the law is unknown to him, who knoweth not the REASON thereof.' An axiom, which cannot fail to command the assent of every intelligent mind.

Id. at viii-ix. Similarly, Warren admonished the student to study books "of a scientific and elementary character" before attempting books written "for practical use." S. WARREN, *supra* note 22, at 372.

42. The position that legal education best occurs "*where the student extracts general rules and principles*" by "searching out the proper *principles* in confused and complicated cases" was stressed a century before Langdell. S. WARREN, *supra* note 22, at 411 (quoting Starkie, *Law Lecture*, 2 LEGAL EXAMINER & L. CHRONICLE 517, 518 (1833)). Contrary to popular belief, Langdell's *Cases on Contracts* (1871) was not the first casebook. *See* E. BENNETT & F. HEARD, A SELECTION OF LEADING CASES IN CRIMINAL LAW (1856).

43. *See* J. HURST, THE GROWTH OF AMERICAN LAW 261 (1950). Some evidence exists from which we can discern the use of the case method prior to Langdell. Clerke, who advocated the case method in 1846, *see* Clerke, *supra* note 23, at 628-29, conducted his own law school, *id.* at 630, and may well have used the method there.

John Norton Pomeroy's "method was not unlike the case system later perfected by Langdell. The students were expected to read cases and then to be questioned on them in classes." 1 P.C. JESSUP, ELIHU ROOT 61 (1938). Elihu Root recalled his teacher, Pomeroy, at NYU in the late 1860s:

Into the fields of conflicting decisions . . . he would lead us with amazing vigor and enthusiasm, and presently order would appear, compelled by . . . high intelligence in the application of fundamental principles to confused conditions . . . . His method of working was an especially valuable example of thoroughness in the collection and testing of all necessary data before beginning to reason towards conclusions, and of breadth of view in determining what data were necessary . . . .

Letter from Elihu Root to John Norton Pomeroy's son (1906), *quoted in id.* at 62. Henry McPike, Class of 1881 at Hastings College of the Law, recalled that Pomeroy used a case method at Hastings. Even in first-year courses, which were primarily lectures, Pomeroy would sometimes "pause and quiz the class, passing questions around indiscriminately, and treating all answers with gravity, no matter how far off any of them might be." In an upper year, Pomeroy "taught by 'the actual case method' referring constantly to the 'leading cases, from which the text rule was deduced, and urged and encouraged the constant reading and study of them.' " T. BARNES, HASTINGS COLLEGE OF THE LAW: THE FIRST CENTURY 113 (1978) (quoting HASTINGS COLLEGE OF THE LAW OF THE UNIVERSITY OF CALIFORNIA, GOLDEN JUBILEE BOOK 1878-1928, at 41 (1928)). Barnes explains that in the "Pomeroy System" the second year of courses was "inductive . . . (working from the particular of cases to generalities of doctrines)." *Id.* at 110.

the whole program of a school upon these ideas.[44] After Langdell's disciple Ames, the archetypal law teacher was a cross-examiner and discussion leader—a style we term Socratic.[45]

Langdell's Harvard, a school devoted to "pure law,"[46] was actually a mixture of the models of legal education. His colleagues were less devoted than he to Langdellian purity,[47] and even he did not totally eschew the methods of the Rules Model.[48] Nor was his method of legal scholarship totally devoid of a policy-oriented approach. It is true that in the 1879 second edition of his casebook, Langdell rejected the notion that the logical integrity of a system of laws could be superseded by policy considerations. Though one might frame an argument on "substantial justice," the understanding of the contracting parties, or the avoidance of "unjust" and "absurd" results, Langdell wrote, "[t]he true answer to this argument, is that it is irrelevant."[49] Seizing upon Langdell's statement, Oliver

---

44. J. HURST, *supra* note 43, at 264.
45. The notion that law teaching is Socratic seems based on the Socrates of the *Meno* *81-85 who teaches geometry to a slaveboy by asking questions. 1 THE DIALOGUES OF PLATO 279-84 (4th ed. B. Jowett trans. 1953). In the same vein, Socrates calls himself a midwife of the mind in *Theaetetus* *150, "and the triumph of my art is in thoroughly examining whether the thought which the mind of the young man brings forth is false and lifeless, or fertile and true." 3 *id.* at 245. In the *Sophist* *230-231, the "Stranger" describes those educators whose method is to "cross-examine a man's words when he thinks that he is saying something and is really saying nothing, and easily convict him of inconsistencies in his opinions." 3 *id.* at 378. This is a purging of prejudices through refutation. The Stranger also speaks, however, of other methods of instruction. Some attempt to educate through admonition, by roughly reproving errors. And, while the Sophists have a certain likeness to the "cross-examination" sort of education described, it is "the same sort of likeness which a wolf, who is the fiercest of animals, has to a dog, who is the gentlest." 3 *id.* at 379. Moreover, the Sophists teach an art of disputing about all things, and therefore erroneously appear all-wise to their disciples. 3 *id.* at 380-82. Socratic legal education is sometimes accused of being more like that of the Sophists. *See* J. OSBORN, THE PAPER CHASE (1973); Kennedy, *supra* note 19, at 72-73.
46. *See, e.g.*, F. ELLSWORTH, LAW ON THE MIDWAY: THE FOUNDING OF THE UNIVERSITY OF CHICAGO LAW SCHOOL 92 (1977).
47. *See* Hand, *Foreward* to S. WILLISTON, LIFE AND LAW (1941), *reprinted in* I. DILLARD, THE SPIRIT OF LIBERTY: PAPERS AND ADDRESSES OF LEARNED HAND 106 (1959).
48. Langdell included an appendix to the second edition of his casebook that consisted of a set of rules, albeit systematically arranged (as was, of course, Judge Gould's text). *See* 2 C. LANGDELL, A SELECTION OF CASES ON THE LAW OF CONTRACTS (2d ed. 1879) [hereinafter cited as LANGDELL ON CONTRACTS]. The rules were also published separately. C. LANGDELL, A SUMMARY OF THE LAW OF CONTRACTS (2d ed. 1880). Indeed, textbooks were widely used along with the case method. *See* J. REDLICH, *supra* note 16, at 49-50. A search for principles through cases may have occupied Langdell's class time, but the students could not be weaned so easily from the old method.
49. 2 LANGDELL ON CONTRACTS, *supra* note 48, at 996.

Wendell Holmes, Jr., concluded: "He is, perhaps, the greatest living legal theologian. But as a theologian he is less concerned with his postulates than to show that the conclusions from them hang together."[50] With all due respect, however, Holmes was unfair in his analysis. Although Langdell may have regarded logic as the touchstone of legal analysis, he also engaged in policy analysis of the most modern sort.[51] Thus, the "ideal type" of the Principles Model seems never to have existed as such, even under Langdell.

D. THE POLICY MODEL

Throughout this century, there have been attempts to shift the emphasis of the law school from the Langdellian vision to what may be called a Policy Model.[52] As early as 1909, Roscoe

---

50. Book Note, 14 N.Y. L. REV. (previously AM. L. REV.) 233, 234 (1880) (unsigned, by Holmes). Holmes also noted:

[I]n this word "consistency" we touch what some of us at least must deem the weak point in Mr. Langdell's habit of mind. Mr. Langdell's ideal in the law, the end of all his striving, is the *elegantia juris*, or *logical* integrity of the system as a system. . . .

If Mr. Langdell could be suspected of ever having troubled himself about Hegel, we might call him a Hegelian in disguise, so entirely is he interested in the formal connection of things, or logic, as distinguished from the feelings which make the content of logic, and which have actually shaped the substance of the law.

51. Langdell continued, immediately following the text which Holmes quoted, to write, "but, assuming [the argument about just results] to be relevant, it may be turned against those who use it without losing any of its strength." 2 LANGDELL ON CONTRACTS, *supra* note 48, at 996. Langdell then presented detailed policy arguments: when a hardship must be imposed on one of two innocent parties it is preferable to leave the situation in status quo; it is improper to impose a liability on which no limit can be placed; and liability should be placed on the party for whom it is easiest to make provision for the contingency. *See id.* The last of Langdell's policy arguments, in particular, has a modern ring. *Cf.* Calabresi & Hirschoff, *Toward a Test for Strict Liability in Torts*, 81 YALE L.J. 1055, 1060 n.19 (1972) (imposing accident costs on "the cheapest cost avoider"). Thus, the very exemplar of the Principles Model, Langdell's casebook, approached both the Policy Model and the Rules Model far more than is generally appreciated.

52. Johnson views 1930 as the date by which the "scientific historicism" of Langdell was widely abandoned for an approach that emphasized the social sciences, law as it actually functioned in society, sociological jurisprudence, or legal realism. (He finds that 1930 is also the first date by which legal education had become centered in the law schools.) W. JOHNSON, SCHOOLED LAWYERS: A STUDY IN THE CLASH OF PROFESSIONAL CULTURES 154 (1978). Dickinson still felt the need to argue in 1931 that "the time has come" to bring students into contact with more noncommercial fields of law, and to promote their taking a "legislative" attitude toward the law. Dickinson, *Legal Education and the Law School Curriculum*, 79 U. PA. L. REV. 424, 436 (1931). Gilmore wrote that by 1940, the jurisprudential revolution had succeeded and the "conceptualism" of Langdell was held up to scorn. G. GILMORE, *supra* note 32, at 86-87. Today, Langdellian conceptualism survives, *see* note 82 *infra*, along with scorn of it.

Pound called for the abandonment of the "method of deduction from predetermined conceptions" and for the adoption instead of a sociological jurisprudence emphasizing the human factor and the social structure within which law operates.[53] This jurisprudence implied that the curriculum should be reorganized in response to social change and that law students should be trained for roles as decisionmakers. The legal realists further undermined the jurisprudential bases of the Principles Model by focusing attention on the factual realities of law and government.[54]

Several law schools led the way in curricular changes after World War I.[55] Columbia initiated an early round of extensive curricular debates on a "functional" legal education.[56] Yale attempted the great experiment of bringing social scientists into the law school.[57] The Johns Hopkins University made a short-lived attempt to treat law in the manner of a graduate school

---

53. *See generally* Pound, *Scope and Purpose of Sociological Jurisprudence* (pts. 1-2), 24 HARV. L. REV. 591 (1911) and 25 HARV. L. REV. 140 (1912).

54. *See generally* Gilmore, *Legal Realism: Its Cause and Cure*, 70 YALE L.J. 1037 (1961). For the conclusion that we are all realists now, see C. AUERBACH, L. GARRISON, W. HURST & S. MERMIN, THE LEGAL PROCESS 361 (1961).

55. In 1937, the University of Chicago curriculum received widespread attention when the school compressed and shifted private law material to make room for new courses. E. BROWN, LAWYERS, LAW SCHOOLS AND THE PUBLIC SERVICE 98 (1948). Earlier, when the University of Chicago law school was organized in 1902-03, the planners "were influenced by the German system of legal education as they put together a curriculum committed to the 'whole field of man as a social being,'—a curriculum that extended beyond the 'pure law' of the Harvard model." F. ELLSWORTH, *supra* note 46, at 110. However, Beale, the funding dean, insisted that the Chicago curriculum be limited to "strictly legal subjects," and courses such as American Political Theory and Jurisprudence were abandoned. Levi, *The Political, the Professional, and the Prudent in Legal Education*, 11 J. LEGAL EDUC. 457 (1959).

56. The Columbia curriculum reforms of the 1920's turned away from law as a body of technical doctrine. Dean Stone noted the need for "re-arranging and organizing the subjects of law school study to make more apparent the relationship of the various technical devices of the law to the particular social or economic function with which they are concerned." Stone, *The Future of Legal Education*, 10 A.B.A.J. 233, 234 (1924).

57. In 1916 a committee issued "A Program for the Expansion of the Yale School of Law into a School of Law and Jurisprudence." Stevens, *supra* note 10, at 470-71. After World War I, there were movements to revise curricula, include social science approaches in courses, and take account of realist jurisprudence. "The new approach assumed . . . that the traditional categories of law are irrelevant . . . ." *Id.* at 475. In 1950, the Yale law curriculum of a later generation was reviewed by a committee of lawyers that concluded that there was justification for including in the curriculum courses from outside the traditional legal fields. Embree, *How Should Lawyers be Educated? A Report on the Yale Law Curriculum*, 37 A.B.A.J. 655, 657 (1951).

discipline.[58] Northwestern perhaps carried the functional approach farthest.[59] Harvard held out for decades for the "straight law" of "traditional 'casebook courses,'" until it too finally yielded, giving its influential imprimatur to the newer approaches.[60] Today, what may be called the Policy Model of legal education has widespread influence[61] and is particularly significant in those schools with upwardly-mobile aspirations.

The Policy Model has several facets. The law library, Langdell notwithstanding, is not the law's only laboratory. Lawyers must master data on society beyond the scope of case reports. The designation "casebook" has become a misnomer for what are often "heterogeneous collections of diverse materials,"[62] commonly labelled "Cases and Materials on Contracts," rather than merely "Cases on Contracts." Legal study often becomes

---

58. The research approach is embodied in the legal studies that were produced. See, e.g., JOHNS HOPKINS UNIVERSITY INSTITUTE OF LAW, STUDY OF CIVIL JUSTICE IN NEW YORK: SURVEY OF LITIGATION IN NEW YORK (1931); JOHNS HOPKINS UNIVERSITY INSTITUTE OF LAW, STUDY OF THE JUDICIAL SYSTEM OF MARYLAND (1930-32); JOHNS HOPKINS UNIVERSITY INSTITUTE OF LAW, STUDY OF JUDICIAL ADMINISTRATION IN OHIO (1930-32).

59. See E. BROWN, supra note 55, at 101.

60. A well known law school myth (albeit much exaggerated) labels the old and new approaches with the names of Harvard and Yale. See Navasky, *The Yales vs. the Harvards (Legal Division)*, N.Y. Times, Sept. 11, 1966, § 6 (Magazine), at 47. Harvard's curriculum after the Langdellian reforms of 1877 was considered to be based on the "fundamental plan . . . to teach law in the strict sense of the word," excluding social science. Levi, supra note 55, at 464. When the curriculum (which had been revised in the interim in 1915) was revised again in 1934-37, the draftsmen acknowledged it might be criticized for over-emphasis on traditional law. See Simpson, *The New Curriculum of the Harvard Law School*, 51 HARV. L. REV. 965, 980-81 (1938). Harvard's "new" curriculum was still characterized as three years devoted to "what our English brethren call 'straight law.'" Simpson, *Developments in the Law School Curriculum and in Teaching Methods*, 8 AM. L. SCH. REV. 1038, 1040 (1938). The new approach eventually had significant influence, even at Harvard: for example, what during the 1920s were "separate traditional 'casebook courses'" in negotiable instruments, sales, and security devices, were combined in a single commercial law course. A. SUTHERLAND, supra note 35, at 327.

61. While aspects of a policy perspective have achieved widespread acceptance, far more fundamental changes in the schools were called for by Lasswell & McDougal, *Legal Education and Public Policy: Professional Training in the Public Interest*, 52 YALE L.J. 203 (1947), and McDougal, *The Law School of the Future: From Legal Realism to Policy Science in the World Community*, 56 YALE L.J. 1345 (1947). Notwithstanding the many post-World War II curricula changes, Stevens concluded that the McDougal-Lasswell challenge was largely ignored. Stevens, supra note 10, at 512-13, 526-27, 529-42. But see, e.g., Miller, *Revising the Torts Course*, 21 U. MIAMI L. REV. 558, 559-60 (1967); *A Symposium in Honor of Hardy C. Dillard: Legal Education*, 54 VA. L. REV. 583 (1968) (articles responding to Lasswell and McDougal).

62. Wilson, *Book Review*, 25 CORNELL L. REV. 653, 655 (1940). See also A. HARNO, supra note 17, at 69.

an interdisciplinary enterprise,[63] with courses and research on law and some other discipline being commonplace. There is increased attention to public law and legislation,[64] to field experiences,[65] and to such "cultural courses" as Jurisprudence, Law and Society, and Comparative Law.[66] As part of this trend, old course boundaries are redrawn, the traditional pigeonholes are discarded, and "new" courses are created.[67]

In this model, the recognition of a new field in the law is a "phenomenon [which] takes place in response to dramatic shifts in technological, political and cultural organization of our society. Law, by its nature, reflects what is . . . ."[68] This functional reorganization of the curriculum has been described by Brainerd Currie as the most important single development in legal education in half a century.[69]

E. THE FIFTH MODEL: A NEW VISION?

A new vision of legal education may be emerging, though we may not yet be able fully to comprehend what it entails. Some find the clinical movement to be the most significant among recent developments. They see clinical education as not just skills training, but as education for professional responsibility.[70] In the view of these educators, one key contribution of

---

63. In the functional approach, the economic, social and philosophic setting of doctrine is considered. E. BROWN, *supra* note 55, at 99.

64. Arthur S. Miller, in analyzing "the impact of public-law on legal education," discussed such items as the addition of new courses to the curriculum, the change in teaching materials, increased attention to the legislature and the bureaucracy, and nonlitigation skills and techniques. Miller, *The Impact of Public Law on Legal Education*, 12 J. LEGAL EDUC. 483 (1960).

65. The values of the Practice Model have been increasingly incorporated into the former law school program. In recognition that lawyers need a broader range of skills than case analysis alone could provide, there have been improvements in moot courts, and increased course offerings in drafting instruments, legal bibliography, and office and trial practice. Clinical courses are now widely available; in connection with these offerings many schools offer field experiences. *See* the early developments reported in A. REED, *supra* note 16, at 260, 283. *See also* Committee on Curriculum of the Association of American Law Schools, *The Place of Skills in Legal Education*, 45 COLUM. L. REV. 345 (1945); Frank, *Why Not a Clinical Lawyer-School*, 81 U. PA. L. REV. 907 (1933); Frank, *A Plea for Lawyer-Schools*, 56 YALE L.J. 1303 (1947).

66. *See* D. JACKSON & E. GEE, BREAD AND BUTTER: ELECTIVES IN AMERICAN LEGAL EDUCATION (1975).

67. *See* E. BROWN, *supra* note 55, at 134-56.

68. G. GILMORE, *supra* note 1, at 9. "If seashells are currency, we will have a detailed, intricate and comprehensive law of wampum." *Id.*

69. *See* Currie, *The Materials of Law Study*, 8 J. LEGAL EDUC. 1, 73 (1955).

70. *See, e.g.*, Marden, *Introduction* to COUNCIL ON LEGAL EDUCATION FOR PROFESSIONAL RESPONSIBILITY, LAWYERS, CLIENTS & ETHICS: USING THE LAW SCHOOL CLINIC FOR TEACHING PROFESSIONAL RESPONSIBILITY at viii (1974)

clinical education is that it immerses the student in the realities of responsibility for an individual client. This experience helps the student become a "people-oriented counselor and advocate."[71] Other recent law school trends emphasize the insights of humanism and psychology.[72] The Langdellian model is rejected, not so much for its narrow vision of the law, but for its dehumanizing effects on the student, effects that are thought to result from harsh versions of the Socratic method.[73] A third current in the law schools includes attention to theories of justice,[74] providing a rival to the scientific and instrumentalist orientation of the law-economics approach to law. This jurisprudence directs the student's attention to problems of values.

"Current," "movement," and "trend" are terms which suggest that it remains unclear whether our age is giving rise to a Fifth Model of the law school. It may be that clinical, humanistic, psychological, and ethical orientations are part of a coherent whole. If so, moral concern for the individual may be a theme that connects all of the orientations that are a part of the Fifth Model.

F. THE FIVE VISIONS TODAY

Schools approximating each of the five visions or models of legal education coexist today; moreover, a law student at any school may be exposed to each. The office apprenticeships of the nineteenth century survive in such modified forms as certi-

---

("One of CLEPR's principal aims in sponsoring clinical education is to expose the law student to ethical problems as they arise in the context of live cases in which the student is participating under faculty supervision as a para-lawyer.").

71. *See* Burger, *The Future of Legal Education*, in SELECTED READINGS IN CLINICAL LEGAL EDUCATION (1973).

72. *See generally* Black, *Some Notes on Law Schools in the Present Day*, 79 YALE L.J. 505 (1970); Cohen, *Toward Radical Reform*, 24 J. LEGAL EDUC. 210 (1972); Paisley, *Moral Basis of Legal Education*, 44 N. DAK. L. REV. 1053 (1969); Redmount, *Humanistic Law Through Legal Education*, 1 CONN. L. REV. 201 (1968); Reich, *Toward the Humanistic Study of Law*, 74 YALE L.J. 1402 (1965); Savoy, *Toward a New Politics of Legal Education*, 79 YALE L.J. 444 (1970).

73. *See* Kennedy, *supra* note 19, at 73; Stone, *supra* note 19, at 392; Watson, *supra* note 19, at 93.

74. *See* Englard, *The System Builders: A Critical Appraisal of Modern American Tort Theory*, 9 J. LEGAL STUD. 27 (1979). John Rawls's *A Theory of Justice* (1973) is perhaps the most commonly discussed theory of justice in law schools today. For other important jurisprudential works which seem to be part of the curriculum in the emerging Fifth Model of legal education, see R. DWORKIN, TAKING RIGHTS SERIOUSLY (1977); R. NOZICK, ANARCHY, STATE AND UTOPIA (1974).

fied student practice[75] and clinical[76] programs. The Practice Model also underlies other experiences that are important parts of many students' legal education, though not always regarded as such by curriculum planners: summer legal employment,[77] post-graduation judicial clerkships,[78] and the informal instruction of new lawyers by their seniors in larger firms or in the courthouses.[79] The nineteenth century system of lectures, or lectures and texts with rules to be memorized, survives in bar review courses. Continuing education programs for lawyers sometimes also employ a nineteenth-century Rules Model of legal education.[80] Most first-year courses, and many upper-year courses, stress a system of logically organized principles taught through cases by Langdellian methods in accordance with the Principles Model.[81] Following the Policy Model, many courses are also likely to supplement case analysis with considerations of policy.[82] Moreover, unlike their predecessors of a hundred years ago,[83] lawyers now generally precede their formal legal training with four years of liberal arts or technical

---

75. On certified law student programs, see COUNCIL ON LEGAL EDUCATION FOR PROFESSIONAL RESPONSIBILITY, STATE RULES PERMITTING THE STUDENT PRACTICE OF LAW (2d ed. 1973).
76. See note 65 supra.
77. On the rise of the custom of student clerkship in law firms, at least for better students and better schools, see J. SELIGMAN, supra note 33, at 91.
78. See generally Oakley & Thompson, Law Clerks in Judges' Eyes: Tradition and Innovation in the Use of Legal Staff by American Judges, 67 CALIF. L. REV. 1286 (1979).
79. One group of educators, for example, came to the conclusion that it is the function of the bar or others, not of the law school, to provide practical instruction bridging the gap to practice. UNIVERSITY OF MICHIGAN LAW SCHOOL, THE LAW SCHOOLS LOOK AHEAD: 1959 CONFERENCE ON LEGAL EDUCATION 11 (1959).
80. See Stumpf, Continuing Legal Education: Its Role in Tomorrow's Practice of the Law, 49 A.B.A.J. 248, 249 (1963).
81. See text accompanying notes 32-51 supra. In 1950 a law professor, whose views are not atypical of teachers of basic courses, wrote, "Yes—I am an old-fashioned fellow; I am still foolish and orthodox enough to believe in the 'first principles of our common law,' as a medium of class instruction." Wormser, "Cases on Private Corporations", 2 J. LEGAL EDUC. 485, 487 (1950).
82. But see Cohen, Introduction to THE LAW SCHOOL OF TOMORROW 3 (D. Haber & J. Cohen eds. 1968) (stating that there is still a "widespread and deeply felt notion that the law schools of today [1968] are, in the main, trade schools concerned more with sharpening how-to-do-it skills than with the consequences of doing it, or with why or whether the how-to-do-it should be done").
83. In the nineteenth century, it was not customary for law schools to require any prior college work. See L. FRIEDMAN, supra note 23, at 527. While it has been said that the Harvard of Story's and Greenleaf's era consisted mostly of college graduates, id. at 528, the Harvard rules for the Story-Greenleaf years declared "No examination and no particular course of previous study are necessary for admission . . . ." D. HOFFMAN, supra note 40, at 556.

studies at college,[84] which may facilitate their ability to understand legal doctrine in its social and cultural context. Liberal arts education, clinical experiences, humanistic teacher-student relationships, and emphasis on individual-oriented law and on ethical questions, all contribute to an appreciation of the human dimension of the law consistent with the emerging Fifth Model of the law school.

Education matching any of the five visions has its value. The purposes of each model are varied and complex, but if one were to characterize each in a phrase, one might say that the Practice Model eases the student's transition into the day-to-day role of his craft; the Rules Model facilitates entry into the profession by supplying information useful for passing bar exams and for analyzing basic legal questions; the Principles Model teaches how to "think like a lawyer"—it instructs students in one of the modes of analysis useful for lawyering; the Policy Model provides education for a legal career recognizing that lawyers are, of necessity, lawmakers; and the Fifth Model helps the student function in the human context of legal practice.

II. CRITERIA FOR RECOGNIZING A LEGAL FIELD

In the past, the recognition of subjects for inclusion in the curriculum of law schools has not always been approached systematically.[85] One law school will respond to a major new social development by adding a course in Law and Atomic Energy, others will not. Predilections of individual textbook writers have been followed by some professors, but not by others. How systematically does the usual faculty, for example, consider the questions raised by one professor about instituting a course in Art and Law:[86] does the proposed course define a field and do legal activities involving the subject frequently

---

84. *See* Blaustein, *College and Law School Education of the American Lawyer* (pts. 1-2), 3 J. LEGAL EDUC. 409 (1951) and 4 J. LEGAL EDUC. 294 (1952); Vanderbilt, *A Report on Prelegal Education*, 25 N.Y.U. L. REV. 199 (1950).

85. *See* note 9 *supra* and accompanying text.

86. *See* Merryman, *A Course in Art and the Law*, 26 J. LEGAL EDUC. 551 (1974). "A related source of interest in this field was a desire to determine whether it really was a field. I took a great deal of razzing from colleagues who thought the whole enterprise frivolous and insubstantial . . . ." *Id.* at 552. *See also* Kelly, *A New Nominee for the Curriculum—Food, Drug and Cosmetic Law*, 3 J. LEGAL EDUC. 97 (1959); Rabin, *Administrative Law In Transition: A Discipline in Search of an Organizing Principle*, 72 Nw. U. L. REV. 120 (1977); Rasco, *The Need for a Latin-American Program in the Law School Curriculum*, 2 J. LEGAL EDUC. 180 (1949).

arise in real life? This section considers criteria, appropriate to each of the five models of legal education, that help in determining whether a separate field of study should be recognized. The proposed field of Law and Aging will be tested against each of the criteria.

A. CRITERIA UNDER THE PRACTICE MODEL

"Law is what lawyers do" reads the simplest, if somewhat circular, definition of law.[87] A change in the role of lawyers would thus justify, even require, revision of law school curricula under the Practice Model, which recognizes a new field of law on the basis of practical considerations rather than on any unifying conceptual theme.

Lawyers today in both private and government practice do increasing amounts of Law and Aging work that requires a special expertise.[88] Much of this work involves the public benefit programs: Social Security,[89] disability,[90] Supplemental Security Income,[91] Medicare,[92] Medicaid,[93] and veterans' benefits.[94] Government social service agencies that distribute benefits to the elderly employ lawyers to write regulations and adjudicate appeals. Legal services programs and others use lawyers to challenge rules and awards.[95] There are also opportunities for remunerative private practice under the Employee Retirement Income Security Act of 1974[96] and the Age Discrimination in Employment Act of 1967.[97] The laws are complex and the amounts involved are vast: pension funds of over $470 billion,[98]

---

87. Compare the idea that law (i.e., the rules of law) consist of what judges (or law officials generally) do. *See* K. LLEWELLYN, THE BRAMBLE BUSH 12 (1960 ed.).
88. *See* INSTITUTE OF LAW AND AGING, SURVEY OF NATIONAL LAW SCHOOL PROGRAMS AND MATERIALS in LAW AND AGING (1978).
89. Social Security Act, 42 U.S.C. §§ 401-431 (1976 & Supp. II 1978).
90. *Id.*
91. *Id.* §§ 1381-1383c.
92. Social Security Amendments of 1972, §§ 1396-1396k (1976 & Supp. II 1978).
93. *Id.* §§ 1395-1395qq (1976 & Supp. II 1978).
94. Act of Sept. 2, 1958, 38 U.S.C. §§ 101-3857 (1976 & Supp. II 1978).
95. *See generally* Marlin & Brown, *The Elderly Poor: An Overview of the Legal Services Attorney's Responsibilities*, 6 CLEARINGHOUSE REV. 192 (1972); Nathanson, *Legal Services for the Nation's Elderly*, 17 ARIZ. L. REV. 275 (1975).
96. 29 U.S.C. §§ 1001-1381 (1976 & Supp. II 1978).
97. 29 U.S.C. §§ 621-634 (1976 & Supp. II 1978).
98. At the end of 1978, the combined assets of private pension funds amounted to $321 billion; the retirement systems of state and local governments had assets of $148.5 billion. Raskin, *Pensions Funds Could be the Unions' Secret Weapon*, FORTUNE, Dec. 31, 1979, at 64. Another estimate of the assets of the state and local systems, as of 1975, put the figure at over $100 billion. PEN-

1980]   LEGAL EDUCATION   285

social security payments of almost $93 billion annually,[99] and other government programs for the elderly of over $24 billion annually.[100]

Another criterion for recognizing a field of law under the Practice Model is the existence of a distinct group of clients. There are perhaps thirty-two million potential clients for lawyers expert in Law and Aging.[101] The size of this group, along with the increased militancy of the elderly in asserting their rights, indicate that Law and Aging is a growth area for the practice of law.

In addition, if a field of law is administered by separate courts, it can profitably be considered a separate field of law under the Practice Model. The legal realists of forty years ago suggested that we recognize specialized government administrative agencies as "courts" of a new kind and establish new courses for each one. Although there are no special courts dealing with problems of the elderly, there are administrative tribunals that frequently rule on the specialized claims of the elderly.[102] By recognizing Law and Aging as a field of study, law schools could prepare students for practice in these forums.

B. CRITERIA UNDER THE RULES MODEL

Under the Rules Model, students learn rules that are stated in didactic texts. The existence of a distinct body of knowledge is a criterion for the definition of a field of law under this model. The volume of research in Law and Aging increases each year. The Law and Aging bibliography prepared by the University of Southern California Law Center Library shows that the number of works published annually in this area has doubled and redoubled each year since 1975.[103] The American

---

SION TASK FORCE, SUBCOMM. ON LABOR STANDARDS, HOUSE COMM. ON EDUCATION AND LABOR, 94TH CONG., 2D SESS., INTERIM REPORT ON ACTIVITIES 1 (Comm. Print 1976). *See generally* P. DRUCKER, THE UNSEEN REVOLUTION (1976); W. GREENOUGH & F. KING, PENSION PLANS AND PUBLIC POLICY (1976).
    99. In 1978, the Old Age, Survivors and Disability insurance program of Social Security paid out cash benefits of almost $93 billion. *Current Operating Statistics*, 43 SOC. SEC. BULL. No. 5, 30, at 31, Table M-1 (May 1980).
    100. Estimates for 1979 indicate that Supplemental Security Income paid out $1.8 billion, the Federal civilian retirement systems paid out about $12.2 billion, and veterans' payments were about $10.7 billion. Samuelson, *supra* note 15, at 258-59.
    101. *See* note 13 *supra* and accompanying text.
    102. *See generally* H. MCCORMICK, MEDICARE AND MEDICAID CLAIMS AND PROCEDURES (1977).
    103. J. MUBURAK, D. SAPIENZA & R. SHJIMANE, GERONTOLOGY AND LAW: A

Civil Liberties Union series of handbooks dealing with the rights of various groups has been extended to the elderly,[104] and two series of teaching materials for Law and Aging are being issued.[105] These materials[106] help to create the very field they deal with by facilitating legal research and the teaching of courses.[107]

Traditionally, under the Rules Model the definition of law courses has also been influenced by considerations of educational practicality and convenience which, regardless of the model that predominates, remain important considerations today. For example, as David Riesman has said, there is a division of labor among courses as well as a balancing of personnel, library resources, and such.[108] Moreover, law schools are not immune to factors causing overall trends in universities today: the rise of multi-disciplinary activities; the stress on "relevance," defined as short-term practicality; the willingness to engage in public service activities; the responsiveness to the availability of outside non-tuition funding; the search for programs attractive to new student populations in the face of pro-

---

SELECTED BIBLIOGRAPHY (1979); see Cohen, *Legal Research Issues on Aging*, 14 GERONTOLOGIST 263 (1974); Levine, *supra* note 11. *See generally* Levine, *Themes and Issues in Gerontology and Law*, 73 L. LIB. J. 259 (1981) [hereinafter cited as *Themes and Issues*].

104. *See* R. BROWN, THE RIGHTS OF OLDER PERSONS (1979).

105. The Senior Adults Legal Assistance program in Palo Alto, California, is preparing, under Federal grant, a series: *S.A.L.A. Curriculum Materials on Aging and the Law*. The Institute of Law and Aging of George Washington University has prepared a Law School Series of materials on *Legal Problems of the Elderly*, regarded as "unpublished" but available upon request.

106. Additionally, the *NSCLC Washington Weekly* of the National Senior Citizens Law Center publishes current case law, legislative, and agency developments; the *Gerontologist* regularly runs law-related articles; the *Journal of Gerontology* has a regular update on periodical literature in Law and Aging; and a new series of reprints and monographs, *Papers in Law and Aging*, is forthcoming from the University of Southern California. Among manuals and symposia available on the subject, see DUKE UNIVERSITY CENTER FOR THE STUDY OF AGING AND HUMAN DEVELOPMENT, LEGAL PROBLEMS OF OLDER AMERICANS: PROCEEDINGS OF A CONFERENCE (1975); NATIONAL COUNCIL ON SENIOR CITIZENS, INC., THE LAW AND AGING MANUAL (1975); J. WEISS, LAW OF THE ELDERLY (1977); *Special Section on Legal Problems of the Elderly*, 9 CONN. L. REV. 425 (1977); *Symposium: Law and the Aged*, 17 ARIZ. L. REV. 267 (1975).

107. A number of themes can be identified that raise questions fundamental to the field of Law and Aging. Can the nation "afford" the increasing number of retired persons? How should government programs for the aged be organized and financed? Is it legitimate for the law to deal with older persons in terms of their age, or does such a practice constitute age discrimination? Is it possible to provide older persons with autonomous, independent lifestyles comparable to those enjoyed by them throughout their adult years? For a discussion of the major substantive topics and themes in Law and Aging, see *Themes and Issues*, *supra* note 103.

108. *See* Riesman, *supra* note 5, at 643-44.

jected declining numbers of traditional university-age students; the attempt to combine vocational usefulness with other, liberal, academic goals; the attempt by upwardly-mobile schools to stake out areas in which distinction can be achieved, taking account of social need, weakness of competition, and existing strengths; and so on. While these items may not give rise to an intellectual justification for any given course or activity, they nevertheless reflect pressures actually at work. No extensive discussion is needed to demonstrate that teaching, research, and related activities in Law and Aging are responsive to these demands.

C. CRITERIA UNDER THE PRINCIPLES MODEL

Under the Principles Model, axioms of law are studied through case analysis, and each conceptual field of law is thought to have its own set of principles. This model of legal education requires that fields of study have theories and concepts that are so interrelated that they appear to stem from an original set of axioms. This can be considered a Langdellian requirement.[109] Law and Aging has certain unifying themes,[110] but may not meet this criterion of rigor. There exist other fields of law that are already recognized, however, that may not meet this axiomatic standard either. Moreover, there is more than one way to achieve axiomatic rigor. Langdell himself discarded cases that were not in accord with the principles he had perceived.[111] Thus it may be that some subset of the cases on Law and Aging would satisfy the Langdellian requirement of axiomatic rigor.

A post-Langdellian version of this criterion may also be proposed. Although legal scholarship today still strives for sci-

---

109. Langdell's curricular divisions at Harvard have been contrasted with those adopted contemporaneously by Pomeroy at Hastings. *See* note 43 *supra*. A Pomeroy partisan writes that for Langdell, the law was "reduced to so many discrete groupings of doctrines reflecting a practical development that was principally jurisdictional and 'remedial.' . . . What parts should be taught was, of course, a matter of curriculum planning, though largely dictated by the practical dimension . . . ." T. BARNES, *supra* note 43, at 111. By contrast, "[t]he Pomeroy System was above all a systematic, logical structuring of branches of the law . . . . [T]he arrangement and relationship of one branch to another . . . allowed for creative systematization." *Id.* at 101-02. In every branch of law, Pomeroy built an architectonic structure differentiating primary rights and duties and remedial rights and duties, with increasingly fine and detailed subdivisions. *Id.* at 102-03, 107.
110. *See Themes and Issues, supra* note 103.
111. "The vast majority [of cases] are useless, worse than useless, for any purpose of systematic study." C. LANGDELL, *supra* note 34, at viii.

entific principles with intellectual coherence, it has largely abandoned Langdell's nineteenth-century model of natural science, and has substituted the analogy of the twentieth-century social sciences. The prototype of this trend was the use of field observation methods by Underhill Moore at Yale to study the effects of various permutations of parking regulation schemes.[112] In contemporary scholarship, Richard Posner has called for "the application of scientific methods to the study of the legal system . . . to discover and explain the recurrent patterns . . . —the 'laws' of the system".[113] In this approach, a field would be an appropriate unit of "legal science" if regularities were discoverable through a social science method.

Law and Aging may well satisfy this criterion. Economists have found gerontology an "important [though still] relatively unexplored, area of economic analysis."[114] Against this demonstration of interest, however, some have expressed disillusion.[115] Law and Aging as a field, if established by virtue of this criterion, thus runs the risk of standing or falling with the fortunes of the reputation of the external social science employed.

Another criterion for determining if an area represents a distinct field of study is if the substantive rules of the subject matter differ from those in other fields. The existence of differing rules implies differing underlying axioms, even if the axioms themselves cannot yet be perceived. This criterion was applied by the initiator of Stanford's Art and Law course to determine whether the subject matter constituted a field.[116] He found that works of art, artists, and institutions in the art world were treated, for legal purposes, differently from those in other spheres of society, and thus concluded that special rules of law

---

112. *See* U. MOORE, LAW AND LEARNING THEORY: A STUDY IN LEGAL CONTROL (1943).

113. Posner, *Volume One of the Journal of Legal Studies—An Afterword*, 1 J. LEGAL STUD. 437, 437 (1972).

114. Clark, Kreps & Spengler, *Economics of Aging: A Survey*, 16 J. ECON. LIT. 919, 949-50 (1978).

115. Professor Gilmore has written:
> After two hundred years of anguished labor, the great hypothesis [that there are observable regularities in social behavior or in societal development] has produced nothing. . . .
> One lesson which we can draw from all this is that the hypothesis itself is in error. . . . So far as we have been able to learn, there are no recurrent patterns in the course of human events; it is not possible to make scientific statements about history, sociology, economics—or law.

G. GILMORE, *supra* note 32, at 99-100. *See also* Leff, *Economic Analysis of Law: Some Realism About Nominalism*, 60 VA. L. REV. 451, 458-59 (1974); Leff, *Law and*, 87 YALE L.J. 989, 1007-08 (1978).

116. *See* Merryman, *supra* note 86, at 552.

applied to the art world.[117] Applying this criterion to the elderly, there are many statutes that treat older people differently than the young.[118] In addition, many statutes that are age-neutral on their face have special applicability to the elderly, such as the laws on inheritance, wills, probate, estate tax, civil commitment, conservatorship, and guardianship.[119] The existence of a distinct body of law relating to the elderly suggests the possibility that underlying axioms may be derived and that Law and Aging is an appropriate candidate for recognition as a field.

D. CRITERIA UNDER THE POLICY MODEL

Under the Policy Model, sociological considerations are integrated into the study of law in an attempt to deal with public policy issues. Legal and nonlegal data supplement case analysis. The primary criterion for the recognition of a field under this model is the determination of whether society faces a significant group of interrelated problems that could benefit from unified legal treatment. Proponents of this model maintain that the traditional formal categories of law, shaped by accident and maintained by tradition, obscure the social problems with which law actually deals; the traditional framework thus yields an artificial perspective. Under the Policy Model, law is reorganized along more functional lines, corresponding to the types of human activity involved.

The problems of the elderly encompassed in a course on Law and Aging represent a body of study suitable for a functionally defined course. Legal questions affecting the elderly involve broad questions of social policy. Their solution requires knowledge of legal and nonlegal data and an understanding of the social, economic, historical, and philosophical issues raised. Thus, for example, the laws affecting mandatory retirement should not be altered without an understanding of the relationship between retirement policies and issues of inflation, unemployment, and education.

---

117. *Id.*
118. *See* notes 89-94 *supra*; R. HAROOTYAN, ANNOTATED INDEX OF FEDERAL LEGISLATION IMPACTING ON THE ELDERLY (1977) (listing over sixty statutes). At present, however, there are no constitutional principles which treat the elderly differently from young people. *See generally* Vance v. Bradley, 440 U.S. 93 (1979); Massachusetts Bd. of Retirement v. Murgia, 427 U.S. 307 (1976); Levine, *"Age Discrimination" as a Legal Concept for Analyzing Age-Work Issues*, in WORK AND RETIREMENT: POLICY ISSUES (R. Ragan ed. 1980).
119. *See generally Themes and Issues, supra* note 103.

Another criterion under the Policy Model might be whether the client group in question sees itself as deserving new "rights" and separate legal treatment. This is a related, but less mundane, version of the Practice Model criterion,[120] which dealt with the existence of clients. Here the clients not only meet Marx's criterion for a class objectively having a common interest, but also that for a class subjectively recognizing themselves as a separate social group.[121] For example, it became necessary to train lawyers in the field of race relations and, more recently, in the field of women's rights, not because of any sudden shift in the ethnic and sexual demographic statistics, but because members of the relevant groups increasingly recognized themselves in such terms when considering legal claims, and turned to the law for specialized legal protection.

Analysis linking a change in ideas to the emergence of the elderly as a self-conscious group belongs to the perspective of the sociology of knowledge, or social construction of reality, as propounded by thinkers like Karl Mannheim.[122] Different groups have their own unique historical experiences, which give rise to different interpretations of the world, and therefore ultimately to different systems of knowledge. Although it has been argued that the elderly retain their lifelong political orientation and are too disparate in interest and ideology to consider themselves part of a unity,[123] there are evidently large numbers of elderly who recognize a shared interest.[124] Under a sociology of knowledge approach, the development of the elderly as a social group sharing certain experiences explains the emergence of such ideas as age discrimination, elder's rights, "gray power," and the field of Law and Aging. Lawyers and scholars, since they are groups dependent on their clients and subjects, come to share these concepts with the elderly.

E. Criteria Under the Fifth Model

Under what may be an emerging Fifth Model of the law

---

120. See text accompanying notes 87-102 supra.
121. See K. Marx, The Poverty of Philosophy 146-47 (1963 ed.). See also 2 K. Popper, The Open Society and its Enemies 115 (3d rev. ed. 1957); Glantz, Class Consciousness and Political Solidarity, 23 Am. Soc. Rev. 375 (1958).
122. See K. Mannheim, Ideology and Utopia: An Introduction to the Sociology of Knowledge (1929). See also P. Berger & T. Luckmann, The Social Construction of Reality (1966).
123. See Hudson & Binstock, Political Systems and Aging, in Handbook of Aging and The Social Sciences 372 (R. Binstock & E. Shanas eds. 1976).
124. See Ragan & Dowd, The Emerging Political Consciousness of the Aged: A Generational Interpretation, 30 J. Soc. Issues 154-56 (No. 3, 1974).

school, the student is trained to focus on the individual human needs and rights of the client. Perhaps an appropriate criterion for recognizing a field under this vision of legal education is whether the candidate field requires the individual lawyer to develop a particular interpersonal capability. Some fields, for example, require particular sensitivities if the lawyer is to interact successfully with clients—perhaps poverty law, prison law, and similar fields. Law and Aging, as a field for counseling and advocacy on behalf of individual clients, satisfies this criterion. Many professionals—including lawyers, psychiatrists, social workers, and others—exhibit a bias or personal distaste that inhibits them from effectively serving old and infirm clients.[125] A course enabling lawyers to overcome this limitation on their professional capacities would thus serve a special function.

A different criterion that might be associated with the Fifth Model is whether a candidate field encompasses distinct issues of values and justice. Under this criterion, Law and Aging can make a contribution to the law school curriculum. Treatment of the elderly by society raises many complex ethical issues, such as whether differential treatment of the elderly constitutes invidious discrimination.[126] A number of unique factors bear on this question and render the issue of discrimination against the elderly analytically distinct from discrimination against other groups. The middle-aged majority makes laws for the elderly, but each member of the majority hopes or expects to become old some day. In addition, the old have had their turn at whatever special advantages the middle-aged enjoy and they are, moreover, often different in important ways from the middle-aged. At the same time that the elderly receive group-specific disabilities, they also receive group-specific benefits. As a result, we find the seeming paradox of advocates of the rights of the elderly condemning "discrimination" while they affirm "reverse discrimination."[127] Because quite different arguments are voiced in the factual context of age discrimination than are raised in the context of race relations, the question of

---

125. *See* R. BUTLER, WHY SURVIVE? BEING OLD IN AMERICA 233-34 (1975); W. SCHOFIELD, PSYCHOTHERAPY 133 (1974) (discussing "yavis syndrome"—the tendency of psychotherapists to treat young, attractive, verbal, intelligent, and successful (which means well-paying) clientele); Mutschler, *Factors Affecting Choice of and Perseveration in Social Work with the Aged*, 11 GERONTOLOGIST 231 (1971).
126. *See* Levine, *Four Models for Age/Work Policy Research*, 20 GERONTOLOGIST 561(1980); *Themes and Issues, supra* note 103.
127. *See Themes and Issues, supra* note 103.

discrimination in the context of the elderly makes a special contribution to the student's education in issues of values and justice.

A third criterion for a new field under the Fifth Model may be whether recognition of the field makes some special contribution to assisting *individuals* with their legal concerns. Law and Aging satisfies this criterion as well. Lawyers, whether informed or not, will be making important decisions affecting elderly persons in the years ahead.[128] The youth-dominated culture of America leads many persons to ignore the problems of the elderly until they face such problems personally. Adding a course in Law and Aging to the law school curriculum would be a step towards educating lawyers to make decisions affecting older people intelligently, would encourage research, and would help enlighten the growth of legal doctrine and legislation. It is hoped that after taking such a course the next generation of lawyers would be better able to deal with problems affecting tens of millions of Americans.

III. CONCLUSION: DOES IT MAKE ANY DIFFERENCE?

Within the criteria imposed by the five different visions of the law school, Law and Aging is a suitable topic for recognition as a separate field of study. Within a Practice Model of legal education, if law is what lawyers do, then indeed many lawyers already "do" Law and Aging, and the number of specialists, both within and without government agencies, is increasing.[129] There is a large and growing clientele with needs to be served. Under the Rules Model, it was noted that there is a considerable and increasing body of knowledge on Law and Aging.[130] There are also many practical considerations which may tip the scales in favor of separate offerings in Law and Aging for law schools of all orientations. Although there may be doubt under the Principles Model as to whether there are underlying principles approaching Langdellian axiomatic rigor evident in the case law on Law and Aging, a post-Langdellian criterion of law as science may be met in the social scientific treatment of Law and Aging.[131] There is also a substantial body of law treating the elderly differently from other persons

---

128. Levine, *People-Oriented Law Confronts Problems of the Elderly*, 1 CITES—(1980).
129. *See* notes 88-97 *supra* and accompanying text.
130. *See* notes 103-07 *supra* and accompanying text.
131. *See* notes 112-14 *supra* and accompanying text.

that may some day be organized in axioms of a traditional Langdellian type. In considering the Policy Model, it was argued that the problems of aging should have available the fullest contribution the law can make, especially since the elderly are increasingly vocal in their demands for specialized treatment.[132] Within the Fifth Model, recognition of Law and Aging as a new field of law would help the future lawyer handle professionally a distinct set of interpersonal relations with a special client group and would raise unique issues of values.[133]

It may be objected that it is not very meaningful to consider whether one set of topics or another should be recognized as a separate field of law. Since the goals of law schools can be achieved through any of a variety of course offerings,[134] it is understandable that a good deal of ridicule has been leveled at the renaming of courses. After all, as Walter Wheeler Cook suggested in another context, line drawing between classifications is more or less arbitrarily done for the purposes of convenience: any given material can be organized according to various schemes.[135]

Moreover, even if a new field of study, like Law and Aging, is recognized, there is no guarantee that a course will be listed in a law school's bulletin or that anyone will take it. The three-year substantive law curriculum is already overcrowded;[136] skill courses and courses intended to provide broad perspective on law in society make further demands on student time. Observers remark that most law students prefer "bread and butter" courses which give "pure, old-fashioned Hessian-training"[137]—rule-oriented courses that will meet client demands.

Nevertheless, questions about the "proper" subdivisions in the law curriculum are important. Historically such questions

---

132. See notes 123-24 *supra* and accompanying text.
133. See notes 125-28 *supra* and accompanying text.
134. The use of specific subject matter courses for wider curricular goals arose once law schools abandoned the mission of teaching all of the law. See Kelso, *supra* note 7, at 529. When the goals of the law school curriculum are expanded to go beyond the teaching of specific legal doctrines, such as contributing to reform of the legal order by training lawyers to advance the cause of social justice, most any course may be used as a vehicle to this end. See Allen, *One Aspect of the Problem of Relevance in Legal Education*, 54 VA. L. REV. 595, 605 (1968); Pincus, *Reforming Legal Education*, 53 A.B.A.J. 436, 437 (1967).
135. Cook, *"Substance" and "Procedure" in the Conflict of Laws*, 42 YALE L.J. 333, 352 (1933).
136. See Prosser, *The Ten Year Curriculum*, 6 J. LEGAL EDUC. 149, 151 (1953).
137. Stevens, *supra* note 10, at 526-27 (quoting Bergin, *The Law Teacher: A Man Divided Against Himself*, 54 VA. L. REV. 637, 643 (1968)).

have played a crucial role in the evolution of legal culture. Differences in the organization of curricula are decisive for law because they establish and endorse different epistemological categories and values. As David Riesman said:

> Whether we go all the way with Kant or not, the categories in which we view "reality" are obviously of vital importance. . . . A division of a criminal law course into categories of "larceny," "arson," and "insanity" will tend to engender one kind of attitude, and "prevention of socially undesirable behavior" and "the problem of conflicting values" another, preferable, point of view.[138]

Thus, Riesman regards the choices made by law professors not only as necessary, but as important in guiding legal thinking towards a selected matrix of social issues. The enterprise of reflecting upon how and why we categorize our intellectual universe in the law and come to recognize new fields may stimulate similar questioning about established courses and fields. The major remapping of the law a century ago that gave us such fields as contracts[139] and torts[140] may now be due for reconsideration to reflect changes in legal practice and society. The curriculum of the future[141] may be conceived less in terms of corporations and property as reified entities, and more in terms of the needs of individual human beings and of the society.

---

138. *See* Riesman, *supra* note 5, at 642.
139. *See* text accompanying note 37 *supra*.
140. There was no law book on the subject of torts until 1859. *See* White, *The Intellectual Origins of Torts in America*, 86 YALE L.J. 671, 671 (1977).
141. On the future of legal education, *see generally* McKay, *Legal Education* in AMERICAN LAW: THE THIRD CENTURY 1 (B. Schwartz ed. 1976).

Name Index

Abbott, Chief Justice 20
Abel, Richard 86
Ackerman 360
Adams, Henry Baxter 80
Adams, Henry Brooks 129, 159, 289
Agassiz, Professor 44
Alexander the Great 313
Allen, Professor Francis 515
Ames, James Barr xiv, 81, 160–1, 162, 169, 209, 220, 428, 429, 571, 572
Anscombe, G.E.M. 484
Anson, Sir William R. 25
Aquinas, Thomas 159, 321
Archimedes 79, 86
Aristotle 39, 54, 57, 159, 321
Arnold, Thurman W. 188, 189
Ashby, Sir Eric 421, 423
Auerbach, Jerold 507, 520
Augustine, St 10, 309
Augustus, Emperor 10, 315
Austin, John 321
Austin, Regina 412
Averch, Harvey 351
Ayer, A.J. 333

Bacon, Francis 40–1, 61, 66
Baldwin, Simeon E. 33–47, 158
Bankowski, Zenon 488
Banks, Taunya 381
Barnett, H. 479, 491, 492, 493
Barrett, Brenda 523–34
Barrett, E. 326
Bates, Henry Moore 165, 169
Beale, Joseph Henry 163, 169, 170, 204, 429
Bellow, Gary 230, 231, 232, 242, 243, 244, 245, 247–51, 280
Bentham, Jeremy 362, 435, 437
Bergman, Paul 233
Berle 189, 223
Bernard, Claude 66
Bessey, Charles Edwin 159–60
Bickel, Alexander 328–9, 360
Bickenbach, Jerome E. 503, 504
Binder, David 231
Bishin, William R. 281, 321–4, 333
Black, Charles 92, 171–7, 330
Black, Donald 496

Blackstone, Sir W. 8, 34, 35, 135, 159, 426, 488, 504
Boaz, Franz 80
Bok, Derek xix, 513
Bolyai, Janos 54
Boyer, Barry B. 507
Bracton, Henry de 39, 161
Brandeis, Justice Louis D. 62, 277
Breyer, Stephen 361
Bridge, Caroline 556
Brierly, J.N. 399, 401
Brougham, Lord 426
Brown, E. 326
Brown, Louis M. 253–8
Brown, Norman O. 282, 338
Bruton, P. 326
Burgess, John W. 80
Burton, Justice 336
Butler, Justice 62

Cain, Patricia 412–13
Calabresi, Guido 359–64
Camus, Albert 289
Cardozo, Justice Benjamin 58, 104, 115, 120, 321, 516, 517
Carlin 440
Carlyle, Thomas 424
Carnap, Rudolf 153, 333
Carrington, Paul D. 87–9
Cassirer, E. 333
Choper, J. 325, 333
Cicero 10
Clark, Charles 86, 189, 204
Clerke xiv
Coase, Ronald H. 350, 476
Cohen, Judge Maxwell 509–10
Cohen, Morris 55
Coke, Lord Edward 16, 17, 18, 19, 25, 305
Condlin, Robert 240, 247–9, 251
Cook, Walter W. 53–9, 164, 165, 188, 430, 589
Cooper, James Fenimore 51
Corbin, Arthur 188, 361, 430
Costigan, George Purcell 164
Cover, Robert 93
Cramton, Roger 87, 507
Crane, Judge 189

Crenshaw, Kimberle 412
Currie, Brainerd 431–2, 576

Darwin, Charles 55
Davie, Dr George 480, 481
Davis, Justice 336
Dession, Professor George 154
Detmold, M.J. 483, 487
Dickinson 189
Dollard 153
Dostoevsky, Fyodor 298
Douglas, Justice William O. 86, 189, 204, 223, 330
Dowling, W. 326
Dreiser, Theodore 298
Dworkin, Ronald 487, 493

Einstein, Albert 56, 289
Eliot, President 182
Ely, Richard T. 80, 360
Emerson, Thomas 92
Emslie, Lord 484
Epstein, Cynthia Fuchs 371
Euclid 54, 55, 56
Evans, Mr 16

Ferri 137
Fitzherbert, Mr 41, 42
Ford, Henry 82
Fox, Mr 9
Frank, Judge Jerome xv, 64, 181–97, 321, 430
Frankfurter, Justice Felix 189, 330
Freud, Sigmund 128, 129, 144, 153, 159, 338, 547
Freund, Ernest 81, 188
Freund, P. 325
Froissart, Jean 307
Fromm, Erich 153
Fuller, Lon L. 263–78, 321, 333

Garrison 215
Gellhorn, Walter 473, 476
Gilmore, Angela D. 407–13
Gilmore, Grant 362, 570
Ginsburg, Justice Ruth Bader 369–72
Glanville, Mr 7, 12, 39
Glennester, M. 544
Glueck, Sheldon 137
Goetz, Charles 360, 361, 364
Goff 488
Gold, Dean 557–8
Goldstein, Professor 441
Goodpaster, Gary 237

Gould, Judge 570
Gray, John Chipman 160–1, 162, 195, 220, 429
Green, Dean 189
Green, Kate 535–41
Greenleaf, Professor 568
Gregory, Duncan 481
Grotius, Hugo 34, 315–16
Gunther, G. 326

Hägerström, A. 484
Hailsham, Lord 484, 496
Hale, Sir Matthew 34
Hall, G. Stanley 80
Hall, James Parker 164, 166–7, 169
Hall, Jerome 134
Hallam, Mr 14
Hamilton, Sir William 481, 488
Hamilton, Walton 196
Hammond, Chancellor 42
Handler 189, 204, 213
Hanna 223
Hantzis, Catharine Wells 373–82
Hardwicke, Lord 20, 426
Harris, Angela 412
Hart, H.L.A. 321, 496
Hawthorne, Nathaniel 298
Hay, Douglas 289
Hegel, G.W.F. 158, 159, 165
Henry I, King 7
Henry II, King 7, 12
Hobbes, Thomas 315
Hofler, Anthony 536
Hofstadter, R. 338
Hohfeld, Wesley Newcomb 159, 164–5, 321, 430
Holland 161
Holmes, Justice Oliver Wendell xv, 58, 104, 105, 114, 158, 212, 305, 312, 321, 336, 401, 429, 517, 572–3
Honnold, J. 326
Houston, Charles 403
Howe, M. 325
Hughes, Everett C. 283
Hull, Cordell 153
Hume, David 470
Hunt, Alan 491–501, 530
Hurst, Willard 428
Hutchins, Robert Maynard 61–8
Huxley, Thomas 53

James, Fleming 92
James, King 17
James, William 56

Jamison, J. Franklin 80
Jencks, Christopher 279
Jhering, Rudolf von 313
Johnson, Leland L. 351
Jones, James 395
Joseph, Sir Keith 526
Jowett, Benjamin 442
Justinian, Emperor 34, 43, 161, 316

Kafka, Franz 298
Kairys, D. 547
Kales, Albert 195
Kamisar, Yale 325, 333
Kant, Immanuel 54, 133, 159, 321, 470, 486, 590
Keener, William 81, 160, 161–2, 164, 169, 429
Kelland, Philip 481
Kelsen 321, 486
Kelso 437
Kennedy, Duncan 85, 373, 375–82, 543
Kent, James 39, 307, 308
Kessler, Fritz 92
Kettleson, Jeanne 243, 244, 245
Keynes, John Maynard 364
Keyser 54–5, 56
Keyserling, Leon H. 101–25
Kingsfield, Professor 373–5, 378–80
Kitch, Edmund 345–57
Klare, Karl E. 385–92, 516
Konefsky, Fred 85
Konenkov 212
Korzybski, Alfred 153
Kuhn, T. 333
Kyer, C. Ian 503, 504

Langdell, Professor C.C. xiv, 25–7, 29–31, 36, 37, 61, 81, 82–3, 84, 111, 181–4, 186, 190, 191, 193, 195, 197, 209, 275, 253, 427–30, 432, 433, 437, 438, 440, 448, 503, 504, 568–73, 575, 577, 578, 583, 584, 588, 589
Langer, S. 333
Langley, Samuel 57
Larson, Magali 81, 84
Lasswell, Harold xv, 151, 281, 435–8, 440, 448, 506–7, 510–12, 515
Lefcoe, George 281
Leighton 530
Levine, Martin 281, 563–94
Lewis, Gilbert 55
Lim, Hilary 535–41
Lindblom, Professor C.E. 363
Littleton, Sir Thomas 25, 41

Llewellyn, Karl N. xv, 189, 199–226, 286, 321, 430, 432–5, 437, 438, 440, 530
Lobachevski, Nikolai 54
Lockhart, W. 325, 326–8, 333, 338
Lorde, Audre 409, 411
Lorimer, James 481–2
Love, Jean 409
Lowenstein, Allard 247
Lyons, David 485

McCormick, Neil 479–89, 491–500
McDonald, P. 544
Macdonald, Roderick A. 451–72
MacDonald, Vincent 505
McDougal, Myres S. xv, 145–55, 435–8, 440, 448, 506–7, 510–12, 515
MacGuigan, Justice Mark R. 503–20
Mach, Ernst 54
Mack 189
Mackenzie, Lord 161
McLaughlin 213
Maclaurin 481
MacRae, Donald A. 504–5
Magill 189
Maine, Henry 44
Malinowski, Bronislaw 153
Manne, Henry 475
Mannheim, Karl 586
Mansfield, Lord 426
Marcuse, Herbert 338
Marshall, Leon C. 431
Marshall, Justice Thurgood 403
Martineau, James 46
Marx, Karl 128, 129, 144, 153, 158, 377, 586
Maslow, Abraham 246
Masseres, Baron 15
Mathiesen 543
Matsuda, Mari 412
Medina, Judge Harold 189
Melamed, Douglas 362
Mellinkoff, David 508
Melsner 238
Melville, Herman 298
Menkel-Meadow, Carrie 227–46
Michael, Jerome 127–44, 189
Michelman, Frank 362
Michelson, Albert 55
Mill, John Stuart 54, 56, 362–3, 536
Millikan, Robert A. 56
Montaigne, Michel de 470
Montesquieu, Charles de 34, 465
Moore, Underhill 188, 430
Morgan 189
Morris, Charles W. 153

Morris, Judge Hugh M. 195
Moulton, Beatrice 230, 231, 232, 243, 245
Mungham, Geoff 488

Newman, Cardinal 442
Newton, Isaac 56

O'Connor, Justice Sandra Day 370
Oliphant, Herman 188, 196, 204, 430
Olivecrona, K. 484

Paley, William 138
Pareto, Vilfredo 153
Parke, Justice James 217
Pearson, Karl 54
Peirce 333
Pigou 364
Plato 321, 437
Poincaré, Jules 54
Pomeroy xiv
Posner, Richard 85, 288, 584
Pothier 16
Pound, Roscoe xv, xx, 116, 157–70, 204, 305–19, 430, 454, 507, 573–4
Powell, Richard 204
Powell, Thomas Reed 188
Priest, George L. 85, 287–91
Pryke, R. 544
Puffendorf, Samuel 34

Quine, W. 333

Radin, Max 196
Rashdall 423
Read, John 505
Reed, Alfred Z. 505
Reeves, Judge 183, 187
Reich, Charles A. 295–301, 454
Richards, I.A. 153
Richardson, Sir Ivor 555–60
Richardson III, Henry J. 395–405
Riemann, G.F.B. 54
Riesman, David 127–44, 279–86, 445, 582, 590
Rivera, Rhondra 413
Robert, Justice 330
Robinson 473, 476
Romano, Dr 277
Romilly, Sir Samuel 138
Rorty, Richard 86
Rosenblum 508
Ross, E.A. 80
Rostow, Professor 154
Royce, Josiah 158

Russell, Bertrand 54, 55, 333

Sacks, Al 250
Sacco, Nicola 143
Sapir, Edward 153
Sartre, Jean-Paul 298
Scales-Trent, Judy 412
Schiller, J.C.F. 55
Schlegel, John Henry 79–86, 505
Schrag 238
Schwartz 359, 360, 362, 364
Scott 170
Scruton, Roger 482
Searle, J.R. 484
Shaffer, Thomas 237
Shakespeare, William 298
Sheinman 530
Shklar, Judith 548
Simmonds, Nigel 488
Simpson, Brian 483
Singer 136
Small, Albion 80
Smith, Adam 345
Smith, Barbara 410
Smith, Lumley 189, 204
Smith, Sidney 505
Socrates 54, 276, 577
Sohm 161
Solomon, Harold 280, 281, 285
Spencer, Herbert 159
Spiegel, Mark 236, 245
Stair, Justice 488
Stalin, Joseph 399
Stanley, Christopher 543–51
Starkie, Thomas 5–25
Stephen, James 136
Stewart, Richard 361
Stone, Christopher D. 281, 325-42
Stone, Justice Harlan F. 97-9, 195
Story, Judge Joseph 307, 308, 424–7, 430, 437, 438, 440, 442, 568
Stowell, Lord 426
Sturges, Wesley 189
Summers, Claude 359
Sumner, Charles 129
Sutherland, A. 325
Swinnerton-Dyer, Sir Peter 482
Sylla 10

Thatcher, Margaret 492
Thayer, Ezra Ripley 167–8, 169, 429
Tiberius, Emperor 10
Trebilcock, Michael 364, 473–8
Tur, Richard 486

Twining, William 419–49, 483, 488, 545, 546

Unger, R.M. 543

Valens, Emperor 11
Valentinian, Emperor 10, 11
Vanderbilt, Chief Justice Arthur xviii
Vanzetti, Bartolomeo 143
Vattel, Emmerich de 34
Veblen, Thorstein xiii, xvi, 129
Vining, Joseph 470

Waite, Professor 137
Wambaugh, Eugene 169
Ward, Lester 10
Warner, Charles 153
Weber, Alfred 130
Weber, Max 129, 153, 547
Webster, Daniel 309
Wechsler, Herbert 127–44
Weinberger, Ota 484

Weldon, Richard Chapman 504
Wellington, Harry H. 91–4
Wellisz, Stanislaw H. 351
White, James 69–78
Whitehead, Alfred North 54, 57, 67, 333
Wigmore, John Henry 164, 166, 169, 170, 224
Williams, Patricia 412
Williston, Samuel 162–3, 169, 170, 429
Wilson, President Woodrow 265
Wisdom, J. 333
Wittgenstein, Ludwig 333
Wood, H.G. 34–5

Yach, D. 479, 491, 492, 493
Yette, Samuel 395
Yntema 196
Young, Dr Warren 556

Zemans 508
Zilboorg, Y. 136